RELIGIOUS PLURALISM, HERITAGE AND SOCIAL DEVELOPMENT IN AFRICA

Editors

M. Christian Green

Rosalind I. J. Hackett

Len Hansen

Francois Venter

Religious Pluralism, Heritage and Social Development in Africa

Published by SUN MeDIA Stellenbosch under the Conference-RAP imprint.

All rights reserved.

Copyright © 2017 ACLARS

No part of this book may be reproduced or transmitted in any form or by any electronic, photographic or mechanical means, including photocopying and recording on record, tape or laser disk, on microfilm, via the Internet, by e-mail, or by any other information storage and retrieval system, without prior writen permission by the publisher.

Views expressed in this publication do not necessarily reflect those of the publisher.

First edition 2017

ISBN 978-1-928314-27-1
ISBN 978-1-928314-28-8 (e-book)

Set in 10.5/13 Palatino Linotype

Cover design and typesetting by SUN MeDIA Stellenbosch

Conference-RAP is an imprint of AFRICAN SUN MeDIA. Conference proceedings are published under this imprint in print and electronic format. This publication may be ordered directly from www.sun-e-shop.co.za

Produced by SUN MeDIA Stellenbosch.

www.africansunmedia.co.za
africansunmedia.snapplify.com (e-books)
www.sun-e-shop.co.za

CONTENTS

FOREWORD ix
    Rosalind I.J. Hackett

INTRODUCTION xi
    M. Christian Green

I. RELIGION, PLURALISM AND HERITAGE IN ETHIOPIA

1   Religious tolerance in Ethiopia: Rhetoric and reality 3
    Mohammed Dejen Assen

2   Contested heritage: The "cul-touristic" turn in the celebration
    of Irreecha ritual in Ethiopia 21
    Serawit Bekele Debele

3   Religious pluralism and cohabitation in Ethiopia:
    Some critical notes 33
    Theodros Teklu

II. RELIGION AND STATE IN AFRICA

4   Exploiting state power in support of a "holy cause":
    Conflict and schism in the Baptist Church in Ghana 1986-1991 51
    Abamfo O. Atiemo & John G. Esubonteng

5   Religion, citizenship and the State of Zimbabwe: The politics
    of Zimbabwe's First Lady Grace Mugabe 71
    Prosper Muzambi

6   10 January: Political calculation or response to a
    socio-anthropological requirement in Benin? 91
    Jean-Baptiste Sourou

III. ISLAM AND CONSTITUTIONAL LAW IN AFRICA

7   Religious preaching and state regulation of the free exercise
    of religion by Shi'a Muslims in Kaduna State, Nigeria:
    A constitutional and human rights discourse 101
    Ahmed Salisu Garba

8   Muslim and Christian contestation over the entrenchment
    of the Kadhi Courts in the Constitution of Kenya:
    Challenging the principle of a secular state 121
    Hassan Juma Ndzovu

IV. INDIGENOUS RELIGION AND MINORITY RELIGIONS IN AFRICA

9   The media coverage of political and religious relations in Côte d'Ivoire: An analysis in light of the role of the *glaè* mask among the Wê people 139
Célestin Gnonzion

10   Individual and collective rights in Africa: Dual worlds of law, religion and African traditional heritage 157
Nokuzola Mndende

11   The National Policy on Religion and Education, and religious dress observances in South African schools 171
Abdulkader Tayob

V. HERITAGE OF LAND, WATER AND GREAT ZIMBABWE

12   Rastafari perspectives on land use and management in postcolonial Zimbabwe 189
Fortune Sibanda

13   African traditional religion in postcolonial Zimbabwe: A sustainable heritage for water resources management 205
Bernard P. Humbe

14   The Great Zimbabwe Monuments and challenges in African heritage management 221
Edmore Dube

VI. RELIGION, HATE SPEECH, DIVERSITY AND EQUALITY

15   Taming rogue clergy and churches: God, scandals, government and religious regulation in Kenya 241
Damaris Seleina Parsitau

16   Hate speech in the United States and South Africa: A legal and comparative analysis 259
Johan D. van der Vyver

17   "Rhodes Must Fall" – An alternative approach to statues in the South African public sphere 271
Georgia Alida du Plessis

18   Homosexuality and the law in Africa: South African case law as a paradigmatic example 291
Elias Kifon Bongmba

VII. RELIGION, HERITAGE AND DEATH IN AFRICA

19 Protecting the dead: The South African National Heritage Resources Act in context 315
   Dineo Skosana

20 Burial rights: Protecting the religious and cultural heritage of communities in South Africa 333
   Helena van Coller

21 Regulating death and funeral rites in a secular but religiously pluralistic society: The case of the Coroner Law System in Lagos State, Nigeria 353
   Danoye Oguntola-Laguda

22 Discrepancy between the legality of the death penalty and African religious heritage in Zimbabwe................................... 371
   Tobias Marevesa & Fortune Sibanda

INDEX 389

FOREWORD

While heritage is about the past, namely the traditions and practices passed on from generation to generation, and the locations and material culture that provide identity for communities, nations, and humanity in general, its public recognition and appropriation are very much a matter of the present. With the broadening of the scope of the concept in recent years to include intangible as well as tangible heritage, immaterial as well as material culture, moveable as well unmovable objects, natural environments and heritage locations of religious interest,[1] it presented itself as a productive, timely, and culturally relevant topic for the African Consortium for Law and Religion Studies, most especially in the context of Ethiopia.

Ethiopia is internationally known for its rich cultural heritage, with sites such as Axum, Lalibela, and Gondar proving central to the country's tourist industry. Seven of Ethiopia's heritage sites have received the imprimatur of UNESCO World Heritage status. The question of cultural heritage in Africa more generally, particularly heritage of religious and spiritual interest, needs to be understood at multiple levels, whether local, national, or international. It also necessitates a range of approaches that address its definition, creation, conservation, management, mobilisation and commodification in the African context. Any one or combination of these areas could have legal implications.

As noted by a leading African scholar of world heritage and development in sub-Saharan Africa, Webber Ndoro, African voices and perspectives in shaping heritage legislation and commemoration have frequently been underrepresented and in fact may be at odds with the "precepts of preservation espoused by UNESCO and its expert groups from the International Council on Monuments and Sites (ICOMOS) and the International Union for Conservation of Nature".[2] He argues that international experts tend to overemphasise certain aspects of heritage such as architectural monuments, archaeological sites of ancient civilisations, and historic sites, while "failing to recognize others that are important to the African traditional definition of heritage, such as those related to African traditional religions, slavery, or colonial resistance".[3] Another contentious issue in his view is the need to reconcile heritage conservation with socio-economic development around resource exploitation. He discusses how the development- and energy-oriented projects that African governments frequently promote "have come into conflict with the prospects for protecting

---

1   See the UNESCO Initiative on Heritage of Religious Interest. Online at: http://whc.unesco.org/en/religious-sacred-heritage
2   Ndoro W. 2017. "World Heritage and Development in Sub-Saharan Africa", *American Anthropologist* 119(1):129.
3   Ndoro, "World Heritage and Development", 129.

and conserving World Heritage Sites".[4] Other negative factors in the case of Africa include illegal activities, civil unrest, war and deliberate destruction of heritage. There are, however, signs, according to Ndoro, of greater awareness by African state parties of the 1972 World Heritage Convention and more visible actors on World Heritage issues at the local level.

Thus, it was not insignificant that the main conference theme on law, religion and heritage in Africa also included social development. For perceptions and appropriations of sacred histories, artifacts and heritage sites can be instrumental or antithetical to the goals of development and nation-building in Africa. As many of the essays in this volume demonstrate, attention to these questions provides much needed perspectives on the local dynamics of diverse African contexts. They also confirm the merits of the interdisciplinarity afforded by the fields of law and religion studies, with their attention to the sub-fields of education, media, and tourism, for example, where understandings of heritage can be naturalised and commodified.

Several of the chapters also attest to the value of considering the potential of national heritage policy and legislation to affirm or destabilise religion-state and/or interreligious relations in African states. Heritage should be viewed in relation to national, cultural, and global citizenship, as well as freedom of religion or belief. Preservation laws may be instrumental in shaping standards of authenticity, antiquity and aesthetics, which, in turn, may have consequences for the incorporation of religious, especially indigenous, perspectives in African settings. Sacred objects, symbols, and sites can be legitimated or de-legitimated through heritagisation processes. As David Chidester has shown for South Africa, the political mobilisation of heritage can provide, sometimes controversial, opportunities for memorialising the past and recognising Africa's indigenous peoples.[5] The negative influence of more revivalist forms of Christianity and Islam in many parts of contemporary Africa in this regard is also noted by several of the contributors. In sum, this timely publication brings new research and fresh perspectives on the legal and development ramifications of cultural and religious heritage for Africa and its peoples.

Rosalind I.J. Hackett
Professor and Head, Department of Religious Studies
University of Tennessee, Knoxville, U.S.A.

---

4   Ndoro, "World Heritage and Development", 130.
5   Chidester D. 2012. *Wild Religion: Tracking the Sacred in South Africa*. Berkeley and Los Angeles: University of California Press.

INTRODUCTION

"Religious Pluralism, Heritage and Social Development" – at the fourth annual African Consortium for Law and Religion Studies (ACLARS) held in Addis Ababa, Ethiopia, the concept of heritage was truly at the centre. Heritage – what it is, who decides, and how to preserve it – is a theme that is not only garnering interdisciplinary attention around the world, but also one that, if attended to well, can harness Africa's rich pluralism of religions and cultures in service of broader social, political and even economic development. The essays in this year's conference book illustrate this point in diverse ways.

Ethiopia was an extraordinarily rich site for holding a conference on heritage, as it is the site of some of the oldest communities of three world religions – Judaism, Christianity, and Islam. Last year's conference book on religious freedom and religious pluralism concluded with three strong chapters by Ethiopian authors, and this year's publication similarly begins with a trio of Ethiopian essays describing the ways in which heritage both complicates and is sustained by religious freedom and religious pluralism. Mohammed Dejen Assen's chapter provides a critical examination of the Ethiopian heritage narrative of religious tolerance and the way in which this narrative has been sustained particularly from Muslim forbearance from resistance and accommodation to the status quo. Serawit Debele's chapter explores how the rituals associated with a nature-based thanksgiving Irreecha ritual of the Oromo people has been "cul-touristically" appropriated by the secular Ethiopian state in service of the tourism industry. This has occurred against a backdrop of historical dominance by the Ethiopian Orthodox Church, in ways that have defined the ritual as culture in a way that has despiritualised its meaning. Her essay thus focuses on heritage as both process and discourse. Theodros Teklu's chapter describes the relationship among religions in Ethiopia, like Assen's essay, taking up the narratives of marginalisation and victimisation of Ethiopian Muslims and emphasising the need for a moral pedagogy of "cohabitation", rather than tolerance, to promote both plurality and responsibility in the heritage of religions among religious "others".

From Ethiopia, the volume moves to consider the implications for heritage of relations between religion and state in three very distinct national contexts. The chapter of Abamfo Atiemo and John Esubonteng uncovers the history of the Baptist Church heritage in Ghana, particularly the way that Ghanaian Baptists created a distinctly Ghanaian Baptist tradition, rooted in Africa and separate from the history of influence by American church missionaries. Prosper Muzambi explores the use of religion and the Bible as sources of political legitimation by Grace Mugabe, the spouse of long-term Zimbabwean president Robert Mugabe, in the context of Zimbawe's ongoing definition of the concept of citizenship. Jean-Baptiste Sourou examines the establishment, in 1997, of 10 January as a national day in the Republic of Benin for the celebration of traditional religions. This had significant roots in the Ouidah 92 festival reuniting Africans and Africans in America, but was controversial, too, for lifting up traditional religions as a site of Benin's African heritage – despite the apparent blessing of Pope John Paul II of African religious traditions in his notable engagement with the African continent.

A duo of essays explores the contribution of Islam to Africa's religious and legal heritage, followed by additional essays on the particular struggles of indigenous and minority religions. Ahmed Garba's essay examines the position of Nigeria's Shia Muslim community in the face of a law proposed that would place bans on religious preaching. Hassan Ndzovu's essay analyses the history of constitutional wrangling in Kenya over the status of Muslim Kadhi Courts and how this debate illustrates that religion and politics, religion, and the state remain deeply intertwined despite constitutionally professed secularism.

From a specific focus on African Islam, the essays then shift to examinations of Africa's diverse traditional religions and of the plight of minority religions, more generally. Writing about Côte d'Ivoire, Célestin Gnonzion provides a remarkable heritage-infused analysis of media coverage of religion through the trope of the *glaè* mask worn by leaders of the Wê people as a symbol of the unity of political power and religious authority. It is a relationship in which the former unity of political and religious leadership in the *glaè* has given way in the contemporary Ivorian context to a situation in which religious leaders, particularly the Catholic bishops, have been publicly criticised for refusing to exercise their power in challenging the state in a prophetic way. Nokuzola Mndende's essay examines how the juxtaposition of modern individual rights and traditional collective rights in the South African Xhosa community, and in other parts of Africa causes today's Africans to inhabit dual worlds, but with the collectivity of the African tradition manifest even in the most basic language of everyday greetings. Abdulkader Tayob provides an analysis of South Africa's ongoing debate over its National Religious Education Policy (NPRE), and how religious diversity in schools has been manifested – and highly scrutinised by the courts – particularly in the religious practices and bodies of girls.

A particular set of heritage questions is presented by the connection of indigenous groups to land, water, and local monuments, and is the focus of the essays contained in the volume's next part. Fortune Sibanda's essay on Rastafarian land use practices showcases not only the Rastafarian reverence for the earth, but also its profound interconnection to dietary, medicinal, and spiritual practices of the Rastafarian tradition. Equally important to land in Africa, as elsewhere, is proper management of the water resources that flow above and below it. Bernard Humbe's discussion of water use practices in Zimbabwe shows how central water and its management are to the spiritual practices of the indigenous Shona people, and how these practices have been affected by pre-colonial and postcolonial laws that took water rights away from the indigenous people in ways that threaten their spiritual practices, their ecology of sustainability, and even resources for peace and conflict reconciliation – all of which derive from their connection to and management of water resources. Edmore Dube's essay, the third in this Zimbabwean trilogy, examines policies surrounding the management of the Great Zimbabwe monuments, and how these policies, too, have involved disjuncture from systems of local management that are key to the monuments' physical and cultural preservation.

The book's next section focuses on controversies to do with religion, hate speech, diversity and equality. Damaris Parsitau provides a moral and ethical assessment of the sociological reality of Kenya's proliferating Pentecostal and charismatic churches, many of which stand accused of emotional and financial exploitation of followers, who seek solace in these ministries to deal with a welter of problems affecting contemporary Kenyan society. Johan van der Vyver takes up the important question of hate speech, in a comparative analysis of African laws prohibiting offence to religious feelings. These occupy a notably different terrain in a South Africa constitutionally committed to fostering equality in diversity than they do in the United States where "free speech" is given much wider latitude. Diversity and equality are also central concerns in Georgia du Plessis's chapter on the controversy over colonial monuments exemplified in the "Rhodes Must Fall" that spread across South African universities, as well as to Oxford University in the U.K. This is, indeed, a global phenomenon that has also manifested strongly in the United States, where universities and municipalities, particularly in light of the #BlackLivesMatter movement, have raised questions about monuments to the Confederate leaders whose move to secede prompted the U.S. Civil War in the nineteenth century. These "monumental" questions are deeply implicated in peoples' and nations' ongoing politics of identity, recognition, memory, and reconciliation. Questions of diversity and equality are also raised in stark form today by debates over homosexuality, homosexual relationships, and same-sex language. The subject of prohibitory laws in many African nations, the dignity and equality of LGBT people, and the relationships and families that they form was recognised in South Africa in the decision in the *Minister of Home Affairs v. Fourie* case. Judge Sachs's decision in the *Fourie* case is analysed through the lens of Protestant Reformation leader Martin Luther's essay "The Freedom of a Christian" in the chapter of Elias Bongmba, who provides a theological argument for recognition of dignity, equality, and the "right to be different" in the African context.

The book ends where all life ends, namely the social and spiritual reality of death, and the laws that we make to address it. Chapters by Helena van Coller and Dineo Skosana take up the regulation of death and burial in the South African National Heritage Resource Act (NHRA). Skosana argues that the NHRA, in seeking to protect the "tangible heritage" of monuments, graves and burial sites, does not sufficiently protect the "intangible heritage" of indigenous beliefs and practices around death, because it permits and does not sufficiently compensate indigenous people for incidents of grave disturbance. Van Coller discusses these issues from the perspective of law, arguing that indigenous communities should avail themselves of religious rights arguments, alongside claims of property rights, to claim their rights to burial places and practices that are often poorly understood by law. From South Africa, the chapters then move to Nigeria and Zimbabwe. Danoye Oguntola-Laguda, employing a blend of religious, legal, and sociological analysis, examines objections of Nigerian Muslim communities in Lagos State to a proposed Coroner Law System (CLS) whose prescriptions regarding postmortem autopsies were seen to conflict with Islamic burial practice. The case study is used to shed further light on the state of religious pluralism in Nigeria. In the volume's concluding chapter Tobias Marevesa and Fortune Sibanda provide an Afrocentric argument against the death penalty, particularly as imposed in pre-colonial and postcolonial Zimbabwe.

The topic of heritage – situated between, drawing upon, and contributing to Africa's religious pluralism and development – was an important topic for ACLARS to take up at this time. It has taken us into a realm of anthropological, political, and policy-laden topics that have not been heretofore addressed in the halls of ACLARS conferences, but in continuity with questions of religious freedom and human rights that have been our organisational hallmark. What and who constitute heritage? What forms of tangible and intangible heritage count? How can minority religious heritages be preserved amidst the at times homogenising and hegemonising forces of the majority? How is law, with its normative power to shape society, involved in "authorising heritage discourses"?

With rapidly developing societies, but also rapid technological developments in our abilities to preserve and curate heritage for our own and future generations, these questions are of great religious, legal, and cultural significance today. In the back of the minds of the organisers of our Ethiopia conference was the specter of ISIS blowing up the great monuments of Syrian civilisation, particularly the ruins of Palmyra, a UNESCO World Heritage Centre site. Along with the explosion of the Bamiyan Buddhas in Afghanistan and the sacking and desecration of Iraq's museum and antiquities treasures in the last decade's wars, the destruction of heritage looms as a unique form of cultural genocide directed at past, present, and future. And yet Africans have loomed large as heritage heroes in recent years, as in the salvation of some of the world's greatest manuscripts from terrorist attacks in the ongoing conflict in Mali, as recounted in the recent and robustly named book, *The Bad-Ass Librarians of Timbuktu*.[1] Our exploration of the many dimensions of African heritage from the vantage points of law and religion will, we hope, be a contribution to heritage debates and to

---

1 Hammer J. 2016. *The Bad-Ass Librarians of Timbuktu: And Their Race to Save the World's Most Precious Manuscripts*. New York: Simon & Schuster.

efforts to prevent heritage atrocities on the African continent and beyond. For as the Timbuktu librarians illustrate – not to mention the magnificent heritage sites at Lake Tana, Gondar, Lalibela, and Axum that some of us were privileged to visit after the Ethiopian conference – heritage preservation is clearly an area in which Africa can lead!

M. Christian Green
Senior Editor, Center for the Study of Law and Religion
Emory University, U.S.A.;
Special Content Editor, Journal of Law and Religion;
ACLARS Publications Committee Chair

I. Religion, Pluralism and Heritage in Ethiopia

1 RELIGIOUS TOLERANCE IN ETHIOPIA: RHETORIC AND REALITY

Mohammed Dejen Assen[1]

INTRODUCTION

In academia, especially of Christian writers of Ethiopian religious history, contemporary politicians and the Ethiopian Orthodox Church (EOC), there seems to be a general consensus that Ethiopia's religious past is characterised by peaceful coexistence and tolerance between Muslims and Christians.[2] Although partly true, the emphasis only on the consensual aspect of the relations not only distorts the conflictual relations,[3] but also undermines contemporary claims of Muslims for more parity and freedom, as the government and Christians associate their claims with religious intolerance and extremism. The author of this chapter subscribes to the general assertion of peaceful coexistence and tolerance, noting however that it was largely attributable to the forbearance of Muslims and the acceptance of the status quo with no or minimal resistance. Whenever Muslims become assertive in political and economic affairs of the state, their relations with the state and Christians deteriorate.

This chapter examines the religious history of the country in relation to the tolerance and forbearance narratives advanced by the Christians and Muslims respectively. In doing so, the first part of the chapter highlights the religious demography of the country by focusing on Islam and Christianity. The second section will deal with the conflicting narratives of Ethiopia's religious past mainly drawn from the Muslim and Christian perspectives. The third part provides a conceptual framework of tolerance and forbearance in the Ethiopian context and explains the Ethiopian experience of religious coexistence. It also discusses the various discourses of religious coexistence advanced by different sets of actors. Finally, it examines contemporary trends of religious (in)tolerance and appraises some of the policies of the government towards religion.

---

1 The author is an assistant professor at Addis Ababa University, College of Law and Governance Studies.
2 For the purpose of this chapter, Christianity is to mean only Orthodox Tewahedo Christianity of Ethiopia. It does not include Protestantism, Catholicism and other denominations of Christianity as they were excluded from the benefits that the Ethiopian state provided for Orthodox Tewahedo Christians. According to the 2007 population census, Protestants comprise about 18.6% of the religious figure of Ethiopia and Catholics are around 0.7%.
3 Hussein A. 2006. "Coexistence and/or Confrontation? Towards a Reappraisal of Christian-Muslim Encounter in Contemporary Ethiopia", *Journal of Religion in Africa* 36(Fasc.1):4-22.

THE RELIGIOUS MAP OF ETHIOPIA

Orthodox Christianity

Based on the population and housing census of 2007,[4] Orthodox Christianity constitutes 43.5% of the total number of the religious composition of the Ethiopian people. Their number decreased roughly by 7% from the 1994 census results.[5] Ethiopia was the first country in Africa to host Christianity. It entered the country in the middle of the fourth century CE[6] through the "two brothers, Frumentius and Aedesius [of Syria]",[7] which makes Ethiopia the third country in the world to adopt Christianity after Constantinople and Armenia.[8] King Ezana, the Axumite King, who was believed to be the first convert to Christianity, established the religion at the state level. A political scientist and historian, John Markakis states that Orthodox Christianity was introduced in the country after the Monophysite doctrine was "condemned as a heresy" by the Catholic Church at the religious Council of Chalcedon. Some groups subscribing to this dogma fled to Axum from the Church of Alexandria, from where the Ethiopian Church used to import Patriarchs until 1959. Those who came to Axum include the nine saints from Syria who later translated the Bible into Ge'ez.[9] As Markakis noted, the Ethiopian Church then followed the Monophysite creed and later incorporated some indigenous elements in it in an attempt to "indigenise" the religion.

After that time, Orthodox Christianity was the established state religion of Ethiopia. It continued with this status up to the close of the twentieth century. Emperor Haile Selassie I (1930-1974) was the last of the so-called Solomonic Dynasty rulers who legally intertwined Christianity and the Ethiopian state in an "unholy marriage".[10] He did his level best to blend Christianity, the Ethiopian nation and the Solomonic throne as if they were one and inseparable.

---

4   Central Statistics Agency (CSA). 2007. "Summary and Statistical Reports of 2007 Population and Housing Census: Population Size by Age and Sex." FDRE Population Census Commission, December 2008, Addis Ababa.
5   The decrease in the number of Orthodox Christians is mainly attributable to the "re-conversion" of Orthodox Christians into Protestantism. The number of increase in Protestants, who were about 11% in the 1994 census but reached to 18.6% in 2007, is roughly equal to the number of decrease in Orthodox Christians.
6   Markakis J. 1974. *Ethiopia: Anatomy of Traditional Polity*. London: Oxford University Press, 27.
7   Trimingham JS. 1952. *Islam in Ethiopia*. London: Oxford University Press, 38.
8   Erlich H. 2010. *Islam and Christianity: Can They Coexist? The Answer Lies in the Horn of Africa*. Boulder, CO: Lynne Rienner, 12.
9   Markakis, *Ethiopia: Anatomy of Traditional Polity*, 44. Ge'ez was the official language of Ethiopia until the middle of the 19th century and now used as the language of liturgy in the Ethiopian Orthodox Church (EOC).
10 Constitution of the Empire of Ethiopia, 1931 (Preamble), Revised Constitution of the Empire of Ethiopia, 1955 (article 26) Article 126 of the 1955 Revised Constitution, the 1960 Civil Code of the Empire of Ethiopia Proclamation No. 165 of 1960. The term "unholy marriage" is used to indicate the incompatibility

This trinity of church, state, and monarchy was so intrinsic that none could be separated without destroying the others. Moreover, Ethiopia's nationhood was consciously defined in terms of religion. Those who professed Christianity were considered to be Ethiopians and all others to be non-Ethiopians. This is illustrated in Markakis's observation when he states that, "according to tradition, Ethiopian nationality is theologically defined, its primary criterion being faith. A non-Christian could not be an Ethiopian, nor could an Ethiopian adhere to any other creed."[11] This was nothing but an advancement of the myth of a "Christian island Ethiopia" agenda. Semitic culture (including the Amharic language and Christianity) were the sole criteria for acquiring Ethiopian nationality. A person had to speak Amharic and profess Christianity to be an Ethiopian. Religion, by its nature, is exclusive where it excludes non-believers and followers of other religions from its domain. The rulers deliberately coined terms like "Christian Ethiopia", "an island of Christianity"[12] etc., making Ethiopian nationhood synonymous with Christianity in order to exclude the vast majority of the Ethiopian population who were non-Christians.

The overthrow of the Emperor in 1974 and the coming into power of the military regime (popularly called Derg[13]) heralded the final divorce of the state from religion and destroyed the unholy trinity of church, state, and throne. The Derg regime declared the secular socialist state of Ethiopia in which cultural, linguistic and religious equality could flourish. In practical terms, however, its religious policies were only superficial and later on focused on its atheist policies that antagonised religious communities in the country. The military junta itself was overthrown in 1991 by an ethno-nationalist force, which later came to be known as Ethiopian People's Revolutionary Democratic Front (EPRDF) and the new government further strengthened the separation of state and religion in the supreme law of the country that contributed to the constitutional equality of all religions.

Islam

Islam is the second largest religion in Ethiopia after Christianity. It consists of 34% of the country's total religious composition.[14] Islam came to Ethiopia at the beginning of the seventh century CE, which makes Ethiopia the first country in

---

    of goals for religious and political institutions as the first is working more for the life in the hereafter while the latter for this world.
11   Markakis, *Ethiopia: Anatomy of Traditional Polity*, 46.
12   "The Christian Island" rhetoric is believed to be coined by the religiously "moderate" Emperor Menelik II at the end of the 19th century due to the inclusion of large numbers of Muslims and traditional believers by the war of conquest. It was advanced by Haile Selassie I with his systematic official and unofficial policies of exclusion.
13   Derg is an Amharic term to denote Committee. Derg ruled the country from 1974 to 1991 with socialism as official state ideology.
14   Central Statistics Agency (CSA), 2007.

the world to accept Islam after Saudi Arabia, where the religion originated. Some scholars, such as constitutional lawyer and renowned scholar of federalism Assefa Fiseha,[15] consider Ethiopia as "the first country to recognize Islam at state level in the world" substantiating his argument with mention of the Ethiopian king Nejashi, who in 615 CE welcomed the first Muslim immigrants from Arabia to his palace to practice their religion freely.

When the Prophet Mohammed and his companions faced persecution from their own Qurayish Arab tribes in Arabia, the Prophet advised them to go to Ethiopia in 615 CE.[16] The Prophet told his disciples to obtain asylum from an Ethiopian king until things become stable in Arabia. Around twelve disciples (numbers are controversial, some say seventeen, others two hundred) of the Prophet arrived in Ethiopia in 615 CE, which is regarded in history as the date of the first *hijrah* (emigration) in Muslim history – in this case taking some of the first followers of Prophet Mohammed from Mecca to the Axumite Kingdom.[17]

The special status of Islam in Ethiopia is attested to by numerous writings, video and audio recordings. In a video recording by the Al-Habesha Islamic Club[18] in cooperation with the Addis Ababa Islamic Affairs Supreme Council, Ethiopia has a special place in Islam mainly for the following reasons: (1) Ethiopia is the first country after Saudi Arabia to accept Islam following the first *hijrah*; (2) Among all the Meccan *sahabas* (followers),[19] Bilal bin Rabah was the first black person to accept Islam and the first *muezzin* (prayer caller) who was of Ethiopian descent; (3) The first Muslim king was the Ethiopian king As'hama (Muslims used to call him Nejashi);[20] (4) The Prophet's nurse was an Ethiopian woman named Baraka Umm Ayma;[21] and (5) Ethiopia was freed from any use of force by Muslims in the words of the Prophet, "leave Abyssinians alone as long as they do not take the offensive".

---

15 Assefa F. 2007. *Federalism and the Accommodation of Diversity in Ethiopia*. Revised Edition. Nijmegen: Wolf Legal, 22.
16 Al-Habesha Islamic Club, "The historic relationship between Islam and Ethiopia", prepared by al-Habesha Islamic Club in cooperation with Addis Ababa Islamic Affairs Supreme Council. Online at: www.youtube.com, "Islam and Ethiopia (Amharic)".
17 Ahmedin J. 2011. *Etyopiyawiyan Muslimoch ke 615-1700: Yechiqonana yetigil Tarik* [Ethiopian Muslims from 615 to 1700: A History of Oppression and Struggle]. Fourth Edition. Addis Ababa: Merewa, 34.
18 Al-Habesha Islamic Club, "The historic relationship between Islam and Ethiopia".
19 The *sahabas* are those followers of the Prophet Mohammed while he was alive.
20 There are some controversies about the king's conversion to Islam. See, for example, Dereje F. 2011, 4, who states, "The EOC recognizes the coming of the companions of the Prophet Mohammed (the *sahaba*) to Ethiopia in 615 AD. What it rejects, and does vehemently, is the Muslims' claiming that the Christian king Armha (As'hama) who hosted the *sahaba* was converted to Islam." This rejection of the EOC is also corroborated by writers like Sergew Hable Selassie, Tadesse Tamirat, Trimingham and others.
21 Erlich H. 1994. *Ethiopia and the Middle East*. Boulder, CO: Lynne Rienner, 5.

In light of the peaceful relations between the Muslim refugees and the Christian king of Ethiopia, the Prophet instructed his followers not to use any force against Ethiopia in the expansion of Islam. Hence, Islam was disseminated in the country through the peaceful means of missionary activities and long-distance trade.[22] However, this does not mean that Muslim-Christian relations were always peaceful throughout history. There were series of conflicts and in some instances deadly clashes between them which will be discussed below.

ETHIOPIA'S RELIGIOUS PAST: CONFLICTING NARRATIVES

> Contemporary Christian-Muslim relations in Ethiopia have become gradually defined by an (assumed) historical tradition of religious tolerance, rather than by the conflict model. This is, to a large degree, contested by Muslims, who maintain that coexistence was made possible only by Christian dominance and the subsequent marginalization of Muslims.[23]

The above quotation indicates the existence of, at least, two perspectives on Ethiopia's religious past: one is largely drawn from Muslims and the other from non-Muslims, mainly the Orthodox Christians. From the Muslims perspectives, considering Ethiopia as a model of religious tolerance were tantamount to accepting the normality of structural and institutional oppression imposed on Ethiopian Muslims and acknowledging oppression as a normal way of life. For them, there had not been religious tolerance or equality in the true sense of the term where the Muslim and Christian communities accepted religious differences as a normal social phenomenon and respected one another's faiths. However, the narratives advanced by Christian writers deliberately excluded the views of the Muslims and totally controlled the definition of "what is meant by religious tolerance in the Ethiopian context". Due to their political, economic and social dominance, Christian writers excluded the views of the Muslims who offered counter-evidence in re-writing their own history. Some Muslim as well non-Muslim writers, who tried to refute the country's Christian-oriented history and reconstruct it in a more balanced way were given nicknames as *yetarik lapis* (an Amharic term to mean "eraser of history").

Muslim activists and writers argue that, the history of Islam and Muslims was either not included in the general Ethiopian history, or, if included, mostly distorted and misrepresented. A Muslim activist and historian Ahmedin Jebel, for example, argues that Ethiopian Islamic history is excluded from Ethiopian history through three major strategies – selection, omission and demonisation.[24] Christian Ethiopian historiographers have deliberately selected certain periods,

---

22 Abbink J. 1998. "An Historical-Anthropological Approach to Islam in Ethiopia: Issues of Identity and Politics", *Journal of African Cultural Studies* 11(2):112.
23 Desplat P and Østebø T. 2013. *Muslims in Ethiopia: The Christian Legacy, Identity Politics and Islamic Reformism*. London: Palgrave MacMillan, 3.
24 Ahmedin, *Etyopiyawiyan Muslimoch ke 615-1700*, 11-12.

historical events, places and cultural phenomena which amplify the interests of the dominant group while omitting or sometimes demonising certain events and activities that have the potential to undermine Christian interests and promote the deeds of their opponents.

Muslim writers and activists challenge the religious tolerance model and forward their own alternatives as "forbearance of Muslims to the status quo better captures the religious past of Ethiopia".[25] However, some contemporary foreign and domestic scholars consider it as equivalent to "re-writing the religious history of the country".[26] Others, on the other hand, praise the Muslims' assertiveness as an effort to construct "a more balanced account of Ethiopia's religious past."[27]

In spite of the long years of marginalisation and discrimination against Ethiopian Muslims, institutionalised by subsequent imperial rules, the long-held view of Ethiopia's religious past inclined towards the religious tolerance model that has defined the religious history of the country though contested by Muslims. It is, of course, inappropriate to put all Muslims in one box and argue that all reject the tolerance model in favor of the forbearance model. For the non-Muslims, on the other hand, Ethiopia's religious past has generally been understood to mean "tolerance and peaceful coexistence", but it would also equally wrong to include all non-Muslims in the religious tolerance model.

Defining tolerance

Tolerance can be difficult to define. The Oxford English Dictionary, eleventh edition, defines tolerance as "the ability, willingness, or capacity to tolerate something".[28] It then defines the word "tolerate" as "to allow the existence or occurrence of (something that one dislikes or disagrees with) without interference; [or allow] to endure (someone or something unpleasant) with forbearance." From this definition, tolerance is understood to mean that people accept or are prepared to accept something which is different from their thinking or worldview. It is also stated in the definition that forbearance is included within the domain of tolerance. Nonetheless, tolerance is more positive than

---

25 Ahmedin, *Etyopiyawiyan Muslimoch ke 615-1700*, 11-12.
26 See, for example, Abbink Jon. 2011. "Religion in Public Spaces: Emerging Muslim-Christian Polemics in Ethiopia", *African Affairs* 110/439:253-274.
27 Dereje F. 2011. "Accommodation, tolerance or forbearance? The politics of representing Ethiopia's religious past". Paper presented at The 4th European Conference on African Studies, Uppsala, Sweden, 1-2. Dereje wrote that "there are few countries [in the world] as burdened by their past as Ethiopia. It is no wonder thus history has been one of the major sites of political contestation." He added that "Ethiopian historiography, like history writing elsewhere, is a contested terrain. [Moreover], historiography is acutely contested particularly in countries where history is one of the cores of political legitimacy."
28 2008. *Concise Oxford English Dictionary*. Eleventh Edition. Oxford: Oxford University Press.

forbearance in that the former entails restraint on both groups to respect the views of one another while the latter implies accepting oppression from one side. In forbearance, one group is forced to accept the views of the other without necessarily requiring reciprocity. The Amharic terms *mechal* (forbearance) and *mechachal* (tolerance) are used throughout this chapter to explain the Muslim forbearance and the Christian tolerance narrations respectively. In *mechal* (forbearance), one group is subjected to accept the superior position of another and duty-bound to respect the values of the other group. However, in *mechachal* (tolerance) both are equally required to respect one another.

Joan Wallach Scott, a historian who has written on conflicts over the Muslim veil in France, does not like to use words such as "tolerance" or "toleration" to express the recognition of diversity or differences since the word has negative connotations for those who are tolerated in implying their inferior position. Instead, Scott convincingly proposes that acknowledgement of differences by the state or those in power, particularly of minority groups, is a better term for capturing a sense of equality. Acknowledging differences instead of tolerating them, serves to "call into question the certainty and superiority of the established views".[29] Scott recommends negotiation of differences non-hierarchically on common grounds of shared differences, since these are an unavoidable phenomenon in pluralistic social life. Others also categorise tolerance into pseudo and genuine. The former being rooted in skepticism towards others while the latter is based on "respect for truth and the dignity of others".[30]

Religious tolerance and forbearance narratives in Ethiopia

The religious tolerance of the past in Ethiopia is subject to different and perhaps contradictory interpretations by different groups. For some, it was *mechachal* (tolerance), for others it was accommodation and still for others it was *mechal* (forbearance).[31] The Amharic term *mechachal* (tolerance) signifies mutual restraints from both groups (in our case Muslims and Orthodox Christians) from upsetting the other group and respect the views and religious values of others. *Mechal* (forbearance), on the other hand, imposes a duty on the one group to respect the other without reciprocity.

Some writings indicate that, Ethiopia is considered to be a model of religious tolerance and peaceful coexistence of Christians and Muslims. It is said that, what makes Ethiopia unique among the countries of the world is not only its early reception of the two major Abrahamic religions (Christianity and Islam), but also the unprecedented peaceful coexistence of these religions

---

29 Scott JW. 2007. *The Politics of the Veil*. Princeton, NJ: Princeton University Press, 19.
30 Tyler A. 2008. *Islam, the West, and Tolerance: Conceiving Coexistence*. New York: Palgrave Macmillan, 73.
31 Dereje, "Accommodation, tolerance or forbearance?", 14-19, 3-9.

in the country.³² Despite this peaceful pluralistic image, scholars like Dereje Feyissa³³ identify three sets of actors advancing three competing discourses for interpreting Ethiopia's religious past – specifically, the EOC, Muslims and Ethiopian government discourses. The EOC discourse is of religious accommodation; the Muslim discourse is of forbearance; and the government is one of religious tolerance.

Ethiopian Orthodox Church discourse

The Ethiopian Orthodox Church, considering itself to be the most "indigenous" of Ethiopian religions, has always presented itself as tolerant towards other religions and that they hosted and accommodated their existence in the country. As discussed above, Orthodox Christianity entered into the country in the fourth century CE, roughly some 300 years prior to Islam, which came in the seventh century CE. Inevitably, this historical priority, even though both came from outside, created a sense of "nativity" on the side of the EOC, while Muslims were regarded as "exotics". The "indigenous" consider themselves to be hosts – and hence accommodative – of the "newcomers". Moreover, due to the intimate relationship between the Ethiopian state and the EOC from the fourth century CE till the last quarter of the twentieth century, it created a sense of ownership on the part of the EOC of the state. It also created the impression that the survival of other religious communities depended, to a large degree, upon the goodwill of the EOC. The EOC also possessed a third of the land of Ethiopia and the power to bless and anoint emperors to govern the people. The symbiotic relationship between the emperors and the EOC gave the latter the clout to exclude other religious competitors from the field, unless it chooses to accommodate them. In this regard, accommodation of different religious communities was largely attributable to the "high moral ground" of the EOC,³⁴ and is considered as one of the defining features of Ethiopia's religious past.

Accommodation, however, entails a meaning of "superior position", and if the need arises, it could eliminate others by withdrawing its accommodation. Thus, accommodation, like forbearance, does not encompass mutual coexistence, but rather the will of the "dominant group" as a precondition for others to survive. Even so, the EOC usually narrates Ethiopia's religious past in terms of accommodation, so much so that, the EOC is praised for its "generosity" in accommodating Muslims and other Christian denominations by its own will.

---

32 *Ewunetu Yih New* [This is the Truth]. 2012. *Lehizbe Muslimu Weqtawi Tiyaqewech Meftihe Lemafelaleg Yetemeretew Komitie Yasalefachew Hidetochina Lemengistina Lebaledirsha Akalat Yasigebachew Ye-Abetuta Debdabewech Sibsib*. Unpublished Collection Works of the Muslims' Solution Finding Committee, 6.
33 Dereje, "Accommodation, tolerance or forbearance?", 2.
34 Dereje, "Accommodation, tolerance or forbearance?", 4.

Ethiopian government discourse

The incumbent government of Ethiopia explains Muslim-Christian relations in terms of mutual tolerance in a way that, to some extent, resembles the EOC's narrative of accommodation.[35] Through state media and various policy documents,[36] the government has advanced the discourse of religious tolerance as the defining feature of Ethiopia's religious past. In so doing, it has been able to re-enforce a myth of religious tolerance and to portray religious tolerance as the unique trademark of Ethiopia to be exported to the rest of the world, which suffers from the infections of religious intolerance and conflict.[37]

The EPRDF government always praises the Ethiopian experience in terms of peaceful coexistence and romanticised the past as mutual tolerance among different religious groups. The government acknowledges the misdeeds of Ethiopian rulers, but the people are usually described as displaying cooperation and respect to one another which has no parallel in other parts of the world. In a 2011 document entitled, *Yehaimanot Akrarinetinina Yegosa Gichitochin Yeminfetabet Agerawi Eqid Meneshawechina Aqitachawech* (A National Plan, Bases and Directions to Solve Religious Extremism and Ethnic Conflicts), the government maintained that:

> Although there were conflicts for power, territorial expansion and controlling trade routes in Ethiopia under the cover of religion, the Ethiopian people always exhibited mutual religious tolerance, respect and cooperation that made us [Ethiopians] proud. While rulers struggled for their own interests, our people displayed religious tolerance and cooperation that can be transmitted from generation to generation and lived peacefully for centuries in one roof.[38]

The culture and history of religious tolerance practiced for centuries in Ethiopia can, according to this view, be taken as an exemplary model for other countries. While the EPRDF-led government designated all Ethiopian emperors, with few exceptions, as "nation-destroyers", who destroyed nationalities and peoples in the name of "nation-building", it never mentioned the religious misdeeds of the rulers for fear of stoking religious tensions. The EPDRF's current religious tolerance discourse can, therefore, be challenged as to its "sincerity" and its use and misuse of history to its own advantage. The government has a strategy of deconstructing and reconstructing Ethiopian history in its own favour. It is a

---

35 Addis Raey. 2012. *Adis Raey Ginbot-Sene 2004* [Addis Raey from May to June 2011]. 2nd Year, 3(9).
36 "*Yehaimanot Akrarinetinina Yegosa Gichitochin Yeminfetabet Agerawi Eqid Meneshawechina Aqitachawech* [A National Plan, Bases and Directions to Solve Religious Extremism and Ethnic Conflicts]". 2011. Unpublished Government Document prepared for creating awareness for government officials.
37 Prime Minister Meles Zenawi's speech to the FDRE Parliament, 17 April 2012.
38 "*Yehaimanot Akrarinetinina Yegosa Gichitochin Yeminfetabet Agerawi Eqid Meneshawechina Aqitachawech*", 3.

meaning imposed on a phenomenon that takes political advantage of power at the centre, despite being contested by some groups.[39]

The religious tolerance narrative, which Muslim activists and elites see as being advanced by the government, lacks sincerity because it provides no empirical evidence of past deeds and it is used only to deflect the contemporary legitimate claims of Muslims for religious parity and freedom, equating their demands with religious intolerance and extremism. The deliberate use of Ethiopia's past religious history as a history of religious tolerance and mutual peaceful coexistence is a tactic of the government to label the present Muslim generation as fundamentalist and extremist. Put differently, the end result of the past religious tolerance discourse is to interpret the Muslim activists' protest or movement for more freedom and rights as a sign of religious fundamentalism, intolerance of diversity, and a threat to the present and future of Ethiopia's unity. The terms Islamic fundamentalism and extremism and the logical steps that flow from "fighting terrorism" is used deliberately by the government to crackdown on Muslim protest and to delegitimise the demands of Muslims for independent Islamic institutions and religious equality and non-interference in their religious affairs. The myth of the history of Ethiopia's religious tolerance is widely contrasted by the government discourse with the intolerant practices and actions of Muslim activists of the present generation.

Muslim discourse

For many Muslims, it was *mechal* (forbearance) of Muslims to the political, social, economic and cultural domination of Christians that explains better Ethiopia's religious past than accommodation and *mechachal* (tolerance).[40] One of my interviewees described the relationship between Muslims and Christians or otherwise the state in three ways: submissiveness, fatigue (exhaustion) and tolerance.[41] In my interviewee's view, it is the first and to some extent the second scenario that better explains Ethiopia's religious past, in which Muslims submitted to Christian superiority and accepted the status quo with minimal or no challenge. So long as Muslims remained subordinate to the Christian-dominated state and accepted it without contest, the state tolerated them for the economic advantage they could provide – for example, by engaging in trade, which was despised by Christians at the time, or by providing cheap labour for the land owners.[42] The fatigue or exhaustion, my interviewee[43] explained, is related to the exhaustion of the two religious communities to engage in constant competition where their numbers are equivalent in some parts of the

---

39   *Addis Raey Megazin* [New Vision Magazine]. 1998.
40   Ahmedin, *Etyopiyawiyan Muslimoch ke 615-1700*.
41   Interview with Mohammed Ali by MD Assen, Addis Ababa University, 14 June 2014.
42   Hussein, "Coexistence and/or Confrontation?"
43   Interview with Mohammed Ali.

country. He mentioned Wollo as an example of where Muslims and Christians came to terms with one another to live in *de facto* peace out of a realisation that it could be disastrous to go into conflict. The third stance of tolerance, for him, was a means toward mutual understanding of differences and respect for one another's identity. In his view, this had never happened in Ethiopia, outside of the official rhetoric advanced by the government and the EOC. For Muslim activists, therefore, the government's narrative of the past as a model of religious tolerance is interpreted as "pressing them to accept the status quo – meaning the religious inequality and their second-class status and undermining the legitimate demands of Ethiopian Muslims".[44]

Taking into account the views of various actors, particularly the Muslims, some writers question whether Ethiopia's religious past was really *mechachal* (tolerance) or *mechal* (forbearance).[45] For Muslims, it was the total submission to hegemonic rule by the Christian kings and acceptance of their marginalised status that maintained peaceful coexistence between the two communities. This situation could not be interpreted as religious tolerance on the basis of equality. Ahmedin Jebel, for example, out-rightly rejects the religious tolerance narratives forwarded by the state media, government and other sources, which simply amplify the religious tolerance message without corroborating through empirical evidence that support their claims. Ahmedin argues that, Muslims "tolerated" the Christian domination and accepted their subordinate status in the Ethiopian body politic.[46]

Orthodox Christianity was always a state religion, from its first appearance in the fourth century to the 1974 popular revolution that swept away the last imperial government. Inevitably, other religions were subordinated and their followers were regarded as second-class subjects, even aliens.[47] In the period from the seventh century to the end of the twentieth century, Islam was seen as a religion of "non-privileged" people and Muslims were destined for second-class status. Muslims were only a useful source of revenue for the imperial governments and linkage with the outside Muslim world, but Muslims should remain impotent in domestic political and social affairs. Muslims were denied access to land ownership, and they were prevented from serving in the army and participating in political and social affairs. They were not allowed to build mosques and celebrate their religious holidays publicly. Muslims were only involved in trade and other "low status" activities like weaving, woodworking and trade, since these activities were despised by Christian elites and commoners.[48] Christians, on the other hand, participated in the so-called "privileged activities", such as farming, soldiery and in governmental posts

---

44   Dereje, "Accommodation, tolerance or forbearance?", 20.
45   Dereje, "Accommodation, tolerance or forbearance?".
46   Ahmedin, *Etyopiyawiyan Muslimoch ke 615-1700*, 30.
47   Hussein, "Coexistence and/or Confrontation?", 6.
48   Hussein, "Coexistence and/or Confrontation?", 6.

as civil servants and political appointees.⁴⁹ Muslims were deprived of land to plough, and prohibited from working in government offices or becoming soldiers, unless they were converted to Christianity.⁵⁰ All these were done through the collaborative effort of the Ethiopian state and the EOC.

Arguably, Ethiopia's religious past was seen superficially through the lens of the religious accommodation and tolerance narratives without critically examining the reality on the ground. Rhetorically, it was portrayed as an ideal example of religious tolerance in the world and even to be exported to other nations – but this narrative only amplifies one side of the story without fully appraising the views of the other.

NEW TRENDS OF RELIGIOUS (IN)TOLERANCE

Once seemingly taboo claims in Ethiopian history started to be raised by Ethiopian Muslims in post-1991 Ethiopia. Muslims of Axum, who constitute around 11% of the total population of the town,⁵¹ along with Lalibela – both of which are perceived to be Christian "holy places" by the EOC – invoked their constitutional rights and requested plots of land from the local governments to establish mosques. The EOC vehemently opposed these demands, stating that these places are "sacred places" for the Christians. Hence, according to the views of Christians, Muslims should not be allowed to construct mosques in Christian holy lands as "Mecca would not allow the construction of any Church there".⁵² The analogy between Mecca and Axum is weak – for one thing, the practice of prohibiting Christians from constructing churches in Saudi Arabia is unjust and criticised by almost all democratic states, and for the other, the laws of Saudi Arabia and federal Ethiopia are different, which makes Saudi Arabia irrelevant for the debate in Axum and Lalibela. It does, however, indicate that the EOC considers Axum to be its "exclusive property" which "others" (Muslims, Protestants, Catholics, Jews, etc.) have no right to claim, irrespective of their numbers of believers in the vicinity.

It is to be remembered that, Axum was the first place in the world to receive Muslim refugees from Arabia and King As'hama (Nejashi, according to his Muslim name) was the first Christian king on earth to allow Muslim asylum-seekers to live peacefully in his kingdom. It is the first instance of peaceful coexistence between the two monotheistic religions. The current "Axum Paradox"⁵³ mainly emanates from the "wrong" assumption about the

---

49 Abbink, "An Historical-Anthropological Approach to Islam in Ethiopia", 112.
50 Markakis, *Ethiopia. Anatomy of Traditional Polity*, 63.
51 Dereje F. 2013. "Religious Conflict Analysis in Ethiopia". Research Report Submitted to the Norwegian Church Aid. Unpublished, 3.
52 Dereje, "Religious Conflict Analysis in Ethiopia".
53 The term "Axum Paradox" is my own usage to show the paradox which happened in Axum town with regard to Muslim-Christian peaceful coexistence in the past and today. In history, Axum Christian leaders were best remembered in Muslim narratives as accommodative for Muslim asylum-seekers from Arabia

prohibition of construction of mosques in a historically Christian "holy land" where the Ark of the Covenant is placed. Ironically, Axum is also claimed by Muslims as their holy land historically, since the first companions of the Prophet Mohammed practiced Islam freely in the Axumite kingdom and some Muslims are buried in and around the city of Axum. The tomb of Nejashi is found near the town that many Muslims visit every year as a local *hajj* or pilgrimage.

Although not fully substantiated by evidence, "nearly all members of the EOC believe that the original Ark of the Covenant is hidden in the Axum Zion Church in northern Ethiopia",[54] and that it was brought by Emperor Menelik I from Solomon's Temple in Jerusalem – this is the origin of the Solomonic myth.[55] Of course, no one has ever seen the Ark, but "believing without seeing", as the religion orders its believers to do, has prevailed.

In an interview conducted by Ahmedin Jebel with local Axum Muslims, they complained that "Muslims of Axum are prevented from constructing mosques in and around the city".[56] The prohibition of mosque construction extends up to an 18 km radius from the town.[57] The reasons for prohibiting Muslims from building mosques, as the interviewees said, were that the Christians opposed it, because in their perspective "Axum is a town of the historical Axum Zion Church and the land of Muse Zion".[58] The Christian tradition regards Axum as "the second Jerusalem, where God's Ark came to rest".[59] However, historian Wudu Tafete argues that, "the principal objective of this 'invented tradition', formulated by the church, was to give political legitimacy to the 'Solomonic dynasty, which came to power in 1270".[60] From the Christians' perspective, it is only wasting money and time for Muslims to seek to establish their worshipping houses in a "Christian holy land"[61] The Muslims of Axum are, therefore, forced to pray in private houses which are given for the Friday congregational prayer as *waqf*, meaning voluntary donation by Muslims of use of their own houses. The belief that Axum is a holy place for Christians originates from the aforementioned assumption, but it has nothing to do with the location of the area.

---

    and respectful of the religion of Muslims. Today, the same Axum is becoming less accommodative of the claims of Muslims and the local rulers in the town are less responsive to the claims of Muslims for plots of land to construct mosques.

54 Craig EJ. 2010. *Haile Selassie and the Religious Field: Generative Structuralism and Christian Mission in Ethiopia*, MA Thesis, Temple University, 22.

55 Erlich, *Ethiopia and the Middle East*, 22.

56 Interview with local Muslims of Axum by A Jebel, 2009. *Yemuslimoch Guday Metsihet* [Muslims' Affairs Magazine] 1(1):31-33.

57 Dereje, "Religious Conflict Analysis in Ethiopia", 3.

58 *Yemuslimoch Guday Metsihet* [Muslims' Affairs Magazine]. 2012. Ummu Ayman Publishing and Advertisement Private Ltd. Co., 1(1):12.

59 Wudu TK. 2006. *The Ethiopian Orthodox Church, the Ethiopian State and the Alexandrian See: Indigenizing the Episcopacy and Forging National Identity, 1926-1991*, PhD Diss, University of Illinois, 7.

60 Wudu, *The Ethiopian Orthodox Church, the Ethiopian State and the Alexandrian See*.

61 Interview with local Muslims of Axum by A Jebel.

Moreover, there are different sayings in Ethiopia which have their own implications for the Axum controversy over securing land for Muslim worshipping houses. As stated earlier, Muslims have been totally prohibited from acquiring land for a living, let alone for mosques. That is why most Muslims today still pursue trade over other activities. An old Amharic saying in the community illustrates how difficult accessing land was for Ethiopian Muslims: *"Yemuslim hageru Mecca, Yewef hageru warka"* – literally "A Muslim's land is Mecca, as a bird dwells on a tree". The saying implies that, there is no place for Muslims in Ethiopia. It is only in Mecca that Muslims can claim their land to construct a mosque. This saying, however, does not work in present-day Ethiopia, especially since the overthrow of Emperor Haile Selassie in 1974. The military Derg regime redistributed the land of Ethiopia owned by feudal lords to the Ethiopian people, irrespective of their religious and ethnic background. Ethiopian Muslims benefited from that policy like many other poor peoples of the country. The 1991 regime change further consolidated the rights of groups and individuals to access land for different purposes, including land for the construction of houses of worship, irrespective of the location within the country. The Ethiopian laws, particularly those laws enacted after 1991, allowed the construction of mosques or churches for believers irrespective of the location, so long as legal procedures are followed. The Constitution of the Federal Democratic Republic of Ethiopia provides in Article 27(2) that "believers may establish institutions of religious education and administration in order to propagate and organize their religion."[62] This right is only restricted to keep education secular and free from "religion, political partisanship or cultural prejudices.[63] It does not prohibit the construction of mosques or churches for the mere reason of the area being regarded as a "holy place" by Christians or Muslims.

The local governments of the regional states of Amhara and Tigray reacted in a mixed way that did not prohibit, but also did not allow, the Muslims to build mosques. The regional governments are aware of the rights of Muslims, but are also trying not to disappoint Christians, particularly the powerful EOC. Despite their efforts not to openly deny access to land for Muslims of Axum and Lalibela, which would violate their constitutional rights, their silence in response to the requests of Muslims amount to denial. The statement made by the United States State Department in 2007 best illustrates the denial of land for the Muslims of Axum and Lalibela to construct mosques:

> Local authorities in the northern town of Axum, a holy city for EOC, continued to deny Muslim leaders' repeated requests to allocate land for the construction of a mosque, even though the Constitution provides for freedom to establish institutions of religious education and administration. Tigray and Amhara regional government officials

---

62 Constitution of Federal Democratic Republic of Ethiopia (FDRE), Proclamation No. 1/1995.
63 Constitution of the Federal Democratic Republic of Ethiopia, art 90 sub art 2.

choose not to interpret this provision liberally in the towns of Axum and Lalibela respectively and the Federal Government did not overrule them.[64]

The denial of plots of land for mosque construction in Axum and Lalibela is not without a backlash effect on Christians in the southern and eastern parts of Ethiopia, where Muslims are numerically dominant. Muslims raised another weak but similar logic with their Christian counterparts, claiming that, Harar and Jimma are "holy places" for Muslims and hence Christians should not be allowed to construct churches. Some even went to the extreme demanding that, "the already constructed churches should be demolished from these areas."[65]

With regard to the denial of plots of land for the construction of mosques, Hussein Ahmed even argues that, it is not only in Axum and Lalibela that Muslims faced opposition from the EOC and ordinary Christian residents for constructing mosques but in all parts of the country. On this point, he noted that:

> The construction of almost all the major mosques in Addis Ababa (and those elsewhere in the country) was invariably preceded by opposition from the Christian residents and churches of the areas in which the mosques were intended to be built, and a protracted legal battle with the government departments responsible for granting the plots of land, issuing the necessary title deeds and the permission for construction.[66]

Even after securing permission from relevant authorities to construct mosques, their heights were limited to a certain number of meters in order not to create psychological influence over the residents and to hide the visibility of Muslim presence. For example, minarets were not allowed to be constructed, in order to keep mosques as short as possible and to limit the reach of the *muezzin*'s prayer call to a very short distance. As Hussein puts it, the minaret of Nur Mosque in Addis Ababa was added much later after its construction since the rulers of the time were unhappy to see Muslim presence in the heart of the capital "dominating the city's skyline".[67]

In the construction of mosques, Muslims nearly always face popular protest, bureaucratic delay and obstruction. In many instances, this has led to violence and open conflict with the Christian community. A case in point was the problem that occurred during the construction of Gullele Mosque in Addis Ababa. While Muslims started constructing the mosque in the 1980s, work was suspended due to opposition from the nearby church. Moreover, the rulers of the vicinity claimed that the site was chosen for the construction of a school.

---

64 2011. "Where is Justice for the Muslims of Axum? Ethiopian Muslims from Tigray-Diaspora", *Badr Magazine*, 25.
65 Interview with former local official in Jimma town currently residing in Addis Ababa by MD Assen, 26 November 2014.
66 Hussein, "Coexistence and/or Confrontation?", 12.
67 Hussein, "Coexistence and/or Confrontation?".

The construction of the mosque was then delayed for years and was resumed only after the coming to power of EPRDF in the 1990s.[68]

In an informal discussion with a 70-year-old Muslim elder in Nefas Silk Lafto, a sub-city of Addis Ababa, he remembers some of the opposition they faced in the construction of mosques during the last days of Emperor Haile Selassie I.[69] My interviewee came to Addis Ababa from Wollo in 1972 with his elder brother. Upon their arrival, they settled around the outskirts of the city constructing "slum" houses from plastic and wood. As he remembers, they had very nice Christian neighbours who invited them over to drink coffee during Christian holy days. However, considering the lower status of Muslims in the public, their neighbours always exerted pressure on them to convert to Christianity, saying "why don't you convert to Christianity for us to eat meat together?"[70] They resisted the pressure and remained Muslim. As he reported, gradually many more Muslims came to the area from different parts of the country to settle. They secured permission from the governor of the area to construct a mosque, but they faced strong opposition from the local Christian residents. When they started construction, Christian residents all of a sudden built a "house" on the same site during the night, what is publicly called as *yechereqa bet* – literally "moon-house" to show its illegal nature constructed at night using the light of the moon. Subsequently, Christians claimed the property to construct a church. Due to the conflict between the Muslims and the Christians, the construction of both groups was delayed for a while. The revolution came in 1974 before the dispute was settled, and the Muslims initiated the matter for decision by the new Derg officials. The Christians also claimed the area. Finally, the problem was settled by providing two plots of land, one for the mosque and the other for the church. Today, the mosque and the church stand side-by-side as "living witnesses".

Compared with the past, the acquisition of land for the construction of mosques has become relatively easier under the EPRDF government. Although some problems of bureaucratic bottlenecks and popular protests persist, Muslims are in a far better position in both legal and practical terms to satisfy their spiritual needs. In the last two decades (1991-2010), the government and Ethiopian Muslims have had generally good relations. Muslims appreciate the efforts of the government in guaranteeing their religious rights and are supportive of the government.

CONCLUSION

The religious tolerance narrative of Ethiopia's religious past is complex to understand, since it is understood in different ways even among Muslims

---

68   Hussein, "Coexistence and/or Confrontation?", 6.
69   Interview with Sheikh Endris by MD Assen, 2012.
70   Based on Ethiopian tradition, Muslims and Christians could not eat together meat slaughtered by a person of the other faith.

themselves. In the long history of Ethiopia, religious tolerance and peaceful coexistence of Muslims and Christians were more prevalent than conflict, but mainly owing to the submissiveness of Ethiopian Muslims and the deliberate action of the successive rulers of the country to make Muslims politically impotent. In one way or another, all the rulers of Ethiopia employed different mechanisms to discourage and possibly eliminate Islam from the country until the 1991 regime change. Some used openly aggressive policies and forced conversion, whereas others pursued a more systematic way of eliminating Islam in the name of pseudo-religious tolerance policies. The intolerant faces of Christian elites were observed several times when Muslims asserted their rights and became politically aware.

In sum, in the long history of Muslim-Christian coexistence, tolerance and forbearance were the common features of Ethiopia's religious past. At the state level, Muslims were denied access to land, government positions and important economic sectors, but at the same time they were tolerated as long as the Christian dominance was unchallenged. There have been legal and practical improvements in the post-1991 Ethiopia but tensions are high between the two religious communities regarding control over the public space. This in turn affects peaceful coexistence negatively.

2 CONTESTED HERITAGE: THE "CUL-TOURISTIC" TURN IN THE CELEBRATION OF IRREECHA RITUAL IN ETHIOPIA

Serawit Bekele Debele[1]

INTRODUCTION

Until the 1974 outbreak of the revolution that led to the end of the imperial regime, religious freedom in Ethiopia was not enjoyed by all. For centuries since its introduction, the Ethiopian Orthodox Christianity was recognised as a state religion with a significant socio-political, cultural as well as economic influence. The same church also had the privilege of defining national identity to the extent that, until recently, Ethiopia was depicted as an "island of Christianity". Other religions like Islam, Evangelical and Catholic Christianity as well as indigenous religions were marginalised. The case with the indigenous religions was even more problematic, because they were not only marginalised, but also made objects of criticism as backward practices. Thus, the Ethiopian Orthodox Church was the only institution that was strictly regarded as a national heritage with which many proudly identify.[2] Nevertheless, with the emergence of a socialist-oriented regime in 1974, this assumed a different form as the government introduced certain reforms that recognised all religions and also declared secularism as a governing principle.

Since then, there has been a relative freedom enjoyed by all religions, although repression on religious groups and institutions was more often than not characteristic of the military regime.[3] After seventeen years of civil war, an ethnic coalition called Ethiopian People's Democratic Revolutionary Front (EPRDF)

---

1 Serawit Bekele Debele is a Fritz Thyssen Stiftung postdoctoral fellow at the department of religious studies: University of Bayreuth, Germany.
2 For instance, Islam was introduced to Ethiopia in the seventh century, thus having a history as old as that of Ethiopian Orthodox Christianity. Until very recently, its status as a national historical heritage that has shaped the country's past was less acknowledged, although of late there is a re-emergence of Islam in the public debate about what makes a national identity in Ethiopia, owing to the vibrant scholarship that focuses on the religion.
3 The military regime introduced certain reforms that were greatly commended by the public. For instance, Islamic holidays like Ramadan were accepted as public holidays like Easter, Christmas and other Christian celebrations. However, the regime was also known for repressing certain religious institutions like Evangelical churches on allegations of relationships they were assumed to have with political organisations. The Mekane Yesus Evangelical church was one such victim due to its alleged association with the Oromo Liberation Front. Thus, regardless of the reforms, the regime was rather ambivalent in the way it related to religious institutions, making the insertion of secularism a superficial government intervention to demarcate the separation of religion and politics.

took power in 1991. The new regime introduced a constitution in 1995 in which religious freedom was granted. Ethnic federalism also became the organising principle of the federal state of Ethiopia. The era of ethnic federalism in post-1991 Ethiopia provided a legal framework that promoted and celebrated ethnic, religious and cultural diversity. Owing to this, identity politics took centre stage; which in turn necessitated the revitalisation of ethno-nationalist sentiments that found expression in most of the previously marginalised and now reviving cultural and religious practices.

Irreecha, the annual ritual of thanksgiving, is a religious festival that gained prominence and visibility following the change of regime in 1991. There are two major seasonal rituals. The first, known as Irreecha Tulu (meaning hilltop), takes place to pray for rain, and it is held just before the rainy season commences. People gather at the top of a sacred mountain to plead with Waaqa (the creator) to give them enough rain for the harvest and also to protect them, their family members, the cattle and everything else that he created. The second one is what is called Irreecha Melka (lake). This is held to express gratitude to Waaqa, who has given the people and the cattle enough rain and also transited them from the foggy and rainy to the sunny and beautiful spring. Irreecha Tulu and Melka may take place at different sacred sites. In this chapter, I am focusing on the major Irreecha Melka that is held as an opening before all others take place. It takes place on a Sunday at the end of September or first week of October at Hora Arsedi, a sacred lake located in the Bishoftu city of Oromia Regional State. It is an important event among the Oromo[4] and other ethnic groups, as it is a season of change from the dark to the sunlight. It is a transition to the season of harvest, a time when the rivers and streams settle and communication among relatives and friends resumes. As a way of appreciating Waaqa's (sky God) kindness for his protection and provision, it is held to extend appreciation and also pray for further prosperity, health and success throughout the year. It is a time to celebrate nature. On this occasion, participants carry freshly cut grass and trek to the lake, where they dip the grass inside the holy water and sprinkle it on themselves, because the water is believed to have a healing and cleansing effect.[5]

---

4 The Oromo are the largest ethnic group in Ethiopia. They live in the Oromia Regional State of the Federal Democratic Republic of Ethiopia. In the current political setup, they are represented by the Oromo People's Democratic Organisation (OPDO), a member party to the ethnic coalition that currently rules the country called Ethiopian People's Revolutionary Democratic Front (EPRDF). They are followers of Waqqeffana, Islam and Christianity (of various denominations). Since change of regime in 1991, there has been an active cultural and religious revival and as will be dealt with in my forthcoming book, the revival has political overtone, which is also what makes Irreecha an interesting entry point to understand the complex and dynamic interaction of Oromo national identity, cultural revival, articulation of political demands and aspirations.

5 While conducting my fieldwork in Bishoftu, I have been told by many participants that they come to fetch the holy water on ordinary days, not just on the main day, to keep it at home to fend off bad spirits and any other sources of ailment

Irreecha brings together thousands of participants from all religious (some of which are Ethiopian Orthodox Christians, Pentecostals, Evangelicals, Catholics, Muslims, followers of the Oromo religion called Waqqeffana) and ethnic backgrounds (for example Amhara, Tigre, Gurage), although the Oromo are predominant. The ritual is also characterised by various colourful events like votive offerings (gifts offered when someone's acknowledges that her or his prayers are answered), spirit possession, invocation songs and ululations, trance, coffee ceremonies, libation and so on. In addition to such ritual performances, it is also commonplace to observe modern music bands performing on a stage built by the city municipality. Folk songs by a group of Oromo females and males are also a noticeable feature of the ritual celebration. Given its ever increasing popularity, its socio-political and economic significance, political dignitaries, including the regional state's president, attend the ritual and address the public through their speeches. Of late, it has also become a site of curiosity for both local and foreign tourists as a result of which millions flock to the sacred lake on the day of the celebration. Since 2007, the Oromia Regional State's Culture and Tourism Bureau has involved itself as a custodian and organiser of the ritual. Although the civil society association called Mecha and Tulema Association was responsible in making Irreecha popular at in the 1990s and early 2000s, the role of the regional state's tourism bureau is paramount in elevating Irreecha into a tourist attraction that is no longer confined to the local celebrants.[6]

This active government involvement through the bureau has led to the gradual shift in the articulation of Irreecha from a "religious ritual" to a "cultural festivity". Under the auspices of the bureau, Irreecha is reinvented as an intangible cultural heritage that mobilises the Oromo across religious

---

and affliction. Many also shared testimonies in which they said that they have witnessed some healing being conducted. The most common problem is related to child bearing. Barren women come to the lake and immerse themselves with the water in the hope that they get children. For some, so I was told, it worked and the next year they return with their offerings to extend their gratefulness.

6   A more detailed account of the ritual is available in my forthcoming book titled *Managing Irreecha: Religion and Politics in post-1991 Ethiopia*. The main finding of my research is that Irreecha is appropriated by political groups, both the state and its opponents, as a space of self-presentation and/or airing resistance against the current political goings on in the country. It is a site that is managed by political actors for the production of governable subjects. It is also where political engagement by the people is actively taken to manifest ambivalent political practices which fall in the spectrum of supporting and resisting the regime. This interplay of celebrating national identity and political engagement reached its climax in the celebration of 2 October 2016. During this time, the nationwide #Oromoprotest that has been going on in the country since 2014 found expression at Hora Arsedi. The youth seized the opportunity to unanimously express their protest and resistance against the continued government crackdown including other fundamental political demands. This eventually culminated with the death of hundreds following the firing of teargas in an attempt to contain the protesting youth. This incident is both a reflection of past state-society relation and will have significant ramifications for the country's political developments in the years to come.

backgrounds to celebrate their collective national identity. This reinvention is predicated on the exclusion of spirit mediumship and practices to that effect. Whereas reverence to Waaqa and the benevolent spirits is central to Irreecha, government officials and some educated elites assert that the practice of revering such entities should not be considered as a constituting element. Particularly, spirit mediumship as it happens at Hora Arsedi is depicted as a backward practice by some and the worship of evil spirits by others.

Such association of spirit mediumship with backwardness and evilness is readily accepted by officials and experts in the tourism bureau, which shows a will to involve itself into the process of redefining the ritual. By redefining Irreecha as a cultural expression, the officials dissociate the ritual from the spiritual practices. This is accompanied by what I call a "cul-touristic"[7] turn, meaning a process of commodification and commercialisation of the ritual in a manner that makes it, as well as the city of Bishoftu, a tourist attraction, not only to local consumers but also to foreigners.[8] This brings in the economic dimension of appropriating and editing the ritual by the culture and tourism bureau. The "cul-touristic" turn is important, as it makes Irreecha marketable to a wide range of Oromo participants who do not necessarily subscribe to everything the ritual delivers. For instance, Protestant and Evangelical Christians and some conservative Muslim and Ethiopian Orthodox Christians are ardent critics and opponents of such practices like possession trance.[9] Some even reject Irreecha in its entirety. Emphasising on the cultural and touristic aspects of Irreecha makes it accessible to this group of critics, because it is articulated in a manner that does not contradict with their religious convictions. However, the redefinition is not simply accepted by all. It is contested and challenged by those who passionately defend the ritual's spirituality.

---

7   I coined the term "cul-touristic" in order to better capture the involvement of the Oromia Regional State's Culture and Tourism Bureau and the change and continuity experienced in the articulation and celebration of the thanksgiving ritual. The term is driven from culture and tourism. It is used to show the gradual expansion of Irreecha into a cultural event and narrowing scope of the spiritual aspect owing to the involvement of the bureau in addition to the active promotion of the ritual as a tourist attraction.

8   Such representation of indigenous religious practices like spirit mediumship and possession cults has a historical foundation, since the Ethiopian Orthodox Church, Islam and Evangelical Christianity uprooted local practices and converted people who were incorporated within the Christian empire. The success of Christianity's expansion partly depended on denigrating such local practices as things of evilness that people have to break away from. While this is the historical basis of their denigration as backward and evil, the recent outreach by the Evangelcals and Pentecostals in the country has made the mediums' marginalisation even higher than before. There seems to be an implicit alliance between these religious groups and some officials in the bureau.

9   For more on the religious demography of Ethiopia, see online at:
    http://www.globalreligiousfutures.org/countries/ethiopia#/?affiliations_religion_id=0&affiliations_year=2010&region_name=All%20Countries&restrictions_year=2014

As a result, two antagonistic groups are at loggerheads. On one hand, there are those who advocate Irreecha as a purely cultural event, while on the other there are those who contest this as a "despiritualisation" of the ritual which otherwise revolves around Waaqa and the spirits. These two groups have actively contested – at times even violently – the shift in meaning and significance of Irreecha. The role of the culture and tourism bureau in establishing the shift towards what I call the "cul-touristic" tone is significant. Given that the proponents of possession trance are subordinated both historically and currently and also because they are a minority, suppressing their stories is much easier compared to the risk the government takes of losing a larger number of Oromo participants who ultimately reject the mediumship and possession trance at Hora Arsedi. Drawing on ethnographic research conducted over the last five years in Oromia, this chapter reflects on the role of "secular" institutions in the contestation, reconstruction and/or transformation of intangible heritages.

HERITAGE AS PROCESS AND DISCOURSE

Laurajane Smith, a professor of heritage studies,[10] conceptualises heritage in a manner that makes it break away from "thing-ness" with an intact and timeless essence by articulating it as a discourse, process, work and performance. She defines it as a socio-cultural process of connecting to an object and a practice that is located in the experience of people in relation to certain performances (like rituals) or objects (like sites). Emphasising its performative aspect, Smith combines heritage with doing something and states that it is a work of "being in place, renewing memories and associations, sharing experiences with kinswomen to cement present and future social and familial relationships. Heritage wasn't only about the past – though it was that – it also wasn't just about material things – though it was that, too – heritage was a process of engagement, an act of communication and an act of making meaning in and for the present."[11] As such, it is a political process that involves diverse interest groups and bound to a set of power relations. Smith further establishes that heritage as a process is mostly created and recreated in the interest of the powerful groups, which have the means to legitimise or delegitimise what is regarded as heritage. Its creation becomes possible in response to various nationalist and political agendas, making it "a dynamic process which involves competition over whose version of the past, [the present and the future]" to preserve and designate as heritage.[12] This might result in the subordination of some discourses propagated by people who have less or no power compared to the authorities who demarcate the boundaries and limits of what heritage entails who in turn contest the imposed version of heritage.

---

10   Smith L. 2006. *Uses of Heritage*. New York: Routledge.
11   Smith, *Uses of Heritage*, 1.
12   Smith, *Uses of Heritage*, 8.

To capture such a complex and dynamic process and practice of heritage formation, Smith developed the notion of "authorised heritage discourse", which rests on the argument that heritage is a discourse in its own right. Smith states that, "authorised heritage discourse" is a notion that encapsulates such a political and power-imbued process of de/nominating heritages.[13] Arguing along this line, archaeologist Rodney Harrison writes that authorised heritage discourse "is a set of ideas that works to normalise a range of assumptions about the nature and meaning of heritage and to privilege particular practices, especially those of heritage professionals and the state. Conversely, the 'authorised heritage discourse' can also be seen to exclude a whole range of popular ideas and practices relating to heritage".[14] It is also, I argue, as much concerned with challenging the powerful agents, namely experts and professionals who are behind what is designated as heritage and whose say in delineating heritage is regarded as valid. It is in this conceptual context that I look at what I call the "cul-touristic" turn in the articulation of Irreecha and the role authorised experts from the regional state's bureau play in removing certain elements as irrelevant while recreating others as authentic expressions of ethnic identity.

AUTHORISING IRREECHA AS CUL-TOURISTIC FESTIVAL AND THE ENSUING DEBATES

As it stands now, Irreecha has secured nationwide popularity not only in the Oromia region, but also in the whole country, as well as in the diaspora. It has become a point of curiosity, and questions regarding whether it is a cultural or religious celebration are increasingly debated. One of the multiple manifestations of the spirituality of the ritual is the spirit possession and trance that take place under the sacred tree, following the process of people dipping the freshly cut grass into the sacred lake and spreading it on their bodies. The possession and trance, accompanying coffee ceremony and votive offering are points of contention for many. While there are people who clearly understand it to have a religious intonation, others utterly discard the notion of Irreecha as religious and hence reject the aforementioned rituals. The bureau has a stance towards spirit mediums and the rituals that go on under the tree. They are regarded as grotesque which makes them unwanted additions to the "pure" Oromo cultural and religious tradition. They are also considered as alien practices that are not supposed to be viewed as part of the celebration. If, according to the bureau's statements, Irreecha accommodates such ritual performances, then instead of attracting, it repels a significant number of Oromo and loses its currency as a unifying celebration. It becomes confined to a few who regard it as a gathering to appease the divine. In this case, the place also

---

13 Smith, *Uses of Heritage*.
14 Harrison R. 2010. "What is Heritage?", in Harrison R (ed). *Understanding the Politics of Heritage.* Manchester: Manchester University Press, 5-42, 27.

becomes nothing more than a pilgrimage site that caters to the spiritual needs of only a certain group of people who subscribe to practices of mediumship at Hora Arsedi. Particularly, the main organiser of the ritual celebration, the regional state's bureau of culture and tourism, is of the view that Irreecha should be understood as a "neutral ground" that is conveniently accessible to all Oromo regardless of their religious convictions. Framing it as a cultural festivity that is removed from the spirituality some attribute to it makes the celebration open to a wide range of attendants. Portraying it as a cultural festival is predicated on the assumption that, compared to religion, culture is viewed as less compelling and to take part in such a colourful festival like Irreecha, one does not have to accept the spiritual aspect of the ritual as its integral part. Such a privileged and essentialised narrative is justified because it presents Irreecha in connection with ethnic identity and as a symbolic event that cements the Oromo across religious and cultural differences. In this way, Irreecha is linked to the broader notion of imagining the Oromo as a homogenous nation.

For instance, the commissioner of the regional state's bureau is clear in his assertion that it is not for the bureau to accommodate the spiritual aspect of the celebration, even more so because it is a secular institution whose task is not to promote religions. Promoting Irreecha as a cultural festivity serves as a pragmatic "strategy" because it brings together a religiously diverse but "ethnically homogenous" group of people. In the words of Oromo official Mohamed Jilo, "since Irreecha is very much connected with the Oromo identity; we are using Irreecha as a platform to create unity among the Oromo."[15] Along this line, an expert in the bureau by the name Alemu Serbesa, who is an anthropologist and a historian, argues that permitting spirit mediums and their practices during the celebration of Irreecha defeats the objective of appropriating it as an authentic heritage of the Oromo who have diverse confessions since not every participant subscribes to spirit possession activities. Most importantly, the mediums' act is seen rather as a source of "aesthetic deformation", to use Serbesa's own expression. For him, this deformation, unless removed, keeps at bay a large number of participants by disfiguring an otherwise pleasant ethno-cultural event.[16] Using such narratives, the authorities and experts in the bureau eschew accommodation of practices that are not acceptable to the elite. Moreover, in the service of making it attractive by erasing the spiritual dimensions from Irreecha and thereby secularising it, the government justifies its claims of distancing itself from religious affairs. This is so because if Irreecha's secularity is highlighted by the bureau, then the government could not be

---

15 Interview with Mohamed Jilo, Addis Ababa, Ethiopia, 24 October 2013.
16 Interview with Alemu Serbesa, Addis Ababa, Ethiopia, 22 November 2013. It is also important to mention that the office is organising certain movements to reform Irreecha in line with the "unifying" culture oriented definition the office ascribed to it. For instance, until September 2012, mediums used to gather on the eve of Irreecha by the lakeside to perform an all night long ritual of pleading with Waaqa and the spirits. Since 2012, however, they have been banned by the police from spending the night at Hora Arsedi.

blamed for violating its own constitutional provisions on secularism which dictate state non-intervention. To achieve this, the experts and authorities are invested with the power to define and legitimise the "cul-touristic" narrative which makes the ritual both marketable as a tourist attraction and accessible to non-believing Oromo participants. Needless to say, the secularising narrative privileges and expands only a certain strand of the ritual as its normal and natural definition. Hence, in addition to socio-economic mobilisation, there is a clear political motive and benefit to promoting it as a cultural heritage.

Smith rightly asserts that such authorised narratives, like the one propagated by the bureau as pronounced by professionals, privilege "expert values and knowledge about the past and its material manifestations, and dominates and regulates professional heritage practices".[17] The experts at the tourism office resort to certain discursive universes to define Irreecha as a cultural heritage and delegitimise other meanings attributed to the ritual by describing them as sources of "aesthetic deformation". Such expressions are readily accepted by many, because they are coming from experts, who seem to be more trusted than others given that they have the professional input to normatively delimit what is right and wrong. As it appears, Irreecha and the discourse regarding its meaning are perpetuated by experts, whose professional intervention in the construction of its new meaning is thereby endorsed.

Such experts focus on promoting what they believe is "normal" and aesthetically pleasing to certain sections of the elite and they seem to have the support of the bureau to perpetuate the discourses. This tendency of appropriating Irreecha as a "cul-touristic" event that mobilises the Oromo across religious backgrounds and also attracts tourists from elsewhere, entails a reinterpretation, and leads to the emergence of conflicting views on whether Irreecha is a religious ritual or a cultural event. However, the bureau's authorities, as well as its experts, have the political and symbolic capital to enforce and promote the interpretation that presents Irreecha as a "cul-touristic" festival. Promoting the ritual as an authentic Oromo culture presupposes the removal of some practices, which are labelled as additives that are not fitting with the tradition. Removing certain practices in turn narrows Irreecha's wider and complex meaning. This development is a clear indication that heritage is a discourse in the sense that it goes beyond the use of language for communication. It is a practice informed by power relations in which ideologies, knowledge and meaning are embedded. In such a hegemonic context of knowledge production, dissenting or alternative voices regarding heritage discourse are not permitted to flourish

CONTESTING THE "CUL-TOURISTIC" TURN

Heritage is about the construction, negotiation, expression and contestation of multiple identities and socio-cultural as well as religious values. Despite this,

---

17 Smith, *Uses of Heritage*, 4.

widening the cultural aspect of Irreecha as an Oromo heritage has understated these multiple meanings and interpretations. By inflating and authorising the cultural aspect of the ritual, the authorised experts have reduced it to something that has a single meaning with which all participants should identify. This imposes on participants a uniform take on and relationship to the ritual. The experience that emerges from being there is ultimately dictated by the experts, leading to the contestation of Irreecha as an intangible cultural heritage. The contestation emerges out of the fact that heritage, as highlighted by Smith,[18] is as much a point of promoting consensus about the past as challenging the status quo imposed presently by the hegemonic authorities.

For instance, articulating Irreecha in culturalist manner has resulted in the marginalisation of the spirit mediums of which the Oromo are a significant constituency. On the other hand, this hegemonic categorisation of sites, cultural and/or religious traditions as heritage changes their relationship to the local people. It becomes set apart, foreign, special and far from the everyday because of its redefinition as a heritage that either contradicts the local perception of the practice and its objectives or does not respond to the needs of the locals. In the case of Irreecha at Hora Arsedi, this authorised reformulation of Irreecha as a cultural semiotics is knitted with the tensions that emerge from the religious tones of the ritual and are brought to the fore by mediums and their followers.

While the culture and tourism bureau is attempting to widen up the cultural semiotics, those who define and relate to Irreecha in strictly spiritual terms are not passively receiving the imposed definition of the ritual that downplays its spiritual tone. For instance, spirit mediums and their followers assert themselves as patrons whose relationship to and experience with the event need to be taken as seriously as the one proposed by the authorised experts who emphasise the elitist notion of Irreecha as a symbol of ethnic identity. In their assertions, they stress that what makes the ritual what it is, including its increasing popularity, is the spiritual force that is attributed to the sacred site and the event.[19] They also make reference to the provision of the Constitution of the Federal Democratic of Ethiopia, which equally grants religious freedom at both individual and associational levels.[20] Based on the constitution, they accuse the authorities of intervening in what should not be their concern. By making reference to the constitutional provision of state non-intervention in religious affairs, spirit mediums and their constituencies challenge the experts of the bureau for imposing their view on the religious event using their power while it is outright wrong to do so as far as the constitution goes. In the mediums' view, this obviously contradicts the constitution and showcases the gap in the implementation of the legal provisions on religious freedom both as an individual and in association.

---

18   Smith, *Uses of Heritage*.
19   Interview with Kuma Ide'a, Dukem, Ethiopia, 16 February 2013.
20   Constitution of the Federal Democratic Republic of Ethiopia, art 11.

CONCLUSION

By flattening out the diversity into singularity, the authorities have attempted to regulate the definition of Irreecha as a cultural heritage that has less or even nothing to do with religion. This action has led to the tension, since a significant number of people challenge the value the authorities have ascribed to it. This tension is a reflection of alterations in the popular understanding of cultural and religious values and also the resistance against manifest dictatorial approaches in delimiting what is and is not heritage. The redefinition of Irreecha by the bureau as a "cul-touristic" event that does not necessarily endorse and reflect the spiritual aspect mirrors also the fact that heritages are instrumentalised by regimes in the contested arena of identity formation and expression. It also shows that the reaction by the subaltern to such an imposition is another sign of the agentive role actors play to challenge and even reject imposed values that do not necessarily reflect their view of heritage.

Clearly, the way Irreecha is reframed as an intangible heritage by the bureau feeds on and responds to the demands of the privileged few. This way of approaching Irreecha by the experts and authorities does not account for diverse participants' diverse senses of being there and taking part in the ritual. This is a clear indication of the role of secular institutions in the reconstruction of certain events in the interest of an ideology which is geared towards managing the public into a homogenised set of categories in the name of "celebrating ethnic identity unanimously". This, however, is not to imply that there is absolute uniformity in the way the authorised narrative is received even within the bureau. There are some experts and ordinary participants who, along with spirit mediums, contest this narrative that makes the spiritual significance of the ritual irrelevant. These sections of Irreecha participants lament the ritual's increasing commodification and also that it is losing its spiritual might. Some even go to the extent that at some point Waaqa and the spirits might withdraw from supporting the Oromo. Thus, the "cul-touristic" turn is not lightly taken by those who fear detrimental consequences that stem from disregard to the spirits Waaqa assigned.

Irreecha is a multifaceted and complex ritual that takes place in a site which is imbued with different meanings that are informed by experiences of participants from different walks of life. It is where various religio-cultural works and multiple identities are performed and expressed. As much as a site for leisure activities of touristic interest, it is an event which is connected to spiritual convictions of certain groups of people. It caters to the aesthetic pleasure and identity affirmation of an elite class as much as it attends to the religious needs of the local celebrants of the ritual. As such, one could assert that Irreecha is an event in which more complex and nuanced socio-cultural as well as religious processes and formations are at work. However, as far as the bureau is concerned, Irreecha is a means of celebrating a seemingly secularised Oromo national identity; it is a site of celebrating Oromo-ness. Thus, there is no interest in endorsing the multiplicity of perspectives that emerge from different positions. Through the culture and tourism bureau of the Oromia region, the state's constitution of the ritual fixes it within the confines of the cultural and touristic interests which lead to the emergence of one dimensional and static meaning. It simply becomes an elitist orthopraxy that is cut off from other developments within various perspectives.

The bureau, relying on the power vested in it, is producing social, political and religious norms by inventing a certain narrative and undermining other alternatives as nonexistent or wrong. It downplays diversity by censoring and controlling narratives, while making us believe that there is singularity of meaning which all have accepted. There is an apparent lack of room to take into account multiple perspectives coming from different subject positions towards Irreecha as heritage. This shift in discourses and narratives has ramifications for the manner in which heritages are used to express identities and belongingness. Instead of allowing multiplicity of meaning through which various identities are constructed and expressed, heritage becomes confined to the meanings ascribed to it by the dominant groups. Such confinement of heritage to the powerful few makes it lose its connectivity with broader section of participants. The crucial part of this problem is also related to the question of preservation and sustainability of a given heritage. If people lose interest in it because it does not represent them and if they do not identify with it, they care less to preserve it and pass it on to the next generation.

Irreecha is appropriated for claiming an Oromo cultural space in the wider politico-cultural landscape in Ethiopia. Its reformulation in this manner is attributed to ethnic federalism that encourages the spectrum of ethnicity as a substantive aspect of national identity. It is under this landscape of competing for cultural spaces and representation in the wider national context that Irreecha became appealing for appropriation as an affirmation of Oromo national identity by expanding on its cultural traits. This "cul-touristic" turn expands the ritual's meaning in the national politico-cultural landscape by giving the Oromo a source of self-assertion and representation. However, this discourse and practice operate at the risk of narrowing down the pluralities of experiences, meaning-making and relationships observed with regards to Irreecha. While such an appropriation of Irreecha empowers the Oromo as a great nation with a proud culture that can assert itself in the national arena, it is disempowering for those whose view of Irreecha is linked to its spirituality. Thus, Irreecha's instrumentalisation as a secular rubric of national representation is made possible at the risk of the subalternisation of indigenous religious traditions as it involves the modification and inflation of the ritual to make it befitting to a national culture. This in turn manifests the tension and contradictions between constitutional implementation of religious freedom versus prioritisation of identity politics which comes from the state's commitment to ethnic federalism.

Finally, linking Irreecha to the tourism office and redefining it in cultural terms has multiple implications in broadening the understanding of religion in relation to politics. The current state is praised for the religious reforms it introduced, championing secularism by clearly stating that the state shall not intervene in religious matters and religions shall not interfere in state related affairs. However, the Ethiopian state has not completely broken with the past in the way it is implementing secularism as a governing principle. While state-religion interplay is the continuation of a legacy from the past, the contemporary Ethiopian state has brought more religions to the fore – this is the new development the change of regime introduced. However, the regime is afraid of religion and sees it as a danger to state, despite the enormous power wielded by the state. In response, the state meddles in religious affairs in manifold ways. Where necessary, it defines by setting the parameters and boundaries to decide what amounts to religious and at which point something becomes cultural. The discourses revolving around Irreecha as a national heritage provide evidence to show that the link between state and religion is much more complex and, in fact, opposed to the dictates of constitutional provisions on secularism.

3 RELIGIOUS PLURALISM AND COHABITATION IN ETHIOPIA: SOME CRITICAL NOTES

Theodros Teklu[1]

INTRODUCTION

Religious diversity is a typical feature of many societies, including African ones. Religious identities are, arguably, shaped not only by societies' "heritage" (including cultural, religious, legal and historical dimensions), but also by social developments. By social developments, I mean those global processes that enter the subjectivities of Africans, in general, and Ethiopians, in particular, such as the socialist movement, neoliberal order, and Islamic radicalisation or "universal" declarations of human rights. Drawing on contemporary social developments that shape the religious identities of Ethiopians, this essay discusses radical religious imaginations that simultaneously institute identity and obliterate the invisible heritage, understood as the diverse ways in which different religious identities, mainly Islam and Christianity, developed together with the sense of mutual respect.

Although a competitive relationship should not be established between heritage and social development, because of their overlapping spheres and potential for synergy, it is important to note that the tension between them can at times be non-constructive, even devastating. In studying the Ethiopian experience, one can observe both. The purpose of this essay is not to offer a full-fledged account of radical religious and political imaginations in Ethiopia. It is rather to present some ideas developed by social theorists, sociologists, anthropologists and historians, which may prove profitable for conceptually reflecting on religious pluralism and heritage in light of legal and social developments in Ethiopia. Consequently, this study aims at encouraging attentive reflection on the current tension in Christian-Muslim relations towards paving the way for an ethos of cohabitation and responsibility.

Cohabitation can be captured by the semantic range of the Latin words *habito*, *habitare*, *habitavi*, and *habitatus* that mean "inhabit, dwell" and also "live, stay".[2] The immediacy or elemental nature of cohabitation, which is primordial to any form of contract or covenant, has a great significance to consider the habitat as a common (Gk *koinos*) fostering human togetherness and fellowship (Gk *koinonia*). My use of the concept has an affinity with the use of the term by philosophers such as Judith Butler and Charles Taylor who appeal not to the

---

1 Lecturer in Philosophical Theology and Ethics, Ethiopian Graduate School of Theology.
2 Online at: http://latin-dictionary.net/definition/21820/habito-habitare-habitavi-habitatus

notion of toleration but "cohabitation".³ Cohabitation implies that all people are cohabitants on earth, and that "We are given to each other. We can't choose."⁴ More on this later.

To this end, I shall focus on imaginations at the intersection of local and global processes that shape the subjectivities of Ethiopians and their implications for religious freedom, rights and responsibilities. I shall begin by delineating the contemporary religious tension in Ethiopia by drawing attention to the relationship between the two main religions in the country – Christianity (63%) and Islam (34%).⁵ This part of the discussion aims at explaining how religious identities are being (re)constructed – between heritage and social development – in a manner that advances religious cleavages. Second, I will critically examine the syntax (grammar) of the public and the crisis of civility within the Ethiopian context. By civility, I mean the culture of mutual recognition and respect.⁶ Here, I will analyse the Muslim narrative of marginalisation and victimisation *contra* the narrative of peaceful coexistence and tolerance that has dominated public discourse in Ethiopia. I will further develop the analysis by focusing on the crisis of civility manifested by the public visibility of religion. Before concluding, I will emphasise the need for a moral pedagogy that accentuates the imperative of peaceful and harmonious cohabitation as an antidote to the "mad dream of a world without others".⁷

RELIGIOUS PLURALISM BETWEEN HERITAGE AND SOCIAL DEVELOPMENT

> As far as the question of religious ... equality is concerned, the result is a mixed affair. Islam, one of the oldest religions in the country, has come to enjoy since 1975 the kind of recognition and respect it deserves. Nevertheless, one could notice a feeling of "It is getting too far" on the part of the Christians and "It is only the beginning" on the part of Muslims. Wise and prudent leadership is required on both sides

---

3   Butler J. 2011. "Is Judaism Zionism?", in Mendieta E and Van Antwerpen J (eds). *The Power of Religion in the Public Sphere*. New York: Columbia University Press, 71-91.
4   Cf. The words of the well-known philosopher, Charles Taylor; Butler J, Habermas J, Taylor C and West C. "Concluding Discussion", in Mendieta E and Van Antwerpen J, 111.
5   Based on Census 2007, Orthodox (43.5%), Muslim (33.9%), Protestant (18.6%), traditional (2.6%), Catholic (0.7%), other (0.7%); cf. Central Statistical Agency, "Population and Housing Census Report-Country – 2007". Online at: http://www.csa.gov.et/
6   Charles Taylor refers to civility as the culture of "human rights, equality and non-discrimination and democracy", which are norms around which democratic societies are organised. See Petersen HS. 2013. "Political Engagement of Historic Churches in Eastern Africa", *Swedish Missiological Themes*, 101:67-106.
7   Mbembe A. 2002. "African Modes of Self-Writing", *Public Culture* 14(1):252.

to make sure that these two old religions would not abandon their tradition of mutual tolerance.⁸

Taking our cue from this passage from one of the most prominent Ethiopian historians, Bahru Zewde, we recognise that religious equality and the question of entitlement are contested issues in Ethiopian history. Muslims feel that the Orthodox have been privileged throughout history and consider it relevant to demand plots of land, for example, to construct mosques. As the above quote establishes, the current situation is characterised by a tension that has the potential to intensify polarisation between Christianity and Islam in Ethiopia. This, in turn, corresponds to the tension between heritage and social development. First, the fact that Islam has gained recognition reflects that remarkable social development has taken place in Ethiopia; and second, the erosion of the culture of mutual respect signifies the obliteration of heritage – "pan-Ethiopian traits", as will be explained below. Although subject to contradictory interpretations, both the culture of recognition and respect, as well as legal recognition, are part of the historical reality of Ethiopia.

A cursory review of the scholarly discussion reveals academic arguments for the peaceful introduction of Islam into historic Ethiopia and its subsequent indigenisation, in contrast to other scholarly voices emphasising Muslim marginalisation and victimisation. The latter perspective utilises the metaphor of a "Christian island" a metaphor ostensibly depicting historic Ethiopia as a Christian country surrounded by Muslims – to make a case for the historical victimisation of Muslims.⁹ Along these lines this metaphor is deployed to reconstruct Ethiopian history as one characterised by a fault-line and power asymmetry between Christianity and Islam.¹⁰ Given the complexity of "Ethiopia" and the various forms the state has taken throughout history – and more specifically, the modern (re)construction of the Ethiopian State – such trends can be rendered problematic.

Contra such a reductive account of history, one may draw attention to how Ethiopians developed as a people. To be sure, it was not merely because of their historical subjection to a common law under the single polity of Ethiopia that Ethiopians – of diverse religious backgrounds – developed as a people. Indeed, there have been micro-levels of social relations that made possible the interaction of Ethiopians across ethnic and religious divides. As Donald Levine,

---

8 Zewde B. 2008. *Society, State and History*. Addis Ababa: Addis Ababa University Press, 353.
9 Østebø T. 2010. "Islamism in the Horn of Africa: Assessing Ideology, Actors, and Objectives". CMI Working Paper 2:52. The idea of Ethiopia being, or depicted as, a "Christian island" might show how it countered attacks of Islamic intrusion (e.g. external enemies such as Turks and Mahdist Sudan), but not necessarily internal Muslim sultanates – without suggesting that there was always a peaceful relationship between them.
10 Desplat P. 2005. "The Articulation of Religious Identities and Their Boundaries in Ethiopia: Labelling Difference and Processes of Contextualization in Islam", *Journal of Religion in Africa* 35(4):482-505, 486.

rightly, points out, there are pan-Ethiopian traits that cut across ethnic and religious groups in Ethiopia: "beliefs about supernatural beings; ritual practices; food taboos; the cult of masculinity; aspects of social organization; insignia of ranks; and customs regarding personal status and the home."[11] According to this view, Ethiopia can be considered a "culture area" that fosters inter-religious interaction. Religions – Christianity, Islam and Judaism – have long coexisted and indigenised in Ethiopia developing common features over time. It suffices here to mention common traits between both Islam and Christianity such as views on religious conversion, veneration of saints, and pilgrimages.[12]

Underlying the above-stated convergent histories of these major religions are expressions of a heritage of peaceful coexistence and mutual respect.[13] Levine notes the substantial proof of a greater degree of tolerance and mutual respect that has developed as a distinctive feature of Ethiopian religions.[14] Arguably, this is not possible without convergent histories and the development of a commonly-held ethos of togetherness. Exploring the frontiers of commonality between these religious groups could be an interesting and important academic exercise.[15]

To argue for cultural and religious coexistence, however, one should not whitewash the grimier historical realities.[16] The opening quote from Bahru Zewde's work indicates the efforts of previous and current governments, which have sought to bring constitutional remedies in order to address past imbalances which largely resulted from the status of the Ethiopian Orthodox Tewahedo

---

11 Levine D. 1974. *Greater Ethiopia: The Evolution of a Multiethnic Society*. Chicago; London: University of Chicago Press, 47.
12 Østebø T. 2007. "The Question of Becoming: Islamic Reform-Movements in Contemporary Ethiopia", *Journal of Religion in Africa* 38(4):416-446. Levine, *Greater Ethiopia*, 44.
13 Levine D. 2007. "Notes on Ethiopia's Distinctive Religious Heritage", *Ethiopian Review*. Online at: http://www.ethiopianreview.com
14 See Levine, "Notes on Ethiopia's Distinctive Religious Heritage".
15 The work of Meron Zeleke could be exemplary in this regard. Based on ethnographic research done on the former centres of Sufi and the courts of sheikhs, Meron Zeleke explicates the various kinds and aspects of rituals that foster conflict resolution and peaceful coexistence at the micro-level of existence integrating people across ethnic and religious cleavages. See Zeleke M. 2010. "The former Sufi Centers of Learning and Their Contemporary Courts", *Journal of Religion, Conflict & Peace* 3(2):1-34. Online at: http://connection.ebscohost.com/c/articles/66621024/former-sufi-centers-learning-their-contemporary-courts. Works that expound the syncretistic nature of religion sometimes can positively challenge ideas of purity and exclusivity, cf. Debele SB. 2009. *Hybridization and Coexistence of Qallu Cabsa Institution with Orthodox Christianity in Debrelibanos Area*, Master's Thesis, Institute of Ethiopian Studies, Addis Ababa University.
16 Freedom and rights discourse is a modern-day problem that should not be stretched beyond the emergence of territorially defined nation-states aiming at the total control of populations which, depending on the specific context, is a modern phenomenon that goes back only to a few centuries or decades.

Church as the state church until 1974.[17] The following articles enshrined in the current Constitution of Federal Democractic Republic of Ethiopia adopted in 1995 (ratification in 1994)[18] are pertinent to religious freedom: "Article 11: "1. State and religion are separate. 2. There shall be no state religion. 3. The state shall not interfere in religious matters and religion shall not interfere in state matters." This article is rightly considered as one that guarantees the secular status of the state. Of course, this kind of secularisation can be understood as secularisation for the sake of religion because (a) the absence of a state church implies the equality of all religions and (b) the separation of religion and state safeguards the autonomy of the two (the freedom of religion is further elaborated in Article 27:1-5).[19] From this perspective, such secularisation seems to be more "procedural" rather than "programmatic" and has its own merits for achieving what Rajeev Bhargava calls "principled distance" between religion and the state.[20] State neutrality however has its own advantages in religiously diverse countries such as Ethiopia.

Such constitutional reforms are not only manifestations of internal phenomena, but also social development that insinuates global processes. Accordingly, the enactment of equality and juridical recognition in Ethiopia are results of internal processes intersecting with global processes such as socialism. Indisputably, "the socio-political history of Ethiopia had seen much Marxist thinking immersed into its intellectual self-understanding."[21] Hence, the above articles are reminiscent of both the fruit of egalitarian socialist ideals and "universal" declarations of human rights. But, this should not suggest that peaceful religious cohabitation and

---

17 At this juncture, it is important to note that the imbalance was not particular to Islam but, as a matter of fact, Protestant Christianity was highly persecuted as outlandish. See Constitution of the Federal Democratic Republic of Ethiopia, 1994.
18 Cf. The Ethiopian Constitution (1994) and (1984).
19 Article 27: "1. Everyone has the right to freedom of thought, conscience and religion. This right shall include the freedom to hold or to adopt a religion or belief of his choice, and the freedom, either individually or in community with others, and in public or private, to manifest his religion or belief in worship, observance, practice and teaching. 2. Without prejudice to the provisions of sub-Article 2 of Article 90, believers may establish institutions of religious education and administration in order to propagate and organize their religion. 3. No one shall be subject to coercion or other means which would restrict or prevent his freedom to hold a belief of his choice. 4. Parents and legal guardians have the right to bring up their children ensuring their religious and moral education in conformity with their own convictions. 5. Freedom to express or manifest one's religion or belief may be subject only to such limitations are prescribed by law and are necessary to protect public safety, peace, health, education, public morality or the fundamental rights and freedoms of others, and to ensure the independence of the state from religion."
20 Williams R. 2008. "Secularism, Faith and Freedom", in Ward G and Hoelzl M (eds). *The New Visibility of Religion: Studies in Religion and Cultural Hermeneutics*. London & New York: Continuum, 48; Taylor C. 2011. "Why We Need a Radical Redefinition of Secularism", in Mendieta and Van Antwerpen, 34.
21 Teklu T. 2014. *The Politics of Metanoia: Towards a Post-Nationalistic Political Theology in Ethiopia.* Peter Lang GmbH, Internationaler Verlag der Wissenschaften, 85.

mutual respect are purely outcomes of the legal recognition of religions. As the scholarly perspectives indicate in the above discussion, before the drafting and implementation of legal charters, there were already-existing practices of mutual recognition – albeit to differing degrees and despite some occasional challenges that disturb mutuality.

Granted, juridical recognition has its own benefits; thus, the freedoms and rights enshrined in the Ethiopian Constitution must be accompanied by good governance that ensures the rule of law. But this needs to match cultural values that make the implementation of the rules possible. Ethiopians of various religious affiliations have yet to mature in this respect. Religious identities in Ethiopia are held in the tension between heritage and social development. What further complicates the Ethiopian case at this juncture in history is the presence of another phenomenon of global processes – that is, Islamic identity discourse informed by Islamic reformism and, arguably, radicalism. We now look at this in greater detail.

THE CRISIS OF CIVILITY AND THE SYNTAX OF THE PUBLIC

As the foregoing discussion attempted to briefly demonstrate, a tension between heritage and social development characterises religious identities in Ethiopia. In what follows, I wish to spell out the tension in terms of the crisis of civility, in particular, the discursive disrespect as manifest incivility. In Ethiopia, since such a crisis is interlinked with the narrative construction of identities and their enactment in public, I will discuss the narrative of Muslim marginalisation and victimisation. An important caveat at this stage is that: (a) I do not claim to establish a unilinear causal relation between the narrative, which I am going to analyse, and discursive disrespect in the public sphere since the influence likely goes in both directions and (b) the fact that I will primarily deal with a Muslim narrative should not give the impression that there are no problems with other narratives, Christian or otherwise.

The narrative of Muslim marginalisation and victimisation

Debates over the meaning of the past and ways of taking the past forward have dominated political discourse in Ethiopia for some decades now. In the wake of the upsurge of ethnic sentience which resonates in ethno-nationalist historiography, Muslim scholars and popular writers have embarked on a project of reconstructing the history of Islam in Ethiopia.[22] Such new sensibility has led to the questioning of the "conventional" idea that there has been

---

22 Crummey D. 2001. "Ethiopian Historiography in the Latter Half of the Twentieth Century: A North American Perspective", *Journal of Ethiopian Studies* 34 (Special Issue):7-24.

a peaceful coexistence between Christians and Muslims in Ethiopia.²³ As Dereje Feyissa notes, the idiom of coexistence is already exhausted because of its susceptibility to contrary interpretations: the Ethiopian Orthodox Tewahedo Church is said to understand it as *accommodation* (how Christian Ethiopia historically welcomed Muslims), while Muslims opt to understand it as *forbearance* (how Muslims endured the historical marginalisation and victimisation under Ethiopian Christian rulers).²⁴ In this respect, the work of Ahmad Hussien, the late professor of history at the Addis Ababa University, can be a good representative that demonstrates this trend. I shall briefly examine his work, which offers a narrative construction of Ethiopian Muslim identity, and will forward some critical remarks.

First, the narrative construction starts by drawing attention to the *hijrah* – the emigration of persecuted followers of Muhammad from Mecca to seek asylum in Axum in 615 AD – in order to assert that Islam, in Ethiopia, is as old as Islam itself. The discourse proceeds to substantiate the presence of peaceful coexistence in the period following *hijrah*, thereby constructing an idealised religious past, which highlights not only the accommodation of Islam, but also a joyous embrace of Islam, symbolically illustrated by the conversion of the Axumite Christian king Nejashi to Islam.²⁵ The narrative depicts this period as the Golden Age. Until the thirteenth century peaceful coexistence continued, but the factors that contributed to the peaceful coexistence are never elaborated – in fact, the possibility of a development of pan-Ethiopian traits are rejected.

Second, the period following the Golden Age – from the thirteenth to the sixteenth century – is characterised by conflict between the Christian kingdom of Ethiopia and the Muslim sultanates. This period is considered to have contributed to the resurgence and military resistance against the Christian kingdom by Muslim sultanates of Ifat and Adāl with the climax of Imām Ahmad b. Ibrāhīm (nicknamed, Ahmad Grañ, meaning Ahmad the left-handed) (1506-1543), who attacked the Christian kingdom of Ethiopia, forcefully converting Christians to Muslims and destroying churches and manuscripts. This conflict is said to have oscillated with some Islamic victories, but ultimately the Muslims were defeated, leading to a subsequent period of the pacification of Muslims, who "seem to have accepted their subordinate position as part of the natural order of things."²⁶ It is due to the brutality of Christian Ethiopia's conquest of Muslims that the Muslim subject has been exposed to a politically exploitative system. The narrative holds Ethiopia's hostility and brutality

---

23   Hussein A. 2006. "Coexistence and/or confrontation? Towards a reappraisal of Christian-Muslim encounter in contemporary Ethiopia," *Journal of Religion in Africa* 36:4-22.
24   Feyissa D. "Accommodation, tolerance or forbearance? The politics of representing Ethiopia's religious past". Online at: http://www.aegis-eu.org/archive/ecas4/ecas-4/panels/41-60/panel-43/Dereje-Feyissa-Dori-Full-paper.pdf
25   Hussein, "Coexistence and/or confrontation?", 5.
26   Hussein, "Coexistence and/or confrontation?", 6.

towards the Muslims responsible for the decline of the Golden Age culminating in the ultimate domination of Muslims by Christians.

Third, the eighteenth and nineteenth centuries are cited as another period of Muslim dynasties of Warra Himano and Yajju in Wollo in north central Ethiopia.[27] The narrative celebrates the leaders of these dynasties as "devout Muslims committed to the enhancement of Islam at the regional level and generous patrons to the *ulama* (religious scholars). They encouraged the teaching of Islam in the royal courts and throughout their territories."[28] The encounter between trans-regional Muslim traders and contemporary Muslim thinkers and reformers is used to account for the development of "organized resistance to the forced imposition of Christianity – led by nineteenth-century militant Muslim scholars in Wallo".[29] Such encounter is regarded as positive and liberating. This narrative employs the logic of difference to idealise Islamic rule over that of Christian rule – the former's commitment to is said to have followed a less or non- Evangelism coercive means through mystical orders, whereas the latter's efforts are regarded as coercive (e.g. the reign of Emperor Yohannes IV between 1872 and 1889).[30]

Fourth, the narrative inscribes the Muslim subject as being caught in a series of conspiracies and subjugations by successive regimes. Lost opportunities such as the reign of Lej Iyyāsu (1913-16) who was pro-Muslim and who sought to "accommodate and integrate Ethiopian Muslims;" and the Italian occupation of Ethiopia (1936-1941) are cited.[31] The overthrow of Lej Iyyasu and the "harsh measures"[32] against Muslim leaders after the restoration of the monarchy in 1941 resulted in the eclipse of any emerging Muslim. Although the imperial regime allowed Islamic courts to function, "Muslims continued to be second-class citizens" during the rule of Haile Selassie.[33]

In this narrative, we encounter a reading of the 1974 Ethiopian revolution as a revolt of Muslims and other marginalised groups. Nevertheless, the narrative asserts that the changes instigated by the revolution were not radical enough to significantly affect the fate of Muslims. The period from 1974 to 1991 is considered as the first phase of Islamic revival, and 1991 to the present as the second phase of Islamic revival in Ethiopia.[34] However, both governments are criticised for failing to adequately respond to Muslim concessions. In this context, it is argued that although Islam has enjoyed legal recognition and has

---

27 Hussein, "Coexistence and/or confrontation?", 7.
28 Hussein, "Coexistence and/or confrontation?", 7.
29 Hussein, "Coexistence and/or confrontation?", 7-8.
30 Hussein, "Coexistence and/or confrontation?", 8.
31 Hussein, "Coexistence and/or confrontation?", 7-9.
32 Hussein, "Coexistence and/or confrontation?", 9.
33 Hussein, "Coexistence and/or confrontation?", 10.
34 Hussein, "Coexistence and/or confrontation?", 10-18.

gained greater visibility in the public sphere, what has been achieved thus far is deemed as insufficient.[35]

Generally, the narrative laments that Muslims were victimised under successive regimes and are still suspected of having relations with external radical groups. Ahmad Hussien draws attention to various localised moments of conflict between Christians and Muslims and the competitions, contentions and polemical exchanges between leaders and lay adherents of the two religions and the intervention of the government in order to precipitate issues of inequality. The situation is further complicated by the contemporary discourse of terrorism, as the result of which Muslims are now policed and placed under continued surveillance. Therefore, the Muslim subject is now under the threat of securitisation, and of losing its recognition and respect.

At this point, I would like to offer some critical remarks beginning with a critique of the new trend of self-writing (i.e. writing about oneself or one's history by oneself), which leads to radical subjectivity. Its resonance remains self-absorbed (in-group or in-tradition tendency) leading to a psychology of distrust, a paranoid relation to the other. In the narrative of Muslim victimisation discussed above, anachronistic historical reconstruction is being undertaken without sufficient attention being given to contextual interpretation. Consequently, it becomes guilty of reading past history using present lenses. Moreover, although the multiple meaning-makings are not as such a negative development, the absence of epistemic humility that should accompany such endeavours is quite disturbing. Most of all, while self-assertion – as an enactment of equality in solidarity with others – is not wrong in itself, the triumphalist undercurrent to win inevitably seems to damage the reciprocity between the Muslim-self and the non-Muslim-other.

Second, in this narrative, binary categories – Christians versus Muslims – are evoked not to challenge strains of relations, but rather to account for moments of the absence of peaceful cohabitation. The juxtaposition of these categories maps onto political identities thereby rendering Ethiopian history as a history of war between Christians and Muslims. The purpose of such juxtaposition is not to offer a myth of religious wars that provides justification for the rise of modern states, as was the case in Europe, but rather to show the historical disadvantages of Muslims in Ethiopia.[36] In order to assert that Muslims are marginalised, should Muslim scholars create binary categories that reduce the entire history of Ethiopians to that of conflict? I would argue that simply demonstrating the constraints hampering ideas of consensus and cohabitation cannot in itself be constructive.

Third, the narrative is caught in the tension between victimisation and voluntarism. In the struggle for the religious freedom of Muslims, two

---

35 Hussein, "Coexistence and/or confrontation?", 18-20.
36 Cavanaugh WT. 2009. *The Myth of Religious Violence*. Oxford: Oxford University Press.

categories are being mobilised: the figure of the Muslim-self as victimised and the assertion of Islamic power (heroism). In the narrative, we find a reading of the Muslim self as victimised and vulnerably exposed to a series of brutal systemic socio-political subjections under successive regimes. It is claimed that the religious identity of Muslims, and its potential as a system of governance, has been historically degraded by Christian Ethiopian rulers. The narrative makes certain aspects remembered, while others are systematically forgotten or muted. To be precise, the narrative makes Muslim victimisation remembered, but Muslim political participation in the Ethiopian state apparatus and Muslim integration and interaction with the Christian people of Ethiopia are systematically explained away, de-emphasised or sometimes denied and ignored altogether.

Finally, although the narrative rehearses a number of historical and contemporary violent incidents, violence itself is not subjected to any kind of critique. Undeniably, the narrative is completely silent on Islamic radicalisation that has been a factor for securitisation (Islam vis-à-vis the state) and the evolvement of an internal caesura within Islam dividing adherents of indigenous Islam and radical groups. In an ideological manoeuvring, it simply reverberates an idea of Muslim homogeneity. It justifies historical acts of violence by Muslim agents as acts of resistance or struggle against marginalisation. In the process, the narrative systematically bypasses the moral question of violence. Consequently, it becomes obvious that the mobilisation of the figure of the Muslim victim is a rhetorical device to advance questions of entitlement and hold onto triumphalism, which manifests in rivalries between Christians and Muslims.

Discursive disrespect as manifest incivility

Historical discourses are not only the focus of the scholarly domain, but are also constitutive of popular level narratives and polemical exchanges. According to Anwar Mehammed, who examined the Salafi movement in Addis Ababa, "The historical discourse also became the basis for the Salafi interaction and relations with Christians."[37] The historical narrative appears to be a powerful rhetorical device in the hands of the Salafis for it instigates both victimhood and voluntarism. To be sure, the victimisation of Ethiopian Muslims is remembered in order to mobilise Muslims to a struggle – a struggle aimed at reversing past "subservience."

Current practices reveal the fact that there are pervasive rivalries between the opposing groups – Christians and Muslims – that strive to control *space* (building mosques, churches, media representation) and *time* (public celebrations, historical

---

37 Berhem AM. 2015. *The Salafi Movement in Islam: An Examination of the Development of its Teaching in Addis Ababa with Special Reference to its Effect on Christian-Muslim Relations*, MTh Thesis, Ethiopian Graduate School of Theology, 90.

national narratives).³⁸ What takes centre-stage in such processes are polemical exchanges between Christians and Muslims, which are symptomatic of the crisis of civility. Such polemical exchanges can be captured by the following sample derogative words used by both Muslims and Christians against each other:³⁹

By Christians:

> "The Strange [Hazardous] Quran"
>
> "… the vagabonding Quran"
>
> "If one looks at the Quran, it is not the word of the creator, but a military camp of terrorists"

By Muslims:

> "*kufār*, infidels"
>
> "Life without power is meaningless … the disastrous striking arms of Cain against the meek Abel should be gathered by power"
>
> "… the enemies of Islam of our times"

Such exchanges have a negative impact on Christian-Muslim relations: "This grievance [is] combined with competition for public visibility," and consequently, the "aspiration for political dominance of the Salafi Muslims played a key role in the deterioration of the legacy of peaceful coexistence of different faith communities in Addis Ababa."⁴⁰ The vectors of the Salafi Muslims entertain a vision of creating "a homogenous and unified community" as a consequence of which they "denounce other Muslims as *munafiq*, meaning hypocrites, and Christians as *kufār*, meaning infidels."⁴¹ Polemical exchanges via social media reveal a new trend of incivility that derides local practices of peaceful coexistence.

Anwar affirms that "The Salafi movement is often associated with intolerance and violence towards local culture while other Ethiopian Muslims are generally tolerant and nonviolent." He continues, "This development of intolerance

---

38 Abbink J. 2011. "Religion in Public Spaces: Emerging Muslim-Christian Polemics in Ethiopia", *African Affairs* 110:2.
39 These exchanges appear in the essay written by Abakiya B. 2012. "Brief Review of Books Written in the Amharic Language Focusing on Christian-Muslim Relations in Ethiopia with Reference to Their Role in Strengthening Peaceful Christian-Muslim Relations", in *Proceedings of the Academic Consultation on Christian Muslim Relations in Ethiopia (Amharic and English)*, Addis Ababa, 1-5 August 2011; Klein J. 2005. *The Ethiopian Evangelical Church Mekane Yesus and Its Understanding of Islam and Approaches to Muslims in Ethiopia from 1969-2004*, MPhil Thesis, Missionsseminar Hermannsburg (Germany), 212-231.
40 Berhem, *The Salafi Movement in Islam*, 65. For an account of peaceful coexistence in Addis Ababa, confer to the study conducted by Beyene A. 2009. *Religious Tolerance in Addis Ababa, 1991-2008*, Master's Thesis, Institute of Ethiopian Studies, Addis Ababa University.
41 Berhem, *The Salafi Movement in Islam*, 66.

towards local culture gave rise to the conflict between the Salafis and other Muslims."[42] Many Muslims, for example, contend against "the Arabization of their society" with respect to dress codes and the "Salafis' rejection of the *Maulid*".[43] Above all, the "insulting" and "provoking" of Christians by the Salafis instigates violence and intolerance between Christians and Muslims.[44] Of course, the focus on discursive disrespect as manifest incivility is not to deny the existence of spectacular violence, as expressed in the mutilation and killing of people and burning of churches. This situation demands a focus on an ethic of togetherness in which themes such as cohabitation and responsibility are figured in.

TOWARDS A MORAL PEDAGOGY OF COHABITATION AND RESPONSIBILITY

So far, we have seen where we are in relation to new religious developments and old heritage. Where, then, does this discussion lead us? As a preface to my answer, I must note that the idiom of tolerance, as noted above has been exhausted. The language of tolerance strongly depicts the other as an object of hate to be tolerated, and this has an intrinsic incompatibility with the idea of religious pluralism. In this section, I wish to propose "cohabitation" as an alternative to tolerance, and explore its potential to transform the syntax of the public. Let me briefly elaborate the notion of cohabitation using the following three points.

First, the *other* is conceived as a *cohabitor*. Cohabitation is about the recognition of the other as a fellow human. World religions teach about welcoming the other. The so-called Golden Rule, which exists in different variants in world religions, is the primordial or fundamental ethic that promotes cohabitation. This rule refers to "the precepts that one should do as one would be done by."[45] Such rule is considered as an "ethic of reciprocity" and the word "golden" refers to "inestimable utility."[46] Several religious texts demonstrate the value of the Golden Rule. In the Christian Scripture, Matthew 7:12 is one of the most cited: "whatsoever ye would that men should do to you, do ye even so to them". The rule is not only one that fosters the ethical aim (the good) but also it can be expressed "negatively", (with a deontological tone) as in Hillel (cf. the Babylonian Talmud, *Shabbat* 31a): "What is hateful to you, do not do to your comrade. This is

---

42 Berhem, *The Salafi Movement in Islam*, 71-72.
43 Berhem, *The Salafi Movement in Islam*, 72.
44 Berhem, *The Salafi Movement in Islam*, 82, 86, 89.
45 1994. *The Chambers Dictionary*. New York: Larousse, 718.
46 1996. *The Compact Edition of the Oxford English Dictionary*. Oxford: Oxford University Press, 188. See also Green WS. 2008. "Parsing Reciprocity: Questions for the Golden Rule", in Neusner J and Chilton BD (eds). *The Golden Rule: The Ethics of Reciprocity in World Religions*. London & New York: Continuum, 1.

the entire Torah. And the rest is commentary. Go and study."[47] We recognise that the Golden Rule has both positive ("Do" unto others) and negative ("Do not do" unto others) formulations.

The Golden Rule exemplifies a religiously-base moral virtue that reminds one of the humanity of the other – that is, the other human being is like oneself and one should not dream of living without the other. The advantage of the Golden Rule is its unique universal accessibility and simplicity. Jeffrey Wattles, professor of philosophy notes:

> The golden rule is, from the first, intuitively accessible, easy to understand; its simplicity communicates confidence that the agent can find the right way. The rule tends to function as a simplified summary of the advocate's moral tradition, and it most commonly expresses a commitment to treating others with consideration and fairness, predicated on the recognition that others are like oneself.[48]

As explicated in the quotation above, the Golden Rule is simple, accessible and is concerned with justice as fairness. The last sentence, in particular, highlights philosopher Paul Ricoeur's notion of "oneself as another".[49] Even so, there are scholars who question the practicality of the Golden Rule on the basis that it cannot offer a clear guidance in ethical and practical conduct. Critics argue that the Golden Rule is too general and plastic insofar as two opposing groups inhabiting mutually exclusive moral positions can use it to reach different, often divergent, conclusions. For example, historically, both the pro-slavery as well as the abolitionist preachers used the Golden Rule in their rhetoric, albeit in divergent ways. For abolitionists, the Golden Rule sanctions the elimination of slavery. In contrast, for proslavery ministers, the abolition of slavery might cause the disruption of the social order and the economic system; therefore, the Golden Rule is meant to endure slavery.

Nonetheless, while such a positive ethic of reciprocity might work negatively, I contend that the Golden Rule has a critical and reparative capacity that can shape and inform our ethos, the ethical *between*, and ultimately the rule of law. The ethical between is the common ethos that binds us together. The ethical between assumes a primal and primordial nature that is intertwined with living together as cohabitants – thereby, manifesting the worth of beings who cohabit. This becomes possible by drawing attention to "the preconditions, contexts, settings, frameworks, stipulations, etc. that give the Golden Rule its concrete and substantive significance."[50] In the work of Paul Ricoeur, we find

---

47 Green, "Parsing Reciprocity", 1. For the Golden Rule in Islamic sacred scriptures, see Homerin E. 2008. "The Golden Rule in Islam", in Neusner and Chilton (eds). *The Golden Rule*, 99-115.
48 Wattles J. 1996. *The Golden Rule*. Oxford. Oxford University Press, 188 cited in Green, "Parsing Reciprocity", 1.
49 See Ricoeur P. 1992. *Oneself as Another*. Blamey K (trans). Chicago: Chicago University Press, 218-239.
50 Green, "Parsing Reciprocity", 5.

a philosophically rich argument for how the Golden Rule can be understood within the discourse of self-esteem, respect, juridical-recognition and equality before the law.[51]

Second, *cohabitation* fosters genuine *religious plurality*. The "unchosen" nature of cohabitation already assumes heterogeneous peaceful inhabiting of the earth.[52] The contemporary understanding of religious pluralism – inclusivism juxtaposed against exclusivism – already assumes an implicit homogeneity or sameness of religions. This logic of sameness is embedded in comparative study of religions and some trends of theological studies. Here, a case in point could be the work of philosopher and theologian John Hick who attempts to deride the uniqueness of the incarnation (and hence, the Trinity) in order to demonstrate the sameness or non-uniqueness of Christian religion from others. Such an approach claims to be in support of pluralism – while it is against it implicitly. Cohabitation can avoid such reductive tendency – the reduction of all religions or pluralism by the logic of sameness – within contemporary trends that accentuate pluralism.

Cohabitation is distinct from integration, which inclines towards homogenising multiplicity. It is also distinct from radical exclusivism or difference, which rejects any attempt to explore commonalty. Cohabitation is a midway proposal equidistant from inclusivist integration and exclusivist fundamentalism. Unlike the former, cohabitation encourages claims to uniqueness, and in contrast to the latter, it promotes exploring convergences of history and creating frontiers or sites of commonality. Its modality advances an understanding of politics as an art of togetherness and works contrary to economies of exclusion, on the one hand, and visions of homogenisation, on the other.

Finally, the *risk* entailed by cohabitation is rather a summons to *responsibility*. Cohabitation and the spirit of religious pluralism imply that self-esteem and respect will have to be translated into juridical recognition that makes possible religious pluralism and mutual recognition. Concomitant to cohabitation is equal treatment guaranteed by juridical recognition.[53] Nonetheless, juridical recognition and the rule of law may not be the ultimate solution for a troubled coexistence. There are certain risks involved in practices of cohabitation and in cases of disturbed cohabitation, post-juridical reconciliation has to be in place. All these point towards the necessity of responsibility that must be undertaken by each religious group.

---

51 Ricoeur, *Oneself as Another*, 218-239.
52 Bulter, "Is Judaism Zionism?", 84.
53 Ricoeur P. 2005. *The Course of Recognition*. Cambridge, Massachusetts and London: Harvard University Press, 197-246.

CONCLUSION

Social developments in Ethiopia have led to the legal norm of equality in the recognition of all religions. Acts of rights assertion or the enactment of equality, in Ethiopia, as practiced by religions are grounded in the rights and freedoms enshrined in the Ethiopian Constitution. Demands for more concessions problematises the religion-state relations. Here, the Muslim protests in Ethiopia of 2011 that went on for about two years – which eventually became a threat to security – may shed some light. The scope of this study has been delimited to the analysis of narratives. However, narratives of victimisation and marginalisation have the potential to produce even more problems in the public sphere. Unfortunately, the radical imaginations fostering religious identities that operate under the logic of hate-of-the-other neither sanction the rule of law nor cultivate the heritage of mutual respect. The critical notes, forwarded in this essay, on the Muslim narrative of identity are not meant to reject the self-assertion of Muslims, but to critique the inherent and implicit violence underlying that narrative. In the narrative analysed above, we demonstrated the implicit polemic against Christianity.

As a discourse of inversion, Muslim narratives of victimisation and marginalisation draw their categories in contradistinction to the historical narrative of Christian Ethiopia. In doing so, the discourse replicates old opposed binaries (Christian-Muslim) insofar as it – paradoxically – mobilises the figure of the victim and celebrates heroism, in which case the immorality of violence escapes critique. Such victimisation amplifies resentment and replicates violence, and becomes a site for the cultivation of radical imaginations that lead to the crisis of civility. In this chapter, we have focused on discursive disrespect and manifest incivility as an alarm that summons reflective sobriety. The way out of this crisis is through advancing a religiously-informed moral pedagogy of cohabitation and responsibility.

II. Religion and State in Africa

4 EXPLOITING STATE POWER IN SUPPORT OF A "HOLY CAUSE": CONFLICT AND SCHISM IN THE BAPTIST CHURCH IN GHANA 1986-1991

Abamfo O. Atiemo[1]
John G. Esubonteng[2]

INTRODUCTION

Historically, the Baptist brand of Christianity arrived in Ghana in two waves. The first wave is associated with the work of Rev Mark C Hayford towards the end of the nineteenth century. By 1904, he had built the first Baptist church in Cape Coast. Church records indicated he raised forty-five churches in the Gold Coast and Côte d'Ivoire. However, at his demise, the work suffered drastically.[3] The second wave is attributable to the efforts of Nigerian Yoruba immigrants, who came to the Gold Coast mainly for economic reasons. They had an organised presence by 1920[4] and subsequently formed an association of churches in 1935.[5] They joined the Nigerian Baptist Convention (NBC) which was set up by the Nigerian Baptist Mission (NBM), the latter consisting of American missionaries sent by the Southern Baptist Convention (SBC). By 1947, Rev and Mrs HR Littleton had been commissioned by the NBM to set up indigenous churches in the Gold Coast.[6] In 1953, the Gold Coast Baptist Mission – today the Ghana Baptist Mission (GBM) was formed by the SBC. Meanwhile the Baptists association of churches in the Gold Coast was inaugurated as a conference within the NBC in 1954. It separated to become a full convention, the Ghana Baptist Convention (GBC), in 1963,[7] still operating almost completely as an immigrant Nigerian entity which used the Yoruba language for its services.

Perhaps it is important at this juncture to explain the relationships between the various bodies mentioned above. In keeping with the spirit of Baptist congregational church polity, the American Southern Baptist Convention missionaries (SBC) when they got to their destinations became known as the

---

1 Senior Lecturer, Department for the Study of Religion, University of Ghana, Legon.
2 PhD Candidate, Department for the Study of Religion, University of Ghana, Legon.
3 Boadi JA. 2008. *A Brief History of the Ghana Baptist Convention.* Unidentified publisher, 19-21.
4 Boadi, *A Brief History*, 24.
5 Baptist Minutes Book of 1963.
6 Kpobi DNA. 2008. *Mission in Ghana: The Ecumenical Heritage.* Accra: Asempa, 91.
7 Brackney WH. 2009. *The A-Z of the Baptists.* Plymouth, U.K.: Scarecrow, 250.

"Mission" hence the NBM and the GBM. The churches they planted aggregated to form the "Conventions", and therefore the NBC and GBC. The missions were provided for and supervised by their sending bodies. In Ghana, there was close collaboration between the GBM and the GBC to grow the Baptist denomination nationally. In practice, the missionaries belonged to both the GBM and the GBC in their capacity as members of their local churches. They therefore could participate in the proceedings and programmes of both bodies. On the other hand, GBC personnel who were not missionaries did not belong to the GBM and could not participate in its deliberations.

The nature of the membership of the Baptist denomination in Ghana was altered radically after the Aliens Compliance Order of 1969, which expelled all illegal immigrants out of Ghana including many Nigerians who were the principal adherents to the Baptist faith.[8] Consequently, most Baptist congregations became significantly depleted in membership with the churches nearly collapsing. The GBM intervened in the running of convention churches at this stage to save the situation. It accelerated the indigenisation of the denomination by raising new Ghanaian pastors and shoring up collapsing churches.[9] These developments produced a new dynamic which eventually led to a bitter conflict between the GBM and the GBC in 1986. Such conflicts were not strange among Baptists globally. Baptists have been known to engage in internal and external church conflicts over the centuries. Externally, they have been characterised as dissenters, who have had to endure state-sponsored persecution, name calling and harassment, as they sought to follow faith and conscience.[10]

These situations led Baptists to the embedded belief in the necessity and desirability of the separation between church and state. Indeed, it was in his correspondence with a group of Baptists that American President Thomas Jefferson made his metaphoric "wall of separation" between the church and the state.[11] This idea of the separation of church and state is believed to have informed the First Amendment of the United States Constitution. Basically, this concept implies that the state does not hold any religious belief and allows the individual to practice his or her faith without falling foul of the law.[12] It guaranteed peace for the Baptist Church in the years that made it and the Methodists together the largest denominations in America next to the

---

8 Kpobi, *Mission in Ghana*, 91. See also Henckaerts JM. 1995. *Mass Expulsion in Modern International Law and Practice*. The Hague: Martinus Nijhoff, 6.
9 Interview with Kojo Amo by J Esubonteng, Winneba, Ghana, 13 April 2016. Transcription/recording on file available from the authors. Amo is a former member of the General Secretary Council and retired Secretary General of the GBC.
10 Bakker H. 2009. "Baptists in Amsterdam", *Baptist Quarterly* 43(4):229.
11 Letter "From the Danbury Baptist Association" [1801], *The Papers of Thomas Jefferson* 35(1):407-409. Online at: https://jeffersonpapers.princeton.edu/selected-documents/danbury-baptist-association
12 Kirwan M. 2008. *Political Theology, A New Introduction*. London: Darton, Longman and Todd, 12.

Catholics.¹³ By that logic the church then was not to expect special privileges, protections and favours from the state other than was available for all citizens.

Baptist conflicts have not only involved church-state concerns, but have also led to internal conflicts and schisms. Baptists, according Gerald Mark Breen and Jonathan Matusitz, were as suspicious of internal domination as they were of interference.¹⁴ For different reasons and over various issues, internal disagreements culminated in schisms and the formation of different Baptist strands and denominations.¹⁵ These internal conflicts and disagreements were usually premised on the need for each congregation to be independent in its thinking and beliefs. Sometimes, cultural, economic and nationalistic sentiments were misrepresented as being the scriptural position to be defended.¹⁶

It was in the context of one such conflict that the Southern Baptist Convention in the U.S. seceded from the Triennial Convention over the right to own slaves.¹⁷ This racial history notwithstanding, the SBC foreign mission effort has been renowned for the scale of its global outreach, in the course of which it set up schools, hospitals and other social facilities, in addition to preaching the gospel in several parts of the world, including Ghana.¹⁸ Even so, the SBC sometimes became embroiled in conflicts with the churches they founded because of what their African counterparts saw as their paternalistic and domineering attitudes.¹⁹ It is against this historical background that the conflict between the GBC and SBC's missionaries (GBM) may be appreciated.

This chapter examines this conflict by analysing the relationship dynamics between the GBM and GBC that led to their falling out, the anatomy of the rupture and method of its resolution. It identifies and discusses its remote and immediate causes. Its methodology of inquiry involves documentary evidence

---

13 Leonard BJ. 2005. *Contemporary American Religion Series: Baptist in America.* New York: Columbia University Press, 34.
14 Breen GM and Matusitz J. 2012. "Spiritual and Religious Communication: Intragroup Conflict among Southern Baptist Pastors", *Journal of Human Behavior in the Social Environment* 22(3):351-374.
15 Althouse MT. 2010. "Reading the Baptist Schism of 2000: Kierkegaardian Hermeneutics and Religious Freedom", *Atlantic Journal of Communication* 18(4):177-193.
16 Mathis JR. 2005. *The Making of the Primitive Baptists: A Cultural and Intellectual History of the Antimission Movement 1800-1840.* New York & London: Routledge, 6-7.
17 Althouse, "Reading the Baptist Schism of 2000", 180.
18 In the mission history of Christianity in Ghana, the involvement of the various bodies in the provision of social amenities has been observed as a significant dimension of what it means to be in Mission. See Odamtten SK. 1978. *The Missionary Factor in Ghana's Development up to 1880.* Accra: Waterville House; Kwamena-Poh MA. 2011. *Vision and Achievement: A Hundred and Fifty Years of the Presbyterian Church of Ghana, 1828-1978.* Accra: Waterville House.
19 Kleinig J.1983. *Paternalism.* Manchester: Manchester University Press, iv-xiii. See also Akpoigbe SA. 2014. "The Aftermath of Foreign Missionaries Policies on African Missions: The Nigerian Baptist Convention as a Case Study", *Global Journal of Arts and Humanities and Social Sciences* 2(5):95.

and interviews with key figures in or witnesses to the schism. The chapter is intended to contribute to the recorded history of Baptists in Ghana, to provide information on the American foreign mission enterprise in Ghana, and to show why and how the GBM and GBC's disagreement over administrative, cultural and heritage issues boiled over into a conflict which resulted in a temporary schism.

CAUSAL FACTORS OF THE SCHISM

The causes of the Baptist conflicts in Ghana can be put in two categories: remote and immediate. The immediate causes are the factors which directly sparked off the conflicts. They were mainly based on a letter the GBM issued to the GBC. The remote causes included attitudes and perceptions, whose existence, though real, are difficult to associate directly with the conflict.

Remote causes

The GBC survived the Aliens Compliance Order of 1969, but with a smaller number of mainly Ghanaian members. It began to grow steadily, planting new churches in collaborative Evangelistic efforts with the GBM. Generally, and on the surface, the dynamics of the relationship between the GBM and GBC were peaceful and cooperative. The missionaries belonged to churches that were led by Ghanaian pastors and were therefore integrated fully into their communities. There did not seem to be any differences at that stage; however, later events revealed that beneath the calm were serious tensions.

Over time, some of the American GBM members came to be perceived as being paternalistic, in their interactions with the GBC elements.[20] Certain of the Ghanaians resented the impression that some American missionaries paternalistically believed they knew what was good for them. Of course, this was driven by the GBC's heavy dependence on the GBM for financial support and other ministerial inputs. Consequently, some members of the GBC thought they were treated as children without the requisite intelligence and capacity for good decision making.[21]

Another issue of concern to the GBC churches was the alleged racist tendencies of the American missionaries. The Ghanaians leaders of the Convention expressed this concern with nationalistic fervour, demanding that the Ghanaian Baptist denomination be Ghanaian in character. Though the opinions of informants were divided, those who saw racist acts and tendencies among the American missionaries were rather forceful in their claim. For example, while

---

20   Taiwo O. 2010. *How Colonialism Preempted Modernity in Africa*. Bloomington, IN: Indiana University Press, 50-59.
21   Interviews with Kojo Amo and Steven Asante by J Esubonteng, Kumasi, Ghana, 20 April 2016. Recording on file available from the authors. Asante is Senior Pastor, Asokwa Baptist Church, and a former member of Secretary General Council.

the GBC accused the GBM of institutional racism bordering on apartheid,[22] the leadership of the Faith Community Baptist Church congregation in Accra specifically rejected this charge.[23] They were therefore described as being colour-blind by those who accused the GBM of racism over their inability see such a real phenomenon. Otherwise, they had not dealt with the missionaries well enough for them to have developed necessary sensitivity.[24] It was obvious that apart from their personal experiences, the general classification then of the American Southern Baptists as racists fed into local considerations within the GBC.[25]

Another concern was the control of missionary funds. There had been the suspicion among the Ghanaians that the missionaries abused funds. In particular, some members of the GBC accused the American missionaries and their agents of using pictures or stories of the most shocking nature to solicit funds supposedly for the benefit of the suffering Ghanaian people.[26] They therefore demanded an account of the funds. The GBC leadership charged:

> The existent relationship has been unsatisfactory in terms of the roles the indigenous people play. Though we work hand in hand, the missionaries have on a number of occasions failed to provide us with relevant information concerning support which they receive for the work. Money and other necessary support are collected in our name but no accountability is given to us the local body. They only account to their sponsors. We have attached herewith a malicious article written by one of the missionaries about Ghana, "Ghanaian wants are few; he asks only for salt."[27]

The GBM's response was that it was a wing of the SBC. As a practice, their budgets, lines of reporting and work assessments were directed by their sending mission and not the national conventions. Indeed, according to Baptists' ethics and doctrine, the SBC/GBM and GBC were independent of each other; therefore, the GBM/SBC could not account to the GBC.[28] On the matter of property management, some GBC members thought that money was an overriding decider in who got the second-hand property the GBM sometimes sold. Instead of allowing GBC members the first right of purchase, they were sold to others

---

22 GBC resolution of 19/09/86, 28/09/86, ICCC53, PRAAD, Accra.
23 Faith Community Baptist Church resolution of Convention Mission relationship, 28/09/86, ICCC53, PRAAD, Accra.
24 Interview with Kojo Osei-Wusu by J Esubonteng, Kumasi, Ghana, 20 April 2016. Recording on file available from the authors. Osei-Wusuh is Principal of Ghana Baptist University and a former member of the General Secretary Council.
25 Stricklin D. 1999. *A Genealogy of Dissent: Southern Baptist Protest in the Twentieth Century*. Lexington: University of Kentucky Press, 49-60.
26 Interview with Kojo Amo. See also Interview with Kojo Osei-Wusuh.
27 GBC letter to PNDC; Dissociation from the Ghana Baptist Convention, 1/10/86, ICCC53, PRAADA, Accra.
28 GBM response to GBC, 4/08/86, ICCC53, PRADA, Accra.

outside the denomination.²⁹ Furthermore, some GBC members accused the GBM of using funds and property sales as a whip against those perceived as troublemakers.³⁰ It is therefore not surprising that author Roland Allen's summary of real, imagined or perceived financial abuse by the missionaries was ever so succinct: "A poor fund, if administered solely by a missionary, only tends to produce misunderstanding and discontent."³¹ Frank Adams, a former GBC president, vindicated this position in 2008, when he described the GBM-GBC relationship as cordial following the establishment of joint expenditure and monitoring committees after the conflict.³²

The most unlikely and paradoxical remote cause of the conflict was the GBM's involvement in a variety of education programmes.³³ The GBM offered direct Christian education through church growth materials and also trained prospective ministers at its seminary at Abuakwa. In addition, indirect support for secular education took place on campuses of tertiary educational institutions in Ghana, which had GBM-assigned personnel to help run the Baptist Student Unions (BSU). These forms of education made the minds of their recipients flourish both in knowledge and analysis, which evidently inured to the benefit of the wider church, as these intellectuals also served in various capacities in their congregations. Nevertheless, education also became a double-edged sword that engendered in these same positive contributors a dissatisfaction which precipitated a challenge of the status quo. Certainly, the role of education in aiding the conflict between the GBC and the GBM evokes parallel memories in African independence narratives. It is repeatedly cited as the instigator for resistance against colonialism, much to the chagrin of its providers.³⁴

Immediate causes

Parallelism

During the 1985 GBC convention in Tema, Dr JA Boadi, then the General Secretary of the GBC, employed the concept of parallelism to characterise the operational relationship between the GBM and the GBC. Organisational parallelism as described by organisational management scholars Massimo Warglien and Michael Masuch as the situation where two smaller organisations

---

29 Interview with Ernest Adu-Gyamfi by J Esubonteng, Accra, Ghana, 10 May 2016. Recording on file available from the authors. Adu-Gyamfi is current and first Executive President of the GBC.
30 Interview with Steven Asante.
31 Allen R. 2008. *Missionary Methods: St Paul's or Ours?* Cambridge: The Lutterwort Press, 155.
32 Adams F. 2008. "The People Called Ghanaian Baptists", *Baptist Quarterly* 42(7):503.
33 Randall IM. 2012. "Seed-Bed for Baptist Leadership", *Baptist Quarterly* 44(6):324-343.
34 Asante MK. 2008. "Foreword", in Kempf GSS and Dei A (eds). *Anti-Colonialism and Education: The Politics of Resistance*. Rotterdam: Sense, ix-x.

within a bigger one operate separately.³⁵ How did this arrangement work between the GBM and GBC? Practically, the GBM and the GBC were seeking to grow the same Baptist denomination in Ghana through independent organisations; therefore they had issues of duplication and coordination. By strict denominational practice, each Baptist group was autonomous and responsible for its own welfare, though also united by their shared doctrines and beliefs. Thus, the GBC and GBM, while travelling in the same denominational direction, essentially had parallel operational tracks – an untenable situation to Ghanaian Baptists.³⁶

The GBM's role of helping regenerate Ghanaian Baptist churches after the Aliens Compliance Order of 1969, as well as its being the major GBC financier, placed it in an especially advantageous position with regard to decision making. The paradox about the parallelism under discussion is that while the GBM as a group was independent of the GBC, its members worked in local Baptist churches across Ghana where they enjoyed membership as any church member did. Consequently, they participated in local churches wearing two hats, both as GBM and GBC members. They then acted as the authorisers of activities. Thus, when decisions were made at the local church level with the active participation of everybody, the American minority membership belonging to the GBM would ask them to wait until they consulted their GBM compatriots for approval. The GBC claimed that this phenomenon was akin to the relationship between the bird and the house fowl. When the fowl got its food, the bird could partake, because it would perch on the ground to eat, but when the bird got its grain, it flew away with it, leaving the fowl stranded. The GBC thought that cooperation meant a prevalent GBM agenda. This situation led to cases of duplication of efforts. For instance, one of the interviewees pointed to a day when the GBM sent a cinema van to the same place where the local assembly was also organising an outreach programme.³⁷ In the end, it looked like a disjointed competition instead of a single concerted Baptist effort.

The GBC leadership complained to the GBM about these unacceptable situations. They then proposed that the two organisations unite administratively, so that there would be a single line of decision making and reporting. Their main argument was that this would remove the duplication and domination associated with parallelism³⁸ and ensure that resources would be more efficiently disbursed. The origins of this proposal can be traced to the 1985 GBC convention, which took the decision of formally approaching the GBM to resolve the existing structural parallelism.³⁹ Subsequently, a joint committee to discuss the issue and recommend an outcome was set up without making much

---

35 Warglien M and Masuch M. 1996. "Introduction", in Warglien M and Masuch M (eds). *Logic of Organizational Disorder*. Berlin: Walter de Gruyter, 7.
36 Adams, "The People Called Ghanaian Baptists," 503-504.
37 Interview with Kojo Amo.
38 Interview with Kojo Amo.
39 Letter signed by Rev Dr JA Boadi, General Secretary GBC, 4/09/86.

headway. It was evident, within a year's work, that the supposed consolidation was not going to be possible. One of the important and contentious reasons why it was not possible was that each group's proposed organograms in the negotiations were mutually unacceptable. The GBC believed that as the mother convention and future inheritor of Baptist work, its personnel should lead the organisation.[40] These suggested structural changes looked more like a takeover bid by the GBC – and this the GBM resisted stubbornly. They were not willing to subsume their SBC identity and work under the GBC banner. On 8 July 1986, after a joint meeting attended by the West African Area Director of the Foreign Mission Board, Rev Dr John Miller, the GBM decided to listen and consider more closely what the GBC was saying.[41] Consequently, the GBM put forward a counterproposal on 4 August 1986, in response to which GBC General Secretary Boadi commented, "We are impressed because for the first time, the Mission seems to have made genuine efforts to understand and respond in a positive way to the demands of the Convention."[42] A month later, an abrupt decision was taken by the GBM to suspend all structural talks in what it described as a prayerful consideration in response to actions by the GBC leadership.[43]

Worship, identity and heritage

Beyond the contentions over structural parallelism came the more fundamental issues of worship, identity and heritage. The GBM's bombshell of a letter to the GBC dated 17 September 1986, re-evaluating their long-standing relationship and suspending all talks on structural relationship mentioned earlier, elicited an equally belligerent response from the GBC. Among other things, the GBM cited the "unacceptable doctrinal drift in some Convention's churches" as an important concern. The GBC, of course, understood what practices were being referenced – practices such as the use of Ghanaian musical forms in favour of Baptist hymns and Pentecostal charismatic practices which included glossolalia (the speaking of tongues). The GBC was neither apologetic nor repentant on any of the scores. Rather, they counter accused the GBM of imposing American Baptist ways of worship on them: "we do not have any doctrinal conflict whatsoever with the mission except for the unacceptability of the imposition of American Baptist traditional way of worship on our churches."[44]

The accusation of deviation from Baptist beliefs and doctrine, on one hand, and its rebuttal, on the other, raises some interesting perspectives in the appropriation of faith and doctrine within national contexts.[45] First and less

---

40 Interview with Kojo Amo.
41 GBC-GBM meeting with Dr John Miller, 8/07/86, ICCC53, PRAAD, Accra.
42 GBM Counter Proposal to GBC, 4/08/86, ICCC53, PRAAD, Accra.
43 GBC letter to GBM, 4/09/86, PRAAD, Accra.
44 GBC resolution No 5, 19/09/86, in response to the GBM's suspension of relationship with the GBC, ICCC53, PRAD, Accra.
45 Omenyo CN. 2006. *Pentecost Outside Pentecostalism*. Second Edition. Zoetermeer: Boekencentrum, 194-198. See also Briggs J. 2013. "Viewing Baptist Heritage and Identity A Review Article", *Baptist Quarterly* 45(1):49-55.

contentiously, the GBC leadership argued that the adoption of Ghanaian music forms, the clapping of hands and congregational prayer was as good as using Baptist hymns in worship.[46] The second and more contentious issue had to do with Pentecostal charismatic expressions of worship. In the middle of the 1970s and continuing through the 1980s, Pentecostal charismatic forms of worship swept through Ghanaian Christian youth groups, including the Baptists.[47] Typically, Evangelicals like the GBM condemned these expressions as demonic and unscriptural. Third, the GBC posture resonated with the position of African intellectuals' demand for a moratorium on missionary activities to allow for the indigenisation of the African Church.[48]

The GBC on its part saw the acceptance of Pentecostal charismatic expressions not only as an authentic African response, but ones that touched on their heritage as Ghanaian Baptists. As former Secretary General Kojo Amo said in relation to African pneumatic expressions during our interview, "We knew the church did ultimately belong to us as Ghanaians and with the understanding that the missionaries would leave we did sincerely what we believed was best for the future of Baptist Christianity."[49] What then in Pentecostal charismatic form of worship made it resonate with African heritage to the extent that some GBC churches adopted it as its form of legitimate indigenous religio-cultural expression? The answer lies in a combination of religious and anthropological factors that will be explored presently. A priori, the understanding that Baptist doctrines and faith could be transferred in the purity of its American cultural expression was a non-starter. As Lamin Sanneh and others have shown, every transmission of faith in Christianity across cultures mostly passes on only the essentials of the faith to be cladded by local culture.[50] Consequently, the faith being practiced by the GBC was a rendition of Ghanaian Baptist expression with important heritage implications.

In this matter, the Americans were concerned about protecting aspects of the Baptist heritage, which were threatened by GBC's shift toward Pentecostalism, while the Ghanaians faced a dilemma about which heritage to preserve and promote: the Baptist doctrinal heritage of deemphasising personal experience or the African heritage of emphasising the manifestation of spirits in religious practice which has found powerful affinity in the Pentecostal revival. In the end, the Africans inclined toward the latter. Thus, the Africans discarded one

---

46 Interview with Fred Deegbe by J Esubonteng, Accra, Ghana, 6 April 2016. Recording on file available from the authors. Deegbe is Senior Pastor, Calvary Baptist Church, and former President of GBC.
47 Tishken JE. 2009. "A Brief History and Typology of the African Reformation", *Nova Religio: The Journal of Alternative and Emergent Religions* 13(1):8.
48 Shepherd LM. 2014. "From Colonization to Right Relations: The Evolution of United Church of Canada Missions within Aboriginal Communities", *International Review of Mission* 103(1):169.
49 Interview with Kojo Amo.
50 Sanneh L. 2009. *Translating the Message: Christian Impact on Culture*. Maryknoll: Orbis, 50-60.

of the marked doctrinal and liturgical characteristics of being Baptist in favour of the then fast-spreading Pentecostal influence which was overwhelming Christianity in Ghana. This is the context in which the GBM appeared to wring its fingers helplessly like a wailing parent that had lost its child to a destructive youthful epidemic.

Cogently, since indigenous culture is the recipient of transmitted faith there is the need to examine the aspects that resonated with Pentecostalism. In a seminal work, theologian and scholar of religion Kingsley Larbi contends, "From the human perspective, the single significant factor that has given rise to a boom in Pentecostal activities in Ghana is that Pentecostalism has found a fertile ground in the all-pervasive primal religious traditions, especially in its cosmology and in its concept of salvation."[51]

This contention is important, because it identifies the very roots of cognition, epistemology, beliefs and emotion – their reality – the worldview with which Ghanaian Baptist Pentecostals negotiated the journey of their daily existence. This is a worldview in which the agents of good and evil – that is, God and the Devil with their associated angels and demons – have real influences on daily causalities. It indeed is a worldview in which the supernatural, in this context God's power, is daily relied upon in effecting healing and deliverance from misfortunes, and enabling believers to cope with life's struggles. Certainly, God's power to save and heal within the context of this worldview is believed to encompass his ability to materially bless and prosper his people.[52] This worldview manoeuvres contours typified by the stressing on the Holy Spirit's power, glossolalia, biblical literalism, forceful Evangelism and lively worship forms which included local music and loud ecstatic modes of prayer.[53] Hence, this religious response to the daily life was considered more appropriate and relevant than the GBM's enlightenment detachment, based in scientific reality.[54]

THE ANATOMY OF THE RUPTURE

The 1985 GBC convention elected Rev Stevenson Williams the black American pastor of Calvary Baptist Church in Accra, as president and Dr JA Boadi the first Ghanaian Baptist pastor as the General Secretary. The general secretary's position was later occupied by the Reverends Kwadwo Osei-Wusuh, Kojo Amo and Steven Asante, who as full time ministers of different Baptist churches jointly acted on part time basis as the General Secretary Council (GSC) to fill in

---

51 Larbi EK. 2001. *Pentecostalism: The Eddies of Ghanaian Christianity*. Accra, Ghana: Center for Pentecostal Charismatic Studies, 7.
52 Larbi, *Pentecostalism*, 7-12.
53 Anderson AH. 2001. *African Reformation: African Initiated Christianity in the Twentieth Century*. Trenton, NJ: Africa New World, 167-169.
54 Topham JR. 1999. "Science, Natural Theology, and Evangelicalism in Early Nineteenth-Century Scotland: Thomas Chalmers and the Evidence Controversy", in Livingstone DN, Hart DG and Noll MA (eds). *Evangelical and Science in the Historical Perspective*. Oxford: Oxford University Press, 137.

the vacancy created when Dr Boadi left for sabbatical leave. The posture of the GSC, alongside that of their president towards the GBM, resulted in a dramatic deterioration in relations between the GBM and GBC. The case was that these officials insisted that the working relationship between the GBC and the GBM change to become more egalitarian. They had a mandate from the Ghana Baptist Convention to work towards changing the operational relationship with the GBM. It is important to recognise that these persons elected to lead the GBC had been known critics of the GBM. Their election reflected the widespread resentment in GBC circles against the GBM's position. A year of unsuccessful negotiation between the GBC and GBM over their relationship had gone by.

It was within this background that the entire membership of the GBM, which numbered more than twenty, walked out during the GBC president's convention address on the morning of the 19 September 1986. This protest was precipitated when Rev Williams commented on the failed negotiations between the GBC and GBM. The GBM's action was followed in the afternoon session by its letter to the GBC significantly dated 18 September 1986, portions of which read:[55]

> Because of the attitude and actions of the present Convention leaders ... the Mission Executive Committee feels that the Mission must re-evaluate its relationship to the Convention. In light of this we suspend further discussion on structural relationships. The Mission will, however, continue to work with any associations, churches, and individuals of like mind and faith and will continue its on-going programs in medical work, theological education, church development, student work, publications and music ministry.[56]

Though the letter was apparently occasioned by Rev Williams' harsh criticism of the relationship between the GBC and GBM, Rev Kojo Amo, a former member of the General Secretary Council has argued otherwise. It is evident from the 18 September date of the GBM letter that it had either been back-dated or pre-written. Whichever one was true, it indicated that the GBM had pre-planned a course of action which deliberately sought to precipitate a crisis of leadership in the GBC while the president gave his address on the 19 September.

Furthermore, the unanimity of the missionaries' walk-out indicated that there had been a prior discussion about a possible collective response action should the president behave in a certain way. That response was likely intended to cause the removal of the convention's executive, as the on-going convention provided the necessary quorums to constitutionally orchestrate leadership change. It was also possible that the GBM was just flexing its muscles as a way of calling the GBC to order, since it bore most of the financial responsibility for Baptist work at the time. The prospect of the loss of GBM resources could have forced the GBC executives to toe the GBM's line. If this was a gamble, the GBM lost it.

---

55 Interview with Kojo Amo.
56 GBM relationship revaluation letter, 17/09/86, ICCC53, PRAAD, Accra.

Surprisingly, the GBC not only threw down its gauntlet, but ratcheted up its reaction in a way that probably was not anticipated by the missionaries. All convention activities for the afternoon session of 19 September were suspended and the GBM letter was discussed at length. The GBC believed the GBM acted in bad faith following its counterproposal put out by the GBM a few days earlier in the negotiations. Consequently, the convention crafted a tersely-worded resolution in response to the GBM letter and walkout. Portions of their correspondence stated that

> ... all foreign Missionaries of the Ghana Baptist Mission are automatically restrained, with immediate effect, from working with Ghana Baptist Convention Churches, Associations, and auxiliaries in all Convention activities.[57]

The letter further indicated:

> By that letter, you have automatically, individually and corporately suspended yourselves from the Ghana Baptist Convention ... We have seen through your diabolical plans to split the loyalty of our member churches as can be seen from paragraph three of your said letter.[58]

It is evident from above that the GBC communication to the GBM on 20 September was emotionally charged, unsavoury in parts and uncompromisingly deepened the schism.

Essentially, the GBC decided to take its destiny into its own hands and to craft a future without the GBM. This decision was prompted by two important additional considerations. The first of these were the nationalist sentiments expressed by sections of the GBC membership and leadership. The leadership was articulating the long-held desire by some Ghanaian Baptists to oversee their own affairs at the highest level. They were against the situation when major decisions concerning Ghanaian Baptist work were made by the GBM alone. They found the constant assessment before the implementation of Ghanaian decisions by the GBM unacceptable.[59] The GBC claimed that it had the knowledge and expertise to do things better because it knew and understood the Ghanaian cultural landscape more. Additionally, it wondered why funds for spreading the Gospel should be interfaced by Americans whose personal living costs were higher.[60]

On receiving the GBC's letter cutting them off from the convention, the GBM tried on 21 September to clarify that its 18 September action had only been intended to cause a re-evaluation and not a severance of relations. It justified its stance by pointing to the caustic manner of the GBC president's address and further cited previous instances of name-calling, which the GBM was no longer

---

57 GBC Suspension Resolution, 19/09/86.
58 GBC Suspension Resolution.
59 Interview with Kojo Amo.
60 Interview with Kojo Osei-Wusuh.

willing to countenance. They indicated that the GBC leadership had accused them of racism, paternalism, lying, corruption, demonic influence, laziness, divide-and-rule tactics and bribery with vehicles and other material goods.[61] In further defence, the GBM provided a litany of offences caused by the GBC. It cited concerns which included the relocation of GBC offices from the Baptist headquarters building and the abolition of the joint strategy committee by the GBC. There was also the deliberate GBC executive action that prevented Dr WE Verner, a missionary, from serving as a GBC official despite being elected at the 1985 GBC convention. These were followed by discussion of doctrinal issues among them the tilt of the Convention towards both Arminianism and Pentecostalism in which personal experience was elevated above biblical doctrine.[62] Finally, they complained about an emerging hierarchical governance system which was not Baptist in nature.[63] However, these explanations were late in coming, as the GBC had acted immediately on the 18 September letter.

The second stream which fed into the conflict seems to have been a proxy war based on the historically acidic American racial relations. Because of the historical and cultural mistrust between whites and blacks in the Baptist Family in the U.S., the relationship between GBC's African American President Williams and the GBM was one filled with tension. The stage was set then for a possible showdown over the GBC-GBM disagreement. Pastor Williams did not see why Southern Baptists in America should be imposing their will on the Baptist churches in Ghana.[64] Though, it seems, he regretted his actions some years later, his personal relationship with the GBM members as GBC president was mutually antagonistic.[65] Rev Williams's contribution to this unequal situation was to encourage the GBC churches to move away from missionary dependence to self-sustainability during the course of his presidency. This is one of the legacies he left to the Convention, whose churches by and large grew in leaps and bounds financially in the years following.[66]

Internal rumpus and schisms of the GBC

The dispute between the GBC and the GBM seemed to have taken a good number of GBC members by surprise. There were pacifists within the GBC who

---

61 Letter Explaining GBM Revaluation Decision, 29/10/86, ICCC53, PRAAD, Accra.
62 Arminianism is a doctrinal position built on the theological ideas of the Dutch theologian, Arminius. The relevant aspect of the doctrine referred to here, is that salvation is dependent on the grace of God, but human free will also plays an important role. This is in opposition to the Calvinist position that salvation depends entirely on the grace of God. Pentecostalism teaches that the outward manifestation of the gifts of the Holy Spirit is for Christians of all ages, as opposed to the traditional Baptist position that the operation of the gifts ceased after the death of the last Apostle.
63 Explaining GBM Revaluation.
64 Interview with Fred Deegbe.
65 Letter from Rev Stevenson Williams to GBM, 27/02/98.
66 Interview with Kojo Amo.

had hoped the GBC would have been more accommodating. There was also a constituency in the GBC who did not see anything wrong with what the GBM had done. These people hoped that there would be an amicable settlement of the issues. Some thought about the loss of benefits and largesse provided by the missionaries and did not want to change the status quo.[67] Some informants claimed, though it was vehemently denied by some ex-GBC executives, that a delegation of GBC members from various churches and associations sought to have a meeting with the GBC leadership over these matters. With their leadership allegedly rejecting this meeting and feeling left without any recourse, they decided to curtail the powers of the GBC executive by initiating a processes of leadership change.[68] On 11 October 1986, a meeting to this end was held at the Ebenezer Baptist Church at Akwatia line, a suburb of Kumasi, and those in attendance recommended the dismissal of the GBC executive at the time, as well as the convening of new elections, citing the following premises for their actions:

a. Failure of GBC to have cordial relations with the mission.
b. The GBC executives' attitudes and actions, such as going to the press did not bring peace.
c. The GBC had disgraced the GBM.[69]

When the GBC leadership refused to resign, they carried out their threat and seceded.[70] They subsequently held an emergency convention from 7 through 9 November 1986 and called themselves the Ghana Baptist Convention-Southern Baptist Convention (GBC-SBC), thus indicating they were loyal to the GBM.[71] The GBC-SBC elected then Deacon Joseph Quansah, a professional accountant, to be their leader and fully cooperated with the GBM in their programmes.

The GBC-SBC churches had a simple belief that the Baptist work in Ghana originated from the SBC-GBM and anyone who joined the denomination had to agree to the doctrines and other rules it sets up. The inclusion of SBC in their name was important to them, because it portrayed the GBM and its staff as simply the representatives of the SBC and not arbitrary actors towards Ghanaians.[72] In line with this understanding, they were of the conviction that the changes the GBC leadership was seeking could not be offered only to GBC which belonged to the global SBC work. If changes were to come, they had to be made gradually and within the legal framework governing Baptist work.[73]

---

67 New Tafo Baptist letter on Convention Mission Relationship, 1/10/86, and Faith Community Baptist Church resolution, 28/09/86, ICCC53, PRAAD, Accra.
68 Interview with Joseph Quansah by J Esubonteng, Kumasi, Ghana, 2 May 2016. Recording on file available from the authors. Quansah is a retired GBC Accountant and Leader of GBC-SBC.
69 Dismissal Letter, 16/10/86, ICCC53, PRAAD, Accra.
70 Interview with Joseph Quansah.
71 Petition of 112 Churches of GBC-SBC, June 1987, ICCC53, PRAAD, Accra.
72 Interview with Joseph Quansah.
73 Interview with JA Boadi by J Esubonteng, Kumasi, Ghana, 20 April 2016. Recording on file available from the authors. Boadi was the first Ghanaian General Secretary

This contention was countered by members of the GBC executive, who were persuaded that a thirteen-page letter they later wrote to the SBC headquarters in Richmond, Virginia, ultimately resulted in changes in its relationships with missions.[74]

One interesting thing about this split was that the GBC-SBC faction claimed they had 112 congregations, compared to 58 that remained loyal to the GBC.[75] The GBC-SBC therefore claimed its legitimacy in the greater number of its churches. Practically, however, the 58 churches that remained with the GBC included all the big churches in the country at the time, and these had both more financial influence and greater numbers of members. It thus appeared that the dynamics of this internal split were not just about the relationship with the GBM, but also about church status and financial ability in the long run. Another point to note was that the splinter group GBC-SBC claimed legitimacy by arguing that each Baptist congregation could form any association they wanted.[76]

Exploiting state power

The idiom "all is fair in war and love" does best capture the behaviour of the three Baptist factions – GBC, GBC-SBC and GBM – as the Ghanaian state eventually intervened in the raging conflict in a way that transformed it from being a purely internal church struggle. In 1986, Ghana was under the revolutionary People's National Defence Council (PNDC) government, which actively promoted nationalism within the ambit of grassroots as the people's power. It had an "anti-imperialist" stance and encouraged the overthrow of social injustice and exploitation by the upper class. It was also unfavourable towards the West – with America as its bitterest enemy.[77] The summary of the actions of the GBC towards the GBM ironically had this PNDC revolutionary nationalist fervour. The irony lay in the reality that the PNDC at this time had an basically anti-Christian posture, and as a result many Christians would avoid dealing with it wherever possible. Unsurprisingly, some GBC-supporting informants vehemently denied having being influenced by the démarches of the era, which saw populist takeovers of private institutions in a so-called revolutionary style as well as an anti-imperialistic rhetoric.[78]

The GBC felt it justifiable and necessary on the 1 October 1986 to ask for the intervention of the PNDC member in charge of education and culture, demanding that the activities of the GBM in Ghana be regulated or terminated by withdrawing the immigrant visa quota, which had been operative since the

---

    and President respectively at different times of the Ghana Baptist Convention.
74 Interview with Kojo Amo.
75 Petition of 112 Churches of GBC-SBC.
76 Petition of 112 Churches of GBC-SBC.
77 Azindow Y. 2005. "Why Ghana Opted for SAP", *Ghana Web*. Online at: http://www.ghanaweb.com/GhanaHomePage/features/Why-Ghana-Opted-For-SAP-93436
78 Interview with Kojo Osei-Wusuh.

1950s.[79] While emphasising their nationalistic aspirations, the GBC harped on the foreign composition of the GBM and demanded that their right to freely operate in Ghana be limited. As expected, the initial inclination of government officials was to grant the GBC's request.[80] The GBC's tactical disposition at this time was to force the GBM to either cooperate or be thrown out of Ghana. The only hindrance was the support the GBM was receiving from the United States government.[81] The GBC-SBC faction was not favourably regarded by governmental officials, but it nonetheless counted as an important organisation.[82]

In response to the GBC's protest, the PNDC member for Education and Culture tasked the Secretaries (ministers) of Interior and Education and Culture to investigate and submit a report.[83] They, in turn, referred the matter to their undersecretaries, but not before the Secretary for Education and Culture had met with the GBC executives. The GBC in its presentations held itself as the legitimate representative of the Baptist churches in Ghana litigating with GBM foreigners.[84] At the same time that the GBC was talking to the government, some of its members in typical PNDC era revolutionary style took over the Abuakwa Baptist Seminary. The allusion to "revolutionary style" is because all assets, personnel, and programmes of the school had always legally belonged to the GBM. Nevertheless, the GBC executives and their followers claimed the seminary was built out of missionary money for Ghanaian Baptists and they therefore had the right to legitimately annex and operate it since the students belonged to Baptist churches. They instructed the students to boycott classes organised by the GBM administration until staff sent by the GBC replaced the existing one. In forcibly taking over the institution, they wrote a letter to its principal, WE Verner, terminating his appointment. He responded by resorting to a legal action.[85] The school remained shut for several weeks before reopening and readmitting students who were made to append their signatures to a document committing them to a pledge to be "of good behaviour".[86] Police reports indicated that the security situation on the campus was volatile.[87] This

---

79 Letter: Dissociation from the Ghana Baptist Mission, 9/10/86, ICCC53, PRAAD, Accra.
80 Letter: The Ghana Baptist Church Affairs, 16/01/87, ICCC53ICCC53, PRAAD, Accra.
81 Informant who saw documents tying the GBM to the United States Embassy.
82 Letter: The Ghana Baptist Convention and the Ghana Baptist Mission Issue, 12/06/86, 1CC53, PRAAD, Accra.
83 Letter re: Dissociation from Ghana Baptist Mission, 2/10/86, ICCC53, PRAAD, Accra.
84 Letter re: Dissociation from Ghana Baptist Mission.
85 Letter: Termination of Appointment, 26/09/86, ICC53, PRAAD, Accra.
86 Protest Against the Arbitrary Actions of the Principal, Ghana Baptist Seminary, Abuakwa, 27/02/87, ICCC53, PRAAD, Accra.
87 Ghana Education Service Headquarters: Wireless Message, 17/10/86, ICCC53, PRAAD, Accra.

takeover bid further deepened the conflict between the GBM and the GBC and added to the issues the government was already dealing with.

The Ashanti Regional Secretary, Colonel Osei Owusu, who became seventh high-ranking government official to be involved with the ongoing rupture, subsequently set up a committee headed by Anglican Church Bishop EK Yeboah to examine the issues that led to the closure of the school as Abuakwa was under his jurisdiction. The Yeboah Committee (YC) concluded that the GBC executives had no business taking over the school the way they did. In tackling the root cause of the unrest at Abuakwa, the YC recommended that new elections be held by Baptists throughout the country to end the existence of two parallel conventions. That prescription, by implication, meant the dismissal of the GBC executives. Critically, the YC also accepted the continued existence of structural parallelism which had been one of the stickiest points of the GBC-GBM conflict.[88] The GBC-SBC and the GBM felt vindicated. It was not surprising that the YC was favourable towards the GBM, because it had no nationalistic ideological position. Reacting to the YC report in typical nationalist tone, the GBC accused the YC of bias and wrote that "the committee failed to appreciate that a wholly alien group existing exclusively on their own without supervision from any indigenous body in 1987 revolutionary Ghana is not anything different from apartheid in South Africa".[89] These sentiments notwithstanding, the report was accepted by the Ashanti Regional Secretary, who forwarded it to Accra for action. Ultimately, the Abuakwa Seminary was reopened under the control of the GBM and the students were made to sign pledges of good behaviour. This frustrated the GBC, who complained that the government was being too soft on the seminary authorities. They consequently wrote, concerning alleged unacceptable actions of WE Verner, Principal of the Abuakwa Seminary: "The convention is utterly dismayed, Sir at the seemingly helplessness of the three departments of Government in the face of such intrigue and manoeuvres of an individual (Principal Verner) to defy orders, in order to foment strife and insecurity among Ghanaian nationals."[90]

Consequently, the Regional Secretary went on to try implementing the recommendations of the YC report. The National Commission of Democracy was instructed to conduct the nationwide GBC leadership elections and a date was fixed. The importance of the election was that the GBC executives who were seen as rabble-rousing were going to be removed. However, much to the annoyance of the GBC-SBC the Ministry of Education and Culture cancelled the proposed election, because the government did not want to be seen getting

---

88 The Report of the Committee of Enquiry on the Ghana Baptist Seminary, 3/02/87, 1CCC53, PRAAD, Accra.
89 GBC Petition against the findings and recommendations of the committee on the Ghana Baptist Seminary, Abuakwa, 11/02/87, ICCC53, PRAAD, Accra.
90 Letter: The Attitude of Rev Dr WE Verner (Principal) and the Re-opening of Ghana Baptist Seminary, Abuakwa, 17/12/86, ICC53, PRAAD, Accra.

"directly involved" in religious affairs.[91] The GBC-SBC in frustration cried foul but this was ignored.[92] The excuse was that Accra was carefully considering the YC report before taking decisions.

Next, the government set up another investigative committee, which after several meetings came out with its report followed by the issuance of a white paper whose details leaned towards the GBC position.[93] The government rejected the continuance of structural parallelism, agreeing that the GBM divided and ruled the Ghanaian Baptist community. Additionally, it demanded that the GBM prepared to handover its role to the Ghanaian Baptists. Furthermore, it forbade the GBM from disposing of any of its assets, while it prepared for the handover to the Ghanaians. In addition, it directed the GBM to submit to leadership talks a month after the release of the white paper. Triumphant theoretically, the GBC was offered the right to administer the immigration quotas held by the GBM upon receiving the notification. "The Ministry of Interior was satisfied that the Ghana Baptist Convention was now the appropriate body to hold the quota held by the Foreign Missionaries to enable it exercise the necessary supervisory role over the activities of the Missionaries. The Ghana Baptist Mission might be given only a token quota when things have been regularised."[94] Practically, however, the quota, which was the key item of legal immigration into Ghana by the GBM, could not be taken over by the Ghanaian Baptists, as further interventions had to come from diplomatic sources. The representatives of the United States government were believed to have intervened.

Based on the documentary evidence available, one can conclude that the thinking of the Ghanaian government that made it employ the state's apparatus was two-fold. First, the government had interest in regulating religious issues where religion mainly meant Christianity or churches,[95] and second, it was unfavourably predisposed towards missionaries, particularly those ones perceived to be imperialistic.[96]

Of practical expediency and pragmatism

From historical, doctrinal and practice perspectives, it is evident that both GBC and GBM actions and reactions were departures from the typical Baptist position of promoting the separation of church and state, and they were made out of expediency and pragmatism. Both the GBC and GBM really should not

---

91 Letter: Election to the Various Offices of the Ghana Baptist Convention, 9/06/87, ICC 53, PRAAD, Accra.
92 Letter: Petition Against Ministry of Education Interfering in Our Elections from GBC-SBC, 29/06/87, ICCC53, PRAAD, Accra.
93 A government white paper is the government's position on a committee's reports.
94 Ghana Baptist Convention and the Ghana Baptist Mission Affair – PNDC Undersecretary's correspondence, ICCC53, PRAAD, Accra.
95 Measures for Containing the Churches, ICCC53. PRAAD, Accra.
96 Catholic Church's Letter of Appeal Against Reduced Missionary Immigrant Quota, ICCC53, PRAAD, Accra.

have resorted to the use of state apparatuses for their protection, yet in the quest for obtaining advantage in the conflict they did. One would have expected that the GBM, which had principally trained the GBC personnel in the essentials of Baptist doctrine on church-state relations, would have done so to the point that its protégé would have avoided state intervention. More importantly, the steps the GBM took to continue to keep its quota drew directly on the protection of the United States government, contrary to the typical Baptist stance on church-state relations. It appeared that expediency and pragmatism had taken the place of the belief in separation of church and state in the face of practical pressure. This act is not completely surprising to congregational and community development scholar Jon Singletary, who reports that some Baptists posit a distinction between the tenet of religious liberty and the separation of church and state, even when the two appear to have the same result. He discusses how Baptists have received public funds to support faith-based social interventions such as the running of schools, hospitals and others throughout the church's history.[97] In this thinking, the GBM's continued presence in Ghana depended then on foreign and diplomatic help in order to fulfil its public ministry. Indeed, United States Consulate even went as far as allowing the GBM to vest its assets comprising landed properties and equipment in the U.S. until they were disposed of or turned over to the GBC in later years.[98]

In 1992, the conflict was finally resolved Rev Dr Fred Deegbe, currently the pastor of Calvary Baptist Church in Accra, convened peace talks. He had good relationships with all of the factions and had not participated in the proceedings that precipitated the conflict because he was outside of Ghana when it erupted.[99] The GBC-SBC executives ultimately disbanded, paving the way for new GBC national elections and a reunification service in Kumasi in August 1992.

CONCLUSION

It is evident that what was initially a purely internal church disagreement engaged state actors at the highest level, because the GBC protagonist who had some measure of nationalism appealed to a similar posturing of the government. Both the GBC and GBM, as the principal actors, were pragmatic in their approaches to surviving the conflict. They forgot about the typical Baptist conviction regarding the separation of church and state and did not employ Christian methodology in resolving their conflict. Considerable time, energy and state resources were employed to fashion a resolution. Much as the YC in the city of Kumasi gave favorable rulings to the GBM, the government in Accra was predisposed towards the GBC. Yet some of the rulings of the government's

---

97 Singletary J. 2004. "Baptist Perspectives on Faith-Based Initiatives and Religious Liberty", *Journal of Religious Gerontology* 16(1-2):81-98.
98 Information according to a document found in a GBM office at Tesano in Accra during 1990s.
99 Interview with Fred Deegbe.

white paper on the conflict could not be carried out, because the GBM also appealed to the American government. It was obvious that peace could not be legislated, but had to be achieved through dialogue. Many of the points raised in this paper deserve further investigation. For example, we do not know the inner workings of the GBC and GBC-SBC conventions when they operated independently between 1986 and 1991. In-depth investigation of the processes of conflict resolution between the GBC, GBM and GBC-SBC is also needed. Finally, it will be interesting to know the fate and thoughts of the principal actors after thirty years.

A manifest concern underlying the postures of the parties in this conflict was about the preservation and promotion of heritage. The GBM, representing historical American Baptist interests, not only felt threatened by the challenge to its hegemony, but also felt it was their responsibility to defend the tradition's heritage. But their insistence on preserving this heritage was resented and resisted by the GBC, who explicitly appealed to the Ghanaian religious culture of belief in spirits and indigenous practices of worship, including rhythmic clapping of hands, drumming and dancing as legitimate elements to be incorporated in Christian worship. That the Baptist churches in Ghana have since then experienced steady growth and have become self-sustaining and self-financing is a testimony to how the changes that occurred as a result of the conflict have been rooted in Ghana's religious heritage. This, perhaps, is also a vindication of those who proposed a moratorium on missionary activities to enable the Church in Africa prove its worth.

5 RELIGION, CITIZENSHIP AND THE STATE OF ZIMBABWE: THE POLITICS OF ZIMBABWE'S FIRST LADY GRACE MUGABE

Prosper Muzambi[1]

INTRODUCTION

The Constitution of Zimbabwe Act, 2013 has, as one of its fundamental human rights and freedoms, the freedom of conscience, which includes freedom of thought, opinion, religion or belief.[2] Despite having this constitutional element of citizenship in Zimbabwe, I argue that the various theories of a theologically informed citizenship that offer what an ideal society ought to be are largely unrealised in the Zimbabwean context.[3] This is particularly the case because those in authority manipulate religion to give legitimacy to their rule. In addition, they make use of scriptural texts that advocate subjection of citizens to those in power and a perpetual maintenance of the status quo. In this connection, the political enunciations of First Lady Grace Mugabe, despite her lack of expertise in the area of biblical hermeneutics, are the focus of this study.

THEORIES OF CITIZENSHIP

Towards the end of the 1970s, it was argued that "the concept of citizenship has gone out of fashion among political thinkers".[4] However, political theorists Will Kymlicka and Wayne Norman assert that there has been an explosion of interest in the concepts of citizenship among political theorists.[5] Historian of civic engagement David Scobey has referred to this revival as the "'return of the citizen' in public and policy discourse."[6] Moreover, this efflorescence is a reflection of a growing belief in many quarters that we are living in what sociologist and former President of Brazil Fernando Henrique Cardoso has

---

1 Prosper Muzambi is a lecturer of Theology at Great Zimbabwe University, Masvingo, Zimbabwe, and also a PhD student in Theology and Development at the University of KwaZulu-Natal, South Africa.
2 Constitution of Zimbabwe Amendment (No. 20) Act, 2013, Chapter 4, Part 2, Section 60.
3 The research in this chapter is guided by the conceptualisation of this term by Kymlicka W and Norman W. 1994. "Return of the Citizen: A Survey of Recent Work on Citizenship Theory", *Ethics* 104(2):352-381. These two contend that a citizen is "someone who has democratic rights and claims of justice". The researcher argues that such ingredients constitute a "healthy state of belonging by inhabitants of any community".
4 Van Gunsteren H. 1978. "Notes towards a Theory of Citizenship", in Dallmayr F (ed). *From Contract to Community*. New York: Marcel Decker, 9.
5 Kymlicka and Norman, "Return of the Citizen", 352.
6 Scobey D. 2001. "The Specter of Citizenship", *Citizenship Studies* 5(1):11-26, 20.

referred to as "an age of citizenship".[7] This change came about in the mid-1990s when the concept of citizenship became a "buzzword" in the realm of political thought.[8] Political historian Richard Bellamy expressed it succinctly when he asserted that "interest in citizenship has never been higher. Politicians of all stripes stress its importance, as do church leaders, captains of industry, and every kind of campaigning group – from those supporting global causes, such as tackling world poverty, to others with a largely local focus, such as combating neighbourhood crime."[9] Governments across the world have promoted the teaching of citizenship in schools and universities and introduced citizenship tests for immigrants seeking to become naturalised citizens.[10] "Types of citizenship proliferate continuously, from dual and transnational citizenship, to corporate citizenship and global citizenship." A list of types of citizenship is provided by Peter Kivisto and Thomas Faist.[11] Whatever the problem, be it the decline in voting, increasing numbers of teenage pregnancies, political polarisation, intolerance of others' conceptualisations of the world values, gripping onto power for too long, or climate change, someone has canvassed the revitalisation of citizenship as part of the solution.

Articles in a book edited by theologian David Kaulemu offers some insights on how citizenship is conceptualised in the Zimbabwean context.[12] In his editorial note, Kaulemu notes that those who responded to his call for contributions to a book on citizenship in Zimbabwe were quite telling. His reading of the responses revealed that there was a general reluctance to talk explicitly about the ontological and spiritual identity of Zimbabwe and how that identity informs the way in which citizenship is imagined. There are many questions that Zimbabweans still hesitate to talk about in public, even though we will sometimes admit to our prejudices in private. As Zimbabweans, we shy away from public discourse unless we are assured of acceptance and victory. The universal common good is alien to our psyche. Since colonisation in 1890, the culture of fear can be found in the majority of Zimbabwean citizens.[13] This fear has helped some politicians' hold to power by appealing to a fallacy that their being in power is God-ordained. To this regard, I focus on the constitutional community of Zimbabwe, rights of freedom of conscience, and social and

---

7   Cardoso FH. 2000. "An Age of Citizenship", *Foreign Policy* 119:40-42.
8   Heater D. 1990. *Citizenship: The Civic Ideal in World History, Politics, and Education*. London: Longman, 293; Vogel U and Moran M. 1991. *The Frontiers of Citizenship*. New York: St. Martin's, x.
9   Bellamy R. 2008. *Citizenship: A Very Short Introduction*. Oxford: Oxford University Press, 1.
10 Mavhunga PJ, Moyo N and Chinyani H. 2012. "Towards a Citizenship Education for Zimbabwe", *Zimbabwe Journal of Educational Research* 24(1):47.
11 The summary of various treatments of citizenship is found in Kivisto P and Faist Thomas. 2007. *Citizenship: Discourse, Theory, and Transnational Prospects*. Malden, MA: Blackwell, 2.
12 David K. 2013. *Imagining Citizenship in Zimbabwe*. Harare: The Konrad-Adenauer-Stiftung (KAS).
13 David, *Imagining Citizenship in Zimbabwe*, vi.

political development. These three components are important in pointing out the need for social and political flexibility and the need to bring out opportunities for change, evolution, and an advancement of a citizenship that is not enslaved by the culture of fear which is part of the Zimbabwean inheritance from the colonial past.

THE CONSTITUTIONAL COMMUNITY OF ZIMBABWE

The background of the Constitution of Zimbabwe, 2013 stretches to the colonial period. Though Zimbabwe was colonised in 1890, it operated as a British Protectorate until 11 November 1965, when the Rhodesian Front (RF) led by Ian Smith made a Unilateral Declaration of Independence (UDI).[14] This was a political declaration made by the RF to cut legal ties with the British Crown. The British government and the majority of black nationalists wanted to have a constitution guaranteeing recognition of the rights of the majority, who were the blacks of Zimbabwe before the declaration of independence. Despite its being designated "a blow for the preservation of justice, civilisation and Christianity"[15] by Ian Smith, the UDI was a legal instrument only representing the interests of the colonials. There was no referendum to come up with this political stance. Instead of establishing peace, it created a rise of nationalistic politics of resistance by blacks and a few white people who were against the injustices of a minority white regime. After a protracted struggle for independence, a new Constitution was crafted through negotiations of political parties of Zimbabwe under the guidance of the British government in 1979 at Lancaster House, and it came to be known as the Lancaster Constitution (LC).[16]

The current Constitution was ushered in as a result of the need to replace the LC, which came into operation on 18 April 1980. The LC was subsequently amended, mainly due to its being archaic and thus irrelevant and inapplicable to the contemporary trends challenging the Zimbabwean community. Though Zimbabwe declared itself independent in 1965, its independence was not recognised until 1980. Thus, the LC became the first constitution of independent nation, but it still reflected colonial terms, since it was a negotiation and compromise between representatives of warring factions namely the whites of the Rhodesian Front led by Ian Smith, on one hand, and by black nationalistic movements, including Zimbabwe African People's Union-ZAPU, the Zimbabwe African National Union-ZANU of Robert Mugabe and Abel Muzorewa's United African National Council – UANC.[17] The drafting of the Constitution

---

14   Lapsley M. 1986. *Neutrality or Co-option? Anglican Church and State from 1964 until the Independence of Zimbabwe.* Gweru: Mambo, 15.
15   Lapsley, *Neutrality or Co-option?*, 15.
16   This Constitution of Zimbabwe was published as a Schedule to the Zimbabwe Constitution Order 1979 (S.I. 1979/1600 of the United Kingdom).
17   ZAPU and ZANU are revolutionary parties that were particularly instrumental in the liberation struggle from colonial rule. These two parties entered into an agreement to have a common cause in the fight against colonialism. However,

mainly involved three political parties that were then part of the Government of National Unity (GNU), namely, the Zimbabwe African National Union Patriotic Front (ZANU-PF), the Movement for Democratic Change-Tsvangirai (MDC-T), the Movement for Democratic Change-Mutambara (MDC-M).[18] After the violence, and political struggle of the last decade (2000-2010), and thirty years of one-party rule, Zimbabwe embraced coalition government and the multi-party sharing of power.[19] In 2008, the power-sharing deal provided the structure for much of the government. Establishing the conditions for the sharing of that power, the Global Political Agreement (GPA) was fostered by the "quiet diplomacy" of former South African President Thabo Mbeki and the Southern African Development Community (SADC). Since the adoption of the GPA, and as it dictated, Zimbabwe underwent a participatory constitution-making process, the culmination of which was a new draft constitution for its people to adopt or reject by referendum, led by the Constitutional Parliamentary Select Committee (COPAC). This is the background of the constitutional inheritance, whose various successes and failures are not part of the scope of this research. However, the fact that the exercise of coming up with the draft constitution involved the consultation of citizens shows an embrace of participatory democracy during the constitution-making process in Zimbabwe. It was thus a people-driven constitution, which was a positive response to the call of Lovemore Madhuku, who is one of the leading constitutional lawyers in Zimbabwe.

Consultations at grassroots level were made and a number of civic groups that also included religious organisations. Examples of these civic groups include the National Constitution Assembly (NCA) led by Lovemore Madhuku, the Catholic Commission for Justice and Peace (CCJP), Coalition Zimbabwe (CZ), the Zimbabwe Council of Churches (ZCC) helped in educating the Zimbabwe populace on key constitutional issues. A referendum that ushered in the new Constitution was held on 16 March 2013. The parliament approved it

---

in 1980, they contested the elections separately. Joshua Nkomo's ZAPU was defeated by Robert Mugabe's ZANU. A struggle for political space between these two political parties claimed several lives. A truce was reached and sealed by the signing of what is now celebrated as the Unity Accord on 22 December 1987. The unity of these two culminated in the formation of Zimbabwe African National Union Patriotic Front (ZANU-PF).

18 Various splinter parties from the original Movement for Democratic Change (MDC) of 1999 came about as a result of internal disagreements among the leadership. Welshman Ncube, the Secretary General of the Movement, and Gibson Sibanda, who deputised Morgan Tsvangirai and others, formed a splinter group of this movement. Besides the power sharing matrics issues, some analysts saw a regional card at hand to this breakaway due to the fact that the top brass of the splinter group were from the southern part of Zimbabwe, a region that mainly consists of Ndebele-speaking people.

19 Sokwanele. 2012. "Reflecting on Zimbabwe's constitution-making process", August. Online at: http://archive.kubatana.net/docs/demgg/sokw_reflect_constitution_making_120808.pdf

on 9 May 2013.[20] It is this 2013 Constitution that I make use of to inform the findings of this study on the place of citizens in light of the right to religion from a Zimbabwean perspective.

RIGHTS OF FREEDOM OF CONSCIENCE AND POLITICAL DEVELOPMENT

From a global perspective, the right to religion is traced from the 1948 Universal Declaration of Human Rights (UDHR), which asserts that "everyone has the right to freedom of thought, conscience and religion; this right includes freedom to change his or her religion or belief, and freedom either alone or in community with others and in public or private, to manifest his or religion or belief in teaching, practice, worship and observance."[21] Many states around the globe have similar sections on freedom of thought, conscience, opinion, religion or belief for various reasons.[22] First, many states are members of the United Nations and signatories to the Universal Declaration of Human Rights (UDHR). The UDHR is also the most immediate progenitor of Article 18 of the International Covenant on Civil and Political Rights (ICCPR), which guarantees religious freedom.[23] As of 7 July 2003, 149 states, representing approximately three-quarters of the world's states, had signed and ratified the ICCPR.[24]

---

20   Wikipedia, "Constitution of Zimbabwe".
21   Universal Declaration of Human Rights, G.A. res 217A (III), UN. Doc A/810 at 71 (1948), art 18. See also Vinod S (ed). 2002. *Human Rights Violations A Global Phenomenon*. New Dehli: A.P.H. Publishing Corporation, 36; Roth Hans-Ingvar. 2016. "Freedom of Religion as a distinct human right", in Coertzen P, Green MC and Hansen L (eds). *Religious Freedom and Religious Pluralism in Africa – Prospects and Limitations*. Stellenbosch: African Sun Media, 15.
22   An elaborate coverage of issues on legal instruments focusing on religion and secular beliefs is found in Lerner N. 2006. *Religion, Secular Beliefs and Human Rights – 25 Years After the 1981 Declaration*. Boston: Martinus Nijhoff. As a way of concretising the issue of similarity, I have singled out the South African context because of its close proximity and ties with Zimbabwe. For this, the book chapter by Denise Meyerson is helpful. See Meyerson D. 2005. "Religion and the South African Constitution", in Radan P, Meyerson D and Coucher RF (eds). *Law and Religion: God, the State and the Common Law*. London & New York: Routledge, 107.
23   The principal international law provision for the protection of an individual's right to freedom of religion is found in Article 18 of the International Covenant on Civil and Political Rights, G.A. res. 2200A (XXI), 21 U.N. GAOR Supp. (No. 16) at 52, U.N. Doc. A/6316 (1966), 999 U.N.T.S. 171, *entered into force* Mar. 23, 1976. A further in-depth discussion can be found in Radan et al. (eds), *Law and Religion: God, the State and the Common Law*, 12-15.
24   Radan et al. (eds), *Law and Religion: God, the State and the Common Law*, 8. Ratification of a treaty binds a State Party to its terms, subject only to reservations made by the ratifying State Party. A reservation has the effect of rendering as non-binding that part of the treaty that is the subject of the reservation. Zimbabwe signs some international, continental or regional treaties, but it requires further legislative ratification.

Populous states that have not signed and ratified this treaty include China, Indonesia, Pakistan, Saudi Arabia and Turkey.[25]

Second, states may belong to continental and regional blocks with treaties that require them to respect peoples' freedom of conscience, belief, thought or opinion. For instance, Zimbabwe is a member of the African Union (AU), formerly known as the Organisation of the African Unity (OAU).[26] On the African region, the guidance is drawn from the African Charter on Human and People's Rights (ACHPR).[27] Part of the ACHPR addresses on rights and duties of both the States and citizens. Human rights law scholar Bronwen Manby considers obligations of Member States to recognise and give effect to the rights in the ACHPR, to non-discrimination and equal protection of the law, to life, to dignity, to liberty and to fair trial.[28] This is enshrined in Articles 1 to 7 of the Charter. Member States are obliged to recognise the rights, duties and freedoms enshrined in the ACHPR and are also obliged to undertake to adopt legislative or other measures to give effect to them.[29] Citizens are protected by Article 2 of ACHPR, which states that "Every individual shall be entitled to enjoyment of the rights and freedoms recognised and guaranteed in the present Charter"

On the social and religious fronts, citizens are protected by Article 8 of the ACHPR, which specifically spells out that there is "freedom of conscience, the profession and practice of religion shall be guaranteed. No one may, subject to law and order, be submitted to measures restricting the exercise of these freedoms" and Article 27.2 of the Charter which spells out that "the rights and freedoms of each individual shall be exercised with due regard to the rights of others, collective security, morality and common interest." In a discourse on citizenship in Zimbabwe, freedom of conscience and religion is of paramount importance, not least because its enjoyment adds value to the dignity and self-respect of the individual. It is also an essential complement to the guarantee of

---

25 Radan et al. (eds), *Law and Religion: God, the State and the Common Law*, 8.
26 The African Union (AU) is a continental union consisting of all 55 countries on the African continent. It was established on 26 May 2001 in Addis Ababa, Ethiopia, and launched on 9 July 2002 in South Africa with the aim of replacing the Organisation of African Unity (OAU). The most important decisions are made by the heads of state and government of its member states. The AU's secretariat, the African Union Commission, is based in Addis Ababa. See Wikipedia, "African Union".
27 African [Banjul] Charter on Human and Peoples' Rights, adopted 27 June 1981, OAU Doc. CAB/LEG/67/3 rev. 5, 21 I.L.M. 58 (1982), *entered into force* Oct. 21, 1986.
28 Manby B. 2008. "Civil and Political Rights in the African Charter on Human and People's Rights: Articles 1-7", in Evans M and Murray R (eds). *The African Charter on Human and People's Rights – The System in Practice*. Second Edition. New York: Cambridge University Press, 171. See also Kolawole O. 2008. "Civil and Political Rights in the African Charter 8-14", in Evans and Murray (eds), *The African Charter on Human and People's Rights*, 215.
29 Taken from Article 1 of the ACHPR. This should be read in conjunction with Article 25 of the same Charter, which spells out the duty of States to promote these rights and obligations through education.

the right to freedom of expression and opinion guaranteed by Articles 60 and 61 of the Constitution of Zimbabwe.

Malcolm Evans and Rachel Murray assert that the ACHPR is unique in that it lacks a precedent in Africa.[30] In an earlier publication, Murray contends that the provisions of the earlier OAU Charter make little express mention of human rights.[31] Instead they reflect the dominating concerns of Africa at that time, namely to ensure the independence of those African peoples who were still colonised, condemnation of apartheid regimes in southern Africa, and protecting the newly acquired statehood.[32] Baricako asserts that more than thirty years passed after the adoption by the General Assembly of the United Nations of the UDHR before the African continent equipped itself with a regional mechanism for the promotion and protection of human and peoples' rights.[33] However, the idea of drafting a human rights convention, with an organ charged with its implementation, began to take root in the 1960s. Nothing immediately followed this initiative. Instead, it took three decades since the establishment of OAU before the ACHPR became a reality. This shows that the OAU Charter was more focused on states rather than the citizens, hence the need for an ACHPR. This was an incomplete conceptualisation of the ideals of citizenship by African nationalists and a pointer to the challenges of human rights abuse in many parts of Africa including Zimbabwe today.

Third, the influence of the United States in its quest to protect fundamental human rights cannot be ignored and has been influential in the African context. This has been one of its founding principles dating back over 200 years. A central goal of U.S. foreign policy is the promotion of respect for human rights as enshrined in the 1948 UDHR. Vinod Sharma avers that "the United States understands that the existence of human rights helps secure the peace, deter aggression, promote the rule of law, combat crime and corruption, strengthen democracies, and prevent humanitarian crises."[34] The U.S. Embassy in Harare, Zimbabwe plays a human rights monitoring role, despite being accused by

---

30 Evans and Murray (eds), *The African Charter on Human and People's Rights*, unpaginated note to the second edition of the book done by the editors of the book.
31 See OAU Charter, Addis Ababa, 25 May 1963.
32 Murray R. 2004. *Human Rights in Africa – From the OAU to the African Union*. Cambridge: Cambridge University Press, 7. The same view is also in an introductory preface by Germain Baricako, former Secretary of the African Commission in the same volume. See Baricako G. 2008. "The African Charter and African Commission on Human and Peoples' Rights", in Evans and Murray (eds), *The African Charter on Human and People's Rights*, 1. Furthermore, it has been suggested that the OAU was not initially willing to consider human rights, labelling them "one of the main elements in the ideological armoury of imperialism". Shivji IG. 1989. *The Concept of Human Rights in Africa*. London: CODESRIA Book Series.
33 Baricako, "The African Charter and African Commission on Human and Peoples' Rights", 1.
34 Sharma V (ed). 2002. *Human Rights Violation, A Global Phenomenon*. New Delhi: A.P.H., 209.

the Zimbabwean authorities of interfering in internal affairs of a sovereign state. A recent statement by the U.S. Embassy maintained, "The United States notes with concern reports of the abduction, assault, and harassment of civil society leaders".[35] Within Zimbabwean civil society, Pastor Evan Mawarire is an example of a religious figure whose Christian principles made him become a conscientious objector. His call for the government to be accountable to its citizens earned him an arrest. The U.S. Embassy in Harare called for his immediate release.[36]

The Constitution of Zimbabwe quoted verbatim categorically states:

60 Freedom of conscience

(1) Every person has the right to freedom of conscience
   (a) Freedom of thought, opinion, religion or belief;[37]
   (b) Freedom to practice and propagate and give expression to their thought, opinion, religion or belief, whether in public or in private and whether alone or together with others.

Freedom of religion is thus enshrined in the supreme law of the land. There is no prescribed religion for Zimbabwean citizens. Zimbabwe is a multi-religious state,[38] though Christianity is the dominant religion. The religious demographic breakdown in 2012 estimates of religious affiliation in Zimbabwe is as follows: Christianity (including syncretic forms): 85%; African traditional religions: 3%; Islam and other religions: less than 1%; and non-religious: 12%. Percentages are based mainly on the 2010-11 demographic survey. The government does not require registration of religious groups. These affiliations assume a population of 12 million. Due to emigration during the recent years of crisis, estimates of the nation's current population varies between 11 and 13 million.[39]

In light of this, chances are that political gatherings in Zimbabwe are likely to be constituted by adherents of religion – with Christians occupying a staggering figure of around 85%. With this background in mind, it is easy for politicians to deliver speeches coloured with religious undertones to an already religion-gullible

---

35 United States Embassy in Zimbabwe. 2017. "US Statement on deteriorating Human Rights Situation in Zimbabwe", 6 February. Online at: https://zw.usembassy.gov/statement-deteriorating-human-rights-situation-zimbabwe/?_ga=1.46040100.1624371614.1491931553
36 2017. "US Embassy Harare calls for immediate release of Pastor Evan Mawarire", *Pindula News*, 4 February.
37 This is similar to the Constitution of the Republic of South Africa, 1996, s 15. See Meyerson, "Religion and the South African Constitution", 107.
38 Chitando E. 2011. "Prayers, politics and peace: The church's role in Zimbabwe's crisis". Online at: http://www.osisa.org/sites/default/files/sup_files/Prayers%2C%20politics%20and%20peace.pdf. In this presentation, Chitando asserts that although Zimbabwe is a multi-religious country, Christianity controls a major share of the spiritual market. As a result, the institution of the church will always play a role in social, political and economic issues – whether it actively seeks to or not.
39 See "Religions in Zimbabwe: Major Religions". Online at: https://relzim.org/major-religions-zimbabwe

audience. Indeed, biblical scholar Masiiwa Ragies Gunda maintains that "the Christian Bible has been extensively used in the public sphere by politicians, judges, industrialists and religious functionaries in such ways as to raise critical questions about the nature of development we aspire for as Zimbabweans."[40] In this context, the use of the Christian Bible by First Lady Grace Mugabe in the public sphere raises particular questions: Is her resort to religion for the promotion of tolerance and respect of voices that challenge the status quo? Or is it for the perpetuation of the status quo and a blind following of a leadership that some see as incompetent, retrogressive, corrupt and oppressive? At the very centre of these questions is a suspicion of the utilisation of religious and theological positions by politicians as they try to legitimise their authority to remain in power.

From their socio-political reading of the Old Testament, biblical scholars Robert B Coote and Mary P Coote have argued that David used religion to legitimise his authority.[41] Respect for the king was conversely related to respect for Yahweh. The few literate people in David's court marketed this ideology to the general public. I argue that today we can re-read the story of David and his successors and assert that these leaders imposed on their subjects the equation that good citizenship was equal to loyalty to the rulers and consequently to Yahweh. Transposing this to the Zimbabwean context, does this re-reading of the Bible promote the protection of freedoms by advancing both civil and political rights and also economic, social, and cultural rights in the sense of the two key U.N. covenants on these rights categories? Are there any tensions around these that cause people to think that their rights as citizens are not being respected and advanced?

Political scientist Frans J Vestraelen has written on religion-state relations in Zimbabwe. Vestraelen's studies focus on the condition of the state in Africa, investigating particularly why and how Christianity relates to politics. Verstraelen describes religion-state relations during the various eras of Zimbabwe's history from a historical and missio-theological perspective. On the precarious state of the state in Africa, Verstraelen writes, "Unfortunately, in the process of nation-building, the State became more or less coterminous

---

40 Gunda RM. 2012. "Rewriting" the Bible or De-biblifying the Public Sphere? Proposals and propositions on the usage of the Bible by public figures in Zimbabwe", in Gunda RM and Kugler J (eds). *The Bible and Politics in Africa*. Bamberg: University of Bamberg Press, 22. Masiiwa Ragies Gunda holds a PhD from Bayreuth University in Germany. He taught Old Testament Studies at the University of Zimbabwe and is one of the founding editors of the Bible in Africa Studies (BiAS) series. His main research interests are on the Bible as an ancient living text.

41 Coote RB and Coote MP. 1993. "Power, Politics, and the Making of the Bible: The Torah", in Gottwald NK and Horsely RA (eds). *The Bible and Liberation: Political and Social Hermeneutics*. Maryknoll, NY: Orbis, 347, 348.

with its leaders, who considered the State as their political earning"[42] – and a heritage which cannot be passed on to the next generation during their lifetime.

Today, almost twenty years after Verstraelen's findings, the situation has not changed for the Zimbabwean context. If anything, the credentials of being war veterans of the liberation struggle in Zimbabwe are an indispensable prerequisite for those who harbour ambitions to occupy leadership positions – a passport to have the "right" to walk in the corridors of power. Being a war veteran gives one the aura of being a privileged citizen. Such voices have become louder within the ranks and files of ZANU-PF. If one does not have this in one's curriculum vitae, at least a close relationship with those who have it can work in one's favour. As far as ZANU-PF is concerned, election campaigns are "incomplete" if the liberation struggle is precluded.[43] The liberation struggle, popularly known as Chimurenga, came in two phases. The first was the 1896/7 Shona/Ndebele Uprisings against colonial rule. The second started in the 1960s and ended in 1979 after the Lancaster-negotiated talks that brought in the first constitution of independent Zimbabwe. Even so, not all members of ZANU-PF leadership are veterans of the struggle for liberation, hence the call to revisit and redefine citizenship in Zimbabwe. This is needed if the state is to forge ahead with an all-inclusive citizenship. Inasmuch as the heritage of the liberation struggle is not to be discarded, the contributions of a generation that did not participate in the struggle can also help in shaping a citizenship that respects the freedoms referred to in this paper.

A further interrogation of generational clashes can also be transferred to other sectors of the Zimbabwean populace. This means that present day Zimbabwe is made up of the liberation generation and the post-liberation generation. ZANU-PF is now made up of those who were born in the 1970s and could not have participated in the struggle for liberation. Some of these are now in their forties in terms of age and they see themselves as inheritors of the political heritage that brought independence. As they keep close relations with the old guard of the liberation, they are very much conscious of the need to take the reins of power from the aging participants of the liberation struggle. Grace Mugabe, who is now in her early fifties, fits within the post-liberation generation. Alex Magaisa, a U.K.-based lecturer in law who was one of the authors of the current Constitution of Zimbabwe, argues that ZANU-PF is now faced with a generational conflict and that the military has not been spared. He says that the "generals are involved in a war of generations. The liberation

---

42 Verstraelen FJ. 1998. *Zimbabwean Realities and Christian Responses: Contemporary Aspects of Christianity*. Gweru: Mambo, 45.
43 The liberation struggle (also known as Chimurenga/Umvukela) to which I am referring is the protracted fight against white colonial rule which began in the early 1960s and ended in 1979 after the 1979 Lancaster Talks. This noble war to restore justice is acknowledged in the preamble of the Constitution of Zimbabwe 2013 in the commendation: "Exalting and extolling the brave men and women who sacrificed their lives during the Chimurenga/Umvukela and national liberation struggles". See also Wikipedia, "Chimurenga".

generation wants to hold on to power against the post-liberation generation, which wants to wrest control of the party leadership."[44] I argue that this has been exacerbated by the rise to power of Grace Mugabe, who belongs the post-liberation generation, but is closely associated with one of the icons of the liberation generation by virtue of marriage.

In religious circles, marriage is held in high esteem. The Bible tells stories of people who strategically married to advance political interests. Solomon is an example. He married many foreign women. He thus formed political alliances to foreign nations by marriage (1 Kings 3:1-2).[45] Religiously, the women brought along with them to the king's palace their religious heritage from foreign lands (1 Kings 11:1-3). In a similar way, but across generations instead of nations, Grace Mugabe married Robert Mugabe, the President of the Republic of Zimbabwe, in 1996.[46] The marriage was done in accordance with both the traditional customary law and the canons of the Catholic Church in a Christian ceremony which emphasises the importance of the sacrament of matrimony.[47] Grace brought along with her the post-liberation generation ideology. The moral implication of the marriage of Grace to Robert Gabriel Mugabe is not the issue of this chapter. However, it suffices to say that the importance of religion in the union cannot be overlooked. It was a precursor of how the biblical text would be used by the First Lady as she launched her political career.

THE POLITICS OF CITIZENSHIP IN ZIMBABWE: A HERITAGE OF THE (AB)USE OF RELIGION

Reflecting on the politics of citizenship in Zimbabwe, one is faced with a number of issues. For this study, I note that it is important to ask if the Bible is not being used to abuse the public in attendance at political rallies or those who sit at home and watch the national television channel which beams live coverage of these rallies. Closely related to this is the need to probe whether this is a heritage of the (ab)use of religion by wielders of political power. Recent scholarship on religion and politics indicates an intermingling between religion and politics around the globe, in general, and Zimbabwe, in particular. Catholic theologian Joachim Kugler argues that "in antiquity ... there is no kind of religion without political dimension and I even dare to doubt that a non-political religion exists

---

44 2016. "'Military fracturing as ZANU-PF wars intensify' in Newsdzezimbabwe", *News Journal Search South Africa Edition* 12 September.
45 Hill AE and Walton JH. 2009. *A Survey of the Old Testament 3rd Edition*. Grand Rapids, MI: Zondervan, 295.
46 Though some sections of society have reservations about this union, which started off as adulterous due to the fact that these two had a child, whilst Sally (Robert Gabriel Mugabe's first wife) was still battling with kidney problems, I have no intention to deal with the moral implications of this marriage.
47 1994. *Catechism of the Catholic Church*. London: Geoffrey Chapman, 358-372; 1983. *The Code of Canon Law*. London: Collins Liturgical, Canon 1055-1165.

today".⁴⁸ It therefore comes as no surprise that politicians in Zimbabwe, despite their lack of authority in biblical hermeneutics, freely carry out their political campaigns with an appeal to religious texts and theological positions. Masiiwa Ragies Gunda, whose ideas on this topic have already been referenced above, further contends that political leadership of today borrowed the colonialist tools of utilising religion where it fits them so as to give religious legitimacy in "abuse of office".⁴⁹

Bearing in mind that Christianity has the largest number of adherents in Zimbabwe and that the Bible is often quoted in public addresses, I assert that Zimbabwe is a "biblified state".⁵⁰ Political public addresses in Zimbabwe are also referred to as rallies if the gathering is meant to address huge crowds. This is to make a distinction between a political meeting of a few people and that which is well publicised to attract huge audiences or supporters. It is at such gatherings that politicians sell their ideologies to the people. One of the biggest of these rallies was held in 1980 at Zimbabwe Grounds in the high-density suburb of Highfield in Harare to mark the independence of Zimbabwe on 18 April 1980. The use of religious undertones is realised at both rallies and meetings that may not necessarily be for huge crowds. It was so in colonial Zimbabwe. As for instance, upon announcing the UDI, Ian Smith said "We have struck a blow for the preservation of justice, civilisation and Christianity, and in the spirit of this belief we have this day assumed our sovereign independence. God bless you all."⁵¹ According to Lapsley, a rebellion against the British crown to perpetuate white supremacy was carried out in the name of the Christian Gospel.⁵² In postcolonial Zimbabwe, Robert Mugabe's speech reflects the words

---

48   Joachim Kugler is a Roman Catholic Priest since 1988 and holds the Chair for New Testament Sciences at Bamberg University (Germany) since 2008. Before that he was Professor of Biblical Theology at Bayreuth University (1999-2008). He is one of the founding editors of "Bible in Africa Studies (BiAS)" series and has worked intensively with African postgraduate candidates in the last decade. His numerous works can be accessed online at: http://www.joachim-kuegler.de/4.html

The views of a number of BiAS scholars are collected in Gunda and Kugler, *The Bible and Politics in Africa*. See especially Tofa E. "The Bible and the Quest for Democracy and Democratization in Africa: The Zimbabwe Experience", in Gunda and Kugler, *The Bible and Politics in Africa*, 42.

49   Gunda, *The Bible and Politics in Africa*, 23, 26.

50   I do acknowledge usage of this term by Masiiwa Ragies Gunda when he discusses the need to be wary of an uncritical biblification of the public sphere. He contends that the Bible can be offensive, and to this I add that politicians and also other members of society have a tendency of extracting a single line of the biblical text that justifies their intentions and actions. Thus, when a person says "according to the bible", what it translates to is that the person has found a line that "legitimises" his or her action without engaging in the proper hermeneutical exercise.

51   Linden I. 1979. *The Catholic Church and the Struggle for Zimbabwe*. Salisbury: Longman, 87.

52   Lapsley, *Neutrality or Co-option?* 15.

of the prophet Isaiah 2:4[53] when he said, "Surely this is the time to beat our swords into plowshares."[54]

On Independence Day, 18 April 1980, the Archbishop of the Roman Catholic Archdiocese of Harare blessed the new flag of Zimbabwe and the proceedings of the night of 18 April 1980. Prayer precedes almost every political gathering in Zimbabwe. Grace Mugabe seems to have taken a cue from this, as she had the audacity to say that "I think he (Mugabe) is the only gift from God that Zimbabwe has. He is the biggest gift we have."[55] What remains a challenge is the level of sophistication that the audience have as recipients of religio-political messages coming from politicians. Some of the audience still hang on to the inherited mentality from the colonial era that what the leadership says is a reflection of the truth, and if they are to be regarded as good citizens the only option they have is to be gullible to the utterings of the politicians. Gunda contends that the Bible is used to benefit an inefficient and corrupt public institution.[56] There is an element here of an uncritical biblification of the public sphere, whereby the confessional use of the Bible is more of a smuggling of the divine in areas and events that are supposed to be judged in terms of efficiency and not religiosity.[57]

Just as Robert B Coote and Mary P Coote argue that the dominant idea behind the making of the Torah and several other Old Testament books is the legitimation of the ruling regime,[58] is it not possible to assert that today politicians use the Bible to legitimate their hold onto power? The Cootes argue that despite the variety of their contents, the Hebrew Scriptures have one main subject, namely, rulers of Jerusalem between 1000 and 150 BCE and the people of Palestine under their rule. In similar fashion, the history of Zimbabwe is that of those who participated in the liberation struggle and those under their rule. The Hebrew Scriptures consist mainly of the scriptures of the temple cult of the god Yahweh in Jerusalem. The purpose of this cult was to legitimate rulers in Jerusalem, and this is what the scriptures are mostly about. Indeed, the writers of the scriptures became particularly active when rule changed hands and a new version of legitimacy had to be devised.[59]

There are parallels here not only to the religious rhetoric of Zimbabwe's ruling couple, but also to the news items that emanate from media under the control

---

53 Isaiah 2:4: "And He will judge between the nations, And He will render decisions for many peoples; And they will hammer their swords into plowshares and their spears into pruning hooks." New American Standard Bible.
54 Mugabe R. 2010. "What Mugabe Promised Thirty Years Ago" (Text of speech by Zimbabwe's Prime Minister designate), *PoliticsWeb*, 4 March.
55 2014. "Mugabe is a 'pastor' anointed by God, says Grace", *New Zimbabwean*, 7 October. Grace Mugabe made this claim while addressing about 300 pastors and their spouses who had visited her children's home in Mazowe.
56 Gunda, *The Bible and Politics in Africa*, 26.
57 Gunda, *The Bible and Politics in Africa*, 35.
58 Coote and Coote, "Power, Politics, and the Making of the Bible: The Torah".
59 Coote and Coote, "Power, Politics, and the Making of the Bible: The Torah", 344.

of the state in Zimbabwe. This shows that in Zimbabwe there is a relationship between religion, state, and media. The state media selectively publish those religious events that are pro-government and in this case, it means pro-ZANU-PF. As expressed earlier on in this chapter, the Constitution of Zimbabwe states that every citizen has a right to practice and propagate and give expression to their thought, opinion, religion or belief, whether in public or in private and whether alone or together with others.[60] Borrowing ideas from Denise Meyerson's,[61] analysis of religion and the South African Constitution, to what extent, if any, does the guarantee of freedom of religion contained in Section 60 of the Constitution of Zimbabwe prevent politicians from involving themselves in religious matters especially if this is done selectively and discriminatively? Further, is it "healthy" to extract and uncritically make use of those religious texts to promote a personal and political agenda?

Commenting soon after the First Lady's "meet-the-people campaign" of 2014, which saw her address political rallies in Zimbabwe's ten provinces, journalist Thomas Chiripasi concluded that Grace Mugabe's entrance into national politics has generated a lot of debate about President Robert Mugabe's succession plans at a time when his ruling ZANU-PF party is being torn apart by internal fissures. The First Lady believes that she has a calling from God to lead the country, although many Zimbabweans have mixed feelings over her surprise inclusion in the succession equation.[62] Similar sentiments are expressed by journalists Peta Thornycroft and Damien McElroy, who argue that Robert Mugabe's much younger wife, a 49-year-old former typist, stepped into the battle to succeed the Zimbabwean president in an address to a ruling party rally in which she proclaimed she was the "chief advisor" to the nonagenarian leader.[63] In her first full-length address to the ZANU-PF faithful, Mugabe vowed that her husband would seek re-election at the congress which is held once in five years due to be held in Harare in December 2014 and lashed out at unnamed cabinet colleagues of the Zimbabwean leader for what she called secret plots to force him from office.[64] In her opinion, the ZANU-PF party would collapse without her husband in the top post.

The First Lady's "meet the people" campaigns were coloured by an incessant appeal to religion as she announced her entrance into the political realm.[65] At

---

60   Constitution of Zimbabwe Section 60, 1(b). Cf. ACHPR, art 8; UDHR, art 18; ICCPR, art 18.
61   Meyerson D. 2005. "Religion and the South African Constitution", in Radan P, Meyerson D and Croucher RF (eds). *Law and Religion – God, the State and the Common Law*. London and New York: Routledge Taylor and Francis Group, 107.
62   Chiripasi T. 2014. "Grace Mugabe's Political Ambitions Spark Debate on Mugabe Succession Plans", *VOA Africa*, 22 October.
63   Thornycroft P and McElroy D. 2014. "Grace Mugabe launches her political career at rally", *Telegraph* (U.K.), 4 October.
64   Chidza R and Manayiti O. 2016. "Mugabe to Rule from Grave – Grace", *Newsday Zimbabwe*, 26 May.
65   The "meet the people" campaigns were done in all the ten provinces of Zimbabwe soon after Grace Mugabe was elected as the Secretary of the Women's League

a rally in Masvingo, her fourth one in the "meet the people" campaign, she announced that politicians such as Mrs Joice Mujuru, whose political demise she devised, was rejected by both God and the people because *ange ave kunhuwa* (she was stinking) before God.[66] Joice Mujuru is a war veteran of the second Chimurenga. She served in the government of Zimbabwe from independence and by the time of her expulsion from ZANU-PF, and she had deputised Robert Mugabe in government for the past ten years. Reasons for her expulsion were spelt out by Simon Khaya Moyo, who was and still is the ZANU-PF secretary for information and publicity: "The grounds for Joice Mujuru's expulsion from ZANU-PF include but limited to the following; plotting to unconstitutionally remove the President and First Secretary of the party from office; orchestrating the 'bhora musango' (shoot the ball away from the goal target) campaign to the detriment of the party's interests … engaging in behaviour unbecoming of a Vice President and second secretary of the party."[67] Grace Mugabe emphasised that people voted for her husband because he is God ordained to rule. She further claimed that even if her husband were to become physically incapacitated, she would have the strength to "push him to the office in a wheelbarrow as he is the only one chosen by God to rule Zimbabwe",[68] that "Mugabe will even rule from the grave" and that people should "vote for Mugabe's corpse in 2018".[69]

However, some Zimbabweans do not share her views. The most recent voice against the (mis)rule of Mugabe is that of the war veterans, who published a communique on the state of Zimbabwe's economy, the ZANU-PF party leadership and the way forward for the people of Zimbabwe. The fifth article of this communique states, "We note, with concern, shock and dismay, the systematic entrenchment of dictatorial tendencies, personified by the President and his cohorts, which have slowly devoured the values of the liberation struggle in utter disregard of the Constitution."[70] The top leadership of the war veterans consists of Christopher Mutsvangwa (Chairman) and Victor Matemadanda (Secretary General). They have openly declared their support for Vice-president Emmerson Munangagwa to be Robert Mugabe's successor. An analysis of this shows that these people are defying the claims of Grace Mugabe that Robert Mugabe will "rule from the grave". It is also a real enjoyment of the constitutional right of freedom of conscience which allows people to freely express themselves. Be that as it may, concerted efforts were made to remove

---

of ZANU-PF.
66 Machiwenyika F and Maponga G. 2014. "'Faction leaders are appointees' – First Lady warns supporters against being used, condemns abuse of power by bigwigs", *The Herald*, 10 October.
67 2015. "Zanu-PF expels Joice Mujuru; Slew of allegations cited; Plots traced as far back as 2004", *The Herald*, 3 April.
68 See Dawber A. 2015. "Zimbabwe's Robert Mugabe will rule until he is 100 from special wheelchair, his wife claims", *Independent* (U.K.), 22 November.
69 2017. "Grace says 'Zimbabweans will vote for Mugabe's corpse in 2018 or I take over ZANU-PF if Mugabe leaves'", *YouTube*, 17 February (posted).
70 2016. "Full Text: War veterans statement in dumping Mugabe", *Nehandaradio.com*, 21 July.

the Mutsvangwa-led executive. This did not materialise. The only loss suffered by Mutsvangwa was that of being disappointed from war veterans cabinet post by Robert Mugabe.

There is also a widespread conviction that Robert Gabriel Mugabe did not win elections on a level political ground. Eliot Tofa asserts that it is important for any government anywhere to respect the sacrosanct right of citizens to elect a government of their choice and that for years, the people of Zimbabwe have been divested the right to elect people of their choice on the basis of an uneven political ground.[71] Violence has been used especially in 2000 parliamentary elections, the 2002 presidential elections and in the pre-electoral period of 2008 harmonised elections.

Besides Grace Mugabe's self-understanding as a "God-send", other members of the ZANU-PF party also appeal to religion to justify the existence of the party leadership. At a rally in Mazowe, Sarah Mahoka read and interpreted the Bible in a way of setting the stage where Grace Mugabe was the guest of honour.[72] She read from the Shona Bible: *"Munhu nemunhu ngaazviise pasi pevakuru"* (Let every person be subject to the governing authorities, Romans 13:1, RSV). She said that people should respect the leadership of Robert Mugabe, since "people are going around saying *VaMugabe vakura* (the President is old) but the truth is that those who are saying so are not young either".[73]

At the same Mazowe rally, Vice-president Phelekezela Mphoko expressed reservations for those in the party intending to accede to power. He said that those who are power hungry will fall: "In the Bible, Satan had a beautiful voice but he was not satisfied. He wanted to be God. Because of that, he fell by the wayside."[74] He says people should learn to be satisfied, and what this meant is that replacing and succeeding the current leadership should not occupy the thoughts of the party's followers.

Outside the leadership of ZANU-PF, some people are trying to influence the young to believe that Grace Mugabe is a godsend. Some have changed the traditional popular hymns into Grace Mugabe songs. An example is the National Association of School Heads which has approved a new version of "Amazing Grace! How Sweet the Sound". Tavonga A Chipadza has given it a new meaning by adding some lines of the "wonderful acts" done by the First

---

71 Tofa, "The Bible and the Quest for Democracy and Democratization in Africa". Eliot Tofa is a Zimbabwean academic. He is currently a lecturer of the Old Testament at the University of Swaziland.
72 Sarah Mahoka is an outspoken member of the ZANU-PF party and Hurungwe East member of the National House of Assembly. She has also been ZANU-PF Mashonaland West women's league chairperson. She is a strong supporter of Grace Mugabe. See http://www.pindula.co.zw/Sarah_Mahoka
73 Mlevu S. 2016. "Live from Chiweshe: Dr Amai Mugabe 'Meet the People Rally'", *The Herald*, 12 February.
74 2016. "Grace says not fooled by Mnangagwa's games, Kasukuwere throw weight behind her", *New Zimbabwe*, 2 December.

Lady and his sign off reads, "The song is a Special Dedication to Her Excellence The First Lady Amai Dr. Grace Mugabe".

Judging from the huge crowds that gather at rallies addressed by the First Lady, it is easy to get the impression that she is enjoying a lot of support by members of the party. This is not the case! Instead, signs of polarisation within the party have never been more conspicuous. For instance, veterans of the second Chimurenga have shown their discomfort with the First Lady's political rise. The leadership of the Zimbabwe War Veterans Association has called for the banning of slogans and songs that praise anyone other than Robert Mugabe. This includes any pro-Grace Mugabe slogans and songs. With regards to succession, their preferred candidate is the 70-year old Emmerson Dambudzo Mnangagwa.[75] Emmerson Mnangagwa is a Zimbabwean politician and personal aid to Robert Mugabe during the liberation struggle. He has been the vice-president of Zimbabwe since 2014 after the sacking of Joice Mujuru from the same post.

The use of religious rhetoric is not a prominent feature of Mnangagwa's political addresses. However, he has also inherited the art of the importance of bearing in mind that Zimbabwe has a religious landscape dominated by the Christian religion. On 26 September 2015, he addressed hundreds of Christians at the Harare Pan-African Leadership Initiative's National Presidential Prayer Breakfast. He quoted Bible verses and emphasised that those in leadership should shun corruption.[76] Just as was the case in pre-Independence and post-Independence Zimbabwe, the post-Mugabe era is most likely to witness a continued manipulative use of religion. The danger of this is that religious texts are selectively used to maintain the status quo. Texts that are deemed subversive to the authority of those in power are avoided. Such usage of the biblical text is discouraged by what has come to be popularly known as Kairos Theology today.

KAIROS THEOLOGY THEOLOGY AS A MODEL FOR CITIZENSHIP IN ZIMBABWE

It is important to note that historically, Kairos Theology is traceable to the 1985 Kairos Document, which was drafted by leaders of the South Africa Council of Churches in apartheid South Africa.[77] The political crisis of the then-apartheid

---

[75] Emmerson Dambudzo Mnangagwa has been Robert Mugabe's right-hand man since the days of the struggle. As Grace Mugabe was celebrating her fiftieth birthday, Mnangagwa pointed out in his congratulatory and happy wishes speech that he has been with Robert Mugabe for more than fifty years. This was probably meant to remind Grace Mugabe that her marriage to Robert Mugabe could not take away the closeness that he has with Robert Mugabe, and this was also to send the message that Grace Mugabe remains a novice in the political game.

[76] Nyakwenda L. 2015. "We must be righteous leaders: VP Mnangagwa". *The Sunday Mail*, 27 September.

[77] "*Kairos*" is a Greek word used in the Bible meaning a time to repent, a moment of truth.

South Africa prompted the church leadership to introspect and spell out what the church was supposed to do amidst strife. The Kairos Document was a critique of theological models that were operative in South Africa at the time. It also made an attempt to propose an alternative biblical and theological model that would bring out the relevance of the Christian religion to society. Out of this, three models of theology came out. These are:

1. *State Theology*, which "is simply the theological justification of the status quo with its racism, capitalism and totalitarianism. It blesses injustice, canonises the will of the powerful and reduces the poor to passivity, obedience and apathy".[78]
2. *Church Theology*, which came from the speeches and statements of church leaders about the regime and the crisis of apartheid South Africa. These did not capture the faith of the majority of South Africans affected by the repressive laws of the government. Nevertheless, the speeches and statements of these church leaders were regarded by the media and generally society as the official opinions of the churches. Despite being critical of apartheid, the voices of these leaders relied more on stock ideas derived from Christian tradition and then uncritically and repeatedly applying them to the situation prevailing at the time. They spoke of reconciliation without truth, peace without addressing issues of justice and non-violence.[79]
3. *Prophetic Theology*, which was a call to have a spiritual, pastoral, and above all, prophetic response by Christians. In as much as it embraced the rich tradition of the Christian religion, it called for boldness and incisive responses to the present realities. It called for a response that did not give an impression of sitting on the fence but to clearly and unambiguously take a stand against all forms of oppression.[80]

Today, Kairos Theology is no longer restricted to the Kairos Theology of the South African context. It has spread its tentacles around the globe. As of 2010, Gary SD Leonard had managed to compile and edit thirteen theologies crafted out of the spirit of the original South African document. Among these is the 1998 Zimbabwean Kairos Document. This document specifies that it is a call to faith communities, civic organisations and all movements and individuals working for positive social, economic and political transformation of society for delivery from poverty, social inequality and to promote good governance. The "prophetic theology" model of the Kairos Document emphasises the need to remain true to tradition, true to the present needs, and shape a future characterised by justice – and not by enslavement to religious interpretations that perpetuate the status quo. For the Zimbabwean context, it becomes imperative that responsibility in the use of religious texts be guided by the consciousness to refrain from manipulatively appealing to religion and tradition when it comes to the choice of leadership.

---

78 Leonard GSD (ed). 2010. *The Kairos Documents*. Durban: Ujamaa Centre for Biblical and Theological Community Development and Research, University of KwaZulu-Natal, 9.
79 Leonard, *The Kairos Documents*, 15.
80 Leonard, *The Kairos Documents*, 23.

A close analysis of the speeches by Grace Mugabe shows that the notion she advances is that it is not the ZANU-PF women that invited her to lead the women's league, thereby catapulting her into the powerful organ of ZANU-PF. Instead, she says it is the "voice of God" that has spoken. This is a way of inculcating into undiscerning minds the idea that what politicians say and do is from God. This is a dangerous position that creates political messianism and fundamentalism. It is therefore not proper for humans to use the name of God and that of religion to cover up for personal projects that may not be holy. Furthermore, the notion that some individuals are God-ordained to rule stifles the aspirations of those who did not take part in the liberation struggle, yet aspire to enter into the corridors of governance. At her political rallies, Grace Mugabe makes audacious claims of being rightly positioned to lead because she has been an apprentice of her husband in the political heritage of Zimbabwe.

CONCLUSION

Religion and the political heritage of Chimurenga are being used to render legitimacy to the rule of Robert Mugabe. Religion is being manipulated to justify the political rise of Zimbabwe's First Lady. However, this is coming at the backdrop of who really has the "'right" machinery to advance his or her interests. For the Zimbabwean case, it is the President who has this. It is a question of those in power being in charge of the systems that allow them to remain in comfort zones. Since this cannot be shouted about, the only acceptable way to justify their hold on power is to appeal to a deity being the source of their authority. It is politics devoid of the ideals set out by the dictates of responsible citizenship. A model of citizenship for Zimbabwe calls for shunning the fallacy that those in power are elected by God. The general populace of citizens who are mainly religious are misled into imbibing a hasty generalisation of religious claims that those in power are God-ordained to do so. This shuts the door for opportunities of change, evolution, and an advancement of a citizenship critical of leadership. The culture of fear inherited from the colonial past has to be replaced by ideals of citizenship that restore social, religious, economic and political freedoms as enshrined in the Constitution of Zimbabwe. As noted above, there is a tradition of undue appeal to and (ab)use of religion by politicians as a way of maintaining the status quo. This renders it impossible to apply the tenets of citizenship, which call for democracy, social justice, efficiency and competency as a yardstick for the moral right to rule. The model of "Prophetic Theology" from the Kairos Document can be adopted for advancing a citizenship theory for Zimbabwe.

6   10 JANUARY: POLITICAL CALCULATION OR RESPONSE TO A SOCIO-ANTHROPOLOGICAL REQUIREMENT IN BENIN?

Jean-Baptiste Sourou[1]

In Benin, on 10 January of each year, the annual festival of traditional religions is celebrated. The institution of this date was promulgated on 20 August 1997 by President Mathieu Kérékou. This is Law No. 97-031 of 20 August 1997, which was previously deliberated and adopted by the National Assembly. The law is a first in Africa, if not in the world. Under the law, traditional religions, have their holiday, paid and unpaid, following the example of the great Christian and Muslim religious festivals, which were the subject of a law enacted seven years earlier, on 18 July 1990, by the High Council of the Republic, the transitional parliament. That law was the Law No. 90-019 of 27 July 1990.

Far from being unanimously endorsed, the institution of this feast of the traditional religions has been much criticised. On the one hand, it would consecrate the resurgence of ancestral practices, sometimes occult and opposed by the Christian faiths (Catholic, Protestant and especially Evangelical) as well as Muslims during the revolutionary period in Benin.[2] On the other hand, it was simply the result of pure political calculations to attract the votes of a large number of voters, since the traditional cults – in particular, the Vodoun – remain very anchored in the morals of good number of Beninese.

The purpose of my research is to analyse and assess these matters. Is 10 January the fruit of pure political calculations, or is it a response to a social and anthropological demand with the intention of rehabilitating these traditional cults and their arts, their Beninese and global heritage and to allow the many Beninese followers of these cults celebrate their community and social identity publicly like the believers of other religions in democratic and secular countries? Contemporary and historical actors in Benin can help us to identify, analyse the facts and draw the necessary conclusions. This study necessarily begins with a detour through the Ouidah 92 Festival in Benin.

OUIDAH 92 FESTIVAL: AMERICAS-AFRICA HOMECOMING

From 8 to 18 February 1992, the first Americas-Africa Homecoming Festival took place in the coastal town of Ouidah in Benin. For ten days, personalities from

---

1   Professor of Communications, Saint Augustine University of Tanzania; Founder and President, Center for Documentation and Research on Art and Social Sciences, Republic of Benin.
2   Sourou JB. 2016. "State and Religion under the 1977 Constitution in Benin", in Coertzen P, Green MC and Hansen L (eds). *Religious Freedom and Religious Pluralism in Africa: Prospects and Limitations.* Stellenbosch: African Sun Media, 29-35.

the world of culture, arts, research, as well as politicians from Benin, Africa, Europe and especially the Americas (USA, Haiti, Brazil and other Caribbean countries) met for a "manifestation of memory, an appropriation of this tragic page of our collective destiny as the slave trade".[3] It was an occasion for the indigenous people and Africans of the diaspora and descendants of the victims of the Atlantic slave trade to meet together in the same places where some gave up their brothers and where others left for a tragic adventure, to look at each other, to do a work of memory, to go beyond the past and to seek together what could unite them in spite of the betrayal, the shame, the inevitable resentments that the treaty has generated for several centuries. According to Nicéphore Soglo, then president of Benin, Ouidah 92 was "also an invitation to weave active solidarity with the descendants of those who survived the ordeal and with whom we want to live our community of destiny fully".

In the same speech, President Soglo highlighted the role of traditional religions in maintaining a common identity between the Africans who remained on the continent and those trafficked by detainees. He said, "It is easy to see that traditional religions, 'vodoun' in particular, formed the framework of the culture of the black peoples of the diaspora, the element that allowed them to safeguard their identity in a universe of physical, economic and cultural degradation. As for the Africans who remained on the continent," he continued, "it was in the same way that they learned their survival under foreign occupation. While the powerful machine of the colonial administration carried out its pitiless wager in the condition of the conquered territories," President Soglo explained, "it was still through the sources of cultural tradition that the movement of refusal, arising in different parts of the continent, drew its mobilizing force and the means of its organization ... The ancestral culture thus presents itself as the natural link between the black peoples scattered throughout the world," he concluded. In sum, beyond all, physical distance, centuries and sufferings of all kinds, the peoples of Africa and the diaspora have an important element that unites them, brings them together and maintains them in a communion of identity. It is traditional religion, Vodoun worship, in particular. And this is what Ouidah 92 wanted to highlight as the basis of a true reconciliation and as a springboard to forge more fraternal bonds that will mark a new era in the relations between Africans on the continent and the diaspora.

For his part, the philosopher and former Benin Minister of Culture, Paulin Hountondji declared, concerning the place of religion in the preservation of the identity of deported Africans, that "of all possible forms of cultural identification, religious identification is the most spectacular. The vitality of the 'vodoun' cult in Haiti and the cult of the 'orisha' in Brazil is proof of this. It is known that the Haitian 'vodoun' is the heir of the 'vodun' cults of South Benin and South Togo and that the cult of the 'orisha' is inherited from

---

3   Soglo N. 1993. "Ouidah 92 est avant tout une manifestation du souvenir" [Ouidah 92 is above all a manifestation of memory], *La Nation*, 10 February:3. All quotations in this paragraph and the next are taken from this source.

the Yoruba cultural area in South Nigeria and South Benin. Thus," he observes, "in these diaspora communities, there is a fierce desire to preserve ancestral religion or to recreate it, a passionate effort to keep alive this tradition that saves them from anonymity more accurately and gives them their own personality. Identification of self through identification with a collective imagination: one must understand this process and recognise it in what it has legitimate."[4] Clearly, in the view of President Nicéphore Soglo and his Minister of Culture, the role played by traditional religion was undeniable in past centuries in terms of the consolidation of the two African peoples. It can continue to occupy this place in both communities: local and diaspora. And if Africa has something noble to offer to the world of the twenty-first century, it can only be through a recovery and appropriation of the values of its traditional religion.

It is understandable that in order to celebrate the "Americas-Africa reunion", a special emphasis has been laid on this important element, the substance that has united the two continents over the centuries: traditional religion. Traditional African religion is not limited to *vodoun* or *orisha* and similar manifestations, but it is a container whose cults are contents. To borrow mathematical language, one would say that the traditional religion is the whole and the Vodoun, Orisha, Shango and other spirits are the elements. "To try to understand Africa and the African without the contribution of the traditional religion would be like opening a large cabinet emptied of its precious content," said the philosopher and anthropologist from Mali, Amadou Hampaté Bah.[5]

In Africa, religion is omnipresent and affects all areas of the individual's life from birth to death and through the various stages of life: initiation to adulthood, marriage, failures, important decisions, illnesses, funerals. The whole life is explained by the crucible of an attachment to the Creator, the spirits and the ancestors. By letting his daily life permeate by the presence of the sacred, the African grounds a cosmovision, an anthropology, a culture. Hence arises a plastic art, music, dance, literature, theatre. For "African religion is a cultural religion; African culture is a religious culture".[6] The reference to traditional religion is strong in the African culture – it is its most valuable defense and attack weapon.

As a whole, Ouidah 92 also sought ways for the promotion of traditional culture, including traditional religion. With the Ouidah 92, a movement of reconquest and reappropriation of a traditional culture, which goes beyond the physical limits of Benin and Africa and which unites millions of people all over the world took form. But this reconquest cannot be achieved without state support

---

4   Hountondji P. 1992. "Le ministre de la culture déclare: 'Non, les cultures du Bénin se sont pas de cultures du Vaudou'" [The Minister of Culture declares: "No, the cultures of Benin are not cultures of vodoun"], *La Nation*, 27 November:5.
5   Bah AH. 1965. *Textes sacrés d'Afrique noire* [Sacred texts of black Africa]. Dieterlin G (ed). Paris: Gallimard, 8.
6   Tossou R. 1977. Presentation to the Pan-African Conference of Theologians of the Third World, Accra, Ghana.

and without a favourable legal framework. During the revolutionary period in Benin, religions as a whole, especially traditional religions, experienced a difficult period, if not outright persecution. But the democratic wind that has blown on Benin from the National Conference of Living Forces in February 1990 and the further establishment of the rule of law promoted the will "to give substance to the permanent quest for identity of the black man".[7] It is in this climate, in fact, that Ouidah 92 was able to stand.

DEMOCRACY IN BENIN: SECULARISM OF THE STATE

The Beninese Constitution of 1990 stipulates in Article 2 that the Republic of Benin is secular and democratic. Article 23 states that the exercise of worship and the expression of beliefs are carried out within the framework of state secularism. In the second paragraph, it is written: "Institutions, religious or philosophical communities have the right to develop without hindrance." This is quite contrary to the Basic Law of 1977.[8]

It was in the climate of the democratic era that Law No. 90-019 of 27 July 1990 was promulgated, designating legal holidays, both paid and unpaid, in Benin. The Christian Churches have six holidays: 15 August, Day of the Assumption; 1 November, All Saints Day; 25 December, Christmas Day; as well as Easter Monday, Whit Monday and Ascension Day. The Muslim community has three holidays: the day of Ramadan, Tabaski Day,[9] and the Day of Maouloud.[10] Until then, traditional religions had no officially recognised feast day.

It is, in fact, this secular character of the Republic of Benin on which the organisers of Ouidah 92 relied to justify the holding of the festival and the place they accorded to the traditional religions. Such a festival could not have seen the light of day in the days of the Marxist-Leninist revolution in Benin between 1972 and 1989. "Secularism, of course, requires the state to stand at an equal distance from all beliefs and confessions,"[11] said President Soglo during the closing ceremony of the festival. "Nevertheless," he continued, "neither did we feel that we were breaking this rule by receiving with joy and fervor his

---

7   Soglo N. 2013. "Pourquoi la fête des religions traditionnelles au Bénin? Les explications du Président-Maire Nicéphore SOGLO" [Why a festival of traditional religions in Benin? The explanation of President-Mayor Nicéphore SOGLO], *Jolome News*. Online at: http://bj.jolome.com/news/article/pourquoi-la-fete-des-religions-traditionnelles-au-benin-les-explications-du-president-maire-nice-336
8   Cf. Sourou, "State and Religion under the 1977 Constitution in Benin".
9   Eid al-Adha "Festival of the Sacrifice", also called the "Sacrifice Feast", is the second of two Muslim holidays celebrated worldwide each year, and it is considered the holier of the two. It honours the willingness of Ibrahim (Abraham) to sacrifice his son, as an act of submission to God's command.
10 This is Prophet Muhammed's (also known as Mohammed or Muhammad) birthday.
11 Soglo N. 1993. "Il nous faut jeter les passerelles nécessaires entre les communautés noires des Amériques et de l'Afrique" [We need to build the necessary bridges between the black communities of the Americas and Africa], *La Nation*, 22 February:5.

Holiness Pope John Paul II.[12] Did not believe we betrayed this duty of neutrality by going to meet Beninese and African religions. The rest is just a matter of words. We must now go beyond any vain polemic and underline the essential convergences."[13]

10 JANUARY: POLITICAL CALCULATIONS?

The organisation of Ouidah 92 has prompted gnashing of teeth in several religious spheres in Benin. Many feared that it was a mock cultural event to promote the Vodoun and other cults.[14] President Soglo alluded to it in his closing speech. Another fear was the fact that traditional cults also sometimes include manifestations that are not respectful of human rights: forced internment in convents, abusive marriages, witchcraft, unorthodox rituals and entanglements. Such behavior violates the integrity of the human person on the one hand, and the Constitution of Benin 1990,[15] on the other. The Catholic Church and other religious communities have struggled and struggled in Benin as pretty much everywhere else in Africa. Their fear is well and truly justified.

In the literature I consulted for this research, it appears that Ouidah 92 was not the result of political calculations. Some argue that Soglo's illness, which occurred shortly after his election as head of the country in 1991, brought him closer to traditional healers and enabled him to appreciate the importance of culture and Traditional religions.[16] It should also be borne in mind that Ouidah 92 was organised by Soglo in 1993 and that the law instituting the Feast of Traditional Religions was passed by parliament and promulgated in 1997 by Mathieu Kérékou, whose election in 1996 was not very much supported by his predecessor.

CONCLUSION

Without sweeping aside the conclusions of Cédric Mayrargue, I believe, based at least on the sources that I have consulted, that the real reasons for the institution of the day of 10 January in Benin can be found in the firm will of the organisers of Ouidah 92 – namely, to "celebrate together with the Diaspora the

---

12 Pope Jean-Paul made a pastoral visit to Benin for the second time from 3 to 5 February 1993, a week before the opening of Ouidah Festival.
13 Soglo, "Il nous faut jeter les passerelles nécessaires", 5.
14 Soglo, "Il nous faut jeter les passerelles nécessaires".
15 Cf. Articles 15, 16 and 18, para 1. In particular, Article 15 reads: "Everyone has the right to life, liberty, security and the integrity of his person."
16 Mayrargue C. 1997. "Démocratisation politique et revitalisation religieuse, l'exemple du culte vodun au Bénin" [Political democratistion and religious revitalisation, the example of the Vodoun cult in Benin], in Constantin F and Coulon C (eds). *Religion et transition démocratique en Afrique* [Religion and democratic transition in Africa]. Paris: Editions Khartala, 135-162.

density and humanistic value of traditional religions, the foundation of African spiritualism ... to give substance to this permanent quest for the identity of the black man. On this land of nourishment and steeped in history and culture ... after four centuries of slave trade and a century of colonisation that had blackened the black man, time had finally come to claim with Aimé Césaire and Léopold Sédar Senghor, our personality, our dignity and our negritude. For an enslaved and colonised soul cannot be carried on indefinitely. We must be proud of our culture, our history, our people, our race."[17] Soglo said recently, "Africa, the cradle of humanity and the source of its origins, is a land of welcome, a land of tolerance and respect for differences."[18] And these values undoubtedly come from African traditional religion, understood as a culture that has shaped, nourished, maintained and consolidated the unique identity of the peoples of Africa throughout the centuries. There are actually some ways of seeing the world that we find only on our continent.

The great Pope John Paul II, during his second visit to Benin recognised the importance of this during his meeting in Cotonou with the leaders of traditional religion,[19] when he declared, "It is legitimate to be grateful to elders who have transmitted the meaning of the sacred, the belief in a unique and good God, a taste for celebration, esteem for moral life and harmony in society."[20] Then the two synods devoted to Africa in 1994 and 2009 largely reversed the role and place of traditional African religion in the formation and maintenance of a Christian conscience in Africa.[21]

Soglo emphasises,

> This position on traditional religions in our policy, is only fair, not only are these religions practiced by a large part of the Beninese population, they are a real factor of identification, understanding and integration. The foundation of this strength lies in the deeply pacifist nature and the exceptional open-mindedness of our endogenous religions. They do not engage in any proselytism and do not engage in any war against other religious denominations, except to defend themselves against the attacks to which they have been subjected.[22]

Those who seek at all costs to condemn the Ouidah 92 initiative and the institution of the National Feast of Traditional Religions also show, in my

---

17 Soglo, "Pourquoi la fête des religions?"
18 Soglo, "Pourquoi la fête des religions?"
19 I believe, without deceiving myself, that this is the only meeting of the kind that John Paul II had during his whole pontificate.
20 Pope John Paul II. 1993. "Rencontre du pape Jean-Paul II avec une délégation des disciples du vaudou" [Meeting of Pope Jean-Paul II With a delegation of vodoun disciples]. Online at: http://w2.vatican.va/content/john-paul-ii/fr/speeches/1993/february/documents/hf_jp-ii_spe_19930204_vodu-cotonou.html
21 Sourou JB. 2014. "African Traditional Religion and the Catholic Church in light of the Synods for Africa: 1994 and 2009", *African Human Rights Law Journal* 14(1):142-149.
22 Soglo, "Pourquoi la fête des religions?"

opinion, a certain lack of knowledge of the geography of religions. If all the peoples of this world have their religion, why should Africans not have theirs? And, yet, among those who fight initiatives like 10 January can be found many Beninese and Africans. All peoples of the world are committed to their cultures, their traditions and their religions. This is true of Shintoism in Japan, Confucianism in China, Buddhism in India, Christianity in Europe (if there is anything left of it) and Islam in the Middle East. And we in Africa where is our religion? What have we done? And what do we want to do?

I think that modern Africa – without hiding behind scientific progress and its achievements and without any shame, if it wants to preserve its soul, its lucidity and its genius – must return to traditional religion, to its cradle, to its true values, and think that even in the face of the problems of today's world. lies its strength, vigour, sap and progress in all fields: political, scientific and cultural.

III. Islam and Constitutional Law in Africa

7 RELIGIOUS PREACHING AND STATE REGULATION OF THE FREE EXERCISE OF RELIGION BY SHI'A MUSLIMS IN KADUNA STATE, NIGERIA: A CONSTITUTIONAL AND HUMAN RIGHTS DISCOURSE

Ahmed Salisu Garba[1]

INTRODUCTION

The Shi'a group otherwise called the Islamic Movement of Nigeria emerged on the Nigerian scene as the insidious effect of a combination of three things. These are the expulsion of Ibrahim Yaqoub al-Zakzaky from Ahmadu Bello University, Zaria; the influx of Islamic books from countries such as Egypt,[2] Iran, Saudi Arabia and Turkey into Nigeria; and their accessibility to Ahmadu Bello University students, particularly after the Iranian revolution of 1979.[3] The Shi'a began as a group in Nigeria in the early 1980s with Ibrahim Yaqoub al-Zakzaky as their leader. Al-Zazaky was a product of Muslim Student Society of Nigeria (MSSN),[4] and his name came into the public domain when the management of Ahmadu Bello University, Zaria, expelled him from the university as a result of the key role he played in the popular "Islam Only" demonstration organised by the Muslim Student Society of Nigeria (MSSN) in 1977, in which the group called for the adoption of an Islamic government in Nigeria.[5] His expulsion from school paved the way for him to visit Iran to explore Shi'a doctrines.[6] It should be noted that before his expulsion from Ahmadu Bello University, Zaria, Zakzaky had already become radicalised and exposed to Shi'a, as a result of contacts with different Islamic writings coming into the country from radical groups in Egypt, Iran and Turkey.[7] It was this scenario that provided the fertile ground for the emergence of Shi'a movement in Nigeria.

The main obsession of the group has always been protesting against what they termed the anti-Islamic posture of the Nigerian government, and at various times they called for the establishment of government similar to that of Iran in

---

1 The author teaches law at the Faculty of Law of the Bauchi State University, Gadau, Nigeria and is a final-year PhD Candidate at the Faculty of Law of the Bayero University, Kano in Nigeria working on the regulation of Religious Preaching in Nigeria.
2 See Hassan IH. 2015. "An Introduction to Islamic Movements and Modes of Thought in Nigeria", in Denzer L and Shereikis R (eds). *PAS/ISITA Working Papers No. 1*. Evanston, IL: Program of African Studies, Northwestern University, 24-26.
3 See Hassan, "An Introduction to Islamic Movements", 24-26.
4 See Hassan, "An Introduction to Islamic Movements", 24-26.
5 Hassan, "An Introduction to Islamic Movements", 24-25.
6 Hassan, "An Introduction to Islamic Movements", 24.
7 Hassan "An Introduction to Islamic Movements", 24-26.

Nigeria.⁸ To achieve their aims, they adopted the well-known methodology of *Taqiyya*, or disguise of religious conviction.⁹ They maintain a strong opposition to secularism and seek to establish an Islamic government in Nigeria headed by their fellow Shi'a members. In addition, they insult and attack the first three Caliphs – Abu-Bakr, Umar and Usman – as being usurpers of the succession to Prophet Muhammad which they believe rightfully belonged to Ali. This is classical Shi'a doctrine. The Sunni Muslims that constitute the majority in Nigeria despise the Shi'a for these allegations and disrespect. Their belief, however, is that the time to take up arms is not ripe in Nigeria and nobody knows when the time will be ripe for them to take up revolutionary arms to change the government as occurred Iran.

The adoption of the *taqiyya* methodology has created fear in the minds of other Nigerian Muslims, on one hand, and of the Nigerian government, on the other. This is a possible explanation for why the Shi'a are always under strong suspicion by government and the people. It may also be true to say that it is this suspicion that triggers conflict between the group and government security outfits at various times.¹⁰ For example, during its silver jubilee celebration on 10 April 2005, the movement affirmed its ultimate aim to establish an Islamic government in Nigeria, but this brought them into conflict with the government.¹¹ They also clashed with Nigerian security outfits at several times resulting in the destruction of the group's headquarters in Sokoto in July 2007 and in Zaria in 2009 and 2014.¹²

Their latest clash with the security in Nigeria was on the 12 December 2015 in the city of Zaria in Kaduna State. The members of the Islamic Movement of Nigeria were doing their usual *tattaki* (a religious procession) in the city of Zaria, with thousands of their members out on the major streets of Zaria City. This blocked public ways and made it difficult for other road users to access the roads. Coincidentally, the Nigerian Chief of Army Staff was on his way to visit the emir of Zazzau, and he was forced to stop on the road because members of the Shi'a group blocked the way and refused the Army Chief access despite entreaties from the army officers. The logjam led to a conflict between the two groups, as a result of which many people died and the Shi'a group's

---

8   Hassan, "An Introduction to Islamic Movements", 25.
9   Hassan, "An Introduction to Islamic Movements", 25-26.
10 Hassan, "An Introduction to Islamic Movements", 25-26.
11 See the official website of the Islamic Movement of Nigeria (IMN) for more information on their activities, at: http://islamicmovement.org, with a Hausa version at: http://www.harkarmusulunci.org, and an Arabic version at: http://www.alharka.net. The websites discuss such important Shi'a ideas and rituals such as Ashura, the birthday of Zahra (*Maulud*), *idul Ghadir*, and others. Furthermore, the discourses of Imam Ruhollah Moosavi Khomeini, Imam Ali Hosseini Khamenei, and other Shi'a scholars are presented on the websites, as well as Shi'ite perspectives of Sunni Islam, radicalism, terrorism, nationalism, and secularism. The websites also post material from the English-language *Pointer Express* and the Hausa (*Mizan*) news magazines of the Zakzaky group.
12 Hassan, "An Introduction to Islamic Movements", 25-26.

headquarters at Gyellasu in Zaria City, a complex building called "Hussainiya Bakiyatullah" serving as the group's headquarters and centre of their activities, was destroyed by the Nigerian Army.

In reaction, the Kaduna State government introduced social control measures to control members of the Shi'a in the state. Firstly, the state proscribed all forms of road blockage, obstruction of public highways, and occupation of public facilities in a manner that disturbs other people in the state. It further directed people to apply and get permission before they engage in any form of procession in the state. Secondly, the state established a commission of inquiry to investigate the remote and immediate causes of the collision between the Nigeria Army and members of the Shi'a. Thirdly, the state introduced the Religious Preaching Bill, 2016, with a view to controlling religious preaching in the state.[13] As a final blow in a series of measures taken prior to proposal of the Religious Preaching Bill, 2016, the state banned and declared the Islamic movement of Nigeria to be unlawful on the basis of the report of a Commission of Inquiry it set up to investigate the confrontation between the Nigeria Army and the Shi'a.

This chapter discusses these various measures, arguing that they are not reasonable in a democratic society like Nigeria and that the state in employing them is not achieving its overall aims regarding the Shi'ite population in Kaduna State. To succeed in its objectives, the state's response must be designed in accord with the Nigerian Constitution and other democratic norms of rights and freedom of religion in societies around the world. To establish this thesis, the chapter investigates the following questions: Firstly, how reasonable and justifiable are these measures in a democratic Nigeria? Secondly, what judicial review mechanism would be employed to determine their reasonability in a democracy and why? And thirdly, how do the measures accord with the freedom of religion clause in the Constitution of the Federal Republic of Nigeria?

To achieve the objectives of this chapter, I provide a detailed analysis of the proposed Religious Preaching Bill, 2016.[14] First, after reviewing some literature on the regulation of religion generally to see the experience in other democracies, I examine the history of regulation of preaching in Nigeria and its effects on various religious groups. Second, I analyse the provisions of the Religious Preaching Bill, 2016 and their likely effects on religious groups in Kaduna State, particularly religious minorities. Third, I examine the particular effect of the law's ban on the Islamic Movement in Nigeria, the nation's main Shi'ite organisation, and the declaration that it was an unlawful society. The overall aim of the chapter is to recommend a theoretical framework for the purpose of ascertaining the reasonability of these religious regulation measures in a democratic Nigeria, along with a practical framework to resolve the conflict

---

13 The full title of the bill was "A bill for a law to substitute the Kaduna State Regulation of Religious Preaching (amendment) Edict No. 6 of 1996".
14 Kaduna State Regulation of Religious Preaching (amendment) Edict No. 6 of 1996.

between the regulatory power of the state and the Shi'ites' freedom of religion as citizens under the Nigerian Constitution.

REGULATION OF FREEDOM OF RELIGION

Regulation of freedom of religion refers to the exercise of state regulatory power to limit citizens' rights to enjoy freedom of religion using laws that are reasonably justifiable in a democratic society generally in the interest of defence, public safety, public order, public morality, public health and in order to protect the rights and freedom of other persons.[15] It is in exercise of this constitutional power that the Kaduna State government introduced the measures under scrutiny to control the Shi'a group that are the focus on of this chapter. Debates on conflicts between the regulatory power of the state and freedom of religion in democratic orders have generally been investigated from five different perspectives using a wide range of methodologies.

Firstly, American constitutional law experts Audrey Peltze[16] and Kenneth Lasson[17] argue that the government should regulate freedom of religion because of the perceived incivility and incitement that religious persuasion contains. Peltze's work, for example, argues that the state can restrict the right to religious preaching, so long as it is done through neutral laws that support government interests while preserving citizens' free exercise rights. How can this be achieved? And through what balancing mechanism can this achieved? These questions are largely unanswered in the theory that Peltze and Lasson describe.

Secondly, American experts on regulation of religion, such as Brian J Grim and Roger Finke,[18] along with experts on religion and politics, such as Monica Duffy Toft, Daniel Philpot and Timothy Samuel Shah,[19] argue that it is unreasonable and unwise to place restrictions on citizens' freedom of religion rights in a democracy, because doing so has grave consequences. These works also focus on the religious economy thesis, which posits that in a free market of ideas, religious ideas should be allowed to compete with one another in the available public space so that in the end the truth prevails. Grim and Finke's work particularly demonstrates that most restriction placed on free exercise rights in democracies are a result of collaboration between the state and dominant religious groups to suppress minority religious groups.[20]

---

15 Constitution of the Federal Republic Nigeria, 1999, sec 45(1).
16 Peltze A. 1982. "A Survey of Constitutional Challenges to Municipal Regulation of Religious Solicitation and a Suggested Legislative Compromise", *Fordham Urban Law Journal* 11:845.
17 Lasson K. 2005. "Incitement in the Mosques: Testing the Limits of Free Speech and Religious Liberty", *Whittier Law Review* 27:3-59.
18 Grim BJ and Finke R. 2011. *The Price of Freedom Denied*. New York: Cambridge University Press.
19 Toft MD, Philpott D and Shah TS. 2011. *God's Century: Resurgent Religion and Global Politics*. London: W.W. Norton & Company.
20 Grim and Finke, *The Price of Freedom Denied*, 25-30.

The suppression of minority groups is a practice which should be discouraged. There are relevant scholarly works in Nigeria to support this point. For example, Nigerian historians, Auwal Anwar and Haruna Wakili argue that dominant Islamic groups in collaboration with governments in Kaduna and Kano States acted under the pretext of control of religious preaching to repress minority Islamic groups that they regarded as dissidents.[21] These works are relevant and evidence-based in support of their thesis, but none of them provide any particular balancing mechanism to test the reasonability or otherwise of laws enacted to restrict the free exercise rights of citizens in a democracy. None of them apply legal approach to study the phenomenon. Grim and Finke are engaged in empirical political science research. Toft and colleagues also write from the perspective of political science.

Thirdly, Nigeria-based legal practitioners, such as Sam Amadi and Inibehe Effiong, argue that the state should not regulate religious preaching at all – despite the provision of Section 45 of the Nigerian Constitution, which clearly allows the state to derogate from such rights on the basis of defence, public order, public morality and other factors.[22] Their studies were done in response to the Kaduna State's effort to amend the Kaduna State Regulation of Religious Preaching Law of 1996.[23] For example, Effiong's argument, through Nigerian constitutional law, is that some specific sections of the Religious Preaching Bill, 2016 offend provisions of the Nigerian Constitution, particularly Section 10 on prohibition of the adoption of a state religion by any state in the country, Section 38 on freedom of religion, and Section 42 which allows the state to limit or derogate from these rights. Effiong does not, however, acknowledge the fact that the freedom of religion clause in the Nigerian Constitution is not an absolute right.

A fourth area of scholarship is the one that uses balancing mechanisms or proportionality tests to resolve conflicts between the regulatory power of the state and the right to religious freedom of its citizens. International agreements propose a "three-step" standard of judicial review designed to strike balance between state regulatory power and citizens' freedom of religion in a democratic society.[24] The three-step balancing mechanism requires that for any limitation on freedom of religion to be legitimate in a democratic

---

21 Anwar AA. 1997. *Gardawa, ulama and the State of Northern Nigeria: The Maitatsine phenomenon, 1962-1985*, PhD Diss, University of Maiduguri. See also Wakili H. 1997. *The Phenomenon of Revolts and Riots in Kano, 1983-1995: An Historical Perspective*, PhD Diss, Bayero University Kano.
22 See Constitution of the Federal Republic of Nigeria 1999, sec 45(1).
23 See Effiong I. 2016. "Kaduna Preaching Bill: Resolving the Constitutional Controversy", *Nigeria Today*, 30 March; Amadi S. 2016. "Kaduna anti-preaching Law: A regulatory mistep" *The Cable*, 12 April.
24 These three standards are provided for under Article 18 (3), the provisions of the International Convention on Civil and Political Rights (ICCPR). See also European Convention on Human Rights, Article 9.2, which is similar to the provisions of the ICCPR.

society, it must satisfy these three standards of prescribes by law requirement, furtherance of a legitimate state interest qualification and the requirement of proportionality. American constitutional law scholar Jeremy Gunn, however, questions the adequacy of the three-legged standard of review as a means for resolving conflicts between the two competing rights. His argument is that the test lacks guiding principles on the kind of evidence to admit or the question of which of the two rights is more important than the other and why and on which of the parties as between the state and the citizen the burden of proving what evidence lies and why.[25] Gunn therefore recommends four standards of review instead of three. According to him, a tribunal faced with the task of interpreting derogatory clauses with respect to freedom of religion should, first, understand its role, second, properly identify the burden of proof of each of the parties, third, apply the less restrictive alternatives with correct evidentiary obligations placed on both parties, and fourthly, understand the relevant degree of scrutiny to apply.[26]

Gunn's argument, however, negates the role of the overall religion-state pattern, especially in a country like Nigeria, as a guiding principle in the interpretation of freedom of religion cases. This relationship is relevant when assessing the nature of the protection of freedom of religion in a country, especially since that religion is indispensable in the maintenance of public order. Particularly in the case of Nigeria, Gunn's fourth recommendation raises the question of how to determine the relevant degree of scrutiny. And this is where the main problem is. What degree of scrutiny should be applied in striking balance between state regulatory power and freedom of religion? How? Why? When?

Addressing these questions is particularly important in Nigeria. This is because the Nigerian Constitution protects a citizen's right to "freedom of thought, conscience and religion, including freedom to change his religion or belief, and freedom (either alone or in community with others, and in public or in private) to manifest and propagate his religion or belief in worship, teaching, practice and observance."[27] The Constitution also protects "freedom of expression, including freedom to hold opinions and to receive and impart ideas and information without interference" and to "assemble freely" and "associate with others."[28] As law and religion scholar W Cole Durham Jr has observed, freedom of religion is a "core doctrine" amongst other fundamental human rights in the world today.[29] However, the Nigerian Constitution also allows the state to derogate from these rights when "reasonably justifiable in a democratic society" on the

---

25 Gunn TJ. 2011. "Permissible Limitations on Freedom of Religion or Belief", in Witte J (Jr) and Green MC (eds). *Religion and Human Rights: An Introduction*. Oxford: Oxford University Press, 263-264.
26 Gunn, "Permissible Limitations on Freedom of Religion or Belief", 266.
27 Constitution of the Federal Republic of Nigeria, sec 38(1).
28 Constitution of the Federal Republic of Nigeria, secs 39 and 40.
29 See Durham WC (Jr). 1996. "Perspectives on religious liberty: A Comparative Framework", in Van der Vyver JD and Witte J (Jr) (eds). *Religious Human Rights Global Perspective: Legal Perspectives*. Boston: Martinus Nijhoff, 1-44.

grounds of "defence, public safety, public order, public morality, public health" and for the purpose of "protecting the rights of others."[30] The Constitution, however, does not define the phrase "democratic society", the criteria for its determination, or what qualifies a law to be "reasonably justifiable" in a society such as Nigeria. The lack of definition creates a legal normative space that ought to be filled by either the court through the exercise of discretion in the event of conflict between the two competing rights, or by the legislature through the enactment of the law. A solution to this definitional dilemma requires the application of a suitable balancing mechanism or proportionality assessment technique to understand the meaning of the phrases which this works seeks to provide.

THE PROPOSED PREACHING LAW IN KADUNA STATE

In order to appreciate the controversy surrounding the proposed revision of the preaching law in Kaduna State, it is helpful to have an understanding of the pre-independence and post-independence history of religious preaching and its regulation in Northern Nigeria generally and in Kaduna State in particular. This includes effects of earlier efforts to modify the Religious Preaching Edict of 1984 through the amendment edicts of 1987 and 1996.

Pre-independence period control of religious preaching in Northern Nigeria

Regulation of Islamic religious preaching is an old phenomenon in Northern Nigeria.[31] It was largely centreed in areas such as Sokoto, Zaria, Kano and Nupe land in Northern Nigeria. During this period, Kaduna was not made the capital of the northern region. The potential danger of Islamic religious preaching motivated authorities in northern Nigeria to regulate the practice. Historically, the attempt by the king of Gobir, Bawa Jan Gwarzo, in the late eighteenth century to control the Islamic religious preaching of jihadist Usman dan Fodio was the first effort to regulate Islamic religious preaching in the region.[32] After the demise of King Bawa, his brother King Nafata continued along the same line but was even stricter. King Nafata restricted Islamic religious preaching in the land of Gobir,[33] barred people not born to Muslim families from converting to Islam[34] and ordered the converts to return to their traditional religion.[35] He also proscribed the wearing of turbans and veils by men and women respectively.[36]

---

30   Constitution of the Federal Republic of Nigeria, sec 45.
31   Gwandu A. 1986. "Aspects of the Administration of Justice in the Sokoto Caliphate and Shaykh Abdullahi ibn Fodio's Contribution to It", *Islamic Law in Nigeria*, Rashid KS (ed). Kaduna: Islamic Publications Bureau, 10-27.
32   Laremont RR. 2011. *Islamic Law and Politics in Northern Nigeria.* Trenton, NJ: Africa World, 64-65.
33   Laremont, *Islamic Law and Politics in Northern Nigeria*, 64-65.
34   Laremont, *Islamic Law and Politics in Northern Nigeria*, 64-65.
35   Laremont, *Islamic Law and Politics in Northern Nigeria*, 64-65.
36   Laremont, *Islamic Law and Politics in Northern Nigeria*, 64-65.

Usman dan Fodio resisted the orders of the king, and this confrontation ended in the well-known jihad that began in 1804.[37] The success of the jihad gave rise to a new administration with Usman dan Fodio as the leader. He then appointed emirs as his deputies in many parts of today's northern Nigeria, including places such as Sokoto, Zaria, Kano and Nupeland.[38]

The second attempt to regulate Islamic preaching took place under the colonial administration in 1926, as a reaction to incessant disagreements between the dominant Islamic religious groups in the region. These conflicts were essentially between the Qadiriyya and Tijjaniyya Sufi orders, but they also included friction associated with the emergence of new Islamic religious groups such as the Ahmadiyya and the Wahhabiyya in the region.[39] At that time, moreover, the region had witnessed a rise in the presence of Christian religious missionaries, who were struggling to win more souls for Christianity, against the wishes of the northern Muslim emirs.[40] As a result, the colonial government issued circulars directing resident governors of Kano, Zaria, Sokoto and Niger to issue proclamations to control religious preaching generally in their areas, in order to avoid any possible infringement of law and order.[41] This was the situation up to 1950, and then through 1960 when Nigeria became independent and gained a new Constitution. That Constitution provided, for the first time, full liberal rights including freedoms of religion, expression and association.[42]

Post-independence period control of religious preaching in Kaduna State

The post-independence history of regulation of religious preaching started in Kaduna State, and it was probably the consequence of a form of "religious gerrymandering", a situation where the law is enacted with the aim of burdening specific religious groups. In the case of Maitatsine and Izala in the late 1970s, this practice favoured the Sufi orders, who were the dominant religious groups in the region. The premier of the Northern Region, Sir Ahmadu Bello (Sardauna of Sokoto) formed what was known as the Council of Ulama on 23 August 1963 in Kaduna State which was the capital city of Northern Nigeria.

This council was mainly composed of members of the dominant Qadiriyya and Tijaniyya Sufi groups.[43] The council was to advise the northern regional

---

37 Laremont, *Islamic Law and Politics in Northern Nigeria*, 64-65.
38 Laremont, *Islamic Law and Politics in Northern Nigeria*, 64-80.
39 Wakili, *The Phenomenon of Revolts and Riots in Kano*, 38-45.
40 Afolayan F. 2009. "Religion and Politics in Colonial Nigeria: The Life and Career of Sir Walter Miller, 1782-1952", in Adekunle JL (ed). *Religion in Politics: Secularism and National Integration in Modern Nigeria*. Trenton, NJ: Africa World, 37-66.
41 Anwar, *Gardawa, ulama and the State of Northern Nigeria*, 88-90.
42 See Constitution of the Federal Republic of Nigeria, 1999, ch 4.
43 Laremont, *Islamic Law and Politics in Northern Nigeria*, 3. See also Umar MS. 1993. "Changing Islamic Identity in Nigeria from the 1960s to the 1980s: From Sufism to anti-Sufism", in Brenner L (ed). *Muslim Identity and Social Change in Sub-Saharan Africa*. Bloomington and Indianapolis: Indiana University Press, 154-178.

government on Islamic affairs, with emphasis on disagreements among different Islamic religious groups and on grass-roots Islamic preachers in the region.⁴⁴ On 7 January 1964, the youth movement Fityanul Islam, which was linked to the Tijaniyya leadership, wrote a complaint to the Sardauna against certain minority Islamic religious group whom they labelled as Gardawa (a Hausa term for graduates of Quranic schools without further Islamic training), urging him to form a committee of scholars to license the group before they were allowed to preach. They further wrote to the Council of Ulama on 25 July 1964, calling for the banning of Gardawa from religious preaching.⁴⁵

In reaction, the Sardauna issued a circular to all the northern provinces, directing them to make the possession of a preaching license a precondition for Islamic religious preachers before they were allowed to preach in the region. This was a sort of "de facto" religious regulation through the indirect influence of the dominant religious groups. That measure forced the Gardawa out of the preaching scene for nearly two years and tended to favour the dominant religious groups in the religious marketplace. Although the Sardauna belonged to the Qadiriyya Islamic religious group and his actions impacted negatively on the Gardawa group, records indicate that he was fairly liberal and ecumenical in matters of religion, until he was killed in the military coup of 1966.⁴⁶

It is in this context that Izala, a Wahhabi-oriented Islamic religious group which was close to anti-Sufi reformism Shaykh Abubakar Mahmud Gumi and strongly opposed to Sufi doctrines and practices, emerged on the scene in 1978.⁴⁷ The emergence of Izala changed the nature of Muslim intra-religious conflict in northern Nigeria from Qadiriyya versus Tijaniyya, to a competition between Tariqa and Izala, with including both Qadiriyya and Tijaniyya groups collectively. It immediately began a campaign of offensive preaching directed against Sufi doctrines, which it labelled as *bid'a* (heretical innovation) and *shirk* (polytheism). In their preaching, Izala preachers used to mention openly the personal names of the founders of Sufi orders. They engaged in *takfir* and even split their mosques from those of the Sufi orders, as they did not allow their members to follow an imam affiliated to a Sufi order. This led to a series of skirmishes between the two groups.⁴⁸ While the imbroglio between Izala and Tariqa groups continued, some of the disgruntled Gardawa re-emerged on the scene under the form of the Yan Tatsine in Kano State. The Yan Tatsine were the followers of Muhammadu Marwa Maitatsine, a peripatetic preacher from northern Cameroon who had settled in Kano, where he engaged in belligerent public preaching against all the existing Islamic groups in the region.⁴⁹

---

44 Umar, "Changing Islamic Identity in Nigeria", 154-178.
45 Anwar, *Gardawa, ulama and the State of Northern Nigeria*.
46 Kuka MH. 2011. *Religion, Power and Politics in Northern Nigeria*. Ibadan: Spectrum, ix-xiii.
47 Kuka, *Religion, Power and Politics in Northern Nigeria*, ix-xiii.
48 Kuka, *Religion, Power and Politics in Northern Nigeria*, ix-xiii.
49 Kuka, *Religion, Power and Politics in Northern Nigeria*, ix-xiii.

Military officers headed by Major General Muhammadu Buhari toppled the civilian administration in 1983. This regime took a cue from the past civilian administration and placed a "blanket ban on religious activities especially open-air preaching".[50] In addition, it forbad the building of new mosques without the permission of emirate authorities. In order to prevent preachers from circumventing any ban imposed by the preaching board of a particular emirate by applying to a neighbouring one, the government also introduced a requirement according to which authorisation for religious preaching must be obtained both in the preacher's emirate of origin, as well as in any other emirate where he might wish to preach. Most of the preaching boards were constituted by scholars affiliated with the Sufi orders, which at the time represented most of the country's religious scholars, Izala found the new measures to be burdensome. Because of this, the founder of Izala, the late Shaykh Ismaila Idiris, was reported to have said in one of his preaching sessions, after both regimes were out of office, that "Allah will not forgive the regimes of Shagari and that of Buhari because they blocked the way of Allah."[51]

It was under this regime that the Regulation of Religious Preaching Edict of 1984 was first enacted.

ANALYSIS OF THE RELIGIOUS PREACHING BILL, 2016

At the time of writing this chapter, the government of Kaduna State had introduced the Religious Preaching Bill, 2016, seeking to replace the state's Regulation of Religious Preaching Edict No. 1 of 1987. This proposed law was part of the reaction of the Kaduna State government to control the Shi'ite-Army imbroglio and other similar problems in the state. My analysis of the content of the proposed law demonstrates that the proposed law is designed by the state to target the Shi'a groups.

Definition of a religious preacher

Section 3 of the proposed Religious Preaching Bill, 2016 defines a religious preacher as any person licensed by the Jama'atu Nasril Islam (JNI) or the Christian Association of Nigeria (CAN) to preach in the state. The JNI is a body established by the late premier of Northern Nigeria in the 1960s to serve as an umbrella body for all Muslims in Northern Nigeria. It has branch offices in all the states of Northern Nigeria headed by emirs or persons appointed by them. These emirs are members of the dominant Sufi dominant religious groups, either Qadriyya/Tijaniyya or Tariqa. They are also mostly Sunni Muslims and do not recognise the Shi'a as Muslims. The JNI played a role in the regulation of Islamic religious preaching in Northern Nigeria in the 1960s and 70s. For example, in 1970, when the *ulama* in Kano State, which consisted of members of

---

50   Umar, "Changing Islamic Identity in Nigeria", 154-178.
51   Umar, "Changing Islamic Identity in Nigeria".

the dominant Sufi orders, influenced the enactment of a law to regulate Islamic religious preaching in Kano State, the minority Gardawa groups suffered.[52] They were denied preaching license to preach in the areas under the jurisdiction of Kano State, but they moved to Kaduna State and obtained preaching licenses from the JNI.[53]

Again, Section 3 of the proposed Religious Preaching Bill, 2016 states that any person not licensed by the JNI or the CAN may not be recognised as a religious preacher in the state. In the case of Muslims, this requirement has favoured dominant religious groups who are mostly Sunni who do not recognise Shi'a as Muslims. This is an obvious example of state favouritism extended to the dominant sects through the proposed law.

Recognition of Islam and Christianity as major religions

Section 4 of the Religious Preaching Bill, 2016 recognises Islam and Christianity as the two major religions in the state, and it establishes three committees to regulate the two religions. The law recognises the strength of Izala as an Islamic organisation in the region. In recognition of the status that the group achieved in the region in the 1970s and 1980s, the proposed Religious Preaching Bill, 2016 gives Izala equal representation with Tariqa at the Interfaith Ministerial Committee appointed by the governor. It does the same thing in terms of recognising the authority of CAN member over other Christian groups. But there are questions about into whose purview minority groups within the broader categories of Islam and Christianity fall. Christian Jehovah's Witnesses and Muslim Shi'a and Ahmadiyya are examples of these intra-religious minority groups. Section 4(2) of the Religious Preaching Bill, 2016 provides for the establishment of a ministerial committee to be composed of: (1) a chairman appointed by the governor, (2) a special adviser to the governor on internal security, (3) a senior adviser to governor on interfaith matters, (4) a member from the JNI and CAN, (5) representative of the Ministry of Justice and (6) one representative each from the Nigerian Police, Department of State Security Service, and the Civil Defense Corps. In addition, the JNI and CAN are to record of churches and mosques including data of all preachers. Minority religious groups are not contemplation as having representation or a role on the committee.

JNI and CAN power over issuance of preaching licenses

Section 5 of the Religious Preaching Bill, 2016 empowers the committees of the JNI and CAN to issue licenses to preachers for a period not exceeding one year, as approved by the ministerial committee. Although these two bodies existed

---

52   Kano Local Government Authority (Control of Quranic Interpretation and Admonishing) Rules 1970. This became Kano Local Government Law No. 3, 1970.
53   Anwar, *Gardawa, ulama and the State of Northern Nigeria*, 4.

long before the Kaduna State government designed its preaching laws, the bodies had no power in law to issue preaching licenses in Nigeria. The JNI had done this in the past but it had no official power to do so under law. However, the preaching laws in Kaduna State had never been enforced, so there was no real way to know whether minority religious groups would have been able to preaching licenses in the state under this system. It does, however, suffice to say that the proposed law, along with the previous ones seems not to contemplate the Shi'a, Ahmadiyya and other minority religious groups as likely recipients of a preaching license.

Local Government Area screening committees

Section 6(1) of the proposed Religious Preaching Bill, 2016 establishes in each Local Government Area a committee to screen applications for licenses and recommend same to the ministerial committee. Section 6(2) provides for composition of the committee which shall consist of the following members: (1) the chairman and co-chairman each representing one of the two major religions (one Muslim and one Christian) to be appointed by the governor on the recommendation of the chairman of the Local Government Council, (2) a representative of the police, (3) two Muslims with one each representing Izala[54] and Tariqa[55] religious groups, and (4) two representatives of CAN.

Compliance with the proposed law

Section 7 of the bill empowers the Local Government Area committees to ensure compliance with the terms of the license so issued and register accredited preachers of all religious groups and organisations operating in the Local Government Area.

Regulation of communication

The Religious Preaching Bill, 2016 also contains a number of provisions regulating communication by religious groups. Section 9 allows all cassettes, CDs, flash drives or any other communication gadgets from accredited preachers to be played inside one's house, *azure* (entrance porch), church, mosque of any other designated place of worship. Section 10 provides that any cassette containing religious recording in which abusive language is used against any person or religious organisation or religious leaders past or present is prohibited in the state.

---

54 A Sunni Muslim group.
55 A Sufi Muslim group.

Punishment

The proposed Religious Preaching Bill, 2016 has a section for prescribing punishments for contravention of the law. Section 12 provides that:

> A person shall be guilty of an offence who in contravention of this law; (a) preaches without a valid license; (b) plays religious cassette or uses a loudspeaker for religious purpose after 8 pm in a public place; (c) uses a loudspeaker for religious purpose other than in a mosque or church and the surrounding areas outside the stipulated prayer times; (d) uses a loudspeaker in vehicles plying the streets with religious recording; (e) abuses religious books; (f) incites disturbance of the public peace; (g) abuses or uses any derogatory term in describing any religion; or (h) carries weapons of any description whether concealed or not in places of worship or to any other place with a view to causing religious disturbance shall be guilty of an offence.

The legal implication of this section as it relates to the Shi'a and other religious groups in the state is that they may not be able to get preaching licenses, because they are not considered to be Muslims by the majority Sunni groups who control over the committees set up to enforce the proposed law. In addition, Section 13 provides, "A person who commits an offence under the provision of this law shall be liable on conviction to a term of imprisonment not exceeding two years or fine of two hundred thousand naira or both; and shall have his license revoked." Section 14 vests jurisdiction over punishment in the Sharia Courts and Customary Courts.

Effects of the interim measures and the proposed preaching bill

The first major effect of the proposed Religious Preaching Bill, 2016 involves the measures of social control introduced by the state in banning all forms of road blockages, obstruction of public highways and occupation of public facilities in a manner that causes inconvenience to other citizens in the state, and the second major effect has to do with the requirement that people seek and obtain the protection of the police before they embark on any procession in the state. These measures may look good for the maintenance of peace and order in the state, especially under Section 45 of the Nigerian Constitution, which allows the state to use its regulatory power to limit citizens' freedom of religion in the interest of defence, public safety, public order, public morality or public health or for the purpose of protecting the rights and freedoms of other persons. It should be noted that in some respects there is not much difference between the proposed Religious Preaching Bill, 2016 and the 1996 edict that it would replace. The key difference is that the 1996 edict was enacted under military rule, while the Religious Preaching Bill, 2016 has been proposed by a democratically elected government. When scrutinised in the context of democracy, measures such as the ones above may not qualify as reasonable measures in a democracy, for several reasons.

Firstly, the interim measures taken prior to the proposal of the Religious Preaching Bill, 2016 were not prescribed by law as required in a democracy. Secondly, the measures were vague in every way and lacked procedures for religious groups to apply for permission to conduct religious activities, such as the procession or other religious gatherings that may interfere with public roads and buildings contained in the first social control measures mentioned in the beginning of this chapter. Thirdly, the measures lacked mechanisms for protecting religious groups from discrimination, especially when such groups apply to embark on their religious activities. Fourthly, the measures did not define the phrase "obstruction of public high ways" or specify who would be competent to determine it. Fifthly, the proposed Religious Preaching Bill, 2016 itself provides no information as to what would amount to inconveniencing other citizens and how to determine it, or what balancing mechanism the authorities would apply to balance the competing rights without burdening the right of the citizen or compromising the neutrality of the state. Sixthly, there is no specification of the punishment for contravention of the law. In the absence of a specified punishment, it is not constitutional to punish a citizen of Nigeria for an offence that is not written down in law under Section 36(8) of the Nigerian Constitution. Finally, it is not clear what type of evidence would be required to prove contravention of these measures in a court of law and by what means. This is especially important, because research into matters of this nature indicates that the process of exercise of discretion in different legal orders is found to be susceptible to bias, especially where it involves groups whose ideologies disagree with predominant ideologies of majority groups in the state, as in the case of the Shi'ites in both Kaduna State and Nigeria as a whole, where Sunni Muslims are the dominant group.[56]

Ban and declaration against the Islamic Movement in Nigeria

The Kaduna State government responded to the faceoff between Shi'a groups and the Nigerian Army in 2015 by introducing social control measures, the introduction of Religious Preaching Bill, 2016 to replace the earlier edicts and the issuance of a declaration order that baned religious preaching. The final crackdown on the Shi'ite group known as the Islamic Movement of Nigeria came on 7 October 2016, when the Kaduna State government issued an order titled the *Kaduna State Official Gazette* No. 21 of 7 October 2016 which banned and declared the Islamic Movement in Nigeria as an unlawful society in Kaduna State.[57] The Kaduna State government relied on Section 45(1) of the Constitution of the Nigeria, which gives the state its regulatory power to restrict limit citizens freedom of religion in the interest of defence, public safety, public order, public morality or public health or for the purpose of protecting the rights and

---

56 See Richardson JT (ed). 2004. *Regulating Religion: Case Studies from Around the Globe.* New York: Kluwer Academic/Plenum, 1-15.
57 See 2016. *Kaduna State Official Gazette* No. 21, 7 October.

freedoms of other persons, and Section 97(A) of the Penal Code Law, Cap 110 Laws of Kaduna State 1991, which gives the governor the power to declare as an unlawful society any organisation whose activities are dangerous to the security and good governance of the state. To justify the declaration, the government based its decision on the finding of the judicial Commission of Inquiry it set up. According to the government, the Commission of Inquiry found that the Islamic Movement in Nigeria is not a registered organisation, has a paramilitary wing and its members do not respect the laws of the country and duly constituted authorities, has overtly continued with unlawful processions, obstruction of facilities including schools without regard to the rights of other citizens and the public peace and order of the state. The governor further stated that the group's actions acts if allowed to go unchecked will constitute danger to the peace, tranquility, harmonious coexistence and governance of Kaduna State.[58]

It should be noted, however, that two days after the issuance of this declaration, the governors of Kano, Plateau, Katsina and other states in Northern Nigeria issued similar declarations against the Shi'ites in their states. These declarations came with devastating consequences for the members of the Shi'a and for Nigerian democracy at large. This is because many people, including members of dominant religious groups in Kaduna, Plateau, Kano and many other states in Northern Nigeria, took the law into their hands and attacked members of the Shi'a group in various states. As a result of this violence, many were killed and their property wantonly destroyed.[59]

TOWARD JUDICIAL REVIEW OF SECTION 45 OF THE CONSTITUTION IN NIGERIA

The social control measures taken by the Kaduna State government were a reaction to the collision between members of the Islamic Movement of Nigeria and the Nigerian Army. These government measures have had effects on the freedom of religion of the Shi'a in Kaduna State and in Nigeria at large. These government actions and their effects have constitutional and human rights implication of regulation of religion in a democratic order like Nigeria.

As we have seen, the Constitution of the Federal Republic of Nigeria makes provision for freedom of religion. Nonetheless, these rights are not absolute. Section 45(1) of the Nigerian Constitution gives the state powers to derogate where necessary for the "defence, public safety, public order, public morality or public health; or for the purpose of protecting the rights and freedoms of other persons". This leaves plenty of room for the state to use penal laws and other legislation to restrict citizens' enjoyments of these rights.

The problem is that the Constitution does not define what a reasonably justifiable law is or the criteria for its determination in a democratic society.

---

58 *Kaduna State Official Gazette* No. 21.
59 *Kaduna State Official Gazette* No. 21.

Analogously, it does not even define what a democratic society is. Herein lies the problem, since without an accurate definition, it becomes increasingly difficult to determine how one can reasonably justify the actions of a state set forth in the proposed religious preaching law, especially as regards these measures taken against the Islamic Movement in Nigeria by the Kaduna State government. Moreover, the question arises as to how the reasonability will be determined.

The absence of an appropriate definition for the phrase "reasonably justifiable law" and the criteria for its determination may be an explanation for why Nigeria has been responding to religious movements such as the Maitatsine, Darul Salam and Boko Haram with the use of force.[60] Nigerian courts have not, thus far, developed any coherent standard of review that can be applied in the event of conflicts between these two competing rights. Would Nigerian courts use foreign precedents for this purpose? If the answer is yes, which country's standard of review would they choose? What criteria would they consider in making the choice? If the answer is no, what alternative interpretative technique would they apply? Will Nigeria continue to crack down on any person whose "search for separate meaning and value in life"[61] differs from that of the majority established religious groups? In the process, will the Nigerian state kill innocent citizens extra judicially for holding opinions different from others?

This chapter's main focus has been not on the faceoff between the Shi'a and the Nigerian Army per se, but rather on the post-conflict measures of social control introduced by the Kaduna State government in reaction to the collision between the two groups. The measures introduced by the Kaduna State government to control the situation were designed to target the Shi'a group possibly. Even so, this chapter maintains that the Nigerian Constitution protects the right to freedom of religion of members of the Shi'a. No judicial pronouncement yet on Section 45 of the Constitution has been made, as it relates to freedom of religion. The Constitution does not define permissible derogation from freedom religion rights and the approach of the Nigerian courts in the area has created gap which should be filled to enhance societal order. What test will the Nigerian courts adopt respecting this conflict?

First, it should be pointed out that the courts in Nigeria will generally invalidate laws made contrary to the procedure laid down in the Constitution as decided in *A.G. Bendel State v. A.G. Federation and Ors*;[62] where the legislature was found to have exceeded its powers in the making of a law, as in *Lakanmi v. A.G. (West)*

---

60 See Adekunle JO. 2009. "Government Reaction to Religious Violence", in Adenkunle JO (ed). *Religion in Politics: Secularism and National Integration in Modern Nigeria*. Trenton, NJ: African World Press, 329-342.
61 Reitz JC. 2005. "Freedom of Religion and Its Limitations: Judicial Standards for Deciding Particular Cases to Maintain the State's Secular Role in Protecting Society's Religious Commitments", in Ostien P et al. (eds). *Comparative Perspectives on Shari'ah in Nigeria*. Ibadan: Spectrum Books, 207-210.
62 See (1982) 3 NCLR 358.

and Ors;⁶³ where a legislation was determined to contravene fundamental human rights, as in *Shugaba Darman v. Minister of Internal Affairs and Ors*;⁶⁴ where it was determined that exercise of powers of one organ in a manner that usurped the constitutional powers of another organ was contrary to the provisions of the Constitution, as in *A.G. (Ogun) State v. A.G. Federation and Ors*;⁶⁵ and finally where any legislation ousts the jurisdiction of the courts, as in *Ademolekun v. University of Ibadan*.⁶⁶ The conclusion to be drawn is that the social control measures taken with respect to the Islamic Movement of Nigeria under the proposed Religious Preaching Bill, 2016, were not backed by Nigerian constitutional law or international human right standards. The rationale for the social control measures are vague and designed to favour the dominant religious groups in the state.

Secondly, the proposed Religious Preaching Law, 2016 contains a contradiction in its very content in recognising Islam and Christianity as the only two religions in the Nigerian state. After all, the same state has banned the Shi'ites and declared them an unlawful society even though they claim to be Muslims. The law has also favoured dominant sects within the dominant religious groups in the state. In this regard, the law conferred power on the Jama'atu Nasril Islam (JNI) and the Christian Association of Nigeria (CAN) to examine aspiring religious preachers concerning their qualifications and to issue preaching licenses to those applicants found to be qualified and to that extent it is anti-religious pluralism and diversity as bedrocks of any democratic order. Conversely, the laws also criminalised preaching without a license or in contravention of the terms of the license. This raises a constitutional challenge. In a constitutional democracy where the rule of law is entrenched, the state is expected to enact laws of general application, not laws that target a specific religion or sect.⁶⁷

The conclusion can that be drawn is that Sections 3, 4, 5, 6 and 7 of the proposed Religious Preaching Law, 2016 allow room for the exercise of uncontrolled discretion by men in authority, contrary to the requirement of laws in democratic legal orders. In addition, the law creates room for discrimination against minority religious groups in the state and negates the principle of religious autonomy claims in a democracy. This can be seen, especially, in the composition of the religious preaching committees where only the JNI and the CAN were recognised in the proposed law.

Another trend that can be inferred is that state regulation of religious preaching in Nigeria has been characterised by violence and discrimination against minority religious groups, which has led to incessant conflicts for years in the

---

63 (1971) U.I.L.R. 201.
64 (1982) 2 NCLR 459.
65 (1982) 3 NCLR 166.
66 (1968) NMLR 253.
67 Reitz, "Freedom of Religion and Its Limitations", 180.

region. Here, the history of the proposed Kaduna State Religious Preaching Bill, 2016, intended to replace the earlier edicts is relevant. The history of the regulation of religion in Northern Nigeria indicates the influence of established religious groups in the enactment and composition of the religious preaching committees has led to injustice against minority religious groups in the state. The resort to violence by the Nigerian government as a means of social control in intervening in the clash between the two groups also indicates absence of democratic culture. It is the same trend that provided the impetus for the 2009 Boko Haram insurgency in Nigeria. Nigeria cannot afford to continue with the current extra-judicial means of resolving conflicts between two constitutional rights.

A final conclusion that can be drawn is that the proposed Kaduna State Religious Preaching Law, 2016 gave the local authorities power without defining its scope in the discharge of their function. The consequence of this was arbitrariness, abuse and violation of the right to freedom of religion of the citizens. It may thus be difficult to secure true religious pluralism, which is an inherent feature of the notion of a democratic society, under the present provisions of the proposed Religious Preaching Bill, 2016. It is valid therefore to conclude that these measures need to be redesigned to agree with free exercise norms in democratic orders in order to qualify as reasonable in a democratic Nigeria. Finally, to be able to determine their reasonability, an appropriate balancing mechanism based on Nigeria's religion-state relations should be applied in resolving conflict between the two rights.

CONCLUSION

The analysis in this chapter calls for a recommendation of a balancing mechanism based on Nigeria's religion-state relations and local experience that may be useful to courts and legislators in handling conflicts between the two competing rights in Nigeria. This balancing mechanism calls for attention to the principle of substantive due process, the existing religion-state pattern and the local experience of countries to the existing criteria used as standards of review in the resolution of conflicts between the two rival constitutional rights. The re-assertive nature of the role of religion in the public domain in Nigeria and the world at large indicates that religion must be involved in the maintenance of public order and security at the global level.[68] Therefore in the event of conflict between these competing rights in the modern world today, this balancing mechanism that is the most appropriate is the one that recognises the current role of religion, the local experience of countries and the need to do justice through the application of the principle of procedural due process.

Part of the local experience of Nigeria for the past twenty years has been managing crises related to religion. Government restriction of the free exercise rights of some religious groups in favour of dominant religious groups in some

---

68 See Toft MD et al., *God's Century: Resurgent Religion and Global Politics*, 207-223.

states of northern Nigeria has contributed to the crises. Neither the government nor any of the victims has approached the court for judicial determination of the conflict. Even if they had approached the courts, only God knows what would have happened considering the mindset of the judges and generally the people of Nigeria on minority religious groups and their ideologies, especially Shi'a group. Another challenge for Nigeria is whether in the light of the present experience surrounding the proposed Kaduna State Religious Preaching Bill, 2016, which seeks to substitute the state's Regulation of Religious Preaching Law of 1996, the Nigerian Shi'a movement and the military clash that resulted, the government will allow members of religious groups full self-determination and right to freely practice religion. Whatever may be the case and as far as democracy is concerned, governments in democracies anywhere in the world have no right to determine to anybody or group of persons what to believe and what not to believe.

8 MUSLIM AND CHRISTIAN CONTESTATION OVER THE ENTRENCHMENT OF THE KADHI COURTS IN THE CONSTITUTION OF KENYA: CHALLENGING THE PRINCIPLE OF A SECULAR STATE

Hassan Juma Ndzovu[1]

INTRODUCTION

Islam and Christianity are the two religions that dominate the religious realm in Kenya. Generally, there are conflicting reports regarding the religious affiliation of Muslims and Christians in the country. Statistics on religious population tend to be varied depending on the source of information. The politics of numbers is contested between the Muslims and the Christians segments of the population.[2] The figures from the 2009 national population census, which had questions dealing with the religious affiliation of a person, indicated Christians to be around 81% of the population and Muslims about 11%.[3] Muslims have rejected this figure and viewed it as a grand design by the government to deprive them of adequate resources and positions of power in a government in favour of Christians.[4] Being a minority religious group vis-à-vis Christians, Muslims have viewed their Christian counterparts with suspicion thereby critical of every move and statement made by either the government or their non-Muslims compatriots.

Despite the Muslims' suspicion, they have always collaborated with their Christian compatriots to participate in their country's political discussions on matters of national interest. For instance, during the reign of Daniel arap Moi (1978-2002), the religious sector and professional bodies jointly challenged his alleged repressive government, leading to the ushering in of multi-party politics

---

1 Hassan Ndzovu is a Senior Lecturer in the Department of Philosophy, Religion and Theology, Moi University, Kenya.
2 Kettani AM. 1982. "Muslim East Africa: An Overview", *Journal Institute of Muslim Minority Affairs* 4(1,2):104-119; Constantin F. 1993. "Leadership, Muslim Identities and East African Politics", in Brenner L (ed). *Muslim Identities and Social Change in Sub-Saharan Africa*. London: Horst and Company; Bakari M. 1995. "Muslim and Politics of Change in Kenya", in Bakari M and Yahya SS (eds). *Islam in Kenya*. Nairobi: MEWA Publication; Cruise DB. 1995. "Coping With the Christians: The Muslim Predicament in Kenya", in Hansen HB and Twaddle M (eds). *Religion and Politics in East Africa*. London: James Currey.
3 See Kenya National Bureau of Statistics, "Overview of 2009 Census". Online at: http://www.knbs.or.ke/index.php?option=com_content&view=article&id=149&Itemid=635; Jamah A. 2010. "Over 27 Million Kenyans are Christians", *The Standard*, 1 September:11.
4 2010. "Census Uproar: Leaders Dismiss Alleged 4.3 Million Figure for Muslims", *Friday Bulletin: The Weekly Muslim News Update*, 3 September:1, 3.

in early 1990s.⁵ This opening of democratic space was followed by the agitation for a new constitution, which culminated in the enactment of the Constitution of Kenya Review Commission (Amendment) Act in 1997. Doubting the government impartiality in the constitution-making process, religious groups came together under the banner of the Ufungamano Initiative to assist the government in producing a new constitution for the country. Since 2010, the country has witnessed Christian and Muslim religious leaders come together in an (un)holy alliance to dominate the public debate in castigating homosexual relations. The perceived unity of the various religious traditions is sometimes challenged when the issue at hand does not bind them to shared community of believers. Thus, when it comes to pursuing objectives that are not related to all the religious communities, the religious sector tends to abandon their shared religious unity and appear divided along specifically religious lines. This situation shows a dialectic play of factors, some creating unity and others creating division – and the case of Kadhi Courts has fallen into the category of divisive forces.

The entrenchment of the Kadhi Courts in the Kenyan Constitution has been a subject matter of dispute between Muslims and Christians in Kenya. The main issue under scrutiny in this chapter is the interplay of religion and state matters in Kenya, as demonstrated through the institution of the Kadhi Courts. As a result, my contribution in this chapter examines the legality of the Kadhi Courts in the Kenyan Constitution, arguing that the entrenchment of the Kadhi Courts in the country's Constitution did not contravene the secular state premise of the Constitution. To establish the above thesis, the chapter addresses the following questions: What are the Kadhi Courts under the Kenyan Constitution? How constitutional are the Kadhi Courts? And how congruent are they with Kenya's secularity principle under the Constitution? While answering the foregoing questions, the chapter seeks to attain two main objectives: (i) to understand the constitutionality or otherwise of the Kadhi Courts, and (ii) to understand their (in)-compatibility within the secular state premise in the Kenyan Constitution.

Whereas the policy in secular states is supposed to be based on the formal distinction between religion and the state, this does not imply complete absence of interaction and influence between religion and politics. In secular states, the incorporation of religion into politics varies and can be described as either moderate or even very little.⁶ The genesis of the word secularism is attributed

---

5   The active professional bodies that aligned with the religious sector together with opposition political organisation to condemned Moi's alleged poor leadership included the Law Society of Kenya (LSK), THE Justice and Peace Convention (JPC), and the National Ecumenical Civic Education Programme (NECEP).
6   Adams CJ. 1982. "Background of the Contemporary Islamic Resurgence", *Islamic Order Quarterly* 4(1); Mazrui AA. 1993. "African Islam and Comprehensive Religion: Between Revivalism and Expansion", in Alkali N et al. (eds). *Islam in Africa*. Ibadan: Spectrum; Hansen HB and Twaddle M (eds). 1995. *Religion and Politics in East Africa*. London: James Currey; Haqnadvi SH. 1995. *Islamic Fundamentalism: Theological Liberation and Renaissance*. Durban: The Centre for

to, the late nineteenth-century British atheist and freethinker, George Jacob Holyoake (1817-1906) in describing a social order independent of religion, but where all religions are respected equally.[7] In Holyoake's view, secularism is not a negation of religion, but argues that societies should not entirely rely on "theological premises and faith", which are "supernatural and non-scientific" in seeking truth.[8] This view can be contrasted by JC Barnet, who posited that "secularism is life organized apart from God, as though God did not exist."[9] Barnet's observation of secularism envisaged a society in which religion had no place in public life. A similar "anti-religious element to secularism" is described by Holyoake's contemporary, an atheist and political activist, Bradlaugh H Bonner (1833-1891), who considered the influence the Church held over certain governments in Europe "as a threat to freedom of all kinds."[10]

A study of the evolution of secularism reveals a long history of competition between religion and the state. The secular political authorities of Europe resented the encroachment of the papacy into the political domain, setting a bitter struggled between the two institutions. The outcome of the struggle was the Church agreeing to confine its activities to spiritual matters, according the state independence to deal with political affairs.[11] This policy of non-interference has been adopted in the constitutions of a number of countries in the world today, including Kenya, which declare themselves explicitly or implicitly to be secular states.

At this stage a question can be asked: what are the principles of a secular state? It is not easy to ascertain the ingredients of a secular state, as they differ from one state to the other. This is attributed to the variant interpretations of the concept of secularism which secular states incorporate into their constitutions. There is no consensus on whether secularism is anti-religious or non-religious in essence, and as a consequence there are many variations of a secular state.[12] Religious studies scholars, Carl F Hallencreutz and David Westerlund argue that a secular state "presupposes that there is at least a formal separation between religion and state", in which the liberal form of this policy respects religion as an important resource in society and accord individual as well as corporate

---

  Islamic, Near and Middle Eastern Studies Publication; Oyediran O and Agbaje A (eds). 1999. *Nigeria: Politics of Transition and Governance 1986-1996.* Basford: Russell Press Ltd; Lincoln B. 2003. *Holy Terrors: Thinking about Religion after September 11.* Chicago: University of Chicago Press.
7 Balasubramanian M. 1980. *Nehru: A Study of Secularism.* New Delhi: Uppal Publishing House; Monshipouri M. 1998. *Islamism, Secularism and Human Rights in the Middle East.* London: Lynne Rienner.
8 Beard RT et al. 2013. "Secularism, Religion, and Political Choice in the United States", *Politics and Religion* 6(4):1-25.
9 Balasubramanian, *Nehru: A Study of Secularism*, 2-3.
10 Beard et al., "Secularism, Religion, and Political Choice in the United States", 1-25.
11 Balasubramanian, *Nehru: A Study of Secularism.*
12 Kuru AT. 2007. "Passive and Assertive Secularism: Historical Conditions, Ideological Struggles, and State Policies toward Religion", *World Politics* 59:568-595.

religious freedom.[13] On the other hand, the Marxist version of secularism is an ideology that views religion negatively and has the core objective of banishing religion from people's consciousness, presumably leaving them with only politics.[14] Nevertheless, such policies have not been successful, as citizens have usually risen to challenge them.

When Kenya attained independence in 1963, the primary concern of the post-independence leaders was to build a strong nation out of the numerous ethnic groups in the country. As a consequence, the country adopted a constitution that did not elevate any religion to the status of a state religion. An examination of the various sections of the Kenyan Independence Constitution reveals the nature of the secular state that obtains in Kenya. Though the Independence Constitution did not specifically stipulate that Kenya is a secular state, as Article 1 simply described Kenya as "a sovereign Republic", most Kenyans understood their country to be secular one.[15] Arguably, this view is based on the two core principles that define a secular state: (1) lack of institutional religious control of the legal and judicial processes; (2) establishment of neither an official religion nor atheism.[16]

However, the form of secularism observed in Kenya is not anti-religious, as Article 78 of the Independence Constitution provided for freedom of religion to all citizens, guaranteed under the general protection of freedom of conscience. Under this section of the Constitution, the state is not allowed to interfere or control religious affairs. Clearly, the policy of the state is to accord equal freedom of religious association to Kenyans. Like the United States Constitution, the objective of the Kenyan Independence Constitution was not to promote one religious conviction at the expense of others, but to provide an enabling environment for all creeds, thereby demonstrating that religion is respected by the Kenyan state. The intention of this policy was to separate religion from the politics of the country and to confine it as a private matter, outside the scope of state legislation or policy. Based on these provisions of the Independence Constitution, if the state supports the religious activities of a particular group, then it is interpreted as a violation of the Constitution.

Nevertheless, attempts to separate religion and state in Kenya have not entirely succeeded, as there is official public visibility of religion in Kenya, for instance the country's national anthem opens with the words "Oh God of all creation", and the opening ceremony of every parliamentary session or national public event is preceded by prayers offered by the representatives of the various religious groups. It is common that when the president, members of parliament, judges and other constitutional officers take the oath of office, they hold the

---

13   Hallencreutz CF and Westerlund D. 1996. "Anti-Secularist Policies of Religion", in Westerlund D (ed). *Questioning the Secular State: The Worldwide Resurgence of Religion in Politics*. New York: St. Martin's, 3.
14   Hallencreutz, and Westerlund, "Anti-Secularist Policies of Religion", 3.
15   *Laws of Kenya: The Constitution of Kenya*. 2001. Nairobi: Government Printers.
16   Kuru, "Passive and Assertive Secularism", 568-595.

Bible or the Quran, depending on their religious affiliation, and add the words "so help me God" at the end of the oath. There have also been instances when the government has had to withdraw certain public policies and legislation for fear of antagonising a particular religious group.[17]

This illustrates that religion in Kenya is respected and ultimately plays a significant role in the public and political life. Despite its secular status premise, Kenya is intensely apprehensive about religion and regulates it on various levels. Therefore, within the Kenyan context, "the old ideas of the separation of church and state … do not signify the separation of religion from politics."[18] Despite the implicit claim in the Independence Constitution that Kenya is a secular state constitutionally, one never fails to notice the presence of religion in government policies and state functions. It is this reading of the relationship of religion and politics that informs my analysis on the debate of the Kadhi Courts and whether their inclusion in the Independence Constitution and the Bomas Draft Constitution contravenes the secular state premise.

KADHI COURTS IN THE KENYAN INDEPENDENCE CONSTITUTION

Before the introduction of the colonial administration, the Kenya coast was under the rule of a political model partially inspired by Islam and administered by the Sultan of Zanzibar. In Kenya, the Zanzibari hegemony covered the cities of Mombasa, Malindi and Lamu, together with parts of Sabaki North Bank, Chonyi, Kauma, the Bajun area south of Kiunga and parts of Digo.[19] Under the rule of Seyyid Said bin Sultan (1806-1856), the Zanzibari hegemony extended its realm of influence, and by the end of eighteenth century the sultanate had emerged as a dynastic kingdom with an Arab (or Muslim) at the top.[20] Although Seyyid Said exercised little direct control, his agents were established along the whole of what is now the Kenya coastline.[21] Thus, coastal Kenya had a long tradition of sultanate rule prior becoming a British protectorate. Before Seyyid Said shifted the capital to Zanzibar, the sultanate was based in Oman, where it had grown out of the original Ibadi imamate.[22] According to the Ibadi Muslims

---

17 Due to strong opposition and to avoid conflict with the religious communities, the Kenya government have on different occasion been forced to drop certain public policies. These unpopular policies included recognition of abortion and homosexuality, as well as the regulation of religious bodies in the country.
18 Voll JO. 1982. *Islam, Continuity and Change in Modern World*. Essex: Longman, 276.
19 PC/COAST/1/22/22, Kenya National Archives.
20 Mazrui AA. 2002. "The Triple Heritage of the State in Africa", in Laremont RR and Seghatolislami TL (eds). *Africanity Redefined: Collected Essays of Ali A. Mazrui, Vol. 1*. Trenton, NJ: Africa World, 37-138.
21 The Kenya Coastal Strip, Report of the Commissioner, December 1961.
22 The Ibadi (Ibadiyya) is a subsect of the Kharijite Islam that is neither Sunni nor Shi'a, and exists mainly in Oman, Zanzibar, Tripolitania in Libya, Mzab in Algeria and Jerba in Tunisia. The righteous imamate is a significant subject in Ibadi legal literature, which considers the Imam as a pious person who is chosen into the leadership position by the elders of the community, who are also obligated to

their political system was viewed as an imamate, and the sultanate was actually a concession to Ottoman traditions of government in the eleventh century.[23] The Ibadi imamate ensured that the religious community was politically established, providing for an intimate interaction between religion and politics.

However, in the eleventh century, internal reforms facilitated changes into the Oman imamate that included transition in the highest political office from imam to sultan. With the changes the sultan's office assumed a purely political position and delegated the religious duties to another office.[24] Although a clear separation of mosque and state evolved in Oman, the sultan retained most of the prerogatives that had formerly been the privilege of the imams. For that reason, when the Oman sultanate ultimately established its base in Zanzibar, efforts were made to maintain the same political system. Therefore, the *liwali* and *kadhi* systems of administration were introduced in the Zanzibar sultanate to represent the sultan in various capacities.[25]

The end of the nineteenth century, during the rule of Sultan Barghash (1870-1888), brought the transition from precolonial Arab Muslim hegemony to Arab Muslim dominance under colonial overlordship. During this period, the British policy of indirect rule used the native institutions of government as means to exert colonial control. The colonial administration was reluctant to tamper with local native institutions that had recognised their authority, preferring to use those institutions instead of inventing new ones.[26] Following this arrangement, freedom of religion was guaranteed, though no extra effort was made to encourage Islam. Supposedly, at least, the British colonial power respected Muslim sensitivities in so far as religious practices were concerned. This was evident with the recognition of the sultan's administrative and legal institutions. A clear illustration of this recognition is evident in a report by a British colonial officer, Commissioner James W Robertson (1899-1983):

> Within the administration there is a special cadre of Arab administrative officers [read also Arab Muslims] headed by the Liwali for the Coast (who is also Adviser on Arab affairs to the Governor) and consisting, apart from him, of four Liwalis and ten Mudirs. These officers also had subordinate Courts of the second and third class with jurisdiction

---

depose him if he acts unjustly. The last "true Imam" to unite the entire country of Oman under his power was Ahmad ibn Sa'id (ruled 1754-1783 CE), the founder of the BuSa'idi dynasty. His descendants later took the title not of Imam, with its connotations of religious leadership, but Seyyid, an honorific title held by any member of the royal family. Later, they used the title Sultan, implying purely coercive power.

23 Pouwels RL. 1979. *Islam and Islamic Leadership in the Coastal Communities of Eastern Africa, 1700 to 1914*. London: University Microfilms International, 363.
24 Pouwels, *Islam and Islamic Leadership*, 394.
25 The Kadhi were judges expected to interpret the Islamic law (*sharia*) in the religious courts on behalf of the Sultan, while the Liwalis were governors administering specific areas of the coastal region with authority from the Sultan.
26 Mazrui, "The Triple Heritage of the State in Africa", 37-138.

in both civil and criminal cases. There are, in addition, Kadhis who are magistrates specialising in questions of Islamic law in relation to inheritance, marriage and divorce, and other personal matters. Jurisdiction is limited to Arabs, Somalis and Africans [Muslims]. These posts were in existence before British administration and to the Muslim peoples of the Coast they are, on nationalist, religious and historical grounds, of very great importance.[27]

However, all the three Arab officials, *liwalis*, *mudirs* and *kadhis*, were not appointed by the sultan, who was also not consulted in their appointments.[28] This Arab cadre of officers was now on the payroll of the colonial administration. Since, for instance, in the precolonial period, the *kadhis* were expected to interpret the Islamic law as judges on behalf of the sultan, this was retained for continuity and smooth transition.

Immediately, the colonial administration took over the governorship of the sultan's dominion, it initiated a number of changes that had far-reaching implications. The changes started with the promulgation of East Africa Order in Council of 1897, which entrenched British rule, as it legally established institutions of state, power and authority. The Order in Council established the Legislative Council, which in turn enacted the Native Court Regulation that empowered colonial officials to make rules and regulations for the administration of natives. The Native Courts Authority (1897) established the Native Courts Ordinances (NCO) that contained statutes like the *liwali*, *mudir* and *kadhi* courts ordinances.[29] After the establishment of the NCO, the Legislative Council enacted the Mohammedan Marriage Divorce and Succession Ordinance 1897, which institutionalised selected aspects of Muslims personal law, such as marriage, divorce and succession. The unfolding events indicated the colonial authority's eagerness to fulfill the agreement made between Zanzibar and Britain. In the agreement, the British had promised to continue recognising the authority of the religious institutions in the protectorate. It was the sultan's wish that "all affairs connected with the faith of Islam will be conducted to the honour and benefit of religion, and all ancient customs will be allowed to continue."[30]

---

27 The Kenya Coastal Strip, Report of the Commissioner, December 1961.
28 The Kenya Coastal Strip, Report of the Commissioner, December 1961.
29 Mwakimako HA. 2006. "The Ulama and the Colonial State in the Protectorate of Kenya: Appointing *Shaykh al-Islam Sharif* Abd-al-Rahaman b. Ahmad Saggaf (1884-1922) and Chief Kadhi *Shaykh* Muhammad b. Umar Bakore (c.a.1932)", in Loimeir R and Seesemann R (eds). *The Global Worlds of the Swahili*. Hamburg: LIT.
30 The Kenya Coastal Strip, Report of the Commissioner, December 1961.

After independence in 1963, the constitutional status of the Kadhi Courts could be found in Article 66 (1) to (5), which provided for their establishment. Specific articles on the Kadhi Courts in the Independence Constitution stated:

Article 66 (1)

There shall be a Chief Kadhi and such number, not being less than three, of other Kadhis as may be prescribed by or under an Act of Parliament.

Article 66 (5)

The jurisdiction of a Kadhi's court shall extend to the determination of questions of Muslim law relating to personal status, marriage, divorce or inheritance in proceedings in which all the parties profess the Muslim religion.

At independence, the Kadhi Courts were three in number, but in 1967 the Kadhi Courts Act allowed the establishment of the courts in other parts of the country, and the number of the courts subsequently increased. Today, the Kadhi Courts are scattered and can be found in all the major towns in the country. According to the Independence Constitution, these courts are to be presided over by either a Chief Kadhi, or a Kadhi appointed by the Judicial Services Commission. It also outlined the jurisdiction of the courts over issues related to personal status (marriage, divorce and inheritance) in which the individuals involved practised the Islamic faith. In the early 2000s, during the debate over a new constitution, the Bomas Draft Constitution that emerged retained the provision entrenching the Kadhi Courts, to the dissatisfaction of the opposing churches. Passionate and emotional campaigns supporting and opposing the courts emanated from both the Christian and Muslim sides. It was a debate that, to a certain extent, polarised the country.

THE BOMAS DRAFT BILL CONSTITUTION AND THE RETENTION OF THE KADHI COURTS

After more than three decades of independence, Kenya began a search for a new constitution. The Independence Constitution was alleged to have allowed the suspension of human rights in many circumstances and also to have permitted a range of oppressive laws to continue. There was the feeling among many Kenyans that the laws in the Independence Constitution were similar to those used by the colonial government to oppress Kenyans and were no longer relevant in postcolonial Kenya. Despite the numerous amendments to the Independence Constitution, there were increasing calls for its complete overhaul.[31] As the clamour for constitutional reform reached a climax, the government insisted that the drafting of such an important document was a

---

31 Okondo PH. 1995. *A Commentary on the Constitution of Kenya*. Nairobi: Phoenix.

task that was best done by foreign experts.³² Reform advocates disagreed with the government, however, arguing that foreign experts could not offer solutions to local problems and demanding that the process to be driven by the people in order to be to be valid.

This is the constitution that its advocates referred to as the Wanjiku Constitution. Wanjiku is a common Kikuyu female name, and like elsewhere in Africa, the female in Kenya is often the most underprivileged person in society. The name Wanjiku was borrowed to symbolise the common person in the country. The call for a Wanjiku Constitution implied a constitution where the ordinary citizens of the country were consulted about the type of government they desired. Consequently, in 1998, the Constitution of Kenya Review Commission (CKRC) was established, and was charged with the responsibility of collecting views of Kenyans on what they would want reflected in the new constitution. The commission endeavoured to hear as many voices as possible to ensure that the recommendations they made were representative of the common person. On 27 September 2002, the CKRC unveiled a Draft Bill that came to be popularly known as the Bomas Draft Bill Constitution. Upon publication of the CKRC's Draft Bill, a group of Christian churches highlighted a number of issues that were of concern to them in the draft constitution, most notably the entrenchment of Kadhi Courts abortion and same-sex marriage.³³

In the Bomas Draft Bill Constitution, the Kadhi courts were retained and additional changes incorporated based on Muslim recommendations. The provisions on Kadhi Courts in the Bomas Draft Bill were as follows:

> Kadhi courts:
>
> Article 199
>
> (1) There are established Kadhi's Courts, the Office of Chief Kadhi, Office of Senior Kadhi and the Office of Kadhi.
> (2) There shall be a number, being not less than thirty, of other Kadhis as may be prescribed by the Act of Parliament.
> (3) A Kadhi is empowered to hold a Kadhi's court called a District Kadhi's Court, having jurisdiction within a district or districts as may be prescribed by, or under an Act of Parliament.³⁴

---

32 Owino RL. 2003. "Whose Constitution will it be, finally?", *Daily Nation*, 11 December:5.
33 Musibi P. 2004. "How the Kenya Church got Involved in the Constitutional Process", *The Eagle*, August:8.
34 See the Draft Bill, The Constitution of the Republic of Kenya, 27 September 2002. Online at: http://www.ogiek.org/sitemap/constitution-kenya.pdf

Jurisdiction of Kadhi courts:

Article 200

(1) The Jurisdiction of a Kadhi's court extends to (a) the determination of questions of Muslim Law relating to personal status, marriage, divorce, including matters arising after divorce, and inheritance and succession in proceedings in which all the parties profess Islam; (b) the determination of civil and commercial disputes between parties who are Muslims, in the manner of a small claims courts as by law established, but without prejudice to the rights of parties to go to other courts or tribunals with similar jurisdiction; (c) the settlement of disputes over or arising out of the administration of *wakf*[35] properties[36].

With respect to the Kadhi Courts sections of the Bomas Draft Bill, Muslims had recommended that the existing Kadhi Courts be reformed and made efficient. Some of the recommendations that were incorporated into the Bomas Draft Bill, such as Article 202, included the requirement that Kadhis be trained in both Islamic and common laws. In addition to their Islamic credentials, the Kadhis were required to be experienced advocates with a common law degree. Also recommended was the provision for a Kadhi Court of Appeal to address appeals from the lower Kadhi Courts. The draft pointed that only after these appeals have passed through the Kadhi Court of Appeal would cases from the lower Kadhi Courts be heard in the national High Court of Appeal. And lastly, the Bomas Draft Bill Constitution recommended that the jurisdiction of the Kadhi Courts be expanded to hear minor commercial disputes among Muslims.[37]

When these recommendations were published in the Bomas Draft Bill of the CKRC, they raised concern among Christians, particularly those drawn from the Anglican and Pentecostal churches. Their opposition in the plenary was uncompromising. The controversy instigated an intense debate between Muslims and Christians over religion and state. Following the unresolved discussion in the plenary, the chairman of CKRC called a meeting of Christian, Muslim and Hindu leaders to find ways of resolving the impasse. The meeting agreed to appoint a committee charged with the responsibility of solving the issue amicably. After several meetings, the committee accepted a number of amendments that Muslim representatives refused to endorse. While Muslims insisted on having the Kadhi Courts entrenched in the constitution, the church

---

35 *Wakf* (or *waqf*) is any valuable (non-)item that an individual voluntarily cedes private ownership and consecrates it to God through a management system that holds it in trust during which period its value would be improved, sustained, and appropriated for the specified objective(s) in the service of God.
36 See the Draft Bill, The Constitution of the Republic of Kenya, 27 September 2002.
37 See sections 200, 201 and 202 of the Draft Bill, The Constitution of the Republic of Kenya, 27 September 2002.

led opposition wanted the entire institution of the Kadhi Courts removed from the Bomas Draft Bill Constitution.[38]

Leading this opposition was a group of church clergies who identified themselves under the banner of the Federation of Churches in Kenya, or simply the Kenya Churches. The demand by the Christian clergy for the abolition of the Muslims courts was based on the following provisions in the Bomas Draft Bill of the Constitution:

> State and Religion
>
> > Article 10
> >
> > (1) State and religion shall be separate.
> > (2) There shall be no state religion.
> > (3) The state shall treat all religions equally.[39]

According to the opponents of the Kadhi Courts, the Bomas Draft Bill had provided that Islamic personal laws would be a source of laws in Kenya despite the provisions in Article 10. They argued that Islamic laws are religious laws and thereby contradict the three provisions stated in Article 10. They further pointed that the Bomas Draft Bill had created a parallel judicial system for Muslims, which was tantamount to favouring one religion and contravened the principle that the state should treat all religions equally. This line of argument was to reappear many times during the debate, and it became the basis of reference for the opponents of the Kadhi Courts.

In this regard, the group of clergies requested all provisions on the Kadhi Courts be removed and replaced by a provision establishing subordinate courts with limited jurisdiction on issues of personal laws relating to marriage, divorce and inheritance, between parties of the same religious faith or persuasion and who submit to that jurisdiction.[40] Consequently, the proposed provision by the opposing churches would allow the Parliament of Kenya to establish subordinate courts for any religious community, including Muslims, to deal with their personal laws if so desired. This approach, in their view, would ensure equal treatment of all religions.

After a wide debate at the constitutional review conference, three issues related to the Kadhi courts were removed. These were: (1) the provision on Islamic laws being a source of laws in Kenya, (2) the creation of a parallel judicial system for Muslims, and (3) determination of civil and commercial disputes according to Islamic law. This implied that the provision entrenching the Kadhi Courts in the Bomas Draft Bill Constitution would be retained, to the dissatisfaction of the

---

38 2003. "The Kenya Church: The Federation of Churches in Kenya", *Daily Nation*, 15 September:15.
39 See section 10 of the Draft Bill, The Constitution of the Republic of Kenya, 27 September 2002.
40 Musibi, "How the Kenya Church got Involved", 8; 2003,"The Kenya Church", 15.

opposing churches. As a result, in July 2004, twenty-six applicants representing a group of Kenyan churches went to the High Court over the entrenchment of the Kadhi Courts in the Independence Constitution and the Bomas Draft Bill Constitution.[41] The federation argued that the historical reasons for which the Kadhi Courts were given constitutional protection are no longer tenable. They claimed that after several years of independence, the former "subjects" of the sultan of Zanzibar should no longer require any constitutional protection, as Kenya was now a unified sovereign state where all enjoyed equality irrespective of race, gender, or religion.[42] They contended that the entrenchment of the Kadhi Courts in the Bomas Draft Bill and the Independence Constitution was a step towards introducing *sharia* in Kenya, which was unacceptable, in their view. They also pointed that any financial maintenance of the Kadhi Courts from the public resources was unjust and amounted to development of one religion. They interpreted this practice as Islam being declared a state religion, contradicting the provision in Article 10 that there shall be no state religion.

Therefore, they wanted Section 66 of the Independence Constitution, which they argued introduced and entrenched the Kadhi Courts to be declared unconstitutional and expunged from the Bomas Draft Bill.[43] In responding to the argument raised by the Federation of Churches of Kenya, the Muslims insisted that the inclusion of Kadhi Courts in the Independence Constitution was not because the beneficiaries were merely "subjects" of the sultan of Zanzibar, but because the courts are a core institution in the practice of Islam. Muslims claim that the laws, rules and regulations applied by the Kadhi Courts are not a creation of the sultan of Zanzibar, but a product of the teachings of Islam. In their view, the Muslims felt insulted by the claim that the courts are outdated and have no place in a modern constitution.[44] Six years later, when an application was submitted in the Constitutional Court challenging the legality of the Kadhi Courts, the judges presiding over the case gave their verdict, declaring the Kadhi Courts to be unconstitutional.

THE SECULAR STATE PREMISE AND THE CONSTITUTIONALITY OF THE KADHI COURTS

In 2004 a section of church leaders had sought several declarations in the High Court with regard to the entrenchment of the Kadhi Courts in the Independence

---

41 Nyamboga N. 2004. "Clerics sue over Kadhis' Courts", *East African Standard*, 15 July:11.
42 2009. "Constitution Review: Experts should be Honest to Issues Agreed Upon in the Previous Process", *The New Dawn*, 1 June-1 July:4, 7.
43 Nyamboga, "Clerics sue over Kadhis' Courts", 11.
44 "Constitution Review: Experts should be Honest to Issues Agreed Upon in the Previous Process", 4, 7. See also the High Court Judges Nyamu JG, Wendo RVP and Anyara Emukule MJ. "Judgement". Online at: http://www.nation.co.ke/blob/view/-/924724/data/162900/-/m44lw9z/-/Kadhi+Ruling.pdf

Constitution. The judges presiding over the case declared the Kadhi Courts to be illegal and unconstitutional in May 2010. In their verdict, the judges concluded:

> (1) In view of the discussion above, we grant the declarations sought in prayer 1 limited to declaring that section 66 is inconsistent with sections 65 and 82 and in respect of section 82 is discriminatory to the applicants in its effect.
>
> (2) As regards to paragraph 2 of the prayers, we find and hold that sections 66 and 82 are inconsistent with each other, and that section 66 is superfluous but it is not the court's role to expunge it. It is the role of Parliament and the citizenry in a referendum.
>
> (3) As regards prayer 3, we hold and declare that any provision similar to section 66 in any other draft of a constitution in word or effect is not ripe for determination.
>
> (4) The enactment and the application of the Kadhis' courts to areas beyond the 10 miles coastal strip of the Protectorate is unconstitutional.[45]

Following the High Court's verdict on the Kadhi Courts, their judgment was received differently and widely debated by various sections of the Kenyan population. For their, part the church leaders welcomed the ruling and urged the government to implement it.[46] The government through the attorney general termed the verdict unconstitutional and appealed to the High Court challenging the ruling.[47] And for the Muslims, a section of the community went to court to challenge the ruling declaring the Kadhi Courts illegal and unconstitutional. The petitioners were aggrieved by the decision of the court claiming their constitutional rights had been violated. They argued that the Kadhi Courts provided an essential dispute resolution mechanism, without which a vacuum would be created in administering justice. Through their lawyer the Muslims argued: "If the effect of the judgment would be to disband Kadhi Courts, which is a section of the judiciary established by the Constitution of Kenya, it would disrupt their proceedings thus creating a sense of insecurity and disillusionment with the administration of justice for a large sector of the population."[48] Muslim leaders rejected the view that the Kadhi Courts are discriminatory on the basis of Section 62 of the Independence Constitution. They claimed that the ruling was faulty and that the judges had ignored the provisions of the same section they had quoted, which said that issues of divorce, adoption, marriage and inheritance are excluded from the definition of discrimination.[49] As illustrated

---

45 2010. "Judges' Ruling that Threw Cold Water on Draft", *Daily Nation*, 26 May:9.
46 Benyawa L. 2010. "Muslim Challenge Ruling on Kadhi Courts", *The Standard*, 4 June:7.
47 Benyawa, "Muslim Challenge Ruling on Kadhi Courts", 7.
48 Benyawa, "Muslim Challenge Ruling on Kadhi Courts", 7.
49 "Judges' Ruling that Threw Cold Water on Draft".

earlier, Section 66 of the Independence Constitution gave the Kadhi Courts the jurisdiction to deal with matters of personal law among Muslims.

The main foundation of the judges' ruling was that Section 66 of the Independence Constitution (which allows for the creation of the Kadhi Courts) is inconsistent with Section 65 (which gives parliament the power to establish courts subordinate to the High Court) and Section 82 (which outlaws discrimination in law making) thereby declaring Section 66 to be superfluous. Despite making the correct conclusion that the role of the court is to interpret the law, and not to amend it, their verdict seem to have been the opposite. They made categorical pronouncements that declared a section of the Independence Constitution illegal. For instance, they granted the request, which had sought for Section 66 to be declared discriminatory, oppressive, unconstitutional, and null and void.

However, the attorney general argued that the High Court had no jurisdiction to declare Section 66 of the Independence Constitution as being unconstitutional. His position was that Section 66 of the Constitution was an existing provision and could not be struck out on the basis that there is no provision of the constitution that is superior or inferior to the other. For the constitutional court to nullify any provision of the constitution would itself be unconstitutional. According to the attorney general, the court's jurisdiction would be to strike out a law (ie. Act of Parliament) other than a provision of the constitution.[50] Consequently, it was wrong to declare the Kadhi Courts illegal if the Independence Constitution provided for them. In their pronouncement, the judges emphasised that they had made a declaration that religious courts should not form part of the judiciary, as this would offend the doctrine of separation of state and religion.

The High Courts' decision was clear advocacy for "assertive secularism", a form of secularism that intends to eliminate any symbol and expression of religion from the public sphere. According to the judges, secularism implies lack of religiosity and therefore, the absence of religious authorities. The interaction of religion and politics is a subject that has been widely debated by scholars. While not reaching a definite position on the subject the High Court dealt with the issue as if there were a conclusive position in the international law. Countries that allow the interaction of religion and politics have embraced different approaches peculiar to their unique situation.

According to Ahmet Kuru, "state policies toward religion are the result of ideological struggles", which manifests in competition between "passive secularists" and "assertive secularists."[51] "Passive secularism", in Kuru's description, is a political principle that attempts to uphold state neutrality toward various religions, thereby allowing for the public visibility of religion: whereas "assertive secularism" is a "comprehensive doctrine" that intends

---

50 Kamau NG. 2010. "Religious Courts go Against the Secular Nature of the State", *Daily Nation*, 7 June:11.
51 Kuru, "Passive and Assertive Secularism", 568-595.

to purge religion from the public sphere.[52] Due to the realisation that it is difficult to have a complete separation of religion and politics, countries that regards themselves as secular states, including Kenya, have grappled with the question of the extent this interaction should be accepted. Therefore, the Kadhi Courts were provided for in the Independence Constitution under the peculiar historical circumstances of the moment, which its defenders have argued should be put into consideration when debating about them.

The High Court judges also held that the enactment and application of the Kadhi Courts beyond the ten-mile coastal strip specified in their establishment to be unconstitutional. This judgment attempted to limit the Kadhi courts to the ten-mile strip whose expansion outside the strip was sanctioned by an act of Parliament. In light of this, the High Court knew they had the jurisdiction to declare illegal any law made by an Act of Parliament if it is in conflict or inconsistence with the constitutional provision. Nevertheless, it was necessary for the judges to examine the history of the Kadhi Courts before giving such a verdict. Though the Kadhi Courts were mostly associated with the coastal region, during the colonial period, the British had recognised the importance of this institution and extended it outside the ten-mile strip. This was illustrated by the British appointing the first state funded Kadhi for the Somali Muslims of the North Frontier District (NFD) in 1927.[53]

During the early years of the first president of Kenya, the expansion of the Kadhi Courts to the Somalis of the NFD was used as one of the conditions in ending the Shifta War.[54] As part of the peace agreement brokered in Arusha by Zambia's President Kenneth Kaunda in 1967, the government of Kenya accepted the expansion of Kadhi Courts to the residents of the NFD.[55] The decision was significant in pacifying the Somalis' agitation to secede as it made them feel that their religious and cultural welfare was taken into consideration by the postcolonial government of Jomo Kenyatta. This is an important part of the background that should have informed the decision of the judges. Other analysts argued that at minimal, the expansion of the Kadhi Courts should have been informed by the justification that "Kenya is not a federal state and that it will be wrong to expect a citizen to enjoy a right in Mombasa and not have the same right in other parts of the country."[56] This view implies that Muslims

---

52   Kuru, "Passive and Assertive Secularism".
53   Kerrow B. 2010. "Are some of our Churches Playing the Devil's Advocate", *The Standard*, 30 May:16.
54   When the Somalis of the NFD were denied their desire to secede and join the Republic of Somalia, they resorted to armed resistance to sabotage the Jomo Kenyatta leadership (1963-1978). Through the support of the Somilia government, the Kenya's Somalis uprising which came to be known as the Shifta insurgency was fought in sporadic ways by employing a guerrilla tactic warfare that targeted government convoys and personnel.
55   Kerrow, "Are some of our Churches Playing the Devil's Advocate", 16.
56   Muganda I and Biriq B. 2010. "Ruling on Kadhis' Courts was Judicial Impunity", *The Standard*, 2 June:15.

in Kenya also live outside the ten-mile strip, and it is the responsibility of the government to ensure that they continue enjoying their rights as Muslims wherever they choose to live. On the issue regarding financial maintenance of the Kadhi Courts by the government, the High Court declared that it is discriminatory and sectarian. Such a conclusion was informed by perceiving the Kadhi Courts as religious courts and not part of the judiciary. According to the Independence Constitution, the Kadhi Courts form an integral part of the official judiciary, and this is why the public coffers are used to fund and maintain them, their proponents hold. Undoubtedly, the ruling by the judges against the Kadhi Courts set off a religious tension threatening the Muslim-Christian relations in Kenya.

CONCLUSION

The debate over the Kadhi courts revolves around the question of whether the courts should be entrenched in the Kenyan constitution or not. Opponents of the Kadhi Courts, chiefly a section of Christian church leaders, claim to have embraced the ideal of secular state against the adoption of religious laws. On the other hand, the supporters of the Kadhi Courts, most of whom are Muslim, are oblivious to the implications of religious laws in the national context characterised by pluralism and freedom of expression. Nevertheless, the Kadhi Courts saga has at the moment been resolved. In August 2010, Kenyans voted for a new constitution that entrenches the Kadhi Courts as part of the judicial system. The passing of the 2010 Constitution of Kenya in a referendum illustrated support for the Kadhi Courts by most Kenyans. Amidst opposition from a section of church leaders, the referendum results showed that there was acceptance of the Kadhi Courts in the country as stipulated in Section 170 of the 2010 Constitution.[57]

Therefore, this chapter has demonstrated that the Kadhi Courts have a long history in Kenya. Despite the adoption of the secularity principle in the Kenyan Constitution, the Kadhi Courts have been accepted as part of the country's legal system. Consequently, the entrenchment of the Kadhi Courts did not contravene the secular state premise in the Kenyan Constitution since the form of secularism observed in the country is not anti-religious, but rather values the role of religion in formulating public policies. There is need for more public awareness of the Kadhi Courts to guard against future opposition to them, and possibly challenge the idea that they are a threat to the secular state premise in Kenya. Clearly, secularism is not purely about the absence of religion, and there is also no single ingredient of a secular state since secularism is a social category, containing numerous dimensions.

---

57 *The Constitution of Kenya*. 2010. Nairobi: The Government Printer.

IV. Indigenous Religion and Minority Religions in Africa

9 THE MEDIA COVERAGE OF POLITICAL AND RELIGIOUS RELATIONS IN CÔTE D'IVOIRE: AN ANALYSIS IN LIGHT OF THE ROLE OF THE GLAÈ MASK AMONG THE WÊ PEOPLE

Célestin Gnonzion[1]

INTRODUCTION

This chapter discusses the interactions between politicians and religious leaders in Côte d'Ivoire. These constitute one of the aspects of the bipolarisation of public space in this country since the return to multiparty politics in 1990. It has to do with the reality of a duality observable, first of all, at the political level, between the former Party, the Democratic Party of Côte d'Ivoire – the African Democratic Rally (PDCI-RDA) and the parties that originated there, and then the opposition party, the Ivorian Popular Front (FPI) and the political groups that identify with it or that are close to it on the ideological level. This political duality influences other social institutions such as the media and religions.

The chapter also establishes a relationship, in the form of a socio-historical heritage, of the interactions between politics and religion in an African traditional society. It is possible to attempt to interpret what is observed in the Côte d'Ivoire on the politico-religious scene in the light of the connection, in the Wê society of the west of Côte d'Ivoire, between the holder of religious power in the form of the mask, or the *glaè*, and those of the political powers in the Assembly of Initiates and the Head of Lineage.

There are, however, notable differences – in the size of populations, territories and media – between the public space in Wê society and the modern public space of politico-religious affairs in Côte d'Ivoire. But several lessons from the management of politics and religion in traditional Wê country can inform the governance of Côte d'Ivoire today. The chapter begins with a discussion of methodological points, then inquires into the context and the problem, leading into an analysis of extracts of the problematic discourses by religious leaders. A final part is devoted to analysis of the place of religion and politics in the traditional society Wê through the specific example of the *glaè* mask.

ELEMENTS OF METHODOLOGY

From a methodological point of view, this chapter analyses a corpus of press articles. These can be divided into two categories. First, there are articles on

---
[1] Université Felix Houphouet Boigny d'Abidjan, Côte d'Ivoire UFR, Information, Communication et Arts.

the speech of Cardinal Bernard Agré, former Archbishop of Abidjan and a privileged witness to several important moments in the socio-political life of Côte d'Ivoire. This first section of the corpus includes the declaration of the Episcopal Conference of Côte d'Ivoire. Secondly, the corpus includes press reports on the criticism of the intervention of the Cardinal Agré and the declaration of the Ivorian bishops. These criticisms were made by journalists as well as by ordinary citizens. The corpus of articles was then analysed according to Èmile Benveniste's linguistic method of enunciation.[2]

Regarding the link between religion and politics in Wê society, the writings of historian Angèle Gnonsoa were the main documentary source of the oral tradition Wê.[3] Gnonsoa's work is here revisited through observation of the Wê society and the role played by the *glaè*. This inquiry is animated by concern for the cultural, linguistic and ethical issues of public communication in countries.[4]

THE CONTEXT AND THE PROBLEM

Bipolarisation of political public space and its influence on media and religions

Since the year 1990, which marked the return to a multiparty system in Côte d'Ivoire, there has existed a political duality between the former ruling party

---

2   Benveniste È. 1974. *Problèmes de linguistique générale* [Problems of general linguistics]. Paris: Gallimard, 86. Enunciation, as defined by Benveniste, is "the operation of the language by an individual act of use". This act of enunciation has characteristics and properties. Among these, one can retain the referential and modal dimensions and the parameters of the situation of enunciation.
   - The referential dimension (the *dictum*)
     The referential dimension or mechanism of reference or referential universe brings back to the fact that when one speaks, one speaks of something. We are referring to something when we speak. Anaphoric contextual repeats can be used in the referential dimension.
   - The modal dimension (the *modus*)
     If, when one speaks, one speaks of something and one refers to some, one also expresses his position in the act of speaking. So we have a way and a way of referring to something. This is the modal dimension of the act of enunciation. There is thus in the utterance, the *dictum* (what is said) + the *modus* (attitude of the speaker in relation to what he says).
   - The parameters of the situation of enunciation
     In addition to its two characteristics of the act of enunciation, we also have parameters of the enunciation situation, namely: time (context), place (place of enunciation), actors (the speaker(s) and the person(s) they are addressing).
3   The work of the historian Angèle Gnonsoa, herself Wê, is authoritative on the problem of the *glaè* in Wê country. She spent many years, almost all her career as a researcher, in understanding the society Wê from the political and religious point of view and the role played by the *glaè*.
4   The present author is a member of the Monitoring Committee of the Council of Traditional Chiefs and Communities.

and the political parties allied to the political group Assembly of Houphouëtists for Democracy (RHDP) and the opposition parties gathered around Laurent Gbagbo's Ivorian Popular Front (FPI), known as the Presidential Majority (LMP) during the 2010 presidential elections.

This bipolarisation can be seen first of all at the level of the media, especially the written press. Indeed, as Aghi Bahi[5] shows so well, we have blue papers, which are close from an editorial point of view to the parties gathered around the FPI, and green papers, which are close to the parties that comprise the RHDP.[6] The production of newspapers and their mode of processing information are negatively influenced by the ideologies of the parties to which they are close. In Côte d'Ivoire, we are witnessing a partisan press, xenophobic writings and incitement to hatred and violence. This situation has been amply described by Samba Koné,[7] Zio Moussa,[8] and in previous research by the present author.[9]

Newspapers tend to appropriate politicians' quarrels by treating the political opponents of their bosses with negative names and qualifiers. Francis Nyamnjoh has raised this problem with regard to the press in Cameroon. In his view, between 1990 and 1993, the media were highly politicised in Cameroon and polarised between two diametrically opposed camps. Each camp pretends to know and to represent the interests of the society and the people. According to Nyamnjoh, "For each camp, the God, the angels and the saints on the other side are nothing but Lucifer and demons."[10]

Beyond this great politicisation of the press, there is processing of non-professional information. The rules of journalistic writing, namely the separation of genres, the balance in the processing of information, are trampled underfoot. Yet the journalistic ethics outlined in the various codes of ethics and duties of journalists in Côte d'Ivoire recommends in some of these articles independence in journalistic work.

---

5   Bahi AA and Theroux-Benoni LA. 2013 "À propos du rôle des médias dans le conflit ivoirien" [Concerning the role of the media in the Ivorian conflict], in Ouedraogo JB and Sall E (eds). *Frontières de la citoyenneté et political violence in Côte d'Ivoire* [Frontiers of citizenship and political violence in the Ivory Coast]. Dakar: CODESRIA, 199-217.
6   Bahi and Theroux-Benoni, "À propos du rôle des médias dans le conflit ivoirien".
7   Koné S. 2015. *Information & Désinformation* [Information & Disinformation]. Abidjan: Samgraphic. See also Tiesse C. 2005. "Une presse injurieuse et anti-confraternelle", *Fraternité Matin*, 26 September.
8   Zio M. 2012 "The Media and the Political Crisis in the Ivory Coast". Legon: Media Foundation for West Africa.
9   Gnonzion C. 2008. *Les facteurs de décisions éthiques et de construction de l'identité des journalistes ivoiriens* [The factors of ethical decisions and the construction of the identity of Ivorian journalists], PhD Diss, Gregorian University of Rome.
10 Nyamnjoh FB. 2000. "West Africa: Unprofessional and unethical journalism", in Kunczik M. 2000. *Ethics in journalism: a reader on their perception in the Third World.* Bonn: Friedrich-Ebert-Stiftung/FES Library, 31-77.

The bipolarisation of public life with respect to religions has manifested itself in a different way. It was felt that every head of state had a type of religious guide who enjoyed the graces of the palace and whose councils were the most credible of those of the others. Researchers such as Bony Guiblehon[11] have already noted this phenomenon. For example, during the reign of Presidents Houphouët-Boigny (before the appearance of then Prime Minister Alassane Ouattara) and Henri Konan Bédié, the Catholic Church and the bishops received greater attention than Protestant churches and Muslims. Large Catholic buildings were built, including Saint Paul's Cathedral in Abidjan Plateau, the Basilica of Our Lady of Peace in Yamoussoukro, which is a replica of St. Peter's in Rome, and mosques were also built, such as the Mosque of the Plateau.

During the reign of Laurent Gbagbo, it was the pastors of the Protestant churches who were the religious guides of the palace and whose counsels and prayers had more meaning for the regime than those of the other religious leaders, even if some Catholic leaders were welcomed for various reasons. Laurent Gbagbo is a former seminarian, and the nationalist ideas or national sovereignty he defended were taken up by some priests and bishops in their public speeches, both mediated and not. Under the regime of President Ouattara, it is the Muslim leaders who have defended the regime in place and prayed for its longevity in their sermons.[12]

It is in this context of bipolarisation that the presidential elections of 2010 were held, and the challenge of their results by the main protagonists will led to a post-election crisis.[13] The media staging of Catholic leaders during the 2010 post-electoral crisis in Côte d'Ivoire is the tip of the iceberg of interactions between religious leaders and politicians since the country's independence in 1960. This media staging was the manifestation of a two-dimensional secularism: the secularism of "collaboration" and the secularism "separatist" type that Rubin Pohor[14] explains well:

> In the case of Côte d'Ivoire, particularly, as elsewhere in several African countries, two aspects of these types of secularism coexist in varying degrees. This is the secularity of "collaboration" and secularism of the "separatist" type. Thus, some have a perception of secularism tending

---

11 Guiblehon B. 2011. *Le pouvoir-faire: religion, politique, ethnicité et guérison en Côte d'Ivoire* [The power-to-do: religion, politics, ethnicity and healing in the Ivory Coast]. Paris: L'Harmattan, 150.
12 2015. "Côte d'Ivoire: Carton rouge à l'imam Ousmane Diakité de la mosquée du Mont Arafat à Cocody", *ConnectionIvoirienne.net,* 18 July.
13 The results of the presidential elections of 2010, according to the institution that proclaims them, would be challenged by either side. The results of these presidential elections proclaimed by the Independent Electoral Commission (CEI), which gave Ouattara the victory, would be challenged by the Gbagbo camp. And those of the constitutional council which invalidated the results of the CIS and gave Gbagbo victory would be contested by the Ouattara camp.
14 Pohor R. 2013. "Points de tensions, laïcité et cohésion sociale". [Points of tension, secularism and social cohesion], *Revue théologie Africaine, Église et Société* 3:77-105.

to emphasize the independence of the State from religions or the autonomy of the region from politics. Separatist secularism, although less obvious, is often mentioned when there is a collision between religion and politics.

The bipolarisation of the public political-religious space was the first problem. The second problem (and the starting point of this chapter) is the public disavowal of the Catholic religious leaders.

Public disavowal of Catholic leaders

The media coverage of the interactions between politicians and Catholic leaders was the occasion to observe a sort of discredit and public disavowal of the latter by ordinary citizens, journalists and even other religious. This media coverage has thus exposed certain limits inherent to the human being: fragility in the face of adversity and a tendency to make partisan judgments and to give unbalanced information. But these supposed limits of men consecrated or anointed by the power of the people through popular, democratic or diplomatic choices raises in varying degrees the question of the credibility of the religious and political leader in Ivorian public space. In the collective social imagination of some citizens, for example, politicians are tainted with certain adverse or derogatory qualifications. Some are even identified as "thieves", "liars" and "demagogue", who promise mounts and wonders, just to be elected and remain in power. And that does not move anyone – or at least not many people.

On the other hand, the case of the religious leader is different. The latter is perceived as a model of truth, justice and love – in short, a man of God – therefore a credible and reassuring man.

In his context of life and the exercise of his spiritual and divine activities, the religious leader is seen as caring for things that bear meaning to the heavens. He is "in the world but not of the world". This is one of the foundations of his teachings to the faithful, whether the latter are Christians or Muslims.

The religious man is perceived in the national community as a credible man, because he is a member and representative of a credible institution – namely, the Church. His word embodies a word of authority borrowed from justice and truth, because it is supposed to be influenced and inspired by the teaching of the Good News of the Gospel. One of the foundations of the credibility of the Catholic leader is the Lord Jesus Christ, of whom he is the representative and in whose name he derives all his legitimacy and announces the Good News. In other words, this Jesus incarnates and identifies himself with the message (the good news) that he announces to the people of God. The encyclical of Pope John Paul II, *Redemptoris Missio*, is explicit in this regard:

> Jesus himself is the "Good News", as he declares at the very beginning of his mission in the synagogue at Nazareth, when he applies to himself the words of Isaiah about the Anointed One sent by the Spirit of the Lord

(cf. Luke 4:14-21). Since the "Good News" is Christ, there is an identity between the message and the messenger, between saying, doing and being. His power, the secret of the effectiveness of his actions, lies in his total identification with the message he announces; he proclaims the "Good News" not just by what he says or does, but by what he is.[15]

Catholic leaders, bishops and cardinals, as the constituents of Christ, also have the mission of continuing this work of announcing the Good News as written by Pope John Paul II:

> My brother bishops are directly responsible, together with me, for the evangelization of the world ... In this regard the Council states: "The charge of announcing the Gospel throughout the world belongs to the body of shepherds, to all of whom in common Christ gave the command."[16]

Clearly, for bishops, as for Christ, it is this intrinsic bond, "the identity between the messenger and the message, between saying, acting and being", which for us is the important element in which is based on the legitimacy and credibility of the men of God and of the Catholic leaders in Côte d'Ivoire. This is what Marshal McLuhan was referring to when he said "The medium is the message."[17] But this identity link is not something fixed. It is a link that is created, develops and consolidates in time and across social contexts. It strengthens the faith and credibility of faithful and observers to Catholic leaders.

In light of the above, we are able to ask ourselves a series of questions arising from the entry into the electronic media and their use by religious leaders in Côte d'Ivoire during the period of the post-election crisis of 2010. How religious leaders expose themselves to the media? Why and for what purpose? What message and what speech was it conveyed in the media? What is the context of this presence in the media? What are these media and what were their perceptions of religious discourses and representations of religious leaders in their productions? Finally, what answers did the discourses and messages of religious leaders generate in the media? The following should help to answer to all these questions.

---

15 Pope John Paul II. 1990. *Redemptoris Missio* [On the permanent validity of the Church's missionary mandate] 7 December, para 13.
16 Pope John Paul II, *Redemptoris Missio*, para 63.
17 From the title of the book of McLuhan M. 1967. *The Medium is the Message: An Inventory of Effects.* London: Penguin.

The televised intervention of Cardinal Bernard Agré

Table 9.1: The referential dimension and parameters of the enunciation of the cardinal's discourse

Actors	Time (context)	Place	What the Cardinal said (*dictum*)
· Cardinal Agré · National community · International community	The programme was broadcast on 23 December 2010 at one of the highlights of the post-election crisis.	Cardinal Agré was interviewed on the first channel of Ivorian television, the RTI. He was the guest of the programme "Raison d'état".	· "For me, the right has been said, and has given a victor, it is necessary to stick to that." · "In all countries of the world, the Constitutional Council is the body responsible for resolving electoral disputes and proclaiming final results." · "… the international community, accused of 'wanting to put the fire' on the Ivory Coast." · "I ask President Laurent Gbagbo and Mr Ouattara to meet somewhere to hear."

The choice of the RTI, more than three weeks after the outbreak of the post-election crisis, cannot seem fortuitous. The RTI has always been under the control of the political regime in place. It proved it even more clearly at the beginning of the post-election crisis, especially with its "Raison d'état" broadcast, which sought to legitimise the victory of the camp and candidate Laurent Gbagbo. Accepting to participate in this media broadcast can be seen as political support brought by the cardinal to one of the camps in conflict. Through his speech, Cardinal Agré takes a clear position in supporting the verdict of the constitutional council which recognises Laurent Gbagbo as winner.

Critical reactions to Cardinal Agré's speech

Table 9.2: The first reaction

Actors	Time (context)	Place	Manner of criticising the Cardinal's discourse (*modus*)
• An Ivorian citizen • Cardinal Agré • National community • International community	A few days after the interview with Cardinal Agré	In the lines of the daily *Patriot*	• "The international community's affair is heartless: the questionable positions of Cardinal Agré" (title of the article) • "He should have been the Ivorian Desmond Tutu. Bernard Cardinal Agré, former Archbishop of Abidjan, would have had, in the crisis that shook the Ivory Coast, statements from the Anglican Archbishop of South Africa that the country would not be where it is today." • "In the name of truth and clerical priesthood, the prelate should have simply asked Laurent Gbagbo to leave power." • "Bernard Cardinal Agré appears and defends the one who hires mercenaries to kill his compatriots. Worse, Monseigneur Agré uses the ultra-nationalist theses of Laurent Gbagbo and his supporters who treat this international community as people who do not think about tomorrow."

To support his criticisms, this citizen recalls the example of South African Archbishop Desmond Tutu, who played a positive and constructive role in his country. He regrets that Cardinal Agré did not follow the same path. He also stresses the duty of truth of a man of God and ends by recalling that, according to him, the cardinal supports a personality who "hires mercenaries to kill his compatriots". These criticisms were published in the daily *Patriot*, which close to one of the parties, namely, camp Ouattara.

Table 9.3: The second reaction

Actors	Time (context)	Place	Manner of critiquing the Cardinal's discourse (MODUS)
• The journal *Venance Konan* • Cardinal Agré • National community • International community	29 Dec. 2010, about a week after the televised interview with the Cardinal	• A forum in the French newspaper *Libération* • The information portal Abidjan.net • The article was reprinted by the Ivorian dailies	• "Your Eminence, should I remind you that one of the cardinal values of Christian doctrine is Truth? This doctrine says that God sent his son Jesus to earth to tell the Truth to the Men. And it was not by chance that Jesus punctuated all his sermons with these words: 'Verily I say unto you.' It is written in the sacred book of Christians, John 14, 'And the Word was made flesh and dwelt among us, full of grace and truth; And we have beheld his glory, a glory as the glory of the only begotten of the Father.'" • "The accession of Laurent Gbagbo to power in 2000 resulted in the deaths of hundreds of people. To this day I have not heard you condemn these massacres. It was in the basement of your cathedral that Robert Guei took refuge on September 19, 2002, and it was there that Laurent Gbagbo's soldiers went to fetch him as a dog on the Corniche of Cocody, without it being known to this day who had informed them of his presence in your premises. I have not yet heard you condemn this assassination." • "You ask that you pray for all these victims, but you do not condemn the perpetrators you know well." • "What kind of pastor are you, Cardinal Bernard Agré?" • "Your Eminence, if you were a man of truth, a man who loves his country, you would use your authority to make Laurent Gbagbo understand that he is driving the Ivory Coast to chaos by wanting to cling to a power that The Ivorians refused him by the votes of the urns. We who fall under the bullets of the Gbagbo killers while men like you are silent, have no choice but to call for help from this international community that you seem to hate."

The author grounds himself in the biblical texts, and in notions of truth and justice to criticise the intervention of Cardinal Agré. He recalls a biblical passage and accuses the silence of Cardinal Agré in the face of several facts in the history of the country, which he cites in his testimony. These are the facts of massacres and the death of a man. In so doing, he accuses the Cardinal of being a partisan and not a judge and an impartial man of God. He wonders ironically about the type of pastor that Cardinal Agré is.

Table 9.4: The declaration of the bishops of Côte d'Ivoire

Actors	Time (context)	Place	What the Ivorian bishops said (*dictum*)
• Bishops of the Côte d'Ivoire • National community • International community	On 3 Jan. 2011, about a month after the onset of the post-election crisis	The Ivorian dailies	"We Bishops of Côte d'Ivoire recommend the following: - That the two candidates undertake to find through the means of dialogue a peaceful settlement of the dispute so as not to endanger the lives of the people. - That they accept to meet to dialogue in spite of their resentment; it would be an act of courage, humility and love for our country. - That they call their militants firmly to calm and restraint. - That the United Nations comply with the fundamental principles which govern it and which are respectful of the rights of man. That it makes use of the peaceful means of settlement of the dispute with a view to contributing to the resolution of the crisis and strictly to the maintenance of peace. We urge him to respect the sovereignty of our country. - That our brothers, the Africans of the AU and ECOWAS, recall the principle of African solidarity which means that when the neighbor's hut burns, it is helped to extinguish the fire. We would therefore like to respectfully draw attention to the incalculable consequences of military intervention for the country and the West African subregion. We say no to such an intervention. We are all embarked in the same ship and no one has any interest in seeing it sink into the formidable waters of violence and civil war."

Two essential points have been criticised in this statement by the bishops of Côte d'Ivoire. First, it comes a little late, almost a month after the outbreak of the post-election crisis. Second The bishops urge the UN to respect the sovereignty of Côte d'Ivoire. In the context of the post-election crisis, this request was seen, rightly or wrongly, as a stand in favor of the Laurent Gbagbo camp. Thus, they were treated of bishops close to the party of the latter.

Table 9.5: Critics of the Bishops' Declaration

Actors	Time (context)	Place	Manner of critiquing the discourse of the Cardinal (MODUS)
· The daily *North-South* · Bishops of the Côte d'Ivoire · National community · International community	8 Jan. 2011	The columns of the daily *North-South*, close to the Ouattara camp	"Episcopal Conference of Ivory Coast - All Bishops Are Not Pro-Gbagbo" (title of article)
· The daily *Patriot* · Bishops of the Côte d'Ivoire · National community · International community	11 Jan. 2011, one week after the declaration of the bishops	An edition of the daily newspaper *Patriot*, close to the Ouattara camp	"Electoral coup d'etat – These political bishops who deceive Gbagbo" (title of the article)
· Ivorian citizen · Bishops of the Côte d'Ivoire · National community · International community	11 Jan. 2011	The columns of the daily newspaper *Le Nouveau Réveil*, close to the Ouattara camp	"After the declaration of the pro-Gbagbo bishops / Pr. Koné Abu Bakary denounces the seductive and dangerous speech of the bishops of Côte d'Ivoire" (title of the article)
· An Ivorian citizen · Bishops of the Côte d'Ivoire · National community · International community	13 Jan. 2011	The columns of the daily newspaper *Le Nouveau Réveil*, close to the Ouattara camp	"After the declaration of the pro-Gbagbo bishops / A citizen asks: 'Why are you blind?'" (title of article)

The statement of the Ivorian bishops was strongly criticised in the national press. The dailies that published these criticisms are those close to the Ouattara camp. These criticisms emanate from journalists as well as ordinary citizens.

THE PLACE OF RELIGION AND POLITICS IN TRADITIONAL SOCIETY WÊ: THE EXAMPLE OF THE GLAÈ MASK

Who are the Wê?

The Wê are an Ivorian people living in the mountainous west of the country. They are distinguished by their different dialect between the Wê of the south, called *gueré* by the government and the Wê of the north, who are called *wobe*. But these different dialects do not greatly influence inter-comprehension within the Wê country.

From the point of view of organisation, Wê society is not governed by a central power, of the monarchical type, as among certain Akan peoples, for example. But as Gnonsoa notes, three important points can be taken into account in the social organisation of the Wê:

1. Lineages as small political units culminating in federated clan lineages (*tche*);
2. Autonomy of the village cell; and
3. Submission of the life of lineage members to sacred institutions (*kwi, dji, glaè*, according to clan).

And among the sacred institutions present in Wê country, the one we are interested in in this chapter is the mask that the Wê call *glaè*. But who is this *glaè*, and what is its religious and political place?

What is the glaè mask of the Wê?

The term mask can refer commonly to an object of any form whatsoever which serves to hide the face. It is in this context, moreover, that this term is used in the expression masked ball. But among the Wê people, the mask does not refer to this.

Here it is not a vulgar object, whose sole function is to conceal something, the human face. Instead, the Wê people use the term of *glaè*[18] to refer to the person who wears the mask. This *glaè* in Wê society and civilisation represents a "living reality", an institution of the order of the sacred which incarnates religious and political powers. Christophe Wondji better explains the reality of the institution of the mask when he writes:

> The universe of the Wê masks ... a mysterious world with appearances and scenic manifestations that are often confusing for the profane: mysteries of forms and colors, mysteries of songs and lyrics, mysteries of gestures and acrobatics whose decoding introduces us to one of the most symbolic civilizations of Black Africa. Indeed, this approach to masks and their role in society aims, in a way, to highlight the structures and functioning of a traditional civilization marked by the permanent

---

18 The reader of this chapter has to consider that the use of the term "mask" refers to the wearer of the *glaè* mask as an important figure in the Wê society.

search for harmony between man and the divinity, between nature and culture, between society and the cosmos. It is not a question here of opposing man to nature and divinity, but of harmonizing his relations with entities in order to integrate him into the world system. For if Greek Prometheus has taken fire from the gods to ensure the mastery of men on earth, the ancestors have used masks to establish the reign of the gods over men.[19]

To speak of a Wê mask is to touch on a leading institution for this people. As Angèle Gnonsoa writes, "Omnipresent in the life of Wê, the masks fulfilled various functions. They had the upper hand on religion, politics, economics, knowledge and art."[20]

But from the religious point of view, the power of the *glaè* is based on the fact that it serves as an intermediary between God and men.

The religious power of the glaè as an intermediary between God and men

The Wê believe in the existence of a single God and creator of heaven, earth and all living beings, visible and invisible. For them, this God is the beginning of all things, for being the most ancient and pre-existent before all. The name used in Wê to designate God shows it easily. Indeed, in different dialects, God is designated by "Gnonsoa", that is to say "ancient", in the Wê of the north, or by "Guela", that is to say "old" in the Wê of the south. But as Gnonsoa the historian observes,

> The Wê invoke God only in the last instance, when all remedies have been exhausted. That is why they only come into contact with Gnonsoa through intermediaries such as the *glaè* to whom a collective and popular cult is dedicated.[21]

Indeed, Gnonsoa further notes,

> The Wê addresses the supernatural powers to ask them to keep the cosmic and social balance. Worship serves to render these powers favorable. The Wê wants to obtain from God, through his mediators, what can make his life pleasant and as long as possible.[22]

It is also important to note, as Gnonsoa points out, that for the Wê, "religion here is not contemplative; it is always the communion of men among themselves, it is communion between men, ancestors and supernatural forces. It is essentially aimed at satisfying the needs here below: food, health, wealth, fertility, power,

---

19 Gnonsoa A. 2007. *Le masque au cœur de la société wê*. [The mask at the heart of Wê society]. Abidjan: FratMat Editions, 73.
20 Gnonsoa. *Le masque au cœur de la société wê*, 73.
21 Gnonsoa, *Le masque au cœur de la société wê*, 77.
22 Gnonsoa, *Le masque au cœur de la société wê*, 77.

peace."²³ In addition to religious power, the *glaè* is also a preponderant holder of political power.

The glaè as predominant holder and co-holder of political power

One of the distinctive features of the political and religious system of the Wê is that the same institution can embody two types of powers – namely, religious power and political power. This is the case with the *glaè*, which, as a sacred institution, holds exclusively religious power, but at the same time is at the top of the list and a preponderant means among the holders of political power. Indeed, among the Wê, political power is divided hierarchically between, initially, the *glaè*, then the Assembly of Initiates²⁴ and finally the Head of Lineage.

The *glaè* is the preponderant holder of political power because, as Gnonsoa explains, he is "well placed to know the rules that govern society, since he is himself a legislator. His antiquity and immortality make him an inexhaustible source of experience and wisdom. In addition, he is a spirit and therefore not inhabited by the human feelings which make most of the arbitrators biased in their judgment."²⁵

We note, therefore, that from the point of view of protocol and politics, the *glaè*, the Assembly of Initiates and the Head of Lineage. But this preponderance does not make the *glaè* a dictator or an autocrat. Gnonsoa teaches us that he is a spokesman accepted by all the people, starting with the Assembly of the Initiates. But in reality, the person who exercises power on a daily basis is the Head of Lineage, because the mask is still not in the village.²⁶ There is therefore an interdependence between the *glaè*, the Head of Lineage and the Assembly of the Initiated.

On the other hand, one of the foundations of credibility in the *glaè* lies in the particularity of the political units in Wê country, which are governed by the blood relationship and not on the basis of an ideology. The *glaè* to better ensure its role of social control, benefits from its attribute of representative of ancestors and of God. As Gnonsoa observes,

> To disobey him is to enter into dissent with the cosmic order, it is to consign himself to death, social and even physical. Only the initiates are capable of discernment in order not to submit blindly. Other

---

23   Gnonsoa, *Le masque au cœur de la société wê*, 77.
24   The Assembly of Initiates is composed of all the men adults and some women who serve the *glaè*. The young men can be part of this Assembly if they are 18 or 19 years old and have undergone the rite of circumcision.
25   Gnonsoa, *Le masque au cœur de la société wê*, 88.
26   A *glaè* represents the person and his full costume (mask and raphia robe). The *glaè* lives in some sort of camp near the village, or in the village but apart from the rest of the inhabitants of the village. The *glaè* comes to the village when necessary. The Head of Lineage or a member the Assembly of the Initiated can call him. The *glaè* can also come to the village in case of some problems.

members of the lineage, especially women and youth, must accept without discussion.[27]

Discrediting Ivorian Catholic leaders during the post-election crisis: Lessons to be learned from the legacy of the glaè mask tradition

As we have shown during this chapter, Catholic leaders were sharply criticised and disavowed following their positions during the post-electoral crisis of 2010 in Côte d'Ivoire. They were accused of having taken sides for one of the camps in conflict, namely that of the outgoing president, Laurent Gbagbo, and in disfavour of the other camp, that of the then opposition candidate and now current president, Alassane Ouattara. For that reason, citizens bestowed hostile statements upon the men of God, hitherto respected by all.

But in the light of the example of the relations between religion and politics of the Wê, we can note certain points worthy of interest, which bring politics and religion together for the same interests of the community, nut at different levels. At a time when certain societies have made the choice of separation between religious and political power, the Wê have found it necessary to link these two powers in a certain way. Some aspects of the management of religious and political power, in particular through the institution of the *glaè*, can be noted here. At the religious level, for example, it can be said that the basis of faith in the *glaè*, the importance for this institution of the questions of justice and equity, as well of social cohesion and peace.

Foundations of faith in the glaè at religious level

There are two bases for faith in the *glaè* in Wê society considerations for: (1) justice and equity; and (2) social cohesion and peace. They are reviewed in order here.

1. *Justice and equity.* The *glaè* as exclusive holder of the religious power in Wê country was the guarantor of justice and equity. The other members of society had faith in the mask because they were convinced that these decisions could not be arbitrary because they are themselves based on the fear of ancestors and God. The organisation of social and political institutions in the country was such that the mask could not be a dictator or impose its ideas, because the society had specific mechanisms of removal or banning the mask from going out publicly. And these mechanisms can be triggered by the assembly of insiders and elders. The fear of social punishment and the ban on escape resulted in the *glaè* being an institution for the promotion of social justice and equity.

The lesson to be learned here is that the exclusive holder of religious power, the intermediary between God and man, had to work for justice and cohesion in the

---

27   Gnonsoa, *Le masque au cœur de la société wê*, 94.

community. If he did not do so, he could be banished by the Assembly of the Initiates and punished by the ancestors. Another lesson is that the Wê believed firmly in the religious power of the *glaè*, convinced that the latter cannot be arbitrary because it is based on the fear of ancestors and God. Social cohesion and peace as the second foundation of credibility and faith in the *glaè*.

2. *Social cohesion and peace*. Another lesson to be learned from the Wê is that the religious power of the *glaè* is also based on the preservation of social cohesion and peace. One of the roles of religion in Wê country is to bring and maintain the balance of man with nature and with God for a better life here below. It is a matter of social cohesion and peace in the community. The cult of the *glaè* serves to ward off wars, conflicts and calamities, to mitigate them or to manage them.

As Angèle Gnonsoa writes, "When a community is experiencing trouble or conflict; When catastrophes such as famine, epidemics or war break down, the cult of the *glaè klaa* (the oldest or the head of the *glaè* in Wê language) serves to distance or mitigate them. The purpose of worship can also be the prevention of evils or thanks for favors received."[28]

Foundations of faith in the glaè at the political level

The greatest legacy of the institution of the *glaè* in Wê country lies in the choice of a fusion between politics and religion. This is the mixed management of religious and political power and the fact that the same authorities jointly hold political and religious powers. At the political level, there was a distribution of roles in a hierarchical way that made political power not a single entity, a single institution. The facets of power were shared by different institutions and different social groups. There was therefore a division and a separation of power. Thus, a lesson to learn from the Wê, and of course to discuss at the political level, is that we should not be afraid to institute a mixed politico-religious power between politicians and religious leaders.

CONCLUSION

The media treatment of Cardinal Agré's speeches and the declaration of the Episcopal Conference of Côte d'Ivoire during the post-election crisis showed that these were disavowed through criticisms reported by the newspapers. The Catholic leaders have been criticised for not sufficiently incarnating the "identity between the message and the messenger, between saying, acting and being", as recalled in the encyclical of Pope John Paul II, *Redemptoris Missio*. Some observers, even if they have chosen media channels close to a political camp, have criticised the great collision between the Catholic leaders and former Ivorian President Laurent Gbagbo. In fact, what was reproached in the Catholic

---

28 Gnonsoa, *Le masque au cœur de la société wê*, 77.

religious leaders is that they did not sufficiently played the role of arbitrator, whose word is authoritative because neutral and impartial.

This media coverage of the interventions of Catholic leaders highlights some of the problems that have plagued public life in Côte d'Ivoire for several decades. Primary among these problems is political bipolarisation, has influenced other institutions, such as the media and religion. The second problem is the reality of an ambiguous and hybrid secularism. These problems, which are problems of power, legitimacy and credibility, also manifest themselves traditional communities, which are of cours, smaller in number and in terms of geographical space. But societies like the Wê have found answers to these problems. The solution found by the Wê is that the *glaè*, the exclusive holder of religious power, is also one of the holders of political power.

The main question for Côte d'Ivoire today is whether the religious should be separated from politics in the management of the affairs of the city, or whether, on the contrary, as in the Wê, the two must manage a symbiosis between the populus and the city in a joint fashion. The second important issue is the credibility of religious leaders. How can one explain that Catholic leaders who have benefited from the trust, fear and respect of all members of the community, all confessions combined, have come to be publicly criticised for being contradicted and decried? An early reply may come from lines of the encyclical of Pope John Paul II:

> Since the "Good News" is Christ, there is an identity between the message and the messenger, between saying, doing and being. His power, the secret of the effectiveness of his actions, lies in his total identification with the message he announces; he proclaims the "Good News" not just by what he says or does, but by what he is.[29]

To put it another way, the credibility of the disciple and the apostle of Christ must be inspired by the example of the latter. And the Wê who believed in the Father of Christ founded the credibility of their religious leaders on the fact that the latter, like the *glaè*, could not act in the interest of the community, for they were convinced that the contrary would provoke the anger of the Ancestors and God, the ancestor of their ancestors.

---

29 Pope John Paul II, *Redemptoris Missio*, para 13.

10 INDIVIDUAL AND COLLECTIVE RIGHTS IN AFRICA: DUAL WORLDS OF LAW, RELIGION AND AFRICAN TRADITIONAL HERITAGE

Nokuzola Mndende[1]

INTRODUCTION

At independence, the new African regimes run by native Africans surprisingly perpetrated the contempt imposed by Western systems on indigenous society. Instead of using the opportunity of independence to reinstate the supremacy of indigenous law over and above Western law and society, native African rulers became even more aggressive in suppressing their own civilization.[2]

As African states had been under colonial rule for a long time, it was a dream of most Africans that when their fellow Africans took the leadership in postcolonial era, Africans would be holistically free. It was very unfortunate that after a lot of blood was spilt fighting for the liberation of the oppressed, such leaders continued to perpetuate the very Western stereotypes that were entrenched in the foreign religions and the laws that were introduced in the respective countries. To cite one example, South Africa was incorrectly declared a Christian country, suppressing the indigenous spirituality and causing anyone who resisted Christian to be regarded as an atheist, pagan or heathen; hence African names were called heathen names. The indigenous law was suppressed and Roman-Dutch law took the centre stage. The restoration of the religion and the law of the land was supposed to be the first priority of the indigenous people after liberation. But the opposite happened – the leaders just became white souls in black skins. To date in South Africa, Christianity and Roman-Dutch law still take the centre stage – thus suppressing the indigenous law and spirituality.

As a result of the above, in any attempt to try to discuss an African perspective on many issues – for instance, individual rights in conjunction with collective rights within the sphere of African culture and spirituality – the debate always ends up reflecting the ongoing conflict between African culture and Western culture. African culture is, rightly or wrongly, perceived as specialising in collective rights; whereas Western culture is, rightly or wrongly, perceived as specialising in individual rights. Such perceptions always put each culture in a

---

1 Dr Nokuzola Mndende, Icamagu Institute, University of the Free State, South Africa.
2 Hansungule M. 2014. "Culture, Governance and African Human Rights in Critical Perspective", *International Journal of Arts and Commerce* 3(1):69-86.

box, as the concept of "nuclear family" is associated with Western culture and the concept of extended family is associated with African culture.

Defining rights laid down by customs and rituals is a very complex exercise, as it cannot be defined in simplistic terms. This is due to the fact that, though individual rights do exist in the African communities and are also fundamental rights for all individuals, they are defined and applied in a manner that is dictated by the customary law of the land. Since the foundation of all customs and rituals is believed to be grounded in the concept of *ubuntu*, which dictates that whatever one is doing for the benefit of humanity, before taking any decision one must make sure that it is not going to affect others negatively, and the decision must benefit the surrounding community. In order to be reminded of the basis of *ubuntu*, there are rules and regulations that are to be adhered to in all activities in the course of human life, and these are taught in daily activities by the elderly who, in turn, are believed to be "students" or "ambassadors" of the ancestors. These rules and regulations, as they focus on the collective and communal, may be unfair to some people at the individual level, especially those who occupy positions by birthright, because they have to comply with the dictates of the customs or traditions. Individual rights are accepted only if they have positive effects both for the individual, and also for the people and environment in which the individual resides.

In this chapter, I will discuss the understanding of individual rights as compared with collective rights in African traditional communities. The focus will be on the South African experience, specifically that of the Xhosa community, which is my lived experience. Though this is my point of departure, one will notice that there are many commonalities with other African countries. With respect to the context of South Africa, it will also be important to examine how such a multi-cultural and multi-religious country unequivocally blends together the application of both individual and collective rights, without marginalising or dictating to any group within its pluralistic country, as per the Constitution. One must understand that South Africa has accommodated many religions, such as African Traditional Religion (ATR), Buddhism, Baha'i, Christianity, Islam, Judaism and many more. With the presence of these religions, South Africa is a multi-cultural society, but all these cultures and religions must abide by one Constitution and one rule of law.

LAW, RELIGION, AND CULTURE IN AFRICA

The Constitution of the Republic of South Africa, 1996,[3] is the supreme law of the land, drafted by lawmakers in Parliament and enacted through statutes. However, the Constitution's enactment has not always been received without controversy among South Africa's indigenous peoples. South African legal

---

3   Constitution of the Republic of South Africa, 1996.

scholar Michelo Hansungule mourns the domination of Western culture in Africa's Constitution after independence, arguing that:

> The perpetuation of alien law and systems in independent Africa has dealt a severe blow to the whole idea of independence in Africa. Constitution after constitution while proclaiming the importance of traditional African values nonetheless subordinated these values to Western values in the form of the bill of rights in fact nothing more than a simple act of "cutting and pasting" from the foreign documents to equally "foreign" but domesticated instruments.[4]

The South African Constitution has, for example, used civil marriage as a basis of the law of succession; yet the law of the land makes customary law the basis of a recognised marriage. In the traditional leadership of South Africa's indigenous cultures, succession is based on the status of the mother, if she is from a royal family and is married the indigenous way. Many Africans in indigenous communities have lost their rights because the recognised marriage is one from the magistrate's court irrespective of having no recognition by the family.

Another example is a pending high court case in Mpondoland area of Ngqeleni district in South Africa. The case involves a polygamous chief who passed on in 2015 and yet had not been buried as of this writing in April 2017. He left the main homestead and stayed with his junior wife, but the junior wife is refusing to release his body, claiming that it was his will that he must be buried in her homestead. According to custom, however, a chief must be buried in the main homestead where his father and grandfather were buried. There is now a dispute between the family and community, who believe that he must be buried at the main homestead, and his junior wife, who is claiming otherwise. He is still in the mortuary. The junior wife cited her individual rights at the high court, because she knew very well that the traditional court would favour the senior wife.

This is the problem of the limitations of the Bill of Rights in the South African Constitution. The Bill of Rights deals with individual rights and does not explain how these rights, if applied irresponsibly, could affect the rights of the people around. A critical analysis of some of the statutes relating to individual and collective rights in South Africa is important in order to assess whether they emphasise individual rights more than collective rights or vice versa, and whether they are applied in a balanced manner.

Most Africans now find themselves caught up in an environment where they experience an identity dilemma, because they are now living in pluralistic societies and have to adjust and represent themselves as progressive and modern. The government has passed many laws without advice and advocacy

---

4   Hansungule, "Culture, Governance and African Human Rights in Critical Perspective".

from the communities. The Children's Act, for instance, focuses on the rights of the child only and is silent on the rights of the parent to raise a morally stable and responsible child. The parent will only be involved when the child commits a crime and is underage, in which case the child must be under the care of the parents. Another example is the Civil Union Act, 2006, which permits same-sex marriage. This is cast as an individual right to be respected. But it creates problems where there is lack of sexuality education within the communities and when there is a clash with the set norms of their communities and their religions when they get married. In most African communities, marriage is solely for procreation, and the communities have set gender roles which exclude homosexual or intersex people. LGBT citizens feel that the Constitution covers them, but their home communities and many families violate their rights by denying them the right to marry freely. These circumstances have resulted in people living in two worlds: the rural world and the urban worlds. In the rural world, customary law still dictates, but in the urban or city world there is a blend of the two laws.

But living in two worlds has made some Africans feel like quasi-citizens in their own land, coerced into being voiceless and disenfranchised participants, as decisions are taken by members of parliament without the majority being given an opportunity to be active participants in the debates. Laws such as the legalisation of abortion,[5] the Civil Union Act,[6] and the Children's Act,[7] to cite a few, were never discussed at the grass-roots level with people in their communities in their indigenous languages, but only in Parliament and city and town halls, which are areas that people could not afford to attend. What made things worse was that even in those town halls, the medium of instruction used was always English, which is not the mother tongue of the local people. This was done despite awareness that the majority of the people are not in the cities, but in rural areas where indigenous languages are used. One must not think that I am advocating for the abolition of these laws. Rather, what I am saying is that the discussions were and are still one-sided, and as a result the rural people and indigenous people are still on the receiving end of injustice. Most of the time, they hear it first from the media of the laws that are passed in Parliament, and it is complete news to them.

Everyday Africans in their ancestral land are made to live in two worlds. At home they live a communal way of life, which is foundational and not a choice, but rather dictated by tradition to all members of the community. At work, they inhabit another world in which Western-style individualism is central and imposed by the Constitution and law. Though it is true that culture evolves, it is also clear that culture on its own is not a single-layered entity, but instead made up of three layers, which can be considered as clothes or skins shed with different degrees of difficulty.

---

5   Choice on Termination of Pregnancy Act, 1996 (Act No. 92 of 1996).
6   Civil Union Act of 2006 (Act No. 17 of 2006).
7   Children's Act (Act No. 38 of 2005).

The first layer is a superficial culture, which is easy to adjust and unclothe, including such matters as housing, transport, cosmetics and many other public dimensions of life. The middle culture is difficult to shed unless one compromises one's identity by renouncing practices, such as individual naming, religious affiliation and language, just to name a few. The deep culture, which cannot be shed or peeled off includes one's race, roots, identity and ethics. In nearly all indigenous African societies, these are based on the communal way of life; hence it is rare to find an African being individualistic instead of acting as a representative of his other family and broader community. For example, in the African way of life, it is regarded as foreign when an individual concentrates on the "nuclear family" consisting of only the father, mother and biological children.

When it comes to matters of freedom of religion and belief, Africans also have a different perspective. In African culture and spirituality, no one is converted into a way of life, but they are born into an already existing tradition. People do not apply to belong to it or decide to abandon it. Even if one chooses to ignore tradition, it is believed that there are ways to remind the individual of their roots, either through physical sickness or escalation of behavioural imbalances. Even those Africans in diaspora have ways of showing their nostalgia by creating new forms of acting out the communal way of life.

The complexity of defining an individual as separate from the surrounding community can also be seen in his life journey of his participation in social and spiritual activities. In a religious and spiritual sense, it is believed that life is a journey from conception to the life hereafter – that is, the world of ancestors. No individual lives alone, but rather among other people, hence the Xhosa saying *"umntu ngumntu ngabantu"* (a person exists amongst other people and his or her wellbeing depends on other people). Through all of the stages of life, including birth, initiation, marriage and death, rituals expressing the communal and social aspect of human life are performed by and for individuals, with clan and community as witnesses.

One could wonder why African traditional communities always link the individual rights and those of the collective. The answer is simple: it is based on the relationship between the individual and the ancestors. The two cannot be separated, as they are believed to constitute what is called a family. In African tradition, the interaction between individual rights and those of the collective begins at birth of each individual. The rites of passage, which are the rituals of birth, puberty, marriage and death, for example, reflect this sense of spiritual collectivity. A newborn baby is formally incorporated into the community of the living and the departed when the *inkaba* (umbilical cord) is buried at the ancestral home by the elderly. The place where the *inkaba* and the ancestors are buried is referred to as one's "home" – that is, one's roots. Home, in this particular case, does not only refer to the infrastructure, but also refers to the ancestral land. The incorporation of an individual into the wider community is also a process that is done after death, with many communities performing the mourning rituals for the deceased relatives.

African philosopher and theologian John Mbiti clearly shows how an individual is made to be part of the whole in the rituals of the African spiritual world. In this regard, Mbiti observes:

> We have seen that birth is the first rhythm of a new generation, and the rites of birth are performed in order to make the child a corporate and social being. Initiation rites continue that process, and make him a mature, responsible and active member of the society. Marriage makes him a creative and reproductive being, linking him with both the departed and the generations to come. Finally comes death. Death stands between the world of human beings and the world of the spirits, between the visible and the invisible.[8]

In all these stages, there are teachings, taboos and responsibilities dictated by traditions and customs for a peaceful society. There are admonitions, advice, and emphasis on sharing and feelings of empathy toward the person next to you in the rites of passage and one's behavior in daily life in relation to age groups. All of these rituals and social practices make it very difficult to isolate individual rights from collective rights, as they are always intertwined.

THE SOCIAL WORLD OF AFRICAN RIGHTS

Clan and kinship

As many African-societies are clan-based, and the clan is what identifies an individual, no individual leaves in isolation of their clan. Clan names are derived from the names of the leading ancestors who, because of their birth rights, were either chiefs or heads of their respective clans. These, together with other deceased members of the family, are believed to be in spiritual communication with the living. In the process of self-definition, an individual is expected to recognise that he or she is a product of basically four clan names which are the paternal (father), maternal (mother), maternal grandmother and paternal grandmother. It is believed that the genes of these clans are in each individual's blood; hence he or she shares the joys, burdens and sorrows with them and calls them family members. Another typical example of an individual living within a collective is the way of greeting another person. This involves inquiries into the health and wellbeing of the individual, but also his or her relatives and environment.

---

8   Mbiti JS. 1969. *African Religions and Philosophy*. London: Heinemann, 149.

Greetings

Though I am not going to deal comprehensively with all of the nuances of African language in this chapter, the language of greetings is a key example of how collective rights often supersede individual rights in African culture. When two individuals greet each other, the responses from each always reflect the collective. Any individual who responds in an individualistic manner, such as, "I am fine", to the question of how they are doing, is labelled as an urban or city person, or as a Westerner or a white person. A typical African response is always inclusive of others; hence it takes a longer time to finish. A typical example below is cited between Person A and Person B. One must also observe that this is a two-way communication in which one must confirm that he or she understands or is listening. As these specific speakers are using isiXhosa (one of the indigenous languages) "Ewe" (yes) is constantly used as an affirmation or is uttered through the nose with a closed mouth as "Mh" or as "Mh-mh". These responses are just a common communication between two people and not based on gender or age or status. It is an individual explaining the situation within the self and of those in the surrounding community.

PERSON A	PERSON B
Ninjani? (How are you [plural]?)	Siphilile. (We are fine.)
Ewe/Mh. (Yes.)	Namahlaba sihamba nawo. (We are going forward with our body aches.)
Ewe/Mh. (Yes.)	Nasekhaya ndishiye kungekho nto. (Even at home they were fine when I left.)
Ewe/Mh. (Yes.)	Ngaphandle kukamama osoloko enkenenkene. (Except my mother who is always weak.)
Ewe/Mh. (Yes.)	Nembalela isiphethe kakubi. (This drought is killing us.)
Ewe/Mh. (Yes.)	Imfuyo iyafa. (The livestock is dying.)
Ewe/Mh. (Yes.)	Ninjani nina? (How are you?)
Hayi Nathi siphilile. (We are also fine.)	Ewe/Mh. (Yes.)

In this exchange, Person B will also reflect not only his/her own personal health, but also that of his/her family and the environment.

Blood and marriage relations

To be related by blood *ukuzalana* (blood) is very important in African culture. In the central rituals of African culture, participation is exercised not only at the level of the relationship by paternal side only, but also by the maternal side;

hence, the *umtshana* (nephew/niece) has a special role in her/his maternal side. In Xhosa culture, the term *umtshana* is a neutral term referring to "one's sister's child". My sister's child (boy or girl) is my *mtshana*, but my brother's child is my child, since we are of the same blood and hence we share the same clan names. This again, explains how an individual should always be in connection with those around him/her before thinking about personal rights.

Through marriage, another level of relationship is that of the parents of the married couple, who are also united by the marriage ritual. These parents call each other *mkhozi* and share joys, sorrows and burdens together. The term *mkhozi* "not only refers to parents links to their biological children, but also to the parents of their child's spouse" The parent of my brother's daughter-in-law for instance is my *mkhozi* though my brother's son has his own parents, but the fact that my brother's son is a Mndende, makes him my son, too.

In this context, no individual lives in what is called a "nuclear family". An individual is a product of at least four families, the one of the father (paternal and maternal), and that of the mother (both maternal and paternal). The individual must understand that he or she is the product of at least four ancestries, including those of the mother, father, maternal grandmother and paternal grandmother. By this knowledge, an individual is related to these families. No individual in African culture could claim monopoly of one parent family line or count as siblings only those born from the same biological parents. In the example below, the children of the three brothers cited below all call the brothers their fathers and the difference is the time each was born. Each of the fathers is considered as what would be referred to as "uncle" in English.

BROTHER	TITLE
Xuza	*Tata omdala* (eldest father)
Mzimkhulu	*Tata ophakathi* (middle father)
Wele	*Tata omncinci* (young Father)

The above table shows what the children of the three brothers call their "fathers". Those of Xuza for instance call him *Tata*, but call Mzimkhulu *Tata ophakathi*, and call Wele *Tata omncinci*. All of the children of these brothers regard themselves as siblings. Moreover, to be a sibling does not only extend to the families of these "biological" brothers, but goes beyond to all those who share the same surname and clan names.

These types of relationships amongst community members are clearly described by Mbiti, who observes of this notion of family or kinship through blood and betrothal, "It is kinship which controls social relationships between people in a given community, it governs marital customs and regulations, it determines the behaviors of one individual towards another."[9] The scope of kinship does

---

9   Mbiti, *African Religions and Philosophy*, 104.

not only extend to the relationship between relatives by blood and marriage, but goes beyond and involves the vertical aspect of the relationship. It goes to those who have departed, – that is, the ancestors as a collective (matriarchal and patriarchal) whose influence is highly respected in the lives of the living. Ancestors are the point of departure in all activities of the living and the environment and they are believed to be intermediaries between the living and the Creator. As Mbiti describes it:

> The kinship system also extends vertically to include the departed and those yet to be born. It is part of traditional education for children in many African societies to learn the genealogies of their descent. The genealogy gives a sense of depth, historical belongingness, a feeling of deep rootedness and a sense of sacred obligation to extend the genealogical line.[10]

What Mbiti explains above clearly indicates that an individual is an entity that is defined from a very broader perspective both horizontal (living clan members) and vertical (those who have departed which are ancestors). This clearly indicates that an individual is an ambassador who must be careful that his/her action are a reflection of not only his/her but his family of the living and the departed. This means that s/he may fall in love with a specific action but if the act is against his family, that means s/he must abstain from it though s/he thinks it falls within his/her rights.

Firstborn children

As there are different levels in the social structure in African communities, there are also different duties and responsibilities which an individual does not perform only for himself or herself, but also for the broader community. These are the natural duties dictated to those who are born within certain levels in the family or community. Among the amaXhosa for example, the firstborn male is not allowed to build his own homestead. He must remain at the communal home, as he will be expected to take over the responsibilities of his father when he passes on. A firstborn male in my community has to be the representative of their father, therefore his rights are dictated by tradition. His wife, too, must know the expectations and limitations of marrying a firstborn male, hence she must also be from a royal family. The wife of a firstborn male knows that she is to also take the responsibilities of the mother in law, she is going to be practically the "mother" to all the children of her husband's younger brothers and sisters. She has to help in solving some problems of her husband's paternal aunts.

One may ask what happens if the firstborn is a girl? The answers is that even if a firstborn male means is born after girls, he is still a firstborn male. Because the Xhosa are a patriarchal society, it is assumed that girls will marry and leave home, so the firstborn male will be the one to remain at home. All his siblings are

---

10   Mbiti, *African Religions and Philosophy*, 105.

free to go and establish themselves elsewhere, but come back to perform rituals at their communal home, when the need arises. In an ideal situation, if one of his sisters separates from her husband and comes back home, the firstborn male (her brother) should take responsibility of her and her children. The firstborn woman's *umafungwashe* (responsibilities) are mostly spiritual to her brothers' children. Even if she is married, during ritual activities she is obliged to come back home to perform her responsibilities. She will only go back home after the ritual has been finished.

If one of the brothers of the firstborn male passes on at an early age and leaves behind small children, it is the responsibility of the firstborn male to provide for his brother's children as they are also regarded as his responsibility. This may involve either be taking responsibility of all of them or discussing with extended family members how to share this responsibility. This when close relatives may decide to *ukuthatha* (take responsibility or adopt) each depending on the agreement with the clan members. This would be what the west calls adoption. Taking on the responsibilities of the father does not, however, entitle the first born to expropriate the intestate to his or her personal use, as happens in some modern societies where, upon the intestate death of a relative, family members descend like greedy vultures onto his or her property without any thought to surviving children or spouse.

The question that needs to be asked is how far does the right to freedom of religion for instance go when an individual occupies a position in traditional leadership whose duties are prescribed by his birth right and not by his personal rights? In fact, in many parts of Africa, a firstborn son has both religious and cultural duties and is, in fact, a sacred person since he leads all the religious activities in his family. Customary law scholar, TW Bennett explains the customary law of succession in African societies as follows:

> The African system of succession is invariably patrilineal. The rules of succession to a deceased are the same for all systems of customary law in South Africa. The guiding principle is always primogeniture in the male line. The ideal candidate for heir is therefore the deceased's eldest son or, failing him the eldest son's eldest male descendant, namely, the eldest surviving grandson. Failing any male issue in the eldest son's line, succession passes to the second son and his male descendants, and so on, through all the deceased's sons.[11]

Customary law scholar Alastair James Kerr agrees with Bennett, stating:

> If the deceased had no descendants the whole range of male ascendants are considered in order of "seniority". It is governed by the principle of primogeniture that even in polygamous marriages prevails. The rules are plain, straightforward and part and parcel of their system of family

---

11 Bennett TW. 2004. *Customary Law in Southern Africa*. Cape Town: Juta & Co, 337.

law, catering among others for the status and wellbeing of all members of an extended family.[12]

What Bennett and Kerr show above is that those who are born within the royal families (chiefs and kings) find themselves in a difficult situation when it comes to individual rights, when they have a right to adopt the religion of their choice for instance, but when it comes to their birth rights, they also have to comply with the rights of the people they lead without denouncing those cultural rights. As a chief is not chosen but born, he is bound by the customary law which is based in African Traditional Religion (ATR), this situation makes the chief to be ATR at home and Christian outside home.

INDIVIDUAL RIGHTS, COLLECTIVE RIGHTS AND HUMAN RIGHTS.

The question that needs to be raised from this examination of individual and collective rights in African cultures in the global human rights context is the sphere within which we should begin to talk about nature of human rights. Should we first think locally then globally or vice versa? If we talk of global human rights, how do we define global when the globe is made up of countries in which are localities that are also part of the global village? Talking about international human rights without considering the heritage of the people concerned is also a violation of their human rights. Multiculturalism should be recognised, as culture defines the identity of the people. What is needed is a dialogue on the commonalities and cultures.

An individual is a complex entity whose blood is a product of different clans. The individual is an ambassador of those clans and communities, since the concept of a "nuclear family" does not exist in Africa. Even an evolving culture cannot erase the practice of a collective, as even in cities Africans are practising their cultures adapting them into their new environment. In most cases, an individual is identified not by his personal name, but by those close to him by blood or by the clan.

Individual rights are never isolated from collective rights. In fact individual rights are dictated by collective rights. That is why even those Africans who decide to convert to other religions besides their indigenous one, either choose to isolate themselves from their roots, which is a very difficult situation as they are neither here nor there, or they choose to be syncretic, that is, practising both worldviews. If they accept syncretism, then at home they are African, but outside the home, for various reasons, they live in two worlds – the indigenous world to satisfy spiritual and cultural interests and the corporate world in order to satisfy economic needs. An individual is moulded by family, kinship and clan, using the culture and spirituality of that specific group based on the prescriptions from the spiritual world. Deviation from prescriptions is believed

---

12 Kerr AJ. 1990. *The Customary Law of Immovable Property and Succession*. Third Edition. Grahamstown: Grocott & Sherry, 99.

to anger the Creator and ancestors. Leaders are expected to lead by example and to take on from what their ancestors left. As there are different levels of leadership, there are also different expectations regarding rights and freedoms.

Multiculturalism and democracy have led to people to make choices that fulfil their internal interests. The interaction of African customary law with the new legal systems that came with evolving history has also opened up a scope to learn about human rights of other nations of the world. Though the insiders in any culture see their ways as supreme, there are sometimes areas where one fills coerced to follow a certain path in fear of the collective even if that path violates some personal beliefs. The issue of patriarchy and gender stereotyping for instance has caused some modern women to be labelled in very negative terms. Now that women are part of the corporate world and political hierarchies, they are no longer expected to be confined to their houses where gender roles are expected to be followed.

The other challenge is the limited scope of an individual to choose not to follow traditional customs and to adopt new beliefs. An example of a young man in the area of Ciskei in the Eastern Cape province of South Africa who did not want to undergo the traditional male initiation as a puberty rite is one to be cited. In African culture this rite is compulsory, as it is believed it's a transition from boyhood to adulthood, and the young man was forced by his father to undergo it. When he came back from this rite, which was against his beliefs, he took his father to court and won the case – yet he was labelled in many ways as an outcast. On the other hand, South Africa is now experiencing an increase in the number of white boys who decide to undergo this rite an African way, and they are allowed to do so as long as their parents agree. This indicates that in a balanced society it is difficult to separate the individual rights from the collective. Each one must listen to the other and sometimes, for the sake of peace, a compromise must be reached.

CONCLUSION

To sum it up, it is important to highlight that though there is a recognition of individual rights in modern African societies, they must not threaten or undermine the rights of other people who may be affected. The question is how far can an individual compromise personal rights because of the obligation to satisfy the collective rights? Also, it becomes more complex if there is no interest in balancing up the rights and a changing society. Now that societies are expanding from local to global in their perspective, there is a need to consolidate the rights of the community as a foundation – embracing those that promote morality and unity, excluding those that are discriminatory, and making peace within and among communities.

Ultimately, individual rights must make others comfortable, too. Rights must be accompanied by responsibility, compromise for the sake of others and an ethical concern to have positive output for all. This approach is consistent with *ubuntu* – the African heritage of collective concern for others, aimed at developing the whole society.

11 THE NATIONAL POLICY ON RELIGION AND EDUCATION, AND RELIGIOUS DRESS OBSERVANCES IN SOUTH AFRICAN SCHOOLS

Abdulkader Tayob[1]

INTRODUCTION

In 2003, the South African Minister of Education, Kader Asmal, proclaimed a National Policy on Religion and Education (NPRE) for the teaching of religion in public and independent schools in South Africa. The new policy came at the end of almost a decade of public debate and deliberation on the value of religion in schools.[2] The NPRE proposed some clear guidelines on the teaching of religion as an educational activity for a nation marked by diversity. It set aside decades of an apartheid policy that promoted and favoured Christian National Education. But the NPRE did not proscribe religious practices and religious observances in schools.[3] It empowered School Governing Bodies, together with religious authorities, to set up local policies guided by the constitutional values of equity and respect for diversity.

This dual aspect of the NPRE, accommodating religious observances in schools, while focusing on a new educational approach to teaching religion, has led to an unexpected anomaly. While most schools maintain an ethos where Christian hymns, prayers and homilies occupy a dominant place in assemblies and school associations, learners from minority religious traditions have been routinely suspended or dismissed for displaying attire that they claimed formed part of their religious practices and obligations. Such religious attire and dress have been rejected for not conforming to school dress codes. A sample of such issues indicates the extensiveness of this phenomenon. In 2002, a learner at Settler's High School in the Western Cape was suspended for five days for wearing a cap and dreadlocks in conformity with her Rastafarian conviction.[4] Sunali Pillay,

---

1 Professor, Department of Religious Studies, University of Cape Town, South Africa. This work is based on the research supported in part by the National Research Foundation of South Africa (Reference number (UID) 85397). The opinions, findings and conclusions or recommendations expressed are that of the author, and the NRF accepts no liability whatsoever in this regard.
2 Chidester D. 2006. "Religion Education and the Transformational State in South Africa", *Social Analysis: The International Journal of Cultural and Social Practice* 50(3): 61-83.
3 National Policy on Religion and Education (NPRE), 2003. Online at: http://www.gov.za/sites/www.gov.za/files/religion_0.pdf, para 59.
4 Roos R. 2003. "Physical Appearance of Learners in Public Schools – Antonie V Governing Body, Settlers High School 2002 4 Sa 738 (C)", *Tydskrif vir die Suid-Afrikaanse Reg* [Journal of South African Law] 4:792-796.

a Grade 11 learner at the Durban Girls High School, was suspended in 2005 for wearing a nose stud in conformity with Hindu practice.[5] In 2010, Lerato Motshabi was ordered to cut the dreadlocks on her head or face expulsion at Navalsig High School in Bloemfontein in the Free State.[6] In 2011, Odwa Sitayaya faced the same threat for wearing dreadlocks at Joe Slovo Engineering High School in the Western Cape.[7] In 2013, the Leseding Technical Secondary School in the Free State demanded that Lerato Radebe cut her dreadlocks before being admitted into class. In 2013 and 2014, two schools in Cape Town were forced to revise their uniform policy to accommodate learners wearing headscarves.[8] Three of these cases, all of them involving girls, were serious enough to be taken up by parents or by members of the Department of Education with the highest courts of the land.[9]

These controversies point to a significant articulation of the NPRE at schools. Looking closely at two of these controversies that have been taken up in South African courts since the promulgation of the NPRE, this essays examine how school administrators, parent bodies and the courts of the land have responded to these irregular and unfamiliar religious practices. The media reports, combined with the court records, show a general reluctance on the part of schools and parent bodies to promote or allow cultural and religious diversity in schools. Dress and uniform codes are rigidly monitored and justified, and indicate a bias against minority religious expressions and observances. But the record also shows justifications proposed to limit these religious observances, and counter-arguments offered by the judges. The justifications and judgments demonstrate a deliberation over learner religious observances on issues of conformity, freedom and religious diversity. This essay shows that while the value of religion education as prescribed by the NPRE is still under debate, the dress observances of some learners are extending its articulation as far as religious observances in concerned. They are dramatically showing religious diversity at schools.

THE NATIONAL POLICY ON RELIGION AND EDUCATION (NPRE) OF 2003

Academics are divided on the value of the NPRE. Most scholars in education and religious studies support the NPRE with regard to its educational vision,

---

5   2005. "Durban Teenager Fights School over Nose Stud." *Mail & Guardian*, 19 July.
6   Vena V. 2011. "Battle of the dreads rages on". *Mail & Guardian*, 15 September.
7   Vena, "Battle of the dreads rages on".
8   2013. "W Cape School Denies Muslim Siblings Entry for Wearing Head Dress", *Mail & Guardian*, 15 September.
9   *A v. Governing Body, The Settlers High School and Others* (3791/00) [2002] ZAWCHC 4 (8 February 2002); *MEC for Education: Kwazulu-Natal and Others v. Pillay* (CCT 51/06) [2007] ZACC 21; 2008 (1) SA 474 (CC); 2008 (2) BCLR 99 (CC) (5 October 2007); *Radebe and Others v. Principal of Leseding Technical School and Others* (1821/2013) [2013] ZAFSHC 111 (30 May 2013).

and they point to its value in introducing and exposing learners to the religious diversity of the country. A second group argues that the NPRE is potentially and actually unconstitutional. They say that it violates the constitutional guarantees for religious observances in schools, ignores the value of confessional education and takes away the right of parents to determine the religious education for their offspring. The learners' observances of religious dress and attire stand between the two positions. Their dress and attire are religious observances that the second group would support, but they are not formal educative expressions which the first group promotes. In the following review, I show how these observances have escaped the attention of scholars writing on the NPRE.

Since the early 1990s, South African religion scholar David Chidester has consistently promoted a new approach to religion education for South African schools emerging out of apartheid. Chidester was actively involved in the formulation of the new policy with Minister of Education Kader Asmal.[10] He made a clear distinction between religious instruction that was confessional and religion education that was comparative and educative. Chidester regarded religion education as a core component of citizenship education for the twenty-first century. It was directed at educating citizens on the diversity of religious beliefs and practices on both national and global levels.[11] Like the building and transformation of museums, parks and events that commemorated the past and projected a new future, religion education was similarly constituted to celebrate the South African nation.[12]

Working with school teachers over more than a decade, Cornelia Roux in theological studies and Rene Ferguson and Janet Jarvis in education, have shown how teachers can and have created spaces in schools where learners were exposed to the diversity of religions in their schools and in South Africa in general. With regard to religion education, they offer a positive prognosis for the implementation of the NPRE. They recognise the obstacles facing the implementation of the NPRE, but remain hopeful that teachers and learners can be enriched by dialogue, hermeneutical engagement and a sensitivity to diversity.[13]

---

10   Chidester D. 2002. "Religion Education in South Africa: Teaching and Learning About Religion, Religions, and Religious Diversity". *Oslo Coalition on Freedom of Religion and Belief*. Online at: http://folk.uio.no/leirvik/OsloCoalition/DavidChidester.htm
11   Chidester D. 2002. *Global Citizenship, Cultural Citizenship and World Religions in Religion Education*. Cape Town: HSRC.
12   Chidester D. 2008. "Unity in Diversity: Religion Education and Public Pedagogy in South Africa", *Numen* 55:272-299.
13   Roux C. 2010. "Religion and Human Rights Literacy as Prerequisite for Interreligious Education", in Engebretson K, De Souza M, Durka G and Gearon L (eds). *International Handbook of Inter-Religious Education, Part Two*. Dordrecht: Springer, 991-1015; Ferguson R. 2011. "Thinking about how Student Teachers Think about Religion, Religious Diversity, Knowledge and Meaning", in Ter Avest I (ed). *Contrasting Colours: European and African Perspectives on Education in a Context of Diversity*. Amsterdam: Gopher B.V. Publishers, 110-133; Jarvis J. 2013. "Paving the Way to Transformation: Student Teachers' Religious Identity and

Not all scholars agreed with the policy and its vision for South Africa. Educationists Albertina Ntho-Ntho and Jan Nieuwenhuis pointed to some of the obstacles facing the implementation of the NPRE in schools. Based on the research done by the former, they found school principals deeply committed to their own religious traditions and unable to deal with the diversity that they encountered in schools. Christianity for the most part remained a "moral compass" for principals, teachers and learners. Principals complained that they were not supported or prepared by the Department of Education to implement the new policy. Ntho-Ntho and Nieuwenhuis concluded that principals should be trained in mediation skills to deal with the demands made by a diverse body of learners.[14]

One of the first critical articles on the values of the NPRE was composed by constitutional law expert Rassie Malherbe in 2002. Malherbe commented on the document entitled "Manifesto on Values, Education and Democracy", published by Kader Asmal in 2001.[15] Malherbe focussed on the proposal made by Roman Catholic priest Albert Nolan in this document that religious observances for specific religious groups should only be performed outside school hours, and that a non-confessional religion education should become part of the school curriculum. Focusing mainly on the former point, Malherbe argued that religious observances at schools were an essential part of the freedom of religion guaranteed by the Constitution of the Republic of South Africa, 1996, in Sections 15(1) and 15(2):

> 15 Freedom of religion, belief and opinion
>
> (1) Everyone has the right to freedom of conscience, religion, thought, belief and opinion.
>
> (2) Religious observances may be conducted at state or state-aided institutions, provided that –
>
> (a) those observances follow rules made by the appropriate public authorities;
>
> (b) they are conducted on an equitable basis; and
>
> (c) attendance at them is free and voluntary.[16]

According to Malherbe, Section 15(1) was a declaration of the freedom of religion, while 15(2) was an elaboration of that freedom.[17] Religious observances

---

Religion Education", *Alternation: Interdisciplinary Journal for the Study of the Arts and Humanities in Southern Africa* (special issue), *Research in Religion and Education* 10:131-147.

14 Ntho-Ntho AM and Nieuwenhuis J. 2015. "Religion in Education Policy in South Africa: A Challenge of Change", *British Journal of Religious Education* 1-13.

15 Asmal K. 2001. "Manifesto on Values, Education and Democracy", *Ministry of Education, South Africa*. Online at: http://www.dhet.gov.za/Reports%20Doc%20Library/Manifesto%20on%20Values,%20Education%20and%20Democracy.pdf

16 Constitutions of the Republic of South Africa, 1996. Online at: http://www.gov.za/DOCUMENTS/CONSTITUTION/constitution-republic-south-africa-1996-1

17 Malherbe R. 2002. "The Constitutionality of Government Policy Relating to Conduct of Religious Observances in Public Schools", *Journal of South African Law* 3:398.

at state institutions were, thus, an essential manifestation of the freedom of religion. In Malherbe's view, no justification was provided by Nolan or the Manifesto for what Malherbe called a limitation of the freedom of religious practices. According to Malherbe, religious observances at schools should be equitable and voluntary, but they should not be taken out of the regular hours of the school. Malherbe also believed that the use of "equity" and not "equality" in the clause was significant. He saw no obligation on schools to support everyone's prayers.[18] Furthermore, Malherbe did not recognise the distinction between religion education and religious instruction that was made by Nolan in his presented, and adopted in the NPRE in 2003. Ignoring this distinction, he believed that religion education should be voluntary since it would potentially impose a perspective that was not shared by learners and their parents.[19]

The key points made by Malherbe in 2002 have been further elaborated and developed by others in their response to the NPRE. Raj Mestry, from the Department of Education at the University of Johannesburg, found the policy on religious observances "vague" and without "specific direction", and thus not binding.[20] Education expert Johannes L van der Walt and his fellow researchers reminded readers that the government had initially accepted that School Governing Bodies would be responsible for determining religious education policy at schools.[21] They believed that when Kader Asmal became the Minister of Education in 1999, he reneged on this promise by shifting the focus from the rights of parent to the inculcation of common values. Erika Serfontein, a professor of law, follows Malherbe's hint that the state may be using religion education for its own ends, observing that "neither the state nor schools are allowed to impose a set of multi-religious convictions on individual learners".[22] The NPRE, Serfontein maintains, promotes a set of common humanistic values in contravention of both the constitution and international law.[23] It spreads a "dull uniformity" rooted in secularism. Its approach to religion is not based on "religious views" but a general outlook that stresses a "comprehensive and fundamental orientation in the world."[24] Such values, Serfontein argues,

---

18 Malherbe, "The Constitutionality of Government Policy", 408.
19 Malherbe, "The Constitutionality of Government Policy", 405.
20 Mestry R. 2006. "The Constitutional Rights to Freedom of Religion in South African Primary Schools", *Australia & New Zealand Journal of Law & Education* 12(2):63-64.
21 Van der Walt J, Wolhuter CC and Potgieter FJ. 2009. "Sosiale Kapitaalskepping deur middel van Die Suid-Afrikaanse Beleid oor Godsdiens in Die Onderwys (2003): 'n Skriftuurlik-Prinsipiële Beoordeling" [Social Capital Creation By means of the South African Policy on Religion in The Education (2003): A Textual Principal Evaluation], *Tydskrif vir Christelike Wetenskap* [Journal for Christian Scholarship] 45(1/2):226; Department of Education, Republic of South Africa. 1995. "White Paper on Education and Training." Online at: http://www.education.gov.za/LinkClick.aspx?fileticket=855fT9w3A2U%3D&tabid=191&mid=484
22 Serfontein EM. 2014. "Education and Religion in South Africa: Policy Analysis and Assessment Against International Law", *Journal of Law and Criminal Justice* 2(1):129.
23 Serfontein, "Education and Religion in South Africa", 121-122.
24 Serfontein, "Education and Religion in South Africa", 127.

are harmful to learners: "a learner['s] human dignity is harmed when he/she is ignored or his/her religious heritage based on religious values is demeaned [sic] to common values."[25]

Serfontein's criticism of "dull" common values is matched by other critics of the NPRE who believe that the state should allow confessional education in schools. Van der Walt, Potgieter and Wolhuter claim that parents in many parts of the world have rejected a multicultural approach to religion education. They believe that values are learnt through deep immersion in a religious tradition, and do not see how the policy could prepare learners for church, and for social and civic engagement.[26] Moreover, in another publication in this debate, Van der Walt takes exception to the implicit definition of religion used in the NPRE. Here, he prefers Rudolf Otto's definition that stresses the numinous dimension of religion in contrast with the NPRE, which leaves out the experience of the holy.[27] In an earlier article with Stuart Fowler, Van der Walt favours dialogue that would mediate "different visions of the good society" in schools.[28] In this dialogue, Van der Walt wants to bring "universal" norms to the school "for social life that are grounded in the revelation of God in Christ."[29] Another commentator on the NPRE, canon law expert Pieter Coertzen, has argued that the new policy deprived religions to pursue education and freedom as envisaged by *them*. While supporting freedom for all religions in schools, Coertzen also justified some churches being "free to preach the Gospel, for the freedom of conscience to serve God according to his Word and for the guarantee that every anti-Christian power that would threaten the Church in the exercise of its holy ministrations will be resisted and prevented".[30] This freedom, exercised in the way framed, implies that religious observances should be permitted to oppose or proselytise others in schools.

Scholars who have emphasised the freedom of religious observances at schools say that the NPRE takes away this right. They insist that religious observances and practices, while voluntary, may not be limited or threatened by schools or government policy. Some go so far as to demand a freedom to demonstrate belief, to proselytise and to assert convictions. But in all their deliberations, they have not seriously considered the religious practices of those learners that do not come from a Christian background. They do not discuss the dominance

---

25 Serfontein, "Education and Religion in South Africa", 127.
26 Van der Walt JL, Potgieter FJ and Wolhuter CC. 2010. "The Road to Religious Tolerance in Education in South Africa (and Elsewhere): A Possible 'Martian Perspective", *Religion, State & Society* 38(1):29-52.
27 Van der Walt JL. 2011. "Understanding the Anatomy of Religion as Basis for Religion in Education", *HTS Theological Studies* 67(3):426-432.
28 Fowler S and Van der Walt JL. 2004. "Chaos and Order in Education", *South African Journal of Education* 24(1):68.
29 Fowler and Van der Walt, "Chaos and Order in Education", 68.
30 Coertzen P. 2002. "Freedom of Religion and Religious Education in a Pluralistic Society", *Nederduitse Gereformeerde Teologiese Tydskrif* [Dutch Reformed Theological Journal] 43(1/2):185-196.

of Christian religious symbols and practices that prevail at schools, and how these would or should be adjusted to the new Constitution and the NPRE. Their arguments are based on absolute constitutional values and principles, on Christian theology or on general educational theory.

Supporters of the NPRE have not addressed the place and nature of religious observances. In their enthusiasm for a new approach to teaching religion prescribed in the NPRE, they have not discussed the value and place of religious observances in assemblies, in schools and classrooms. The typical religion education approach assumes a position of learning *about* religions, and avoids a discussion of observances that assumes a confessional bearing.[31] They have so far ignored religious observances that are part of schools, and that the NPRE supports.

As far as the religious observances are concerned, the NPRE stands between its supporters and objectors. It did not follow the suggestions of Catholic theologian Nolan that religious observances should be limited to outside school hours. It unequivocally supports religious observances for learners, and for schools as a whole. It lists several ways in which these may be permitted, including school assemblies, and through learner religious associations in which teachers may be involved.[32] Moreover, while the policy promotes religion education, it does not completely reject the value of religious instruction. While it states that religious instruction is the "responsibility of the home, the family, and the religious community", it admits that "more needs to be done to strengthen this role [religious instruction]".[33] In line with this favourable view of religious education, it advises schools to "allow ... the use of their facilities" for programmes of religious instruction.[34] The NPRE, thus, does not reject the place of religious observances and the value of religious instruction, but favours religion education in the formal curriculum in an unequivocal way.

The religious practices of learners in the form of dreadlocks, nose studs and head coverings provides a unique vantage point to assess the articulation of the NPRE. Such practices are religious observances but they are not formal educational lessons. They deserve the attention of those who support and oppose the NPRE. It will now be shown that their effects in schools, parent body meetings and court judgments are far-reaching. Schools and parents deliberate on the value of religious observances, putting forward arguments and justifications against their manifestation. In contrast, court judgments show how to celebrate or accommodate diversity. The religious observances of learners show an articulation of the NPRE that deserves greater attention.

---

31 NPRE, para 22.
32 NPRE, para 58-59.
33 NPRE, para 55.
34 NPRE, para 60-62.

RELIGIOUS OBSERVANCES AT SCHOOLS

The court records provide an opportunity to look closely at how schools, parent bodies and judges respond to religious dress observances at schools. They include affidavits, justifications, and intermediary and final judgments. These provide information on the religious observances of the learners, and justifications and reasoning offered by schools, parents, parent bodies, and court judges. The first case concerns a girl prohibited from joining her class for wearing Rastafarian dreadlocks. And the second one concerns a girl suspended from school for insisting on wearing a nose stud.

The Lerato Radebe case: Rastafarian dreadlocks

Lerato Radebe was a 13-year-old girl admitted to Leseding Technical Secondary School. When she presented herself at school in 2013, she was not allowed to join class unless she cut her hair in conformity with the school's dress code. Some mornings, she would be forced to sit in the staff room throughout the day. Supported by the NGO Equal Education, Lerato's father raised the matter with the school, then with the local office of the Department of Education, and then eventually in the Free State High Court.

According to an affidavit presented in court, the school argued that Lerato's dreadlocks were merely a hairstyle and in conflict with the school's code. It also argued that Lerato could not be a Rastafarian, since she attended church where she took Holy Communion and had two siblings who did not wear dreadlocks. The school also contested the representation of Lerato's father, who insisted that she be allowed to wear dreadlocks as a right guaranteed by the Constitution of the Republic of South Africa, 1996. The school maintained that the grandmother raised Lerato and her siblings and also registered Lerato at the school. Unlike the father, who challenged the school, the grandmother seemed more willing to cut Lerato's hair. Apart from the religious justification offered against Lerato, the school in its affidavit also argued that the "machines and chemicals" used in classrooms posed a danger to Lerato's dreadlocks. The school claimed that it attempted to find an alternative school for Lerato, but it also admitted that no other schools in the vicinity would have permitted Lerato to keep her dreadlocks. At a general meeting called by the principal, parents allegedly supported the school's policy on Rastafarianism. At the meeting, parents were allegedly appalled at the consumption of cannabis in Rastafarianism and agreed that the school should not make special provision for dreadlocks. The affidavit of the school was also supported by the local office of the Department of Education.[35]

---

35 *Lerato Radebe, Lehlohonolo Radebe, Selloane Motloung, Equal Education vs. Principal of Leseding Technical School, Chairperson of the School Governing Body, Leseding Technical School, District Director, Lejweleputswa District, Head of Department, Basic Education, Free State, MEC For Education, Free State, Minister of Basic Education*, 2013, Case no. 1821, *Free State High Court*, Respondents' Brief Heads of Argument.

The matter was heard at the Free State High Court, where Judge Phalatsi ruled that the school should modify its school uniform code and accept learners like Lerato, who chose dreadlocks. The judge urged the school and the Department to deal with the evident discrimination at the school, since "religious intolerance could ruin the country." The judge feared for South Africa if it ignored what "religious intolerance can do … in our own African continent, as in Northern Mali and Northern Nigeria".[36] Media reports indicate that learners and parents were unhappy with this decision.[37]

The Sunali Pillay case: Hindu nose stud

Sunali Pillay at the Durban Girls High School decided to wear a nose stud when she turned fifteen. The school objected to this, as it conflicted with the school's dress code. Sunali's parents supported her choice and asked that the school protect her constitutional right.[38] The school consulted experts in education and in the Hindu tradition and were assured that the wearing of a nose stud was not a compulsory observance in Hinduism. At a disciplinary hearing held at the school, Sunali was ordered to conform to the dress code at the school. The parents took the matter to the Equality Court in Durban, which upheld the school's decision. The latter found that Sunali did not face *unfair* discrimination. The matter was then taken up at the High Court and then heard on appeal at the Constitutional Court. There the judges ruled that Sunali had a right to wear a nose stud as part of a cultural right and that the school should modify its dress code for the future.[39]

RELIGIOUS OBSERVANCES IN SOUTH AFRICAN SCHOOLS

The full court records, including the judgments and the affidavits provided by various parties, provide material for reflection on how these minority religious practices are perceived and received in schools. In this essay, such practices are compared with the religious observances that are permitted by the NPRE. Based on these two cases, the following discussion looks closely at schools and their general response to minority religious observances. From a religious studies perspective, it examines the analysis and recommendations made by

---

36 *Lerato Radebe and others vs. Principal of Leseding Technical School and others*, 2013, Judgment of the Court, 13 May 2013.
37 2013. "Leseding learners protest over Radebe's return to school." Online at: http://www.bloemfonteincourant.co.za/leseding-learners-protest-over-radebes-return-to-school
38 *MEC for Education (Kwazulu-Natal), Thulani Cele (School Liaison Officer), Anne Martin (Principal of Durban Girls' High School), Fiona Knight (Chairperson of the Governing Body of Durban Girls' High School) vs. Navaneethum Pillay with amici curiae Governing Body Foundation, Natal Tamil Vedic Society Trust, Freedom of Expression Institute*, 2007. Constitutional Court of South Africa, CCT51/06, para 131.
39 *MEC for Education (KZN) and others vs. Navaneethum Pillay and others*, 2007. Constitutional Court Judgment, CCT 51/06, 5 October.

the judges for religious and cultural practices. This closer reading of the cases shows how religious diversity is extended at schools, often against the initial wishes of schools and parent bodies. More generally, it shows how diversity that is promoted and supported by the NPRE is articulated through the bodies of learners on schools.

These two cases indicate that learners who adopt religious observances against school norms face censure at school. They confirm media reports that schools have not been very enthusiastic to celebrate the diversity of the country on the bodies of learners, in school uniforms and on school grounds. One of the justifications used for rejecting such practices is that they contradict school codes for uniforms. This was mentioned in both cases elaborated here, and turned down by the judges as insufficient justification to limit the right of learners to observe religious practices. It was also presented as an argument in an earlier case of dreadlocks worn by a learner in the Western Cape, heard by the High Court (Cape of Good Hope Division) in 2002. The school charged the learner of "serious misconduct." The judge in that case challenged the interpretation of the school code offered by the Governing Body of the school and the Head of the Western Cape Education Department. He reminded the respondents (the governing body of the school, the head of the Western Cape Education Department, and the Member of the Executive Council for Education in the Western Province) of the values of the new constitution that should be inscribed in schools.[40]

The idea of a uniform school code is deeply rooted in South Africa, and considered to be a normal part of schooling. Judges and legal scholars who have commented on these cases also assume the value of school uniforms, and recommend only modest departures from the codes.[41] In 2005, the Department of Education issued a set of guidelines on uniforms and expects schools to develop policies accordingly. The guidelines support the value of uniforms, while insisting that the diversity of South African schools be "accommodated."[42] The experience of the learners in these cases suggest that current uniform codes did not fully accept or celebrate the diversity displayed on the bodies on learners. At best, learner observances were expected to be accommodated or accepted under strict conditions. This "tolerant" approach must be contrasted with the value of diversity that is celebrated in the constitution and in the NPRE. Through their bodies, learners at school were disrupting uniform codes set and policed by the

---

40 A v. Governing Body, The Settlers High School and Others (3791/00) [2002] ZAWCHC 4 (8 February 2002). See para 8, 18, 19 on the charge of misconduct and para 14 and 15 on the values of the constitution.
41 Roos R. 2003. "Physical Appearance of Learners in Public Schools – Antonie V Governing Body, Settlers High School 2002 4 Sa 738 (C)", *Tydskrif vir die Suid-Afrikaanse Reg* [Journal of South African Law] 4:792-796; Lenta P. 2012. "Is There a Right to Religious Exemptions?" *The South African Law Journal* 129:303-329.
42 Department of Education, Republic of South Africa. 2005. "National Guidelines on School Uniform, 2005". Online at: http://www.education.gov.za/LinkClick.aspx?fileticket=y%2fNJsnhP8WQ%3d&tabid=333&mid=969

schools and governing bodies. They were not asking for tolerance, but asserting their rights. In a subtle way, the learners with new religious attire were also calling into question the value of school uniforms that are assumed to be the hallmark of good schooling in South Africa.

Learner religious observances stand in stark contrast to the religious ethos maintained by many schools in South Africa. Most South African public schools maintain Christian religious observances like prayer, hymns and Bible readings. Sometimes, other religious groups are invited to participate as well. But the doctoral dissertation of Ntho-Ntho has pointed to the continuing dominance of Christian symbols and practices in schools.[43] And this study is supported by a body of scholarship discussed above that argues for further invigouration of religious observances and confessional religious education. Considering this status quo and academic discussion, the schools' attitudes towards non-Christian observances manifested on the bodies of learners begs comment. The schools are not the bastions of secularism that reject religious observances, but rather characterised by a dominant religious ethos of schooling that continues from the past. The controversial practices of the learners thus suggest a struggle over the bodies of learners. Learners with dreadlocks, nose studs and headscarves are confronting prevailing religious observances in a dramatic way. They were using their bodies to observe minority religious practices in schools where mainly Christian religious observances were the norm.

Schools were not unaware of the NPRE, the constitution and their demands. A closer look at their responses shows a deliberation over these religious practices. Schools offered various forms of justifications to support their rejection of the controversial practices. These were often religious justifications that did not consider the convictions of the learners. Leseding Technical Secondary School put forward two arguments against Lerato's dreadlocks. It made a point on the danger posed to the learner due the "machines and chemicals" used in the school.[44] More significantly, it questioned the veracity of Lerato Radebe's commitment to Rastafarianism. The school questioned the quality of her religious belonging. It pointed out that she "partook of the Holy Communion" at a Roman Catholic church. It further pointed out that her siblings were not Rastafarians.[45] In a more general claim, Leseding Technical Secondary School referred to the public harm posed by Rastafarian religion and practices. In its affidavit to the Free State High Court, the school defended itself by saying that the dreadlocks worn by Lerato pointed to Rastafarianism which might not be a religion, or might be a harmful religion.[46] The affidavit of the school reveals a

---

43   Ntho-Ntho AM. 2013. *School Principals Mediating Change: The Case of Religion in Education*, PhD Diss, University of Pretoria.
44   *Lerato Radebe and others vs. Principal of Leseding Technical School and others*, 2013, Respondents' Brief Heads of Argument, para 3.12.
45   Opposing affidavit, *Radebe and Others v. Principal of Leseding Technical School and Others* (1821/2013) [2013] ZAFSHC 111 (30 May 2013), para 4.14 (d) and (e).
46   *Lerato Radebe and others vs. Principal of Leseding Technical School and others*, 2013, Respondents' Brief Heads of Argument, para 3.20.

desperate attempt to delegitimise dreadlocks. In Sunali's case, the Durban Girls High School also doubted the religious value of her decision and practice of a nose stud. It approached an authority in Hinduism who assured them that wearing a nose stud was not a *compulsory* (my emphasis) practice in Hinduism.[47] With this distinction between obligatory and non-obligatory practices, the schools determined a religious value for Sunali.

These justifications put forward by the schools border on theological deliberations. The Leseding case shows how the school was using its understanding of religion or Christianity, and imposing its consequences on Lerato. It could not believe that Lerato might be experimenting with a new religion, or that her new religion did not oppose taking Holy Communion. The communal and exclusive understanding of Christianity was used to delegitimise Lerato's faith in Rastafarianism. It was used as a justification to prohibit her from wearing her dreadlocks. The school in Durban also found a justification for prohibiting a nose stud. With the support of an authoritative voice in Hinduism, it created a division between compulsory and non-compulsory religious practices. Apparently, only the former would be allowed to stray from the uniform code of the school. In these two cases, schools and parent bodies are engaging in or using religious deliberations and justifications to judge religious practices observed by learners. Based on these arguments, they are limiting religious observances on the body of learners at their respective schools.

When the cases reached the courts of the country, these justifications and arguments were assessed and debated. The courts generally supported the learners, rejecting the justifications, religious or otherwise, put forward by the schools. They all emphasised the new values of South Africa that should guide uniform codes and school norms. In its judgment on the nose stud case of Sunali, the Constitutional Court went one step further. In contrast with the theological or religious deliberation of the schools, the court introduced a more "secular" way of approaching the matter at hand. In particular, it introduced a distinction between religion and culture into its deliberations on the practices brought by the learners to school. The judgment consisted of two opinions, a majority written by Justice Pius Langa and a minority by Justice Kate O'Regan. Both agreed that Sunali as unfairly treated at her school for wearing a nose stud, but they disagreed on how schools should address new religious practices adopted by learners. Their differences, based on a deliberation of the religion and cultural, are significant for the articulation of the NPRE in schools.

The judges introduced the distinction between religious and cultural practices that they felt ought to be considered by schools. They referred to anthropological literature that argued that cultures and religions were not so easily distinguished from each other.[48] Nevertheless, they provided a working

---

47 *MEC for Education: Kwazulu-Natal and Others v. Pillay* (CCT 51/06) [2007] ZACC 21; 2008 (1) SA 474 (CC); 2008 (2) BCLR 99 (CC) (5 October 2007), para 8.
48 *MEC for Education (KZN) and others vs. Navaneethum Pillay and others*, 2007. Judgment, para 54.

definition to help schools think about learners' religious practices on the basis of such distinction: "Without attempting to provide any form of definition, religion is ordinarily concerned with personal faith and belief, while culture generally relates to traditions and beliefs developed by a community."[49] It will be shown that Langa and O'Regan differed on the impact of the distinction between religion and culture.

In leading the majority opinion, Justice Langa saw no material impact of this distinction between religion and culture on the freedom afforded by the Constitution. He stressed that the freedom exercised by a learner to express a cultural practice was equally guaranteed by the Constitution. He stated that the freedom of practising a personal non-obligatory cultural practice was more important that an obligatory cultural practice: "Indeed, it seems to me that it may even be more vital to protect non-obligatory cultural practices ... To limit cultural protection to cultural obligations would, for many cultures and their members, make the protection largely meaningless."[50] Justice Langa was directly addressing the distinction introduced by the school to limit Sunali's right to wear a nose stud. Rejecting this justification, he directed attention to the dignity of all South Africans promoted by the Constitution and the Equality Act of 2000. More significantly, he used the subtle distinction between religion and culture to stress the protection afforded to individual cultural practices.

In the minority judgment, Justice O'Regan argued that the Constitution's clauses on religion implicitly accepted a difference between beliefs and cultural practices. The relevant clauses were absolute on convictions, but subject to deliberation on cultural practices.[51] Based on this distinction, the court may have to determine, O'Regan argued, if "the belief is sincerely held in order to decide whether a litigant has established that it falls within the scope of section 15 [protection of religious freedom]."[52] If the matter under consideration was a cultural practice, then it had to be determined if it was generally shared by a community. Justice O'Regan argued that the nose stud worn by Sunali was a culturally shared practice, and should be permitted by the school. Unlike Justice Langa, however, Justice O'Regan did not accept that a voluntary and personal cultural expression enjoyed the same protection of the Constitution and the Equality Act.[53]

Justices O'Regan and Langa offered different guidelines for religious practices at schools. Justice Langa focussed on how cultural practices, both shared and voluntary *personal* practices, were limited and curtailed in the past in schools.

---

49 *MEC for Education (KZN) and others vs. Navaneethum Pillay and others*, 2007. Judgment, para 47.
50 *MEC for Education (KZN) and others vs. Navaneethum Pillay and others*, 2007. Judgment, para 66.
51 *MEC for Education (KZN) and others vs. Navaneethum Pillay and others*, 2007. Judgment, para 141-143.
52 *MEC for Education (KZN) and others vs. Navaneethum Pillay and others*, 2007. Judgment, para 146.
53 *MEC for Education (KZN) and others vs. Navaneethum Pillay and others*, 2007. Judgment, para 157.

The new constitution supported diversity in schools, including its uniforms. Justice O'Regan was not less mindful of this context, but her opinion offered a different route for schools. Cultural practices were always shared, and could not be held individually in a "society of atomised communities.[54] In her judgment, schools should develop policies on how to deal with practices that did not conform to school uniform codes. Exemptions should be offered in a fair manner, and not impinge on the dignity of any learner. Schools may judge religious practices on the basis of a sincerity of belief, its shared provenance, and the degree of importance given to it by leaders within a cultural tradition.[55]

Justices Langa and O'Regan represented and offered two divergent visions for diversity in schools. Justice Langa offered a reading of the Constitution that supported and promoted diversity at a deep individual level, one that was not unjustifiably restricted or curtailed by schools and religious leaders. Justice O'Regan believed in the distinction between beliefs and cultural practices. Practices that were supported by beliefs were guaranteed. But individual cultural practices should be evaluated by schools and religious authorities. In her recommendation, singular cultural practices were not automatically guaranteed freedom of expression. The two opinions signify a struggle over cultural representations in schools – an exuberance on an an individual level, on the one hand, and a guarded resistance to new traditions, on the other.

Constitutional and jurisprudential theorist Patrick Lenta, who has commented on these cases from a liberal legal perspective, agrees with Justice O'Regan on practices that are adopted by individuals on the basis of religious convictions. Lenta does not see the value of protecting cultural practices in the same way as Justice Langa.[56] Legal theorist Iain Benson responded to Lenta's view, and returned to the issue that Justices Langa and O'Regan opened their judgment on the distinction between religion and culture. Like them, he believed that it was difficult to separate the religious from the cultural in learner practices.[57] It is important to note that Justice Langa's opinion introduced a subtle difference in the discussion of religion rights. His acceptance of the distinction is directed at the freedom of cultural practices guaranteed by the constitution. He does not dwell on the value of conviction on the part of the individual, or the religious or cultural tradition to which a practice belongs. He focusses on the freedom of the individual to adopt a cultural practice. Justice Langa's argument for supporting individual cultural practices was closely related to the particular historical context of South Africa, which the legal scholars tend to forget as

---

54 *MEC for Education (KZN) and others vs. Navaneethum Pillay and others*, 2007. Judgment, para 155.
55 *MEC for Education (KZN) and others vs. Navaneethum Pillay and others*, 2007. Judgment, para 157.
56 Lenta P. 2007. "Muslim Headscarves in the Workplace and in Schools", *The South African Law Journal* 124(2):296-319.
57 Benson IT. 2008. "The Case for Religious Inclusivism and the Judicial Recognition of Religious Associational Rights: A Response to Lenta", *Constitutional Court Review* 1:297-312.

they deliberate on religious rights. The discrimination faced by learners in the past in South Africa were not limited to religious conviction and practices, but also conceptions and practices of African culture.[58] Justice Langa's opinion on individual cultural practices addresses this legacy.

Justice Langa's opinion pointed to another important point that flow from these two cases. His judgment identified the individual agency of the learners in adopting a cultural practice: "Indeed, it seems to me that it may even be more vital to protect non-obligatory cultural practices ..." In the Leseding Technical Secondary School case, the records show that Lerato was not following her grandmother or her other siblings in the adoption of dreadlocks. Sunali adopted the nose stud without the knowledge or prior approval of her parents. They echo the literature on uniform dress codes, in general, that learners explore and experiment with their convictions and their practices. Uniforms, particularly their violations, provide an opportunity to express individuality and personality.[59] Religious observances of individual learners in South Africa pointed to their agency in articulating the NPRE and the Constitution.

CONCLUSION

Since the promulgation of the NPRE in 2003, a debate has been going on between those who see it as a harbinger of a new future on the teaching of religion in schools, and those who thought that it was unconstitutional for limiting religious observances at schools. This essay has shown that the NPRE, in fact, does not proscribe religious observances, even as it promotes a new approach to teach learners about religion. The debate among academics seems to have ignored the fact that the NPRE gives something to both groups. Given this challenge of religious observances in the policy and the academic debate surrounding it, this chapter has turned attention to the religious practices of learners that have been routinely rejected at schools. As religious observances, they provide a vantage point on how the NPRE has been articulated in schools. With a close reading of court documents in two cases, this chapter shows how learner religious practices were resisted, deliberated upon, and accommodated at the behest of the courts. It points to the disruption caused by these learner practices to uniform school codes, and to standard justifications against suspected religious traditions.

Schools and parent bodies resisted these practices by various kinds of religious and non-religious justifications. These justifications revealed prejudice against

---

[58] Leatt AMJ. 2011. *The State of Secularism: Constituting Religion and Tradition Towards a Post-Apartheid South Africa*, PhD Diss, University of the Witwatersrand, 86; Gordon RJ. 1991. "Serving the Volk with Volkekunde: On the Rise of South African Anthropology", in Jansen JD (ed). *Knowledge and Power in South Africa: Critical Perspectives Across the Disciplines*. Johannesburg: Skotaville, 79-97.

[59] Garot R and Katz J. 2003. "Provocative Looks: Gang Appearance and Dress Codes in an Inner-City Alternative School", *Ethnography* 4(3):421-454.

minority traditions, but also religious justifications imposed upon learners. When presented in courts, these prejudices and innovative justifications were turned down by judges. In the nose stud case, in particular, the judges introduced a distinction between religious convictions, shared practices and individual choices to address this and other religious and cultural practices. This more secular approach did not completely avoid the treacherous ground of religious beliefs, but provided an innovative way of navigating the diversity of South African schools. The majority led the way by emphasising the freedom to be enjoyed for individual cultural and religious practices. A minority opinion allowed schools, parents and religious authorities to control the experiments of freedom of learners. In general, their legal deliberation paved the way for greater diversity of religious practices in schools.

While it might too early to tell if these deliberations in schools and courts will create a more accommodating environment for learners to observe religious practices on their bodies, there is no doubt that these practices have pushed the limits of the articulation of the NPRE. Their practices have put the spotlight on existing religious observances in schools. They have revealed religious and non-religious arguments at schools, and among parents. And they have pointed to new legal distinctions to pave the way for the celebration of cultural and religious diversity at schools. In an unexpected way, the learner practices may be more educative on diversity than many a school lesson on religion or religious education.

V. Heritage of Land, Water and Great Zimbabwe

12 RASTAFARI PERSPECTIVES ON LAND USE AND MANAGEMENT IN POSTCOLONIAL ZIMBABWE

Fortune Sibanda[1]

INTRODUCTION

Globally, the land question remains paradoxical as it is heavily steeped in racial, gender, class, ethnic, regional, national and international controversies. In Southern Africa, Zimbabwe provides a typical example of how the land question forms a crucial part of a people's history since all the three Chimurenga wars[2] were the result of issues pertaining to land.[3] Indeed, land is regarded as the mainstay of the country's economy. In contemporary parlance of ZANU-PF, "the economy is land and land is the economy".[4] In recent years, Zimbabwe embarked on the controversial Land Reform Programme (LRP) that was championed by the government as a way of reclaiming a lost heritage and empowering the black majority. The LRP, which placed Zimbabwe under the spotlight, is arguably justified as part of the government's call to "indigenise, empower, develop and create employment" for the benefit of the entire nation.[5] Nevertheless, close to two decades after the commencement of the Third Chimurenga in 2000,[6] the land question remains a contested part of the Zimbabwean heritage with regard to the issue's ownership, use and

---

1 Fortune Sibanda holds a Doctorate in Religious Studies from the University of Zimbabwe. He lectures in the Department of Philosophy and Religious Studies, Great Zimbabwe University, Masvingo.
2 *Chimurenga* is a Shona term which means a war of liberation. The First Chimurenga lasted from 1896 to 1897; the Second Chimurenga war from 1965 to 1979; and the Third Chimurenga was characterised by land invasions that commenced in 2000 and culminated in the Land Reform Programme.
3 See, for example, Sibanda F and Maposa R. 2014. "Beyond the Third *Chimurenga*?: Theological Reflections on the Land Reform Programme in Zimbabwe", *The Journal of Pan African Studies* 6(8), March:54-74. The phrase "Beyond the Third Chimurenga", which is part of the title, refers to the period following the government command to discontinue with illegal land invasions.
4 Team ZANU-PF. 2013. *The People's Manifesto 2013: Taking Back the Economy – Indigenise, Empower, Develop & Create Employment*. Harare: ZANU-PF, 31. See also Mugabe RG. 2001. *Inside the Third Chimurenga: Our Land is Our Prosperity*. Harare: Department of Information & Publicity, Office of the President and Cabinet.
5 See, for example, Team ZANU-PF. 2013. *The People's Manifesto 2013*; Chirenje G. 2015. "Indigenise, Empower and Develop!", *News Day*, 4 August. In essence, the Land Reform Programme was meant to rationalise land ownership between the white minorities who formed 0.6 percent of the population, yet still possessed over 70 percent of the fertile land, to the detriment of the black majority. See also Dube Musa W. 2015. "*A Luta Continua*: Toward Trickster Intellectuals and Communities", *Journal of Biblical Literature* 134(4):890-902, (894).
6 The Third *Chimurenga* started in February 2000 when a communal initiative of the people under leadership of Chief Enock Zenda of Svosve in Mashonaland East

management. Apparently, during the so-called *jambanja* phase,[7] a high degree of euphoria associated with land redistribution to the dispossessed black majority manifested, resulting in reckless cutting of trees and incidents of veld fires with impunity by *varimi vatsva* (the new indigenous farmers) that destroyed natural resources on former white-owned farms. Therefore, the debates on land use and management have attracted the attention of different players, such as agricultural scientists, economists, social and political scientists, literary artists and feminists. This study seeks to contribute to the existing discourse in religious studies on the land issue by focusing on Rastafari.[8]

Specifically, this chapter examines the perspectives of Nyahbinghi Rastafari communities on land use and management in postcolonial Zimbabwe. Rastas in Zimbabwe are an often forgotten and misunderstood Pan-African New Religious Movement, which, nevertheless, is a cardinal player in the land issue on the basis of their contribution to the country's political liberation. Rastas are sometimes located at the margins and have had to grapple with some negative stereotypes in society.[9] However, a lot can be gleaned from the "Rastafari green philosophy"[10] that encompasses the principle of Ital livity[11] to the backdrop of

---

Province forced the government to embark on a revolutionary land resettlement programme that resulted in the LRP.

7   *Jambanja* phase refers to the period when there were haphazard and unpredictable incidents of land seizure from white commercial farmers during the Third Chimurenga, or *hondo yeminda* (war for the land) as it was also known.

8   Etymologically, the term 'Rastafari' is derived from the combination of Amharic words *Ras* (prince, duke, lord) and *Tafari*. In its original use, "Ras Tafari" was the name of His Imperial Majesty (H.I.M.) Emperor Haile Selassie I, who was born as Lidj Tafari Makonen in 1892 and crowned Emperor of Ethiopia on 2 November 1930. In general, Rastafari is the name of the movement and at the same time it is the name of the followers of the movement itself. The adherents deify Emperor Haile Selassie I (referred to as Jah Rastafari) and the religion as well as followers is named after H.I.M. The study uses the term Rastafari to refer to both the religion and those who practise it, notwithstanding that the practitioners are also identified as "Rastafarians" and the short form, "Rastas". See, for example, Salter R. 2008. "Rastafari in a Global Context: Affinities of 'Orthognosy' and 'Oneness' in the Expanding World", *IDEAZ* 7. Special Issue on "The Globalization of Rastafari", 10-27.

9   In most societies, Rastafari are one of the most misunderstood groups and people tend to be sceptical of Rastas. They are sometimes described as "dagga-smokers" (marijuana smokers) and good-for-nothings. See, for example, Sibanda F. 2015. "'Legalise It!': Re-thinking Rastafari-State Relations in Postcolonial Zimbabwe", in Coertzen P, Green MC and Hansen L(eds). *Law and Religion in Africa: The Quest for the Common Good in Pluralistic Societies*. Stellenbosch: African Sun Media, 185-205. See also Salter, "Rastafari in a Global Context", 10.

10 Sibanda F. 2015. "Rastafari Green Philosophy for Sustainable Development in Postcolonial Zimbabwe: Harnessing Eco-theology and Eco-justice", in Chimhanda FH, Molobi VMS and Mothoagae ID (eds). *African Theological Reflections: Critical Voices on Liberation, Leadership, Gender and Eco-Justice*. Pretoria: Research Institute for Theology and Religion, UNISA, 187-206.

11 "Ital" or "I-tal" comes from the words "vital" or "total". It is employed when referring to food, meals, environment, social atmosphere, or way of living that is wholesome, organic, lively and hence nourishing and healthy. "Livity" refers

climate change and the widespread use of chemical fertilisers by beneficiaries of the LRP in Zimbabwe. The chapter argues that organic, conservative farming and natural living, which Rastafari advocate, are vital in protecting the productivity and cleanliness of the land heritage for present and future land users in Zimbabwe. In other words, land justice has become an urgent agenda for action, not merely in terms of its ownership, but also in its sustainable use and management.

THEORETICAL FRAMEWORK AND METHODOLOGY OF STUDY

This study benefited from the insights of the Afrocentric theory. This African-centred theory, also known as Afrocentricity, is associated with Pan Africanist scholars, such as Molefi Kete Asante, who advocated and popularised the Afrocentric genre. In essence, Afrocentricity is a response to the derogatory Western scholarship on Africa, Africans and their cultural heritage. The broader intellectual aim of Afrocentricity is to challenge and deconstruct Eurocentric denial and misrepresentation of African history and culture.[12] It is believed that Western writers and colonialists conveyed a pessimistic perspective on African culture, religion and heritage. African heritage, culture and religion were often misunderstood, misrepresented, distorted and displaced.[13] This created a philosophy of the centre and the periphery which placed Western culture at the centre whilst African culture and heritage were assigned to the margins.[14] This demanded a deconstruction process to be applied in the reclamation of African culture, African heritage, African philosophy, African history, African indigenous religion as well as African land. Along these lines, Asante says Afrocentricity calls for "collective consciousness" among African people, where "all African phenomena, activities and ways of life to be looked at and given meaning from the standpoint and worldview of Africans."[15] Therefore, with Rastafari being Afrocentric in orientation, the Afrocentric theory is ideal for exploring Rastafari perspectives on land use and management. This is because Afrocentricity "stands as both a corrective and a critique"[16] to the attitudes and

---

to one's quality of life, or livelihood that a person or other living things possess. Thus, "Ital livity" is a natural lifestyle that encompasses organic farming, food and diet. See Dickerson MG. 2004. I-tal *Foodways: Nourishing Rastafarian Bodies*, MA Thesis, Department of Geography and Anthropology, Louisiana State University & Agricultural and Mechanical College, 156. Online at: http://etd.Isu.edu/docs/available/etd-06022004-174954/unrestricted/Dickerson_thesis.pdf

12 Adeleke T. 2009. *The Case against Afrocentrism*, Jackson: University Press of Mississippi, 10.
13 See Mndende N. 1999. "From Racial Oppression to Religious Oppression", in Walsh TG and Kaufmann F (eds). *Religious and Social Transformation in Southern Africa*. Minnesota: Paragon House.
14 Sibanda F. 2011. *African Blitzkrieg in Zimbabwe: Phenomenological Reflections on Shona Beliefs on Lightning*. Saarbrucken: LAP, 2.
15 Asante MK. 2007. *An Afrocentric Manifesto: Toward an African Renaissance*. Malden: Polity.
16 Asante, *An Afrocentric Manifesto*, 27.

actions of past and present generations with regards to the land question in Zimbabwe. The corrective element targets the distortions of land distribution and use in the colonial and postcolonial times in Zimbabwe given that Rastafari is interested in ensuring land justice. As a critique, the Afrocentric theory sensitises beneficiaries of the land redistribution to use and manage natural resources in a sustainable way.

This study utilised a poly-methodic approach. In order to collect data, the study used in-depth interviews conducted with information-rich Nyahbinghi Rastafari members, who were purposively sampled from the Marcus Garvey Nyahbinghi Rastafari House in Epworth, Chaminuka Nyahbinghi Rastafari House in Chitungwiza, Marondera Nyahbinghi Rastafari House in Marondera and Dzimbadzemabwe Nyahbinghi Rastafari House in Glen Norah. Participant observation was also used as a data collecting technique. The latter was useful in two ways: On one hand, the researcher was exposed to some homestead gardens and patchy maize field portions cultivated under the urban agricultural land use from open spaces of municipal land. On the other hand, the researcher participated in so-called Rastafari Reasonings where the subject of land was discussed. The study also benefited from a documentary analysis of the print and electronic media of newspapers and television captions as well as from Nyahbinghi Rastafari archival documents that included photographs, brochures and songs.

The study also benefited from the insights of a corroboration of the historical, sociological and phenomenological approaches to describe and interpret data. The historical method involves hermeneutics and has a complementary relation with the phenomenology of religion on the basis of anti-reductionism that promotes the insider perspective. The historical approach was ideal for the study in tracing the history of the land question and bringing out the way Rastafari communities understand the issue in Zimbabwe. The study tapped into phenomenological principles such as *epoche* (bracketing out), descriptive accuracy, eidetic intuition (establishing the meaning) and comparison. Although the sociological method is often accused of reductionism in the study of religion, the research found it useful in as much as the sociological themes in relation to religion enhanced understanding of the dynamics of the land question in Zimbabwe on the basis of class, gender, creed and political affiliation. On the whole, a Rastafari hermeneutics was useful in offering a critique on land ownership, use and management in Zimbabwe.

HISTORICAL BACKGROUND OF RASTAFARI IN ZIMBABWE

Rastafari, a religio-political movement of Jamaican origin, has a fairly long history of existence. It is regarded as a Pan-Africanist and Ethiopianist movement that arose among oppressed, marginalised black former slaves in Jamaica, influenced by the ideas of people such as the Jamaican-born philosopher and Pan-Africanist, Marcus Garvey.[17] Today, Rastafari has grown and spread to become a global phenomenon partly through the contribution of the reggae icon, Bob Marley. Rastafari is one of the religions in Zimbabwe whose emergence may precede the independence of the country in 1980, but whose membership and popularity was arguably accelerated with the coming of the Rastafari revolutionary reggae doyen, Bob Marley, to perform on independence eve.[18] Through Bob Marley's music, Rastafari registered its partnership with Pan-African liberation revolutionary movements, including those of Zimbabwe. Rastafari is characterised by diversity between and among the Nyahbinghi, the Bobo Ashanti and the Twelve Tribes of Israel[19] in both Jamaica and Zimbabwe. Nyahbinghi, which is at the centre of this chapter, is one of the major strands of the Rastafari movement in Zimbabwe that has several branches (houses) mainly in the major cities and towns. This makes it largely an urban phenomenon. The Nyahbinghi Rastafari houses that forms the focus of this study are based in Harare, namely, Marcus Garvey Nyahbinghi Rastafari House in Epworth, Chaminuka Nyahbinghi Rastafari House in Chitungwiza, Marondera Nyahbinghi Rastafari House in Marondera and Dzimbadzemabwe Nyahbinghi Rastafari House in Glen Norah. Among these houses, the Rastas are diverse in their orientation with some being so-called reggae Rastas, environmentalist Rastas and Rasta Italists. All these categories are linked to the Rastafari concern land justice in terms of ownership, use and management.

RASTAFARI THEOLOGY OF LAND

A Rastafari theology of land cannot be isolated from historical experiences such as the African holocaust perpetuated by the transatlantic slave trade, colonial rule and postcolonial contradictions, which were pivotal to Rastafari origins and ideological orientation. Rastafari, as a religio-political Pan-African movement, was also influenced by the ideas of Pan-Africanists such as Marcus Garvey's "back to Africa" call and prophecies about a black king and redeemer for black people. Following Garvey, the crowning of Haile Selassie as Emperor of Ethiopia on 2 November 1930 was regarded as a *kairos* moment for African liberation. Essentially, Marcus Garvey influenced the Rastafari African theology of liberation that made race consciousness and land justice central in the God-talk of Africans in the diaspora.[20] Through Rastafari, an African liberation theology anchored on African identity and land justice was formulated.

---

17 See, for example, Sibanda F. 2012. "The Impact of Rastafari Ecological Ethic in Zimbabwe: A Comparative Discourse", *The Journal of Pan African Studies* 5(3), June:59-76.
18 Sibanda, "Legalise It!".
19 Middleton DJN. 2015. *Rastafari and the Arts: An Introduction*. New York and London: Routledge, 2.
20 Hewitt R. 2016. "Stealing Land in the Name of Religion: A Rastafari Religio-Political Critique of Land Theft by Global Imperial Forces", *HTS* 72(1):a3347. Online at: http://dx.doi.org/10.4102/htsv72i1.3347

In Rastafari philosophy, Ethiopia, Africa, Babylon, Zion and Jamaica are symbols that do not only refer to geographical and physical location but also to markers of ideological and psychological identity formation.[21] Ethiopia and Africa are interchangeable in Rastafari worldview and they are sometimes referred to as "home", "the promised land" and "Zion", whilst Jamaica and Babylon signify places of oppression. The embrace of African land as Zion is the first step in any Rastafari theological reflection. As Roderick Hewitt, theology and ethics scholar, writes, "Rastafari's embracement of Ethiopia as the tangible expression for all of Africa is linked to a biblical reference about Ethiopia, the coronation of Haile Selassie as Emperor of Ethiopia and Garvey's teaching about the centrality of Ethiopia and Africa in the liberation of black people."[22] The above shows how Rastafari theology of land cannot be understood outside Africa and Ethiopia, in particular. The fact that Ethiopia remained uncolonised made it an ideal symbol for African independence and sovereignty. Therefore, the iconic red, gold and green colours of the Ethiopian Lion of Judah flag became a Rastafari emblem, as a way of identifying with Africa and its values. Along the same lines, repatriation of some Africans in the diaspora can also be conceived on this basis.

In the context of land justice, Rastas believe that land constitutes a fundamental resource which forms the identity of a people and the need to deconstruct the historical error on land dispossession by imperial forces. The importance of land is succinctly captured by the Zimbabwean historian, Henry Moyana, when he argues that land is vital for the dead, the living and the unborn.[23] In Zimbabwe, the colonial state alienated land through legislation forcing Africans to leave their historical ancestral lands and thereby propelling the emergence of three Chimurenga wars of liberation. The global Rastafari theology on land dovetails with the next section on land ownership, use and management among Rastas in Zimbabwe.

LAND OWNERSHIP, USE AND MANAGEMENT IN THE PRISM OF RASTAFARI

The issues surrounding land ownership, use and management are very critical in Rastafari. This is because Rastafarians have a high regard for a natural livity or Ital livity, which can be understood from their perspectives on natural land use and diet. Rastas need land to produce Ital food commensurate with their vegetarian diet and gregariousness with nature. Erin David, a Rastafari researcher, puts it succinctly, thus: "In practice, living naturally means producing one's own food, eating an Ital diet and, respecting the sacredness

---

21 Hewitt, "Stealing Land in the Name of Religion".
22 Hewitt, "Stealing Land in the Name of Religion".
23 Moyana HV 2002. *The Political Economy of Land Question in Zimbabwe*. Gweru: Mambo.

of the Earth by refusing to use it commercially or to sell it for profit."[24] The following subsections explore the different elements of Rastafari perspectives and experiences, namely, land ownership, land use and land management.

Land ownership

In Zimbabwe, land ownership is a complex phenomenon, but it is closely linked to official recognition and registration, which has affected the Rastafari movement whenever they wanted to acquire property, benefit from land allocation or publicly gather as an organisation. Therefore, it has to be asked: Can Rastas acquire and own land in Zimbabwe? In an interview, one Rasta elder had this to say:

> In Zimbabwe, President Mugabe said that there is need for communal land for Rastas. However, he stressed that Rastas must first get organised before they are allocated land. [Yet] some Rastas say that we do not want to register because it will be dealing with Babylon. This shows that some have not yet come to terms with the reality that we are not in a foreign nation. Rastas see government as being there to administer on behalf of the people. It is not government but the people running it democratically. Eurocentricity is dividing people through church-state relations which is still strong where State is separate from Church rather than having State and Church working together in unity. Rastafari Churchical Order uses a Theocratic Reign …[25]

A number of issues can be identified in the above narrative on Rastafari land ownership in Zimbabwe. The millenarian tendencies of some Rastafari members are evident from the above where the government leaders operate as politicians who cannot be trusted and thereby being dismissed as "Babylon".[26] At the same time, some put trust in the government showing a shift from a position of isolation and non-involvement to one of political engagement through *routinisation*.[27] Such Rastafari adaptation to contemporary realities is reminiscent of Bob Marley's advice through reggae music for the suffering and oppressed people to "Get up, Stand up! Stand up for your rights! [and

---

24   David E. 1998. "Nature in Rastafari Consciousness". Online at: https://debate.uvm.edu/dreadlibrary/david.html
25   Interview with a Rasta Elder, Harare, 30 December 2012.
26   "Babylon" generally refers to Western hegemony, but also to any system of oppression, both by whites or blacks. Politicians are not always trustworthy and they are often regarded as full of tricks – "polytricks". Edmonds EB et al. (1998. "Dread 'I' In-A-Babylon", in Murrell NS, Spencer WD and McFarlane AA (eds). *Chanting Down Babylon: The Rastafari Reader*. USA: Temple University Press, 24-33) defines "Babylon" as "… that worldly state of affairs in which the struggle for power and possessions takes precedence over the cultivation of human freedom and concern for human dignity", p. 24. For Roderick Hewitt ("Stealing Land in the Name of Religion"), Babylon is life-denying and de-humanising. This is useful in understanding Rastafari views on land ownership in Zimbabwe.
27   Barnett 2012:292 cited in Hewitt, "Stealing Land in the Name of Religion".

never to] give up the fight!"²⁸ Indeed, in recent years, the Nyahbinghi Rastafari got registered by way of a notarial deed of trust, as the Nyahbinghi National Council in Zimbabwe.

The urgent need for land among Rastas has been summed up by the Zimbabwean roots reggae artist and Rastafarian elder, Man Soul Jah in one of his songs on the album *Time*, which featured the popular track, "Mr Government Man".²⁹ In the song, Man Soul Jah chanted in part: "Mr Government Man … Give me the land." "Mr Government Man" was released in 2000 and meant to express the landless people's demand for land as a right and source of livelihood and identity in Zimbabwe. Although this song received generous airtime on the local radio stations, and coming from a reggae artist being an avenue for spreading "Jah message to all humankind", the song resulted in him being ostracised for supporting the country's land reform programme.³⁰ Although the majority of Nyahbinghi Rastas do not own land "beyond the Third Chimurenga", they support the motive behind the Land Reform Programme in Zimbabwe. In the eyes of many Rasta participants, the land reform programme characterised by *jambanja* (land invasion) was a justified struggle to reassert black indigenisation, empowerment, identity and independence.

In support of the LRP in Zimbabwe, one Rasta elder had this to say: "The white settlers took the land by force from our Ancients (elders) in the Ancient of Days. There is nothing wrong in taking back that land in the same way because it is rightfully ours. It's high time that we emancipate ourselves from mental slavery and indigenise through Rastafari."³¹ Similarly, another elder said that the land reform is about reclaiming sovereignty lost to white colonialists and as well as black oppressors – the land barons who own multiple farms. On the basis of multiple farm ownership by the few fellow black elites, Rastas pronounce judgment and a message of denunciation to these contemporary oppressors – sometimes through reggae music or as the subject for dialogue at *binghi*³² (reasoning sessions held in different Rastafari houses every Sabbath).³³

---

28 Bob Marley, 1973. "Get Up, Stand Up", *Burnin*. Bob Marley and the Wailers.
29 Man Soul Jah was born as Joseph Tatenda Nhara. He is a station manager for the Zimbabwe Broadcasting Corporation's Voice of Zimbabwe Radio Station in Gweru.
30 Chakanyuka T. 2014. "Man Soul Jah, Prophet without Honour in His Town", *Gweru Today*, 16 January. Online at: https://www.facebook.com/nhasimugweru/posts/733813733296809
31 Interview with a Rasta Elder, Masvingo, 20 February 2014.
32 *Binghi* refers to the ceremonial gatherings of Rastas at different shrine sites where they participate in ritual activities which they believe facilitate communion and spiritual healing. The *binghis* usually last for more than a day and are sometimes held to commemorate special days on the Rastafari calendar. There is also another sense in which *binghi* refers to the sacred space on which the shrine is located. Among other activities, Rastas engage in "reasoning", in which they participate in intense discussion to inspire and enlighten one another through dialogue.
33 The researcher was part of some of the dialogues held during *binghi* sessions on the subject of land. Rastas are forced to choose where they stand in this struggle

Along the same lines, Ras John of Marcus Garvey House remarks that,

> [l]and reform was good because it fulfils the views of Marcus Garvey that Africa is for the Africans both at home and abroad. Land is a basis of people's identity. Bloodshed is bad, but this was a justified war for the black majority. As far as I know, Rastas did not take part in *jambanja* physically but they supported the struggle heartically and spiritually through word, sound and power. Land is good because we need land for businesses, organic farming for *ital* food, building houses, tabernacles and setting up a Rasta community. Rastas condemn the corruption of multiple farm ownership and wish for equitable land distribution and full utilising the land. Rastas are into indigenisation but are not benefitting because of party politics. We also condemn reckless cutting down of trees by some newly settled farmers.[34]

Rastas call for economic emancipation, indigenisation and sustainable development partly through land ownership and farming as one critical area they see as vital for livelihood. The narrative of Ras John's also shows that most Rastas have not been among the beneficiaries of the land redistribution programme, partly because of politics. Given that the LRP was mainly spearheaded by ZANU-PF, it follows that Rastas who were non-partisan will not find it easy to get land, notwithstanding their pro-indigenisation ideology. In addition, some of the observations of Ras John concerning the abuse of natural resources through the wanton cutting down of trees by some newly settled farmers will be revisited under the subsections on land use and management.

Land use

As has been hinted above, Rastafari perspectives on land use are guided by the Rastafari green philosophy and ecological ethic centred on beliefs and practices that are in harmony with nature. Even as observed at their *binghis*, Rastas want to be as close to nature as much as possible demonstrated when they "sit in the dust" to show their love to Mother Earth.[35] Essentially, "Rastafari is endowed with visions that advocate 'green' theologies as contextual responses to neo-colonialism and the hypocritical western practices driven by greed."[36] Therefore, Rastafari land use upholds the entire earth as an ecosystem that must be kept in balance through stewardship for the plants; animals and humans are constituent parts of the cycle. Building on what Rastas say Emperor Haile Selassie once said about planting a million trees yearly,[37] they are in the habit of

---

between Good and Evil, Zion and Babylon. This is how they encourage one another to build livity or quality life.
34 Interview with Ras John, Marcus Garvey Rastafari House, Harare, 30 May 2014. The term "heartically" is part of Rasta diction to mean "by heart" or "heartily".
35 See, for example, David E. 1998. "Nature in Rastafari Consciousness". Online at: https://debate.uvm.edu/dreadlibrary/david.html
36 Sibanda, "Rastafari Green Philosophy", 187.
37 Sibanda, "Rastafari Green Philosophy", 196.

planting trees, which boils down to the sustainable use of land. In addition, Ibo Foroma, a Rastafarian adherent and writer, quoted Emperor Haile Selassie I's command to Rastas towards taking immediate action against deforestation in Ethiopia as far back as 1958. I quote Selassie's instructions at length as captured by Foroma, thus:

> It is a matter of great concern for us that the forest wealth which God in His mercy has bestowed upon our country is thus being continually reduced and wasted. Hence it becomes the duty and obligation of every single Ethiopian to become aware of the tremendous industrial and agricultural advantages to be derived from our forest resources, and to practise tree-planting, in order that our hills and planes which have been stripped of their wooded cover may once again be clothed in their green mantle … The existence or non-existence of forest wealth in a country is one of the most important factors influencing its development and progress … The increasing pace of de-forestation and the growing dearth of timber in Ethiopia, caused by unregulated tree-cutting and the failure to replace these by new plantings, give us occasion for anxiety that a severe economic problem will confront the coming generation. It is essential that steps be taken here and now to stop this wastage and to check this destruction … In these days when all nations of the world, in recognition of the tremendous importance of forest wealth, have launched intensive programmes for forest conservation and re-forestation, it behoves our country also to take the appropriate measures to solve this problem. It is our wish and our desire that each and every citizen of our country follow the example we set on this Arbour Day in planting this tree, and himself plant as many trees as he can, for his own benefit as well as for the benefit of future generations.[38]

The above quote illustrates the dangers of destroying forests to the planet and humanity at large. Selassie's warning is cogent since trees are the backbone of life on earth. Some Rastas in Zimbabwe, such as Ras John, have taken the wise words of His Imperial Majesty into action by advocating reforestation in Epworth and the country as a whole. Sizzla Kalonji, a Jamaican Reggae artist who once expressed interest to repatriate to Zimbabwe, was spot on when in his song, "The Planet is in Peril", describes how human activity is destroying the environment, flora and fauna, in the name of "development".[39] This provides many lessons for Rastas in Zimbabwe, who are on record for criticising the cutting down of trees by, among others, newly settled farmers. The key message is that planting trees will save the planet, not the other way round.

The Rastafari thrust toward sustainable land use is behind its practising of organic farming that is a source of Ital food for their vegetarian diet and

---

38 Foroma I. 2016. "Save the Planet: Plant Trees", *The Sunday Mail*, 27 November. Online at: http://www.sundaymail.co.zw/save-the-planet-plant-trees/
39 Foroma, "Save the Planet: Plant Trees".

self-reliance. In a brochure at Chaminuka Rastafari House, the following was noted in relation to Rastas:

> We also call for the economic emancipation of the [black] race and support indigenisation. We believe in self reliance, self sustainance, [sic] self awareness … most of us are blessed with different skills. We also very much support Agriculture since we are vegetarians and we need organic farming to keep our temples [bodies] clean … Agriculture has always constituted the fundamental source of wealth for the human race. Agriculture is the bloodstream of industries.[40]

The above citation shows that Rastas practice conservative and organic farming that enhances their vegetarian diet. According to Rastafari philosophy for sustainable livelihood, artificial land use pollutes and poisons the soil, water and air through chemicals and fertilisers, to the extent that both land and people are impoverished. Some Rastafarians note that in their small house-yard gardens they are practising organic farming where they grow vegetables and herbs of different kinds which are food-medicines.

On basis of the above, given that the majority of Rastas do not own farms, they are part of urban communities that are utilising house-yard gardens for growing herbal plants for their families. In this regard, some Rastas have developed the interest in growing herbs and acquiring skills in herbal therapy, thereby operating as Rastafari herbalists.[41] Using limited space, the herbs commonly grown in Rasta herbal gardens include, among others, *zumbani* (*lippia javinica*, or lemon bush), *gavakava* (aloe), *tsangamidzi* (*zingiber officinale*, or ginger), *mowa* (*amaranthus hybridus*, amaranth or pigweed), *guku/tsine* (*bidens pilosa*, or blackjack), garlic (*allium sativum*), lemon grass (*cymbopogon citrates*), *minthi* (*menthe spp.* or mint), moringa (*moringa olifera*), chilli/*mhiripiri* (*capsicum annum*), onion (*allumfistulosum*), *gwavha* (*psidium guajava* or guava), Mexican marigold (*tagetesminuta*), *mupopo* (*carica papaya* or pawpaw).[42] Some

---

40 *Chaminuka Rastafari House Brochure*. No date. Harare. Rastas see agriculture as a cog-wheel of industry. For instance, horticulture sector production, fruit industry and vegetable production, and flower production could be used for producing Ital food-medicines and other products in order create employment and feed the nation at a time when the country is importing from neighbouring countries such as South Africa. Thus, Zimbabwe needs to improve yields and establish a platform for food security. This Rastafari position is in tandem with that expressed by Nyangore FS. 2016. "We don't need billions to fix agriculture", *The Sunday Mail*, 21 February, Extra:5. According to Nyangore, Zimbabwe is an agrarian economy with a lot of potential if effectively used and managed.

41 Herbs are any useful plants which can be used in cooking, for cosmetics, to sooth ailments or repel pests. Many fruits and vegetables have herbal properties. Some Rastas enhanced their knowledge on herbs by attending workshops run by NGOs in urban areas. For a closer look at herbs in urban areas, see, for example, MDP-ESA, *Herbs for Urban Communities: Safe Plants that can be grown and used by families in Towns and Cities*, 7. Online at: http://www.mdpafrica.org.zw/publications/uaherbs.pdf

42 The Shona terms appear first and the Latin and English versions are in parentheses.

of these herbs are propagated through cuttings, vegetative methods, runners, root division, bulbs, layering and seed. In order to further maximise the limited space of their gardens in high density suburbs (where most Rastas reside) they use pots to practice container gardening for herbs that can be placed on a balcony. Therefore, Rastas in towns and cities utilise the advantages of growing herbs as they are able to grow them in small spaces, they are easy to grow, are perennials, can grow in poor soil and are productive.[43] Through observation, the study established that some Rastas establish compost heaps and create mulch using plant matter in their organic farming.

In Epworth, the researcher was shown a well-tendered garden with a lot of bananas, yams and maize (among other crops) that belong to a Rastafari family. The Rastas submitted that they strictly forbid the use of chemicals and artificial fertilisers in their gardens. This is an appreciation and enhancement of naturality that encompassed "conservationism and traditionalism in land use and nourishment strategies".[44] Hence Rastas are environmental friendly in their land use.

Rastas reason that non-organic farming of cash crops such as tobacco and cotton lead to the use of chemicals and artificial fertilisers that pollute land, water, air and exhaust soils through depleting nutrients.[45] On contrary, when Rastas cultivate herbs and crops like soya beans, the fertility of the soil is improved and their Ital food supply is environmentally enhanced through organic farming. Rastas also refer to hemp as a crop that is environmental friendly, but currently still classified as illegal under Zimbabwean law. Paradoxically, industrial hemp is on high demand and in use in some Western countries. The cultivation of this crop would enhance national and global efforts to curb the adverse effects of climate change and increase soil fertility besides the economic benefits of hemp products such as textiles, canvas, hemp rope, oil and pharmaceuticals.[46] This shows that in their practices, Rastas have a lot to teach other nationals on the sustainable use of land just as its management, to which we now turn.

Land management

Land management among Rastas cannot be separated from land use as overlaps exist. The sustainable use of land through conservative organic farming is complemented through land management that encompasses critical methods that can save soil and water and avoids pollution. For instance, the

---

43   MDP-ESA, *Herbs for Urban Communities*, 7.
44   Dickerson, "I-tal *Foodways*", 135.
45   Sibanda, "Rastafari Green Philosophy", 199. Rastas refer to cigarettes as "cancer sticks" in contrast to *ganja* whose leaves were used for medicine to heal the nations (cf. Revelation 22:2).
46   Sibanda, "Rastafari Green Philosophy", 200. Rastas submitted a project proposal document for the country to cultivate industrial hemp that mirrors the "Hooked on Hemp Project" in South Africa where Rastas conducted experiments on farms with government support.

use of contour ridges, healing gullies, terracing and strip cropping are not alien practices to some Rastas. They are conscious of the need to save soil, water, trees, grass and wildlife through conservation. As Ras John explained in an interview, Rastas understand that wanton cutting down of trees leads to soil erosion by both wind and water, which led him to develop a passion for taking care of the vegetation at the Marcus Garvey Hills in Epworth.[47] As part of the care to land, conservation-minded Rastas practice stubble-mulching on their small pieces of land by using plant materials such as leaves and grass, which eventually decompose to form organic matter that makes the soil fertile. According to Rastas, land can also be managed by using grassed waterways. This also protects soil from excessive erosion.

Rastas also pointed to the growing of trees as an agricultural crop that tally with land management. Trees on forestland or farm woodlots must be planted, cultivated, given good care and harvested. Of importance to note is the type of trees that promotes good land management and soil fertility. One Rasta elder expressed concern that exotic trees such as Eucalyptus trees may have the advantage of growing fast, but they do a lot of harm to the soil. These trees impoverish the soils and requires a lot of ground water drying out the land. Rastas also note the disadvantages of Eucalyptus and pine trees, which have poisonous effects on mushroom. Mushrooms that grow in such plantations are inedible in contrast to those that grow under indigenous trees. This is the context in which the Rasta elders seek the promotion of indigenous trees and also advocate the legalisation of hemp, both of which are environmental friendly.

In addition, land management among Rastas includes shunning the use of artificial fertilisers and chemicals on crops. Instead, Rastas they promotes the use of natural fertilisers in the form of organic fertiliser. Research has shown that herbs could be used to improve soil texture and nutrient content of the soil. Moreover, herbs such as comfrey, amaranthus and nettle can be utilised to prepare a strong liquid fertiliser by soaking the leaves for up to two weeks.[48] The same leaves can be used for mulch or may be added to compost. Pests, such as insects, mice, rats and moles can also be successfully managed on the gardens without resorting to artificial chemicals by using strong-smelling herbs to keep them away or reduce their numbers. Such information constitutes knowledge that some Rastas practice in their house-yard gardens with much success.

As part of their land management, Rastas seek to avoid land pollution. This is done mainly by "environmental arts Rastafarians",[49] who are into recycling and reusing used material. Indeed, some Nyahbinghi Rastas are reusing and

---

47 Interview with Ras John.
48 MDP-ESA, *Herbs for Urban Communities*, 22. The study also revealed that here are dusting powders made from chilli and garlic powder useful in repelling ants, crawling insects and soil pests.
49 See, for example, Sibanda, "Rastafari Green Philosophy", 201; Sibanda, "The Impact of Rastafari Ecological Ethic in Zimbabwe".

recycling as part of their "Jah works" through which they make works of art from material they collect on the streets and garbage heaps. In this way, they are directly and indirectly managing the carbon footprint that humanity leaves on the environment. By walking the talk to which most advocates of climate change in high echelons of society are just giving lip service, Nyahbinghi Rastas can help to explain the meaning and need for conservation by living and pronouncing practices and laws related to conservation as well as anti-pollution. Therefore, Rastas can be good partners in land use and management that are environmental friendly.

RETURNING TO EDEN THROUGH RASTAFARI LAND USE AND MANAGEMENT: CRITICAL REFLECTIONS

The metaphor of "returning to Eden" is employed with the intention of promoting the idea of going back to the beginnings in terms of land use and management. Rastas are fond of the past.[50] The Garden of Eden was the place where the first human beings resided and lived on a clean environment and natural food. This imagery has implications for Nyahbinghi Rastafari in Zimbabwe. Firstly, in the eyes of Rastas, land is a God-given basic human right that must be restored into the hands of black majority. The Pan-Africanist philosophies of Marcus Garvey and Bob Marley are invoked creatively by Rastas to show that people are their own liberators from oppression. Rastafari is resolute to challenging white and black oppressors on the land question to ensure its eventual equitable redistribution in Zimbabwe. The land question invokes Rasta-State relations, which have different dimensions in Zimbabwe. Secondly, land gives an identity to people and is a source of their livelihood. Therefore, Rastas support organic farming identified as sustainable use of land as well as a source of Ital food and Ital livity. The vegetables, fruits and herbs, which form their diet, grow on the land. This land must be used with wisdom to preserve its fertility and sustain the ecosystem. Thirdly, Rastas possess environmental consciousness. They denounce the reckless cutting of trees under the land reform programme, manifesting among some of the new farmers. This practice is denounced by Rastas without fear or favour. Fourthly, the Rastas are leading the community in managing the environment through "reducing, recycling and reusing", which matches or even surpasses national trends of land management.

---

50 See, for example, Daynes S. 2010. *Time and Memory in Reggae Music: The Politics of Hope*. Manchester: Manchester University Press, 197, where anchoring on the past is vital for Rastafari as it is meant for liberation. It functions through *identification* which is from the present to the past instead of *inheritance* that comes from the past to the present. However, this anchoring on the past does not imply rejecting modernity because it accommodates a projection to the future. This is applicable to Rastafari views that seek to promote traditionalism and conservative farming as ideal methods identified with the past.

CONCLUSION

The chapter has demonstrated that Rastafari is essentially a Pan-Africanist movement that seeks to promote the empowerment and liberation of Africans through land ownership. Both black and white oppressors are criticised on the land question debates in Zimbabwe, particularly those who are multiple farm owners. Rastafari is a relevant player to dialogues on the spirituality and political economy of land, indigenisation and identity in Zimbabwe. The Rastafari "green philosophy" and conservative farming to preserve the soil, as well as to uphold the purity of land and nature by utilising organic farming and shunning artificial fertilisers/chemicals are ideal for national development. Thus, one may conclude that Rastafari values such as social and ecological justice, stewardship and human rights, when applied to the land use and management, promote indigenisation, economic empowerment and sustainable heritage management in postcolonial Zimbabwe. As such, Rastafari perspectives on land use and management can enhance value addition to the knowledge, culture and sustainable development initiatives in Zimbabwe today.

13 AFRICAN TRADITIONAL RELIGION IN POST-COLONIAL ZIMBABWE: A SUSTAINABLE HERITAGE FOR WATER RESOURCES MANAGEMENT

Bernard P. Humbe[1]

INTRODUCTION

This chapter explores sustainable heritage in the management of water sources by rural communities of Zimbabwe. The problem it addresses focuses on heritage for water resources management in rustic communities. The coming of Christianity as a modern way of worship despised African traditional religious strategies of water resource conservation and management. This was compounded by the introduction of water laws, by both colonial and postcolonial governments that deprived indigenous people of their rights to water management systems. In addition, it must be recognised that many changes have occurred as a result of non-African influential forces that have accompanied globalisation. Bearing in mind that the Zimbabwean rural economy is agricultural in nature, lack of a sustainable heritage for water resources management has retarded socio-economic development in rural areas given the importance of water to agriculture.

It is against the above that this chapter argues for the increased harnessing of indigenous religion by governments and non-governmental organisations (NGOs) toward management of water systems in rural communities. Indigenous religion shall be used interchangeably with African traditional religion (ATR), Shona religion and Mwari religion. It is from their indigenous religious worldview that these communities derive so-called indigenous or traditional knowledge from which laws are extracted to manage water bodies. For the indigenous, water heritage is a cumulative set of knowledge, practices, understandings and interpretations concerning themselves and their environment, passed from generation to generation. Their constant interaction with the environment facilitates development of knowledge about water systems which is preserved in their cultural ambiance.

The inquiry in this chapter is premised on qualitative and descriptive case studies of Buhera and water sources management through integration of African indigenous religion. Field work was conducted over the course of six months, extending from 10 August 2015 to 15 February 2016. Complemented by considerations of phenomenology of religion, the study allowed for a systematic collection of data by investigating the cultural realities of people in the face of water crisis, taking into account that African indigenous religion is

---

1 Department of Philosophy and Religious Studies, Great Zimbabwe University.

an important aspect of the Shona people's way of life.[2] The sampled population included people from the Shona linguistic groups located in Buhera District. Interview responses enabled an understanding of the dynamics of variables[3] within the Buhera District that influence management of water bodies. Through observation, the question of how African indigenous religion is used in water management systems in Shona rural communities was answered with reference to the population's religious worldview.

A cartography of the Shona people

The Shona is a large ethnic group in Zimbabwe. The term Shona was officially ascribed to this group of the indigenous people by the white South African linguist, Clement M Doke in 1929. Doke identified people whose dialects had mutual intelligibility. As a result, the term Shona was meant to embrace five major dialects: Karanga, Zezuru, Ndau, Manyika and Korekore.[4] Michael FC Bourdillon, a sociologist of religion, acknowledges diversity among these groups. He discovered that the term, Shona, while primarily a linguistic classification, is also a convenient term to designate a particular group of people who not only share language, but also have shared religious, cultural and, to some extent, historical links and experiences.[5]

Buhera, one of Manicaland Province's seven districts, is home to 24,072 habitants.[6] The region under study falls within Agro-ecological zone, region 5 with an average annual rainfall of less than 200 millimetre per year. The average temperature for the district annually is 34 degrees celsius.[7] Therefore, Buhera is a hot and dry district. Within the district, special focus is paid on Nyashanu and Chamutsa chieftaincies. The two chiefs preside over communities of indigenous people who migrated from various neighbouring districts, which include Chipinge, Bocha, Chivhu, Gutu and Bikita. It is common to hear the following dialects in the area: Ndau, Zezuru, Karanga and Manyika. The multiplicity of dialects points to the diversity of cultures within these different ethnic groups. However, because these people stay in the same vicinity, there is fusion of traditional cultural practices and even language is shared, such that sometimes

---

[2] Masaka D and Makahamadze T. 2013. "The Proverb: A Preserver of Shona Traditional Religion and Ethical Code", *The Journal of Pan African Studies* 6(5): 132-143.

[3] Maposa RS and Mhaka E. 2013. "Indigenous Culture and Water Technology: A reflection on the Significance of the Shona Culture in light of climate change in Zimbabwe", *Greener Journal of Art and Humanities* 3(2):024-029.

[4] Maposa RS and Humbe BP. 2012. *Indigenous Religion and HIV and AIDS Management in Zimbabwe: An African Perspective*, LAP Lambert Academic.

[5] Bourdillion MFC. 1976. *The Shona People*, Gweru: Mambo.

[6] Buhera District. Online at: www.geoview.info

[7] Chinamasa E and Mavhiza FM. 2014. "Participatory Water Sources management model for schools: Case of Buhera district, Zimbabwe", *Journal of Humanities and Social Science* 19(4):21-32.

it is difficult for an outsider to separate the fine thread which ties these Shona people together.

The above pluralism has both positive and negative bearing on the indigenous people's aquatic cultures, as well. With continued population growth and socio-economic development, water demands in Buhera district are rising. Modern legislation has alienated indigenous Shona people from their heritage of water resources management. This creates a problem, since in their cultural locale, the Shona perceive water as a religious phenomenon, which should be owned and managed by the users. Breakdown of boreholes and drying-up of both surface and underground water bodies results in the villagers' water rights being severely violated. Therefore, in the water policy of Zimbabwe, there is an urgent need for a legal pluralistic framework which should be used to govern water practices in rural areas.

Traditional religious and legal landscape of the Shona people and their water resources

The Shonas' indigenous religion influences their thoughts, feelings, interests, aspirations and actions, as posited by John S Mbiti, author on African traditional religion, when he advanced the now classic expression that Africans are "notoriously religious".[8] The Shona believe in a Supreme Being called Mwari.[9] Because of their strong belief in Mwari, Shona religiosity is widely understood as Mwari religion.[10] Mazambara calls it Mwariology.[11] Mwari is the creator of the universe and is the one who sustains it. He is approached via mediation by through the *vadzimu* (ancestral spirits), who are believed to possess supernatural powers. These ancestral spirits are regarded to be the central to Shona humanity and wellbeing in Zimbabwe.[12] The spirits can bring fortunes or misfortunes to their progenitors, depending on how the living relatives appease them. Shona also believe in guardian spirits, called *mhondoro*, and various wandering alien spirits known as *mashavi*. All these spiritual entities are sources of good or bad aptitudes.

Preoccupation of belief in supernatural forces directs and influences the Shona people's course of life. This idea is further buttressed by Kwame Gyekye, an African philosopher, who argues that even though some Shona people are aware of the purely scientific causal explanations, they do not often consider these as profound enough to offer complete satisfaction in accounting for the

---

8   Mbiti JS. 1969. *African Religions and Philosophy*. New York: Doubleday, 4.
9   Muzorehwa GH. 2014. *African origins of monotheism: challenging the Eurocentric interpretation of God concepts on the continent and in diaspora*. Eugene: Pickwick.
10 Mukonyora I. 1999. "Women and Ecology in Shona Religion", *Word and World* XIX(3):276-284.
11 Interview with P Mazambara, 11 August 2016. Mazambara is a lecturer of Zimbabwean culture at Great Zimbabwe University.
12 See Maposa and Humbe, *Indigenous Religion*.

events of life that they feel need explanation.[13] Rather, they resort to indigenous religion that fully address the "why" and "how" questions with regard to the status of a given water source. Therefore, everything and every act are looked at from a religious perspective.

Shona religion has traditional sacred practitioners (traditional healer, spirit medium, village head, headman and chief), who through use of religious laws act as gatekeepers to sacred reality of water bodies in indigenous communities. Within the context of an indigenous African society, ATR heritage is expressed via a people's beliefs, practices, ceremonies, rituals, festivals, symbols, objects, sacred places, morals, religious leaders and the revered practitioners,[14] but this is not necessarily reflected in Zimbabwe water policies.

Given the above scenario, the Shona give water a religious meaning. Water belongs to the living, the unborn as well as to the dead. In fact, of all the many non-living substances and items in Africa, there is probably no other which shares such rich water symbolism. The overwhelming importance of water lies in its connection with life.[15] Shona pay allegiance to its sacredness when they use it directly or indirectly in performance of their various ritualistic activities that enhance their well-being.

When it comes to the management of water and other resources, the hierarchy of the Shona polity consists of the *Sabhuku* (village head), the *Sadunhu* (headman) and the *Ishe* (chief).[16] Usually, legal proceedings start at the village level. The chief's court is the final court of appeal before entering the state system of district courts presided by professional judicial officers. However, the authority implied by the Traditional Leaders Act of 2013, ensures that the courts of chiefs and headmen have a more positive role in the legal and social frame work of the lives of rural people.

Shona customary law has a number of distinctive characteristics: It is unwritten; customary laws are directly validated by community acceptance; customary laws are not clearly defined and can vary from district to district. Like many groups in Africa, the Shona understand their laws by virtue of being and living as Africans. Customary courts are open to all and there are no restrictions regarding evidence. Shona law also makes little distinction between criminal and civil law and all litigation is aimed at reconciliation.

Customary laws have existed in parallel with statutory water legislation for many years in Zimbabwe. Rights to water resources under customary law

---

13 Gyekye in Chingombe et al. 1997. Online at: http://aessweb.com/journal-detail.php?id=5012
14 Mbiti, *African Religions and Philosophy*, 4.
15 Kriel A. 1989. *Roots of African Thought 2 Sources of Power*, Pretoria: University of Pretoria, 3.
16 The Shona religio-political system is organised hierarchically, starting with the village head, followed by headman and at its apex is the chief. They are all custodians of the indigenous people's cultural heritage.

are conceptualised in a fundamentally different way from the requirements of statutory law. This has implications for the resource use and management model to be implemented. According to customary law and practice, water is treated as a God-given resource that all are entitled to use. By stating that water belongs to God, people are saying it belongs to the land. And, by saying it belongs to the land, they are saying it belongs to them. Therefore, the control and management of water should be in their hands. They see water as a basic human right because it is a source of survival: water is life.[17]

Because these indigenous customary law practices are established over the years, they are critical considerations that need to be reflected in the law for the better management and voluntary enforcement of the laws. In the Shona religious cosmos, the environment includes an interweaving of the spiritual world, humanity and nature. These three are bonded and interdependent. Therefore, the Shona understand themselves as part of the environment. The spiritual world is manifested in the landscape through phenomena such as water bodies.[18] There is no doubt that, as they utilise the water sources overtly and covertly, the people are determined to protect water sources as the abodes of their spiritual beings.

Government of Zimbabwe water policy

Against this backdrop of religious ritual and customary law, the government of Zimbabwe embarked on a reform of the water sector in 1995. This came as a result of the inadequacy of the 1976 Water Act, a revision of the original Water Act of 1927.[19] As will be shown below, the policy on water resources, as highlighted by the Water Act and the Zimbabwe National Water Authority Act (ZINWA),[20] resulted into improved management and use of the country's water resources.

The two water acts provided that:

- All surface and underground water will belong to the state.
- All Zimbabweans must have access to water for primary use.
- All water must be beneficially used.
- Water should be treated as an economic good.
- Water tariffs will need to take cognisance of those unable to pay the full price.

---

17 Latham in Chikozho C and Latham J. 2005. "Shona customary practices in the context of water sector reforms in Zimbabwe." International Workshop on African Water Laws: Plural Legislative Frameworks for Rural Water Management in Africa. Johannesburg, South Africa, January 26-28.
18 Fontein in Maposa and Mhaka, "Indigenous Culture and Water Technology".
19 Chikozho and Latham, "Shona customary practices", 2.
20 It is a wholly government-owned arm that manages water systems. The Authority was formed in 2000 following the promulgation of ZINWA and its functions and mandate are drawn from the same act and the Water Act of 1998.

- Water rights in perpetuity need to be replaced by water permits issued for a specific time period.
- Water management should involve all stakeholders at lowest possible level and
- The environment is to be considered as a consumer in its own right.[21]

Alterations to the water reforms continued and, in December 2012, the National Water Policy was approved by government and publicly launched on 22 March 2013. The policy envisages that, within five years, ZINWA will focus on its core functions of planning, developing and managing the country's water resources in accordance with the provisions of the Water Act of 1998.[22] It reallocates responsibility for water and sanitation services to local governments, both urban and rural. Institutional accountability for rural Water, Sanitation and Hygiene (WASH) will resort under Rural District Councils (RDCs), with the central government providing leadership and oversight.[23]

A close look at the above water policy shows that though there is recognition of traditional leadership in water developmental projects, there is no provision for traditional law and practice as such in the act – except perhaps in the recognition of primary rights to water. Therefore, the postcolonial water policy in Zimbabwe is divesting the indigenous people of their water rights. The latter rights start from ownership of the water sources as per indigenous religious culture, for example the case of boreholes. There is need to also understand boreholes in the context of indigenous religion. They are symbolic in that they connect the underground world with the human world by supplying water that is vital for sustenance of both human and non-human life. The water comes from the underground world where ancestors are buried. The functionality or boreholes is propelled by the spirits of the land.

This has been ignored and maligned by the government, rural district councils and non-governmental organisations.[24] Public opinion has been taken into account in the formulation of these government water laws. However, policymakers and legislators operate from cities, hence they are not well acquainted with traditional laws that, though not codified in written form, have been in existence since time immemorial, are based on long-standing practice, and are essential in rural water governance issues.

CASE STUDIES IN RELIGION AND WATER SOURCES IN ZIMBABWE

Buhera's several water sources are socially and religiously constructed. They vary from natural sources such as rivers, streams, pools and rainwater, to human

---

21 Ibid.
22 The Zimbabwe Water Forum Policy Note 3.0, April 2013, 3.
23 Ibid.
24 Rusinga O and Maposa RS. 2010. "Traditional Religion and natural resources: A reflection on the significance of indigenous knowledge systems on the utilisation of natural resources among the Ndau People in south-eastern Zimbabwe", *Journal of Ecology and the Natural Environment* 2(9):201-206.

made sources such as wells, boreholes and dams. By force of circumstance, communities depend on several sources for water supply, for no single source is capable of supplying all the water needs throughout the year. The majority of the villagers in the region acknowledge that boreholes and hand-dug wells are the major sources of water in their communities. Boreholes constitute 52.3% of the sources, while hand dug deep wells constitute 22.6%. Thus, about 80% of Buhera's water is groundwater.[25]

Case 1: Boreholes and religious ritual

According to the Rural District Council Act 29:17, it is the prerogative of the Ward Development Committee (WADCO) to meet the water needs, via, for example, requests for additional water points and assistance in the maintenance of existing ones. The so-called District Development Fund (DDF) accounts for 55% of the boreholes in the district[26] and any NGO that sinks a borehole is required to hand it over to the DDF. The latter is then is responsible for the management of the borehole as is the case with all boreholes in the district. In Buhera, 40% of the boreholes have been drilled with the assistance of the NGOs which include: Africare, World Vision, Christian Care, Zimbabwe Red Cross and Mercy Corps.[27]

In Ward 27, the majority of the boreholes that function throughout the year are the ones that were sunk during the colonial regime, and they are known as *migodhi yechikare* (traditional boreholes). The following are the names of boreholes from which communities obtain water throughout the year: Mugodhi wekwaMakarara, Muzerengwa, Dakacha, Mugodo and Siyesiye. Traditional leaders were involved in identifying the sites where these boreholes were sunk. The sinking of the boreholes were preceded by the performance of rituals for the success of the drilling and the sustenance that the boreholes would provide. These boreholes are named after the villages in which they were sunk. *Kutumidza zita* (apt naming) constitutes one of the most important indigenous rituals in Africa. In fact, it is a vital *rite de passage* in several indigenous Shona communities in Zimbabwe, as well.[28] The idea behind the naming ritual is that the water is transformed and assumes life embodied in the name. If a borehole is named after a person, the water source becomes incorporated into the family and community of that person. This increases people's sense of ownership of the borehole and translates in turn into maximum care of the water point.[29]

The families who look after these boreholes have implemented various strategies to prolong the lifespan of these boreholes. The water points are, for example, encircled using *mupane* logs. A *mhanda* (V-shape log) is inserted

---

25 See Chinamasa and Mavhiza, "Participatory Water Sources."
26 Ibid.
27 Ibid.
28 See Maposa and Humbe, *Indigenous Religion*.
29 Chambers in Chinamasa and Mavhiza, "Participatory Water Sources".

underneath the hand pipe to prevent water users from smashing it against the ground. People take turns in fetching water in the spirit of community sharing, so *mbawo* (egocentrism) is discouraged. Indigenous communities also have expectations that regulate behaviour of water users at the water points. For example, if anyone has to bring a metal container, it must not contain any soot residue; bathing and laundry should not be done within the radius of hundred meters; the washing of nappies are strictly prohibited. In all, generally high standards of hygiene are to be maintained.

It is told that, in the late 1970s, after a quarrel with her husband, a woman in Nehumambi area defecated at one of the water points and the water dried up instantly. The reason given is that the community and its spirits were angered by such behaviour. Apparently the woman also lost her sanity and traditional healers confirmed that it was due to punishment from the ancestors. In functional terms, this incident served as a deterrent to other would-be transgressors of the customs that prevent the pollution of water sources. This is also a practical example in which the Shona managed their water resources. They are highly conscious of power enshrined in the traditional customs of the people as a collective group and as a cultural unit.

It is well acknowledged in communities that the traditional boreholes are strongly associated with mystical forces. The power of African religious laws rests wholly on the ascription of psychic powers to the water sources as the abodes of ancestral spirits.[30] Unfortunately, as noted by Lekan Oyebande, the priority accorded to indigenous knowledge with regard to water management during the colonial era had not been sustained by post-independence governments of the country.[31] Water has been aligned more to politics than religion.

In 2000, surveys of underground water by a Non-Governmental Organisation in conjunction with traditional leadership were carried out in Shiri area. However, politicians by-passed traditional chiefs in the actual borehole sinking project, by simply instructing drillers to sink the borehole near their homesteads. The boreholes hardly supplied communities with any water and this affected social development in Buhera. Though standards of living are difficult to measure, indicators of social development can be seen in the communities with access to enough water. Unavailability of water means that villagers spend the greater part of their time searching for water, negating other important chores and aspects of their social life. In other words, the availability of water is linked with the improvement of the well-being of villagers so that they can reach their full

---

30 Eneji CVO et al. 2012. "Traditional African Religion in Natural Conservation and Management in Cross River State, Nigeria", *Environment and Natural Resource Research* 2(4):45.
31 Oyebande in Gbadegesin N and Olorunfemi F. 2007. "Assessment of Rural Water Supply Management in Selected Rural Areas of State, Nigeria", *ATPS Working Paper Series* 49:2.

potential. In securing the availability of water, traditional African religion itself becomes a resource toward development.

The above shows that integrating traditional knowledge into modern water resources management practices is crucial. The sinking of boreholes must respect the traditional beliefs of the Shona. Through their cultural heritage, indigenous people are versed with the kind of rituals to be performed before commencement of borehole sinking. In Ward 29, there is an area called Zomba, where several Shona freedom fighters were killed during the Zimbabwean liberation struggle. It is very difficult to start a successful water project in this area without performing proper rituals which appease the spirits of dead liberation fighters. Experiences of villagers show that in situations where traditional religion was overlooked, mysterious loss of equipment and injuries to machine operators occurred. Even for the one borehole which is functional, villagers, through their traditional leaders always communicate with the spiritual world to enhance borehole's sustainability. If spirits of the dead fighters are angered, it is said, they are seen hovering around the water point especially at night. So, the success of any water management strategy rests on the involvement of the traditional belief systems of the beneficiaries of the water point.[32]

Case 2: Hand-dug deep wells and indigenous "water knowledge"

The Shona also have a cultural approach to identifying water sites for *migodhi yemvura* (hand-dug wells). Indigenous peoples possess traditional knowledge and skills concerning the identification of a water source site. These include identifying indigenous trees such as *mubvumira* (*kirkia acuminate*), *muchakata* (*parinaria curatellifolia*), *mupanda* (*lonchocapus capassa*) and *mushuku* (*uapaca kirkiana*) which are associated with rich sources of groundwater.[33] Furthermore, these trees are conserved since they have direct impact on the water sources.[34] Second, *churu* (termite mounds) are also considered a sign of plenty of groundwater as water is needed for the construction of these mounds. Third, a belt followed by a certain type of *chamupupuri* (whirlwind) is understood as a table of groundwater. The belief is that a *njuzu* (a mermaid) is a keeper of water sources in indigenous communities and it travels in whirlwinds. Fourth, indigenous experts in well digging use V-shaped sticks of *mutehwa* (*grewia bicolor*) to detect the availability of groundwater. They hold the sticks firm above the ground and availability of water is detected by vibrations of the sticks. The quantity of the water at the place is determined by the strength of the vibrations.

The Shonas' traditional land management skills often provide the most effective method of water resource management in their settlements. For this reason, water sources on indigenous lands are often considered a sacred element, and

---

32 Ibid.
33 See Maposa and Mhaka, "Indigenous Culture and Water Technology."
34 Mubonani in Chinamasa and Mavhiza, "Participatory Water Sources."

indigenous people may be the holders of "water knowledge". *Kugadzira migodhi yemvura* (ritualising the hand-dug deep wells) is a common practice. Ritualised objects like strings or charms that possess mystical, spiritual and therapeutic powers are placed in or at the water source. They act as protective elements which prevent people from contaminating the water or engaging in other unacceptable practices. They also ensure a perennial supply of water.

Case 3: Chikwengweru Pool as a "sourceless source"

The Chikwengweru Pool is a shallow water source which lies between two granite stones, and is enclosed by wooden. The availability of water is perennial, but water levels decrease if the water spirits are angered. Water from this pool tastes sweet despite the fact that other sources of water in the area have hard, salty water. Water is drawn using utensils that are prescribed especially non-metal objects like gourds, wooden or clay containers, which have not been used for cooking. It serves more than seventy households in five villages. Those in custodianship of the pool belong to Nemadziva family of the Moyo/Heart totem. The pool is heavily associated with the lightning and thunder that occur each time the area receives rainfall. In terms of quantity the Chikwengweru area receives more rainfall compared to surrounding places. Traditional healers and members of use the water to cure barrenness and other various bodily diseases, to wash away bad luck and to exorcise evil spirits.

The people believe that Chikwengweru pool is a mystery which reveals the work of Mwari. They call it *chinyuke/manyuko*. According to Gwinyai Muzorewa, an African theologian, though still metaphorical, *chinyuke* translated as the "sourceless source" or "the source of all sources," means something whose intrinsic existence is bound in and of itself, and serves as the cause of all existence before and yet-to-be.[35] For the Shona people of Buhera, the "sourceless source of Chikwengweru pool is understood in the context of the unexpected coming of waters in form of a pool in an area which is characterised by aridity. Therefore, in their ecological view, Mwari is believed to be *Manyuko*, because he is author of "a beginingless and endless" existence.[36] In everyday life, *chinyuke* signifies a surfacing of water from underground which all of a sudden emerges to the surface collected in a pool that endures drought.

Villagers in Ward 28 use Chikwengweru water in systematic ways and with deep observance of *zviera* (taboos) and assorted practices that are grounded in the religio-cultural system. This body of the belief system shapes the locals' interpretation of their perception of the accessibility and utility of the available natural resources. The quality of Shona taboos is that they are restrictive and not directive. Through their cultural belief systems, the Shona people protect this pool from pollution and running dry since it is a habitat of a mermaid. When

---

35   See Muzorehwa, *African origins of monotheism*.
36   Ibid.

approaching the pool, villagers are encouraged not to harbour bad thoughts. Among other things, this helps to control those who might be nursing grudges to the extent of exacting revenge by poisoning water sources. In addition, people are not allowed to hold meetings at the pool. After fetching water people, should leave the place. Those who come to fetch water must desist from using *zvimonyodzo* (vulgar language). This is a practical way of avoiding conflicts.

People who draw water at Chikwengweru pool use prescribed containers. Villagers are prohibited from drinking water from the pool using open hands or using it to wash their bodies. These practices help to keep the pool purified, by controlling the spread of diseases.[37] Without these rules, some forms of antisocial behaviour might earn the perpetrator the label of *nhundiramatsime*, meaning one who urinates in wells of water.[38] In their beliefs about well-being, the Shona hold that there is a causal connection between the moral condition of the community and its water bodies.[39]

Taboos are an indigenous way of educating and knowing metaphysical issues that are regarded as fundamental to the equilibrium of the social system or to foster order in the society. Reverence to Chikwengweru pool is done as an expression of loyalty to the traditional leaders. Availability of water is only ensured by the ancestors through the role played by traditional leaders, traditional healers, spirit mediums and elders of the community. Ancestral spirits in the area reveal themselves to the indigenous in form of a snake. There is a big, colourful snake about 10 meters long which resides in the pool, and no one is allowed to temper with it. Although the snake is one of the best-known death-dealers in Africa, it is often associated with life-giving water. Presence of the snake is assurance of availability of water which belongs and is given by ancestors.

WOMEN AT THE CENTRE OF TRADITIONAL WATER MANAGEMENT

Women in traditional African culture fulfil roles that are fundamental to the development of water-centred folklore and associated religious beliefs.[40] In Buhera, traditional knowledge of indigenous peoples is often passed on via shared practice and storytelling. Women are the custodians of *ngano* (folklore) used to encourage good water management skills. One such a story is of wild animals in a waterless environment that set out digging a well to survive. All of the animals, including those with great physical strength failed to reach the water table, all except for the despised tortoise. The hare was barred from accessing the well, since it had refused to participate in the digging process. However, the hare used honey to bribe those on guard. After the majority of

---

37 See Maposa and Mhaka, "Indigenous Culture and Water Technology".
38 Ibid.
39 Taringa N. 2014. *Towards an African-Christian Environmental Ethic*. Bamberg: University of Bamberg Press.
40 Mukonyora, "Women and Ecology", 280.

the animals had become victims of the hare's ruse, it was little tortoise's trap which led to the capture of hare and its eventual reprimand. The tortoise had smeared glue upon its body and waited quietly under water waiting for hare's arrival. Later hare came to the well, on its attempt to drink water secretly, and it glued onto the tortoise's body. The tortoise came to be associated with water, and therefore it too is protected by the people.

Through such stories, women use animal imagery to communicate important social values to the young.[41] The values imparted in youth contribute significantly to the way the Shona, and possibly many other African people with a similar cultural heritage, think about bodies of water and their management. Among other lessons, children learn that aquatic creatures are very important in ensuring the availability of water. There is community ownership of the water sources. Every individual must contribute to the source's management despite his or her age or stature. There exists a body of rules used to govern usage of water sources. Anyone who breaks the agreed laws is reprimanded before being admitted again into the community. Within the Shona indigenous communities, folklore plays an important role, as an instrument of socialisation.

The most popular praise name for Mwari is *Dzivaguru,* which means the Great Pool. Sometimes the root word *Dziva* (pool) is used instead of *Dzivaguru*.[42] In a Shona ecological system, water is a key fertility feature. A pool of water symbolises the woman's womb as the fountain and origin of life. *Dzivaguru* is widely associated with feminine aspects of the Mwari belief system. The woman's responsibility is to produce crops for the family; thus, she wants to see the rains fall to replenish the water sources. She is also expected to bear children until *nyoka yagume ura*. The Shona understanding is that the uterus of a woman consists of a snake that, in its active stages, effectuates reproduction and there comes a time when the snake is no longer active. This is menopause stage. A woman who does not bear children is associated with *mhanje* – that is an infertile barren land.[43] Women who are not sexually active also take a central role in rain-making ceremonies in which beer is brewed by *mbonga* (virgin girls) or *vaguma ura* (women of advanced age). These women are considered to be Mwari's wives.[44]

41　Mukonyora, "Women and Ecology", 280.
42　Daneel M. 1970. *The God of the Matopo Hills*. The Hague: Mouton, 16.
43　Ibid.
44　Ibid, 282. Traditionally, rainmaking ceremonies were done at the Matopos cultic centre, where a voice of Mwari was heard communicating with the indigenous people. At this cultic centre there were *mbonga* (virgin girls) who played a mediatory role between Mwari and the people. The concept "Mwari's wives" is understood as a spiritual union between the *mbonga* and Mwari, whom they served at this cultic centre.

WATER, VALUES AND MEANING

Water sources are imbued with values and take on meaning through people's daily lives and struggles.[45] There exists a sense of collective responsibility, meaning that each and every member of the community is bound to ensure that he or she fetches water from the water bodies without compromising the ability of present and future generations to meet their water needs in a sustainable manner. It has been noted that water bodies managed from a traditional approach are given a chance to "rest and recover" instead of being over-used.[46]

Despite the rationale for integrating these knowledge systems into modern management practices, indigenous knowledge related to water is still often misunderstood and ignored in water projects, policies and planning processes. Participatory approaches are required in which traditional religion and water education is linked to human experience particularly in rural areas. It is imperative to involve communities in identifying the cultural and social practices that may increase or decrease the water levels in their sources in formulating water policies appropriate for this existential situation.

There is also a need to take into consideration the values, attitude, preferences and capacities of the different stakeholders in the supply and management of water in rural areas. Human practices related to water relations typically date back many generations: hence, in many traditional societies, people have developed cultural values, attitudes and norms of behaviour in relation to water use.[47]

POLICY RECOMMENDATIONS FOR ZIMBABWE WATER MANAGEMENT

Legal Pluralism: The Shona people's adherence to own water customs and practices suggests that the country should have a legal pluralistic framework that governs water resources. May describes legal pluralism as a situation where the transfer or introduction of one system is superimposed on an existing political structure or culture.[48] Though legal pluralism is not an easy framework to use in governing natural resources, in practical terms, the rural communities in Zimbabwe are governed by systems that have multiple rules (State, RDC and local) with both legal and customary bases of legitimation and different enforcement structures and processes.[49] It is important to acknowledge the vitality of indigenous religion in a legal pluralistic framework for it makes use of customary practices for water resources management. Therefore water policy makers should therefore acknowledge and respect indigenous religious water practices.

---

45   See Rusinga and Maposa, "Traditional Religion and natural resources".
46   *Culture and water – Kunene River Awareness Kit.* Online at: www.kunene.riverawarenesskit.com
47   Ibid.
48   May in Chikozho and Latham, "Shona customary practices", 1.
49   Nemarundwe in Chikozho and Latham, "Shona customary practices", 7.

Customary law and practice. Besides for Roman-Dutch law that is reflected in both the common and statutory law of Zimbabwe, there also exist the customary law and practice. The FAO Legislative Study No. 58 provides an in-depth study of the dynamics of customary law in different African ethnic groups. Customary law is a code of rules approved by the indigenous community that has been observed, recognised, and handed down by ancestors since time immemorial.[50] These laws provide for a set of rights and duties to be observed by the communities. Despite customary law being subjected to pressure from Western religions, colonialism and modernity, its observance is still prevalent in Buhera Shona communities. It is adaptive, which makes it especially resilient as well. Adaptations are iterative, and is found within the shifting landscape of the people's notions of what is culturally acceptable. Culture and customary behaviour are the embodiment of society's legal institutions.

Religious ritual and practice. Closely related to the above, is the fact that the Shona people understand and describe the nature of their Supreme Being in aquatic terms. Their religious world provides tools for identification of water sources and naming and classification of water systems. This rich knowledge source serves as the information base for society, facilitating communication and decision making.

Be that as it may, African indigenous religion dominates the Shona worldview as it does for most Zimbabweans. African well-being is located in its cultural situatedness. Among the Shona, one symbol of their religio-cultural beliefs is water. For this reason, in water-stressed regions, unavailability of water from its sources is understood as a religio-socio-cultural crisis and solutions to these crises are also culturally-oriented. This can contribute to local empowerment, increasing self-sufficiency and credibility of projects and policies.[51]

Water is not only understood as a physical commodity, but also as an inherent religious and cultural value and thus it is associated with the indigenous people's identity. Being understood to be the providers of water, Mawari and the ancestral spirits are contacted when it becomes scarce. This can be done through rain making rituals. These rituals are presided over by traditional religious practitioners who happen to be the living custodians of natural resources including water. The causes of the drying up of water sources are diagnosed through involvement of spirit mediums, and rituals are performed to rectify the problem. Therefore management of water should not be done following legal laws of the government only, for water is a religious substance meant to sustain every human and nonhuman living organism. Through religious observance, there are certain codes of conduct and taboos expected to be followed that serve as a heritage of water resource management as was seen in the aforementioned case studies. Given the prominence of indigenous religious religion in rustic communities, villagers are more comfortable in abiding to a religious water

---

50 Posselt in Chikozho and Latham, "Shona customary practices".
51 Ibid.

life management system which they are acquainted to in this way rather those prescribed by water legislation. Also women, who have been seen as close to Mwari in terms of fertility, are noble inculcators of recommended aquatic practices in their families as they educate children in responsible water use via folktales and proverbs.

CONCLUSION

This study has suggested that management strategies for all water resources include the aim of sustaining and prolonging the life span of water sources in rural areas. Current Zimbabwean water resources legislation does not recognise customary law and practices. As was noted, ZINWA and District Councils are mandated to regulate water systems even in rural communities. In traditional African contexts, such as that of the Shona, natural resource use, management and conservation are products of people's spirituality, culture, practices, taboo systems and knowledge accumulated over centuries.[52] It should be the prerogative of traditional leaders to deal with water issues in wards and not just that of ward councillors. Yet, customary authorities do not have any formal representation in water regulatory bodies. This is one of the gaps that need to be addressed by adopting legal pluralism in management of water resources.

Findings indicate that traditional religious and cultural practices form the sustainable heritage which contributes towards the conservation of water resources by ascribing psychic powers to the boreholes and pools. Reverence for these water sources has been a pragmatic tool for conflict management. As such, the use of African indigenous laws of water management helps in fostering peace and conflict resolution. Villagers are not allowed to have conflicts lest their water sources will dry up. Peace is a vital resource for social development. Relying on traditional African heritage on water management is easy and affordable since it their way of life, therefore it aids in the social development of people and communities that use it. Besides using it for domestic purposes, water is important in advancing the indigenous people's social wellbeing. Finally, in a sense, the sacredness of water "washes away" *minyama* (misfortunes) among the indigenous people. Misfortunes or bad luck barricade indigenous people's quest for a successful life. So sources of water become places of renewal or entrance into a new life.[53]

---

52   Sibanda in Maposa and Mhaka, "Indigenous Culture and Water Technology".
53   Kriel, *Roots of African Thought*, 3.

14 THE GREAT ZIMBABWE MONUMENTS AND CHALLENGES IN AFRICAN HERITAGE MANAGEMENT

Edmore Dube[1]

INTRODUCTION

The chapter examines how colonial policies have affected the Shona forefathers' and their Remba cousins' rites and rituals within the Great Zimbabwe Monuments grounds. In proposing Jewish, Arabic, Persian, Portuguese, Chinese or Indian as opposed to African origins of the structures, the colonial discourse has effected regime change at the monuments.[2] Originating with missionaries and perpetuated by the British colonialist politician Cecil John Rhodes, who employed pseudo-archaeologists armed with the results supporting a case for foreign origins before the excavations commenced, the colonial ideology negating African architectural capacity also includes items such as a 1938 tourism and monuments brochure that includes the shadowy image of the Queen of Sheba against the monuments' conical tower.[3] Though some groups may have resisted colonial classification, the Remba seem to have given in to the "superior discourse" in the form of the Judeo-Christian template[4] (evaluating everything using Jewish and Christian values). The dominant discourse has been such that associating with Jewish or Christian traditions is ranked superior to all other traditional associations tenable in Zimbabwe. Some Remba have even found it prudent to exploit the slightest similarities with Jews to escape the stigma which would accrue from retaining association with "warring" Arabs.

The Remba are a Shona-speaking group found in clusters throughout Zimbabwe with some concentration around Great Zimbabwe, though Mberengwa District is thought to be their spiritual home.[5] They follow dietary laws, circumcision rituals and genetic configurations similar to Jews and Arabs, and scholarly opinion differs on whether such similarities are of Jewish or Arab origin.

---

1 Edmore Dube holds a PhD in Islamic Studies from the Department of Philosophy and Religious Studies, Great Zimbabwe University.
2 Bent JT. 1892. "The Ruined Cities of Mashonaland, and Explorations in the Country", *Proceedings of the Royal Geographical Society* 14(5):42.
3 "The British Museum: The Wealth of Africa Great Zimbabwe Students' Worksheets". Online at: https://www.britishmuseum.org/pdf/GreatZimbabwe_StudentsWorksheets.pdf
4 Mazarire GC. 2013. "Mberengwa, Zimbabwe – Home to the Lemba Tribe. Are they the descendants of Yemenite Jews?" Unpublished paper presented at the Historical Dimensions of Development in the Midlands Seminar, Fairmile Hotel, Gweru, 2001.
5 Mativha MER. 1992. *The Basena, Vamwenye, Balemba*. Johannesburg: Morester, 47.

However, the genetic similarity is only male oriented leading to a scholarly consensus that their mothers are Shona.[6] The chapter will examine this argument in due course, but of critical importance is the fact that the Remba themselves are divided on their paternity, which is also a critical issue in the intangible heritage debate. The existence of Arab material culture together with curved objects symbolising circumcised male organs attributed to the Remba at Great Zimbabwe further complicates their relationship with Arabian origins, just as it does their roles in the building and use of Great Zimbabwe. Even worse, the Remba have not only lost their intangible heritage in the ensuing confusion, but they have also been excluded from any say regarding the monuments, which have been expropriated by the successive governments.

The challenges in heritage management are a result of Western-type legal statutes improperly constituted to "disinherit" the owners of the shrine in favour of the political elite.[7] The political elite are either directly or indirectly (complicit) in collusion with some missionaries and education authorities in appropriating heritage sites for their own benefit. The Solomonic legend has been used as a superior ideological tool to discredit any legitimate local claims. Furthermore, this Solomonic legendary motif within the "Judeo-Christian template" has augmented the non-African origins of the controversy, which resulted in acute nationalism struggling against colonialism. The chapter begins with an examination of the non-African origins controversy before moving on to focus on the African origins and the shrine's religious significance. From there it highlights Arab-Remba interaction, after which it addresses colonialism and nationalism in conflict and the Solomonic legend with its inherent elements of Jewish-Arab conflict. The chapter concludes that the Judeo-Christian template, colonialism and Western-type laws have disinherited the locals of which the Remba serve as an example. Since the heritage managers are fully aware of this, they are in an awkward position in which they have to manage heritage against their consciences. Heritage managers have written extensively to show that heritage should instead be managed for the locals, with the locals.[8]

THE NON-AFRICAN ORIGINS CONTROVERSY

The Great Zimbabwe Monuments are a disputed Iron Age settlement comprising dry bond stone structures located seventeen miles southeast of

---

6   See Beach DN. 1980. *The Shona and Zimbabwe 900-1850*. Gweru: Mambo; Mandivenga EC. 1983. *Islam in Zimbabwe*. Gweru: Mambo.
7   Mawere M, Sagiya ME and Mubaya TR. 2012. "Convergence of Diverse Religions at Zimbabwe Heritage Sites: The Case of Great Zimbabwe National Monument", *International Research Journal of Arts and Social Sciences* 1(2):23.
8   See Ndoro W. 2005. *The Preservation of Great Zimbabwe: Your Monument, Our Shrine*. ICCROM Conservation Studies 4. Rome, Italy; Matenga E. 2011. "The Soapstone Birds of Great Zimbabwe. Archaeological Heritage, Religion and Politics in Postcolonial Zimbabwe and the Return of Cultural Property", *Studies in Global Archaeology* 16. Uppsala: Uppsala University.

the city of Masvingo in central Zimbabwe. The monuments are 159 miles from the Zimbabwean capital of Harare, 300miles south of the Zambezi River and 250 miles west of the Indian Ocean.[9] They are the largest and most magnificent of the more than 250 similar structures scattered across the adjacent Mozambique, South Africa, Botswana and Zimbabwe – collectively known as the Zimbabwe Culture sites.[10] The Great Zimbabwe monuments were strategically located on the southern edge of the so-called Central Plateau, in a commanding position to take advantage of the costal trade with the Swahili and the Arabs,[11] as the most dominant authority south of the Zambezi for 250 years.[12] It was also a metropolitan city of the "ancient" miners.[13] Archaeologist Innocent Pikirayi argues that the term "ancient" has generally been used by antiquarians at the turn of the twentieth century (for example, by Theodore Bent 1892, Richard Hall 1905) to disconnect the present day Karanga locals from the builders of Great Zimbabwe, as an effort at silencing later history.[14] Such silencing has left indigenous people angry.[15] Through the utilisation of *vashambadzi* (trade agents), the Great Zimbabwe state was able to maintain links with traders from Kilwa on the Tanzanian coast, as well as West Africa, Persia and China,[16] and its decline may have been due to the shift of gold trade to the north.[17]

The non-African theory of the origin of the monuments is a Eurocentric assumption based on Western prejudice against the African intellectual and architectural capacity.[18] European travelers were astounded by such an elegant civilisation in the heart of Africa and they refused to accept indigenous architectural capacity for such magnificent construction.[19] The perception, partly sponsored by Christian missionaries and partly by the British colonists, went unchallenged for over thirty years following its initial publication by

---

9 Carroll ST. 1988. "Solomonic Legend: The Muslims and the Great Zimbabwe", *The International Journal of African Historical Studies* 21(2):223-247, (233).
10 Carroll, "Solomonic Legend", 233; Ampim M. 2004. "Great Zimbabwe: A History Almost Forgotten" (April 2004 presentation delivered in Toronto, Canada, sponsored by the G.O.D. Collective); Pikirayi I. 2016. "The True Story of Great Zimbabwe", *New Zimbabwe*, 8 March.
11 Beach DN. 1980. *The Shona and Zimbabwe 900-1850.* Gweru: Mambo; Ndoro W. 1997. "Great Zimbabwe", *Scientific American* 95.
12 Pikirayi I. 2013. "Great Zimbabwe in Historical Archaeology: Reconceptualising Decline, Abandonement, and Reoccupation of an Ancient Polity, A.D. 1450-1900", *Historical Archaeology* 47(1):26-37, (27).
13 Hall RN and Neal WG. 1902. *The Ancient Ruins of Rhodesia.* London: Methuen.
14 Pikirayi, "Great Zimbabwe in Historical Archaeology", 33.
15 Fontein J. 2016. *The Silence of Great Zimbabwe: Contested Landscapes and the Power of Heritage.* London and New York: Routledge.
16 "Ancient Zimbabwe – The Great Zimbabwe Ruins". Online at: http://www.victoriafalls-guide.net/ancient-zimbabwe.html
17 Pikirayi, "The True Story of Great Zimbabwe".
18 Pikirayi I. 2012. "Peter Garlake (1934-2011), Great Zimbabwe and the politics of the past in Zimbabwe", *Azania: Archaeological Research in Africa* 47(2):224.
19 Carroll, "Solomonic Legend", 233.

explorer Karl Mauch.[20] In 1871, Karl Mauch, a German national, categorised the monuments as part of the family of Semitic structures, claiming – with religious overtones – that the structures were modelled on Solomon's temple on Mount Moriah overlooking the Ophir gold mines. This Solomonic theoretical postulation originating from a literary genre of travel and adventure stories was subsequently mistaken by unsuspecting European audiences as actually representing Solomon's reign at the Great Zimbabwe.[21] As Zimbabwean heritage specialist and former site manager of the Great Zimbabwe World Heritage property, Webber Ndoro aptly puts it: "A sample of wood from a lintel bolstered Mauch's rapid assessment: it smelled like his pencil, therefore it was cedar and must have come from Lebanon … This attitude was pervasive in colonialist Africa: the continent had no history, no sophistication; its people and tribes were unchanging, unable to develop, culturally barren."[22]

The physical presence of Solomon at Great Zimbabwe was strengthened by a further comparison of the monuments on the plain to supposed palace lodgings of the Queen of Sheba when she visited Jerusalem during the reign of Solomon, "which must have been replicated here by a civilized mind".[23] The Rhodesia[24] Department of Tourism strengthened the Solomonic legend through its advertisement brochures. As noted earlier, a travel poster of 1938 presented the monuments with a shadowy picture of the Queen of Sheba on the walls of the conical power.[25] The poster represented the official colonial position regarding the history of the monuments. Later travelers, disputing both local acumen and legends based on the Bible, suggested Portuguese, Arab, Chinese, Persian or Indian architectural involvement.[26] This was due to the proximity of the Arabs in the Zambezi valley and the Portuguese on the coast of the Indian Ocean, as well as artefacts of Arab, Chinese, Persian and Indian origin found at the site. These included a fourteen century-Arab copper coin with the seal of Hasan ibn Sulaiman, the sultan of Kilwa (1320-1330 CE) on the Tanzanian coast, glass beads and porcelain from China (mostly from the Ming Dynasty – 1368 to 1644 CE) and Persia.[27] Ceramic ethno-archaeology was used to develop models and chronology of these pre-historic events,[28] though much still needs to be done to improve the description of Great Zimbabwe ceramics.[29] Parallels were drawn

---

20 Ampim, "Great Zimbabwe: A History Almost Forgotten".
21 Carroll, "Solomonic Legend", 238.
22 Ndoro, "Great Zimbabwe", 98.
23 Ampim, "Great Zimbabwe: A History Almost Forgotten".
24 Rhodesia was the colonial name of Zimbabwe.
25 "The British museum: The Wealth of Africa Great Zimbabwe Students' Worksheets". Online at: https://www.britishmuseum.org/pdf/GreatZimbabwe_StudentsWorksheets.pdf
26 Bent, "The Ruined Cities of Mashonaland", 242.
27 Ndoro, "Great Zimbabwe", 98.
28 Nyamushosho RT. 2014. "Ceramic Ethnoarchaeology in Zimbabwe", *International Research Journal of Arts and social Science* 3(2):17-18.
29 Pikirayi I and Chirikure S. 2011. "Debating Great Zimbabwe", *Azania: Archeological Research in Africa* 46(2):225.

with the stone structures of the Indian golden city of Myosore of the Vijayanagar kingdom.[30] This new parallel made further connections between gold and God by associating gold mining with a religious shrine.

Cecil John Rhodes, whose agenda would have been greatly enhanced by looking down upon the indigenous African population and rejecting any significant architectural acumen among them, sponsored James Theodore Bent, a member of the British Association of Science, who was not a qualified archaeologist, to excavate at the Great Zimbabwe Monuments. As might have been anticipated of a paid non-professional, Bent maintained that the artefacts were of foreign origin, Semitic in nurture and most likely Arabian.[31] This position was sustained ten years later by British archaeologist, Richard Hall, who concluded that the ruins reflected the culture of more civilised races.[32] He relegated the African occupation of the settlement to a later date and busied himself removing the layers that told the African story as a later contamination of civilisation. This ideological position remained official throughout the colonial period (1890-1979).[33]

AFRICAN DISCOURSES OF GREAT ZIMBABWE

African discourses celebrate the Great Zimbabwe Monuments as an African contribution to world civilisation. These monuments have tremendous cultural, political and scientific significance.[34] They were proclaimed a national heritage site by the colonial government in 1937, and Zimbabwean nationalists saw them as a pillar of strength,[35] and all colonial efforts to thwart nationalism through 'alienising' monuments failed.[36] This was clear in the renaming of the Zimbabwe National Party from African National Party and the formation of Zimbabwe African People's Union in 1961, Zimbabwe African National Union in 1963 and the adoption of the name "Zimbabwe" at independence in 1980. This Afrocentric view got its initial boost in 1905 through the work of the English archaeologist David Randall-MacIver.

Randall-MacIver, who carried out the first scientific archaeological excavations of the monuments and paid close attention to the mud dwellings on the site was the first to declare the monuments to be "unquestionably African in every detail".[37] This officially-unacceptable conclusion led to the restriction of archaeologists from the site for quite some time. However, the British

---

30 Carroll, "Solomonic Legend", 238.
31 Bent, "The Ruined Cities of Mashonaland", 238.
32 Hall, *The Ancient Ruins of Rhodesia*.
33 Garlake P. 1973. *Great Zimbabwe: New Aspects of Archaeology*. London: Thames & Hudson.
34 Ndoro, *The Preservation of Great Zimbabwe: Your Monument, Our Shrine*, 62-71.
35 "Ancient Zimbabwe – The Great Zimbabwe Ruins".
36 Pikirayi, "Peter Garlake (1934-2011)", 224.
37 Randall-MacIver D. 1906. "The Rhodesia Ruins: Their probable origins and significance", *The Geographical Journal* 27(4):325-336.

archaeologist Gertrude Canton-Thomas was allowed access to the ruins in 1929. She confirmed that the monuments were of African origin with respect to artefacts, nearby dwellings and oral tradition.[38] Archaeologist Peter Garlake, who was a senior inspector of the monuments during the colonial era, must have surprised the establishment by negating the foreign origins position he was employed to defend and market.[39] Instead, he defended the indigenous origin of the monuments on account of the homogeneity of the structures with surrounding styles, and for that he was exiled in 1970.[40] Scott T Carroll aptly notes that the problem lay in that "the suggestion that Black African constructed such grandiose building as the Great Zimbabwe assails tremendous prejudice."[41] Zimbabwean archaeologist Innocent Pikirayi lays blame for the Great Zimbabwe site and landscape contest on lack of representation of local history in literature, museum displays, archaeological narratives and management reports.[42]

Religious symbolism and significance

The Hill Complex (acropolis) was the symbol of royalty and religion,[43] and the elegant stone structures represented prestige and status.[44] Standing on an elevated place, eighty meters above the ground, it is the oldest structure on the site that gradually spread to the valley in phases II and III.[45] Part of the complex had steatite upright posts topped with soapstone birds interpreted as symbols of authority and rituality. The secluded, high-level complex was a symbolic show of authority, as well as to preserve the royal privacy.[46] The sacred enclosure by the king's hill residence, the location where the bird sculptures were found, was excluded from the generality of the people, leaving it as a preserve for the selected practitioners. At this site the king patronised the territorial spirits symbolised by the bird sculptures that lent legitimacy to the state. Spirit mediums have continued to visit the site through the colonial period to the present. It is clear that the sanctuary had a political and territorial aura, though Matonjeni and Njelele shrines in Matopos were regarded as more sacred.[47]

---

38 Caton-Thompson G. 1931. *The Zimbabwe Culture: Ruins and Reactions.* Clarendon.
39 Garlake, *Great Zimbabwe*.
40 Pikirayi, "Peter Garlake (1934-2011), 224.
41 Carroll , "Solomonic Legend", 233.
42 Pikirayi, "Great Zimbabwe in Historical Archaeology", 26.
43 "Great Zimbabwe", *Enyclopaedia Britannica*. Online at: http://www.britannica.com/place/Great-Zimbabwe
44 Pikirayi, "Great Zimbabwe in Historical Archaeology", 26.
45 Chirikure S, Bandama F, Chipunza K and Ndoro W. 2016. "Seen but not told: Re-mapping Great Zimbabwe using Archival data, Satellite Imagery and Geographical Information Systems", *Journal of Archaeological Method and Theory*, 15.
46 "Great Zimbabwe (Eleventh–Fifteenth Centuries)". 2001. Online at: http://www.metmuseum.org/toah/hd/zimb/hd_zimb.htm
47 Ndoro, *The Preservation of Great Zimbabwe: Your Monument, Our Shrine*, 68.

At the centre of the religious system was Mwari, the God of fertility, who communicated to the people through the spirit mediums. Despite the collapse of the state in the fifteenth century, the religious ceremonies continued into the nineteenth century.[48] Zimbabwean archaeologist Roger Summers notes that "Dzimbabwe was a place sacred to the chief and his ancestors where formal supplications were made to the Great God Mwari in times of dire tribal need: drought, cattle diseases and human epidemics".[49] Many myths attest to the religious value of the Great Zimbabwe monuments to this day. Even Karl Mauch witnessed the religious awe the shrine provoked from locals – a religious value that may have helped it make onto the UNESCO list.[50]

African and African American historian Manu Ampim, translates the term *zimbabwe* as the "venerated house", the "ritual seat of the king" and the "home or grave of a chief".[51] The Zimbabwean archaeologist Edward Matenga argues that the interpretation associating *zimbabwe* with the burial place of chiefs was due to the fact that kings were buried in stone structures.[52] Greater veneration in Shona kingdoms went to the graves and ancestors of the chiefs. Such ancestors were referred to *mhondoro* (territorial spirits).[53] The rain-supplication ceremonies included the sweeping of the graves of former chiefs as an integral part.[54] Great Zimbabwe, therefore, implies a great house of the ancestors of the Shona people, the guardians of the land.[55] Discoveries of the ceremonial battle spear and axes in the same place enhanced the ritual nature of the enclosure. Innocent Pikirayi and Shadreck Chirikure maintain that material culture found inside the enclosure reflect what they were used for.[56] The ritual spearhead, iron gongs and soapstone bird effigies attest to the presence of a ruling elite, centralising religion for the benefit of power and order.[57] Cecil John Rhodes' Ancient Ruins Company effectively ended this rich practice, putting the site management into perpetual dispute.

Arab and Remba peoples in the hinterland

But the indigeneity of the Great Zimbabwe monument has a lineage that is intricately connected with the Arab and Remba peoples who inhabited the

---

48 "Ancient Zimbabwe – The Great Zimbabwe Ruins".
49 Summers R. 1971. *Ancient Ruins and Vanished Civilisations of Southern Africa*. Cape Town: Gothic Priniting Company, 2.
50 Mawere, Sagiya and Mubaya, "Convergence of Diverse Religions", 22-31.
51 Ampim, "Great Zimbabwe: A History Almost Forgotten".
52 Matenga, "The Soapstone Birds of Great Zimbabwe", 123-131.
53 Schoffeleers JM (ed). 1979. *Guardians of the Land: Essays on Central African Territorial Cults*. Gweru: Mambo.
54 Dube E. 2013. *A Tradition of Abstinence and Ritual Identity: The Ruling Sadiki Remba of Mposi in Mberengwa*. Lambert: Lambert Academic.
55 Ampim, "Great Zimbabwe: A History Almost Forgotten".
56 Pikirayi and Chirikure, "Debating Great Zimbabwe", 222.
57 Matenga E. 1998. *The Soapstone Birds in Zimbabwe: Symbols of a Nation*. Harare: African Publishing Group, 19.

region.⁵⁸ Within the broader boundaries of the ancient Zimbabwe state, there was a symbiotic relationship between Arabs and Shona middlemen.⁵⁹ From this relationship emerged the name Remba, derived from *chilemba*, a turban worn by Muslims and their local admirers, including African converts to Islam.⁶⁰ The Arabs penetrated Zimbabwe from the East African coast during the era of the Great Zimbabwe state, which rose, peaked and collapsed before 1500 CE.⁶¹ These Arabs intermarried with the coastal and interior people. Islam spread through this direct contact with the Arabs, as a result. The Muslim activities in the vast Mutapa Empire (a successor to the Great Zimbabwe state) were gradually affected by the Portuguese establishment of Sofala in 1505.⁶²

Arab wares and architecture were adopted as standard in some settlements in the Zambezi valley resulting in a hybrid culture. Beach observes that "in this culture, Islam became a dominant religion, and spread from the Arabs to the African people along with some Arabic."⁶³ Barbosa confirmed that some Muslims at "Sofala are black men, some olive, and use the tongue of the land."⁶⁴ The Shona Muslims acted as *vashambadzi* (middlemen) buying gold at a cheaper price on the Plateau to be sold at a competitive price at the coast.⁶⁵ From their large settlement at Sena, the Remba earned the contextual names *Vasena* (of Sena) and *Vashavi* (traders).⁶⁶ During the colonial period the Shona-speaking Remba, were "lumped together with Muslim Indians under the general classification of *mwenye*."⁶⁷

As trade on the Central Plateau was controlled from Great Zimbabw, some of the Islamised "Shona-speaking peoples" spread to Great Zimbabwe, and their presence at Great Zimbabwe affected the local customs.⁶⁸ The Zimbabwean scholar of Islamic Studies Ephraim Chikakano Mandivenga maintains that, "It appears that with the coming of Muslim traders the whole area was turned over

---

58 Dube E. 2014. "Ephraim Chikakano Mandivenga and Tudor Parfitt: Two Scholars at Cross Roads? Reflections on the Remba Origins", *Journal of International Academic Research for Multidisciplinary* 2(9):306-319.
59 Beach, *The Shona and Zimbabwe 900-1850*, 417.
60 Gideon S. 2003. *Community and Conscience: the Jews in Apartheid South Africa*. New York: Brandeis University Press, 178.
61 Mandivenga, *Islam in Zimbabwe*, 1.
62 Mandivenga EC. 1992. "Muslims and the Pre-colonial History of Zimbabwe", *Journal Institute of Muslim Minority Affairs* 13:99-115, (99).
63 Beach, *The Shona and Zimbabwe 900-1850*, 25; Alpers EA. 2000. "East Central Africa", in Levitzion N and Pouwels RL (eds). *The History of Islam in Africa*. Athens: Ohio University Press, 303.
64 Quoted by Beach, *The Shona and Zimbabwe 900-1850*, 107.
65 Beach, *The Shona and Zimbabwe 900-1850*, 40.
66 Muhammad bin-Dohry. 2011. "Great Zimbabwe and the Lemba connection," Online at: http://www1.herald.co.zw; Stayt HA. 1931. "Notes on the Balemba", *Journal of the Royal Anthropological Institute* 61:231-238.
67 Beach, *The Shona and Zimbabwe 900-1850*, 108. "Mwenye" is a Remba praise name which David Beach argues denotes Islamic origin, which is why the Remba were officially classified with Muslims.
68 Mandivenga, *Islam in Zimbabwe*, 2.

to Islamic influence to a large extent. Besides, many of the tribesmen apparently adopted such Muslim names as Ali, Moosa, Kassim, Mustafa, Adam, Yusuf. These indigenous people are today identified as the Varemba".[69] Though Mandivenga may be exaggerating the Islamic influence at the Great Zimbabwe capital, some Remba people inhabit the area around Great Zimbabwe to this day and there is evidence of Muslim presence dating a few centuries back.[70] The Remba use tribal names, such as Madi, Sadiki, Hasani, Hamisi, Haji, Sarifu, Seremani, Bakari, Sarifu and Saidi, which are derived from Arabic.[71] Like Muslims, the Remba circumcise their sons between seven and fifteen instead of at infancy as would be the case if they were following the Jewish culture.[72] This makes the Remba "distant descendants of the Muslims who got 'cut off' from the cost by the Portuguese."[73] As indicated above, the Remba may have helped build Great Zimbabwe, and their presence in the monuments area is marked by the excavated models of circumcised male organs that have been found at the initiation site in the Great Enclosure. The Remba were not necessarily the Great Zimbabwe architects, but may have contributed to its building as did many other groups.[74]

The controversies about Great Zimbabwe did not disappear with the termination of the Arab-Remba intercourse but continued to be imbedded in the colonial discourses of dominance. Colonists failed to acknowledge local acumen even in the presence of obvious local connections exhibited in the similar dwellings visible in the surrounding areas as well as oral traditions. Spirit mediums refused to give up their practices within the complex despite legal ban, which represented the undying African spirit and lack of substitute shrines among the indigenous Karanga people. The traditional connection between religion and politics was clear in that mediums were soon joined by political parties in defying the new authority. This symbiotic relationship between religion and politics in defence of territory (shrine) speaks well of the African discourse. This continued respect for the shrine demonstrated its symbolic meaning to the locals as the abode of their ancestral spirits.

---

69   Mandivenga, *Islam in Zimbabwe*, 2.
70   Mandivenga, *Islam in Zimbabwe*, 30.
71   Hammond-Tooke WD. 1937. *The Bantu-Speaking Peoples of Southern Africa*. London: Routledge & Kegan Paul, 82.
72   Hammond-Tooke, *The Bantu-Speaking Peoples of Southern Africa*, 81-84.
73   Mandivenga EC. 1986. *Islam in Zimbabwe: A study of the Religious Developments from the Sixteenth to the Twentieth Century*, PhD Diss, University of Aberdeen, abstract.
74   Parfitt T. 2000. *Journey to the Vanished City*. New York: Vintage Random House, 1-2; Mufuka K. 1983. *Dzimbahwe Life and Politics in the Golden Age 1100-1500 AD*, Harare: Publishing House; Le Roux M. 2003. *The Lemba – A Lost Tribe of Israel in Southern Africa?* Pretoria: University of South Africa.

POLITICAL DISCOURSES OF DOMINANCE

The Zimbabwean archaeologist Innocent Pikirayi notes that, in the last two decades of colonialism the Great Zimbabwe discourse was influenced a "new antiquarian revisionism, based on what Ian Smith and his apologists thought about the place."[75] Ian Smith, the last Rhodesia Prime Minister, and his government were bent on maintaining white supremacy through the denigration of everything African. They sought to perpetuate the "Pioneer Discourse"[76] by burying heroes of the Pioneer Column[77] in sacred places including briefly at the Great Zimbabwe monuments. Anthropologist Joost Fontein argues that "the site was appropriated to provide historical and moral justification for the imperial projects."[78] The monuments had to be physically, psychologically and spiritually sealed off from the locals. Physically, a police post was put in place to bar locals from having their rites and rituals within the monuments area. This practice effectively revised the centuries old religious (spiritual) use of the monuments by the local population, which lasted until the takeover of the country by the Pioneer Column at the close of the nineteenth century.[79] The successive white regimes put in place legal instruments "protecting" monuments and museums. These instruments were to be administered by an "interested" civil service, which was to disparage the truth that credited the indigenous population with masterminding the construction of the Great Zimbabwe complexes.[80] Its mandate was to advance the theory of the foreign origins of the monuments to discourage any credit being given to locals for such marvellous precolonial achievements.

Colonialism and nationalism in conflict

The situation became more acute with the rise of nationalism which took pride in ancient African achievements for inspiration. Africans could no longer stand the psychological trauma of being looked down upon by colonists, especially being dispossessed of their ancient heritage. The first act of defiance was in reclaiming the Great Zimbabwe Monuments through the political movements' nomenclature: Zimbabwe National Party (1961), Zimbabwe African People's Union (1961) and Zimbabwe African National Union (1963).

To strengthen its ideology of white dominance, the colonial regime had two dominant partners helping it communicate an exclusive model. The

---

75 Pikirayi, "The True Story of Great Zimbabwe".
76 The "Pioneer Discourse" glorified the colonisation of Zimbabwe by a group of armed volunteers sponsored by Cecil John Rhodes, the British imperial tycoon based in South Africa.
77 "Pioneer Column" is the official terminology used to describe the armed volunteers who occupied Zimbabwe at the behest of Cecil John Rhodes.
78 Fontein J. 2006. *The Silence of Great Zimbabwe: Contested Landscapes and the Power of Heritage*. Harare: Weaver, 213.
79 Matenga, "The Soapstone Birds of Great Zimbabwe", 123-131.
80 Garlake, *Great Zimbabwe: New Aspects of Archaeology*.

most enduring partner was education, closely connected with the Christian missionaries, who formed the other pillar of the colonial regime. The missionaries were clear that outside the church there was no salvation.[81] The practice of the African indigenous religion at the monuments would be both misleading and non-salvific. Church doctrine left no room for the traditional use of the monuments. In fact, to complement the authorities who built a police post and placed dogmatic civil servants at the monuments site, the church built a large mission at Mogenster overlooking the ancient site.[82] This was replicated in other places. The famous historian of central Africa, Terence O Ranger, has noted that: "After many years of unsuccessful mission work in the Matopos, the Christian church at Hope Fountain decided to conduct its services at sacred sites including Silozwane national monument that is also near Old Bulawayo another heritage site in an attempt to discredit their use by the local people."[83]

In its exclusive approach, the church further advanced the notion of being chosen in relation to the Jews – and Christians by extension.[84] The theory of election with its resentment for everything African led to an unnecessary assault on the local culture. The church offered the Western version of the Judeo-Christian tradition as an alternative to the local culture which was described as heathenism. The term "Judeo-Christian" refers to "the influence of the Hebrew Bible and the New Testament on one's system of values, laws and ethical code".[85] In the Black and White paradigm, the African ways represented the former while the later signified Western civilisation. Christian villages were built to wean Africans from their heritage. Gokomere Mission, forty kilometers north of Great Zimbabwe, and, to a lesser extent, Mogenster provide good examples.[86]

The Solomonic legend and the Abrahamic religions

The missionaries further hoped to appropriate the African heritage through the Solomonic legend. The idealistic search for the historicity of Solomon's gold mines at Ophir led a member of the Berlin Mission Society, Rev A Merensky, to direct Karl Mauch to Great Zimbabwe on a verification mission and he straightaway appropriated the structures to the Semitic people.[87] Between

---

81 Knitter PF. 1985. *No Other Name? A Critical Survey of Christian Attitudes Toward the World Religions.* New York: Orbis, 121.
82 Mawere, Sagiya and Mubaya, "Convergence of Diverse Religions", 23.
83 Ranger TO. 1999. *Voices from the Rocks: Nature, Culture and History in the Matopo Hills.* Harare: Baobab, 150. "Another heritage site" here refers to "Old Bulawayo" – all quoted.
84 Banana CS. 1996. *Politics of Repression and Resistance: Face to Face with Combat Theology.* Gweru: Mambo; Isabel M, Cox JL and Verstraelen FJ (eds). 1993. *Rewriting the Bible: The Real Issues.* Gweru: Mambo.
85 Lee R. 2009. "Seven Principles of the Judeo-Christian Ethic", *The American Patriot's Bible*. Nashville, TN: Thomas Nelson.
86 Zvobgo CJM. 1996. *A History of Christian Missions in Zimbabwe 1890-1939.* Gweru: Mambo.
87 Carroll, "Solomonic Legend", 236.

1873 and 1876, an interested European press enthusiastically spread the news of Mauch's speculation about Solomon's presence at Great Zimbabwe. Literary works including Hugh Mulleneux Walmsley's *The Ruined Cities of Zululand* and Rider Haggard's *King Solomon's Mines* wetted the appetite of the European audience for success stories of European adventures, while making the subsequent African literature student of the colonial Rhodesia hate or feel uncomfortable with his/her past.[88] By the end of the nineteenth century, the reign of Solomon at Great Zimbabwe had been accepted as proven; and thus "fiction and popular notion had been mistaken for fact".[89]

The Judeo-Christian template not only excluded the Africans and their religion from the monuments, but also negated any other tradition contrary to the propagation of the Christian appropriation of the Jewish Messianism through Christ. In this regard, Muslims, who equally deny the divinity of Jesus Christ, could not have anything to do with the magnificent monuments. Christians "quoted" Muslims as denying any involvement in the monument construction which they attributed to Solomon.[90] The authenticity of these quotations is doubtful since they were written by Christians in an atmosphere of Christian-Muslim competition. The Portuguese were the first to use the technique of forged Muslim quotations in the mid-sixteenth century and this spread to other Christian nations uncritically.[91]

Missionaries also used education to concretise their model, which essentially meant appropriating Western Christian values exclusive of any other "salvation and progressive model". Those who dared challenge this model by words or action risked dismissal in some instances.[92] This dominant discourse that advanced Jewish-Christian superiority and damaged the Remba cultural heritage leaving them with disputed paternity.[93] To fit into the dominant discourse, the Remba close to the monuments claim Jewish ancestry, while some members of the same Remba group residing in Gutu District in eastern Zimbabwe have long embraced Islam leading to the building of a mosque and employment of a professional Muslim imam. Currently plans are afoot to build the Great Zimbabwe Synagogue among the Remba of Tadzembwa close to the

---

88 Walmsley HM. 1869. *The Ruined Cities of Zululand*. London: Chapman and Hall; Haggard R. 1885. *King Solomon's Mines*. London: Thomas Nelson and Sons.
89 Carroll, "Solomonic Legend", 236.
90 De Barros J. 1964. "Da Asia", in Theal GN (ed). *Records of South-Eastern Africa*, vol. VI. Cape Town: Printed for the Government of the Cape Colony, 267-268.
91 Carroll, "Solomonic Legend", 243
92 Teachers were dismissed for marrying more than one wife.
93 Historians David N Beach and Stan Mudenge and Islamic scholar Ephraim Chikakano Mandivenga argue that the Remba circumcision rituals, marriage and dietary laws reflect Muslim heritage acquired as a result of Arab-Shona intermarriages in the Zambezi valley. Even Tudor Parfitt's genetic theory does not exclude Islamic heritage, as he agrees that the Jews and Arabs of Hadramaut in Yemen have similar genetic configurations. Some Remba today accept Islamic heritage, while others claim Jewish origins leaving the tribal group with disputed paternity.

Great Zimbabwe Monuments. The synagogue issue has been necessitated by a sense of belonging. This is particularly so because, by the time the discourse reached out to the Remba, the majority of them were already Christian.[94]

Tudor Parfitt, a British anthropologist born in Wales and bred in England from a non-Jewish family with "an intense admiration for Jewish people", has travelled to the remotest regions of the world looking for the "lost tribes of Israel".[95] Parfitt supports the Jewish theory, regarded as fallacious by a number of local scholars, including David N Beach, Ephraim Chikakano Mandivenga and Stan IG Mudenge. Parfitt advanced a genetic theory which gives the Remba a genetic configuration similar to that of the Jews. He argues that they must have moved from Yemen as a group into Africa. This assumption is problematic because in that case they should have had both male and female genes similar to those of the Jews. Since they have only the male gene in common he has proposed another assumption in which a lone Jew unknown in history must have strayed into East Africa and left children there. This assumption is complicated by the fact that the Arabs in the region of Hadramaut, the postulated region of the "original Sena," have a similar genetic configuration. Moreover many Arabs from the region were in the vicinity of the Great Zimbabwe area, as confirmed by the presence of many artefacts. The Remba also use Arabic and not Jewish names and the marriage and food taboos in question bridge two of the Abrahamic religions: Judaism and Islam.

The proposed Jewish linkage may therefore be an unstable tradition. The British historian Eric Hobsbawm, in discussing invented traditions, notes that "where possible, they normally attempt to establish continuity with a suitable historic past … However, insofar as there is such reference to a historic past, the peculiarity of 'invented' traditions is that the continuity with it is largely fictitious."[96] Hobsbawm further argues that "many practices which are considered traditional are in fact quite recent inventions, often deliberately constructed to serve particular ideological ends."[97] The Jewish link is ideologically linked to the Judeo-Christian template.

---

94   The authenticity of Remba religious heritage took a sharp turn in 1961 when Muslims took an active role to (in Ephraim Mandivenga's terminology)"re-Islamise" the Remba by building mosques and "re-teaching" them Islamic principles. By then many of them were already Christians and reluctant to "re-join" Islam.
95   Online at: www.miamherald.com/2013/05/3389721/religious-studies-professor-is.html
96   Hobsbawm E. 2004. "Introduction: Inventing Traditions", in Hosbawm E and Ranger T (eds). *The Invention of Tradition.* Cambridge: Cambridge University Press, 1.
97   Yee D. 1995. "A Review of The Invention of Tradition by Eric Hobsbawm and Terence Ranger (eds), Cambridge University Press, 1992". Online at: http://dannyreviews.com

The *Ngomalungundu* (the drum that thunders), which Parfitt likens to the Ark of the Covenant,[98] further complicates the authenticity of his argument. The latter posits a lone Jewish ancestor and negates the former theory of the Exodus from Jerusalem with the Ark of the Covenant via Yemen with the subsequent imitations. To say that the drum which has nothing real in common with the Ark of the Covenant except the method of carriage is its replica baffles the mind. The biblical Ark of the Covenant was not a thundering drum. It was the trumpet that sounded and not the Ark of the Covenant. But this claim has resulted in the construction of synagogues in Mberengwa, "the spiritual home of all the Lembas",[99] along with one being proposed in the Great Zimbabwe region. The trend in Mberengwa, though, has been that only those interested in Judaism as "one of the churches", including non-Remba, go to the synagogue.[100] The Jews, however, are not allowed in the Remba initiation venues and are not considered legitimate ritual slaughterers by the majority of the Remba,[101] though Remba culture has come to be managed through a Judeo-Christian template.

By managing the Remba cultural heritage through the Judeo-Christian template, Christians have sown confusion in the Remba ranks. Their aim of discrediting any competing religion has left the Remba with a disputed paternity and in danger of being declared foreigners in their land of birth. Yet in the Shona context, a cousin can actually take over the traditional leadership of his mother's people. If the carvings representing circumcised manhood were made at the behest of the Remba, then they have been lost to the Great Zimbabwe Museum just as the Ngomalungundu which now lies in a Harare museum.[102] The Remba do not benefit from such displays which have been deprived of all religious connotations.

LEGAL PROTECTIONS AND CHALLENGES IN HERITAGE MANAGEMENT

The Great Zimbabwe site has been legally protected since 1893 and is currently protected under the National Museum and Monuments Act Chapter 25:11 (1976), which provides for the legal protection of the resources within the property.[103] The Act does not define the role to be played by local authorities,

---

98 The *Ngomalungundu* is a drum which was also used in sacred performances by the Remba.
99 Mativha MER. 1992. *The Basena, Vamwenye, Balemba*. Johannesburg: Morester, 47.
100 Mariposa Tavengwa, a Remba who goes to one of the synagogues says only those Remba interested can come since it is just one of the "churches" which even accepts *senzi* (non-Remba as in gentiles). The impression from this Remba elder implies that importance is placed on conversion and not heritage.
101 Interview with Maramwidze Tadzoka by E Dube, Danga-Mposi, Zimbabwe 22 April 2016.
102 Parfitt T. 2002. "The Lemba: An African Judaising Tribe", in Parfitt T and Trevisan-Semi E (eds). *Judaising Movements: Studies in the Margins of Judaism*. London: Routledge Curzon, 40-42.
103 Mawere M, Mubaya TR and Sagiya ME. 2013. "Challenges, Dilemmas and Potentialities for Poverty Relief by Heritage sites in Zimbabwe: Voices from

and the ambivalence in this area creates problems for heritage management, especially with regards to determining the relevant stakeholders for the smooth management of both tangible and intangible heritage. The Act affects the traditional interaction between the heritage site and the local community as the legal implementation is more skewed against the indigenous involvement. The monuments were adopted as a UNESCO World Heritage Site in 1986, implying their outstanding universal value. It was one of the most significant civilisations of the medieval period,[104] and one of the only seven in southern Africa to be accorded such respect by UNESCO. Nevertheless, even with the UNESCO World Heritage Site designation, management of the Great Zimbabwe monument site has not been without challenges.

The first challenge is to address is the question: For whom should heritage be managed? Heritage management specialists Munyaradzi Mawere, Tapiwa Mubaya and Munyaradzi Sagiya argue that "the use of heritage sites should be compatible with culture of the people in which the site is located, that is, the use of the sites should respect the cultural significance of a place."[105] But the foregoing discussion has shown that once the Pioneer Column established company rule in what was then Rhodesia, the Great Zimbabwe Monuments became part of the establishment to the exclusion of the indigenous people.[106] This suggests that the adoption of Western formal legislation has had the effect of alienating the local people from the administration of their natural and cultural heritage.[107]

A new appropriation theory was invented in the name of the exotic origin of the monuments. Was this exclusive model fair if the Afrocentric view of the local origins is correct? The function of the place changed from sacred site to tourist centre, which further excluded the locals since they could not afford the fees. It is difficult for the descendants of the builders of the structures to accept the ban, while those with money marvel at what should be their rightful inheritance. This top-down management approach transfers all benefits to the controlling authority. Instead, the bottom-up approach would have allowed the locals to benefit, while the authorities reaped the taxes.

The political parties used the monuments as an inspirational past achievement, and now the country has its very name derived from the Great Zimbabwe monuments. The liberation discourse nationalised the monuments and at

---

Chibvumani Heritage Site Stakeholders", *Journal of Sustainable Development in Africa* 15(1):193.
104 Ampim, "Great Zimbabwe: A History Almost Forgotten".
105 Mawere, Sagiya and Mubaya, "Convergence of Diverse Religions", 29.
106 Mawere, Mubaya and Sagiya, "Challenges, Dilemmas and Potentialities", 187-188.
107 Ndoro W and Kiriama M. 2008. "Management mechanism in Heritage Legislation", in Ndoro W, Mumma A and Abungu G (eds). *Cultural Heritage and the Law. Protecting Immovable Heritage in English Speaking Countries of Southern Africa. ICCROM Conservation Studies* 8, 54.

independence they continued to be controlled by national codes through 1986, when UNESCO codes were also extended to the monuments as a World Heritage Site.[108] These legal regimes have not done better in the restoration of the colonial dispossessions. Heritage management is still done for purposes contra enhancement of local needs. Those with the political muscle utilise the venue without hindrance, thus war veterans from the Harare province brought with them Mashonaland regional mediums Nehoreka and Bhasvi in March 2011 and held their ceremony uninterrupted, and yet ordinary people have to conjure means to enter the monuments area for similar performances.[109]

CONCLUSION

Colonial discourses have negatively affected the ownership and use of both the tangible and intangible heritage at Great Zimbabwe. The colonial government appropriated the monuments and assigned them foreign origins which abrogated the claim to ownership and use by the indigenous people. The "authorised heritage discourse syndrome"[110] did not allow the attribution of any kind of heritage associated with the monuments to its indigenous authors and owners. Laws were crafted specifying the colonial authorities as stakeholders, but they were silent about the place of the indigenous people. Implementation, however, clearly excluded the indigenes. But issues associated with religion do not easily succumb to legal frameworks. For that reason, Great Zimbabwe remains the spiritual home of indigenous aspirations, to the extent that political parties were named after the monuments in the midst of the harsh apartheid laws advocating separate progress for different races. The monuments continued to inspire various spirit mediums from across the country through the colonial, liberation and post-independence periods.

Independence did not bring legal revision and the locals have remained peripheral to the management and use of heritage associated with Great Zimbabwe. Since the nationalisation of the monuments by the colonial government in 1937, they have never reverted to local use – with the result that spiritual use at political or national levels has remained more tolerable to this day than local use. The "authorised heritage discourse syndrome" augmented by the "Judeo-Christian template" has struck a wedge in the Remba cultural heritage leaving them with a disputed paternity; split between Muslim and Jewish fatherhood. The foundations of the Great Zimbabwe Synagogue are currently being laid, even though similar endeavours in Mberengwa have neither attracted committed Remba Christians to synagogue, nor integrated Jews into the Remba cultural milieu. Failure has been the result. Those who

---

108 Mawere, Sagiya and Mubaya, "Convergence of Diverse Religions", 23.
109 Mawere, Sagiya and Mubaya, "Convergence of Diverse Religions", 23.
110 Matenga,"The Soapstone Birds of Great Zimbabwe". The term "authorised" indicates that heritage officials had no leeway to digress from the official position even though they knew its flaws.

maintain the Jewish discourse have had a problem of "telescoping", that is, projecting events too far into the past. As it is, no artefacts discovered at the monuments reflect any period span by the Jewish empire, clearly dissociating the Jewish empire from the Great Zimbabwe Empire.

Successive governments have adopted Western formal legislation which has alienated locals from the administration of their heritage sites. The net result of this has been to put heritage managers in an awkward position, speculating what their actual role should be vis-à-vis what the law says in relation to the realities on the ground. Locals struggle against the law to have access to what is theirs for their own religious enhancement against uncooperative successive political authorities. The government as the legislature- and law-enforcing agent, the local indigenous believers and the Christian exclusivists are locked in endless arguments over the utilisation of the monuments. All these currents make life difficult for the conservationists who value local input as a management tool. Very often heritage managers have advocated for dialogue amongst the competing voices.[111] Closing out locals has been of particular concern to the heritage managers, since the locals are the owners of the heritage. There is a need to re-align the heritage laws in order to re-integrate the locals into the management systems of the heritage sites. This is important because, although this chapter focuses on Great Zimbabwe, the situation obtaining here may be true for all other heritage sites in Zimbabwe.

---

111 See the following works by monuments and former monuments staff. Mawere, Sagiya and Mubaya, "Convergence of Diverse Religions", 22-31; Mawere, Mubaya and Sagiya, "Challenges, Dilemmas and Potentialities", 186-198; Matenga, "The Soapstone Birds of Great Zimbabwe".

VI. Religion, Hate Speech, Diversity and Equality

15 TAMING ROGUE CLERGY AND CHURCHES: GOD, SCANDALS, GOVERNMENT AND RELIGIOUS REGULATION IN KENYA

Damaris Seleina Parsitau[1]

INTRODUCTION

In Kenya, as is the case in many parts of the African continent, religion is both a social and political force. It is therefore not surprising that the religious industry has been booming for the last three decades, with little or no regulations of its activities. In the recent past, Kenyans have witnessed an increasingly high number of religious scandals committed by men and women of God, who are supposedly also keepers of morality and ethics. While rogue clergy are increasingly becoming a panacea to the Kenyan public, they have also attracted significant debates and discourses, with loud calls for stricter regulation of these clergy and their churches. However, relatively little academic attention has been devoted to these phenomena.[2] Based on recent ethnographic research, as well as social analysis and observations of the Kenyan social and religious scene, this chapter highlights and demonstrates through case studies some of the recent scandals involving Kenya's clergy from the Pentecostal churches, with a view to providing a moral, ethical and social critique of the Kenyan social, political and religious scene.

This chapter explores these tensions by highlighting the challenges this phenomenon presents to the public and the Kenyan government, caught between freedoms of expression and attempts to regulate religious organisations and rogue clergy in Kenya. Further, this inquiry attempts to answer the following questions: How can the government tame rogue clergy in an extremely contested social, political and religious sphere like Kenya? Who will hold rogue clergy to account and what is being done? What are the tensions inherent in regulating rogue clergy and political power? The chapter is organised into several sections. Firstly, I discuss the social and religious background in Kenya,

---

1 Damaris Seleina Parsitau is the Director of the Institute of Women Gender and Development Studies and a Senior Lecturer at the Department of Philosophy, History and Religious Studies at Egerton University, Kenya. She is also an Associate Fellow and a Visiting Research Fellow at UNISA, South Africa. This chapter is written courtesy of generous research grants from the Nagel Institute in the USA.
2 For an in-depth analysis of one of these rogue clergy, arguably the biggest of them all, Prophet David Owuor, see Parsitau DS. 2016. "Prophets, power, authority and the Kenyan state: Prophet David Owuor of the National Repentance and Holiness Ministry", in Coertzen P, Green MC and Hansen L (eds). *Religious Freedom and Religious Pluralism in Africa: Prospects and Limitations*. Stellenbosch: African Sun Media, 233-255.

as well as the proliferation of the Neo-Pentecostal churches, some of which have been involved in scandal. This overview is followed by case studies of rogue clergy and their churches, as well as government attempts to regulate the churches. Lastly, I offer a social and moral critique of these churches and their clergy, as well as their gullible members.

WHEN GOD BECAME KENYAN: KENYA'S SOCIAL AND RELIGIOUS LANDSCAPE: SETTING THE CONTEXT

Kenya is a nation with a rich religio-cultural diversity. With its population of 38.6 million people, the country is an embodiment of historical, cultural, ethnic, religious, social, political and linguistic affinities and diversities. Indeed, its religious landscape is quite complex, dynamic and diverse, including African Indigenous Religion (AIR), various strands of Christianity and Islam as well as smaller groups of practitioners of Hinduism, Buddhism, Baha'i and Judaism, among other religions. Demographically, Kenya is predominantly Christian. The Kenyan Population and Housing Census of 2009 revealed that Christians constitute about 31.8 million of Kenya's 38.6 million people. What this essentially means is that about 82.6% of the population in Kenya is Christian, constituting a significant majority compared with other faiths.[3] It is further estimated that 4.3 million of the population are Muslims.[4] The non-religious population is small but nevertheless significant. Accurate statistics for minority faiths are difficult to access and are largely a matter of conjecture. However, the major religious traditions in Kenya are Christianity and Islam, both of which have been influenced by indigenous African religious traditions.

All these religious traditions, to use religion scholar Afe Adogame's words, "have mutually enhanced and transformed each other in a highly competitive context."[5] Besides, they serve as significant sources through which many Kenyans seek to understand their complex reality and existence. For these reasons, religious ideas and worldviews continue to shape the ways in which Kenyans explain, predict, and control the events and life circumstances that surround them. It can correctly be argued that religion and spirituality have served as a significant source through which many Kenyans seek to understand both their complex reality and existence and which serve as a panacea for their various existential problems of day-to-day living. Moreover, Kenya is not the

---

3 Kenyan National Bureau of Statistics. 2010. *Kenya: 2009 Population and Housing Census Highlights.* Nairobi: KNBS, 2.
4 Statistics for Kenyan Muslims have been deeply politicised and highly contested with some Muslim groups suggesting that the population is anywhere between 10 to 30 percent of the population. This claim is however not supported by demographic data, as was evident in the 2009 Population Census.
5 Adogame A. 2010. "How God became a Nigerian: Religious Impulse and the Unfolding of a Nation", *Journal of Contemporary African Studies* 28(4):479-498.

only religious country in Africa, as indicated by report from the Pew Forum on Religion and Public Life.[6]

Given these statistics, it is not surprising that religious actors and institutions have become powerful forces in shaping social, spiritual and political developments on much of the African continent. At the same time, new religious movements such as the Pentecostal and charismatic churches have recently proliferated in Sub-Saharan Africa in recent decades and have completely altered the social and religious landscape of the country.

THE PROLIFERATION OF PENTECOSTAL CHRISTIANITY IN KENYA: SETTING THE CONTEXT

The Pentecostal and charismatic Christian movements exploded onto the Kenyan social and religious scene and have steadily grown from the 1980s, establishing hundreds of churches all over the country. Since the 1990s, these have become perhaps the fastest growing spiritual movements in Kenya today. Similarly, they have attracted thousands of followers, mainly educated youth, women and other social groups. At present, Kenyan Neo-Pentecostalism represents the most visible evidence of religious renewal, as attested by its social and public prominence and constitutes the fastest growing group of churches.[7] A 2006 survey by the Pew Forum suggests that renewalists – including Pentecostals and charismatics – account for more than half of Kenya's population.[8] The survey also shows that approximately 70% of Protestants in Kenya are either Pentecostal or charismatic, and about one third of Kenyan Catholics surveyed can be classified as charismatic.

The Pew Forum's estimates are further validated by newspaper reports that appear to support this immense growth. Alex Ndegwa, for example, reports that "the Registrar General's office is overwhelmed by increasing demands for church registration".[9] The former attorney general, Amos Wako, while speaking in a workshop for church leaders, revealed that the department was overwhelmed by increasing demand for registration of churches and that the facility was facing difficulties in processing 6,740 pending applications by various religious organisations.[10] Wako also revealed that there were about

---

6 Pew Forum on Religion & Public Life. 2011. *Global Christianity – A Report on the Size and Distribution of the World's Christian Population,* Washington, DC: Pew Research Center, December. Online at: http://www.pewforum.org/2011/12/19/global-christianity-exec
7 Parsitau DS. 2011. "Arise, Oh Ye Daughters of Faith: Pentecostalism, Women and Public Culture in Kenya", in England H (ed). *Christianity and Public Culture in Africa.* Athens: Ohio University Press, 131-148.
8 As cited in Parsitau DS. 2014. *Neo-Pentecostalism in Kenya: Its Civic and Public Role,* PhD Diss, Kenyatta University.
9 Ndegwa A. 2007. "Over 6,000 Churches Awaiting Registration", *The Standard,* 4 September.
10 Ndegwa, "Over 6,000 Churches Awaiting Registration".

8,520 registered churches and that about 100 applications are filed every month. According to the Registrar of Societies, pastors and founding clergy register some churches as private properties co-owned with spouse and family, thereby making it personal property. This development partly explains the numerous protracted church ownership tussles that are rampant in the Kenyan courts, as well as a dramatic increase in scandals perpetuated by a section of Neo-Pentecostal clergy.[11] Although not all of these churches seeking registration have Pentecostal and charismatic inclinations, most of them are of Pentecostal persuasion.

These different sets of statistics, while contested, nevertheless point to the tremendous growth of Neo-Pentecostal and charismatic churches in Kenya, many of which have sprung up in major urban centres, some within less than three to five kilometers apart. Some are huge churches with large membership while others are too small to be called churches. They nevertheless add to the numbers. These churches rose sharply to prominence due to a combination of factors. Scholars and Pentecostal leaders alike have linked this sudden growth of Pentecostalism in Africa with the economic crisis and stagnation of the 1980s and the subsequent Structural Adjustment Programmes (SAPs) that led to the worsening material conditions of life for many people during the 1980s and 1990s.[12]

In Kenya, as in many other African countries, religious actors are respected members of society. Religious actors are also increasingly asserting themselves in issues in public life, especially the political life of their countries. They do this through grassroots mobilisation, electioneering processes and peace building, contributing to national debates around constitutionalism and human rights issues,[13] religious pluralism and interfaith dialogue, among others. Yet these countries also offer clear illustrations of how religious actors, particularly those

---

11 Although religious scandals are part and parcel of church history, the majority of scandals in the Kenyan religious scene affect mostly Pentecostal and charismatic clergy. This is based on my own personal observations as well as media reports on religious scandals in Kenya. See, for example, Shupe AD. 2008. *Rogue Clerics: The Social Problem of Clergy Deviance*. New Brunswick, NJ, and London: Transaction.

12 Parsitau DS. 2008. "The Impact of Structural Adjustments Programmes (SAPS) on the Health Status of Women in Kenya", in Sama M and Nguyen VK (eds). *Governing Health Systems in Africa*. Dakar: CODESRIA, 191-200.

13 A variety of Christian churches and faith-based organisations contributed to constitutional reforms in Kenya, while the Pentecostal and Evangelical churches sought to shape the 2010 Kenyan Constitution by vehemently opposing the inclusion of Muslim Kadhi Courts in the new constitution. For more on the Khadi Courts controversy in Kenya, see the essay of Hassan Juma Ndzovu, "Muslim and Christian contestation over the entrenchment of the Kadhi Courts in the Constitution of Kenya: Challenging the principle of a secular state" in this volume. See also Ndzovu HJ. 2014. *Muslims in Kenyan Politics: Political Involvement, Marginalization, and Minority Status*. Evanston, IL: Northwestern University Press, esp ch. 4; Green MC. 2013. "Religious and Legal Pluralism in Recent African Constitutional Reform", *Journal of Law and Religion* 28(2):401-439; Green MC. 2014.

from Neo-Pentecostal Christianity are increasingly involved in moral, ethical and financial scandals.

Over the last one decade or so, religious scandals have proliferated in Kenya. There have been significant numbers of highly publicised cases of outright fraud on the part of some Pentecostal church clergy in the last five years or so. A growing number of clergy, mainly charlatans of Kenya's religious industry, have planted churches variously also called prophetic, deliverance and healing ministries to make money out of gullible members. As the religious industry and prophetic ministries have grown, there has also been a dramatic increase of religious scandals mainly associated though not limited to the Pentecostal and charismatic types.

Yet it is not by accidents that prophets and prophetesses have become an ever-growing feature of Africa's and Kenya's social and political landscape. The proliferation of prophets has made it difficult to tell the genuine ones from the charlatans, especially since there are thousands of gullible followers in need of spiritual guidance and prayers to surmount their daily existential challenges. In the course of ethnographic research carried over the last ten years, I found, for example, that some of these churches' reception desks have shelves full of "anointing oil," "anointing water" and "anointing salts" that are sold according to the nature of one's illness. The items also vary in price depending on the nature of illness. Serious illnesses such as cancer, HIV/AIDS, diabetes and high blood pressure require one to pay more for the anointed items than if one suffers from a cold or flu.

The selling of religious paraphernalia by these clergy to gullible members has only served to increase the vulnerability of those seeking spiritual solutions to their problems, while at the same time enriching some Pentecostal clergy and leading to intense scrutiny by both the print and electronic media, thereby exposing not just the scandals committed by clergy, who seem to exploit the vulnerabilities and gullibility of their followers, but also the gullibility and vulnerability of followers. Indeed, scandals committed by Kenyan leaders, whether religious or political or state agents, are so frequent that it can correctly be said that scandals are part of our daily lives.

RELIGIOUS IMPUNITY AND THE FINANCIAL AND MORAL SCANDALS OF PENTECOSTAL CLERGY IN KENYA

Although clerical scandals span the globe, relatively little attention has been given to understanding the scandals perpetrated by Pentecostal clergy, beyond abundant media scrutiny. In the course of writing this chapter, I found nearly no sociological literature on the scandals perpetrated by Pentecostal church clergy. This is interesting, considering religious scandals are not unique to Pentecostal

---

"From Social Hostility to Social Media: Religious Pluralism, Human Rights, and Democratic Reform in Africa", *African Human Rights Law Journal* 14(1):93-125.

churches. For the present study, I draw on data accruing from intense media scrutiny and legal commentary on the churches, as well as my own personal observations and ethnographic studies. In this section, I explore selected case studies of recent religious scandals that have received significant attention in the Kenyan social and religious scene and led to calls to the government to regulate such churches.

Prophet Victor Kanyari and Lucy Nduta of Salvation Healing Ministry

In 2015, Victor Kanyari, a televangelist and pastor of the Salvation Healing Ministry, who is also the son of disgraced Prophetess Lucy Nduta, was exposed on Kenya Television Network's *Jicho Pevu* (Grim Eye), an investigative television series,[14] for performing dubious miracles, faking healing and coaching his staff to tender phony testimonies of among other things, healing and prayer induced prosperity. The series exposed Kanyari for selling fake miracles and duping believers into giving money and other gifts to the church with the promise that God would look into their issues. Kanyari was further revealed to be a con artist, who preyed on his gullible followers for financial gains. This harrowing video exposé laced with shocking confessions from part of his team, revealed how this church founder obtained money from worshippers in the pretence that they would receive miracles.

The exposé of *Makri ya Injili* (prayer predators) clearly showed the deceptive methods that Salvation Healing Ministry's Victor Kanyari has used to lure and exploit his gullible and trusting followers for the past fifteen years in order to enrich himself. The exposé was supported by witness testimonies given by paid members of the church, who falsely testified that they had been miraculously healed of AIDS through Pastor Kanyari's prayers. Kanyari further washed the feet of his followers with water lased with potassium permanganate. When he did this, the water turned red and he told his followers that this was blood oozing out of their feet as he performed miracles of healing

In another exposé, Kanyari paid women, mostly prostitutes, to come for faith healing services with twisted mouths and faces which would miraculously be realigned during prayer services televised on the national Kenya Television Network. Kanyari was exposed not only as a con man and who used the services of prostitutes, but also as a drunk who cheated on his gospel musician wife in an act that ended their marriage. The story aired in KTN's prime time slot also showed footage in which Kanyari appeared to be falsifying phone calls on his radio programmes recorded from his house. Audiences were urged to send as much as 500,000 Kenyan shillings ($5 000 US) after a single episode. Church members and anybody else who needed prayers had to send him a mandatory

---

14   Kanyari V. 2014. "Makriya Injili" [Prayer predators]. Ali M and Need AN (prod), *Jicho Pevu* [Grim Eye], Kenya Television Network (KTN), 2 November.

310 Kenyan shillings ($4 US) as a mandatory fee for prayer. This clip went viral, prompting government action to regulate these churches.

After the exposé, an unrepentant Kanyari bragged that he had become an instant celebrity, since he was the subject of discussion in Kenya's public and private discourses. He further bragged of his rise from a mere secondary school dropout and a former manual farm labourer to become a prophet whom everyone was talking about. He claimed that every church asks for seed offerings and tithes and all other manner of giving and that he was only fixed by the media which was a common practice in many Pentecostal and charismatic churches.

His mother, Prophetess Lucy Nduta, also of Salvation Healing Ministry and host of a weekly TV programme, was arrested in mid-2006 for extorting money from the faithful – particularly for requiring patients to plant a seed between 200,000 and 400,000 Kenyan shillings ($2,000 to $4,000 US) for her to cure them from AIDS through powerful prayers. Upon receipt of the payment, church elders would allegedly take the AIDS patients to a local AIDS clinic where they would be issued with false medical certificates giving them a clean bill of health. Evidently, many patients had sold their properties or borrowed money from friends and family to raise the seed money.

The prophetess argued that she had cured at least 200 AIDS cases in her church alone. According to religion scholar Paul Gifford,[15] one woman had given a car worth 300,000 Kenyan shillings ($3,000 US) for prayer for her ailing daughter, another nearly one million Kenyan shillings ($10,000 US) for prayer to conceive and yet another 21,000 Kenyan shillings ($210 US) to obtain a visa to the Netherlands. Another follower gave 20,000 Kenyan shillings ($200 US) for a prayer to become rich. The prophetess tried to have the case dismissed, arguing that questions of faith and spirits did not fall within the court's competence. Instead, her plea was rejected and she was jailed for two years. It seems the son learnt from his mother and may have continued to run the church while his mother was serving her sentence.

The story of Victor Kanyari caused significant public outrage, with many calling for his arrest and prosecution, as well as the regulation of churches by the government. Kenyans across all social platforms took to Twitter, Facebook, WhatsApp and Instagram social media platforms to protest, because they were angry at the foolishness of the flock and the clergy taking advantage to fleece their gullible members. Although led to public conversation about the need to regulate the activities of Pentecostal churches, there appears to be a lack of consensus about the actions to take against the clergy.

While many on social media called for prosecution and regulation of the churches, lay members in Kanyari's church continued to attend services. For his part, Kanyari told his followers that the media and his enemies are out to finish him. Kanyari's reasoning not only blamed the work of devil for his misgivings

---

15   See Gifford P. 2009. *Christianity, Politics and Public Life in Kenya*. London: Hurst & Co.

instead of taking personal responsibility, but also served to defuse the story, which was likely the main objective. While a handful of Kanyari's followers left his church after the exposé, others stayed, convinced that the scandal was stage managed and orchestrated to malign the good name of the man of God, their beloved pastor. Nearly two years after the scandal, Kanyari walks around free, drives a top of the range Land Rover Sport and owns a palatial home on the outskirts of Nairobi. More importantly, he continues to preach every week in his church and attracts a modest congregation.

Following this exposé, the Director of Public Prosecution ordered an investigation of the activities of this church and its founder. Kanyari argued that he did not cheat or dupe anyone. Instead, they were willing members who paid for fake miracles and were not forced to but did it out of their own free will. Social media remained awash with mockery of the clergy and gullible members. Nevertheless, after a couple of weeks, the story died and Kanyari was back to business as usual.

Apostle James Maina Ng'ang'a of Neno Evangelism Ministries

Apostle James Maina Ng'ang'a of Neno Evangelism Ministries, a former convict turned televangelist, is a notorious man who runs one of the largest deliverance church ministries in Kenya. Neno Evangelism is largely a deliverance and healing ministry based in Nairobi, with branches spread across major towns in the country. James Maina Ng'ang'a was born in 1954, to a poor family that was not able to give him a stable upbringing or an education. Ng'ang'a moved to Nairobi in 1970 in search of some livelihood and found a job as a house servant. According to Paul Gifford,[16] Ng'ang'a later joined criminal gangs, a move that led to drugs, alcohol and a spiral of crime and many arrests and jail terms. He became a hard-core criminal and served many sentences in prison, during which time he was converted to the faith.

Ng'ang'a founded his Neno Evangelism Ministry, in 1992. In 1997, he opened his Neno Evangelism Centre situated at a central crossroads in one of Nairobi's best locations. His church services have attracted nearly 5,000 to 10,000 followers to his monthly crusades, which have since diminished. Ng'ang'a operates a Bible school, and has had a television programme on Kenya Broadcasting Corporation (KCB) every Saturday morning. He is immensely proud of his deliverance sessions and lays great emphasis on the gospel of prosperity. Thanks to his prosperity gospel, Ng'ang'a himself has grown immensely wealthy. In 2007, his manager estimated his wealth at a modest 100 million Kenyan shillings, according to Gifford. His lavish lifestyle reveals a story of a man who grew from rags to riches thanks to the activities of his church.[17] Yet, Ng'ang'a is increasingly

---

16   Gifford, *Christianity, Politics and Public Life in Kenya*, 193.
17   Wesangula D. 2015. "Apostle James Maina Ng'ang'a: Wealthy man of God with a baffling past", *The Standard*, 9 August. Ng'ang'a past belies a poverty-stricken childhood and several jail terms for theft and other misdemeanours.

arrogant, careless and flashy and loves to court attention and controversy with a careless abandon.

In 2012, a local radio station reported that a drunk Ng'ang'a got into a fight with his second wife and a security guard. His wife alleged in court papers that Ng'ang'a was not only a drunk, but also an adulterous and abusive husband and father. He walks around with a gun and has on many occasions been photographed drunk and rowdy. In early 2016, Ng'ang'a was driving drunk along the Naivasha-Nakuru highway and caused an accident that killed a middle-aged woman and seriously injured her husband. Ng'ang'a quickly left the scene of the accident and a young man appeared and claimed that he was the one driving the red Range Rover Sport. Apostle Ng'ang'a was aided by the police to run away from the scene of the accident, with the police commissioner coming out to defend the man of God. But eyewitnesses had identified a drunk Ng'ang'a and taken pictures of him at the scene of the crime.

This kind of impunity has elicited tremendous public outrage, especially when he colluded with the police to cover up the crime and bring in an impostor, who was paid 300,000 Kenyan shillings ($3,000 US) to falsely state that he was the one driving the vehicle. Eyewitnesses reported that he was driving drunk and recklessly and therefore endangering the lives of other motorists. Ng'ang'a denied the claim through his lawyer. The incident was captured on WhatsApp and widely circulated on social media. When the exposé was aired, there was tremendous public outcry to tame rogue clergy. Social media went ablaze with accusations that the pastor had bribed policemen to release his dented Range Rover after a hit-and-run accidents. It was the action of Kenyans on social media that ultimately saw him arrested and charged in a court of law. After a short public outrage and intense media scrutiny, his case, like that of Kanyari went silent. Today Ng'ang'a continues to run and preach in his church every Sunday as if nothing happened, and many of his followers still patronise his church in search for miracles and deliverance.

Gilbert Deya Ministries International (United Kingdom)

Another much publicised case of outright fraud involving rogue clergy is that of U.K.-based but Kenyan-born Archbishop Gilbert Deya, who claims to have 36,000 followers in Great Britain. Deya established the Gilbert Deya Ministries International in 1997. According to biographical data on his church website,[18] the ministry has church branches in Liverpool, London, Birmingham, Nottingham, Lutton, Reading, Manchester and Sheffield. His church is further claimed to be the fastest growing church in the U.K. and worldwide.

Gilbert Juma Deya is a fugitive wanted by Kenyan authorities for child-trafficking. His organisation claims that Deya is able to help infertile, post-menopausal women to conceive through the power of the Holy Spirit and

---

18 Gifford, *Christianity, Politics and Public Life in Kenya*, 157.

special prayers. In the U.K., one woman claimed to have had three children in less than a year. Allegedly, he would pray for childless and post-menopausal women in London to exorcise the spirits keeping them childless. These women would then travel to Kenya and there deliver miracle babies in slum clinics. They would then take their new born babies back to Britain.

These outrageous claims turned out to be a child-trafficking racket. In 2004, Deya was arrested on charges of kidnapping and trafficking of children. Deya's wife Mary Deya was arrested in Kenya in September 2004 on charges of kidnapping a baby from Nairobi's Kenyatta Hospital. She denied the allegations, claiming she had given birth to the baby herself, although doctors proved that she could not have been the mother. Investigations led to a racket in which twenty-one babies were found in a house operated by these child traffickers. The kids were then placed into foster care in Kenya, after DNA tests found that none of the children were biologically related to the women they claimed to be the biological mothers. Rose Atieno Kiseren, a former pastor with Deya's ministry, was jailed for child-trafficking alongside Mary Deya.[19] Upon her release from jail, Kiseren confessed that miracle babies were a hoax created by the Deyas and their accomplices to deceive her and other God-fearing people. The case dragged on with some of the documentation from the national hospital going missing, witnesses failing to appear and the judge of a new trial admitted she did not understand the delays. In May 2006, Mrs Deya was eventually jailed for two years for child abduction.

Bishop Deya continued to protest his innocence, claiming the miracles which God performed through him are of God and are beyond human understanding and that no man can explain them except God. According to Kenyan police, the ministry is a baby-snatching ring; thus, the authorities have frozen Deya's ministry's accounts, issued a warrant for his arrest in Kenya and petitioned for his extradition from the U.K. Deya is currently fighting extradition and seeking political asylum from his base in Glasgow. He is said to own three homes, as well as a jet and helicopter. He fought deportation from the U.K. to Kenya, but his ministry's accounts were frozen nevertheless.

Allan and Kathy Kiuna of Jubilee Christian Centre (JCC)

Allan and Kathy Kiuna are the founders of Jubilee Christian Centre (JCC) a sleek Neo-Pentecostal church situated in leafy Parklands in Nairobi. This church is modelled on the and is run on corporate principles, like a firm or a blue-chip company. This type of corporate church is complete with a separate administrative arm, a ministry arm and an investment arm – all to further the spread of the Gospel. Bishop Allan Kiuna and his wife Pastor Kathy Kiuna of the Jubilee Christian Centre (JCC) often use "marketplace rhetoric" to teach their flock how to succeed at the work place and how to grow wealthy.

---

19   Gifford, *Christianity, Politics and Public Life in Kenya*, 157.

The Kiunas live an opulent life in the leafy suburb of Runda in Nairobi and are celebrated as Nairobi's most romantic couple, often appearing on TV to give tips on marriage and relationships. Kathy Kiuna runs the *Women Without Limits* programme, a pseudo-empowerment programme that is televised on Nation Television (NTV) as a forum where women open up about their day-to-day challenges and how they overcame them, thanks to the prayers and spiritual mentorship of the Kiunas.[20] Kathy Kiuna courts controversy and loves media attention, appearing in all kinds of magazines and social media. The Kiunas unashamedly preach and promote the gospel of prosperity. Asked if their church is a prosperity gospel, Kathy Kiuna maintains: "We serve a prosperity God, Kathy counters. God wants us to be prosperous in every single way. His desire for us is to walk in abundance. I am praying for church people to show the likes of Bill Gates dust!"[21] Recently pictures of their houses circulated on social media, followed by outraged comments that pastors who serve God should not live extravagant lives. Kathy Kiuna has no apologies, stating: "Those who talk only know the 'after' they should have seen the 'before' To appreciate the work of God. She says. He has raised us up in the church and the church is as good as its flock-if the flock is walking in poverty so will the church."[22]

The latest controversy surrounding the Kiunas was when they announced that the JCC church members had bought Bishop Allan Kiuna a private jet valued at two billion Kenyan shillings ($20 million US) for his birthday. Pictures of the jet published on social media platforms went viral, with many criticising gullible members of prosperity churches, who are eager to feed the opulent lives of prosperity preachers at their own expense and suffering, continuing to live in poverty and want as their clergy grow into billionaires. Kathy and her husband are often pictured playing golf, on holiday in exotic places, and their sleek and expensive cars and sport motorbikes have also caused quite a stir. As with the churches mentioned above, criticism does not appear to lead to pragmatic discussions and national debates that might lead to tangible action. While those who are not overtly religious and can see through the teachings of these churches, thousands of followers turn to such clerics for prayers and spiritual leadership.

TAMING THE BEAST: THE GOVERNMENT AND REGULATION OF RELIGIOUS ORGANISATIONS

While the cases highlighted above are the most high-profile and controversial cases in Kenya, there are many other such controversies that do not receive

---

20 Deacon G and Parsitau D. 2016. "Empowered to Submit: Pentecostal Women in Nairobi Navigation Culture", *Journal of Religion and Society* 19:1-17.
21 Kiuna K. 2011. "Pastor Kathy Kiuna – On her Critics, Marriage, Divorce, Faith and being herself", *True Love*, November:45-47.
22 Kiuna, "On her Critics, Marriage, Divorce, Faith and being herself". See also Ondieki E. 2016. "Keeping up with the Kiunas and their jet-setting lifestyle", *The Daily Nation*, 17 December.

media attention, and the phenomenon of rogue clergy is evident in many other parts of Africa. In Kenya, following the high-profile exposés of the rogue clergy described above, there was widespread public outrage on traditional and social media platforms. The Kenyan government reacted to these stories by imposing an indefinite suspension of registration of new religious and called for fresh registration of existing ones. This suspension was recently lifted after the President of Kenya, Uhuru Kenyatta, declared the ban over.[23] Existing religious bodies were also required to file details of their status and financial returns with the Registrar of Societies.

The Attorney General of Kenya, Githu Muigai, immediately announced that a new framework was in the making to review the Societies Act and establish a special unit to manage religious institutions so that they can operate like trade unions and political parties. In publishing the new framework, Muigai, who has been critical of some of the religious organisations' activities, sought to bring sanity, transparency and accountability to the booming religious sector and reign on rogue clergy. The Religious Societies Compliance Rules, as the framework is called, would define standards for religious institutions as well as local and foreign clergy. For example, in order to become a member of the clergy, an individual would have to obtain a certificate of good conduct from the police and clearance from the Ethics and Anti-Corruption Commission (EACC), while foreign clergy would have work permits and recommendation from their diplomatic missions.

At the organisational level, he government would also be given details, such as the names and locations of committee members and registered trustees of religious institutions. Similarly, religious societies would need to file annual returns of their exemption or non-exemption certificates or they would have their licences revoked. Religious institutions have in the past been registered as charities under the Societies Act. The term "society", in this case, refers to any club, company, partnership or other associations of ten or more persons whatever its nature or objective, established in Kenya or having its headquarters or chief place of business in Kenya and any branch of a society. The looseness of this term has empowered anyone to register an institution and make it a church. Yet for some time now, a section of the Kenyan public has wanted to see a stricter regulation of the churches, especially the newer Pentecostal churches and its leadership.

The proposed rules would have the clergy hold a theological certificate from an accredited theological institution. It is important to note that most of the rogue clergy mentioned above are self-imposed and self-proclaimed and have no known theological training. Instead they claim to have been called and anointed by God to start their churches or ministries. The new rules will affect all faiths, including mainstream churches, mosques and temples. The Kenyan government has additionally proposed a raft of tough new measures aimed

---

23 Mwangi W. 2017. "Uhuru lifts ban on church registration, warns against illegal activities", *The Star*, 12 March.

at radically changing the way religious organisations conduct their business. The new draft rules published by the Attorney General Muigai aim at curbing religious societies that swindle Kenyans and engage in money-laundering, promote terrorism or become a public nuisance.

The rules have drawn sharp reactions from clergy from across the religious sector. A section of the clergy from across various denominational divides fought tooth and nail against these proposed regulations and threatened to vote out the government. They condemned Attorney General Muigai for not consulting them, and it became a political issue. Clergy are very powerful in Kenya and the state does not like to rattle the clerics. The National Council of Churches of Kenya (NCCK) under its current general secretary Canon Peter Karanja cautioned against generalisation and treatment of all churches in the country as law breakers based on action of a few individuals. Ideally, mainline churches in Kenya are structured institutions with system of control. It is however a free-fall for Pentecostal church where democracy of the spirit.

Yet the action or inaction of the government in regulating religious organisation and rogue clergy points to a number of tensions and paradoxes for the Kenyan government. This is because the Kenyan Constitution 2010, Article 32(1) states that every person has the right to freedom of conscience, religion, thought, belief and opinion. Article 32(2) further states that every person has a right to either individually or in community with others in public or in private to manifest any religion or belief through worship, practice, teaching or observance of a day of worship. It is this legal and policy framework that religious clergy have exploited to make sure that they are not held to account.

At the same time, religion is a strong social and political force in Kenya because of its capacity for mobilisation. In Kenya, religion and politics often flows into each other. The church is co-opted by the state and vice versa. When churches feel threatened by the state, they often threaten to mobilise their religious constituencies to vote out the government. This is because, firstly, they enjoy good patronage and have capacities to easily unite different social groups, secondly, have strong national and international links, and thirdly, they enjoy global solidarity, like as witnessed during the 2010 constitutional review process, in which U.S.-aligned Evangelicals supported Pentecostal churches that opposed the passage of the new constitution.

PROPHETS FOR PROFITS OR JUST GULLIBLE MEMBERS! : A MORAL AND ETHICAL CRITIQUE OF NEO-PENTECOSTAL CHURCH CLERGY

Africa is faced with tremendous social, economic and political challenges, as well as a moral and leadership crisis. In fact, since the infamous Structural Adjustments Programmes (SAPs) of the 1970s and 1980s,[24] African nations have

---

24 See Deacon and Parsitau, "Empowered to Submit: Pentecostal Women in Nairobi Navigation Culture"; Parsitau, "The Impact of Structural Adjustments Programmes (SAPS) on the Health Status of Women in Kenya".

faced numerous challenges, including unemployment, increased poverty and collapse of infrastructure, particularly in healthcare and education, that have put tremendous strains on service delivery. Coupled with the lack of social welfare, increased corruption and ethnic tensions, there has been resource-based and politically inspired conflict leading to insecurity, as well as acts of terrorism leading to mass displacement and thousands of refugees, that have produced a total collapse of social structures. The impact of the SAPs was felt across the African continent, but it also coincided with the proliferation of Pentecostal and charismatic churches, which many observers have directly linked to the SAP crisis.[25] Many poor and vulnerable people turned to deliverance and faith healing ministries to cater to their daily existential problems and dull their sufferings.

Since then, Pentecostalism has become a thriving business and the shortest route to wealth and influence on a continent teaming with population, unemployment, poverty and disease, conflict, environmental degradation. Local pastors employ all sorts of tricks and techniques to exhort money from gullible folks. They use this money to build magnificent churches, buy luxurious cars, houses and aircrafts and live openly opulent lives, while their church members languish in poverty, misery and squalor. In most cases, pastors tell the faithful to give money to God, so that God will bless them in return. They dupe people by telling them that divine favours come to those who pay their tithes and offerings regularly. Often, they use biblical injunctions such as "givers never lack" to squeeze money out of people.

Pentecostal pastors also claim they have power to make the deaf hear, the blind see and the lame walk, as in the case of Archbishop Deya discussed above. There have been indiscriminate claims of miracles and divine healing from Pentecostal clergy, in a context of crippled medical facilities often plagued by lack of medicine, medical facilities and equipment, striking health personnel, corruption and the politics of healthcare that exist in many other African countries. This has led to increased suffering for the impoverished masses who cannot afford proper medical care. Amidst this desperation, unscrupulous clergy take advantage of the African healthcare predicament or to total absence of it. Such clergy are cashing on the desperation and gullibility of Africans by offering ineffective prayers and healing crusades to promote and enrich themselves. The healthcare crisis in Africa breeds desperation and foments the desire for miracles, faith healing and deliverance sessions to dull the pain and desperation of the sick and poor.

There is a tendency for many in this sector to claim the ability to cure AIDS, cancers, disabilities, prophesy of impending disasters, conflicts, death and all manner of diseases and conditions. At prayer healing services in some Pentecostal churches, pastors invite people infected with HIV to come forward for public healing prayers after which they burn their anti-retroviral medications

---

25 Gifford, *Christianity, Politics and Public Life in Kenya*, 2009.

and declare the persons healed. The cure is not free, and many spend a fortune to procure it. The controversial prayers continue even as believers' conditions worsen and some die. The situation has even spawned debates over whether science or religion should take the lead in the fight against the AIDS pandemic. Desperation, stigma, family rejection, fears of witchcraft and all other social anxieties drive people into a never-ending search for miracles and cures found in the myriads of healing crusades and prayer rallies. This is particularly worrying and frustrating for people infected with HIV, but more importantly alarming for health practitioners working in the health sector, as this negates the achievement against the HIV/AIDS pandemic.

While Pentecostalism has developed over the years, criticism has also grown, along with the accusation that pastors deceived churchgoers to get rich. At the same time, the growing rise of political power among Pentecostals also makes them untouchable. Many are political actors shaping debates and driving policy. Anyone who is critical of Pentecostal pastors is likely to come across strong opposition, resistance, and condemnation from enthusiastic members and in some cases politicians and governments. For example, when the attorney general published a proposed the aforementioned regulatory framework to control rogue clergy and religious organisations in Kenya, the opposition party, led by the former prime minister criticised the government for unfairly targeting religious institutions based on a few rotten apples.

Even though opposition to certain scandals draw general condemnation from across the board, many people still felt that the religious sector should not be regulated. Yet there is also growing criticism from a significant minority who are gaining voice in social media platforms and want to see religious organisations held to account. For example, Kenyans on social media platforms have criticised Kenyan clergy's activities that are deemed inappropriate. Over time, media and public scrutiny may create a more critical imagination among adherents, who will begin to question their leaders and churches, but the exploitation persists in the short term.

Are Kenyan and by extension African Christians gullible or just desperate? There is a huge section of followers who fall into these categories. These followers are searching for a moral vocabulary in grappling with hard social and economic times. This is what makes them gullible. For many, church is a space to be in community with one another – a space for healing both physical and emotional and spiritual pain and for negotiating relationships and identities. People's involvement in these churches cannot be neatly associated with any particular issues. Instead, it involves complexity of issues that are not just spiritual but are also personal, and communal. During times of crisis, people go to church to be in community.

In Africa, many people are perpetually living in moments of one crisis after another. They feel lost, alone and in need of moral guidance. They look up to their clergy to provide a moral universe and leadership and space for healing.

At the same time, some rogue clergy have taken advantage of this situation, and many attempt to speak the language that the gullible want to hear. This is a huge challenge that many African governments grapple with on a daily basis. It is for such reasons that in 2004, the Nigerian Broadcasting Commission banned the broadcast of miracles on national television. Faith healing is the greatest threat to scientific medicine and healthcare delivery in Africa. Miracles have no basis in science, reason and common sense. Claims of divine cure and healing cannot be reconciled with the dire health situation in many African countries.

The greatest threat to Pentecostalism is its unregulated clergy and the moral failure of its leadership. Although other Christian movements have suffered, Pentecostalism seems particularly rife. Deeply embedded within Pentecostalism's ethos is a cult of personality. Charismatic leaders are put on a pedestal of accountability and often virtually worshipped by many of their followers. At the same time, many are averse to education, especially theological education, instead privileging the power of the Holy Spirit as their sole teacher. However, clergy are powerful and command tremendous respect. You can't touch the church. Laws to regulate the churches are fiercely opposed by the churches themselves, who form a huge voting block. It is particularly difficult in a largely Christian nation.

Thirdly, too many Pentecostal clergy handle church money as personal money and church properties as family business. They travel alone, without having to account for their whereabouts or activities. While many Pentecostal churches such as CITAM have instituted structures and policies to handle cases of pastoral misconduct, ineptitude and financial misconduct and impropriety, many find these policies hard to enforce. In Kenya, Pentecostal and charismatic churches are under the Evangelical Alliance of Kenya, but it is not clear how they handle these issues. There is no body that regulates independent churches in Kenya, and a favourite Pentecostal saying, "touch not my anointed" (Psalms 105:15), is used to forbid or stifle criticism of the movements' leaders.

Sexual promiscuity and financial misconduct are rife and rampant within church ranks and little is done about it unless a scandal becomes public. Yet, Pentecostals tend to be forgiving of their clergy's moral lapses both in Kenya and beyond. Kanyari and Ng'ang'ga are back to preaching. They are a power unto themselves. This has tarnished many Pentecostal churches image and standing in society. Since then, the churches in Kenya have struggled to gain respect, but they also appear to struggle with an identity crisis. Many have decried bad religion in Kenya as the churches continue to grapple with rogue clergy and bad religion, prompting observers to ask if religion is indeed the bane of the Kenyan society. This has attracted a lot of attention to the clergy, their sources of wealth and their morals. Pentecostal clergy's moral and ethical failures are reflective of the general leadership crisis prevalent in much of Sub-Saharan Africa. Corruption is rife in many African nations and integrity of leadership in government, the private sector as well as the religious sector is lacking. Corruption is prevalent in many African countries, including the most religious countries. Kenya and Nigeria, for example, are highly religious countries, but they are also some of the most corrupt countries in the world. This is the paradox that needs further attention. The same scenario is replicated in other countries such as Zimbabwe, South Africa and Uganda. The church leadership is critical in fighting social, economic and political ills, such as corruption, ethnicity, insecurity and lack of good governance. Yet a corrupt church cannot fight these ills when it has itself been co-opted by the state. Instead, the case for rogue clergy is a reflection of the general state of the nation of Kenya, where social, economic and political scandals are part of the country's social and political landscape.

CONCLUSION

In the recent past, Kenyans have witnessed an increasingly high number of religious scandals committed by the so-called men and women of God, who are supposedly also the keepers of morality and ethics. Yet, rogue clergy are increasingly becoming a panacea to the Kenyan public, and there has been significant pressure for the government to tame rogue clergy by introducing regulations to tame the religious industry. At the same time, questions are being raised about the gullibility of Kenya's faithful, who appear to learn a lesson or two from rogue clergy to whom they continue to fall prey. This chapter has attempted to highlight these tensions by focusing on the challenges this presents to the public and to the Kenyan government caught up between protecting freedoms of expression and attempting to regulate religious organisations and rogue clergy in Kenya. The government must protect gullible members from rogue clergy whose sole aim is to enrich themselves at the expense of vulnerable and desperate souls whose only hope seems to be supernatural. The government must engage with faith-based organisations, sensitise the public and find a lasting solution to the problem. Faith-based organisations themselves should also devise internal mechanism to regulate themselves, if they hope to reclaim their integrity and respect.

16 HATE SPEECH IN THE UNITED STATES AND SOUTH AFRICA: A LEGAL AND COMPARATIVE ANALYSIS

Johan D. van der Vyver[1]

My academic career is deeply rooted in distant countries that are worlds apart from one another. I am a member of the faculty in the School of Law of Emory University in Atlanta, Georgia, in the United States of America, and an Extraordinary Professor in the Department of Private Law of the University of Pretoria in South Africa. As far as freedom of speech is concerned, the systems that prevail in the United States and in South Africa are also in substance worlds apart. Whereas freedom of speech is a basic norm of the American constitutional system, South African law is by contrast founded on the protection of human dignity and consequently places radical constraints on the publication of defamatory language; and in order to counteract group rivalries amongst traditionally divided population groups, the "new South Africa" includes radical constraints on speech and action that could be offensive to any of the racial, ethnic, religious or linguistic factions within the South African community.

FREEDOM OF SPEECH IN THE UNITED STATES

Constitutional protection of human rights in the United States is in essence founded on libertarian principles in which the First Amendment freedoms (freedom of religion, freedom of speech, freedom of the press and the right to petition the Government for a redress of grievances) are of special significance. For very special historical reasons, the First Amendment freedoms, notably freedom of speech, constitute *die Grundnorm* (the basic norm) of the entire system of human rights protection.[2] If a conflict between different constitutional rights and freedoms were to emerge, the courts must always attempt to "balance" those conflicting rights or freedoms so as to afford equal protection to all of them. However, should freedom of speech be in irreconcilable conflict with any of the other constitutionally protected rights and freedoms, it would prevail. The First Amendment freedoms have thus been proclaimed to be the "preferred freedoms", defined by Chief Justice Earl Warren as "a scale of

---

1 IT Cohen Professor of International Law and Human Rights, Emory University School of Law; Extraordinary Professor in the Department of Private Law, University of Pretoria.
2 See Van der Vyver JD. 1995. "Constitutional Free Speech and the Law of Defamation", *South African Law Journal* 112:593-594, 595; Van der Vyver JD. 1998. "Universality and Relativity of Human Rights: American Relativism", *Buffalo Human Rights Law Review* 4:60.

constitutional values,"[3] and which means that the presumption of legality of legislation can more readily be rebutted when such legislation restricts First Amendment freedoms than would be the case when economically qualified rights are at stake.[4]

In *Palko v. Connecticut*, Justice Benjamin Cardozo referred to freedom of thought and speech as "the matrix, the indispensable condition of nearly every other form of freedom."[5] In *Schneider v. State*, Justice Owen Roberts accordingly proclaimed:

> This court has characterized the freedom of speech and that of the press as fundamental personal rights and liberties. The phrase is not an empty one and was not lightly used. It reflects the belief of the framers of the Constitution that exercise of the rights lies at the foundation of free government by free men. It stresses, as do many opinions of this court, the importance of preventing the restriction of enjoyment of these liberties.[6]

In *Saxbe v. Washington Post Co.*, Justice Lewis Powell, having noted that "the First Amendment protects important values of individual expression and personal self-fulfillment," went on to say:

> What is at stake here is the societal function of the First Amendment in preserving free public discussion of governmental affairs. No aspect of that constitutional guarantee is more rightly treasured than the protection of the ability of our people through free and open debate to consider and resolve their own destiny ... It [the First Amendment] embodies our Nation's commitment to popular self-determination and our abiding faith that the surest course for developing sound national policy lies in a free exchange of views on public issues. And public debate must not only be unfettered; it must also be informed. For that reason this Court has repeatedly stated that First Amendment concerns encompass the receipt of information and ideas as well as the right of free expression.[7]

Any limitation of First Amendment freedoms, for whatever reason, would be unconstitutional, except in highly exceptional circumstances. Since the American constitutional system subordinates considerations of human dignity to the salience of First Amendment freedoms, it has, for example, found all kinds of constitutional obstacles in well-intended legislative efforts to curtail child pornography,[8] and degraded the law of defamation to almost oblivion.

---

3   *United States v. Robel*, 389 US 258, at 263 (1967).
4   *United States v. Caroline Products Co*, 304 US 144 (1938).
5   *Palko v. Connecticut*, 302 US 319 (1937).
6   *Schneider v. State*, 308 US 147, at 161 (1939).
7   *Saxbe v. Washington Post Co*, 417 US 843, 862-63 (1974).
8   See, for example, *Reno v. American Civil Liberties Union*, 521 US 844 (1997) (striking down the Communications Decency Act of 1996 on First Amendment grounds); *American Civil Liberties Union v. Reno*, 217 F 3rd 162 (3rd Cir, 2000)

For example, in *New York Times Co. v. Sullivan*, the United States Supreme Court decided that a public official must prove "actual malice" if he or she were to claim damages for libel that relates to his or her official acts;[9] that is "knowledge that it [the statement] was false or with reckless disregard of whether it was or not."[10] The court held that "debate on public issues should be uninhibited robust, and wide-open,"[11] and that a malicious motive on the part of the defendant will not be presumed but must be proved by the plaintiff.[12] Needless to say, in countries where human dignity and equality trumps considerations of free speech, the proscription of child pornography and hate speech do not present any constitutional obstacles.

American jurisprudence dealing with hate speech is particularly instructive. It should be borne in mind that "speech" is given a broad meaning in the United States. The concept of constitutionally protected speech has been extended to include saluting or not saluting the national flag by learners at the beginning of the school day,[13] the burning of a cross or Nazi swastika that would arouse anger, alarm or resentment,[14] flag burning or desecrating the flag of the United States as a means of political protest,[15] or wearing a black armband to protest against the Vietnam War.[16]

In 1992, the U.S. Supreme Court was called upon to judge the constitutionality of a municipal ordinance which rendered it a misdemeanor for someone to place "on public or private property a symbol, object, appellation, characterisation or graffiti, including, but not limited to, a burning cross or Nazi swastika" if the person concerned had reason to know that the display would anger or alarm

---

(upholding an injunction relating to the Child Online Protection Act, holding that the legislation will "more likely than not" be found to be unconstitutional as constituting an undue restriction of First Amendment freedoms); *United States v. Playboy Entertainment Group, Inc*, 529 US 803 (2000) (declaring unconstitutional a provision in the Telecommunications Act of 1996 regulating signal "scrambling" to ensure that only paying viewers will have access to Playboy programmes, holding that the provision, being a "content-based regulation of a form of speech that enjoyed First Amendment protection", violated the constitutional free speech guarantees); *Ashcraft v. Free Speech Coalition*, 535 US 234 (2002) (the Court invalidating sections of the Child Pornography Act of 1996 as being "over broad" because they purported to ban sexually explicit images that *appears to depict* or *conveys the impression of depicting* minors).

9 *New York Times Co v. Sullivan*, 376 US 254, at 279-80 (1964).
10 *New York Times Co v. Sullivan*, 280.
11 *New York Times Co v. Sullivan*, 270, See also *Pennekamp v. Florida*, 328 US 311, at 347 (1946) (holding that freedom of discussion should be given "the widest range compatible with the essential requirement of the fair and orderly administration of justice").
12 *New York Times Co v. Sullivan*, 283-84.
13 *West Virginia State Board of Education v. Barnette*, 319 US 624 (1943).
14 *RAV v. City of St. Paul*, Minnesota 505 US 377 (1992).
15 *Street v. New York*, 394 US 576 (1969); *Smith v. Coguen*, 415 US 566 (1974); *Texas v. Johnson*, 491 US 397, at 400 (1989); *United States v. Eichman*, 486 US 310 (1990).
16 *Tinker v. Des Moins Independent Community School District*, 393 US 503 (1969).

others, based on "race, color, creed, religion or gender".[17] The ordinance, the Court found, violated the free speech provision of the First Amendment, because it prohibited "otherwise permitted speech solely on basis of the subject the speech addresses". According to the concurring justices, the unconstitutionality of the ordinance derived from the fact that it only prohibited hate speech delivered by symbols and because the speech that fell outside the scope of the ordinance can only hurt feelings or cause resentment.

Hate speech legislation in America is mostly confined to sanctioning higher sentences than normally prescribed if the crime was motivated by hostile feelings toward a group to which the victim belongs. The U.S. Supreme Court accordingly upheld the constitutionality of a law of Wisconsin that made provision for increased sentences in cases where the crime was prompted by hate.[18] The Court reasoned that the law was directed against conduct and not expression, and that the motivation that prompted a criminal act is a legitimate consideration when determining an appropriate sentence. In another matter, the U.S. Supreme Court struck down a law of New Jersey which authorised a judge to increase a sentence above the maximum prescribed by law in cases where the crime was racially motivated.[19] The Court decided that it was for a jury and not the judge to determine facts – in this instance a racial bias – that would expose an accused to a penalty which exceeds the prescribed maximum.

In a case concerning an anti Ku Klux Klan measure of the state of Virginia, the U.S. Supreme Court again upheld the constitutionality of a state law which created a felony consisting of the burning of a cross "on the property of another, a highway or a public place … with the intent of intimidating any person or group."[20] The Court noted that had the cross been burnt at a political rally, the act would have constituted political speech and would therefore have been protected under the First Amendment free speech provision.

More recently, in the case of *Snyder v. Phelps*, the United States Supreme Court was called upon to consider the legality of the display of offensive placards denouncing, among other things, homosexuality in the military, by members of the Westboro Baptist Church in the proximity of the funeral of an American marine killed in Iraq in the line of duty.[21] The judgment, delivered by Chief Justice John Roberts, proclaimed that speech on a public sidewalk, relating to a public issue, cannot be legally condemned as a tort of emotional distress, even if the speech is "outrageous".

---

17 *RAV v. City of St. Paul, Minnesota*, supra n 13.
18 *State v. Mitchell*, 508 US 476 (1993).
19 *Apprendi v. New Jersey*, 530 US 466 (2000).
20 *Virginia v. Black*, 538 US 343 (2003).
21 *Snyder v. Phelps*, 562 US 443 (2011).

Comparing the American constitutional system with the one of South Africa is particularly instructive in the context of our theme: the one placing a particularly high premium of free speech, and the other subjecting freedom of expression to constraints dictated by the supreme concern for human dignity. It is important to emphasise that American judgments relating to freedom of speech do not constitute "comparable foreign case law" that should be taken into accounts by courts of law when interpreting the Bill of Rights.[22] Statements such as those of Judge Rex van Schalkwyk in *Mandela v. Falati*, proclaiming with reference to American cases, "the primacy of the freedom of speech" and depicting freedom of expression as "the freedom upon which all others depend,"[23] are therefore simply incorrect. Nor can one concede the proposition that "the Constitution creates no hierarchy of fundamental rights."[24]

It is important to emphasise that a strictly libertarian constitutional system, like the one of the United States, is not suited to the needs of a plural society, like the one of South Africa, where polarised group rivalries take on epidemic proportions. A nation in the making must value the demands of reconciliation to be a supreme priority and cannot afford to permit expressions of intolerance, or group-related biases and stereotyping, which counteract that noble cause. It must seek to accomplish a fair balance between freedom to express one's beliefs and the proscription of speech that is offensive and would for that reason prolong the ongoing process of reconciliation.

The South African nation comprises perhaps the most diverse plural composition in the entire world; furthermore, it is known for the polarisation of factions of the population.[25] Group rivalries are still rife in South Africa as a feature of the country's demographic divides. Dealing with such rivalries and orchestrating reconciliation are central to social engineering within that troubled land. Constitutional change in South Africa that took effect on

---

22 See Constitution of the Republic of South Africa, 1996, s 35(1).
23 *Mandela v. Falati*, 1995 (1) SA 251, at 259; 1994 (4) BCLR 1, at 8 (W). See also *De Klerk & Another v. Du Plessis & Others*, 1995 (2) SA 40, at 51; 1994 (6) BCLR 124, at 134 (T) (Van Dykhorst J referring to a similar submission that "our law of defamation can … be reviewed in the light of the approach of the United States Supreme Court", but preferring not to express an opinion as to the legitimacy of this "interesting vista" and its implications); *Gardener v. Whitaker*, 1995 (2) SA 672, at 688; 1994 (5) BCLR 19, at 34 (E) (Froneman J including references to American jurisprudence in his comparative outline to substantiate the importance of freedom of speech, without emphasising the necessity of placing the judgments concerned in a proper comparative perspective).
24 *Gardener v. Whitaker, supra* n 21, at SA 690; at BCLR 36.
25 See *S v. Makwanyane and Another*, 1995 (3) SA 391, 1995 6 BCLR 665, para 308 (CC) (Justice Mokgoro referring to South Africans having "a history of deep division characterised by strife and conflict"); and *Du Toit v. Minister for Safety and Security & Another*, 2009 (6) SA 128, para 17 (CC) (Chief Justice Langa stating that "the South African nation was for decades a deeply divided society characterised by gross violations of fundamental human rights").

27 April 1994 was designed to innovate social, political and legal structures that would be radically different from those of the country's past history. The new constitutional dispensation in that sense emanated from a reactionary response to the evils of the preceding era.[26] The Constitution of the Republic of South Africa, 1996, while thus recognising "the injustices of our past",[27] accordingly depicted the new South Africa as "an open and democratic society based on human dignity, equality and freedom."[28] The constitutional Bill of Rights provided the legally enforceable backing for such a society: Any institution associated with discrimination and repression of apartheid South Africa must be taken to be incompatible with the values embodied in the kind of society the country now aspired to be.[29]

The drafters of the South African constitution accordingly rejected the segregation of rival ethnic, religious and linguistic communities as well as the promotion of cultural, religious or linguistic homogeneity within the nation, as a means of counteracting group-related tensions in the country's social construct. Instead, they opted for creating – in the celebrated words of Archbishop Desmond Tutu – "a rainbow nation". The new constitutional dispensation seeks to promote pride in one's particular ethnic, religious or linguistic identities. However, the South African dispensation is also sensitive to the notion that pride in one's group identity does not elevate one to a superior status in the community. The respect of others for one's cultural values, religious persuasions or linguistic preferences demands full respect for the culture, religion and language of others. The constitutional principle that applies in this regard has been reduced to perhaps the most basic moral directive for a "new South Africa"; one that finds expression in the concept of *ubuntu* (in Zulu) or *botho* (in Tswana) "an idea based on deep respect for the [inner] humanity of another".[30] *Ubuntu* translates into "humaneness" and constitutes "part of our rainbow heritage".[31] It stands in sharp contrast to "dehumanising and degrading the individual".[32] Justice Albie Sachs on occasion referred to *ubunthu-botho* in the sense of "civility" as "a precondition for the good functioning of contemporary democratic societies". He noted that "civility in a constitutional sense involves more than just courtesy

---

26   See Van der Vyver JD. 1991. "Constitutional Options for Post-Apartheid South Africa", *Emory Law Journal* 40:785-787, 789; *Du Plessis & Others v. De Klerk & Another*, 1996 3 SA 850 (CC); 1996 5 BCLR 658 (CC), para 90 (per Ackermann, J).
27   Constitution of the Republic of South Africa, 1996, Preamble.
28   Id., s 36(1), 39(1)(a). See also s 7(1).
29   See *Brink v. Kitshoff NO*, 1996 4 SA 197 (CC); 1996 6 BCLR 752 (CC), para 33 (per O'Regan, J). See also *S v. Makwanyane & Another*, supra n 23, para 218 (per Langa, J), para 262 (per Mahomed, J), para 322 (per O'Regan, J); *Shabalala & Others v. Attorney-General of the Transvaal & Another*, 1996 1 SA 725 (CC); 1995 12 BCLR 1593 (CC), para 26 (per Mahomed, J); *Ferreira v. Levin NO & Others; Vryenhoek & Others v. Powell NO & Others*, 1996 1 SA 984 (CC), 1996 1 BCLR 1 (CC), para 29.
30   *Dikoko v. Mokhatla*, 2006 (6) SA 235; 2007 1 BCLR 1, para 68 (CC). See also id., para 69.
31   *S v. Makwanyane & Another*, supra n 23, para 308 (per Mokgoro, J).
32   Id., para 250 (per Langa, J).

and good manners ... It presupposes tolerance for those with whom one disagrees and respect for the dignity of those with whom one is in dispute."[33]

South African law therefore does not uphold the almost incontestable sanctity of freedom of speech that the American constitutional system does. In South African law, "certain expressions do not deserve constitutional protection because they have the potential to impinge adversely on the dignity of others and cause harm."[34] In South Africa, "the right to freedom of expression is not a pre-eminent freedom ranking above all others."[35] In this respect, it "differs fundamentally from the balance struck in the United States", where freedom of speech constitutes the basic norm of the entire rights regime.[36]

The South African Constitution accordingly subjects the freedom of expression to limitations, which include a prohibition of the "advocacy of hatred that is based on race, ethnicity, gender or religion, and that constitutes incitement to cause harm."[37] Under the Promotion of Equality and Prevention of Unfair Discrimination Act, "no person may publish, propagate, advocate or communicate words ... against any person, that could reasonably be construed to demonstrate a clear intention to (a) be hurtful; (b) be harmful or to incite harm; (c) promote or propagate hatred."[38] The Act, by prohibiting unfair discrimination,[39] hate speech,[40] harassment,[41] and "dissemination and publication of information that unfairly discriminates,"[42] is clearly based on a link between the protection of human dignity and the right to equality. It defines hate speech as words "that could reasonably be construed to demonstrate a clear intention to (a) be hurtful; (b) be harmful or to incite harm; (c) promote or propagate hatred";[43] however, "*bona fide* engagement in artistic creativity, academic and scientific inquiry, fair and accurate reporting in the public interest" do not constitute hate speech.[44]

---

33 *Masetlha v. President of the RSA and Another*, 2008 (1) SA 566; 2008 1 BCLR 1, para 238 (CC).
34 *Du Toit v. Minister for Safety and Security & Another*, supra n 23, para 32 (CC).
35 *S v. Mamabolo (E TV & Seven Others Intervening)*, 2001 (3) SA 409, 2001 5 449, para 41 (CC).
36 Id., para 40; Van der Vyver JD. 1997. "Constitutional Protection of Children and Young Persons", in Robinson JA (ed). *The Law of Children and Young Persons in South Africa*. Durban: Butterworths, 282; and Van der Vyver JD. 2005. "Limitations of Freedom of Religion or Belief: International Law Perspectives", *Emory International Law Review* 19:508.
37 South African Constitution, 1996, s 16(2)(c).
38 The Promotion of Equality and Prevention of Unfair Discrimination Act 4 of 2000, s 10(1). See Krüger R. 2011. "Small Steps to Equal Dignity: The Work of the South African Equality Courts", *The Equal Rights Review* 7:27.
39 The Promotion of Equality and Prevention of Unfair Discrimination Act, s 6, 7, 8 and 9.
40 The Promotion of Equality and Prevention of Unfair Discrimination Act, s 10(1) (c).
41 The Promotion of Equality and Prevention of Unfair Discrimination Act, s 11.
42 The Promotion of Equality and Prevention of Unfair Discrimination Act, s 12.
43 The Promotion of Equality and Prevention of Unfair Discrimination Act, s 10(1).
44 The Promotion of Equality and Prevention of Unfair Discrimination Act, s 12.

VI. Religion, Hate Speech, Diversity and Equality

The "new South Africa" is thus founded on zero tolerance for words and conduct offensive to others. It has therefore been decided that depicting members of particular population groups as "hotnot", "kaffir", "rooinek", "boer" or "coolie" is strictly forbidden since such names "have for decades been used to bring people of different races into contempt."[45] Other cases that have attracted special attention in recent times include one in which the conservative Christian owners of a grocery store open to the public refused to serve a Muslim client wearing a fez were reprimanded because their conduct amounted to unbecoming discrimination based on religion.[46] It was also decided that the media were under legal constraint not to publish cartoons that appeared in a Danish newspaper depicting the Prophet Mohammed as a terrorist, because those comic strips "advocate hatred and stereotyping of Muslims."[47] A newspaper report that likened homosexuality to bestiality could not be tolerated under the assumption of freedom of the press because it promoted hatred against the gay and lesbian communities.[48]

A prominent politician, Julius Malema, has been called on the carpet on several occasions for hate speech transgressions. While he was leader of the African National Congress Youth League (2008-2012), he was reprimanded for the chanting of a "freedom song" that includes the phrase *dibulu iBhunu* (shoot the Boer), because it was found to be offensive to the Afrikaans-speaking section of the South African nation and as such violates the proscription of offensive language.[49] The matter was taken on appeal by Malema and the African National Conference, but was settled on the basis of the appellants agreeing "that certain words in certain freedom songs may be experienced as hurtful by members of minority communities" and "to act with restraint to avoid the experience of such hurt". The settlement was made an order of court.

Malema was also brought to trial in the Equality Court in 2010 by the SONKE Gender Justice organisation for stating in an address of 22 January 2009 to

---

45 Decision of the Broadcasting Complaints Commission in *P Johnson v. 94.7 Highveld Stereo*, Case No 07/2002, 14 February 2002.
46 *Woodways CC v. Moosa Vallie*, Case No A251/05 (HC Western Cape, 31 August 2009).
47 *Jamait-Ul-Ulama of Transvaal v. Johncom Media Investment Ltd and Others*, Case No 1127/06 (W), 3 February 2006. The ban was subsequently lifted because the comic strips were widely published on the Internet.
48 In *South African Human Rights Commission v. Jon Qwulane*, Case No 44/EQ JHB (31 May 2011), the Equality Court at the Johannesburg Magistrate's Court demanded an unqualified public apology to the gay and lesbian community from – and imposed a fine of R100,000 to be paid by – Jon Qwulane (subsequently the South African ambassador in Uganda) for a newspaper article he wrote under the heading "Call Me Names, but Gay Is NOT OK", in which he compared homosexuality with bestiality.
49 *Agriforum and Another v. Malema and Another*, 2011 (6) SA 240; 2011 BCLR 1289 (EqC). The matter was referred to the Equality Court as a matter of great urgency by the North Gauteng High Court in Pretoria. *Agriforum and Another v. Malema*, 2010 (5) SA 235 (GNP). "Boer" means "farmer" but is also commonly used to denote the white Afrikaans-speaking citizens of South Africa.

students of the Cape Peninsula University of Technology that the women who accused ANC President Jacob Zuma of rape actually had a "nice time" with him, and he went on to say: "When a woman didn't enjoy it, she leaves early in the morning. Those who had a nice time will wait until the sun comes out, request breakfast and ask for taxi money." The Equality Court found that the utterance complained of amounted to hate speech and harassment, that Malema must issue a public apology, and that he must pay People Opposed to Women Abuse (POWA) an amount of R50,000 within one month of date of the judgment.[50]

Malema was eventually (for other reasons) expelled from the ANC and subsequently founded a new political party, the Economic Freedom Fighters (EFF), of which he is currently the leader. The EFF is the third most political party in South Africa, having gathered 6.35% of the votes in the 2014 general elections, thereby gaining 25 seats in Parliament. The important point in the context of this essay is that Malema has clearly not seen the last of the Equality Court. Statements such as the following are commonplace in his public addresses: The Afrikaans language must fall; it must not be spoken; we must not be compelled to speak that language; we do not compel you to speak Shangaan or Zulu.

Malema is not the only prominent politician to have been confronted with hate speech complaints. In January 2016, a complaint was lodged with the South African Human Rights Commission against President Jacob Zuma for a statement he made on land reform in Rustenburg on occasion of the ANC's 104th anniversary dinner, saying: "The source of poverty, unemployment, and inequality is land. It was taken … not bought. Stolen. But the government of the people has to buy it back as if it was sold."[51] The complaint was filed by Pieter Groenewald, the Freedom Front Plus parliamentary spokesman on land affairs, who maintained that the reference to "stolen land" in South Africa refers to white people and fuels the racial hatred between whites and blacks in the country. Zuma was required to respond to the complaint by 4 July 2016, which he failed to do.

Earlier, in February 2015, a complaint was lodged by the Freedom Front Plus party with the South African Human Rights Commission against Jacob Zuma for a statement he made at a fundraising dinner, depicting the arrival of Jan van Riebeeck, who in 1652 founded a white settlement on behalf of the Dutch East India Company at what subsequently became Cape Town, as the cause of all the problems in South Africa: "You must remember that a man called Jan van Riebeeck arrived here on 6 April 1652, and that was the start of the trouble in this country. What followed were numerous struggles and wars and deaths and

---

50 *Sonke Gender Justice Network v. Malema*, Case No 02/2009, 2010 (7) BCLR 729; [2010] ZAEQC 2 (15 March 2010).
51 See *Zuma Complaint Lodged with SAHRC*. Online at: http://www.iol.co.za/news/politics/zuma-complaint-lodged-wit-sahrc-1972819

the seizure of land and the deprivation of the indigenous peoples' political and economic power."[52]

Another case that attracted considerable public interest was one involving an elderly lady, Penny Sparrow, a retired real estate agent, who was appalled by the extensive littering of Scottburgh Beach on the Natal coast which she visited on New Year's Day, and on 3 January 2016 posted on Facebook the statement: "Dear, o, dear, from now on I shall address the blacks of South Africa as monkeys as I see the cute little wild monkeys as the same, pick, drop and litter." The defendant did not attend the proceedings because she allegedly feared for her life. The Equality Court decided that the words amounted to hate speech and ordered her to pay damages in the sum of R150,000 to the Oliver and Adelaide Tambo Foundation, plus the costs of the proceedings.[53]

Currently, a case against Judge Mabel Jansen is pending. She was extremely upset by the large number of rape cases that came before her, in many cases involving victims of tender age. She communicated with a certain Gillian Schutte in a private Facebook exchange in an attempt to find a solution to the problem, stating: "Gillian do you believe that I am even propositioned by my black colleagues who tell me they will be in hotel x and expect me to report there at a specific time? I am shell-shocked. In a culture a woman is there to pleasure them. Period. It is seen as an absolute right and a woman's consent is not required. You may find this hard to accept and unpalatable as I did. I still have to find a black girl who was not raped at about 12. I am dead serious." Ms Schutte made the statement public to expose the "deep racism and colonial thinking" prevalent in South Africa.[54] What was perceived as racist stereotyping resulted in Judge Jansen being placed on indefinite leave while further action against her is being contemplated. The matter has been referred by the Democratic Alliance to the Judicial Service Commission with a view to her being defrocked.

It must be emphasised that Judge Jansen does not appear to be a racist. In 1977 she adopted two black African children, who testified what a good mother she was to them. Her concern about the frequency of rape in the country is also not without foundation. It is estimated that 500,000 rape cases take place in the country every year. Women's groups estimate that a woman is raped in South Africa on average every 26 seconds. The South African Police Service disagrees; it estimates that a woman is raped on average every 36 seconds. Statistics provided by the South African Police Service show that in 2014/15 the reported rape cases amounted to 43,195. Reported child rape cases in 2011/12 amounted to 21,128; in 2012/13 to 20,702; and in 2013/14 to 18,528. It is estimated that 40% of South African woman will be raped during their lifetime. These statistics are

---

52 See 2015. "Jacob Zuma under Investigation for Using Hate Speech", *The Guardian*, 19 February.
53 *ANC v. Penny Sparrow*, Case No 01/16, [2016] ZAEQC 1 (10 June 2016).
54 See 2016. "South African Judge Mabel Jansen in Race Rape Row", *BBC*, 9 May.

confined to reported rape cases, and it is estimated that only one in nine rape cases are reported.

Attributing the high rate of rape cases in South Africa to African culture nevertheless constitutes a violation of the hate speech constraints incorporated into South Africa law. However, the objective of those constraints – counteracting group rivalries in the country – presupposes that the offensive statement is brought to the knowledge of population groups that will be offended by the allegation concerned. It would therefore appear that the primary offender was not Judge Jansen, who conveyed the offensive allegation to a fellow white South African in a private communication, but the person who splashed it on the Internet for everyone to see.

CONCLUSION

I have often said that the constitution of a country is its most unexportable commodity. The special significance of freedom of speech in the United States is commendable within the social construct of that country; it is ill suited for a country like the new South Africa which has committed itself to the eventual elimination of group related animosities of the past.

Emphasis on human dignity, rather than individual freedoms, as the most basic premise of human rights protection is clearly in conformity with international-law standards. The Universal Declaration of Human Rights and the Covenant on Civil and Political Rights both proclaim that "recognition of the inherent dignity and of the equal and inalienable rights of all members of the human family is the foundation of freedom, justice and peace in the world.[55] According to its Preamble, the 1981 Declaration on the Elimination of All Forms of Intolerance and of Discrimination Based on Religion or Belief is founded on the basic principles of the Charter of the United Nations that proclaims "the dignity and equality inherent in all human beings".[56]

As far as the elimination of group rivalries is concerned, South Africa has not yet complied with international demands. Despite serious efforts – with constitutional backing – to eliminate group related hostilities in the country, South Africa has not even come close to accomplishing this noble objective. As noted by Chief Justice Pius Langa in 2009: "The process of reconciliation is an ongoing one which requires give and take from all sides."[57] "Our democracy is still fragile," said Judge Eberhard Bertelsmann, adding that "participants in

---

55 Universal Declaration of Human Rights, Dec. 10, 1948, G.A. Res. 217A, Preamble, first paragraph [emphasis added]; International Covenant on Civil and Political Rights, Dec. 16, 1966, 999 U.N.T.S. 173, Preamble, first paragraph [emphasis added].
56 Declaration on the Elimination of All Forms of Intolerance and Discrimination Based on Religion or Belief, Nov. 25, 1981, G.A. Res. 36/55, U.N. GAOR, 36th Sess., Supp. No. 51, at 171, U.N. Doc. A/RES/36/51.
57 *Du Toit v. Minister of Safety and Security*, 2009 (6) SA 128, para 28 (CC). See also *Agriforum and Another v. Malema and Another & Another*, *supra* n 47, para 11.

the political and socio-political discourse must remain sensitive to the feelings and perceptions of other South Africans when words were used that were common during the struggle days, but may be experienced as harmful by fellow inhabitants of South Africa today."[58]

Following the commendable rule of Nelson Mandela that was focused on reconciliation, a reactionary response to the newly established democracy was quite predictable. Gaining political control of the country initially prompted tremendous euphoria in the mindset of the formerly repressed population. However, it soon emerged that although a large number of Africans benefitted quite considerably from the government policy of remedial action, a vast majority of the population soon realised that many of the poor, uneducated and unemployed are still poor, uneducated and unemployed. Poverty, educational degradation and unemployment are exacerbated by the tremendous population increase in less sophisticated communities. The persistent inequalities between the rich and the poor sparked unrest and violent protests in the country, as well as the escalation of tribalism and racism under the rubric of a twisted perception of self-righteousness. The bottom line of it all is that *de facto* inequalities constitute primary obstacles in creating a rainbow nation, and as far as the commendable objectives of the Constitutional Assembly are concerned, South Africa still has many more miles to run.

---

58   *Agriforum and Another v. Malema & Another, supra* n 47.

17 "RHODES MUST FALL" – AN ALTERNATIVE APPROACH TO STATUES IN THE SOUTH AFRICAN PUBLIC SPHERE

Georgia Alida du Plessis[1]

INTRODUCTION

Higher education students of South Africa have recently revived anti-colonial and black consciousness rhetoric with requests for the removal of the Rhodes Statue at the University of Cape Town (UCT) Upper Campus.[2] The Black Consciousness Movement (BCM) swept across South Africa in the 1970s following the Sharpeville massacre in 1960. BCM organisations helped to educate and organise Black resistance, especially amongst the youth. The BCM urged a defiant rejection of apartheid, saw the rise of the South African Student Organisation (SASO – today called SASCO) as well as the organisation of trade unions. The BCM is synonymous with its founder, Steve Biko – one of the icons of the apartheid struggle. He instilled courage among the masses to fight an unjust system under the banner of Black Consciousness. The BCM meant a new framework of student thinking and flowed from Biko's resentment of the influence of white thought on determining an African's future. Biko then began a search for self-identity and hoped to build up the pride of Black culture.[3] He stated that real integration was only possible when once "the various groups within a given community have asserted themselves to the point that mutual respect has to be shown." He further argued, "Each group must be able to attain its style of existence without encroaching on or being thwarted by another … From this it becomes clear that as long as blacks are suffering from an inferiority complex – a result of 300 years of deliberate oppression, denigration and derision – they will be useless as co-architects of a normal society where man is nothing else but man for his own sake … Hence what is necessary as a prelude to anything else that may come is a very strong grass-roots build-up of black consciousness."[4]

---

1   Research fellow in Public Law at the University of the Free State, South Africa.
2   This re-emergence of a Black Consciousness Movement is proclaimed in the media. Leithead A. 2015. "Why South Africa's born-free generation is not happy". Online at: http://www.bbc.com/news/world-africa-34570761. The "rainbow nation" that Nelson Mandela spoke about is being seen as a failed project by many young, particularly black, South Africans and they are demanding more change than South Africa has given them the past 21 years.
3   South African History Online. Online at: http://www.sahistory.org.za/article/introduction-black-consciousness-movement
4   Biko S. 1987. *I Write what I Like*. Oxford: Heinemann Educational, Cox and Wyman Ltd, 21.

It was mostly black South African youths who are part of the "born free generation"[5] who started the "Rhodes Must Fall" (RMF) campaign, which also extended to Oxford University in the United Kingdom.[6] At UCT, the scenes that erupted around the Rhodes statue ended with the statue being hoisted by crane onto a truck surrounded by students cheering its banishment.[7] These students were mostly deeply dissatisfied with the remaining presence of colonial and apartheid symbols and religion within the public sphere of South Africa. The student leaders of RMF stated that the campaign was not directed against a particular historical individual but rather the symbols of institutional colonialism beyond democracy.[8] It was also held that the campaign was not about the denial of a particular history but that the statue continued to exercise power over the present.[9] Religious symbols and some statues are closely connected to South Africa's apartheid past and stand for white supremacy, racism, imperialism and the oppression of black Africans. As stated by Duane Jethro, the controversies surrounding the persistence of apartheid and colonial symbols demonstrate the contemporary role of established cultural heritage forms in mediating complex histories and belonging in post-apartheid South Africa.[10]

In light of a youth disillusioned and angry about the dreams of a "rainbow nation",[11] a dysfunctional government and remaining legacies of apartheid and colonialism (not only in economic circumstances but also in statues, art work, public displays and religion), how is the issue of heritage protection to be dealt

---

5   The "born free generation" in South Africa is the first generation of those South Africans who were born after the end of apartheid in 1994. At national level, South African born frees do not possess uniform views on the psychological, political and economic aspects of democracy. They never lived through apartheid and therefore their experience thereof widely differs along lines of race and class. Deep and pervasive racial cleavages in the psychological, political and economic attitudes of this generation remain as well as tremendous diversity in their lived experiences. Norgaard S. 2015. "Rainbow Junction: South Africa's Born Free Generation and the Future of Democracy". Online at: http://cddrl.fsi.stanford.edu/sites/default/files/stefannorgaard_finalcddrlthesis_0.pdf, iii. In their search for identity, the "born free" tag might do more to obscure than reveal political identity. The "born free" tag is also contested because many still feel that they are not free. Norgaard, "Rainbow Junction", 4.

6   See, for example, Elgot J. 2016. "'Take it down!': Rhodes Must Fall campaign marches through Oxford". Online at: http://www.theguardian.com/education/2016/mar/09/take-it-down-rhodes-must-fall-campaign-marches-through-oxford

7   Kros C. 2015. "Rhodes Must Fall: archives and counter-archives", *Critical Arts* 29(1):52.

8   Kros, "Rhodes Must Fall", 151.

9   Kros, "Rhodes Must Fall", 152.

10   Jethro DH. 2015. *Aesthetics of Power: Heritage Formation and the Senses in Post-Apartheid South Africa*, PhD Diss, University of Utrecht, 2.

11   The concept of a "rainbow nation" was at the time of the end of apartheid a necessary invention as the post-apartheid state tried to mobilise its own social cohesion. The Constitution of the Republic of South Africa provided (and still provides) an important set of inclusive values at a time when suspicion still reigned between different racial groups in the mid-nineteen nineties. Jethro, *Aesthetics of Power*, 14-15 & 17.

with? Can the removal of such heritage be justified by the negative historic connotations of these statues and monuments? How can heritage be protected in a manner that is in line with human dignity, equality and freedom – the cornerstones of the South African Constitution? Although the Constitution of the Republic of South Africa, 1996, promotes human dignity, equality, freedom and diversity, it does not clearly state when public symbols such as statues and monuments infringe these values. Also, although the National Heritage Resources Act (NHRA) 25 of 1999 provides for the legal removal of undesirable monuments by way of obtaining a permit, it does not provide guidelines as to when a monument or statue is undesirable, discriminating or contrary to human dignity.

This chapter seeks to address from a South African Constitutional perspective the manner in which to deal with recent events of "iconoclasm" relating to controversial religious, cultural or historical statues containing and representing negative elements of the history of the South African society. "Iconoclasm" also holds a specific connection with religion (but is not limited to it) in the sense that it was used during the Protestant Reformation (as only one example) as a reaction against the perceived idolatry of the Catholic Church and any iconoclastic act seen as a form of "heresy" against the Catholic Church.

The first part of this chapter investigates the historical narrative that created the controversies around these statues. The second part investigates recent waves of iconoclasm (such as the RMF campaign), the elements imbued therein and the reasons for their occurrence. Third, the South African legal framework and governmental reactions regarding "iconoclasm" are investigated, as well as whether the current South African position provides an adequate way to deal with the emotional and political sentiments surrounding recent iconoclastic acts. Finally, in light of the lack of proper guidelines surrounding such acts, the chapter provides for an alternative way to deal with offensive statues. The alternative method is argued to be in line with human dignity, equality and freedom as provided for in the Constitution of the Republic of South Africa. Two notions developed by Charles Taylor,[12] namely the "politics of recognition" and a "presumption in favour of equal worth", are presented as a bottom-up approach to identity formation. Also, the notion of "deep diversity", as developed by Taylor, is presented as a framework within which these issues should be considered. The parameters of deep diversity and equal worth must enhance and give effect to the notions of human dignity, equality and freedom.

---

12   Taylor C. 1994. *The Politics of Recognition. Multiculturalism: Examining the Politics of Recognition*. Princeton: Princeton University Press, 25-73.

THE HISTORICAL NARRATIVE BEHIND THE CONTROVERSIAL SYMBOLS AND MONUMENTS

In order to understand the anger surrounding the presence of colonial and apartheid statues as remaining legacies of a discriminating South African past, it is vital to understand the history that these statues and religious symbols represent. Cultural and religious identity in South Africa is defined by its history, as well as attempts to escape from such history. Such an escape is partly manifested in setting up statues that contradict or challenge existing colonial statues[13] or the mere removal of religious and cultural symbols, logos[14] and statues. However, in order to understand these attempts to escape, one has to understand the memory from which escape is sought.

During apartheid, schools in South Africa, as elsewhere, reflected society's political philosophy and goals.[15] A group of Afrikaner churches proposed an education programme, Christian National Education (CNE), to serve as the core of the school curriculum.[16] The National Education Policy Act 39 of 1967 at the time, clearly stated that education had to have a Christian character.[17] With the National Party's reign and the enactment of the Bantu Education Act 47 of 1953, CNE became the official education policy during apartheid. Black schools had inferior facilities, teachers, and textbooks.[18] By 1989, hundreds of political activists had been murdered, thousands had died in inhumane conditions in mines, native populations no longer had land of their own and tens of thousands were incarcerated, many of them without trial.[19]

Despite the fact that more than twenty years have passed since the end of apartheid and the beginnings of the pursuit of dreams of a rainbow nation, symbols of religious and racial apartheid and religious and cultural colonialism can still be found in the South African public sphere. South African youths, especially the black youth, still claim to be bound by the shackles of apartheid, colonialism and its legacy. Although born after apartheid, this generation claims that they are legally free but still carry the burden of an identity forged by apartheid and live their lives in a country with elements and demographics that remind them of apartheid's continuing legacy.[20]

---

13 Examples of such monuments are the Blood River Wagon memorial and the Ncome Zulu cultural exhibition in KwaZulu-Natal.
14 Many South African universities recently changed their logos and slogans to remove any religious connotations.
15 South Africa: A country study. Online at: http://www.country-data.com/frd/cs/zatoc.html
16 South Africa: A country study.
17 Horrell M. 1978. *Laws affecting race relations in South Africa: 1948-1976*. Johannesburg: South African Institute of Race Relations, 350.
18 Horrell, *Laws affecting race relations*, 295.
19 Peffer J. 2005. "Censorship and iconoclasm – unsettling monuments", RES: *Anthropology and Aesthetics* 48:46.
20 Norgaard, "Rainbow Junction", 2.

Although South Africa transitioned from an apartheid government to a democracy in the early 1990s, the policies have a continued legacy of significant inequality. The burden of many of these inequalities falls on South African youths in terms of education, employment, poverty, and health outcomes.[21] Approximately 64.5% of children live in households that fall within the bottom two income quintiles with a per capita income of less than R765.00 per month, and 70.5% of black African children live in low income households, compared to only 4.4% of white children.[22] In 2013, the youth unemployment rate was 63% of the youth labour force (3.2 million individuals).[23]

The hopelessness and anger at recurring patterns of injustice and inequality caused by apartheid legacy, and an increasingly incompetent and corrupt South African government, have resulted in a series of events such as the defacing and removal of cultural and religious symbols and slogans from the South African public sphere – especially in institutions of higher education. For students participating in the RMF movements, transformation has not been complete. In their view, they are still trapped in structures of marginalisation, because society is still functioning within the values of colonialism and apartheid. The destruction of images has entailed a process of arguing that what many had been going along with had been a grave mistake. This is also a tough admission to make.[24] At the same time white South African youth are caught between unwillingly or involuntarily carrying the blame and feelings of guilt for the remaining legacy of apartheid. Some of the white youth are able to understand the anger and frustration of fellow black students, while others view the movement as an act of racism and a threat to their culture and the Afrikaans language. This wave of "iconoclasm", rooted in the mentioned anger and accusations of not being heard, needs closer attention and constitutional deliberation.

WAVES OF ICONOCLASM

The defacing of statues is not a new occurrence. In the academic world, it is called iconoclasm. In general, iconoclasm is the destruction or alteration of images, objects and art imbued with some kind of symbolic value, and can extend beyond tangible objects.[25] Since the French Revolution, the breaking of

---

21 Kriel AJ, Whitehead KA and Richter LM. 2005. "Barriers to Conducting a Community Mobilization Intervention Among Youth in a Rural South African Community", *Journal of Community Psychology* 33(3):253-259.
22 Lehohla P. 2013. Statistics South Africa. Social profile of vulnerable groups (2002-2012). Report No. 03-19-00 (2002-2012).
23 Oosthuizen M and Cassim A. 2014. "The State of Youth Unemployment in South Africa". Online at: http://www.brookings.edu/blogs/africa-in-focus/posts/2014/08/15-youth-unemployment-south-africa-oosthuizen
24 Peffer, "Censorship and iconoclasm", 59.
25 Kolrud K and Prusac M. 2014. "Introduction", in Kolrud K and Prusac M (eds). *Iconoclasm from Antiquity to Modernity*. Aldershot: Ashgate, 1.

images and destruction of idols have been linked to the rhetoric of revolutionary politics.[26] Iconoclasm was present from the Byzantine[27] to the Reformation periods.[28] Protestant Reformers such as John Calvin encouraged the removal of religious images by invoking the prohibition of idolatry. The removal of an emperor's visual presence was a means of controlling or depressing debate.[29] In antiquity images of the emperor were destroyed as an act and a means of wiping out his memory, and one may say that the practice has continued and continue to this day.[30] "Iconoclasm depends on the power of the image, in as much as a neglected image, which is no longer the object of either worship or hatred, remains an unlikely target."[31] More recently, on a campus in Texas the words "black lives matter" were spray-painted over three statues of Confederate leaders.[32] The toppling of the statue of Saddam Hussein is another more recent example.[33]

Iconoclasm is not new to South Africa. Following the tumultuous years during the transfer to a democracy, there were several iconoclastic reactions. Initial erasure of the colonial heritage enacted as a form of decolonisation was later followed by a more inclusive redress – such as adding new moments or layers of suppressed history to existing places of commemoration.[34] Statues were removed, art was removed from parliament and original African names were reinstated. Iconoclasm has again reached epidemic proportions between 2014 and 2016. Besides the Rhodes statue at UCT, others statues that were subject to iconoclasm included the Queen Victoria statue in Port Elizabeth and the CR Swart statue at the University of the Free State campus (2016). Since RMF, there have been about twenty other similar incidents in South Africa.[35]

Besides the anger and disappointment of the youth with the continuing legacy of apartheid and a dysfunctional government, these statues also represent a continuing legacy that assists in continuing frameworks of inequality. As

---

26 Clay R. 2012. "Re-Making French Revolutionary Iconoclasm", *Perspective* 1:181-186.
27 Also see the chapter on "Islam, Judeo-Christianity and Byzantine Iconoclasm", in Patricia Crone. *Religion, Law and Political Thought in the Near East, c.600-c.1100.* Aldershot: Ashgate Variorum.
28 Kolrud and Prusac, "Introduction", 4.
29 Kolrud and Prusac, "Introduction", 6.
30 Kolrud and Prusac, "Introduction", 5-6.
31 Kolrud and Prusac, "Introduction", 6.
32 Tani M. 2015. "Confederate Statues at University of Texas spray-painted with 'black lives matter'." Online at: http://uk.businessinsider.com/confederate-statues-defaced-at-ut-austin-20156?r=US&IR=T
33 Axelfod J. 2013. "A decade after Saddam Hussein's statue falls: A tale of two memories." Online at: http://www.cbsnews.com/news/a-decade-after-saddam-husseins-statue-falls-a-tale-of-two-memories/
34 Bakker KA and Müller L. 2010. "Intangible Heritage and Community Identity in Post-Apartheid South Africa", *Museum International* 62(1-2):48.
35 For a list, see http://www.theheritageportal.co.za/thread/vandalisation-statues-south-africa

described by John Peffer, these are images[36] of pain and torture, murder, labour that lobotomise and bury its shattered men.[37] The psychological analyses of iconoclasm and the relationship between statues and the living beings that occupy the space these statues occupy remain complicated. Some are of the opinion that monuments are capable of radiating an impression of "supernatural omnipresence" and the bodily experience of constructed space. There is a vivid intercommunication between monument and spectator.[38] During the RMF protests one student stated that the flinging of human faeces at the statue was so that the statue "feels" ashamed the way he (the student) feels ashamed that these faeces are in his living environment. The attempt was to "desanctify" the statue[39] and to make it human.[40] Irrespective of the psychological reasons for iconoclasm, offensive statues influence human dignity, identity formation and constitutional rights. Monuments and statues are literally markers of conceptual spaces and responsible for mapping a landscape. They serve the present and are designed to preserve memory for the sake of future generations. Therefore, the absence of some monuments, or the representation of only one history, can represent history in a conjured fashion[41] and affect constitutional rights.

Amidst the human rights implications of the effect of such statues on the human dignity of people and their perception of being equal and free in a society, what is the most constitutional manner in which to deal with obscure statues within public spaces? Not only do these statues represent parts of history – albeit very negative parts – their psychological and consequent effects on the human rights of those who are confronted with them daily are of utmost importance. Within public spaces, a balance is to be struck between preserving history and heritage, remaining inclusive of all religions and cultures within South Africa and maintaining an environment representative of equality. This immediately poses the following question – how to balance these factors in the most constitutional manner and in line with the underlying values of the Bill of Rights, such as human dignity, equality and freedom. Do these statues and logos achieve equality, human dignity and freedom? Will the defacing or removal of statues achieve these rights? Does the apartheid and colonial history have a place in the present? In order to answer these questions, the legal framework within which they should be answered is clarified.

---

36 These images are not limited to statues but also include spaces such as the Voortrekker Monument.
37 Peffer, "Censorship and iconoclasm", 46.
38 Kros, "Rhodes Must Fall", 153.
39 Kros, "Rhodes Must Fall", 154.
40 Kros, "Rhodes Must Fall", 155.
41 Marschall S. 2003. "Setting up a dialogue: monuments as a means of 'writing back'", *Historia* 48(1):317.

THE CONSTITUTION, LAW AND GOVERNMENT CONCERNING ICONOCLASM

The Preamble of the Constitution of the Republic of South Africa, 1996 states:

> We, the people of South Africa,
> Recognise the injustices of our past;
> Honour those who suffered for justice and freedom in our land;
> Respect those who have worked to build and develop our country; and
> Believe that South Africa belongs to all who live in it, united in our diversity.

When applying this foundational paragraph to iconoclasm in a complicated country such as South Africa, several questions emerge. How can the injustices of our past be recognised? Can it be done by eliminating all signs thereof? By keeping all signs thereof and remembering the injustices they caused? By recognising and acknowledging the signs of injustice but recreating them to reveal their bias, for example the insertion of a commemorative site, such as the Blood River museum, to provide a more balanced approach to history?[42]

The National Heritage Resources Act 25 of 1999 (NHRA) provides limited answers. Public monuments and memorials are defined as "erected on land belonging to any branch of government or any organisation funded or established in terms of legislation or which is paid for by government funds". Section 37 of NHRA states that public monuments and memorials must be protected in the same manner as places entered in a heritage register. This means that no person may destroy, damage, deface or remove such a monument without a permit issued by the heritage resources authority responsible for the protection of such a site.[43] Therefore, the removal or defacing of statues is possible, but it should follow a specific procedure and can only be done with a permit issued by the appropriate authorities. The NHRA does not give any guidelines as to when such a permit is to be given or not.

The African National Congress (ANC) government has tried to hold a rather rational position in these instances – a position that does not account for the urgency, anger and feelings of indignation of the South African youth. Government holds that heritage sites and monuments have cultural significance and value because of their importance to a community in revealing a pattern of South Africa's history. It demonstrates a particular aspect of a particular time. Government promotes a transformative agenda while accepting that the past cannot be completely wiped away. For this reason, and as part of transformation, the diverse voices of all citizens of South Africa must be allowed to express themselves. A national policy of reconciliation, nation-building and social cohesion is promoted by the government.[44] Therefore, the government's

---

42 Bakker and Müller, "Intangible Heritage", 48.
43 National Heritage Resources Act, section 27(18).
44 Online at: http://www.gov.za/speeches/minister-arts-culture-mr-nathi-mthethwa-defacing-and-or-violent-removal-colonial-statues-8

approach is largely conservative and aimed at racial reconciliation.[45] This policy followed the example of Afrikaner policy during apartheid towards old, offensive and controversial British monuments, which was aimed at establishing a constructive dialogue between older and new monuments.[46] In an attempt to set up dialogue, many post-apartheid monuments have been placed near existing older monuments to seek confrontation with the colonial and apartheid legacy.[47]

Clearly, and based on recent events of iconoclasm, the government's approach has not appealed to the anger and frustration of large sections of South Africa's youth. Furthermore, the South African laws, such as the NHRA, are rather vague in establishing the conditions when a permit for removal will be granted and under which conditions. Who decides what stays and what goes and under what criteria?

Although the South African Constitution provides that all laws and policies should enhance the values and rights of human dignity, equality and freedom, non-racialism and non-sexism,[48] it is not clear how these values will be interpreted and balanced in cases of iconoclasm. Black South African youths may claim that the existing colonial and apartheid statues infringe their right to equality, human dignity and freedom. They may claim that they cannot be free and equal in the presence of these statues and that it causes them to experience unfair discrimination. Section 9 of the Constitution clearly states that, if there is discrimination, it has to be shown that it is unfair discrimination before being declared unconstitutional. When one of the 17 expressly mentioned grounds is discriminated against in Section 9 (including race), the presumption is that such discrimination will be unfair, unless the contrary can be proven.[49] If the presence of a statue leads to racial discrimination, it is presumed that the presence of such a statue is discriminating and contrary to equality, unless the contrary can be proven. The constitutional guarantee of equality must be interpreted contextually, entailing a historical understanding of South

---

45 Marschall S. 2003. "Setting up a dialogue: monuments as a means of 'writing back'", *Historia* 48(1):317. Also see Duane Jethro D. 2014. "Cecil Rhodes, Heritage Formation and Contemporary Popular Culture". Online at: http://historymatters.co.za/content/cecil-rhodes-heritage-formation-and-contemporary-popular-culture-duane-jethro
46 Marschall, "Setting up a dialogue: monuments as a means of 'writing back'", 318. Here "dialogue" means that the political, social or religious history of one statue challenges or confronts the political, social or religious history of another sharing the same public space. Such "dialogue" therefore refers to the historical narrative behind the statues.
47 Marschall, "Setting up a dialogue", 318.
48 Sections 1, 9 and 10 of the Constitution.
49 See section 9(5) of the Constitution. In section 9, the grounds for unfair discrimination are race, gender, sex, pregnancy, marital status, ethnic or social origin, colour, sexual orientation, age, disability, religion, conscience, belief, culture, language and birth.

Africa's past and South Africa's future.[50] In *Pretoria City Council v. Walker*[51] the Constitutional Court of South Africa stated that when determining equality, it has to be assessed against the background of the preceding paragraphs of section 9 and the constitutional and historical context of the developments in South Africa.[52] The presence of discriminatory statues and whether it leads to the infringement of equality should take into account the history of South Africa and how such history enlarges sensitivities to anything that mirrors it – including statues. It should also be determined whether the presence of a statue is conducive for remedying remaining patterns of disadvantage and achieve substantive equality.

A distinction has to be made between formal and substantive equality. South Africa follows an approach that adheres to substantive equality. Law professor Sandra Fredman (University of Oxford, but born in South Africa) states that recent decades show growing acceptance of the limits of formal equality with its focus on the abstract individual, as this has "failed to address deeply entrenched patterns of social disadvantage". This also means that equality requires more than restraint from the state. It requires active transformation to change entrenched patterns of disadvantage. Fredman further states that the abstract individual of formal equality is a myth.[53] As economist and philosopher Amartya Sen argues: "Equal consideration for all may demand very unequal treatment in favour of the disadvantaged. The demands of substantive equality can be particularly exacting and complex when there is a good deal of antecedent inequality to counter."[54]

Equality jurisprudence must thus be truly "transformative" and not merely "inclusionary".[55] It will not be sufficient to simply remove discriminatory statues, laws or practices but, rather, as stated in Sections 7[56] and 9, there are categories of disadvantaged persons who should be advantaged (even by way of differentiation and fair discrimination) and the state should actively promote this. Substantive equality may thus require active removal of statues by the state in order to eradicate remaining discrimination, rather than a negative or passive approach of non-involvement by the state.

---

50 Currie I and De Waal J. 2005. *The Bill of Rights Handbook*, 5th ed. Cape Town: Juta, 231.
51 1998 (2) SA 363 (CC) (1998 (3) BCLR 257).
52 *Pretoria City Council v. Walker* 1998 (2) SA 363 (CC) (1998 (3) BCLR 257): para graph 26.
53 Fredman S. 2005. "Providing Equality: Substantive equality and the positive duty to provide", *South African Journal of Human Rights* 21:165.
54 Fredman, "Providing Equality", 166.
55 Albertyn C. 2007. "Substantive Equality and Transformation in South Africa", *South African Journal of Human Rights* 23:254. See also Fredman, "Providing Equality", 167.
56 Section 7 states the following: "(1) This Bill of Rights is a cornerstone of democracy in South Africa. It enshrines the rights of all people in our country and affirms the democratic values of human dignity, equality and freedom. (2) The state must respect, protect, promote and fulfil the rights in the Bill of Rights …"

Does this mean that, because of past injustices, old colonial and apartheid statues can be removed and merely replaced by new ones advancing the interests of previously disadvantaged racial groups? Has the government's reconciliatory approach towards monuments in public spaces been transformative or merely inclusive? Has the government been radical enough to address and transform persisting patterns and images of injustice in public spaces? Although the South African Constitution provides for a general normative framework on how to deal with obscure statues in the public sphere when it amounts to equality claims and other human rights issues, it is unsure what the outcome would be for each and every monument or statue. The outcome will probably be determined on a case-by-case basis, with special emphasis on remedying past injustices and transforming society. Within the framework of the constitutional analysis applicable to each case concerning an offensive statue, this chapter aims to introduce a number of important factors that are fundamental to consider during this analysis. Hence, subject to the right to equality and the right to human dignity, this chapter wants to establish a new framework for participation and social inclusion concerning statues in the public sphere. These considerations wish, in the manner proposed by law professor Catherine Albertyn, to facilitate or establish new, non-hierarchical, normative frameworks of participation and social inclusion that are transformative.[57] Neither the approach of removing statues, nor the mere addition of state determined cultural artefacts to the public sphere will serve as the most constitutional approach in upholding equality, human dignity and freedom. Mere removal represents an act of censorship and mere additions by the state a lack of deep diversity and transformation. What is needed is a bottom-up approach seeking initiatives from civil society rather than a top-down approach where culture and national identity are determined by the state.

CENSORSHIP AND ICONOCLASM

Although the removal of a statue or monument will depend on and ultimately be determined in light of the Constitution of the Republic of South Africa, 1996, one should be weary of the potential effects of iconoclasm and the complete removal of statues. Although the effects on the human dignity of previously disadvantaged groups might be great, the possibility should be considered that the removal of a statue might have an even greater disadvantageous effect on the human dignity of previously disadvantaged groups.

This possible disadvantageous effect refers to the relationship between iconoclasm and censorship. It is possible that actions of defacing or removal may actually silence and ignore the injustices of the past, rather than dealing with it. It is the same as saying that a subject should not be talked about because it is too painful. Iconoclasm can prohibit a public sphere of active debate

---

57 Albertyn, "Substantive Equality", 260.

because the hurts of the past are removed visually, but not emotionally. By sterilising and silencing the public sphere and history, we are only silencing the pain[58] and preventing dialogue aimed at reconciliation. The possibility exists that completely removing the image creates an emptiness – this is a primary form of iconoclasm.

On the other hand, if a statue is maintained, what is to be done about the politics of memory?[59] Whose memory is to be attached to a statue and what should it say? Because memory is not an undeviating concept and is highly political, ideological and subjective, it is argued that an approach most suitable under a regime of human dignity, equality and freedom is a highly inclusive approach – one that promotes and gives voice to *all* the memories attached to a statue. Even if *one* memory is not preserved, but the debate surrounding the statue is ongoing, it is more important that the diverse voices are recognised and history and political issues constantly reviewed. This is in line with the approach following a politics of recognition proposed below. It is suggested that it might be that between all the different memories about a single event, lies the actual events. Yet, in our pursuit to establish what exactly happened (if that is even possible) all different memories should be honoured. It might seem an impossible task, but democracy is not supposed to be easy and will take hard work, effort and sacrifice. This is a form of the secondary type of iconoclasm promoted in this chapter.

A secondary type of iconoclasm is a way of using the iconoclastic gesture to attack censorship, address the hurt attached to the monument and its imposition on human dignity, without removing or damaging the obscure object. John Peffer suggests that through a secondary type of iconoclasm, memory can also be countered as opposed to officially and unofficially sanitised versions of history.[60] Secondary iconoclasm addresses the reasons why the statue is offensive, rather than ignoring that the hurt is present. One example of a secondary form of iconoclasm (in the form of a protest action) is South African artist Tracey Rose's attempt to unravel doilies (made by the "coloured"[61] community outside Oudtshoorn) at the Klein Karoo National Arts Festival in 1998. She wound the threads around a police monument of an

---

58 Peffer, "Censorship and iconoclasm", 45.
59 See, for example, the politics of memory concerning the Second World War – Ther P. 2006. "The burden of history and the trap of memory." Online at: http://www.eurozine.com/the-burden-of-history-and-the-trap-of-memory/. The issues pertaining to memory and its service to justice can clearly be seen in the South African history and methods of dealing with painful memory – for example, the Truth and Reconciliation Commission (TRC). Here it is important to understand that there are dangers to forgetting but also dangers to the manipulation of memory and presenting it as the "truth". See Duvenage P. "The Politics of Memory and Forgetting After Auschwitz and Apartheid". Online at: http://mobile.wiredspace.wits.ac.za/bitstream/handle/10539/7767/HWS-106.pdf?sequence=1
60 Peffer, "Censorship and iconoclasm", 222.
61 Usually, in South Africa, persons of mixed race origin refer to themselves as coloured.

officer and his dog. Several white male officers demanded that she cease the work until one of them finally cut the doily threads with a knife. The act of unravelling constituted an effort to lay open the past and make visible acts of oppression under apartheid.[62] When she was asked why she used doilies, she stated that when she grew up women were shut up in a women's knitting circle from age sixteen and older, and doilies were the trophy of female worth. Doilies represented repressed and oppressed emotions and self-censorship. Mixed race females in Oudtshoorn during apartheid were seen as sex objects used by men. If you were "coloured" you were the product of some kind of "illicit sex". Wrapping a monument of the police in doilies was meant as an unravelling of the history behind the public image. Rose saw her performance not as destruction, but as re-creation and reformation of the relationship between mixed race women and white men.[63] Other similar acts included for example *Loslyf*'s publication of semi-naked women in front of the Voortrekker monument – ridiculing Afrikaner pride.[64] These secondary means of iconoclasm deprive the image of its power and diminish its political power in the same way as primary iconoclasm does.[65] The secondary approach to iconoclasm is revolutionary in that it does not bury oppressive images in the waste heap of history, but rather keeps them in play.[66] However, these monuments are not kept in play in a static manner. There are many ways to unsettle a monument by revealing a new semantic wealth by opening up previously occluded meaning. The vision can be pulled apart and new possibilities found.[67]

The secondary form of iconoclasm becomes a form of dialogue and debate – a proposal and a reply. When considering the equality considerations explained above, it should also be taken into account that the removal of statues might silence the injustices of the past and amount to censorship, which in turn can cause greater harm to human dignity and equality. The South African government has practised such a secondary form of iconoclasm by inserting commemorative cites within existing sites, representing and highlighting the layers, intricacies and development of oppression. An early example is the Ncome Monument, created in 2000. It corrects the one-sided iconographic representation of the "Battle of Blood (Ncome) River" and intends oppositional content. It does represent Voortrekker artefacts and history but also represents and transforms this history.[68] However, these changes were mostly done by the state, resulting in a hegemonic, dominant voice about culture, and

---

62 Peffer, "Censorship and iconoclasm", 55.
63 Peffer, "Censorship and iconoclasm", 56.
64 Peffer, "Censorship and iconoclasm", 56. *Loslyf* used to be an extremely controversial Afrikaans pornographic magazine. It represented everything the Nationalist apartheid government did not stand for and challenged the ideologies of Afrikaner Nationalism. The word "Loslyf" is a slang Afrikaans word that depicts a sense of freedom pertaining to one's body.
65 Peffer, "Censorship and iconoclasm – unsettling monuments", 58.
66 Peffer, "Censorship and iconoclasm – unsettling monuments", 59-60.
67 Peffer, "Censorship and iconoclasm – unsettling monuments", 60.
68 Bakker and Möller, "Intangible Heritage", 48.

silencing many a dissonant and smaller voice[69] – in other words, an indirect imperial dominance by the state of what the public space should look like. The imposition of a cultural identity by the state, whether by adding or removing statues, supports static conceptions of history, while modification from the local community realises democracy at local level and promotes a bottom-up approach.[70] Therefore, a top-down state imposed cultural identity countering these statues will merely censor dissenting voices and deny groups of persons the opportunity to create their own identity from the bottom-up. A bottom-up approach avoids a single narrative of cultural identity. It will promote democracy at the local level and notions of deep cultural diversity and equal worth, as advocated by Charles Taylor.

DEEP DIVERSITY, THE POLITICS OF RECOGNITION AND EQUAL WORTH vs A SINGLE NARRATIVE

If the state is the main purveyor of heritage and a hegemonic voice in the production of cultural heritage, then fluid and meaningful dialogue between different cultures becomes impossible and minority and diverse cultures are drowned. This amounts to a convergence of cultures and a lack of recognition of diversity. The state has mostly emphasised the use of static monuments while avoiding complex narratives.[71] Although the state should launch initiatives and promote commemoration (and various versions of commemoration) and dialogue through the medium of statues, this should not prevent the freedom of expression of local communities, but rather encourage the creation of cultural identity from the real centre of the narratives – the communities themselves. On various microlevels the struggle should be commemorated from the centre narratives.[72] This adds to authentic dialogue with existing statues and monuments of colonialism and apartheid. Failure to engage the dialogue and expression of the community will result in general apathy and disengagement by the younger generation.[73] Such fluid and open-ended heritage conservation does not place the emphasis on consensus, but rather so that differences and complexity may be continually explored.[74]

Narrow definitions of history and culture should be rejected[75] and the complexities that involve South Africa's history should be represented in statues – not merely the constructed identity of the government. The national identity constructed by the state can be seen in commemorations like the

---

69 Bakker and Möller, "Intangible Heritage", 49.
70 Peffer, "Censorship and iconoclasm", 59.
71 Bakker and Möller, "Intangible Heritage", 50.
72 Bakker and Möller, "Intangible Heritage", 50.
73 Bakker and Möller, "Intangible Heritage", 50.
74 Bakker and Möller, "Intangible Heritage", 54.
75 Wright JP. 2010. *Memory, Monuments and the South African National Imaginary: Constitution Hill and the Fiction of Ivan Vladislavić*, MA Thesis, University of KwaZulu-Natal, 6.

Apartheid Museum. This museum creates a static and simplified history, but not a dialogue entailing disagreement. It rather represents consensus and the inevitability of the current dispensation with its unquestioned legitimacy.[76] The Apartheid Museum speaks a constant monologue that drowns out other voices.[77] It presumes a national imagery and consensus about South Africa without considering the fact that people have different notions of the past and that their present identities are difficult to include in a unitary nation. It does not take account of disagreement and diversity.[78] Such a unifying approach to cultural identity is irrelevant to black youth amidst a collective identity crisis in post-apartheid South Africa. Consequently, they "hark back" to the past (decolonisation of statues) with amplified intensity[79] – as recently seen in the "Rhodes Must Fall" campaign.

What is called for is an opening-up in thinking about South African heritage and apartheid. South Africa has, up to now, been written about as a closed separate space. It should not be viewed as a space separate from other decolonised countries where identity and culture are merely defined by government in light of victimhood. South African culture is more than the liberation narrative and fights over racial supremacy and racial victimhood as a determinant of identity – although this is a very important part of it. Culture and identity in South Africa have always been more fluid. Culture and identity were first restricted by apartheid and are now constrained by the oversimplified discourse of rainbow nationalism, racial victimhood and racial supremacy.[80] Instead of merely removing old statues and adding new ones representative only of a simplistic state-imposed identity – which would undermining the richness of South African culture – a notion of deep diversity and equal worth would enable all groups of society to create a living and vibrant dialogue by way of public representations of statues and monuments. In light of the concept of deep diversity and equal worth, these public spaces should not only represent colonial style statues and monuments, but also commemoration inherent in the represented culture itself.

Merely adding a statue to the already existing one in order to stimulate dialogue, creates a new identity, philosophy and understanding of the public sphere – but one that is currently solely determined by the state. A deeply diverse South African heritage should be presented in the public sphere, and one that is constructed from the bottom-up and not only by the state or via a state-imposed identity. These styles should not merely be similar to those of existing colonial and apartheid statues, but should be authentic to its culture. These monuments should "write back" but not only in the language of the

---

76   Wright, *Memory, Monuments*, 70.
77   Wright, *Memory, Monuments*, 71.
78   Wright, *Memory, Monuments*, 65.
79   Wright, *Memory, Monuments*, 66.
80   Wright, *Memory, Monuments*, 5.

coloniser by way of statues of new heroes cast in bronze.[81] This can be part of it, but should also be a celebration of the aspects inherent in the culture itself. Such an approach is rooted in self-reflection and blocked from falling into a new kind of censorship.[82]

There are two suggested ways of achieving such a public space: (1) by secondary iconoclasm as explained above; (2) by a grass-roots approach taking account of deep diversity and equal worth. Since the first one has already been dealt with, I move now to address the second suggestion.

In his important essay, *The Politics of Recognition*, Canadian philosopher Charles Taylor states that besides the fact that the protection and promotion of plural religions and cultures within the public sphere involve matters of human dignity, equality and freedom, it also concerns what Charles Taylor calls "the politics of recognition".[83] In the present day, we understand the formation of identity and the self as taking place in a continuing dialogue and struggle with others and then in the public sphere, where a politics of equal recognition has come to play a bigger and bigger role.[84] However, the modern notion of identity emphasises equality but also that everyone should be recognised for his or her unique identity.[85] It is argued that our identity is partly shaped by the recognition or absence of recognition of others, and so a person or a group of people can suffer true damage. Misrecognition can inflict harm, be a form of oppression, imprisoning someone in a false, distorted, and reduced mode of being.[86]

Denying any culture or cultural history a part in the public sphere can lead to the misrecognition of that culture and a violation of their human dignity. This can be done by the indiscriminate removal of both statues and monuments because they stem from the pre-1994 period. It could also be caused by a lack of recognising the deeply diverse and complex natures of majority and minority cultures by way of a state-imposed hegemonic identity based on the sole dialogue of racial victimhood and racial superiority. Such recognition should also not be manifested in replicating liberal and colonising methods of commemoration – namely statues. In order to give effect to the recognition of

---

81 Marschall, "Setting up a dialogue", 321.
82 Peffer, "Censorship and iconoclasm – unsettling monuments", 59
83 Taylor C. 1994. *The Politics of Recognition. Multiculturalism: Examining the Politics of Recognition*. Princeton: Princeton University Press, 25-73.
84 Taylor, *The Politics of Recognition*, 37.
85 Taylor, *The Politics of Recognition*, 38.
86 Taylor, *The Politics of Recognition*, 25. According to Duane Jethro, the Rhodes Must Fall Movement questioned these exact ideas of tolerance, the recognition of all histories on equal terms and the unquestioned inclusion of all material pasts. Jethro, *Aesthetics of Power*, 243.

this diversity, Taylor argues for a "presumption in favour of equal worth". He argues that it is:

> ... reasonable to suppose that cultures that have provided the horizon of meaning for large numbers of human beings, of diverse characters and temperaments, over a long period of time – that have, in other words, articulated their sense of the good, the whole, the admirable – are almost certain to have something that deserves our admiration and respect, even if it is accompanied by much that we have to abhor and reject.[87] Perhaps one could put it another way: it would take a supreme arrogance to discount this possibility a priori. There is perhaps after all a moral issue here. We only need a sense of our own limited part in the whole human story to accept the presumption. It is only arrogance, or some analogous moral failing, that can deprive us of this.[88]

Although Taylor here talks about the guilt of Western liberal societies in imposing their views of what is worthy on other cultures,[89] this can be extended to the argument that diverse cultures within South Africa should be seen as having inherent equal worth. It should not be viewed merely from the perspective of the decolonisation and apartheid narrative proposed by government to forge national identity. Although this narrative has influenced various cultures, it is not the only element that defines them. They are equally worthy in their own splendour and richness. Solely because of this they should be commemorated within the public sphere – all of them.

Charles Taylor's concept of "deep diversity" is one that he introduced in an essay, titled "Deep Diversity and the Future of Canada", but it applies equally to South Africa's deeply diverse and complex society. Deep diversity centres on celebrating ethnic, cultural and religious distinctiveness and promotes diversity in deeper layers of identity formation and social relations.[90] In other words, deep diversity acknowledges and celebrates the fact that the identity and memory of a human being is not only one-dimensional. There are religious, cultural, political, economic and historical factors (amongst others) that influence and create memory and identity. Furthermore, it will be a grave injustice to view such identity-formation from only one ideological perspective that is abstracted from the reality of an individual, a cultural group or a religious group of persons. It includes an ethical account that acknowledges and addresses diversity in multicultural societies, without expecting distinct persons to be abstracted from their own distinctiveness and specification.[91] The value and importance of the culture is not judged from outside national identity, but also by that which is inherent in the culture. It is more than mere toleration

---

87 Taylor, *The Politics of Recognition*, 72-73.
88 Taylor, *The Politics of Recognition*, 73.
89 Taylor, *The Politics of Recognition*, 63.
90 Masaeli M. 2013. *The Ethics of Deep Diversity in Multicultural Societies – Part I*. Online at: http://livebettermagazine.com/article/the-et
91 Masaeli, *The Ethics of Deep Diversity – Part I*.

and more than mere acknowledgement of diversity. Rather, it actively engages in the "political recognition of the distinctiveness of different others". It also allows for a more participatory discourse of democratisation and inclusion in multicultural societies.[92]

> This ethics starts from the assumption that all individual persons have the same potential to determine and express their own sense of belonging and, therefore, their own distinctive identity. This sameness, the principle of equality of difference, must become an imperative in acknowledging and recognizing people's differences in their own original way of selfhood and its expression in social relations. The ethics of deep diversity, then, promises a discourse of emancipation from social marginalization and exclusion.[93]

Such an approach provides for a bottom-up notion to build a diverse and complex public space of commemoration rather than a state-imposed one. Public spaces can commemorate cultures from the perspectives of the cultures themselves without anyone being silenced or excluded.

> The ethics of deep diversity ... appeals for a more *rooted* conception of *polity* embracing everyone without ascribing them any sense of being silenced or excluded. That is to say, the ethics of deep diversity broadens gates of participation and encourages open-ended dialogue among all different participants for articulation of the agreed upon and all-encompassing discourse of social life. Hence, at the beginning it appeals to taking into account the ignored and glossed over distinctiveness, passes through a full denunciation of discrimination and downgrading of people as second-class citizens and ends at the full dialogue position with them in an equal manner.[94]

Hence, the notions of deep diversity, the politics of recognition and equal worth eradicate one-dimensional and shallow conceptions of public spaces. Rather, deep diversity calls upon different cultures to build a vital cultural identity and presence in the public sphere. This identity is a project that starts with diverse cultures themselves. It should commemorate those cultures and identities from their own perspectives and not a governmentally or colonially imposed perspective. This approach should open the public space widely for rigorous confrontation through dialogue that addresses and does not avoid the injustices of the past.

---

92 Masaeli, *The Ethics of Deep Diversity – Part I*.
93 Masaeli M. 2013. *The Ethics of Deep Diversity – Part II*. Online at: http://livebettermagazine.com/article/the-ethics-of-deep-diversity-in-multicultural-societies-part-ii/
94 Masaeli, *The Ethics of Deep Diversity – Part II*.

CONCLUSION

South Africa is no idyllic rainbow nation upon which the international world is waiting to succeed. There are nevertheless elements of it, persons who have incorporated this into their daily lives and are striving for it. Then there is the emancipated born-free generation, with only second-hand memories of apartheid. They did not experience apartheid first hand, but they do experience the legacy thereof, which resonates with what they have been told and what has been read in school and in their free time. Statues such as Rhodes and CR Swart reinforce the memory of the legacy and what they have been told. Consequently, the narrative reads as follows: get rid of the statue and then get rid of the memory of apartheid and also attempt to get rid of the legacy. But can one get rid of the legacy and the memories caused by it by eradicating it or neutralising the public sphere? When there is no statue and all names are those of freedom fighters, and there is still poverty and dire socio-economic situations – to which statue will we go to confront these situations?

Hence it is argued that the top-down approach taken by the state has not been transformative enough to give effect to the requirements of substantive equality, freedom and human dignity. The primary iconoclasm approach of mere removal of statues in the formation of national identity may pose an even greater threat to equality. Such removal may amount to censorship. Mere additions by the state will negate deep diversity. A form of secondary iconoclasm that adheres to notions of deep diversity, equal worth and the politics of recognition should be followed instead. Deep diversity acknowledges that there are layers of identity formation in a society and that a top-down imposed state identity does not sufficiently celebrate diversity. Hence, the equal worth inherent in diverse cultures require the state to allow all cultures to develop their own identity formation equally. This should be done from within the specific culture and from the perspective of the culture rather than a top-down approach by the state.

What must be rejected is the removal of one discriminating narrative by replacing it with a superficial state-imposed narrative. What is necessary is a constant dialogue of diversity where issues are debated and diverse cultural identities of South Africa are presented and celebrated from the bottom-up and from their own perspective (or their own narrative). As Charles Taylor theorises, deep diversity should be a discourse that lifts people and groups of people out of social marginalisation and exclusion. Such an approach ends when all persons are in full dialogue on an equal footing.

It is too early to state with any measure of certainty or even to anticipate which direction identity formation in South Africa will take. After the RMF campaign, the eruption of smouldering anger, and the fast-paced dialogue of black consciousness and anti-white privilege, South Africa awaits a restless period of expectation as to emerging forms of identity formation.

18 HOMOSEXUALITY AND THE LAW IN AFRICA: SOUTH AFRICAN CASE LAW AS A PARADIGMATIC EXAMPLE

Elias Kifon Bongmba[1]

INTRODUCTION

The law may not automatically, of itself eliminate stereotyping, and prejudice. Yet it serves as a great teacher, establishes public norms that become assimilated into daily life and protects vulnerable people from unjust marginalization and abuse.[2] – Justice Albie Sachs, Constitutional Court of South Africa

The above statement from the judgment issued by Justice Albie Sachs of the Constitutional Court of South Africa states the role of law in a highly contested debate on homosexuality in the case *Minister of Home Affairs and the Director General of Home Affairs v. Marie Adrianna Fourie and Cecelia Johanna Bonthuys*. This chapter revisits the Sachs decision of 1 December 2005 from a theological perspective to argue that central to the homosexuality debate are human rights, freedom, equality before the law and human dignity. I conclude the chapter with a brief discussion of Martin Luther's essay, "The Freedom of a Christian", to highlight the core values of freedom, responsibility and respect for human dignity as a way of conducting dialogue on contested issues.[3] I am motivated to engage in this analysis as a scholar of African descent who now lives in the United States and does research on the religious traditions of Africa, to explore lessons that scholars can learn from the diverse legal traditions on the African continent and search for a middle ground that draws from case law from South Africa. My intention is not to offer a solution from outside of Africa, but to invite further discussion on homosexuality in light of questions about freedom, human dignity, individual and social responsibility, which the Sachs decision in the *Fourie* case brought to the forefront in the landmark case

---

1   Elias Kifon Bongmba is the Harry and Hazel Chavanne Chair in Christian Theology and Professor of Religion at Rice University in Houston, Texas, U.S. This study was prepared with support of the Dean of Humanities at Rice University. I thank Dean Nicholas Schumway for the research support to carry out this research in relation to my responsibilities as President of the African Association for the Study of Religion. I also thank M Christian Green for reading, commenting and giving me insights on the essay. I also thank two anonymous reviewers for their helpful suggestions.
2   *Minister of Home Affairs v. Fourie* 2006 (1) SA 524 (CC). (CCT 60/04) [2005] ZACC 19; 2006 (3) BCLR 355 (CC); 2006 (1) SA 524 (CC) (1 December 2005) Opinion of Justice Sachs, 86. Online at: http://www.saflii.org/za/cases/ZACC/2005/19.html
3   Luther M. 2015. "The Freedom of a Christian, 1520", in Wengert TJ (ed). *The Annotated Luther Vol 1: The Roots of Reform*. Minneapolis, MN: Fortress, 467-539.

on same-sex relationships in South Africa. I am convinced that the lessons from the Sachs decision in *Fourie* can apply in other parts of the world where there are debates on homosexuality. However, in this chapter, my focus will be on the debates in the African context. I do not presume that all African societies are the same, nor do I imply any South African exceptionalism. The broad but cautious assumption I bring to this interpretation is that South Africa shares some cultural values with other African countries and like many members of the African Union is a constitutional democracy, where the rule of law plays a mediating role on contested ethical questions. I am also convinced that examining the legal decision that legalised same-sex unions in South Africa can open other perspectives on individual and communal beliefs and in doing so invite a dialogical approach that emphasises amicable ways of discussing homosexuality.[4] As M Christian Green has pointed out, some African scholars think religious leaders and politicians have overemphasised homosexuality at the expense of political reforms, a concern for human rights and development.[5]

This approach emphasises a multidisciplinary dialogue on homosexuality that takes into consideration the place of constitutional and legal framework of each country, particularly because marriage is a civil contract and the rules that govern that contract cannot be subjected to claims of religion and culture alone. It should be noted that there is marriage pluralism in some African communities, both because there is no uniformed legal approach to marriage in Africa and because there are indigenous marriage practices that do not require the contracts, as does the modern constitutional legal system. Furthermore, in parts of Nigeria and South Africa, same-sex unions exist that are not grounded in sexuality or procreation but in economic, power, or family reasons.[6] In this chapter, I will privilege constitutional law or the legal system in this discussion, even though in some African countries civil marriages are not the norm, nor are they mandated by law. For example, in some places customary law still governs many marriages, even if both parties still have to go to the municipal authority and sign a marriage certificate. However, even in those contexts where customary marriages are recognised, it is also the case that constitutional provisions and the legal system of the country, as well as statutory law and decisions made by the courts in such contexts, are binding on all citizens.

---

4   *MEC for Education: KwaZulu-Natal & Others v. Pillay & Others*, 2008 1 SA 474 (CC); 2008 2 BCLR 99 (CC), para 47 and 53.
5   Green MC. 2015. "Modern Legal Traditions: Africa", in Strawn B et al. (eds). *The Oxford Encyclopedia of the Bible and Law*. New York: Oxford University Press (citing particularly the writings of Sylvia Tamale). See also Green MC. 2013. "Religious and Legal Pluralism in African Constitutional Reform", *Journal of Law and Religion* 28(2):401-439.
6   Henkeman M. 2014. "Muslim Marriages in South Africa get the long deserving full recognition", SchoemanLaw Inc., 13 June. Online at: https://www.schoemanlaw.co.za/muslim-marriages-south-africa-get-long-deserving-full-recognition/. See also Nkosi G. 2007. "Indigenous African Marriage and Same-sex Partnerships: Conflicts and Controversies", *International Journal of African Renaissance Studies* 2(2):200-216.

HOMOSEXUALITY IN LEGAL LIMBO IN AFRICAN COUNTRIES

Homosexuality, which has been banned in more than 34 African countries, has recently been proscribed in sweeping legislations in Nigeria and Uganda.[7] The new laws in Nigeria and Uganda stipulate stiffer sentences and the death penalty; whereas in Cameroon, the penal code prescribes prison sentences between six months to five years for people found guilty of "sexual relations with a person of the same sex".[8] Nearly all the constitutions of African countries state that the state guarantees the rights and freedoms of the people.[9] Guaranteeing rights, with no barriers, means just that, and one must not single out gays and lesbians for discrimination on religious grounds or support the false perception that homosexuality is foreign to Africa. Even if one were to accept the argument that homosexuality was introduced by foreigners, one must stress that same-sex couples live in Africa today and national constitutions protect their rights. The constitutions of African countries guarantee personal rights to life and integrity, individual growth in a social context, liberty and freedoms.[10] Most countries in the world make the same promises of religious freedom, but these promises are not always realised. Postcolonial states in Africa have had their own struggles with religious freedoms, because political leaders have controlled religious institutions and manipulated belief and religious language to gain support of religious communities and forestall criticisms.[11]

Members of the lesbian, gay, bisexual and transgender (LGBT) community remain in legal limbo in many African communities, even where no anti-homosexuality laws have been passed. Cameroonian laws prohibit homosexuality, and state authorities have actively suppressed gay and lesbian rights.[12] For example, Jean-Claude Roger Mbede, charged with the crime of sending a love text to another man in which he stated, "I'm very much in love with you."[13] He was tried, convicted and sentenced to serve three years in prison. He appealed the judgment and an appeals court in Douala upheld that sentence. Mbede, who had served part of the sentence and was released as the appeal process began, expressed shock and told Associated Press by phone: "I am going back to the dismal conditions that got me critically ill before I was

---

7   International Gay Association (IGA). Online at: http://ilga.org/
8   Ghoshal N. 2013. "Dispatch: Does Cameroon Support Violence Against LGBTI People?" *Human Rights Watch*, September 12.
9   Heyns C (ed). 2004. *Human Rights Law in Africa*. The Hague and Boston: Kluwer Law International, 247.
10 Robertson AH and Merrils JG. 1996. *Human Rights in the World: An Introduction to the Study of International Protection of Human Rights*. Manchester and New York: Manchester University Press.
11 Quansah EK. 2008 "Law, Religion and Human Rights in Botswana", *African Human Rights Law Journal* 8(2):503. See also Goering R. 2004. "Africa's Gays Persecuted as Cause of Ills", *Chicago Tribune*, 9 June.
12 Human Rights Watch. 2011. "Cameroon: Sodomy Law Violates Basic Rights", *Human Rights Watch*, 17 May.
13 2012. "Cameroon jails 'gay' Man for Texting 'I'm in love with you' to a Male Friend", *The Guardian*, 17 December.

temporarily released for medical reasons ... I am not sure I can put up with the anti-gay attacks and harassment I underwent at the hands of fellow inmates and prison authorities on account of my perceived and unproven sexual orientation. The justice system in this country is just so unfair."[14] While in prison, Mbede had a health crisis because of the deplorable conditions in Cameroon prisons, and human and gay rights activists in Cameroon pressed for his release.[15] One cannot miss the fact that there is also a political engagement in these prosecutions. Ghoshal points out, "It's the country that arrests, prosecutes, and convicts more people than any other country that we know of in Africa for consensual same-sex adult conduct ... In most of these cases, there is little or no evidence. Usually people are convicted on the basis of allegations or denunciations from people who have claimed to law enforcement officials that they are gay."[16]

In addition to these legal actions, there is a broad "othering" discourse about homosexuality that is evident in several ways, but two notable expressions of othering are worthy of note. The courts have convicted people on charges that they were "effeminate". What was the evidence? The men were caught with Bailey's Irish Cream, a drink preferred by women and viewed in Cameroon as a drink that gay men also prefer.[17] Judicial activism against homosexuality in Cameroon has been accompanied by violence. Andre Banks, executive director of the gay rights organisation All Out, has pointed out that the anti-gay climate in Cameroon hurt Mbede. "Roger said he had to leave the university where he was studying because of the attention from the case and because of the mounting threats and fear of violence that have been very concerning to him," Banks said.[18] "He's worried that he won't be able to have a normal life in Cameroon because of the amount of attention it's brought to him." Mbede's lawyer, Alice Nkom, has received death threats, and the family of Michel Togue, another lawyer who has defended homosexuals in Cameroon, has also received death threats.[19]

In Botswana, too, the legal system discriminates and proscribes homosexuality, but the prohibition has not been done with the legislative flare that has taken place in Nigeria and Uganda. Section 164 of the Penal Code of Botswana addresses homosexuality under the heading of "Unnatural Offences", as including: "Any person who (a) has carnal knowledge of any person against the

---

14   Associated Press. 2012. "Cameroon Court upholds Sentence for Man who sent 'very much in love with you' text to another man", *CP24.com*, 17 December.
15   Ghoshal N. 2013. "Dispatch: Does Cameroon Support Violence Against LGBTI People?" *Human Rights Watch*, 12 September.
16   Ghoshal, "Dispatch: Does Cameroon Support Violence Against LGBTI People?"
17   2012. Cameroon: UN concerned over reports of arrests of suspected gay and lesbian people, UN News Centre, 16 November.
18   Associated Press, "Cameroon Court upholds Sentence for Man who sent 'very much in love with you' text to another man".
19   Associated Press, "Cameroon Court upholds Sentence for Man who sent 'very much in love with you' text to another man".

order of nature; (b) has carnal knowledge of an animal; or (c) permits any person to have carnal knowledge of him or her against the order of nature, is guilty of an offence and is liable to imprisonment for a term not exceeding seven years."[20] Indecency is described as acts contrary to nature, carnal knowledge of an animal, or carnal nature that violates the order of nature. Therefore, homosexuality is equated with acts that are contrary to nature. The current Penal Code also describes homosexuality as unnatural offences, including indecent assault of boys under age 14 (it is notable that there is no provision for assault of girls under 14); indecency between two people in private or public; incest; as well as different offences relating to marriage and possession of children set forth in in Sections 172-175.[21] Criminalising homosexuality in Botswana violates the laws of Botswana, especially in Section 3 of the Constitution of the Republic of Botswana, which clearly guarantees freedoms, liberty to life, security, freedom of conscience, freedom to assemble, association, and protections of privacy and property under the law, irrespective of race, national origin, political opinions, colour, beliefs or sex.[22]

To understand the role of law, in the contestation over homosexuality, I will turn to case law in South Africa as a paradigmatic example in which the law can offer a middle ground and invite a new theological ethics on the question of homosexuality in the Church. Compared to most countries in Africa, South Africa is seen as a very progressive country on LGBTQ issues. Thus, its inclusive constitution and its Constitutional Courts have issued rulings on sexuality which I consider paradigmatic on same-sex relations.

THE LAW AND HOMOSEXUALITY IN SOUTH AFRICA: THE *FOURIE* DECISION

The role of law in determining the permissibility of homosexuality has received recent legal attention in South Africa, where the courts have affirmed the rights and freedoms of gays and lesbians to choose their lifestyle. In *Minister of Home Affairs and the Director General of Home Affairs v. Marie Adrianna Fourie and Cecelia Johanna Bonthuys*, the contestation raised questions about the role of

---

20 Republic of Botswana, Penal Code, Ch-8:01. Online at: http://www.unodc.org/tldb/pdf/Botswana/PENAL_CODE.pdf
21 See "Bill No. 1 1998", *Government Gazette*, 23 January. See also Tafa AB. 2000. "Right to sexual orientation: The line of the Botswana government", in Conference on Human Rights and Democracy, 17-19 November 1998. Gabarone: Ditshwanelo/Botswana Centre for Human Rights, 129.
22 Constitution of the Republic of Botswana. Online at: http://www.chr.up.ac.za/undp/domestic/docs/c_Botswana.pdf. See also Botswana Network on Ethics, Law and HIV/AIDS (BONELA) and Lesbians, Gays and Bisexuals of Botswana (LaGaBiBo). 2008. "The Violation of the Rights of Lesbian, Gay, and Bisexual and Transgender Persons in Botswana", 10. Online at: tbinternet.ohchr.org/Treaties/CCPR/.../INT_CCPR_NGO_BWA_92_8221_E.doc

religion in the debate, as well as the role of law.[23] I will focus on the role of law, because the legal instruments of the state can and should be used to protect human rights, freedoms, and human dignity; provide the framework for arbitration and set guidelines for responsible citizenship. I do not assume that all religious leaders have adopted an anti-homosexuality position. Some religious leaders support affirm members of the LGBTQ communities. Archbishop Desmond Tutu of South Africa is a strong supporter of sexual minorities in Africa. The Rev Dr Kapya Kaoma of Zambia has been very supportive of sexual minorities and joined other religious leaders in in issuing the KwaZulu-Natal Declaration calling for an end to discrimination against sexual minorities.[24] But objection to homosexuality by members of some religious communities, such as Evangelical religious leaders have done in Uganda and Nigeria, ignores the demands of human rights which African states have pledged to promote and is not the best way forward.

In South Africa, Justice Sachs, in a revolutionary judgment in the *Fourie* case, held that it was unconstitutional and an act of injustice for the state and members of certain religious communities to prevent gays and lesbians from getting married. Following the judgment, the South African Parliament voted on 14 November 2006 to pass the Civil Union Bill by an overwhelming majority of 230 to 41, and Deputy President Phumzile Mlamblo-Ngcuka signed it into law on 30 November 2006. On 1 December 2006, South Africa legalised gay marriage, becoming the first country in Africa to legalise gay marriage and the fifth in the world to do so.[25] In issuing the judgment, Justice Sachs spelled out the full human dimensions of the case:

> Finding themselves strongly attracted to each other, two people went out regularly and eventually decided to set up home together. After being acknowledged by their friends as a couple for more than a decade, they decided that the time come to get public recognition and registration of their relationship, and formally to embrace the rights and responsibilities they felt should flow and attach to it. Like many persons in their situation, they wanted to get married. There was one impediment. They are both women.[26]

The case demonstrated that homosexuality involves desires, choices, commitments, and the freedom to assume responsibility to love and care as a member of the human family – all of them aspects of life that can be recognised as

---

23 Udombana NJ. 2005. "Interpreting Rights Globally: Courts and Constitutional Rights in Emerging Democracies", *African Human Rights Law Journal* 5(1):56.
24 Kaoma K. 2014. *American Culture Warriors in Africa: A Gide to the Exporters of Homophobia and Sexism*. Somerville, MA: Political Research Associates. See 2016 "The KwaZulu-Natal Declaration of the First African Scholars' Consultation on Human Sexuality, Religion and Equality, August 21, 2014" (Special Issue Sexuality in Africa), *Journal of Theology for Southern Africa* 155:8-10.
25 2006. "SA Legalises Gay Marriage", Brand South Africa, 1 December Online at: https://www.brandsouthafrica.com/governance/services/rights/same-sex-marriage
26 *Minister of Home Affairs v. Fourie* 2006 (1) SA 524 (CC), opinion of Sachs J, 2.

religious values. The appellants sought relief before the Constitutional Court because they were excluded from the public rituals and celebrations of their commitment to love and live as a married couple, because Common Law defined marriage as "a union of one man with one woman". This was also complicated by the Marriage Act of South Africa because Section 30(1) contained the specific language "wife and husband", according the formula which was used in marriage ceremonies. This made some people think that same-sex couples were excluded from marriage.

In the trial court, Justice Roux ruled that Section 30(1) of the Marriage Act refers to marriage as a union between male and female and that compelling the Minster of Justice to change it was tantamount to asking him to act unlawfully. The applicants then took their case to the Supreme Court of Appeal (SCA), calling for further development of common law, but they did not link it to a challenge of the Marriage Act. In the majority opinion of the appellate court, Judge Edwin Cameron of the Supreme Court of Appeal, pointed out that "the Constitution grants powers to the Constitutional Court, the SCA and the High Courts to develop the common law, taking into account the interests of justice".[27] A reasonable application of the Bill of Rights would justify the development of common law to limit provisions of Section 36(1) as long as the developments are consistent with the spirit, aims and "object of the Bill of Rights". According to Sachs: "Taken together, these provisions create an imperative normative setting that obliges the courts to develop the common law in accordance with the spirit, purport and objects of the Bill of Rights. Doing so is not a choice. Where the common law is deficient, the courts are under a general obligation to develop it appropriately."[28] That was the background of the appeal that brought the case to Justice Sachs and the Constitutional Court.

Judge Cameron had indicated that the Constitution of the Republic of South Africa, 1996, and the general constitutional structure of South Africa supported incremental legal development. With a changing view of sexual orientation, it was reasonable to think that people would accept further developments of the common law. Cameron argued that the idea of family and family life ought to change to avoid unfair discrimination against homosexuals which denied them their dignity and foundational ideals of the Constitution. However, the majority decision from that court also claimed that the verbal formula prescribed by the Marriage Act cannot be substituted and can only be done by "the constitutional remedy of 'reading-in'.[29] In dissent, Justice Ian Farlam reviewed the history of marriage back to the Council of Trent in 1563 and in 1580 in which marriage which was a civil institution, but received its religious institutionalisation from the period of the Council of Trent. Farlam noted that barring homosexuals from marriage discriminates against them, prevents them from exercising the privileges and responsibilities of marriage, and infringes on their constitutional

---

27 *Fourie*, Sachs J, 8.
28 *Fourie*, Sachs J, 8.
29 *Fourie*, Sachs J, 11.

rights and their dignity. The problematic issue in the *Fourie* case was that in the early court filing, the appellants did not challenge the marriage formula in the Marriage Act. The South African Law Reform Commission (SALRC) had recommended actions that could remedy discrimination against gays and lesbians, but these were incremental changes. The applicants could not be denied relief on grounds that they did not challenge the validity of Section 30(1) of the Marriage Act, because the Marriage Act did not approve the common law definition of marriage and the formula could be changed by updating and changing traditional terms like wife and husband to spouse to conform to the terms of the law. Justice Farlam would also approve suspending the provisions of common law for two years, in order to give Parliament time to pass legislation recognising the rights, equality, and dignity of all people. Both parties in the case did not like the outcome and appealed to the Constitutional Court.

Justice Sachs reiterated that the two interrelated issues in the case were, whether common law and the provisions of the Marriage Act unfairly discriminates against gays and lesbians and what was the appropriate remedy for that unconstitutional act.[30] Justice Sachs began with the first issue: whether the law denied equal protection and unfairly discriminated against same-sex couples by excluding them from the provision of the Marriage Act. Noting that the state argued that the South African Constitution did not protect the right to marry, but the right of individuals to set up their own family life without interference from the state, Sachs maintained that this was a form of negative liberty which historically had denied same-sex couples the right to marry. Sachs argued that "if their form of family life suffered from particular disadvantages, then these should be dealt with by appropriate legal remedies in response to each of the identified problems, not by entry into the global set of rights and entitlements established by marriage. Marriage law appropriately confined itself to marriage, it was contended, and not to all forms of family relationships."[31] This argument was correct because the Bill of Rights in the South African Constitution does not "expressly include a right to marry". Sachs pointed out that one cannot infer from this that the South African Constitution did not protect rights, because in another case the court noted that values of human dignity, equality, and freedom are enshrined in the text and, regardless of how they were interpreted in the future, enforced marriages or prohibitions would not survive a constitutional challenge.

Sachs focused in the case on the argument that dignity, equality, and freedom were the real issues in the case under consideration.[32] This was a tactical move and a display of moral precision in the protection of individual rights and freedoms. It was also a revolutionary perspective, which returned to the core values at stake in all of the debates on homosexuality and same-sex marriage. Past court cases demonstrated the negative impact of social discrimination

---

30 *Fourie*, Sachs J, 27.
31 *Fourie*, Sachs J, 27-28.
32 *Fourie*, Sachs J, 29.

grounded on sexual orientation and asserted that same-sex couples are "permanent minority in society and have suffered in the past from patterns of disadvantage".[33] The courts also upheld the view that gays and lesbians suffered the same pattern of discrimination at a deep level of intimacy and social relations and thus denied constitutional guarantee of equality and human dignity irrespective of differences. This made such discrimination unfair and reducing same-sex couples to a single dimension of sexuality, rather than recognising their wider social relations and civil status.[34]

Taking previous cases into consideration, Justice Sachs argued that LGBT people in same-sex relationships have the same emotional, spiritual, physical and financial capacities to run households. They are capable of adopting children and caring for them. They can establish *consortium vitae* (partnership or cohabitation) and are entitled to the benefits enjoyed by heterosexuals, since Section 10 of the Constitution guarantees the dignity and rights of everyone. Gays and lesbians were portrayed as somehow incapable of doing the same things other human beings do, in a way that perpetuated prejudices and stereotypes, the effect of which was a "crass, blunt, cruel and serious invasion of their dignity".[35] In Justice Sachs's estimation, "The discrimination based on sexual orientation is severe because no concern, let alone anything approaching equal concern, is shown for the particular sexual orientation of gays and lesbians."[36] Sachs argued that although the courts called attention to the seriousness of discrimination grounded on sexual orientation and maintained that protecting marriage as an institution could not be done at the expense of the dignity of gays and lesbians, the Court left two questions open: the status of unmarried people in a heterosexual relationship and whether and how the law should grant recognition to same-sex relationships. Justice Sachs's *Fourie* decision thus stopped short of giving gays and lesbians an umbrella recognition of their relationship. Justice Sachs rejected legal relief that would be administered in bits and preferred that the Parliament enact legislation that would give members of the gay and lesbian community the freedom to marry.

A CORE ELEMENT OF THE JUDGMENT: THE RIGHT TO BE DIFFERENT

Arguing for the right to be different, Sachs highlighted "four unambiguous features" that provide a context for analysing "unfair" discrimination on the basis of sexual orientation. These include the presence of multiple family formations in South Africa, which rules out imposing a specific formulation; the need to recognise the long history of discrimination against gays and lesbians just because they have a different sexual orientation; the lack of a comprehensive

---

33 *Fourie*, Sachs J, 29.
34 *Fourie*, Sachs J, 30.
35 *Fourie*, Sachs J, 34.
36 *Fourie*, Sachs J, 34.

regulation of the rights of gays and lesbians to experience family life of their own; and the fact that the Constitution of the Republic of South Africa, 1996, offers for the respect of the rights and dignity of all people – a move which is significant to break with the past patterns of discrimination.[37] He argued that an important mark of democratic society is accepting everyone as they are. "To penalize people for being whom and what they are is profoundly disrespectful of the human personality and violatory of equality."[38]

The gist of Justice Sachs's decision was that equality requires respect for people despite differences and does not mean people should suppress difference. In no way does equality imply homogenisation. Difference is not the basis for excluding people or promoting stigma and marginalisation. Difference is a cause to celebrate perspectives that promote the vitality of the society rather than ones that perpetuate the historic positions in South Africa. In Justice Sachs's view, "The Constitution thus acknowledges the variability of human beings (genetic and socio-cultural), affirms the right to be different, and celebrates the diversity of the nations."[39] In recognising such a right, the Court called upon South Africans to carry out their duty to affirm the character of the nation by affirming mutual respect and tolerance.[40]

What then is the significance of marriage and the impact of exclusion from marriage as an institution? The law now constructs marriage as a private contract between a man and a woman, but the words "I do" make it also public and state-regulated engagement, registered, and conducted in public and sometimes religious places. Competent witnesses often certify that such a union has been legally solemnised in a manner that indicates that both the individuals and the state have an interest in that solemn transaction.[41] Both parties to a marriage have "reciprocal duty of support", a responsibility which cannot not be abrogated by a pre-nuptial agreement. The point of these rituals is that two people who declare their love for each other and decide to live together as a married couple accept and share responsibility to each other and the rest of the community in which they live. Theys exercise their freedom to marry who they choose, but this is responsible freedom. It is for that reason that one should see public celebrations which include signing legal papers as a free expression and sign of that commitment to one another. The Sachs decision also implied that the stronger party in the union assumes more responsibility to stabilise the union. The idea of freedom and responsibility is what sets aside marriages today apart from common law requirements which some thought were the only way of legitimising sexual relations.

---

37   *Fourie*, Sachs J, 38.
38   *Fourie*, Sachs J, 38.
39   *Fourie*, Sachs J, 39. See also Minow M. 1990. *Making all the Difference: Inclusion, Exclusion, and American Law*. Ithaca: Cornell University Press, 53-74.
40   See *Christian Education South Africa v. Minister of Education* 2000 (4) SA 757 (CC); 2000 (10) 1051 (CC).
41   *Fourie*, Sachs J, 41-42.

Judge Sachs then stated that in light of the proceeding explication of the idea, reality and obligation of marriage:

> ... the exclusion of same-sex couples from the benefits and responsibilities of marriage, accordingly, is not a small and tangential inconvenience resulting from a few surviving relics of societal prejudice destined to evaporate like the morning dew. It represents a harsh if oblique statement by the law that same-sex couples are outsiders, and that their need for affirmation and protection of their intimate relations as human beings is somehow less than that of heterosexual couples. It reinforces the wounding notion that they are to be treated as biological oddities, as failed or lapsed human beings who do not fit into the normal society, and as such, do not qualify for the full moral concern and respect that our Constitution seeks to secure for everyone. It signifies that their capacity for love, commitment and accepting responsibility is by definition les worthy of regard than that of heterosexual couples.[42]

Same-sex couples suffer both material deprivation and intangible damage; live in a state of legal blankness devoid of all the celebrations and commemorations that come from recognition. They also deserve the right to depend on state regulation when things go wrong and the law cannot ignore the needs of people when things go wrong.[43] Justice Sachs called the equal protection from unfair discrimination in the South African Constitution revolutionary. Excluding same-sex couples was only grounded in "historic prejudice". The Marriage Act did not make provisions for gays and lesbians because of this long history of discrimination. The Constitution was clear: "The state may not unfairly discriminate directly or indirectly against anyone on one or more grounds, including race, gender, sex, pregnancy, marital status, ethnic or social origin, colour, sexual orientation, age, disability, religion, belief, culture, language, and birth."[44] Sachs argued that gays and lesbians are "defined out of contemplation as subjects of the law".[45] Sections 9(1) and 9(3) not only protect same-sex couples from punishment and acts that stigmatise and do more than just leave them alone, but also demand that they be treated as equals and be given all the dignity accorded them by the law.

REMEDY TO DISCRIMINATION AGAINST GAYS AND LESBIANS IN MARRAIGE

In consideration of the rights, dignity and freedoms of the applicants Justice Sachs granted the applicants in the cross-appeal and the applicants in the application certain leave to reduce their legal burdens. Justice Sachs ordered that "The common law definition of marriage is declared to be inconsistent

---

42 *Fourie*, Sachs J, 45.
43 *Fourie*, Sachs J, 47.
44 *Fourie*, Sachs J, 49 (quoting Constitution of the Republic of South Africa, sec 9(3)).
45 *Fourie*, Sachs J, 49.

with the Constitution and invalid to the extent that it does not permit same-sex couples to enjoy the status and the benefits coupled with responsibilities it accords heterosexual couples."[46]

What makes this case relevant today is the fact that in addition to weaving a carefully constructed decision based on human dignity, human rights and freedom, Sachs drew parallels with slavery, colonialism, prohibition of interracial marriage and male domination. "All were based on apparently self-evident biological and social facts; all were sanctioned by religion and imposed by law."[47] This statement is pertinent today because the debate on homosexuality in Africa today draws from colonial laws. In the postcolonial era, however African politicians and religious leaders have become even more verbally abusive of gays and lesbians based on what they assume are "self-evident facts".

HUMAN FREEDOM AND HOMOSEXUALITY

Same-sex unions raise questions about freedom, human rights and responsibility. However, in the African context, culture and values have been highly contested in discussion of homosexuality. One can think of culture and values together, but there are also clear distinctions. In addressing the many responses to homosexuality in Africa today, one cannot avoid these claims. On the question of culture, one can say unequivocally that that it has been demonstrated that same-sex relations in Africa are not as new as its critics would have us believe. There are extensive studies of homosexuality in precolonial and colonial African, as well as postcolonial African societies.[48] Insisting that homosexuality is not part of African culture can only be sustained if we assume that because a large majority of Africans are heterosexual, therefore any exception is not part of the culture. From existing literature, we know that this is not historically and anthropologically correct, and it is at odds with the claims made by Africans today for the freedom and the right be different sexually. Therefore, the

---

46 "SA legalizes gay marriage".
47 "SA legalizes gay marriage".
48 See Tamale S (ed). 2011. *African Sexualities: A Reader*. Cape Town: Pambazuka; Tamale S. "Out of the Closet: Unveiling Sexuality Discourses in Uganda", *Feminist Africa* 2:42-49; Epprecht M. 2006. *Hungochani: The History of Dissident Sexuality in Southern Africa*. Montreal: McGill-Queen's University Press; Musisi N. 1991. "Women, 'Elite Polygamy' and Buganda State Formation", *Signs* 16(4):757-786; Mazrui A. 1975. "The Resurrection of the Warrior Tradition in African Political Culture", *Journal of Modern African Studies* 13(1):67-84; Murray SO and Roscoe W (eds). 1997. *Islamic Homosexualities: Culture, History and Literature*. New York: New York University Press; Murray SO and Roscoe W. 1998. *Boy-Wives and Female Husbands: Studies in African Homosexualities*. New York: St. Martins's; Lyons AP and Lyons HD. 2004. *Irregular Connections: A History of Anthropology and Sexuality*. Lincoln and London: University of Nebraska Press; Moodie TD with Ndatshe V. 1994. *Going for Gold: Men's Lives in the Mines*. Berkeley: University of California Press.

question of human freedom to make adult decisions about human sexuality calls for careful consideration, because the historical record demonstrates that sexual minorities have lived and in Africa in the past and did not experience the vitriolic discourse that Africans are engaged in.

Since there have always been homosexuals in Africa, one cannot say that homosexuality is not part of African culture, even though colonial administrations of the past and Christian groups today have so claimed. What the Christian community, in particular, needs to be doing today is to initiate a constructive dialogue to eliminate what legal theorist Sylvia Tamale has described as the instrumentalisation, control and regulation of African sexuality, especially the sexuality of women, through the "intersection of religion, statutory law and reinterpreted traditional customs".[49] In other words, what is necessary is for religious groups can see the legalisation of homosexuality in South Africa as an invitation to rethink the notion of human freedom today. I am convinced that today Christians in Africa can act in a manner that demonstrates Christian freedom.

THE FREEDOM OF A CHRISTIAN AND THE DEBATE ON HOMOSEXUALITY

African communities have faced many challenges, such as the collapse of economies leading to massive poverty, the growing environmental crisis which has led to significant challenges in food production, the HIV/AIDS pandemic and the Ebola virus. However, nothing has generated the sense of apocalypse that has been generated by the debate over homosexuality. The Christian tradition is at a watershed moment in its history in Africa, recording growth at very high levels as Pentecostal and revival movements continue to sweep through the continent. That Christian growth has brought many debates to the forefront, but none has been accompanied by the vitriolic denunciations, sheer hatred and regressive legislative actions as the debate on homosexuality. The debates on homosexuality within the Christian tradition in Africa involves major issues and beliefs concerning how to understand sexuality as part of human nature. The discussions are sometimes heated, because differences in understanding of sexuality make others frame homosexuality as sin. For many of these people, if people of the same sex cohabit, then they have committed a breach of the covenant between God's will for humanity and type of relations that should strengthen society. Those who support same-sex relations think that we live in a very different time and have a rich, diverse understanding of human sexuality which does not necessarily contradict nature. Such relations may rightly have described as revolutionary in the African context, but those calling for an understanding and dialogue do not want to throw away ethics. They just want members of the Christian tradition to figure out how to relate

---

49 Tamale S. 2014. "Exploring the Contours of African Sexualities: Religion, Law and Power", *African Human Rights Law Journal* 14(1):150-177.

to each other in changing times. The idea that the church can understand and address change is nothing new, because throughout its history, Christianity has taken positions that were later changed when scientific discoveries enabled us to understand our universe better.

Sexual ethics today is one of those issues that invites careful theological analysis and dialogue. It calls for a pluralistic approach to dialogue. In this essay, I advocate a middle path which all parties to the conversation can navigate with epistemic and religious humility. In such a framework, our views of human nature, sin and covenant are open to contextual interpretation. It is this dialogical path that is appealing, especially when members of a political community recognise that in addition to their theological and religious positions, they are also bound to the same legal system which is not beholden to any religious position. My appeal to dialogue is one that has been stated by a number of major ethicists of the twentieth century, including leading Christian ethicist James Gustafson.[50] It is my contention here that in seeking that middle path, the Christian community in Africa can learn some lessons today from Reformation theologian Martin Luther's signal essay, "The Freedom of a Christian". Through it, the faith community can make sense of the Sachs decision in *Fourie* and appreciate the role of law in promoting equality, freedom of choice, respect of human dignity and human rights called for the contestations over homosexuality.

Martin Luther's essay, "The Freedom of a Christian", was written in 1520 in his attempt to open up space for a dialogue to resolve tensions within the church.[51] This text contains valuable lessons for dealing with contested issues. Luther obviously did not write this magnificent treatise to discuss divisive issues like homosexuality, but issues of a similarly important nature that the Church faced in his time. The ideas Luther expressed therein and in other writings would lead to his excommunication from the Roman Catholic Church and eventually to the Protestant Reformation. Luther wrote this essay after a meeting with Karl von Miltitz, one of the German Princes who had worked to resolve the conflicts in the church. Von Miltitz urged Luther to write a letter to the Pope that would promote reconciliation, and Luther dedicated "The Freedom of a Christian" to Pope Leo X.[52] This revolutionary background makes "The Freedom of a Christian", an important text to turn to for lessons on how to conduct a dialogue when faced with difficult questions of social and religious division and upheaval.[53]

---

50 Gustafson J. 2007. *Moral Discernment in the Christian Life: Essays in Theological Ethics.* Boer TA and Capetz PA (eds). Louisville, KY: Westminster John Knox, 98-110.
51 Luther, "The Freedom of a Christian, 1520".
52 Wengert, *The Annotated Luther Vol 1*, 468-469.
53 Luther, "The Freedom of a Christian, 1520". For a critical analysis of the history and provenance of the text, see Wengert, *The Annotated Luther Vol 1*, 476 ff.

Stylistically, "The Freedom of a Christian" reflected conventions used in Latin scholarship and followed rules of etiquette and social decorum consistent with documents of that nature. I have turned to this document for several reasons. First, Luther's text offers a model for negotiating and discussing difficult questions. This is apparent because in spelling out his disagreement with the church, Luther spared no effort to state his respect for the office and person of the Pope, whom he called "blessed father". Luther stated: "I have never turned my soul away from your Holiness so as neither to desire with all my powers the very best for you and for your see nor, as far as was in me, to seek the same with earnest and heartfelt prayers to God."[54] He praised the reputation of the Pope, noting that he Luther had defended the reputation of the Pope, and the Pope's reputation was praised all over the world. Luther went further; stating that he would never attack "even those whom public opinion dishonors". Luther was conscious of the fact that he had his own faults and therefore would not be the first person to cast a stone against another offender. He added, "I have never thought ill of your person and, ore over, that I am the kind of person who eternally wishes the very best of things happen to you and for me this strife is not with any person over morals, but over the word of truth alone."[55] Luther admitted though that he had cursed the Vatican Curia because of their depravity and godlessness, stating he did not think anything he said would change them, but he recognised he owed a debt to all Christians to warn them of the dangers posed by the functionaries of the Vatican which he described as chaotic Babylon. Given what was at stake for the global church at the time, Luther adopted a conciliatory tone in addressing the Pope, whose "sublime dignity" he applauded the Pope even though Luther recognised that the Pontiff as a servant of God and a servant of the church, surrounded by a "pestilential" group who had turned the Pontiff into a demigod.

Despite some of the feisty language in the text, Luther's conciliatory approach to a crisis is not what we have seen in the debate on homosexuality in Africa. Instead, homosexuals have been attacked, denigrated, dehumanised and killed; they have been called reprobates, animals or worse than animals; and they have been accused of polluting their communities, of spreading HIV and being responsible for the Ebola virus. Former Zambian President Frederic Chiluba, who declared Zambia a "Christian nation", described homosexuality as the "deepest level of depravity" and said that homosexual acts promote AIDS.[56] In Kenya, former President Daniel arap Moi described homosexuality as a scourge that violates African and Christian values. Homosexuals have been arrested and jailed without trial in Cameroon and other African countries.[57] The anger and rhetoric have not only promoted draconian laws, but led to threats

---

54 Luther, "The Freedom of a Christian, 1520", 474-475.
55 Luther, "The Freedom of a Christian, 1520", 476.
56 1998. "Chiluba Blasts Gays", *Times of Zambia*, 19 October:1.
57 Bongmba EK. 2016. "Homosexuality, Ubuntu, and Otherness in the African Church", *Journal of Religion and Violence* 4(1):15-37. https://doi.org/10.5840/jrv201642622

and the killing of gays and lesbians in some African nations. There is no doubt that Luther reserved some of the harshest words for his theological opponents, and one cannot dignify that either, but in reference to the Pope who had the power to resolve the tensions and introduce changes that could have stopped the disagreement in the church, Luther's treatise offers a model of respect for one's interlocutor that we have not seen in the responses from some members of the Anglican Communion in Africa, who have taken pleasure are deriding the Anglican Communion worldwide.

THEOLOGICAL IMPLICATIONS FOR TODAY

Luther's core argument, offers a perspective on difference that invites reflections on some of the key issues involved in the debate on homosexuality. First, Christians are called to a life of freedom, and this applies to everyone. Luther argued: "The Christian individual is a completely free lord of all, subject to none. The Christian individual is a completely dutiful servant of all, subject to all."[58] This was a subtle but powerful claim from Luther. This freedom consists in righteousness and the "holy word of God, the Gospel of Christ". He cites the Biblical passage that states, "if the Son makes you free, you will be free indeed." (John 6: 36) One therefore is free on the basis of what Jesus has done. For the Reformers, the Word of God, proclaims the message about Jesus as the one who died to justify and save people from the bondage to sin and the law. One is justified by faith alone, and everyone must believe that all have sinned and it is the gift of Christ alone that saves people. The commands to Christians are to guide human beings to understand themselves and knowledge, even knowledge of the human impossibility of keeping these commands. This makes Christians realise that they can only achieve everything through faith, because God is the only one who gives the commands and also fulfills everything.

Luther's emphasis on freedom remains important, because one of the things that makes human beings distinct is the freedoms they have to think, resolve, and take action. Free will involves the totality of what it means to be a self-determining individual who is able to make decisions and make choices. Any created human being is free to be who they are. Human freedom in this sense can only be a problem if it is used to diminish the freedom of others. Luther inserted a note in his argument that is particularly important for our purposes. He pointed out that church leaders cannot exercise power over everything, because such vast powers belonged to kings, princes and human beings on earth.[59] This is an important distinction, which signals a modern argument concerning the separation of church and state, although it is not stated in those terms. Church authorities can offer perspectives, but they cannot dictate their views on public matters addressed by the law. Luther does not promote license to engage in wrongdoing, because believers should not be slaves to sin. Instead,

---

58 Luther, "The Freedom of a Christian, 1520", 488.
59 Luther, "The Freedom of a Christian, 1520", 505.

"the Christian is free from all things and is over all things, so that such a person requires no works at all to be righteous or saved."[60] Therefore, Christian leaders are servants and stewards. They should serve all people, because Christ is the one who gives freedom. In the current debates on homosexuality, Christian ministers ought to see their role as servants called to serve all members of the faith community, including homosexuals, who share a common freedom in Christ.

The member churches of the All Africa Council of Churches (AACC) have focused on freedom for a long time. The first General Assembly of the AACC had as its theme "Freedom and Unity in Christ".[61] At the time of the declaration of the theme, concerns focused mostly on freedom from colonial rule and the need to define an independent or indigenous church in the African context. The immediate concern for freedom at the AACC extended the freedoms Christians experience in Christ to political freedom in Africa, because some African countries were still dominated by colonial powers at that time. In later years, the AACC began to speak of freedom and justice in the postcolonial state, an indication that independence did not really bring full freedoms.[62] It would be a mistake to limit the search for freedom to politics and the economy. The church today cannot afford to ignore the calls for freedom on the question of adult responsible sexuality and allow unjust constitutions and laws continue to oppression of sexual minorities. It is also necessary for theologians of all backgrounds in Africa to focus on human freedom in all aspects of life, because freedom is an indication that one has experienced freedom in Christ and now lives in peace with God and his or her neighbor – acts that promote a rich perspective of human identity and freedom.[63] In articulating freedom, it is important to remember that accepting difference – in our case here, sexual difference – is central to human freedom in our day.[64] It is therefore incumbent on religious and political leaders to promote the freedoms of all people because the goal of power is to work for freedom.[65]

Second, Christians are called to act responsibly towards all people, regardless of their sexual orientation. In the latter part of "The Freedom of a Christian" Luther discussed the notion of the outer person, which he used to articulate a dialectical position anchoring freedom and servitude. We often speak of servitude today in terms of responsibility to the other, an ethical position which Sachs decision in *Fourie* highlighted in pointing out that two people who live

---

60 Luther, "The Freedom of a Christian, 1520", 507.
61 AACC. 1963. *Drumbeats from Kampala: Report of the First Assembly of the All African Conference of Churches, Kampala 20-30 April 1963*. London: Lutherworth, 60.
62 AACC. c1976. *AACC Newsletter*, Special Issue on Liberation.
63 De Gruchy JW. 1995. *Christianity and Development: A Theology for a Just World Order*. Cape Town: David Phillip, 19-20.
64 See also Ukpong J. 1984. "Current Theology: The Emergence of African Theologies", *Theological Studies* 45:501-536.
65 Bongmba EK. *The Dialectics of Transformation in Africa*. New York: Palgrave MacMillan, 126.

each other also assert their freedom and accept responsibility to serve one another. Luther explored this dialectic of freedom and servitude by explaining that a person has two natures: one is spiritual and the other is the bodily. The spiritual person is free and a new person. Here, Luther responds to those who think that faith is license and states clearly that "the Christian is slave to all and subject to all". The Christian, therefore, does all things as long as he or she remains in this mortal life. The heart of the argument is that the Christian disciplines the body to conform to the inner spiritual being and in order to serve God joyfully. The point is that the Christian through faith serves God, because it is faith that restores a person to paradise not good works. However, what is important here is that in doing good works, the Christian does not just serve God alone, but is expected to do good works for the neighbor without discrimination. Homosexuals today are our neighbors. They must be welcomed and treated with dignity because Christians are to serve all people.[66] All Christian work is "ordered toward the advantage of others".[67] In that way, the Christian shares in the mind of Christ which was manifested when Christ took on the form of a servant and died on the cross.

Towards the end of the treatise, Luther argues that church leaders should imitate the example of Christ and serve the neighbor in faith and "live in Christ through faith and in the neighbor through love". The Christian should adopt a middle path that restrains itself from condemning others for what they do or the ceremonialist who insists on laws and ceremonies only. This middle path between condemning homosexuality and discussing it in a respectful manner. Such a dialogue could clarify some of the questions members of the different religious communities might have regarding homosexuality and create a climate for people to accept people who they are and not discriminate against them because of their sexual orientation. Taking a middle dialogical position would ensure that one does not offend others, especially sexual minorities. Luther's argument is complex, but one thing is clear; rather than judge people and create legal structures to prosecute them for their lifestyle, Christians are called to love unconditionally and be servants to all people.

It is therefore important for Christians in Africa today to promote their ethical responsibility for sexual minorities, because it is a rich way of respecting and upholding human dignity. An important theme from the *Fourie* decision of Justice Sachs in the Constitutional Court of South Africa was the issue of dignity of the appellants. Prevailing marriage practices which prohibited homosexual marriages, violated the dignity of homosexuals. Reformation legal scholar John Witte Jr has described "The Freedom of a Christian" as Luther's *Dignitatis Humanae* – his bold new declaration on human nature and human freedom that described all Christians in his world regardless of their "dignity or lack of dignity" as conventionally defined. Pope and prince, noble and pauper,

---

66 Luther, "The Freedom of a Christian, 1520", 519-520.
67 Luther, "The Freedom of a Christian, 1520", 521.

man or woman, slave or free – all persons in Christendom, Luther declared, share equally in a doubly paradoxical nature."[68] *Dignitatis Humanae*, of course, refers to the core religious freedom statement of another revolution, the modernisation of the Roman Catholic Church at the Second Vatican Council. Luther's "The Freedom of a Christian," an earlier statement of human dignity and religious freedom, can with *Dignitatis Humanae* stand as a ringing statement of the centrality of human dignity in the Christian tradition – a call that African churches would do well to heed in addressing homosexuality and homosexual relationships. Human dignity is a given that is grounded in the *imago dei*, that is given to each created being. That sense of dignity cannot be taken away.

African theologians have echoed the quest for human dignity that has shaped the quest for African liberation. They have done so because human dignity has a divine sanction. The death of Christ restored that dignity from the effects of sin. The essence of being a faith community, as well as a political community, lies upholding the dignity of each member of the community and giving them the space to develop their potential regardless of their sexual orientation. When the AACC returned to Kampala in 2013, the quest for human dignity was part of the overall agenda for the church in a continent experiencing political, economic and social challenges that had significantly compromised human dignity. The meeting was preceded by a symposium in Nairobi Kenya that laid out the themes that would be discussed in Lusaka. The delegates called on member churches to respect and nurture human dignity to promote the total development of the human person.[69] Certainly one of those challenges was the heated rhetoric on homosexuality and calls for the death penalty for homosexuals from some of the major religious organisations on the continent.[70] The Church is called to be an advocate for all whose dignity is compromised even by ethical debates in which good people disagree. No one should be treated as less than human because of the sexual choices they have made. In *Rise Up and Act: A Resource Material on Violence against Women*, the staff of the AACC has called on the ecclesial community to "listen to victims of violence with a commitment to creating space for their healing, restoration of their dignity, liberation of the perpetrators and reconciliation of the communities."[71] The larger issues were HIV and AIDS, but we can see how that have implications for all areas of life, especially the highly contextual question of sexuality. The AACC has argued

---

68   Witte J (Jr). 2014. "The Freedom of a Christian: Martin Luther's Reformation of Law and Liberty", *Evangelishce theologie* [Evangelical Theology]74:127-135. Also available as Emory Legal Studies Research Paper no 14-316, 3. Online at: https://papers.ssrn.com/sol3/papers.cfm?abstract_id=2517769
69   AACC. 2012. *The Church in Africa: Opportunities, Challenges and Responsibilities: Proceedings of the International Symposium Held in Nairobi from 5th-7th December*. Nairobi: AACC.
70   Kaoma K. 2016. "I Say, We Must Talk, Talk, Mama!: Introducing African Voices on Religion, *Ubuntu* and Sexual Diversity", *Journal of Theology for Southern Africa* 155:16-29.
71   See AACC. 2006. *Come Let Us Rebuild: A Report of AACC Assembly, Yaoundé, Cameroon, November 22-27, 2003*. Nairobi: AACC, 211-213.

that treating others as less than human for whatever reason is inconsistent with a theology of life and dignity.[72] The AACC took up the question of dignity again at its General Assembly in Maputo and agreed to "campaign for African Dignity" in 2009. This campaign focused on reclaiming the selfhood of the church, but its broad themes included liberation, reconstruction and working to promote sustainability in all areas of African life.[73] It must be stressed that the African notion of *ubuntu* also grounds the notion of human dignity and spells out respect for the humanity of others as a given ethical practice.[74]

Finally, a dialogical approach to homosexuality in the African Church that takes development in constitutional and civil law seriously must embrace equality as a core human value. There is an urgent need for the Christian community in Africa today, to resume a broad, open and cordial dialogue on the differences of opinion on homosexuality. In light of the legal developments in South Africa which I have discussed, it is clear that one of the starting point for such a critical dialogue that will be consistent with a theological and legal framework is to privilege equality. The recognition that all people are equal before the law, was key in the decision issued by the South African Constitutional Court. Equality is a theological position which Christians of most traditions value and appreciate. One of the cardinal beliefs of the Christian tradition is the belief that all people carry the *imago dei*, implying that human beings, regardless of their sexual orientation, carry the image of God. If each individual is created in the image of God, regardless of what one thinks about the other person's personal life, one can respect and treat that person as an equal. The Christian hymn proclaims: "In Christ there is no East or West, in Him no South or North; but one great fellowship of love, throughout the whole wide earth."[75] Christians have always understood equality to also mean that all people, regardless of their spirituality, are equal in the eyes of God and therefore should be treated equally.

The Church in Africa lives with incommensurability on many fronts, including the debate on homosexuality. In this regard, the recognition of equality should serve as an invitation for all members of the political community to find a way of working together. Many Christians in Africa think that this implies coming up with a compromise which would ignore their beliefs on what is right and what is wrong. But one wonders, if our approaches are grounded on equality on these matters, would extending recognition to the rights of others be interpreted mainly as a surrender to a world in which people are now abandoning Christian practices? I do not think that would be the case. Recognising a shared sense of equality calls for mutual respect in dialogue on all questions. Law

---

72   AACC, *Come Let Us Rebuild*.
73   Sukapapa TC. 2017. *Ecclesiology and Ethics: An Analysis of the History of the All Africa Conference of Churches (1963-2013)*, PhD Diss, University of Western Cape, 262 ff. I am indebted to Sakupapa for his rich discussion of human dignity in the conciliar tradition.
74   Bongmba, "Homosexuality, Ubuntu, and Otherness in the African Church".
75   Words of the Hymn by John Oxenham, 1908.

and religion scholar M Christian Green reminds us of how important it is for religious people to take a middle path by pointing out that philosopher Charles Taylor's magisterial volume, *A Secular Age*, characterises some of the positions on the secular side as a loss. "Political compromise, done rightly, entails loss for both sides, in that no side can claim a privileged position and both must give something up in order to achieve peace. But there are another losses in modernity that have come through legacies of colonialism, racism, political and economic underdevelopment, and growing inequality that also plague our contemporary world."[76] Green's larger point is to demonstrate, in agreement with fellow law and religion scholar Cathleen Kaveny, that Christians can take what they consider prophetic position on some social issues, but they should do so without contempt.[77] My point in noting this is that a theological strategy for dialogue should seek eliminate the contempt that currently exists in the debate on homosexuality in Africa and should at the very least begin with the premise that all people are equal.

CONCLUSION

Homosexuality as an orientation that an individual is free to express is supported by the law, as the *Fourie* case in South Africa demonstrated. Sometimes the exercise of freedom can be problematic to others. In such cases, the responsibility of the Christian is to love and serve one another. This is a message for the entire church. Beginning with a brief overview of Luther's seminal text, "The Freedom of a Christian", I have laid down reasons why the Church in Africa should return to dialogue on the question of homosexuality. At a time when the church in Africa is focused on removing gays and lesbians from their midst, claiming that their desires are unnatural and go against African values and the teachings of Christ, it is important to reflect on what it means to be in Christ. Faith in Christ is the basis for freedom and responsibility. Faith in Christ is the basis for living in Christ, and it does not matter whether one is straight or gay. As members of Christ, all Christians share in that perfection and that community of life brought by Christ. The fundamental thing all are the summoned to do is to serve one another in the manner in which Christ has served others. But there is more to this argument, and it lies in Luther's distinction between religious leaders who have jurisdiction over the church and earthly leaders who have jurisdiction over the affairs of this world. Many people around the world are increasingly recognising that other people express themselves and their sexuality in a different manner. This was the decision of the Constitutional Court of South Africa more than twelve years ago in legalising same-sex marriage in the *Fourie* decision and the resulting passage of the Civil Unions Bill in South Africa. In

---

76 See Green MC. 2016. "Loss, Lament, and Prophetic Modernities," *Contending Modernities: Catholic, Muslim, Secular* (Notre Dame, IN: Kroc Institute for International Peace Studies, 30 August).

77 See Kaveny C. 2016. *Prophecy Without Contempt: Religious Discourse in the Public Square.* Cambridge: Harvard University Press.

ruling the way it did, the Constitutional Court of South Africa underscored the fact that the Bill of Rights recognised one's prerogative to experience and to express one's sexuality differently, as long as it does not violate the dignity and rights of another person. In a secular state, the church cannot impose its will, even if Christians form the majority of the people in that state.

VII. Religion, Heritage and Death in Africa

19 PROTECTING THE DEAD: THE SOUTH AFRICAN NATIONAL HERITAGE RESOURCES ACT IN CONTEXT

Dineo Skosana[1]

INTRODUCTION

Although grave relocations are a common phenomenon in contemporary South Africa, not much has been written to reflect on the laws that administer heritage resources and graves. This chapter provides an overview of the development of the South African National Heritage Resources Act No. 25 of 1999 (NHRA). It ultimately considers how this legislation regulates the resting place of certain remains after death. An analysis of the historical background of this Act, illuminates the democratic government's pressure to incorporate all forms of heritage that were previously marginalised by colonial typologies of heritage. The attempt to reform South Africa's heritage resulted in broad yet, undetailed legislative provisions of what constitutes heritage, what is to be protected and how. It is this ambiguity in the legislation, this chapter argues, that the laws governing graves are inadequate to address.[2] When exploited, the existing loopholes, as well as insufficient implementation, violate the cultural constitutional rights of the previously marginalised communities.

To fully comprehend the provisions of the NHRA, how it regulates graves and the limitations of this Act, this chapter first draws attention to the history of law in South Africa. It considers the degree of influence of European legal traditions, as well as the religious basis of Roman and Roman-Dutch legal systems, and ultimately examines how these shaped the regulation of heritage resources – in particular, graves. The chapter concludes that the external legal influence that has its basis in Christian values, and the need to adhere to progressive international legislative standards, constructs a fallacy that South Africa's heritage act is the most progressive in Africa. Scholars suggest that the Act is progressive because it is broad, inclusive and represents a diverse South African nation, when in reality, the legislation does not sufficiently provide for intangible heritage and indigenous beliefs. This, in turn, permits the disturbance of graves from land with contested ownership rights, and also

---

1 Department of Political Studies, The University of the Witwatersrand and The Wits History Workshop.
2 This argument is also articulated by Esterhuysen A and Saccaggi B. 2014. "Sekuruwe Grave Relocation: A Lesson in Process and Practice", *The South African Archaeological Bulletin* 69(200):173-181, who both point to the flaws in the legislation that protects heritage resources and graves in South Africa, and weaknesses in the way that these legislated processes are implemented.

undermines the cultural rights of the previously disadvantaged communities which are endorsed by the Constitution of the Republic of South Africa, 1996.

EXTERNAL INFLUENCE ON THE SOUTH AFRICAN LEGAL TRADITIONS

Much the same as other South African laws, which are a product of interwoven but distinct legal traditions, the laws that regulate heritage and graves in South Africa, are no exception. The foundation of these laws can be found in the early codified Roman law, Roman-Dutch law and English common law, whose provisions have been followed and sometimes betrayed by the South African legislation. South African law scholars, Robert Hahlo and Ellison Kahn, as well as, legal theorist Hosten,[3] share the view that the South African common law has its foundational roots drawn from the earlier Roman law and Roman-Dutch[4] law. That being said, these scholars align with Melbourne Univerisity legal studies scholar, Martin Chanock whose view is that South African law was also constructed internally as a response to local circumstances and the needs of the developing state, economy and ruling classes.[5]

Roman-Dutch law was introduced at the Cape of Good Hope (present day Cape Town) by Dutch settlers in the middle of the seventeenth century.[6] Before then, Netherlands mainly applied a Germanic common law, but also versions of a modified Roman law.[7] South African English-common law coalesced with Roman-Dutch law in the aftermath of Britain's occupation of the Cape in 1806.[8] Chanock details the preservation of Roman-Dutch law and its combination with English law when he explains that, "[a]fter the Union, the creation of Roman-Dutch canon was carried on by the Appellate Division which rolled back the advances that English common-law doctrines had made, particularly in Natal. Paradoxically, however, because judges were the primary agents, they saved the Roman-Dutch law by English common-law methods, case by case."[9] As a result, a mixed jurisdiction that typifies modern South African law developed.[10] Over the years, the influence of English law has been most marked amongst

---

3 See details in Hahlo R and Kahn E. 1968. *The South African Legal System*. Cape Town: Juta; Hosten WJ. 1983. *Introduction to South African Law and Legal Theory*. Durban: Butterworths.
4 See Du Toit F. 2014. "Roman-Dutch law in modern South African succession law", *Ars Aequi*, April:278, who defines Roman-Dutch law as "a legal system developed in the Netherlands through the reception particularly in the sixteen and seventeenth centuries of Roman law and its synthesis with Germanic customary law, feudal law and canon law".
5 Chanock M. 2001. *The Making of South African Legal Culture 1902-1936*. Cambridge: Cambridge University Press, 155.
6 Du Toit, "Roman-Dutch law", 278.
7 Hahlo and Kahn, *The South African Legal System*, 516.
8 Du Toit, "Roman-Dutch law", 278.
9 Ibid, 159.
10 Ibid, 279.

other bodies of law in criminal procedure, civil procedure, evidence and constitutional law.[11] Laws relating to private property and succession preserved their Roman-Dutch character. Of particular interest for consideration of the issue of grave relocation is the remnant influence and application of Roman-Dutch law of ownership and property in contemporary legislation.

THE RELIGIOUS BASIS OF ROMAN LAW

Ancient Rome had no principle analogous to "separation of church and state".[12] For this reason, the same men who were elected public officials could also serve as the highest ranking priests.[13] Central to Roman religious law was the idea of the immortality of the soul, and this served as the basis for the deification of Roman emperors as incarnations of divinity before and after life.[14] Beliefs about resurrection, exaltation and the idea that the head of state is the son of God had a long history.[15] Religious associations with gods would be halted when Christianity became a lawful religion under Constantine's Roman Empire. Before then, however, Christianity was considered blasphemous and persecution was an official policy tended towards Christian and religious beliefs that were considered pagan. After the ascendancy of the first Christian Emperor Constantine to power, laws were passed that prevented the persecution of Christians.[16] Thereafter, cathedrals were rapidly built all over the Roman Empire. Tracing the progression of canon law in Rome, the Roman law scholar, Charles Sherman records in the year 315 CE that Constantine empowered his subjects to bequeath their property to the Church.[17] So freely and frequently was this permission subsequently acted upon, that half a century later, Christian churches and religious orders were found to own vast quantities of property.

The adoption of Christianity gave rise to the formation of congregations with many varying opinions about the Christian doctrine and no centralised way of enforcing orthodoxy.[18] However, a set of guidelines meant to define Christian beliefs and differentiate them from heretical doctrines was proposed after the First Council of Nicaea.[19] Fundamental to the Roman Nicene Creed (a core statement of Christian belief) was the idea of the "Trinity", which refers to the teaching that there is one God who comprises three distinct aspects, the "Father"

---

11 Hahlo and Kahn, *The South African Legal System*, 19.
12 Rüpke J. 2007. *A Companion to Roman Religion*. London: Blackwell, 4.
13 Members of the elite classes held priesthood.
14 Thomson A. 2008. *Bodies of thought: science, religion, and the soul in the early Enlightenment*. Oxford: Oxford University Press, 42.
15 Haasbroek D. 1995. *The Mythology and Political Origins of Christianity*. Cape Town: V & R Printing Works.
16 Kelly C. 2006. *The Roman Empire: A Very Short Introduction*. New York: Oxford University Press.
17 Sherman C. 1919. "Brief History of Imperial Roman Canon Law", *California Law Review* 7:93, 94.
18 Rodney S. 1996. *The Rise of Christianity*. Princeton: Princeton University Press.
19 Morgan J. 2003. *Constantine Ruler of Christian Rome*. New York: Rosen Central.

(God), "the Son" (Jesus Christ, God's earthly incarnation) and the "Holy Spirit", sometimes referred to as the "Holy Ghost") as the maker of heaven and earth.[20] Equally important to this belief is that through the death and resurrection of Jesus Christ, sinful humans can be reconciled to God and thereby offered salvation and the promise of eternal life.[21]

A brief analysis of the religious basis of Roman law illustrates the dominance and influence of Roman political and religious philosophies, which spread across Europe during different historical periods. Not only was this political influence transmitted to European territories through Roman invasion such as the Netherlands, but also passed on to African colonies in the modern age. Fundamental to this chapter is the relationship between state law and religion. The association between the latter and the former was and continues to be one of the primary debates within political theory.[22] In a contemporary edited series, titled *Law and Religion*, editor Gad Barzilai suggests that "modern law and religion are complementary, contradictory and simultaneous sources of rule-making, adjudication and execution. Both embed obedience and obligations, leadership, institutions and legal ideology as foundations of their maintenance and prevalence, based on a strict structure of commands."[23] Considering the historic influence of widespread Christian values on legal systems and on burial laws, to be precise – it is evident that modern legislation, particularly in postcolonial South Africa, neglects beliefs on ancestors and the customary practices related to these. The Heritage Act is broadly framed with the objective of restorative justice, however, its provisions do not thoroughly consider the relationship that African communities have with the dead. The effect of this is evident from a case study of Glencore colliery mine's relocation of ancestral graves that belong to former labour tenants and migrant laborers from the Tweefontein farm, in the Mpumalanga province of South Africa in 2013.[24]

---

20 See for details the Holy Bible: Genesis 1 refers to the Father, verse 2 the Spirit, and verse 3 the Son.
21 See the Holy Bible, John 2:25.
22 The earlier works of Niccolò Machiavelli and John Locke amongst others shaped modern debates on the relationship between state, politics, law and religion.
23 Gad B (ed). 2007. "Law and Religion", in *The International Library of Essays in Law and Society*. Aldershot: Ashgate, xi.
24 Although the case study is central to the ideas and the argument in this chapter, it only reflects on the Heritage Act and its inadequacies which allows the disturbance of graves. The case study was selected to understand why grave relocations are subject to contestations. Phenomenological interviews were conducted with fourteen families whose ancestral graves were relocated. The study found amongst other areas of contestations, that grave relocations are disputed because ancestors are not simply bearers of good and bad omen (spiritual security), but also symbolise the families' history of migration and settlement. Their graves are evidence in South Africa's post-apartheid land restitution programme, while the general sentiment was that Glencore managers (who argue that the graves are on their property), treated the families' remains like objects that stand in the way of production and profit making. Although a wake-fee (compensation fee) of R1,500 was offered to the families, this was not negotiated and not regulated

PROTECTION OF GRAVES UNDER ROMAN LAW AND ROMAN-DUTCH LAW

South African law has in some respects conformed, yet at times disregarded, the laws of the Romans who held much respect for graves. Old sources reveal the Romans' use of the words grave and tomb interchangeably. Occasionally, a clear distinction between the latter and the former was made. A grave was defined as the space occupied by the deceased.[25] Graves, in this regard, were classified as things of religious law that were dedicated to gods of lower regions *res religiosae*.[26] Under Roman law, corporeal objects,[27] were classified into those which are subject to ownership *res commercio* and those not susceptible to ownership *res extra commercium*.[28] Graves were unsusceptible to ownership, and as such, they were inalienable. Analysing the categories of religion and commerce in Roman law, Algerian born historian of French law, Yan Thomas writes that "neither the places reserved for the dead nor the monuments erected above them were heritable or marketable. They could not be sold."[29] That being said, the sculptures of a grave were alienable.[30] Grave violation was measured on the basis of the principle which states that only that part of the soil in which the deceased was actually buried could benefit from prohibition against profanation, and only this particular part was excluded from the market.[31] Usually, however, violation consisted of an alteration to the monument, which was defined as anything built above the religious place, including the tomb itself and the air above it, according to the principle that ownership of the ground carried with it ownership of the upper levels.[32] Elaborating on the laws on grave violation Yan Thomas records that Roman law envisaged the harming of the dead only indirectly through the violation of their tomb. From this perspective, to exhume the body without the state's consent was to put the tomb itself to death.[33]

---

by the Heritage Act. Thus, the families could not afford to perform rituals such as slaughtering, and the gathering of relatives for an official ceremony to inform their ancestors about the relocations. This has left families in a state of spiritual insecurity, in which they think their ancestors will not approve of the process of the relocations and might in turn create social instability for the living.

25 Ulpian, *de sepulchre violato* in Thomas Y. 2004. "Res religiosae: on the categories of religion and commerce in Roman law", in Pottage A and Mundy M (eds). *Law, Anthropology, and the Constitution of the Social: Making Persons and Things*. Cambridge: Cambridge, University Press, 44 records that "the place accorded to the tomb is not religious in its entirety, but only to the extent that a body is inhumed within it. A tomb without the remains was considered as a monument."
26 Thomas Y. "Res religiosae", 40-72.
27 Jonkers J. 2005. *The Silence of the Dead: Ethical and Juridical Significances of the Exhumations at Prestwich place, Cape Town, 2003-2005*, MPhil Thesis, University of Cape Town, 77.
28 *Lawsa* 27 (first reissue), 211-212.
29 Thomas, "Res religiosae",'41.
30 Ibid.
31 Ulpian, *de supulchro violato*, in Thomas, "Res religiosae", 44.
32 Thomas, "Res religiosae", 57.
33 Ibid, 63-66.

Violation laws were concerned with that which constitutes a tomb – for to empty a tomb of its contents was to extinguish the *res religiosae*.[34]

Similarly, Dutch jurist Johannes Voet commonly referred to by South African courts, accepted that the bones themselves were sacred but a cenotaph – an empty tomb erected to those buried elsewhere, or whose bodies are missing – was not.[35] Additionally, burying in the property of another person without consent did not make a place consecrated. However, this did not mean that the landowner might exhume the bones without the permission of the governor. This was because, "the very removal of the bones embraced in itself something of a religious nature" according to the commentaries.[36]

Voet's view, however, differed from that of earlier Dutch practitioners when he suggested that religious things such as graves could be alienated for a just cause; and could be sold together with land, that is, as an accessory to the sale of something larger. This was on condition that the "thing continued to be used for its sacred purpose".[37] Simultaneously, there were Roman-Dutch commentators who differed on whether the Roman *res religiosae* was still recognised by the law of Holland.[38] In an attempt to narrow these contested views, the seventeenth-century Dutch jurist Hugo Grotius wrote that:

> In relation to man, many writers have distinguished things as belonging to God (*res divini juris*) and belonging to men (*res humani juris*); and under things belonging to God the Romans included dedicated things (*res sacrae*), the graves of the dead (*res religiosae*) and the walls of the cities (*res sanctae*): but upon a careful examination it will be found that all these things belong to men.[39]

In this regard, because graves were the private property of individuals, they were subject to commerce. Graveyards on private property formed part of the land; they were not inalienable because of their religious nature. As such, graves belonged to the landowner.[40] This change of religious doctrine, Neville Cloete, who writes the history of the South African judicial system explains, was an outcome of the Reformation that had made itself felt in Holland in the mid-16th century, with "religious freedom" being declared in 1572.[41] With the public practice of Roman Catholicism banned in Holland in 1580, the Roman Church had lost its authority and all things fell under worldly political authority.[42] Yet

---

34 Thomas, "Res religiosae", 64.
35 Voet Commentaries, xi 7 2.
36 Voet Commentaries, xi 7 3.
37 Voet Commentaries, xi 8 6.
38 See for more details in Jonkers, *The Silence of the Dead*, 77.
39 Grotius H. 1926. *The Jurisprudence of Holland*, Oxford: Clarendon Press in Jonkers, *The Silence of the Dead*, 83.
40 *Lawsa* 27(1), note 383.
41 Cloete N. 1987. "*Res religiosae* en die stigtingsfiguur – 'n historiese ondersoek na die juridiese aard en konstitusie van die sogenaamde religieuse sake in die Suid-Afrikaanse reg", *Transkei Law Journal*, 136.
42 Ibid.

paradoxically, the violation of a tomb *sepulchri violatio* was still recognised as wrongful by Roman-Dutch law.[43]

Both Roman law and Roman-Dutch law recognised the sacredness of graves and made provisions to protect them accordingly. Most significant to this chapter is that both legal traditions in some way favoured the landowner. The latter could not exhume a grave without a permit, however, he or she could obtain authorisation from the governor. Noteworthy, are remnants of both legal traditions in contemporary legislations in South Africa. Grave exhumation without a permit remains prohibited. And similarly, in the aforementioned case study, Glencore is in possession of the title deed of the sites that are mined. The mine's land tenure, coupled by a mining permit, gives developers more leverage over communities whose graves are subject to relocations.

FROM THE BUSHMAN RELICS PROTECTION ACT OF 1911 TO THE NATIONAL MONUMENTS ACT OF 1969

By the twentieth century, various cases concerning burial sites which came before the South African courts would illustrate an allegiance to the modified Roman-Dutch law, under which land with the presence of graves could be bought and sold. However, under Roman law the prohibition of desecration of graves and exhumation of remains without authorisation remained in force.[44] This meant that the purpose of graves would have to be retained even after alienation of the land on which they might be situated. Although, the University of Cape Town private law scholar, Julian Jonkers, explains that in then Union of South Africa[45] it was not always a statutory offence to violate a grave. The first such general legislation appeared in the Transvaal in 1925.[46] The Transvaal Ordinance has since been assigned to the Province of Gauteng,[47] Northern Province,[48] North-West Province[49] and the Mpumalanga.[50] Early Natal Ordinances have been consolidated as the KwaZulu-Natal Cemeteries and Crematoria Act 12 of 1996.[51] In the Cape, the first such legislation dates back to 1980.[52]

---

43 De Vos Wouter. 1952. "Grafskending", *South African Law Journal* 296:298-299.
44 See details of the cases in Jonkers, *The Silence of the Dead*, 86-90.
45 Predecessor to the Republic of South Africa.
46 See Jonkers, *The Silence of the Dead* and the Removal of Graves and Dead Bodies Ordinance 7 of 1925 (Province Transvaal) which prohibited the destruction or removal of graves without consent from authorities.
47 Proclamation 114 of 17 June 1994.
48 Proclamation 109 of 17 June 1994.
49 Proclamation 110 of 16 June 1994.
50 Proclamation 112 of 16 June 1994.
51 The provisions on exhumation and reinterment apply throughout the province, as opposed to for example the provisions on cemeteries, which apply in specified areas of the province. Section 2.
52 Exhumation Ordinance 12 of 1980 which now applies to the Eastern, Northern and Western Cape under different proclamations.

Prior to the Union of South Africa, there had not been any formal legislation that regulated cultural heritage.[53] The first heritage agency was organised in 1905, as a result of activism opposing the demolition of a castle in the Cape for new railroads.[54] The earliest statute to regulate heritage, the Bushman Relics Protection Act, was enacted in 1911. This Act sought to protect aboriginal paintings and sites of archaeological and anthropological interest, including burial grounds and skeletal remains, as well as other relics.[55] The Bushman-Relics Protection Act would initiate a series of laws, such as the Natural and Historical Monuments Act 6 of 1923, as well as the Relics and Antiques Act of 1934 (which consolidated the Bushman-Relics Protection Act). These were later followed by the National Monuments Act of 1969. Considering the later heritage legislation, South Africa's heritage specialist Delmont suggests that, this string of legislation was designed to bolster the state ideology of Afrikaner Nationalism and separate development.[56]

As far as burial sites were concerned, the National Monuments Act of 1969 protected the "anthropological or archaeological contents of the graves" used by Bushmen or any other people who inhabited or visited South Africa before the settlement of Europeans at the Cape, alongside other Bushman relics and artefacts. It was an offence under the Act to destroy, damage, excavate, alter, remove, from the original site or export from the South Africa such objects without a permit.[57] Removal of such objects could only take place without felony if found during a normal course of mining, engineering or agricultural activities. However, anything found would have to be immediately reported to a cultural institution by the finder or the owner of the land.[58] In common law, such found objects were regarded as *res nullius*, and ownership would vest in the finder.[59]

The National Monuments Act protected war graves only after it was amended in 1981.[60] Previously, war graves had been covered by separate statutes. The 1981 National Monuments Amendment Act repealed the War Graves Act and included the provisions relating to war graves under the National Monuments

---

53 Richings F. "Historical Monuments, Wrecks and War Graves", *Lawsa* 10(2) (first reissue).
54 See this in Saccaggi B. 2011. *Disenfranchised Heritage, Ancestral Graves and Their Legal Protection in South Africa*, MA Thesis, University of the Witwatersrand, 31, where he points out that that the role of the National Society was to protect colonial relics, as these were considered a vital aspect of the country's genesis. Precolonial structures and objects were given little consideration, with the main focus on imperial heritage.
55 Bushman Relics Protection Act 22, 1911.
56 Delmont E. 2004. "South African heritage development in the first decade of democracy", *African Arts* 34(4):39-94.
57 National Monuments Act 1969, Section 12 (2A).
58 National Monuments Act 1969, Section 12 (2A).
59 Section 12(3)(B). A permit system for excavations was added in 1935, and in 1969 permits became necessary for collecting artefacts and fossils as well.
60 National Monuments Act 13, 1981.

Act, which then became known as the War Graves and National Monuments Act. University of Cape Town scholar of engineering and the built environment, Stephen Townsend, records that there were eleven acts at the time and amendments on the subjects of monuments and war graves between 1967 and 1981.[61] This flurry of legislative activity, according to him, "demonstrates the apartheid's pre-occupation with heritage and its management in this period after South Africa's expulsion from the United Nations and the Commonwealth and its deepening isolation".[62]

This was not the end of statutory protection. The Commonwealth War Graves Act was enacted in 1992 to protect graves of members of the armed forces who died during World War I and World War II.[63] But it is the National Heritage Resources Act of 1999 (NHRA), the most recent heritage legislation, having commenced operation on April 2000, that will occupy the rest of this discussion. Although the Act is relevant in its entirety, only its general aims and specific provisions regarding burials places will be discussed.

TOWARDS THE NATIONAL HERITAGE RESOURCES ACT

The restorative justice "master narrative",[64] was dominant during the constitutional negotiations of 1992-1993, leading to the 1994 elections.[65] This narrative saw the birth of negotiations over reparations for human rights abuses, which led to various programmes such as the Truth and Reconciliation Commission (TRC) and Restitution of Land Rights in 1995.

The very language of loss and restoration was fundamental in the construction of the National Heritage Resources Act of 1999. The NHRA was written in line with the Constitution of the Republic of South Africa, 1996, which states in Chapter 2 of the Bill of Rights that individuals have rights to belong to cultural groups and participate in cultural life. Subsequent sections provide that persons may not be denied their right to enjoy their culture, practise their religion, use their language and join related associations. Considering the background within which the South African Constitution was written, it would seem that the idea

---

61 Townsend S. 2003. *Development rights and conservation constraints. Urban conservations-oriented controls in the city centre of Cape Town*, DPhil Diss, University of Cape Town.
62 Ibid, 62.
63 Act 8 of 1992. The Commonwealth War Graves Act 8 of 1992 prohibits the desecration, damage and destruction of graves, tombstones, monuments and memorials connected with the burials of members of the commonwealth armed forces who died in the First and Second World War (s 1 and 2). The owner of land upon which such a grave is situated, nor any other body in control of the burial place, may disinter or alter the grave, unless three months' notice were given to the commission (s 3(1)). The grave may not be removed except by the commission or with the written permission of the commission (s 3(4)).
64 This notion is borrowed from the work by Walker C. 2008. *Land Marked: Land Claims and Land Restitution in South Africa*. Athens, OH: The University Ohio Press, 34.
65 Ibid, 35.

to encourage individuals to practice their religion is premised on the notion that South Africans are diverse citizens with wide-ranging religious beliefs. Nonetheless, the reality is that the previous and current heritage legislations reflect an endorsement of Christian values, in that they overlook indigenous beliefs in ancestors (intangible heritage).[66]

In its preamble, the NHRA states that "heritage has the potential to affirm our diverse cultures, and in so doing shape our national character".[67] In essence, being a nation and the process of becoming a nation could only be realised if diverse cultural resources were protected and managed by the state in order to promote the nation's well-being. Describing the context under which the NHRA was adopted, Delmont observes that "the program of nation-building that underlies the Act was not without its problems". Drawing from the work of anthropologists John and Jean Comaroff, she suggests that there were obvious anomalies in the formation of modern nation-states in an era of globalisation. South Africa affirmed its sense of national identity at a moment in which currencies were amalgamating, borders were becoming more permeable, trade and industry barriers were being reduced and the global economic landscape was being marked by the logos of the multinational corporations.[68] Therefore matters of development, job creation and poverty alleviation would surpass those around preservation as far as mining and grave relocations are concerned in South Africa.

Janette Deacon, a member of the Arts and Culture Task Group (ACTAG), records that by 1994 out of the 4000 national monuments no less than 98% represented colonial and settler history, with the remainder comprising natural heritage geological, paleontological, archaeological and rock art sites.[69] South African heritage specialist Penny Pistorius explains that the need for better definitions of heritage and the mechanisms of its protection brought about a number of amendments to the National Monuments Act, which was finally repealed in 1999, by the new National Heritage Resources Act.[70] The NHRA was a product of recommendations submitted by the ACTAG, set up by the Minister of Arts and Culture. ACTAG produced two reports that detailed recommendations on arts, culture, as well as heritage policy. As a basis for that, the Department of Arts and Culture put together a white paper in 1996 and adopted principles proposed by the ACTAG. Once the white paper had been published, a public participation process ensued and a draft heritage

---

66 Beliefs such as the treatment of remains (that are symbolic of ancestors) with respect, as well as performing traditional rituals and ceremonies to appease the ancestors.
67 Ibid, (preamble).
68 Delmont E. 2004. "Re-Environing Greater Johannesburg: South African Heritage Development in the first Decade of Democracy", *African Arts* 37(4).
69 Deacon H, Mngqolo S and Prosalendis S. 2003. "Protecting Our Cultural Capital: A research plan for the Heritage Sector". HSRC Working paper.
70 Pistorius P. 1996. "Legislation and the National Monuments Act", in ICOMOS. *Monuments and Sites South Africa*. Sri Lanka: ICOMOS.

bill was developed. Then a member of ACTAG, Janette Deacon recollects that Penny Pistorius, an independent contractor and former National Monuments Council's employee, whose responsibility was to draft the bill, went through other countries' heritage legislations. Australia, New Zealand, Canada, and to some degree the U.K. heritage legislations were the most influential. The Burra Charter[71] principles adopted to create a national and international accepted standard for heritage conservation in Australia, were very influential in drafting the NHRA, according to Janette Deacon.

PROVISIONS OF THE SOUTH AFRICAN NATIONAL HERITAGE RESOURCES ACT

The influence of international definitions and typologies of heritage is very evident on the NHRA. Most international definitions generally continue to equate heritage with built structures, artefacts, or objects from the past. Thus, the material aspect has been paramount in defining heritage. Tangible heritage is defined as "a monument, group of buildings or site of historical, aesthetic, archaeological, scientific, ethnological or anthropological value".[72] This definition, as incorporated into laws, reflects the perception that for heritage to be valued, it had to be ancient. Accordingly, places of significance and objects or items have been equated with monuments, relics or antiques. Surprisingly, even after African independence, the definitions used by heritage laws remained unchanged. In fact, most of the heritage legislation of African countries still dates back to the 1960s and 1970s.[73] Hence the conclusion by some scholars who suggest that heritage legislations and definitions reflect Eurocentric views of heritage that has traditionally valued monuments and sites over the intangible values associated with them.[74]

As a result, rarely was intangible heritage (also named living heritage) incorporated in the definition of heritage. If incorporated, the definitions often emphasised only certain aspects of intangible cultural heritage. Early expert definitions in the United Nations Educational Scientific and Cultural Organisation (UNESCO) focused on artistic creations like performance, but by the late 1990s, emphasis was also being placed on knowledge and values.[75] The Human Science Research Council (HSRC), argued in their findings that definitions at a national level reflect national cultural and political concerns

---

71 First adopted at an Australian small town Burra in 1979; was put together by the Australian International Council on Monuments and Sites (ICOMAS) to identify the principles that should be used for conservation of Heritage Resources.
72 World Heritage Centre, http://whc.unesco.org/
73 Ndoro W. 2005. "Legal definitions of Heritage", in Ndoro W, Mumma A and Abungu G (eds). *Cultural Heritage and the Law: Protecting Immovable Heritage in English Speaking Countries of Sub-Saharan Africa*. Rome: ICCROM.
74 See, for instance, Ndoro, "Legal definitions of Heritage".
75 Human Sciences Research Council Report. 2004. *Definitions of intangible heritage* – HSRC, 27.

and that any national instruments which do not include oral histories in their definition of intangible heritage, such as the NHRA, is unusual in not including them.[76] A further limitation, and more significant to the argument in this chapter, is that definitions of intangible heritage excludes expressions of religion and spirituality.

Like much legislation, the NHRA has its basis in the precedent of the previous National Monuments Act, which was revised to suit the new democratic dispensation. The NHRA set out to redress past inequalities and to promote the management of the national estate in a way that was necessary to define the nation's multi-cultural identity, as well as to promote nation-building. The urgent need to redress what Colette Scheermeyer, Head of South African Heritage Resources Agency, describes as "many years of neglect and disregard for the many facets of heritage and extensive cultural treasures associated with non-white communities",[77] may have compelled the NHRA to employ a broad conception of heritage.[78]

Following the recommendations of the Arts and Culture Task Group, intangible heritage was included as one of the resources that required protection. The NHRA describes living heritage as intangible aspects of inherited culture that may include "cultural tradition, oral history, performance, ritual, popular memory, skills and techniques, indigenous knowledge systems and the holistic approach to nature, society and social relationships".[79]

Janette Deacon recollects that when the NHRA was written, intangible heritage was difficult to legislate, because the UNESCO convention on intangible heritage had not been drafted at that time.[80] Thus, there were no guidelines. On those grounds, intangible heritage is only discussed in the preamble. Janette Deacon concluded that, if the Heritage Act was to be re-written, the part on intangible heritage would be a priority – "be more specific".[81]

One of the limitations of the NHRA stems from its wide-ranging provisions. Although the NHRA incorporates different conceptions of heritage and acknowledges the value of such to those groups who were previously marginalised, such a fluid conceptualisation of heritage poses difficulty in

---

76   Human Sciences Research Council Report, 27.
77   Scheermeyer C. 2005. "A Changing and Challenging Landscape: Heritage Resources Management in South Africa", *The South African Archaeological Bulletin* 60(182): 121-123.
78   A heritage resource or national estate on the Act is defined as any place, building, landscape, geological, archaeological or paleontological sites and graves and burial grounds, as well as objects and records of cultural importance.
79   Indigenous beliefs about ancestors and cultural practices related to ancestors fall within intangible heritage, The National Heritage Resources Act 1999, section 2. Ancestral beliefs are recognised as indigenous knowledge systems.
80   Interview with Janette Deacon by D Skosana, Iziko Museum, July 2015.
81   Ibid.

applying a legal framework.⁸² Zimbabwean heritage practitioner, Webber Ndoro argues that "definitions of heritage in legal instruments have to be very precise so as to avoid ambiguity. Precision leaves no doubt with regard to what falls within the coverage of the law."⁸³ Webber Ndoro also highlights the importance of such precision when he points out that definitions have a direct impact on the scope of the national legislative instruments. They determine the regulation of powers, what is to be protected and how.⁸⁴ Reflecting on heritage definitions in English-speaking sub-Saharan countries, Ndoro records that, except in South Africa, these countries have very narrow and specific definitions.⁸⁵ His evaluation concludes that with narrow and specific definitions, the danger is always that much heritage – including intangible heritage, cultural landscapes, and itineraries – will not be covered. Broader definitions have an obvious advantage in being all-inclusive. However, they may suffer from lack of detail about the types of protected heritage.⁸⁶ The lack of detail in the NHRA for instance, is evident in that ancestral beliefs are protected as "indigenous knowledge systems", without consideration of the contestations about this conceptualisation, who defines indigenous systems or how law should engage with indigenous knowledge systems. This permits any other party which seeks to relocate graves to neglect their importance to communities because their significance is not legally endorsed. The failure to thoroughly articulate the significance of graves and ancestors is partly due to the influence of Christianity in law making.

IMPLEMENTATION OF NATIONAL HERITAGE RESOURCES ACT

The Arts and Culture Department guidelines proposed a three-tier system for the management of heritage resources. This would be a decentralised administrative system in which the decision making was done by central authorities. Critiquing the three-tiered system, the University of the Witwatersrand archaeologist Amanda Esterhuysen writes that, "unfortunately, rather than presenting a strong and united conservation unit, the tiered heritage system tends to be undeveloped, under-resourced and uncoordinated."⁸⁷ She further suggests that "communication between Heritage Departments, Agencies and Councils, the National Provincial and Municipal Departments of health,

---

82 Ndoro W and Pwiti G (eds). 2005. *Legal frameworks for the Protection of immovable cultural Heritage in Africa*, Rome: ICCROM.
83 Ibid.
84 Ibid.
85 Ibid.
86 Ibid.
87 Esterhuysen A. 2009. "Undermining Heritage", *The South African Archaeological Bulletin* 64(189).

environment, and planning, result to slow and questionable decision making."[88] Janette Deacon shared the same view when she said,

> What is happening especially within mining, is that those departments are not working together with other departments. So, the mining people, the Department of Minerals ... are not interacting with the Department of Environmental Affairs for example. And they are not interacting with the Department of Arts and Culture. Ideally, they should be. But it's not happening. And because our constitution doesn't allow for one department to argue with another department, we are stuck in many ways.

The three-tiered system required a change of the Monuments Council, which had four regional branches for the four provinces that existed before 1994. This meant that decisions about the significance of heritage places should ideally be taken at the lowest competent level of governance – in other words ideally at a local level, although it is not clear from the NHRA who constitutes local authorities. At the provincial level, NHRA would be implemented by the Provincial Heritage Resources Agencies PHAHs, except in cases where the South African Heritage Resources Agency (SAHRA), which serves as the national implementation body that manages the functions of NHRA, acts on behalf of the provinces. Heritage resources considered of provincial significance are managed by PRAHs and those regarded as of national significance are managed by SAHRA.

According to NHRA, all levels of authorities must coordinate the identification and management of the national estate that is graded from one to three.[89] This grading system caused an outcry during consultations for the heritage bill. One of the major concerns was that when the bill was put into law, all previous monuments, which included a very large number of colonial buildings, became provincial heritage sites. So, it immediately reduced their significance to provincial level rather than national. Controversy was primarily from the owners of buildings who saw their property as being demoted.[90] Additionally, there was also less funding opportunity across provinces for the heritage resources graded under provincial heritage. According to Webber Ndoro and Donatius Kamamba,[91] the ranking system is used by most countries in order to

---

88 Esterhuysen, "Undermining Heritage".
89 Grade I heritage resources are "those with qualities so exceptional that they are of special national significance", Grade II heritage resources are those "which, although forming part of the national estate, can be considered to have special qualities which make them significant within the context of a province or a region". Grade III heritage resources- are those of local significance and are administered by a local authority. The graves which were relocated by Glencore mine are classified under Grade III heritage resources, whereas, war graves or those of renowned political activists may be classified under grade I or II.
90 Interview with Janette Deacon.
91 Director of the Antiquities Division at the Ministry of Natural Resources and Tourism in Tanzania.

establish priorities for management by heritage organisations.[92] These authors also suggest that heritage ranking in other countries affects property rights and determines public access and management responsibilities of the state. In a ranking system, they argue, cultural heritage is more likely to suffer, because, in Africa, it is not manifested only through monuments.[93]

THE PROTECTION OF GRAVES IN SOUTH AFRICA

The above history of the NHRA is essential to understanding the legal regime governing the protection of graves in South Africa. Graves are protected and regulated under Section 36 of the NHRA. A grave is defined as "any place of interment, including its contents, headstone, or other markers of such a place, and any other structure on or associated with such a place".[94] Graves are categorised according to the following two primary criteria: those inside and outside of a formal cemetery, and those graves that are younger and those older than 60 years. To exhume archaeological graves (older than 100 years old), those of victims of conflict, royal or traditional leaders; historical graves or burial grounds, and any grave or burial ground older than 60 years which is situated outside a formal cemetery administered by the local authority, a permit is obtained from SAHRA.[95] Graves that are less than 60 years old and inside a formal cemetery require permission from the Health Department and or a local municipality to relocate. There are no formalised guidelines for this application process, nor is there a definite understanding of what constitutes a local heritage authority. When asked about why there were classifications of graves by date, Janette Deacon explained that it was partly a carryover from the National Monuments Council, and a desire to separate things which would be defined as archaeological from those defined as historical.[96] On this point, Deacon reasoned that "for archaeological things it is virtually impossible to trace the previous owners of that place so you have got to regard the archaeological things, written in the act as things that belong to the state, in other words not individually owned."

One of the key weaknesses of the NHRA, is that protection is only extended to graves over 60 years of age, graves of victims of conflict and those graves considered as of cultural significance. In essence, only graves that are over 60 years of age are treated as heritage resources. These are relocated in line with

---

92 Ndoro W and Kamamba D. 2005. "The Ranking of Heritage Resources and sites in Legislation", in Ndoro, Mumma and Abungu, *Cultural Heritage and the Law*, 40.
93 Ibid.
94 National Heritage Resources Act, 1999, Section 2.
95 Ibid.
96 Interview with Janette Deacon.

SAHRA's guidelines. Explaining why graves that are 60 years old would be considered heritage resources, Deacon reflects that this is mainly because,

> We felt that 60 years was a kind of cut-off point that you could have lost touch with where the graves of family members were. And would most likely have moved away and would not know about graves being exhumed for one reasons or another. And we felt that it was necessary to put that into law and we also assumed, maybe it was a wrong assumption in some ways, that by 60 years, local authorities would have been organised enough to have made a list of all people who were buried there and so that they would be able to pick up on the consultation process. I don't know if that was a good idea. It's hard to say.

Graves that are less than 60 years old, not of victims of conflict or of cultural significance, fall out of the NHRA and are therefore, regulated through the Human Tissue Act 65[97] and municipal ordinances. These ordinances require an undertaker to remove the grave, although the NHRA does not make provisions for the process that needs to be followed by the local authorities to ensure that the employed undertaker has the necessary experience. On the contrary, graves over 60 years require a qualified archaeologist to remove. Archaeologists are required to conduct research on the grave, record the layout of the grave and objects found, as well as to consolidated into a report. This is a slower and more costly exercise as compared to hiring an undertaker who is also not required to be in possession of an exhuming license. Thus, developers often seek to find loopholes which can make it possible for the relocation to be carried out by the undertakers.

For any development, the developer is expected to contact SAHRA to inform the agency of the intended development.[98] SAHRA then has an opportunity to consider if the development will affect any heritage and instruct the developer to submit a Heritage Impact Assessment.[99] SAHRA can also instruct the developer to contact a provincial or local heritage authority if it decides the heritage should be administered on a provincial or local level. According to the Heritage Act, the permit should only be granted once SAHRA finds that adequate arrangements have been made for the process of alteration or relocation contemplated by the applicant.[100] The latter is obligated to contact and consult with individuals and communities who may have an interest in the

---

97 In sum, the tissue act states that you may not store any human tissues anywhere other than at a medical facility. This was to prevent institutions such as museums from keeping human remains that have been fossilised and technically are no longer remains but turned into stone.
98 National Heritage Resources Act, 1999, Section 38 (5)(b).
99 Section 38 (2). The processes and implications of the Heritage Impact Assessment submissions will be discussed in detail in the next chapter which deals with the provisions of the Mineral and Petroleum Resources Development Act.
100 National Heritage Resources Act, 1999, Section 36.

graves and thereafter, enter into an agreement with them.[101] However, there is no definite framework for consultation with communities; as a result, there is no verification process in place to ensure that the person who gives permission to move the grave is the rightful member of the family.

Explaining the relocation process, South Africa heritage consultant from Professional Heritage Solutions, Henk Steyn, mentioned that meetings related to grave relocations are announced in local newspapers, in a language that communities understand.[102] Families are often offered a "wake fee", which is intended to help prepare for the reburial ceremony. The mine fee covers expenses such as a coffin, transport costs and in other cases, compensates families for the relocation of the graves. Compensation creates family disputes, as members of the families do not always agree on what can be considered a reasonable compensation amount for the relocation of a grave.[103] Wake fees and other forms of compensation are not legislated; as a result, both developers and communities are often at loggerheads.

CONCLUSION

This chapter demonstrates that external legal systems such as Roman law and Roman-Dutch law, both which have their basis in Christian values have had a great influence on South African legislation, in particular the National Heritage Resources Act. Continued adherence to international legislative standards sets the NHRA as the most progressive heritage legislations in Africa. In reality, however, the international typologies of heritage employed do not adequately provide for intangible heritage (non-Christian beliefs). This inadequacy permits the disturbance of graves because the relationship between ancestors and communities is not thoroughly provided in laws protecting graves. Grave disturbances in the brief highlighted case study, were carried out in manner that undermines the cultural rights of the previously disadvantaged peoples. One of the major contestation to emerge out of the case study, was that failure to compensate the disturbed graves made it impossible for the families to perform cultural rituals that provide spiritual security for the living members. Overall, the chapter highlighted that provisions for intangible heritage or beliefs related to ancestors require further development.

---

101 National Heritage Resources Act, 1999, Section 36 (5)(a).
102 Interview with Henk Steyn by D Skosana, 30 October 2014.
103 Interview with Henk Steyn.

20 BURIAL RIGHTS: PROTECTING THE RELIGIOUS AND CULTURAL HERITAGE OF COMMUNITIES IN SOUTH AFRICA

Helena van Coller[1]

INTRODUCTION

Over the years, cultural communities all over the world have experienced constant threats to their sacred sites, and religious and cultural communities in South Africa have experienced the same. Religious heritage sites and religious traditions play a significant role in educating future generations and creating a sense of belonging in communities. The phrase "burial rights" relates to the whole range of death and burial practices in respect of the deceased. The emphasis of this chapter will be in particular on burial places, both on public and private land. This is because among many cultures, a cemetery or burial site is often much more than just a place of final rest for the dead, but also a place of spiritual and cultural reference. In some cultures, particularly in African cultures, it is a place of connecting with ancestral spirits and for ancestral veneration. The chapter will first outline some of the legal mechanisms in place to protect and promote communities' religious rights and heritage espoused in the National Heritage Resources Act 25 of 1999 (NHRA), the South African Charter of Religious Rights and Freedoms (SACRRF), as well as the constitutional protection.

In relation to public land, the chapter will discuss some challenges faced by communities, particularly in relation to the reuse and relocation of graves. With reference to some practical examples, the chapter will highlight some inefficiencies not only with the legislation itself but also with the implementation thereof. A lack of consultation and engagement with stakeholders and a lack of coordination between the different tiers of government seems to be some of the biggest challenges. In relation to burying on private land, a conflict between the right to freedom of religion and property rights is inevitable. With reference to some case studies, the chapter will illustrate how courts have tried to resolve this conflict and also how reliance on legislation assisted communities in asserting their burial rights. Religious communities have a duty to educate and inform the court of their specific religious views or practices. Often there is a lack of understanding on the part of the courts, especially in relation to different, minority and traditional religions, and it has been stated that "[m]uch of the jurisprudence appears to be grounded in a worldview that separates land from religion, history from spirituality, and belief from practice".[2]

---

1 Associate Professor, Faculty of Law, Rhodes University, South Africa.
2 Ratipa MM. 2015. "'Just Piles of Rock to Developers but Places of Worship to Native Americans' – Exploring the Significance of Earth Jurisprudence for South

PROTECTING OUR RELIGIOUS AND CULTURAL HERITAGE: A LEGISLATIVE FRAMEWORK

The National Heritage Resources Act 25 of 1999 (NHRA)

The South African Heritage Resources Agency (SAHRA) is the national administrative body responsible for the protection of South Africa's cultural heritage. It was established through the National Heritage Resources Act (NHRA). The legislation aims to promote good management of the national estate,[3] and to enable and encourage communities to nurture and conserve their legacy so that it may be bequeathed to future generations. According to the preamble:

> Our heritage is unique and precious and it cannot be renewed. It helps us to define our cultural identity and therefore lies at the heart of our spiritual well-being and has the power to build our nation. It has the potential to affirm our diverse cultures, and in so doing shape our national character. Our heritage celebrates our achievements and contributes to redressing past inequities. It educates, it deepens our understanding of society and encourages us to empathise with the experience of others. It facilitates healing and material and symbolic restitution and it promotes new and previously neglected research into our rich oral traditions and customs.

This quotation from the NHRA encapsulates the spirit of the SAHRA. In terms of the Act, "heritage resource" means any place or object of cultural significance. "Cultural significance" includes reference to spiritual value and according to Section 3(1) they are considered part of the national estate. The national estate also includes graves and burial grounds, including ancestral graves.[4]

A place or object will also be considered part of the national estate if it has cultural significance or other special value because of its strong or special association with a particular community or cultural group for social, cultural or spiritual reasons.[5] In addition to the formal protection of culturally significant graves, all graves older than 60 years and not in a cemetery (such as ancestral graves in rural areas) are protected. The legislation protects the interests of communities which have an interest in the graves and require that they must be contacted and consulted before any disturbance can take place. Agreements must also be made with such communities and individuals regarding the future of such grave or burial ground. In this regard, Section 5 of the Act emphasises

---

African Cultural Communities", *Potchefstroom Electronic Law Journal* 18(1):3226.
3   Section 3(1) of the Act states that those heritage resources of South Africa that are of cultural significance or other special value for the present community and for future generations must be considered part of the national estate and fall within the sphere of operations of heritage resources authorities. Section 2 includes a list of such resources, including graves and burial sites.
4   NHRA, s 3(2)(g).
5   NHRA, s 3(3)(g).

the fact that heritage resources form an important part of the history and beliefs of communities and must be managed in a way that acknowledges the right of affected communities to be consulted and to participate in their management.

Section 8 of the NHRA provides for a three-tier system for heritage resources management. National level functions are the responsibility of SAHRA, provincial level functions are the responsibility of provincial heritage resources authorities and local level functions are the responsibility of local authorities. Heritage resources authorities and local authorities are accountable for their actions and decisions and the performance of functions under this system.[6] In the examples discussed below, it will become clear that this three-tier system and the lack of communication and coordination between the different tiers are some of the main reasons for the poor implementation of the Act.

Heritage resources contribute significantly to research, education and tourism and according to the World Tourism Organization (UNWTO), the United Nations agency responsible for the promotion of responsible, sustainable and universally accessible tourism. Approximately 300 to 330 million tourists visit the world's key religious sites every year, including burial sites.[7] UNWTO Secretary-General, Teleb Rifai views religious tourism as crucial in building cultural dialogue and peace. According to Rifai, "Religious tourism can also be a powerful instrument for raising awareness regarding the importance of safeguarding one's heritage and that of humanity, and help preserve these important sites for future generations."[8]

South Africa has many sacred sites, as many as there are cultures and beliefs, ranging from sacred hills, valleys and lakes to mosques, kramats – the holy shrines of Islam – and Hindu temples. These religious heritage sites provide important meeting grounds for both visitors and communities. They can drive economic growth and international tourism, but more importantly they contribute and develop tolerance, respect and mutual understanding between different cultures and religions. There are more than twenty recognised kramats in the Cape Peninsula area, with one of the oldest known gravesites in Constantia.[9] These kramats mark the graves of Holy Men of the Muslim faith who have died at the Cape. Some of the top religious sites in South Africa, according to the travel website Trip Advisor, are the Hare Krishna Temple of Understanding in Durban, St George's Cathedral in Cape Town Central, the Dutch Reformed Church in Stellenbosch, Regina Mundi in Soweto, Nizamiye

---

6   NHRA, s 8(1).
7   Press Release. 2014. "Tourism can protect and promote religious heritage", 10 December. Online at: http://media.unwto.org/press-release/2014-12-10/tourism-can-protect-and-promote-religious-heritage
8   Ibid.
9   Collingridge Lee-Anne. 2015. "The Cape's kramats: A unique religious and cultural heritage", 8 September. Online at: http://www.southafrica.net/blog/en/posts/entry/the-capes-kramats-a-unique-religious-and-cultural-heritage

Mosque in Midrand and the Cathedral of St Michael and St George in Grahamstown.[10]

Heritage resources have the capacity to promote reconciliation, understanding and respect, and contribute to the development of a unifying South African identity. They provide evidence of the origins of South Africa and must be carefully managed, although the challenges outlined below will illustrate that it is indeed not always the case. The NHRA also provides that laws and procedures must be clear and give content to the fundamental rights set out in the Constitution. What follows is a brief outline of the most important constitutional mechanism in place for the protection of the religious rights and heritage of communities in South Africa, followed by specific examples and case studies illustrating some challenges in the legislative content and application experienced by communities.

Constitutional protection

Section 15 of the Constitution of the Republic of South Africa, 1996,[11] provides that everyone has the right to freedom of conscience, religion, thought, belief and opinion. Freedom of religion includes traditional African religions and practices, and this is also reflected in numerous international documents.[12] However, individuals and community may not exercise the right in a manner inconsistent with the other provisions of the Bill of Rights.

Section 31 of the South African Constitution further provides that persons belonging to cultural, religious or linguistic communities may not be denied the right, with other members of that community, to enjoy their culture, practice their religion and use their language, and to form, join or maintain cultural, religious and linguistic associations and other organs of civil society, including therefore indigenous communities. Section 31 of the Constitution reflects Section 27 of the International Convention on Civil and Political Rights (ICCPR) to which South Africa is a party.[13] This section is very important in relation to religious and cultural heritage, since the traditions and culture of indigenous

---

10 Trip advisor. 2016. "Religious Sites in South Africa", November. Online at: https://www.tripadvisor.co.za/Attractions-g293740-Activities-c47-t10-South_Africa.html
11 Constitution of the Republic of South Africa, 1996.
12 Article 18 of both the Universal Declaration of Human Rights, G.A. res. 217A (III), U.N. Doc A/810 at 71 (1948) and the International Covenant on Civil and Political Rights, G.A. res. 2200A (XXI), 21 U.N. GAOR Supp. (No. 16) at 52, U.N. Doc. A/6316 (1966), 999 U.N.T.S. 171, *entered into force* Mar. 23, 1976; article 9 of the Convention for the Protection of Human Rights and Fundamental Freedoms, 213 U.N.T.S. 222, *entered into force* Sep. 3, 1953, as amended by Protocols Nos 3, 5, 8, and 11, *entered into force* Sep. 21, 1970, Dec. 20, 1971, Jan. 1, 1990, and Nov. 1, 1998 respectively; article 1 of the Declaration on the Elimination of All Forms of Intolerance and of Discrimination Based on Religion or Belief, G.A. res. 36/55, 36 U.N. GAOR Supp. (No. 51) at 171, U.N. Doc. A/36/684 (1981).
13 "In those States in which ethnic, religious or linguistic minorities exist, persons belonging to such minorities shall not be denied the right, in community with the

communities are often influenced by spiritual beliefs and these communities have strong spiritual connections to their lands.

Section 9 of the Constitution further provides for the right to equality before the law and the right to equal protection and benefit of the law, non-discrimination on various grounds, including ethnic or social origin and culture. In order to give effect to Section 9(4) of the Constitution, the South African Parliament passed the Promotion of Equality and Prevention of Unfair Discrimination Act of 2000. Indigenous people and communities may therefore not be discriminated against on basis of race, culture, religion or any of the grounds envisaged in Section 9(3) of the Constitution. Various other provisions of the Constitution relate to religion and religious freedom. Sections 185 and 186 respectively provide for a Commission for the Promotion and Protection of the Rights of Cultural, Religious and Linguistic Communities (CRL Commission). Various other human rights such as the right to human dignity, the right to freedom of expression, and the right to freedom of association, relate indirectly to the protection of religious freedom.

Section 7(2) of the Constitution further makes it clear that the state must not only respect and protect the rights in the Bill of Rights, but also promote and fulfil them. It further emphasises the relevance of customary law, in that the Bill of Rights does not deny the existence of any other rights or freedoms that are recognised or conferred by common law, customary law or legislation, to the extent that they are consistent with the Bill.[14] When interpreting the Bill of Rights, a court must also promote the values that underlie an open and democratic society based on human dignity, equality and freedom and must consider international law.[15] In this regard, the International Labour Organization (ILO) Convention 169 is relevant. Although South Africa is not a signatory to this Convention, it provides relevant guidelines and has persuasive value when a dispute of this nature must be resolved by the courts. ILO Convention 169 is the Indigenous and Tribal Peoples Convention of 1989 (ITP Convention).[16] The ITP Convention is based on respect for the cultures and ways of life of indigenous and tribal peoples. It aims at overcoming discriminatory practices affecting these peoples and enabling them to participate in decision making that affects their lives.

The ITP Convention acknowledges the fact that in many parts of the world indigenous people are unable to enjoy their fundamental human rights to the same degree as the rest of the population of the states within which they live, and that their laws, values, customs and perspectives have often been eroded.

---

other members of their group, to enjoy their own culture, to profess and practise their own religion, or to use their own language."
14   Constitution of the Republic of South Africa, 1996, s 39(3).
15   Constitution of the Republic of South Africa, 1996, s 39(1).
16   ILO Convention 169 – Indigenous and Tribal Peoples Convention, 1989 (No. 169). Convention concerning Indigenous and Tribal Peoples in Independent Countries, *entered into force* Sep. 5, 1991. Adoption: Geneva, 76th ILC session (27 June 1989).

The Preamble specifically recognises "the aspirations of these peoples to exercise control over their own institutions, ways of life and economic development and to maintain and develop their identities, languages and religions, within the framework of the States in which they live." Article 14.2 of the Convention gives due and full recognition to "the right of the [indigenous] people to use lands not exclusively occupied by them, but to which they have traditionally had access for their subsistence and traditional activities". Similar sentiments are echoed in Article 26 of the United Nations Declaration on the Rights of Indigenous Peoples (UNDRIP), which provides that:

> Indigenous peoples have the right to own, develop, control and use the lands and territories, including the total environment of the lands ... which they have traditionally owned or otherwise occupied or used. This includes the right to the full recognition of their laws, traditions and customs, land tenure systems and institutions for the development and management of resources, and the right to effective measures by States to prevent any interference with, alienation of or encroachment upon these rights.

UNDRIP was adopted through resolution 61/295 of the General Assembly. While as a General Assembly declaration UNDRIP is not a legally binding instrument under international law, it "represents a commitment on the part of the United Nations and Member States to its provisions, within the framework of the obligations established by the Charter of the United Nations."[17] UNDRIP elaborates on existing human rights standards:

> The Declaration does not attempt to bestow indigenous peoples with a set of special or new human rights, but rather provides a contextualized elaboration of general human rights principles and rights as they relate to the specific historical, cultural and social circumstances of indigenous peoples. The standards affirmed in the Declaration share an essentially remedial character, seeking to redress the systemic obstacles and discrimination that indigenous peoples have faced in their enjoyment of basic human rights. From this perspective, the standards of the Declaration connect to existing State obligations under other human rights instruments.[18]

UNDRIP contains further provisions which traditional communities can refer to in their mission to protect their cultural sites. Article 25 emphasises the rights of indigenous peoples to "maintain and strengthen their distinctive spiritual and material relationships with the lands they have traditionally owned or otherwise occupied or used, and to uphold their responsibilities to future generations". Article 29 further provides for the right to the conservation

---

17 *The United Nations Declaration on the Rights of Indigenous Peoples: A Manual for National Human Rights Institutions*. 2013. The Office of the United Nations High Commissioner for Human Rights, August, 37. Online at: http://www.ohchr.org/Documents/Issues/IPeoples/UNDRIPManualForNHRIs.pdf

18 Ibid.

and protection of the environment and the productive capacity of their lands or territories and resources. Re-enforcing the values expressed in the NHRA, it provides for private access to religious and cultural sites[19] and the right to maintain, control, protect and develop their cultural heritage.[20]

Section 234 of the Constitution of the Republic of South Africa, 1996, provides that "in order to deepen the culture of democracy established by the Constitution, Parliament may adopt Charters of Rights consistent with the provisions of the Constitution". Any such charter of rights will then have the force of law. The Constitution envisages that the rights in the Constitution may be further extended, supplemented and given content by way of such additional charters.

The South African Charter of Religious Rights and Freedoms (SACRRF) is a document that defines the freedoms, rights, responsibilities and relationship between the "State" of South Africa and her citizens concerning religious belief.[21] The Charter expresses what freedom of religion means to those of religious belief and religious organisations within a South African context and the daily rights, responsibilities and freedoms that are associated with this right. These include the right to gather to observe religious belief, freedom of expression regarding religion, the right of citizens to make choices according to their convictions, the right to change their faith, the right to be educated in their religion, the right to educate their children in accordance with their philosophical and religious convictions and the right to refuse to perform certain duties or assist in activities that violate their religious beliefs.

The SACRRF was first signed at a public ceremony in Johannesburg on 21 October 2010, and signatories continue to be added to the open document. Signatories include religious groups and organisations, human rights organisations, legal and academic entities and media bodies. If passed into law, the Charter will ensure that the rights of religious believers are clearly defined and protected under the law of South Africa. The SACRRF may be used as a legal instrument even as the current climate of understanding and tolerance between government and religion may alter. After the public signing of the SACRRF, a Council for the Protection and Promotion of Religious Rights and Freedoms was established to oversee the process of the Charter being formally enacted into South African law. The passing of the SACRRF into law will mean that religious believers have legal impartiality and protection to practice all elements of religious belief under the Constitution. The SACRRF is the first public charter to be developed under Section 234 of the Constitution of South Africa.[22]

---

19   UNDRIP, art 12.
20   UNDRIP, art 31(1).
21   The South African Charter of Religious Rights and Freedoms. 2016. "Explanatory notes on the Charter", 16 May, 4. Online at: http://www.crlcommission.org.za/docs/sacrrf.pdf
22   See further Charter, 4-5.

The SACRRF makes provision for the right of every person to have access to sacred places and burial sites relevant to their convictions. Such access and the preservation of such places and sites must be regulated within the law and with due regard for property rights. According to the Charter:

> 4. Subject to the duty of reasonable accommodation and the need to provide essential services, every person has the right to the private or public, and individual or joint, observance or exercise of their convictions, which may include but are not limited to reading and discussion of sacred texts, confession, proclamation, worship, prayer, witness, arrangements, attire, appearance, diet, customs, rituals and pilgrimages, and the observance of religious and other sacred days of rest, festivals and ceremonies.
>
> 4.1. Every person has the right to private access to sacred places and burial sites relevant to their convictions. Such access, and then preservation of such places and sites, must be regulated within the law and with due regard for property rights.

In accordance with Section 4 of the Charter, anyone is entitled to visit sacred places and burial sites, as long as property rights and other legal considerations are observed. Importantly, any visit to sites on private land must be arranged with the landowner, and may not put an unreasonable burden on the landowner or cause damage of any kind to the property. Emphasis is placed on mutual respect and consideration.[23] Sacred places and burial sites are found on both public and private land and challenges are experienced by communities in relation to both. With reference to some practical examples, the chapter will now highlight some challenges faced by communities specifically in relation to the reuse and relocation of graves.

CHALLENGES

The reuse of graves

In accordance with Section 156(1) of the Constitution of the Republic of South Africa, 1996, a municipality has executive authority in respect of and has the right to administer all the local government matters listed in Part B of Schedule 4 and Part B of Schedule 5 of the Constitution. These are functional areas (for instance education or health services) in which the national, provincial or local government have legislative competence in. Municipalities also have the right to administer any other matter assigned to them by national or provincial legislation and further may make and administer by-laws for the effective administration of the matters that they have the right to administer. Part B of Schedule 5 specifically provides for cemeteries, funeral parlours and

---

23   See Charter, 29.

crematoria. The NHRA supports this section of the Constitution by specifying that local government is responsible for the execution of the NHRA at local level. Municipalities are responsible for declaring which heritage resources have cultural significance at local level. According to the NHRA, the national system for the management of heritage resources applies to a local authority, as well.[24] In terms of making by-laws, the NHRA provides that a local authority may, with the approval of the provincial heritage resources authority, make by-laws in order to regulate the admission of the public to any place protected under the NHRA to which the public is allowed access. The by-laws may also regulate the conditions of use of any place protected under the NHRA which is under its control and the protection and management of a protected area.[25]

In relation to burial grounds and graves, the NHRA does make provision for the fact that where it is not the responsibility of any other authority, SAHRA must conserve and generally care for burial grounds and graves protected.[26] The NHRA, however, follows the principle that heritage resources should be managed by the levels of government closest to the community and therefore these local and provincial authorities should manage heritage resources as part of their planning process.

Recently, a grave fight with Eskom, South Africa's main electricity provider, erupted over burial sites at the R145-billion Medupi power plant, which may have been built on graves of the ancestors belonging to at least 14 families. These families are fighting for the right to visit these graves and allege that they were not properly consulted about the development when construction for the multibillion rand project began more than seven years ago. According to a report by the African Development Bank, "no real effort has been made to identify such unmarked graves and so the risk of desecration remains substantial."[27] In African religious belief systems, it is important to have access to graves as it is custom to visit the sites and perform rituals when people face problems.[28] Many traditional religious communities in South Africa see the world of the ancestors as "analogous" and "contiguous" to the world of the

---

24 NHRA, s 4(a).
25 NHRA, s 54(1).
26 NHRA, s 36(1).
27 Ackroyd Bianca. 2014. "EXCLUSIVE: Grave fight with Eskom over burial sites at Medupi", 4 August. Online at: https://www.enca.com/families-fight-eskom-over-access-graves-medupi
28 Mndende N. 2013. "Law and religion in South Africa: An African traditional perspective", *NGTT* 54(4):75. According to Mndende, African tradition religion means the "indigenous religion of the Africans. It is the religion that has been handed down from generation to generation by the forebears of the present generation of Africans. It is not a fossil religion (a thing of the past) but a religion that Africans today have made theirs by living it and practising it". See further Dopamu PA. 1991. 'Towards understanding African Traditional Religion", in Uka EM (ed). *Readings in African Traditional Religion*. New York: Peter Lang, 19-37.

living.[29] They also believe that the improper care of the dead has more sinister and far-reaching consequences for the community at large.[30] Communities perform rituals for various purposes. These rituals are extraordinary practices performed by the living for the spiritual world, and include special gatherings of the clans aimed at communal religious practices, like the rites of passage and sometimes "special rituals as requested by ancestors, like the bringing back of the spirit of some family member who died far away from home. In these religious gatherings the community acts out its various forms of worship. Through these rituals, unity and healing are achieved."[31]

The Commission for the Promotion and Protection of the Cultural, Religious and Linguistic Rights of Communities (CRL Commission) has also received numerous complaints in relation to the reuse of graves. In September 2015, the eThekwini Municipality called on the public to claim all unclaimed family graves, by renewing grave leases to ensure graves more than 10 years old were legally leased. According to eThekwini cemetery by-laws, the city may reuse graves which are more than 10 years old, where leases have not been renewed, after advertising its intention to allow interested lessees to apply for renewals. Religious and traditional leaders were shocked at the call to claim graves for recycling. According to the chairman of the KZN House of Traditional Leaders, Zulu culture did not allow the practice: "In our culture, we respect graves. Once a person has passed away, we respect that person and we can't do anything to remove the grave except to discuss with the family."[32]

According to the Anglican Bishop of KwaZulu-Natal, "For people of all faiths, death isn't burying someone and then forgetting about them. It is much deeper than that and for most faiths there is still a connection."[33] Early this year, the CRL Commission, during an investigation into religious and cultural leaders and practices, also investigated the policy and practices of the eThekwini Municipality in relation to the reuse of graves. The CRL Commission embarked upon a study on "Reuse of Graves by Local Governments: A Solution or Violation of Cultural and Religious Rights of Communities", after receiving a

---

29 See further Ngubane H. 1976. "Some notions of 'purity' and 'impurity' amongst the Zulu", *African Journal of the International African Institute* 46(3):274-284.
30 Saccaggi B and Esterhuysen A. 2014. "Sekuruwe grave relocation: a lesson in process and practice", *The South African Archaeological Bulletin* 69(200):176.
31 Mndende, "Law and religion", 78. For further readings on this topic, please see Mndende N. 2006. *African Spiritual Journey: Rites of Passage among the Xhosa speaking of South Africa.* Cape Town: Icamagu Institute; Mndende N. 2009. *Tears of Distress: Voices of a denied spirituality in a democratic South Africa.* Idutywa: Icamagu Institute; Mbiti S. 2015. *Introduction to African Religion.* Second Edition. Long Grove, IL: Waveland.
32 Comins Lyse. 2015. "Durban's plan to recycle graves", 14 September. Online at: http://www.iol.co.za/news/south-africa/kwazulu-natal/durbans-plan-to-recycle-graves-1915860
33 Ibid.

number of complaints from the public, particularly from the eThekwini Metro Municipal area. According to the Mayor of eThekwini:

> ... dealing with the issue of cemetery space was difficult because cemeteries are competing with developments such as housing, agriculture and infrastructure. It is really a competition between the dead and the living. As Government we have a responsibility to provide housing and other development infrastructure for our people to ensure that we have a sustainable City. On the other hand we have to meet the demand for cemeteries, as we are finding that some of our communities are still sceptical about alternative burial methods that have been identified.[34]

It is clear that municipalities are facing numerous challenges in finding new burial spaces, but the practice of reusing graves is also violating the cultural and religious rights of people.[35] The CRL Commission was informed that local governments' disregard for the principles regarding religious and cultural rights of most communities, have led them to feel that the practice reuse of graves without their consent, is a violation of their religious and cultural rights.[36]

The South African Local Government Association (SALGA) acknowledged that the demand for land for cemeteries is high and recognised that cultural and religious beliefs attached to cemeteries and burial methods of communities cannot be undermined. However, they have made it clear in a statement that:

> SALGA believes that municipalities are within their own right to exercise their bylaws in line with available legislation and thus alternative burial methods, including multiple internments, are legal as provided for in the legislation.[37]

Some of the solutions and alternatives to conventional burial proposed by SALGA include the use of eco-cemetery concepts, intensive recycling of graves, multiple-use approach to cemeteries and the employing a variety of cost-effective methods as alternatives to traditional/in-ground burial, including cremations.[38] According to African Traditional Religion, "a corpse cannot be kept in the homestead, whether it is in the form of bones or ashes; that is

---

34 CRL report, "Reuse of graves by local governments: A solution or violation of cultural and religious rights of communities". Report compiled by the Commission for the Promotion and Protection of the Cultural, Religious and Linguistic Communities, 18. Online at: http://crlcommission.org.za/docs/reuse-report.pdf
35 Nxumalo Mphathi. 2016. "Reused graves issue could go to court", 3 February. Online at: http://www.iol.co.za/news/politics/reused-graves-issue-could-go-to-court-1979455
36 CRL report, 3.
37 Press release. 2015. "Reuse of graves by local governments: a solution or violation of cultural and religious rights of communities". Issued by the South African Local Government Association (SALGA), 3 June. Online at: https://www.facebook.com/permalink.php?id=165498883507659&story_fbid=916054318452108
38 CRL report, 19.

regarded as *isimnyama* (being under dark cloud). Cremation is out, no one can keep ashes at home, neither to sprinkle it in the sea or river; that is out of the question. A deceased individual should be in a grave."[39]

A lot of the problems that communities have experienced seems to be traced back to poor communication, lack of consultation with communities and various stakeholders and poor implementation of the NHRA and other relevant legislation. Section 5 of the NHRA emphasises the fact that heritage resources form an important part of the history and beliefs of communities and must be managed in a way that acknowledges the right of affected communities to be consulted and to participate in their management. This is no easy task and SAHRA recently briefed the parliamentary Tourism Portfolio Committee on the importance of heritage sites in tourism development.[40] The Tourism Portfolio Committee is responsible for the oversight of the Department of Tourism. According to SARHA, they face numerous challenges, including striking a balance between heritage conservation and development of land and the lack of skills and resources in the heritage management sector. SAHRA is further challenged by limited capacity in its core business and provincial heritage resources authorities that are non-functional. The geographical spread of heritage resources nationally makes it very difficult to manage, and numerous of South Africa's heritage sites are in disrepair and need urgent upkeep and maintenance. In this regard funding and cooperation from government departments are lacking.

As outlined above, Section 8 of the NHRA provides for a three-tier system for heritage resources management. One of the challenges faced by SAHRA is the lack of cooperation between the different government spheres and perhaps legislation is needed to compel provinces and local governments to work more closely with the SAHRA. Esterhuysen is of the view that the tiered heritage system is "undeveloped, under-resourced and uncoordinated' and that the communication between the different heritage departments, agencies and councils, and the department of health, environment, and planning at the various government levels, result in 'slow and questionable decision making.'"[41] Concerns were also raised in connection with this system of collaboration, insofar as it might not be the best thing for SAHRA to hand over a heritage site to a provincial or local authority. The parliamentary Tourism Portfolio Committee is of the view that when a site has been handed over to a province or a municipality, the SAHRA should still have responsibility.[42] It has further been argued that the split in functions can be confusing as the communication

---

39 Mndende, "Law and religion", 80.
40 Presentation by SAHRA to the Portfolio Committee on Tourism. 2015. "Importance of Heritage Sites in Tourism Development", Parliament, 4 September. Online at: https://pmg.org.za/committee-meeting/21461/
41 Esterhuysen A. 2009. "Undermining Heritage". *The South African Archaeological Bulletin* 64(189):1.
42 SAHRA, "Importance of Heritage Sites in Tourism Development".

between authorities can be unreliable and it has the potential for applications or complaints to go missing.[43]

In relation to the relocation of human remains, it is argued that different arms of government (i.e. municipalities as well as provincial health departments) are applying the regulations, with no formal obligation on administrators to crosscheck information with another. It is further argued that "it appears that no one from these departments carries out on-site inspections to check that exhumations are carried out.[44] Often administrators in the various heritage agencies and provincial and municipal departments of health, environment and planning work in isolation and are ignorant of the law. A lack of communication and proper consultation was a repeated theme in many of these cases. Communities are not aware of or not informed about the legislation. Communities are often not kept in the loop in relation to the status of the graves or about the processes involved where graves are in the process of being relocated and it is confirmed yet again that "heritage and social assessments and consultation process are carried out independently form one another".[45] Provisions in the NHRA are also not complied with. There seems to the practice that heritage consultants work independently of communities, however, Section 38(3)(e) of the NHRA places an obligation on the responsible heritage resources authority to make sure that the report contains information about the results of consultation with communities affected by the proposed development and other interested parties regarding the impact of the development on heritage resources.

The CRL Commission remains of the view that the reuse of graves remains a disrespectful way of trying to solve the problem of development.They propose that national legislation that deals with the issue of the reuse of graves must be promulgated by parliament with immediate effect and that local governments should stop this practice of reusing graves. This has been acknowledged by SALGA who stated that they will "continue to facilitate engagements with the CRL Commission as well as other affected stakeholders to explore amicable solutions to the land issues in metropolitan municipalities."[46]

Cultural communities are often deeply connected to certain places in the natural world. These religious or sacred sites often carry with them "a whole range of rules and regulations regarding people's behaviour in relation to a set of beliefs to do with the spirits of the ancestors, as well as of more remote and powerful gods or spirits.[47] Sacred sites form part of a community's cultural and religious heritage. The previous discussion has mainly focused on challenges experienced by communities in relation to burial and sacred sites on public land or where

---

43 Saccaggi and Esterhuysen, 174.
44 Saccaggi and Esterhuysen, 179.
45 Saccaggi and Esterhuysen, 180.
46 See SALGA statement.
47 Ratipa, "Just Piles of Rock", 3198-3199.

conflict has arisen over these sites with public authorities. However, in terms of the constitutional protection of the religious rights and heritage of communities in South Africa, another land issue that religious and cultural communities face is the right to visit sacred places and burial sites situated on private land as well as the right to bury on these lands. This challenge brings two competing fundamental rights – the right to freedom of religion (Section 15) and the property clause (Section 25) in direct conflict with each other. With reference to some case studies, the next section will illustrate how courts have attempted to resolve this conflict but also how communities have managed to rely on the existing legislation in order to assert their burial rights on private land.

The right to bury

In South Africa, both the land owners and occupiers are protected by Section 25 of the Constitution. Under Section 25(9) of the Constitution, an Extension of Security of Tenure Act 62 of 1997 (ESTA) was promulgated in order to specify and regulate the rights and duties of occupiers and land owners. The right to bury on farmland has often proved to be problematic. On the one hand, landowners feel that they have a right to enjoy undisturbed use and ownership of their land. On the other hand, occupiers feel that as occupiers of land they have a right of security of tenure including the right to bury their deceased family members on land where they reside.

The case of *Nkosi and Another v. Bührmann*[48] raised a sensitive and emotionally contentious question involving, on the one hand, the right to religious freedom, and particularly the right to practise one's religion, and, on the other hand, the right not to be deprived of one's land except by law. The appellant, Grace Nkosi wished to have the body of her late son, Petros Nkosi, buried on a farm in the Ermelo district where she resided as an occupier. The respondent, who is the owner of the farm, refused consent for the burial. In relation to the right to freedom of religion, the appellants relied heavily on Section 5 of ESTA,[49] more particularly Section 5(d) that provides that an occupier shall have the right to freedom of religion, belief and opinion and of expression. This clause is similar

---

48 *Nkosi and Another v. Bührmann* 2002 1 SA 372 (SCA).
49 "5. Fundamental rights. –
Subject to limitations which are reasonable and justifiable in an open and democratic society based on human dignity, equality and freedom, an occupier, an owner and a person in charge shall have the right to –
  (a) human dignity;
  (b) freedom and security of the person;
  (c) privacy;
  (d) freedom of religion, belief and opinion and of expression;
  (e) freedom of association; and
  (f) freedom of movement,
with due regard to the objects of the Constitution and this Act."

to Section 15 of the Constitution, which guarantees that that everyone has the right to freedom of conscience, religion, thought, belief and opinion.

The appellant argued that central to her religious practice are the rituals of burying the dead, and that because the land they occupy is the only resource by means of which they can exercise their religious right and manifest its practice, such right must include the right to bury their dead on that land. To that right, therefore, the right of ownership has to yield.[50] With reference to various cases, the court undertook an interpretative exercise by starting with a discussion of the ESTA Section5(d) right to religious freedom.[51] The main question that they had to address in relation to the right to freedom of religion was whether the right to freedom of religion entitled the appellant by law to take some of the respondent's land for a grave. The court acknowledged that funeral and graveside rites, rituals and ceremonies are very much part of religious beliefs and practice[52] and that it is the right of all citizens to observe and carry out their religious practices when burying their dead.[53] According to the facts in that case, the appellant did not claim that funeral and graveside rituals could not be observed in the case of a burial elsewhere. According to the court:

> In those circumstances it cannot be said, without more, that the appellant's constitutional rights to practise her religious and cultural beliefs (that are protected by s 15 and s 31) will be denied to her if the burial is not permitted. That does not exclude the possibility, however, that where religious or cultural beliefs are so inherently attached to particular land that the right to hold and practise them would be denied if the rights of ownership are asserted, the latter rights might be equired to give way. That does not arise in the present case.[54]

The court highlighted the fact that a burial not only requires a piece of ground to be available, but also the necessary permission or consent of the land owner, whether the state, a juristic person or an individual.[55] The court came to the conclusion that the right to freedom of religion and religious practice has internal limits. "It does not confer unfettered liberty to choose a grave site nor does it include the right to take a grave site without the consent of the owner of the land concerned. It follows that s 5(d) of the Act does not, when viewed in isolation, confer the right which the appellant claims."[56] The court subsequently dismissed the appeal.

When the judgment in the *Nkosi* case was given, Section 6(2)(dA) was not yet part of ESTA. As a result of this judgment, the legislature enacted Section 6(2)dA). In terms of Section 6(2)(dA) of ESTA, an occupier shall have the right to bury

---

50 *Nkosi*, para 32.
51 *Nkosi*, para 41-44.
52 *Nkosi*, para 46.
53 *Nkosi*, para 47.
54 *Nkosi*, para 46.
55 *Nkosi*, para 47.
56 *Nkosi*, para 49.

a deceased member of his or her family who at the time of that person's death, was residing on the land on which the occupier is residing, in accordance with their religion or cultural belief, if an established practice in respect of the land exists. In order to enjoy this protection, the occupier must thus establish on the balance of probabilities that:

- he or she is an 'occupier' on the farm where he or she intends burying the deceased on;
- the deceased was a member of his or her family;
- the burial sought would be in accordance with his or her religious and/or cultural beliefs;
- the deceased was residing on land, which the occupier resided at the time of death of the deceased; and
- an established practice on land exists to bury deceased family members.

"Established practice" in terms of ESTA means a practice by which the owner or person in charge or his or her predecessor in title routinely gave permission to people residing on the land to bury deceased members of their family on that land in accordance with their religion or cultural belief.

In the case of *Nhlabathi*,[57] the family of Kiti Elijah Nhlabathi approached the Land Claims Court (LCC) for an order permitting his burial in the Nhlabathi graveyard on the farm Mooifontein. The deceased had been living in the same household with the applicants on the farm. The Nhlabathi family informed the owner of the farm of the death of the deceased and requested permission for his remains to be buried on the farm. The owner firmly rejected the request. The Nhlabathi family then approached the LCC and relied on Section 6(2)(dA) of ESTA. The court ordered that the family is entitled, in terms of Section 6(2)(dA) of ESTA to bury the body of Kiti Elijah Nhlabathi on the farm Mooifontein. The court was happy to conclude that nothing was put before them to substantiate a submission that the proprietary rights of the owner in this case might outbalance the burial rights of the first applicant and that at the time of his death, the deceased was residing on Mooifontein. In the court's view, there existed an established practice to permit the burial of deceased occupiers and members of their families on the farm Mooifontein. The applicants belonged to the Christian Church in Zion. The burial would be conducted in accordance with the rites of that church, just as the burials of the two Nhlabathi children, Zandile and Albert.

In *Dlamini and Another v. Joosten and Others*[58] the family of Gertrude Ntombi Zondia approached the LCC for an urgent order in that they be permitted to bury the deceased at the Dlamini family burial site on the farm Bockenhoud

---

57 *Nhlabathi and Others v. Fick* [2003] 2 All SA 323 (LCC) para 36.
58 *Dlamini and Another v. Joosten and Others* 2006 (3) SA 342 (SCA).

Fontein, a farm owned by the Joosten family. In the LCC, Bam JP refused to permit the burial, but granted leave to appeal against its decision to the Supreme Court of Appeal (SCA). The Dlamini family has resided and worked on the farm for generations, and over the years they had buried their deceased on the farm in accordance with their religion and cultural belief with the consent of the Joostens. However, in 2002 the Joosten family withdrew the permission, and when the Dlaminis sought permission from the Joostens to bury the deceased, this was refused. The Dlaminis submitted that it is a religious or cultural belief that deceased members of their family must be buried close to their homestead so that the spirits of their ancestors might be close to them. According to them, "It was and is extremely important to my late wife and I that we were entitled to bury our deceased family members near our home on the farm, as it is a cultural imperative for us that our ancestors and our family members are buried close to our home."[59]

The Dlamini's based their cause of action on Section 6(2)(dA) of ESTA, which permits a person who occupies land that belongs to another person to bury deceased members of his or her family on that land if permission for burials had routinely been given in the past. They argued successfully that once a practice of allowing burials had been established on the farm, as it had been in the case of the deceased, it could not be withdrawn unilaterally. The SCA upheld the appeal.

CONCLUSION

The chapter has sought to give an overview of some of the legal mechanisms in place to protect and promote communities' religious rights, particularly in relation to burial places. Various factors may have an influence when local communities are involved in disputes relating to their sacred sites. Some of these factors highlighted in this chapter included a lack of communication and engagement with communities and also ignorance of the laws, procedures and practices that are available to communities in order to assert their religious rights. It has been noted that certain stakeholder groups such as the poor, women and the youth are not effectively engaged in cases affecting burial rights, often due to a lack of financial resources to attend public meetings or a lack of access to newspapers in which notices are published. Often there are also language barriers when it comes to notices and communications, Concerns can also not be adequately understood or addressed.[60] In cases where there is a plan to reuse a grave, the CRL Commission proposes that local governments should ask all affected family members to decide which members should be buried together in one grave. Local governments should also appropriately and effectively engage in discussions with all affected communities before closing

---

59 *Dlamini*, para 21.
60 Saccaggi and Esterhuysen, 179.

down cemeteries or reusing graves in their areas.[61] Direction can also be taken from the Regulations on fair administrative procedures, made in terms of Section 10 of the Promotion of Administrative Justice Act 3 of 2000. In relation to public hearings in a community consisting of a considerable proportion of people who cannot read or write or who otherwise need special assistance, an administrator must notify people in that area in a manner and language that will bring the matter to the attention of the community at large, such as group meetings, surveys, the Internet, radio or television broadcasts, posters or leaflets and secretarial assistance to persons. When communities are involved in a dispute, the way in which an argument is formulated and presented to court can also make or break a case. It is essential that communities themselves have input into the process. The various case studies in relation to the ESTA Act have illustrated that communities can be successful in asserting their religious rights where they construct good religious arguments in terms of the applicable laws.

The SACRRF further plays an important role since it states specifically that religious institutions have the right to determine its own religious affairs and that the the state must create a positive and safe environment for the exercise of religious freedom. In approving a plan for the development of land, the state must also consider religious needs.[62] Since the SACRRF provides for the right of communities to access sacred places and burial sites relevant to their convictions, they have to make sure that those involved clearly understand their views and convictions.

The right to freedom of religion provides religious communities with the opportunity, but also the responsibility, not only to give content to this right, but also to formulate and defend their own religious identity within the limitations set by the Constitution and the law. The NHRA provides that laws, procedures and administrative practices must be clear and generally available to those affected thereby. They must serve as regulatory measures but also provide guidance and information to those affected thereby. These laws and procedures must further give content to the fundamental rights set out in the Constitution, set out above.[63] Communities should therefore explore all the possible avenues available to them. This include, but are not limited to the common law, national legislation, local government by-laws, customary law, constitutional provisions, international law and examples of cases decide by various courts.

Churches and religious institutions can also play a role in supporting their communities in preserving and protecting their heritage. Religion is a vital aspect of cultural heritage in South Africa for many individuals and groups. According to the National Heritage Council, "it is imperative that religious organisations (whether churches or traditional religious groups) as part of their

---

61   CRL report, 21.
62   The South African Charter of Religious Rights and Freedoms, s 3.1.
63   NHRA, s 5(3).

obligations, position themselves as positive custodians of social and cultural values of the communities they serve."[64]

---

[64] Mancotywa Sonwabile. 2014. "Critical Conversations about Heritage, Popularising Contemporary Heritage Issues. National Heritage Council of South Africa", 10. Online at: http://www.nhc.org.za/a-book-that-sparks-debate-about-contemporary-heritage-issues-launched/

21 REGULATING DEATH AND FUNERAL RITES IN A SECULAR BUT RELIGIOUSLY PLURALISTIC SOCIETY: THE CASE OF THE CORONER LAW SYSTEM IN LAGOS STATE, NIGERIA

Danoye Oguntola-Laguda[1]

INTRODUCTION

In Nigeria, secularism has been the determining principle for government engagement in religious matters. Section 10 of the 1999 Constitution of the Federal Republic of Nigeria substantiates this claim. However, the realities in the country suggest a religious pluralised environment in which competing religious traditions contest for space and influence of government policies. The political class have also appropriated religion as a tool of negotiation during electioneering campaigns and process.[2] Consequently, the policies and engagements of government have been influenced by religious beliefs and traditions towards the people and international organisations.

Such was the case of the controversy over Nigerian membership of Organisation of the Islamic Conference (OIC) in the 1980s, when the military government had to jettison the planned membership due to protest from the Christians under the auspices of the Christian Association of Nigeria (CAN). The Christian group believed that joining OIC was the beginning of the Islamisation of the country. Muslims in Lagos State also protested the government return of schools to missionary groups in 1999. Muslim groups, such Ahmaddiyah and Ansar-Ud-Deen believed this constituted a process of marginalisation of Muslims in the state, as they lacked the capacity to manage such schools at that time.

Another recent controversy in Lagos State was the reactions of Muslim communities in the state to the Coroner Law System (CLS). The CLS was passed into law in 2007 by the Lagos State House of Assembly.[3] The law was to check cases of questionable deaths and regulate funeral rites and processes in the state, especially in public institutions such as health centres and in cases of deaths of individuals in police custody. The law demands a postmortem examination of all corpses to determine the cause of death. This would necessarily delay

---

1 Department of Religions and Peace Studies, Lagos State University, Ojo, Lagos, Nigeria.
2 See Oguntola-Laguda D. 2015. "Religion, leadership and struggle for power in Nigeria: A case study of the 2003 presidential election in Nigeria", in Coertzen P, Green MC and Hansen L (eds). *Religious Freedom and Religious Pluralism in Africa: Prospects and Limitations*. Stellenbosch, South Africa: African Sun Media, 143-156.
3 Lagos State Coroner Law System. 2007. Lagos: LSPC, August.

funeral process of dead Muslims, who are supposed to be buried immediately after death. This led to protests against the CLS by Muslims communities in Lagos State.

The consternation that the CLS prompted in the Lagos State Muslim community is familiar to anyone who considers the religious and social context of grief and mourning of death around the world. Two decades ago, the American Christian political philosopher Nicholas Wolterstorff mourned the death of his son with the following words: "It's so wrong, so painfully wrong, for a child to die before its parents. It's hard enough to bury our parents. But that we expect. Our parents belong to our past, our children belong to our future. We do not visualize our future without them. How can I bury my son, my future, one of the next in line? He was meant to bury me."[4] Wolterstorff's words upon the death of his child underscore the importance of funeral rites and the pain of death to every human being, especially in cases of the death of a child or a young person in the extended family. The German philosopher Martin Heidegger posited that death marks the end of life of any living thing. Its occurrence is not an accident, but a phenomenon with existential origins. For him, "Dying is not just an event that occurs to man at the close of his life, but a man's mode of being. For Dasein (man) is a being towards death. A being who begin to die the very day he was born and live all his life towards death."[5] This opinion suggests that death is a process humans need to prepare for and to which family and friends must inevitably respond.

In the African context, the Kenyan-born philosopher and theologian John Mbiti argues that death "is something that concerns everybody, partly because sooner or later, everyone personally faces it and partly because it brings loss and sorrow to every family and community".[6] Mbiti underscores the basic implications of death to African people by explaining its universality and effects on the society, particularly as it comes with sorrow, grief and pain. Writing about the Yoruba of South-West, Nigeria, Bolaji Idowu, an anthropologist, posits that death is a creation of God.[7] Death becomes an agent that God uses to call people whose time on earth is fulfilled back to the celestial world. The Yoruba people, like other Nigerian tribes, accept the reality of death with conviction that it is inevitable. However, the Yoruba also believe that death is only good for the aged, but that this is not the case when infants, youth and young adults die. Deaths of the aged are often celebrated, while those of children come with sorrow, grief and plenty of mourning.[8] After death comes the funeral rite. To Nigerians, funeral

---

4 Wolterstorff N. 1997. *Lament for a Son*. London: SPCK, 16.
5 Heidegger M. 1967. *Being and Time*. Macquarie J and Robinson E (trans). Oxford: Basil Blackwell, 8.
6 Mbiti JS. 1982. *African Religions and Philosophy*. London: Heinemann, 8.
7 Idowu EB. 1996. *Olodumare: God in Yoruba Belief*. Sixth Edition. Lagos: Longman.
8 See Oguntola-Laguda D. 2014. "Conceptualizing Death In Yoruba Religion and Philosophy", in Oguntola-Laguda D (ed). *Death and Life After Death in African Philosophy and Religions: A Multi Disciplinary Engagement*. Harare: African Institute for Culture, Dialogue, Peace and Tolerance.

rites are very crucial to the transition of the dead to the celestial world. It is a formal ritual that must be done with care and reverence; otherwise, the dead will not transit properly to the realm of the ancestors.

It is funeral rites and rituals like these that the Lagos State government now proposes to regulate through the Coroner Law System. This law is intended to regulate the process of funeral and burial of dead persons in the state, regardless of the religion that the deceased individual practised while alive. The aim of the CLS is to regulate and check cases of questionable death in public institutions such as police detention, prisons, and hospices. It is, however, the case that religious rights of some Nigerians have been infringed by the CLS. Muslims, in particular, have been the most affected by the CLS, as introduced in Lagos State in 2007. This law was used to investigate the death of people at the Synagogue Church of All Nations (SCOAN) in 2014 in a way that became a matter of controversy. Thus, Asonzeh Ukah, a Nigerian scholar of religion has argued that the SCOAN case "graphically illustrates the complexity and contradictions that exist in the relationship between … the law and the state".[9] Ukah observes that the state promulgates the law and enforces it through its agents for the good of the society. Further, religion also acts in public interest. This suggests that there is a symbiotic relationship between religion and the state.

Even so, this chapter proposes that the nature of religious pluralism in Nigeria does not support secularism. Instead, it allows competing religious epistemologies to seek government attention and interaction to further and protect the interests of particular religious communities. This chapter seeks to re-examine the religious landscape in Nigeria base on the concepts of pluralism and secularisation through analysis of the Coroner Law System introduced in Lagos State in 2007, as it has affected funeral rites for the dead in the multi-religious environment of Lagos State.

RELIGION, PLURALISM AND SECULARISM IN NIGERIA

Religious groups do rise up in protest against government policies when its affects their tenets and doctrines. In Nigeria, there has been ecumenical opposition by religious groups on critical national issues. Such was the case with respect to LGBT rights issues in the Nigerian polity between 2011 and 2014, during the process of formulation and signing into law the Same Sex Marriage (Prohibition) Act, 2013. Muslims and Christian groups together supported the government position to ban homosexual activities in the country. In this instance, the law forbad LGBT advocacy and practices in the country, with jail sentences attached to its violation. The government position with regards to the SSMA was supported by all religious groups in the country, creating an ecumenical

---

9   Ukah A. 2015. "Prophecy, miracle, and tragedy: The afterlife of T.B. Joshua's ministry and the Nigerian state", in Coertzen P, Green MC and Hansen L (eds). *Religious Freedom and Religious Pluralism in Africa: Prospects and Limitations*. Stellenbosch: African Sun Media, 210.

front against the LGBT communities in Nigeria. Indeed, the government, for its part, relied on religious perspectives and religious scriptures as a basis for the law, claiming that LGBT activities are sacrilegious. While LGBT rights are an issue distinct from the CLS, the point here is that even though Christians and Muslims are frequently on opposite sides in their reactions to government policies in ways that lead them to cite the secular nature of the country for their own protection, when they have a perceived common enemy, they are capable of alignment in support of the government.

Secularism in Nigeria, therefore, protects the religiosity of the citizens and allows for government engagement in religious matters. This explains why some scholars have argued that secularism in Nigeria is a ruse, as the government uses public funds to support religious practices. Sections 45 and 145 of the Nigerian Constitution, in particular, permit the government to provide an enabling environment for the practice of religions in the country. This was the justification for the building of both the Christian Ecumenical Centre and National Central Mosque in Abuja, as Nigerian Islamic scholar Is-haq Oloyede has concluded.[10] It is clear, however, that there is a symbiotic interaction between political actors – specifically, government officials – and religious leaders and communities. Public funds have often been used to support religious rituals and rites. The situation has created paradoxes that demand critical evaluation in order to strike a balance between government policy formulation and their influence on religious communities, and how these paradoxes have shaped religious identities in Nigeria.

The term pluralism suggests that there are pluralities of particular ideologies in competition. The ideologies may be competing for political power, economic control or survival. It can be cultural, ethnic or tribal struggle for supremacy.[11] Religious pluralism exists when more than one religious tradition is in competition with each other to gain converts, occupy spaces and seek attention from governments and the people. Gordon Melton, a sociologist, writing about religious pluralism in the West, claims that:

> During the 20th century the West has experienced a phenomenon it has not encountered since the reign of Constantine, the growth of a significant visible presence of a variety of non-Christian and non-orthodox Christian bodies competing for religious allegiance of the public. This growth of so many alternatives religiously is forcing the West into a new situation in which the still dominant Christian religion must share its centuries old hegemony in a new pluralistic religious environment.[12]

---

10 See Oloyede IO. 2014. "Theologising the Mudane, Politicising the Divine: The Cross Currents of Law, Religion and Politics in Nigeria", *African Human Rights Law Journal* 14(1):178-202.
11 See Oguntola-Laguda D. 2004. *Religion: Study and Practice in Nigeria*. Lagos: Free Enterprise Publishers.
12 Melton G. 1998. "Modern Alternative Religions in the West", in Hinnells JR (ed). *A New Handbook of Living Religions*. Harmondsworth, U.K.: Penguin, 594.

Melton's position seems to describe aptly the religious plurality that now permeates the world. It is also relevant to the Nigerian situation, where traditional African religious cosmologies now compete with the cosmologies and epistemologies of Christianity and Islam.

Religious pluralism has made adoption of secularism a necessity for states where more than one religious ideology is prevalent. To my mind, it is to prevent government intervention in religious matters and remove the influence and consideration of religious creeds, doctrines and rituals in government policies and functions. It could be an attempt to avoid conflicts and promote religious tolerance among competing religious ideologies. It could also be to pursue the theories of sociologists like Peter L Berger, who has suggested that secularisation and modernity go hand in hand.[13] The intention of the government of Nigeria, however, at least since independence in 1960, has been to try to be neutral among competing religious epistemologies. The aforementioned controversies over the attempt to join OIC and to return schools to missionaries indicate that such neutrality is subjective.

The reality is that the world is today neither wholly secular nor wholly religious, but religions have affected humanity both more positively and more negatively than has secularity. This is contrary to the position of Norwegian sociologists Inger Furseth and Pål Repstad, who argue that "secularization is the consequence of the differentiation process whereby system in society have become relative, independent from religious norms, values, and legitimations".[14] Secularisation theories are attempts to account for how pluralism has re-shaped religious competitions and also reduced religion to private engagements into which the government should not intrude. In Nigeria, even though the Constitution suggests the existence of a secular state, the state has always appropriated religion in its policies and laws. This new order and the tensions that it has introduced between secularism and religion seems to be fertile ground for competing epistemologies.

In the opinion of sociologist of religion Kevin Christiano and colleagues, pluralism, by its nature, has "multiplicative effects".[15] As they rightly note, ever increasing pluralism does undermine the absolute certainty that has been claimed by some religions, for example, the monotheistic faiths of Judaism, Christianity, and Islam and Judaism. Each new religion spawns more new religions, and these new religions continually arise to test this argument. Thus, Christiano and his fellow researchers conclude: "The more one becomes

---

13   Berger PL. 1997. "Epistemological Modesty: An Interview with Peter Berger", *Christian Century* 114:974. It should be noted that Berger, more recently, has questioned his own secularisation thesis in light of global religious resurgence. See Berger PL (ed). *The Desecularization of the World: Resurgent Religion and World Politics*. Grand Rapids, MI: Wm B Eerdmans Publishers, 1999.
14   Furseth I and Repstad P. 2010. *An Introduction to the Sociology of Religion: Classical and Contemporary Perspectives.* Aldershot: Ashgate.
15   Christiano KJ, Swatos WH (Jr) and Kivisto P. 2008. *Sociology of Religion: Contemporary Development*. Lanham, MD: Rowman and Littlefield Publishers.

aware of more and more religious competition in a marketplace-like setting, the harder it becomes to assert that one religion contains all truth and that the others must be wrong. While it is certainly possible to make comparisons of better and worse, all-or-nothing rigidity simply doesn't hold up."[16] Historically, Islamic nations (such as Iran, Pakistan, Bangladesh, Saudi Arabia) have not permitted the "free commerce" in religion that has become the hallmark of western democracy. In Africa, with its pronounced plurality of religions, it may be difficult for the state to engage in religious monopoly. In Nigeria, for example, the religious landscape is a free-market situation in which demand for spiritual solutions to spiritual needs determines supply. This is simply because of its religious pluralism. Thus, we can submit that monopoly is the antithesis of pluralism of the Nigerian situation.

Religious pluralism creates a marketplace of ideas in which absolute claims for "ultimate truth" are always at some degree of risk. The free-market situation gives freedom to the "buyers" to pick and choose among competing ideologies those that satisfy their "need" – materially and spiritually. Based on the free market model, Christiano and colleagues posit two theories on secularisation as follows: First, there is substantial body of evidence that pluralism of belief (including disbelief) has been intensified due to globalisation. Second, pluralisation forces us to make distinction between secularisation and what might be called new religious movements that may emerge or other world traditions may gain dominance over a traditional historical epistemology.[17] The latter as was the case with Christianity in the West and African Traditional Religions (ATR).

It can be argued that, the market situation proposed by Christiano and his fellow researchers leads inevitably to syncretism. A "buyer" seeking solution to a multi-faceted problem may "shop" to meet his or her needs in different shops or supermarkets where all "products" seem to be available. This syncretism does not make the "buyer" irreligious, but rather makes it more interesting and challenging to choose among the competing "brands". New religious pluralism therefore provokes new syncretism, since it seems the religious "boundaries" have been broken down in the face of pluralism.

It can also be argued that religious pluralism necessitates secularisation, wherein appropriation of values in policies formulation can be done without religious justifications or rationales. In other words, under conditions of religious pluralism, religion loses its capacity to impose its beliefs and practices, and the society claims the capacity to lead its own destiny without religious participation. An individual will therefore be able to examine the ideologies, epistemologies, doctrines, tenets and practices of the competing religions and make his or her choice based on "needs". There are limitations here as to what

---

16   Christiano et al., *Sociology of Religion*, 75.
17   Christiano et al., *Sociology of Religion*, 74.

will be available for sale. This goes to support the thesis of Furseth and Repstad,[18] as well as Berger's thesis that "modern pluralism causes individual perception of reality to lose its self-evident status, becoming a matter of choice".[19] However, Berger now claims that this does not necessarily lead to secularisation.

The Nigeria situations suggest an antithesis of Berger's secularisation thesis, especially when applied to state policies formulation. Government appropriates religious doctrines and values into laws as well as policies. This was the case in the SSMA 2013 against the activities of LGBT communities in the country. However, the situation with the CLS seems a bit different, as religious values were not considered in the formulation of the law. The implication is that the Nigerian government is inconsistent in its appropriation or non-appropriation of religious values.

RELIGIOUS PLURALISM IN NIGERIA

As stated earlier, the Constitution of the Federal Republic of Nigeria of 1999, like other constitutions before it, claims that the state is a secular state. The implication of this claim is that religion shall not be a factor in governance and the responsibility to lead, and that governance rests solely on the constitution, customs, traditions and culture of the federated "groups". However, the realities on ground suggest the contrary. Not only is the country religiously plural, but, as noted above, religion has continually been a factor in government policy formulation and implementation of laws in many cases. It is therefore apposite to consider the religious landscape in Nigeria, as a way to understand how religious diversities play out in the country and the promulgation of the laws that govern it.

There are three competing religions in Nigeria – Islam, Christianity and African Traditional Religion (ATR). These competing ideologies jostle for space in the mind of about 180 million Nigerians. It should be noted, however, that Islam and Christianity are the dominant religions. It is very difficult, if not impossible, to put the religious demography of the country into figures, due to religious politics and the politics of religious statistics in the country. The general opinion is that Muslims are predominant in the North, while Christians dominate the South.[20]

Islamic groups in Nigeria

Islam was introduced into the country through the North and the trans-Saharan trade through the desert of North Africa. Since its introduction, it has spread

---

18 Furseth and Repstad, *Introduction to the Sociology of Religion*, 91.
19 Berger, "Epistemological Modesty", 978.
20 See Adogame A. 2011. "How God became a Nigerian: Religious Impulse and the Unfolding Nation", in Obadare E and Adebanwi W (eds). *Nigeria at Fifty: The Nation in Narration*. London: Routledge.

all over the country. Missions and groups have emerged, propagating Islamic tenets and doctrines. The groups could be divided into three: (1) mission groups (e.g. Ansar-Ud-Deen Society, Nawal-Ud-Deen Society, Zumratul-ul Islamiyah Society), (2) spiritualist groups, who engage in healing and soothsaying for the patrons (such as that of of Shaykh Abdul Hamid Olohungbemi, founder of Shamsu-d-diniil-Islamiyyah[21]) and (3) the so-called Islamic "Pentecostals" (e.g. Nasru-Lahil-Fatil Society (NASFAT), Quareeb Society (QUAREEB), Nadwatul-Ahli Society of Nigeria (NADWAT)).[22] The last group is popular in South West Nigeria where prayers and lectures are organised every Sunday for the faithful. This is what Nigerian religion scholar Abdul Lateef Adetona refers to as the "prayer market".[23]

It should also be noted that Islam and Muslims in Nigeria have used religion as a tool of social identity, political negotiation and economic empowerment. This has led to establishment of groups among students and youths in secondary and tertiary institutions. An example is the (MSSN) to spearhead agitation for emancipation of Muslim youths in the Nigerian polity. Women's groups, such as Federation of Muslim Women in Nigeria (FOMWAN), were also created to seek for the recognition of women in the country. These groups educate Muslims on their social and political rights and encourage Muslims to be active in politics and economic discourses in the country. These groups have become active in the political development of the country. For example, during military rule in Nigeria (1983-1999), Muslims were among those who agitated for the institution of democracy. In this regard the Supreme Council for Islam in Nigeria (SCIN) and National Council of Muslim Youth Organisations (NACOMYO) were in the forefront of the movement. In Nigeria, it would seem the Muslims are more unified compared to the Christians in the "spiritual marketplace".

Christian groups

Christianity was introduced to Nigeria by the mission groups in 1842. Since then, various groups have emerged. These groups have been major social and political advocates in the country. Prime examples of these groups include the African Independent Churches (AICs) and the Pentecostal and charismatic churches. Some of these groups emerged from the mission churches. And, indeed, in the socio-political front, Christian churches played a pivotal role in

---

21 See Bello MA. 2002. *Shaykh Abdul Hamid Olohungbemi and His Dawah Activities in Ado Odo (Ogun state) and Its Environs*, MA Thesis, Lagos State University.
22 Adetona LM. 2005. "Role of Muslim Youth in the Implementation of Shariah in Contemporary Nigerian Society". Paper presented to the African Association for the Study of Religions, Legon, Ghana. See also Sanni A. 2004. "Prayer Youth Movement – A case of NASFAT". Paper presented at the African Association for the Study of Religions regional conference, Legon, Ghana.
23 Adetona LM. 2012. "NASFAT: A Modern Prayer Group and its Contributions to the Propagation of Islam in Lagos", *World Journal of Islamic History and Civilization* 2(2):164.

the movement for Nigeria's independence. Christian churches have continued to seek good governance, corruption-free leadership and good social values for the country. The efforts of the Christian groups are often publicised through the umbrella of the Christian Association of Nigeria (CAN) and the Pentecostal Fellowship of Nigeria (PFN).

It should be noted that there is competition, even among the Christian groups, for the soul of the people. Thus, we can talk about pluralism even among the Christians in Nigeria. Christian groups have turned Nigeria into a spiritual marketplace where "religious trade fairs" are organised regularly to "cater" to the needs of the people. The Christian groups have taking their "wares" to the electronic media, buying airtime for preaching and converting souls. They often give phone numbers, email addresses and internet websites where they can be contacted for prayers. This situation, arguably, has weakened the focus of the groups and made the Christian tradition a means to prosperity, social relevance and empowerment for the leaders, while the congregations continue to wallow in poverty, ignorance, unemployment and disease. To confront these problems, Christians in Nigeria have continuously moved from one church to another in a pluralised Christian environment seeking "products" in a "religious department store", where salvation, miracles, prosperity and healing are the major "goods" on display".

African traditional religions

The third religious tradition in Nigeria is African traditional religion, popularly referred to by many scholars as African Traditional Religion (ATR). This religion has dominated the politics, economics, social and cultural landscape of the people of Nigeria before the advent of Islam and Christianity. It should be noted however, that there still are Nigerians who are patrons and adherents of these religions, even though few. Though there is little demographic data to support this claim, it seems to be the case that the membership base of the ATRs is not increasing as fast as that of the Muslims and Christians. My hypothesis here is based on anecdotal evidence from my 21 years of research of these groups. These religions have been organising and modernising their traditions, so as to attract patronage. In fact, for the last decade, 20 August every year has been declared *Isese* (traditional) Day by the Lagos State government, in deference to traditional religion in Lagos State. This is because Lagos due to its cosmopolitan nature is religiously diversified and pluralised. It should be noted that this is peculiar to Lagos.

There are many variations among the African traditional religious groups in Nigeria. Conservative groups tend to practice pristine forms of traditional religion. Liberal groups are sometimes accused of syncretism for combining traditional religion with Islam or Christianity. There are also those who, in the name of modernity, appropriate Islamic and Christian values to "sell" ATR to Nigerians. In this category, we have Ijo Orunmila Adulawo and Ijo Orunmila or Ato. These groups have appropriated Christian liturgy as part of their tenets and doctrines. They have a creed, hymnbook and standing choir, with leadership patterned after the Anglican Church structure. There is also a notable "syncretic" group known as Chrislamherb. Found among the Yoruba people, this group blends Islam and Christian traditions with ATR. It is interesting to note that the traditional religious groups have become significant forces in the attempt to occupy and dominate the Nigerian religious space.

NEW PLURALISM AND ENGAGED SECULARISM IN THE NIGERIAN RELIGIOUS SPACE

It may not be wrong to claim that Nigeria is a hub of religious rituals and practices on the African continent. Religions in Nigeria play deterministic roles in politics, economy and social engagement of the leaders and followers in a country that claims to be secular. This is also true of government formulation of laws and policies. We can therefore argue that Nigeria is a religiously pluralistic country, where multiple religious traditions compete for the mind of the populace.

This perhaps may contradict the aforementioned constitutional position that Nigeria is a secular state. While it is true that the state has not adopted any religion as official, the rulers have continuously appropriated religious values in policy formulation and implementation. Eleven days are declared public holidays in Nigeria for religious reasons. Political processes and programmes must give due recognition to religion for them to be acceptable to the electorate. For example, it has become a tradition for political parties in Nigeria to always apply "religious balance" in the selection and presentation of candidates for electoral offices.

The idea that pluralism is the cause for secularisation cannot hold true in Nigeria. While religious pluralism can lead to secularisation, or separation of religion and state according to the American model, it cannot be true of the developing nations in Africa as the Nigerian example has shown. On the contrary, secularism in Nigeria allows for and at times manipulation of the values of more than one religion in the making of government policies, legislations and programmes, so that government maintain balance among all religious epistemologies in the polity. This policy of what might be called "engaged secularism" is different from the theories on secularism as discussed above. It is a new model that called for further academic engagement.

Syncretism is one of the attendant effects of religious pluralism. This concept suggests a combination of two or more religious traditions to form one. In fact, in an environment where there are many religions showcasing their "wares", there is bound to be syncretism, since the "needs" of the people will determine what they will "buy" in the "spiritual supermarket". As mentioned earlier, Nigerians are faced with the problems of hunger, disease, ignorance, spiritual attacks and bad governance, among others. Any religion that "displays" solutions to these problems will be patronised by the people.

To examine this phenomenon, research undertaken for the analysis here included a structured questionnaire administered in Lagos by the present writer and some postgraduate students among selected educated upward mobile religious youth between the ages of 25 and 45. About 65% of the respondents to the questionnaire on this issue agreed that they patronise more than one religious group to tackle the challenges confronting them. A solid 30% claimed they are committed to the tenets and doctrines of their religion as a solution to these problems. The other 5% are not bothered about the situation and feel that spiritual solutions to social and economic problems will come naturally.

Therefore, the Nigerian situation suggests that there is no religious monopoly in responding to the myriad of problems facing the country. A combination of two or three religious "wares" may bring the ideal solution to the problems of the people. In a religiously plural society like Nigeria, people will adopt and appropriate multi-religious panaceas to their spiritual and material problems. Where there are alternative epistemologies, people tend to seek multiple solutions to issues confronting them. The implication is that no one religion has solutions to the multi-faceted problems of the modern world. The crux of the matter is to determine how religious groups respond to government policy formulations and how government has often responded to agitations for withdrawal of its policies when it seem to affects the beliefs, doctrines and rituals of some religious groups. The Coroner Law System in Lagos State is an excellent case study for understanding this dynamic.

RELIGION AND GOVERNMENT POLICY AND LAW FORMULATIONS: THE CASE OF THE CORONER LAW SYSTEM IN LAGOS STATE

The Lagos State House of Assembly (LSHA) enacted the Coroner Law System to regulate the process of death investigations and other related matters in the state. The law became operational in 2007, forty years after the creation of the state. A Chief Coroner, Chief Medical Examiner and District Medical Examiners are to be appointed to oversee the implementation of the law. The Chief Coroner (CC) is at the head of the implementation team. The Chief Medical Examiner (CME) is responsible to the (CC), and it is he who determines the cause and circumstances of death. The District Medical Examiners (DMEs) are to work with the CME from the five divisions of the state. Section 14 of the CLS stipulates that a report of death shall be made to the office of the coroner and that deaths may be subjected to postmortem examination where there is reasonable cause to believe that the cause of death was unknown, sudden, unexpected and unnatural. It also involves situation of unreported death, violent, suspicious, accidental, self-neglect, negligence by others, due to medical misconduct, suicide, suspected suicide or assisted suicide.

Section 15 of the CLS mandates that the Coroner hold an inquest whenever he is informed that the death of a deceased person lying within his coroner district was a result of death from one of the possible causes mentioned in Section 14. The Coroner is also empowered by the CLS to order exhumation of bodies that have been buried without postmortem with prior authorisation of the medical examiners, especially in cases where inquest is necessary. Further, Section 23 of the CLS makes it mandatory that all deaths should be reported to the appropriate coroner agencies. This includes deaths of family members and people in the community, as well as death in police custody or jail or in medical hospice. Section 28 permits the medical examiners to perform a postmortem for the purpose of establishing the cause and manner of death, even if it requires retaining any human tissue or other parts from the body of a dead person. In such cases, the medical examiner should apply and obtain the consent of the Coroner and next of kin of the deceased person.

The above are some of the provisions of the CLS. The law became operational in Lagos in 2007 and immediately became a subject of debate among religious groups in Lagos. Muslims have been vehement in their opposition to the implementation of the law. To them, it is against the traditions and doctrines of Islam in relation to death and funeral rites of Muslims. In Islam, a dead person is expected to be buried immediately after death regardless of the time of death. This requirement precludes conducting a postmortem investigation to determine the cause of death. The underlying belief is that Allah gives life at birth and takes it at death. Further, all parts of the body at the time of death must be buried as part of the funeral rites. Consequently, the retention of tissues or other parts of the body, as specified by the CLS, is against Islamic traditions on funeral rites. According to Abdul Lateef Adetona, one of the three imams of Lagos State University's mosque, the enactment of the CLS did not take into cognisance the feelings of Muslims in the state.[24]

In the opinion of Muslim Mahmud of Okepopo Quranic Mosque, the CLS is anathema to Islamic traditions as mentioned above; however, he admitted that the CLS did not violate any specific injunction of the Quran.[25] In his opinion, the Islamic traditions on burial and funeral rites are based on Arab customs and traditions of the prophet. According to these traditions, Muslims bury their death on the same day that the death occurs or if late in the night, then the next morning. Decomposing corpses can also cause environmental and health hazards to the community, thus the tradition of immediate burial. Ustaz Kabir Paramole, the Chief Missioner of Jejewiyyat Islamic Movement in Lagos suggested that the CLS cannot be sustained in a pluralistic and cosmopolitan

---

24   Interview with Abdul Lateef Adetona by D Oguntola-Laguda, Ojo, Badagry Division of Lagos State, Nigeria, February 2009.
25   Interview with Muslim Mahmud by D Oguntola-Laguda, Lagos Division, Lagos State, Nigeria, February 2009.

society like Lagos.²⁶ In his opinion, the formulation of the CLS law should have considered the religious persuasions of the population. He was not surprised that Muslims in the state opposed the implementation of the law from the outset, and when it was withdrawn for review by the governor, he felt the agitation of the Muslims in this regard must have yielded positive results.

Tunde Bajulaye, one of the law officers in the Lagos State Ministry of Justice, opined that there was nothing wrong in the formulation and implementation of the CLS.²⁷ In his view, the law was put in place by government to check the excesses of law enforcement agencies, such as the police, with regard to deaths in their custody, cases of unreported death and deaths due to negligence, among other causes. The state is secular and does not make religious beliefs and practices a factor in its policy-making process. Nonetheless, the Muslims should protest the implementation of the law in court. Since the law was introduced, no Muslim groups or individuals have so far sought judicial redress against the implementation of the CLS in the state.

Christians are not against the CLS. They do not see anything wrong with its implementation in the state. However, one interviewee, Kehinde Babarinde, a pastor at Satellite Baptist Church in Lagos, opined that the only snag in the CLS is the retention of parts of the deceased body by the medical examiner for possible future analysis. In his view, this is not necessary.²⁸ Rather, the state should put in place machinery that will make an inquest or postmortem brief and thoroughly completed within a short time.

But the CLS law remains problematic from the Muslim perspective. The national coordinator of Muslim Right Concern (MURIC), Lakin Akintola, believes CLS is a violation of the right of Muslims to decent burial as dictated by Islamic traditions. He has therefore championed the call for the abrogation of the CLS in Lagos.²⁹ The Lagos State Government reacted to the numerous agitations and protests against the implementation of the CLS by withdrawing the law for further review. The CLS was reintroduced in 2010 with modifications to respect the funeral and burial rites of Muslims in the state.

ANALYSIS OF RELIGIOUS RESPONSES TO THE CLS LAW

In course of the study that underlies the present analysis, we collected data using questionnaire and oral interviews to analyse the religious responses to the CLS law. We distributed questionnaires and conducted 50 oral interviews

---

26 Interview with Ustaz Kabir Paramole by D Oguntola-Laguda, Ojo, Badagry Division, Lagos State, Nigeria, November 2009.
27 Interview with Tunde Bajulaye by D Oguntola-Laguda, Ikeja, Ikeja Division, Lagos State, Nigeria, July 2008.
28 Interview with Kehinde Babarinde by D Oguntola-Laguda, Satelllite Town, Badagry Division, Lagos State, Nigeria, February 2009.
29 Interview with Lakin Akintola by D Oguntola-Laguda, Iba Town, Badagry Division, Lagos State, Nigeria, February 2009.

with Muslims and Christians in Lagos State. The intention was to seek their opinion on how the CLS affected the practice of their religious traditions on funeral rites. Our focus was on Muslims in Lagos, since Muslims voiced the greatest number of objections to the law; however, we also interviewed five Christian clerics. Questionnaires were administered among Muslims in the five divisions of Lagos state. Ten thousand of these questionnaires were distributed in the five divisions of the state evenly among the five regions of Epe, Ikorodu, Badagry, Lagos and Ikeja, and 8,436 were returned.[30] The questionnaires were administered during Jumat prayers which Muslims in Lagos State attend religiously.

The study revealed that illiterate Muslims in Lagos State were not even aware of the CLS. It was only the leaders of Muslim groups who seemed to know of its existence. It was further observed that the illiterate Muslims continued to practice their normal funeral rites without any recourse to the CLS during the brief period it operated. For them, death and burial practice was "From Allah we come and to Him we shall return". But this lopsided distribution of awareness does not demonstrate that religious leaders do not have influence on their followers. In fact, it strongly suggests that leaders could exploit this gap to frustrate the implementation of government policies in the state. Further, part of the problem government encountered then was that government did not adequately research into the sensitivities of religious adherents before the introduction of the CLS. This is confirmed by the following further results of the study.

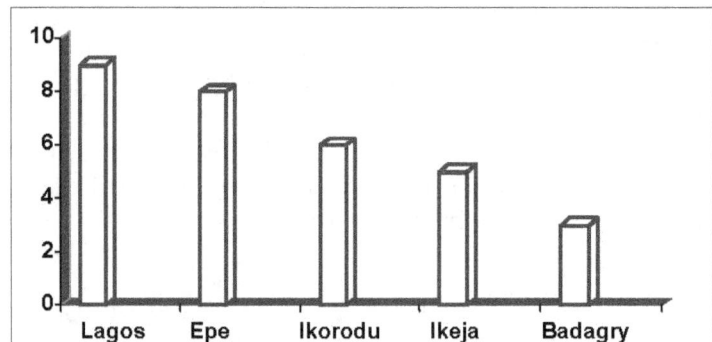

Figure 21.1: Level of awareness about CLS

---

30 It is perhaps worth noting that these divisions are for administrative convenience of the government of Lagos Sate and have been in place since inception of the state in 1967. The population of Lagos State alone has a population of nearly five million people, and these divisions have a reasonable population of over 800,000. Postgraduate students distributed these questionnaires, and brought back the 8,436 completed questionnaires from their respondents. The questionnaires were administered during Jumat prayers which Muslims in Lagos State attend religiously.

The graph distribution in Figure 1 shows that the CLS was more popular in the Lagos division than all other divisions. Badagry displayed the lowest knowledge of the CLS. Muslims in this division were not even aware of the enactment of the CLS, as they continued to bury their death without reporting to the appropriate authorities as stipulated by the law. It should be noted that Muslims in Badagry division are not many compared to Christians. Even those who claimed to be Muslims were syncretic and still patronised traditional religious ceremonies and festivals. In this regard, they are not strict in the application of Islamic funeral rites during burial of the dead. Some even combined the burial rites of ATR with those of Islam. The effect was that they did not necessarily bother about the implications of the CLS in the funeral rites and rituals of their Muslim brothers and sisters. In Epe, most (64%) of our respondents were aware of the CLS and voiced their opposition to it through numerous Islamic groups in Lagos State, as well as among the five divisions. The scenario was not different in Ikeja. However, we observed that the cosmopolitan nature of this division might have been a determining factor about their knowledge and awareness of the CLS. Ikorodu is a division where Muslims are highly syncretic, as in Badagry. They hardly ever attend Jumat service and belong to numerous secret societies of ATR that pervade the area.

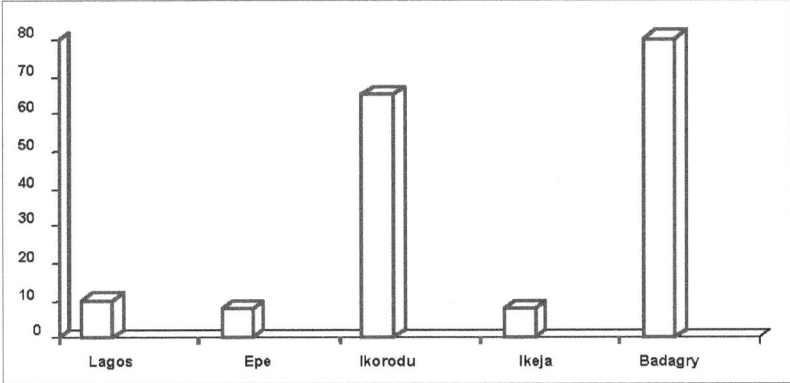

Figure 21.2: Would you allow postmortem?

Muslims in Lagos, Ikeja and Epe would not tolerate a postmortem or inquest about their deceased ones. To them, it is against Islam. They also rejected the idea that the medical examiner reserved the right to retain part of the body of the deceased. In Badagry and Ikorodu, those who claim to be Muslims are not keen on this requirement of the CLS. To them, if it is necessary and imperative they should be done otherwise they careless.

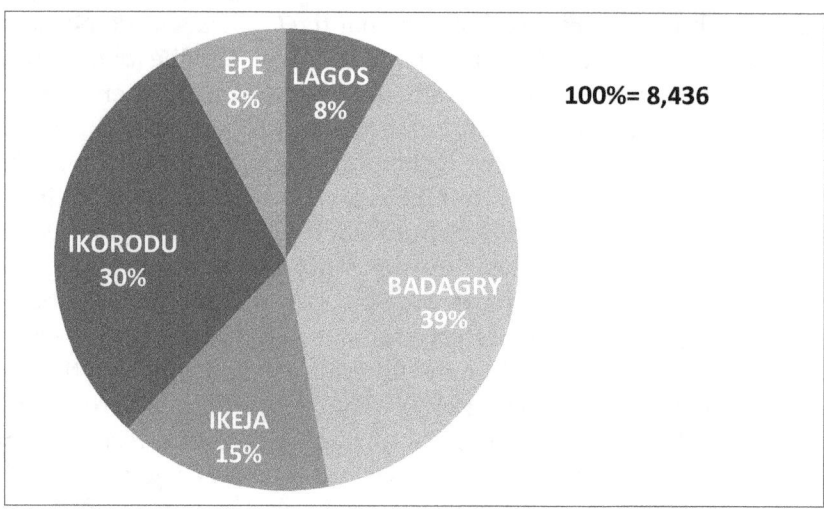

Figure 21.3: Would you want the CLS reintroduced in its old form?

Our respondents in Lagos are not comfortable with the CLS in its old form and therefore called for a review. Of the survey respondents, 91% acknowledged the necessity of the CLS, but they advised that the CLS should take Islamic traditions, tenets and laws into consideration. The same response was derived from Ikeja, with an even higher percentage of 95%. Epe division did not want the CLS at all, only legislation to regulate death from dubious causes. Ikorodu and Badagry were not particularly bothered about the CLS. Thus 65% and 62% of our respondents respectively in Badagry and Ikorodu would want the old CLS.

CONCLUSION

Nigerians are incurably religious. This same mentality is often carried into political engagements. This is reflected in the way religious traditions and tenets have influenced government policies in the country as a whole, even though the country is supposed to be a secular state. This chapter demonstrates that secularism does not suggest non-religiosity, but rather an attempt to push religion out of public domain and to reject its deterministic tendencies regarding state laws and policies. This was the case with the Coroner Law System 2007 before its withdrawal. It further shows that government formulation of laws and policies in a religiously plural state like Nigeria must always put into consideration the doctrines, beliefs, and rituals of competing religious traditions. This was the case when the CLS reintroduced in 2010, with modifications of those sections that were against the funeral rites of Muslims, except for deaths in police custody or prisons, which were still required to be subject to postmortem investigation.

In a religiously heterogeneous state, the scenario would have been different. The CLS would have considered the religious rites as well as the sensibility of the people in formulating the law. The case of the CLS is an example of how religious doctrines, tenets and traditions have affected the formulation of laws and government policies meant for the good of the society. Incidents of dubious deaths, especially in police custody, which are rampant in Lagos, need to be verified by the coroner at an inquest, so that the cause of death can be determined and appropriate sanctions placed on erring police officers, government officials and other persons involved in such deaths.

Due to religious doctrines and beliefs, particularly Muslim objections to the CLS, the law was withdrawn in 2008, following protests and outcries from Muslims in the state. It should be noted that the law has since been reintroduced, and because the government has been silent on its implementation, there has not been any notable protest against it. However, it has been applied to several cases of death in public spaces and religious institutions. The case of SCOAN as earlier mentioned in this chapter is an example. The case of the Dana Air plane crash in 2013 is also a reference point in the implementation of the modified CLS. In these two instances, unsubstantiated reports suggest that Muslims were among the dead.

22 DISCREPANCY BETWEEN THE LEGALITY OF THE DEATH PENALTY AND AFRICAN RELIGIOUS HERITAGE IN ZIMBABWE

Tobias Marevesa[1]
Fortune Sibanda[2]

INTRODUCTION

From time beyond reckoning, the death penalty has been perceived in ambivalence. On the one hand, some people regard the death penalty as inhuman, anachronistic, wild and a barbaric way of instilling discipline that must be abolished. In addition, some consider this law as "un-African" and a legacy of western colonial rule.[3] On the other hand, capital punishment also commands support as a deterrent to potential criminals and in dealing with notorious people in extenuating situations. In Zimbabwe, the legal regime regarding the death penalty is relatively fluid, and this has created uncertainty, confusion and a dilemma amongst citizens.[4] Whereas civic groups, governments and legal experts have grappled with the issue of the death penalty for many years, this chapter uses the religious lens to provide an Afro-centric reading of the African religious heritage on the death penalty in Zimbabwe.[5]

This chapter utilises the Afrocentric paradigm as a theoretical framework to understand the discrepancy between the legality of the death penalty and African religious heritage in Zimbabwe. Afrocentricity was made popular by

---

1 Tobias Marevesa is a PhD candidate with North-West University, South Africa. He is a lecturer in Religious Studies, Department of Philosophy and Religious Studies, Great Zimbabwe University, Masvingo.
2 Fortune Sibanda received his PhD from the University of Zimbabwe in 2015. He is a lecturer in Religious Studies, Department of Philosophy and Religious Studies, Great Zimbabwe University, Masvingo.
3 Agere H. 2016. "Death Penalty Raises Stink", *The Sunday Mail Extra*, 24 January:E1. See also 2016. "Death Penalty is, in fact, a Flagrant Violation of the Right to Life and Dignity", *The Herald*, 23 February.
4 Agere, "Death Penalty Raises Stink".
5 See Verstraelen FJ. 1998. *Zimbabwean Realities and Christian Responses*. Gweru: Mambo Press. See also Parrinder G. 1969. *Africa's Three Religions*. London: Sheldon Press, whose book title is crafted to reflect coverage of African Indigenous Religion, Christianity and Islam on the basis of their long presence on the African continent. Thus, all the three religions constitute "African religious heritage" and it is the sense in which it is used in this chapter. The phrase "African religious heritage" also affirms the spirituality and religiosity of Africans that define them as a people in the sense in which Mbiti JS (1969. *African Religions and Philosophy*. Oxford: Heinemann Books, 2) understood it when he asserted that "Africans are notoriously religious."

African scholars such as Molefi Kete Asante and Maulana Karenga,[6] who are leading scholars and advocates of the Afrocentric genre. The emergence of Afrocentricity came as a reaction to Eurocentric ideology, which universalised European aspects of culture, communication, philosophy, education, rhetoric, linguistics, history, psychology and anthropology.[7] The legal community in Zimbabwe is also steeped in western ideologies, as reference is still made to the Roman-Dutch law and English common law within the legal system of the country to this day. Therefore, an Afrocentric approach to the Zimbabwean legal system would accommodate African traditional law, alongside the views of Christianity and Islam, rather than merely depending on the western-influenced legal systems to deal with issues of capital punishment.

The Afrocentric paradigm has the merit of being both a corrective and a critique. As a corrective, Afrocentricity counters the European meta-paradigm, which denied the agency and action of African people in legal matters. Under colonial rule and in some postcolonial contexts, African customary law and beliefs on matters of human life, death and the hereafter, particularly in the context of phenomena such as the *ngozi* (avenging spirits), there was a tendency to ignore and deny the efficacy of these customary beliefs. One of the present authors (Sibanda), an Afrocentric scholar of the history and phenomenology of religion, asserts that the Eurocentric approach to African beliefs in *ngozi* minimised them, at worst, as mere nonexistent superstition and, at best, as evil spirits, but those who murdered innocent people were often tormented by avenging spirits in cases usually settled through restitution mediated by traditional courts, thereby proving the vitality of African traditional law in this context.[8] This shows the relevance of the Afrocentric theory in countering the Eurocentric predominance in the Zimbabwean legal system. As a critique, the Afrocentric paradigm can sensitise people towards realising that they are their own liberators or oppressors in the context of the issue of the death penalty, given that the Constitution of Zimbabwe should be fair and just to all citizens. Therefore, Afrocentric theory is vital to this study in light of the discrepancy between the legality of the death penalty and African religious heritage in Zimbabwe.

This chapter collects data from interviews with elders, traditional leaders, church leaders, members of the Lemba[9] Islamic community and legal practitioners.

---

6   Adeleke T. 2009. *Case Against Afrocentricism*. Jackson, MS: University Press of Mississippi, 9.
7   Asante MK. 1998. *The Afrocentric Idea*. Philadelphia: Temple University Press, 19.
8   Sibanda F. 2016. "Avenging Spirits and the Vitality of African Traditional Law, Customs and Religion in Contemporary Zimbabwe", in Coertzen P, Green MC and Hansen L (eds). *Religious Freedom and Religious Pluralism in Africa: Prospects and Limitations*. Stellenbosch: African Sun Media, 347.
9   In Zimbabwe, the Lemba/Varemba people belong to the Karanga ethnic group and are mainly found in Mberengwa District, Midlands province, as well as in Gutu and Masvingo Districts, Masvingo province, in Zimbabwe. There has been extensive work undertaken on the Lemba communities. They seem to be distant descendants of a mixed population of Africans, Arabs and others.

Data was also gathered through documentary analysis of print and electronic media covering issues of capital punishment in Zimbabwe. The study also combined insights from the historical, sociological and phenomenological approaches to describe and analyse the data. According to Fredrick J Streng, a historian of religion, the history of religions systematically organises and classifies religious material.[10] Using the historical approach in this study had the merit of tracing the origins and background capital punishment in Zimbabwe and beyond within African Indigenous Religion (AIR), African Christianity and Lemba Islam. In addition, previous and current statistical records of the inmates on death row or whose verdicts were transformed to life in prison are also explored through the historical approach.

Sociology of religion is about how religion affects people and how people are affected by religion.[11] The method focuses on human relationships and interactions in society. Through sociological method, one can explore issues in relation to religion and law, class, gender, economics, change and other aspects of society. Therefore, a socio-historical approach from the history and sociology of religion may provide a favourable platform for understanding the legality of the death penalty in Zimbabwe, given that religious phenomena like existing legal institutions, are socially and historically conditioned. As a method that seeks to promote the insider perspective, the phenomenology of religion provides the study with tools of analysing the views of participants by using *epoche* (bracketing), empathy, descriptive accuracy and *eidetic* intuition, through which the meaning of religion can be approximated.[12] The phenomenological method emphasises the need to avoid terms like "superstition" and "pre-literate" with reference to African beliefs and practices, as well as customary

---

By the sixteenth century, they were engaged in Islamic, some Abrahamic, and local (Zimbabwean) ritual practices. Some of the Lemba are Muslims, whilst others are Jewish in their religious orientation. The Lemba have a syncretic tendency in which they mix Islamic and African traditional practices. A lot of debate has focused on their Muslim or Jewish character. It has been observed that the "Lemba did not retain the 'Islamic' identity of their ancestors, but their distinctive, syncretic forms of circumcision, burial and ritual slaughter perpetuate a sense of 'difference' from surrounding populations", Shaw R and Stewart C. 1994. "Introduction: Problematising Syncretism", in Stewart C and Shaw R (eds). *Syncretism/Anti-Syncretism: The Politics of Religious Synthesis*. London: Routledge, 16. The Zimbabwean scholar Ephraim Mandivenga has argued that the Lemba was a product of earlier Muslim activities enforced through "re-Islamisation". See Mandivenga E. 1989. "The History and 'Re-Conversion' of the Varemba of Zimbabwe", *Journal of Religion in Africa* 19(2):98-124. See also Chitando E. 2011. "VaJudha (African Jews) in Harare: Expressing Contested Identities in Tight Spaces", *African Studies* 64(2):137.

10   Streng FJ. 1985. *Understanding Religious Life*. Belmony: Wadsworth Publishing Company, 220.
11   Bourdillon MFC. 1990. *Religion and Society: A Text for Africa*. Gweru: Mambo Press.
12   See, for example, Chitando E. 1998. "The Phenomenological Method in a Zimbabwean Context: To Liberate or to Oppress?", *Zambezia* 25(1):99-114. In this article, Chitando suggests that, notwithstanding its weaknesses, the phenomenology of religion is ideal for studying African Indigenous Religion.

law. Although the history of religions and phenomenology of religion share an anti-reductionist stance towards religious and social phenomena as *sui generis*, thereby promoting the uniqueness of religion, this is in contrast to the sociology of religion, which "explains away" social and religious phenomena. Therefore, a corroboration of the three approaches in the context of the death penalty is ideal for the chapter, since the weaknesses of one method can be covered by the strengths of other methods.

This chapter focuses on the discrepancy between the legal basis of the death penalty and how it is perceived from the perspectives of African religious heritage in Zimbabwe. It employs a broad understanding of "African religious heritage" to refer to the trilogy of African Indigenous Religion (AIR), African Christian tradition and Lemba Islam. By "heritage", this chapter encompasses the religious, cultural, legal and historical traditions and how they formulate religious identities and societies in contemporary Africa. The chapter posits that capital punishment does not augur well with human rights and religious norms within AIR, African Christianity and Lemba Islam. In other words, there is a discrepancy between the legality of the death penalty and African religious heritage, as it is experienced in Zimbabwe. The chapter further argues that although the Constitution of Zimbabwe currently still provides for the death penalty, the existence of a moratorium[13] is a hopeful stance for an eventual abolitionist position that would be commensurate to African religious heritage.

THE CONCEPTION OF DEATH IN THE AFRICAN WORLD VIEW

The overarching influence of African cosmology goes beyond practitioners of African Indigenous Religion (AIR) to include African Christians and African Muslims, particularly on matters of death and the hereafter. It is from this premise, that this section addresses the conception of death in the African worldview. Africans, including the Shona of Zimbabwe, believe that humanity was created by the Supreme Being, Mwari, who controls life and death. No one, therefore, has the right to take anyone's life except the Creator. Yet, they believe that in society, there are good and bad spirits, with some people harming others through anti-social practices of witchcraft and sorcery. They also believe in life after death, holding that "after the physical death of the body (*nyama*), the soul (*mweya*) continues to live."[14] Thus, there is both the physical and the spiritual existence. According to Canaan S Banana, an African scholar and theologian, "Life is an endless enterprise. Death is not death; it is a vehicle from the ontology of visible beings to the ontology of invisible beings. Death is part of life, it is a

---

13 Moratorium is a constitutional provision in which the state suspends executions as a sort of "halfway measure" between abolition and retention of applying the death penalty. Legally, such a state would still have the death penalty, though probably with a weak resolve. However, the problem is that the state can resume executions at any time.
14 Sibanda, "Avenging Spirits and the Vitality of African Traditional Law", 350.

gateway to life in the here-after."[15] African people perceive life and time in a cyclic fashion, which contrasts the linear western conception of time and life. From this understanding, it is held that "a person exists from an 'it' at birth, without a name, and is expected to live to a ripe old age before passing on to the next spiritual life after death, where the individual eventually develops into an 'it' – a nameless dead".[16]

Among the Shona, the dead are said to have a greater and more mysterious power-force as compared to that of the living, making "death a graduation and a gravitation into a new and higher life".[17] The immortality of the spirit is summed up by the Shona saying that claims: "*Chinoora inyama, mweya hauori*" (what perishes is the flesh, but the spirit is immortal).[18] The saying above contains the traditional beliefs on death and the hereafter, vital to the study of the death through capital punishment and the impact of *ngozi* spirit to the hangman who effects the death on behalf of the government. Ending life through the death penalty may suggest that a person is guilty of a serious crime deserving a moral sanction by society. In such a scenario, performing death rituals like *kurova guva* (to beat the grave) ceremony, which brings back the spirit of the dead home and domesticates it,[19] might be impossible. This is because the state, by law, would not surrender the copse of the hanged person to the family members for a decent burial. In this way, without a proper burial of the body, there is no grave to speak of and there can be no death rituals. The hanged person is therefore likely to be disqualified from the status of being a *mudzimu* (ancestor), where s/he spiritually joins other "living dead" as "guardians of the family affairs, traditions, ethics and activities".[20] Although the power of those who die through capital punishment cannot be underrated, since they can also come back as an avenging spirit to the hangman until they are fully compensated, the question that remains is how justified this move is in light of existing statutes vis-à-vis the abolitionist position attributed to African religious heritage in Zimbabwe.

THE ZIMBABWEAN DEATH PENALTY: A HISTORICAL OVERVIEW

In all societies, the death penalty has a long history of controversy for being employed to end human life. While not all crimes merit the contentious death penalty, cases of attempted murder, murder, conspiracy, treason, rape, attempted rape, aggravated robbery, felony murder, among other offences,

---

15   Banana CS. 1991. *Come and Share: An Introduction to Christian Theology*. Gweru: Mambo Press, 27.
16   Sibanda, "Avenging Spirits and the Vitality of African Traditional Law", 350.
17   Banana, *Come and Share*, 28.
18   Sibanda, "Avenging Spirits and the Vitality of African Traditional Law", 350.
19   Banana, *Come and Share*, 30.
20   Banana, *Come and Share*, 32.

top the list.²¹ In colonial Africa, the death penalty was a prominent feature of legislation for political, religious and social reasons.²² This has spilled over into some postcolonial African countries.²³ Amnesty International has been working towards ending executions since 1977, when only sixteen countries had abolished the death penalty in law or practice.²⁴ Today, about two thirds of the countries worldwide have abolished capital punishment.²⁵ Paradoxically, some countries, like the United States of America, who are key players in the advocacy for human rights through abolishing the death penalty, are complicit in the sentencing and execution of people.²⁶ The American "criminal justice system" is punctuated by a language of justice and injustice, a discourse in which questions of human rights and democratic legitimacy come to the fore,²⁷ marred by the persistence of capital punishment in a globalised world.

In postcolonial Zimbabwe, for instance, the death sentence has been restricted to murder and treason since 1992,²⁸ and it has been retained in the Constitution (Amendment No. 20 of 2013), where in Part 2 under Fundamental Human Rights and Freedoms, Section 48, on the "Right to life", says in subsection (1) says: "Every person has the right to life." However, this fundamental right to life is immediately compromised when, in subsection (2), the death penalty is

---

21 Agere, "Death Penalty Raises a Stink".
22 African Commission on Human and Peoples' Rights (ACHPR). 2011. *Study on the Question of the Death Penalty in Africa*. Banjul, The Gambia: Baobab Printers, 25. Online at: http://www.achpr.org/files/news/2012/04/d46/study_question_ deathpenalty_africa_2012_eng.pdf
23 Examples of these postcolonial African countries that still have the death penalty are Benin, Burkina Faso, Gambia, Ghana, Nigeria, Liberia, Mali, Cameroon, Chad, Democratic Republic of Congo, Equatorial Guinea, Eritrea, Ethiopia, Kenya, South Sudan, Sudan, Somalia, Tanzania, Uganda, Botswana, Lesotho, Madagascar, Malawi, Swaziland, Zambia, Zimbabwe, Algeria, Egypt, Libya, Morocco and Tunisia. These states are *de facto* abolitionist – that is, they have not legally proscribed the death penalty but decline to authorise the execution of those sentenced to death. They have frozen or put on hold all executions of condemned prisoners. In other words, they have put in place a moratorium. See ACHPR, *Study on the Question of the Death Penalty in Africa*, 28, 29, 47.
24 Hersher R. 2016. "Death Sentences and Executions are Down, But Voters Still Support Death Penalty Laws", *NPR.org*, 21 December.
25 Erickson M. 2016. "Death Penalty". Amnesty International Online at: https:// www.amenesty.org/en/what-we-do/death-penalty/. Today, Europe is a death penalty-free zone.
26 Hersher,"Death Sentences and Executions are Down, But Voters Still Support Death Penalty Laws". Ideally, the death penalty is still legal in 37 of the 50 states in the United States. For instance, it has been recorded that out of 30 people who were sentenced to death, 20 were executed in the U.S. in 2016 alone.
27 Isaac JC. 2015. "The American Politics of Policing and Incarceration", *Perspectives on Politics: A Political Science Public Sphere* 13(3):609.
28 Novak A. 2014. "Capital Sentencing Discretion in Southern Africa: A Human Rights Perspective on the Doctrine of Extenuating Circumstances in Death Penalty Cases", *African Human Rights Law Journal* 14(1):32.

announced as applicable in specified offences.[29] The persistence of this statute is indicated by the existence of over one hundred inmates who are currently on the death row.[30] If these people on the death row continue to be "marked for death", this shows an existing historical contradiction and anomaly associated with the issue of the death penalty in Zimbabwe, which can be illustrated through reference to different religious traditions constituting African religious heritage in Zimbabwe.

AFRICAN RELIGIOUS HERITAGE AND THE ENIGMA OF THE DEATH PENALTY IN ZIMBABWE

As intimated earlier, African religious heritage is used in the study underlying this chapter to refer to what the distinguished scholar of comparative religion, Geoffrey Parrinder, described as "Africa's three religions", namely, African Traditional Religion (ATR), Christianity and Islam. The longstanding history of these traditions in Africa qualifies them to constitute African religious heritage. None of these religions can be viewed in monolithic terms in the African religious context. Therefore, this section provides an overview of each of these traditions to demonstrate the discrepancy between the death penalty and the historical and social realities in the religious realm.

African traditional religion perspective

The African traditional perspective is illustrated through reference to Shona traditional religion. There is a claim that, historically, under the Munhumutapa Empire,[31] the Shona did not have the death penalty.[32] Although it might be true for Shona societies to say that the death penalty was nonexistent in precolonial Africa, there is also ample evidence to the contrary concerning its existence in

---

29　Constitution of Zimbabwe (Amendment No. 20 of 2013). Section 48(2) states: "A law may permit the death penalty to be imposed only on a person convicted of murder committed in aggravating circumstances, and – (a) the law must permit the court a discretion whether or not to impose the penalty; (b) the penalty may be carried out only in accordance with a final judgment of a competent court; (c) the penalty must not be imposed on a person – (i) who was less than twenty-one years when the offence was committed; or (ii) who is more than seventy years old; (d) the penalty must not be imposed or carried out on a woman; and (e) the person sentenced must have a right to seek pardon or commutation of the penalty from the President." See also 2016. "Zimbabwe: Death Penalty Violates Human Rights", *Zimbabwe Standard*, 25 September.

30　Agere, "Death Penalty Raises a Stink".

31　This is a precolonial empire set by the Shona people. At the height of its rule, the empire stretched from the western parts of present day Zimbabwe to Mozambique in the East. See Bourdillon MFC. 1987. *The Shona Peoples*. Gweru: Mambo Press for a map of Munhumutapa Empire.

32　Maodza T. 2016. "Capital Punishment Archaic: VP Mnangagwa", *The Herald*. 25 February:2.

other African communities.³³ In precolonial Zimbabwe, the Shona traditional or customary law was an oral law enforced by kings or chiefs and *indunas* (chief's advisors). Its unwritten form presented challenges of ascertaining its exact content and application. However, in Shona society, it appeared to be the case that the death penalty was never applied, unlike the situation in Zimbabwe today. According to Shona tradition, a person guilty of a capital offence was not necessarily executed, but alternative methods of dealing with the criminals were employed. In cases of crimes such as murder, the traditional kings or chiefs would order the perpetrator to compensate by paying "blood money" or a herd of cattle to the victim's family. "Blood money" was paid to assuage the anger of the victim's family for loss suffered and to promote peace and reconciliation.³⁴

If literary works could be read as Shona history, it can be argued that Francis D Hodzongi's *Mhosva Inoripwa*³⁵ and Father Emmanuel F Ribeiro's *Muchadura*³⁶ – both Shona fiction novels – are instructive on how Shona society tried to instil moral uprightness, such that people would avoid killing each other, lest they suffer from the consequences of the *ngozi* spirits. In addition, Shona society could banish the offender from the village permanently or temporarily. In the case of banishment, the guilty person was exiled for a stated period of time and upon return was expected to perform sacrifice that was a form of restitution sanctioned by the elders. It can be noted that among the Shona people, just as in some other African communities, "the execution of criminals for serious crimes must not be confused with cases of deprivation of life for reasons other than a penalty crime".³⁷ Therefore, the Shona traditional religion can be regarded as a system that sought to preserve life at all costs by avoiding retributive justice. This is in tandem with the observation that some African communities, in cases of murder, "saw no point in sacrificing a second life for one already lost because that meant causing the loss of another breadwinner and creating in the process more orphans and widows/widowers".³⁸ So, on the basis of the African

---

33 For instance, scholars' writings on African law refer to the Zulu kingdom in South Africa where adultery with any of the chief's wives attracted a death penalty. In such contexts, the methods of execution included decapitation, spearing to death, administration of poison, and burial of people alive. See, for example, ACHPR, *Study on the Question of the Death Penalty in Africa*, 23.
34 ACHPR, *Study on the Question of the Death Penalty in Africa*, 9, 25.
35 Hodzongi FD. 1981. *Mhosva Inoripwa*. Harare: Longman.
36 Ribeiro EF. 1977. *Muchadura*. Gweru: Mambo Press.
37 ACHPR, *Study on the Question of the Death Penalty in Africa*, 24. For instance, the Shona communities had practices such as 'ritual' murder, killing at birth twins or a child born with teeth, a person guilty of practising witchcraft, death from trials by ordeal, among others.
38 ACHPR, *Study on the Question of the Death Penalty in Africa*, 25. Once again, reference to literary works from a historical perspective shows that Shona fiction novels, particularly Nobert Mafumhe Mutasa's *Mapatya* [Twins] (Salisbury: Longman Rhodesia, 1978) and Ignatius M Zvarevashe's *Gonawapotera* [a deep sacred pool where the ostracised people were thrown to die] (Salisbury: College Press, 1978) are instructive on demonstrating how Shona society eliminated some of its people through death for various reasons, such as ritual murder of

philosophy of *ubuntu* (humanness), the Shona did not practise an eye for an eye principle, because it would make the world blind. This shows that there is a discrepancy between the death penalty, as it is practised today, and Shona traditional religion in Zimbabwe.

African Christian perspective

This section focuses on the African Christian perspective on the death penalty in Zimbabwe. Given that there are diverse Christian groups in Zimbabwe, this chapter uses the case of Christians from African Independent Churches (AICs), with specific reference to Johane Marange Apostolic Church (JMAC). The JMAC is a Hebraist movement influenced by both the Judeo-Christian tradition and African religion in its beliefs and practices. Its adherents are guided by the Bible on the issue of capital punishment, particularly instances where the Old Testament sets capital punishment as a penalty for certain crimes. For example, the biblical teaching in Genesis 9:6, says: "Whoever sheds the blood of man, by man shall his blood be shed," showing an argument in support of capital punishment. Along the same lines, the Old Testament prescribes death by stoning for various sins (Exodus 21:28), with two witnesses required for the punishment to be carried out.

The JMAC places *mitemo iri gumi* (the Decalogue) at the centre of its teachings. For instance, in response to the question of what their perspective was on the death penalty, one of the JMAC leaders had this to say: "*Mutemo waMozisi unoti usauraya*" (The Law of Moses says thou shall not kill, citing Exodus 20:6). This is a biblical teaching is upheld by all members, who therefore find the death penalty to be problematic. In addition, the JMAC refers to similar teachings proclaimed by the Apostle Paul in the New Testament when he denounces retribution for evil. JMAC members referred to where Paul says: "Do not repay evil for evil ... do not take revenge. For it is written 'vengeance is mine says the Lord'" (Romans 12:17-19). Apart from the biblical teaching, the JMAC members were cautious not to kill, because this could invoke the spirit of *ngozi*. This shows how JMAC members as African Christians combine biblical teachings and African traditional beliefs such as those on *ngozi*, or avenging spirits.

The crucifixion of Jesus, the result of a death sentence by the Romans for sedition, is a very important event in the theology of JMAC. This is because *pasika* (Paschal/Passover feast) is a prominent sacrament of the JMAC annual festival gatherings of members from far and wide. Hence, JMAC recognises the passion of Jesus and regards VaJudha (Jews) as blameworthy for the crucifixion of Christ. They hold this view, even though there is scanty constitutional and legal evidence as to why Jesus was executed, and it appears that Jesus was crucified as a political messianic aspirant who wanted to remove the Roman

---

twins deemed a curse to the community and witchcraft accusations. This was deprivation of life rather than the death penalty per se.

rule by force.³⁹ The crucifixion method was only applied to the Jews, which was perceived to be a Roman way of oppressing the Jews by executing them in a degrading, discriminatory and inhumane method. Whereas JMAC members are theologically inspired and influenced by Old Testament prophets like Moses, Elijah and Elisha,⁴⁰ Stephen, who became the first Christian martyr through death by stoning (Acts 7:54-60) following a death sentence by the Sanhedrin for blasphemy, is also a household name to them. Stephen was accused of challenging the fundamental beliefs of Judaism, including regard for Jerusalem as an unparalleled holy place, affirming the sacredness of the Temple, and following the Mosaic Law.⁴¹ All the same, the JMAC's position towards the death penalty is negative, because they say only God has the right to take life and that the death penalty is inconsistent with African religious heritage in Zimbabwe. In order to illustrate their preference towards a position of forgiveness and reformation in contrast to the death penalty, the JMAC members quote scriptural texts such as Isaiah 1:18 (KJV), which says: "Come now, and let us reason together, saith the LORD: though your sins be as scarlet, they shall be as white as snow; though they be red like crimson, they shall be as wool." This shows that the JMAC members prefer rehabilitation to the death penalty. Nevertheless, JMAC members have been under the spotlight in Zimbabwe for causing unnecessary deaths of children by failing to comply with conventional medical practices such as immunisation.⁴² The church believes in faith healing and does not allow its members to be treated in hospitals. Therefore, it can be argued that although JMAC is against the death penalty per se, its position on medical issues makes them guilty of violating children's rights in Zimbabwe.

African Islamic perspective

This section focuses on the Lemba Islamic perspective on the death penalty in Zimbabwe. It particularly focuses on the Lemba Muslims of Sunni disposition belonging to the Karanga ethnic group, located in Chinyika and Hamandishe communities in Gutu District, Masvingo province. Although the Lemba Muslims believe in the efficacy of the Islamic religious law, the *sharia* law,

---

39 Brandon SGF. 1967. *Jesus and the Zealots: A Study of the Political Factor in Primitive Christianity*. New York: Charles Scribner's Sons.
40 See, for example, Sibanda F, Makahamadze T and Maposa RS. 2008. "Hawks and Doves: The Impact of Operation Murambatsvina on Johane Marange Apostolic Church in Zimbabwe", *Exchange* 37:71.
41 Brown RE. 1997. *Introduction to the New Testament*. New York: Bloomsburg, 328; Perin N and Duling DC. 1982. *The New Testament: An Introduction*. London: Harcourt Brace, 320; Kummel G. 1984. *Introduction to the New Testament*. London: SCM Press, 180.
42 Sibanda F and Marevesa T. 2013. "March or Die? Theological Reflections on the Violation of Children's Rights in African Initiated Churches, Zimbabwe", *Asian Academic Research Journal of Multidisciplinary* 1(7):163-175.

which governs the lives of Muslims the world over,[43] they are also influenced by the context in which they are located. For instance, the Lemba Muslims in Zimbabwe say they are guided by the Constitution of Zimbabwe and find it impossible to apply *sharia* in its fullness, but at the same time resort to the *sharia* in their own personal law matters, such as marriage, divorce, inheritance, diet and funeral rites, among other things.[44] Furthermore, the Lemba Muslims are aware that Islamic punishment, as laid out in the Quran, can often seem very harsh, as indicated by punishments such as the cutting off of the hand of a thief or administering a hundred lashes with a whip for being caught in adultery.[45] *Sharia* allows for capital punishment for three offences: murder, adultery and apostasy.[46] In Islamic states, where some Muslims support capital punishment, they base their views on the fact that it is laid down in *sharia*, which incorporates the Quranic injunctions, along with the *sunna*, *hadith* and other sources. The Lemba Muslims interpret the Quran to understand that forgiveness or mercy is preferable to execution.[47] In addition, Lemba Muslims refer to the example of the Prophet Muhammad who agreed to capital punishment and used it to sentence people to death for murder when he was ruler of Medina.[48] However, in Zimbabwe, Lemba Muslims, with their syncretic tendencies that combine Islamic and African traditional religious beliefs, said that they were not comfortable with supporting capital punishment because this could attract *ngozi*, particularly in the case of the hangman.[49] This is one of the moderating forces among Lemba Muslims in Zimbabwe.[50]

---

43 Okon EE. 2014. "Hudud Punishments in Islamic Criminal Law", *European Scientific Journal* 10(14):227-238.
44 Interview conducted by the authors with a Lemba Imam, Chinyika Community, 20 February 2017.
45 See Surah 5:38 and Surah 24:2 for the punishments administered for theft and fornication, respectively.
46 Among the three categories of criminal behaviour and actions in Islamic jurisprudence, the *Hudud* offences top the list and are specified in the Quran and *sunnah*. *Hudud* crimes include rejection of Islam (apostasy), fornication and theft. Prophet Muhammad is quoted in one of the *hadiths* as saying: "The blood of a Muslim may not be legally spilt other than in one of three (instances); the married person who commits adultery; a life for a life; and one who forsakes religion (of Islam) and abandons his community." See Okon, "Hudud Punishments in Islamic Criminal Law", 229.
47 Mumisa M. 2015. *Sharia Law and the Death Penalty: Would Abolition of the Death Penalty be Unfaithful to the Message of Islam?* London: Penal Reform International, 7. Muslims make reference to scriptures suggesting forgiveness and mercy rather than death. For instance, Surah 42:40 states: "Let harm be repaid by an equal harm, though anyone who forgives and puts things right will have his reward from God himself – He does not like those who do wrong."
48 Okon, "Hudud Punishments in Islamic Criminal Law".
49 Interview conducted by the authors with Hasane, a Lemba Elder, Hamandishe Community, 21 February 2017.
50 Another limiting factor when dealing with criminal offences among Lemba Muslims in Zimbabwe, which is a non-Islamic state, is the nonexistence of a *sharia* court that can handle capital sentences. See Okon, "Hudud Punishments in Islamic Criminal Law", 233, where Okon observes: "Life is sacred and cannot

The Lemba Muslims of Zimbabwe also point out that saving life as much as possible was better than destroying it. They interpret the Quran as only suggesting capital punishment, not making it compulsory. The Lemba Muslims also stress that if the court of law sentences the accused to death, perhaps after being convicted of murder, the family of the accused should seek forgiveness or pardon from the family of the murdered victim, so that they may pay compensation or "blood money" to avoid the death penalty. In this sense, Lemba Muslims are not against customary law, which is safeguarded by chiefs and elders who arbitrate cases in which restitution is paid. In these ways, the Lemba Muslims and others are resolutely opposed to the death penalty and prefer punishment based on forgiveness, deterrence and reform in ways that are also Afrocentrically sound. This makes the Lemba Muslims more moderate in their perspective towards the use of criminal punishments than Muslims in Islamic states.[51]

THE LEGALITY OF THE DEATH PENALTY IN ZIMBABWE

Among the Shona people and in the context of Shona traditional religion, the first people to face the death penalty were Sekuru Kaguvi and Mbuya Nehanda after the First Chimurenga War (1896-7) through the ruling of the colonial administrators. They were charged for sedition and causing political mayhem in the country by leading the resistance of the Shona people in Mashonaland.[52] It is said that before they were hanged, the two were asked to confess their sins in the name of Jesus Christ. Whereas Mbuya Nehanda refused, Sekuru Kaguvi accepted Jesus as His Saviour, got baptised and was accorded a Christian name. Paradoxically, the two were ultimately executed by the colonial administrators, under the same charge, which dismisses the efficacy of Christian baptism in the case of Sekuru Kaguvi.[53] Thus, it continues to be asked: How legal was this execution, after all?

During the Second Chimurenga War (1965-1980), the colonial system continued to effect capital punishment, particularly on Africans, for political reasons. Many Africans were imprisoned and sentenced to death for various crimes. The existence of capital punishment in the colonial period is confirmed by the

---

be taken except through a death sentence handed down by a Shariah court of competent jurisdiction in an Islamic state."

51 The moderate stance of Lemba Muslims in Zimbabwe towards the death penalty is reminiscent of the transformation from the harsher side of Islamic law registered in Nigeria in recent years as reported by the *New York Times*. See Polgreen L. 2007. "Nigeria Turns from Harsher Side of Islamic Law", *The New York Times*, 1 December.
52 Beach DN. 1986. *War and Politics in Zimbabwe*. Gweru: Mambo Press.
53 The fact that Sekuru Kaguvi was executed in spite of having been converted to the coloniser's religion seems to suggest a contradiction in the Christian religion of the colonisers – almost a sacrilegious perversion of Christ on the Cross and hardly consistent with forgiveness and redemption, for which Christianity often professes to stand.

experience of the vice president of Zimbabwe, Emmerson Mnangagwa, who escaped the death penalty by a whisker under the Ian Smith regime due to being underage.[54] As a young political activist of 21 years, he had been sentenced to death by hanging. The Catholic priest and Shona fiction literary artist, Father Emmanuel Ribeiro, who was a prison chaplain at that time, saved Mnangagwa after he recommended a medical examination to ascertain that he was under the age of 21. During the colonial period, capital punishment could only be handed down to convicts above the age of 21, and it was originally only applied to nine crimes, which were reduced to treason and murder in postcolonial Zimbabwe.[55] Through his personal experience, Emmerson Mnangagwa is in the forefront of strongly advocating against the death penalty to the extent of proposing the amendment of the Constitution of Zimbabwe. On this basis, it can be argued that the exoneration of some people from the death penalty is a positive development that must be extended to all people in Zimbabwe.[56]

In interviews conducted with traditional leaders, such as chiefs and elders, the majority of respondents felt that the death penalty had outlived its relevance in Zimbabwe. According to the President of the Chiefs' Council in Zimbabwe, Chief Fortune Charumbira, the death penalty was alien to Zimbabwean culture and was a legacy of colonialists.[57] Chief Charumbira added that capital punishment must be abolished, because executing a person created more harm than good. This is because under the Shona traditional religion, killing was wrong as it could invoke *ngozi* and create a cycle of violence.[58] Elsewhere, Chief Charumbira was quoted as saying that when one kills a person, one kills the physical body,

---

54 Maodza, "Capital Punishment Archaic: VP Mnangagwa", 2. See also, for example, Muzulu P. 2016. "Mnangagwa Stance on Death Penalty Influenced by Experiences", *News Day*, 8 February:6.
55 Muzulu, "Mnangagwa Stance on Death Penalty Influenced by Experiences", 6.
56 The reality of equity alongside equality in the issue of the death penalty must be acknowledged in Zimbabwe. In most common law jurisdictions, strict equality is tempered by "equity", whereby women and girls are given exceptions in some cases in order to do justice. Exclusion of women from the death penalty can be regarded as an acknowledgement of their lesser power and greater vulnerability in most sectors of society, such that some of their crimes might be out of self-preservation or self-defence. In addition, the age limits for the death penalties for youth or the aged can be intended to acknowledge the mental frailties of youth or old age.
57 Interview conducted by the authors with Chief Fortune Charumbira, Masvingo, 20 February 2016. Chief Charumbira, a Karanga by descent, stressed the Shona traditional position, which shows that the death penalty was nonexistent. Hence, it is a discrepancy to have it in the Constitution of the country long after colonialism.
58 Interview conducted by the authors with Chief Fortune Charumbira. The cycle of violence from a Shona perspective hinges on the fact that without proper restitution, *ngozi* can torment and wipe out families of the perpetrator of murder. See, for example, Sibanda, "Avenging Spirits and the Vitality of African Traditional Law, Customs and Religion in Contemporary Zimbabwe", where there are illustrations of the havoc that *ngozi* spirits can make when not fully restituted.

but the spirit of the dead lives on. That is why, in Shona traditional religion and culture, a person who kills someone is made to pay compensation to appease the *ngozi* spirits.[59] The chiefs felt that no sane person should accept the job of a hangman,[60] which has not been filled since 2004 in Zimbabwe.[61] Along the same lines, another traditional practitioner, Sekuru Friday Chisanyu, the President of the Zimbabwe National Practitioners Association (ZINPA), said Zimbabweans are not keen to take up the job of a hangman for cultural reasons, particularly the teachings of African traditional religion against the shedding of human blood.[62] In the words of Sekuru Chisanyu, as presented by local media reporter, "In the indigenous African tradition, the death penalty is forbidden. The hangman will surely attract the wrath of the avenging spirits of those that he would have executed. It is for the simple reason that Zimbabweans are shunning this post."[63] On the whole, most of the traditional leaders and elders interviewed took an abolitionist stance towards the death penalty and proposed that sentences of life in prison for those convicted of serious crimes would be inconsistent with African traditional religious perspectives.[64]

In African Christian circles, church deacons, priests and other church elders of the Johane Marange Apostolic Church who were interviewed denounced the death penalty on the basis of its cruelty to human life, which is God-given. In addition, the church elders cited the dreaded question of *ngozi* as a vital retributive and deterring factors against supporting the death penalty. This JMAC position on the death penalty is comparable to that of Pastor Emmerson Fundira of Jehovah Sharma Ministries,[65] who emphasised the same idea when he said that the "Bible is clear on this one – it instructs us not to kill. There is no reason why a human being should take the life of another human being".[66] This statement represents the abolitionist position held by the majority of the African Initiated Church (AIC) Christians interviewed for this study.

---

59 Agere, "Death Penalty Raises Stink".
60 This view from the Chief about *ngozi* and the long absence of a hangman in Zimbabwe may appear simplistic to outsiders, but it forms part of the strong beliefs among the Shona people.
61 Prisoners under death sentence were last hanged in 2004. Zimbabwe's last hangman left the post in 2005 after hanging two notorious armed criminals, Edgar Masendeke and Stephen Chidhumo. See Matabvu D. 2016. "Dying to land hangman's post", *The Sunday Mail*, 1 May:3.
62 Interview conducted by the authors with Sekuru Friday Chisanyu, Harare, 25 February 2016.
63 See Chara T. 2016. "Hangman holding the aces", *The Sunday Mail Extra*, 24 January:E1.
64 The African traditional perspectives on preference for life imprisonment mirror the existing teleological theories in African culture for punishment. These include punishing for retribution, deterrence and rehabilitation, as in many Western contexts.
65 This is a Pentecostal church in Zimbabwe, which believes in the preservation of life by all means necessary, including through performing healing miracles and avoiding the death penalty.
66 Chara, "Hangman holding the aces".

In a similar vein, in 1993, the Catholic Commission for Justice and Peace (CCJP) in Zimbabwe petitioned on behalf of four inmates who had been on the death row for about five years and were soon to be executed. Citing Christian values, the CCJP argued that execution after a prolonged detention on death row was a cruel, inhuman and degrading treatment that contradicted Section 15(1) of the Constitution.[67] Thus, the JMAC, the Roman Catholic Church and other African Christians recognise the duty of the government in protecting society from crime and the punishing of those who breached the law. Nevertheless, they argue that the aim of the punishment was not supposed to be retributive, but to reform and rehabilitate the offender. On this basis, they have asserted that even the most depraved person has the potential of being reformed through systems of confinement and imprisonment organised by the state. As African Christians, they believe in the sanctity of life, such that only God has the right to take life. In this light, the death penalty is inconsistent with African religious values.

The Lemba Islamic perspective on the death penalty in Zimbabwe is also related to the preceding African religious voices covered by the chapter. Unlike the situation in Islamic states in North Africa, where the death penalty continues to be employed with various degrees of enthusiasm,[68] the Lemba Muslim participants in Zimbabwe tended to side more with the abolitionists than with the retentionists. Muslim adherents form about 2% of Zimbabwe's 15 million people.[69] This partly explains why they are often overshadowed by African Christians and African traditional religions in Zimbabwe. Most Lemba Muslims prefer the use of life imprisonment and payment of compensation by the murderer over capital punishment.[70] The majority of Lemba Muslim interviewees in this study stressed that today most people throughout the world have a wrong perception about Islam as a religion of violence, but they do not see capital punishment as mandatory from their reading of the Quran. For example, the Quran states: "Take not life, which God has made sacred, except by way of justice and law. Thus does He command you, so that you may learn wisdom" (Quran 6:151). The Lemba Muslims in Zimbabwe would prefer a constitutional amendment to do away with capital punishment in favour of life imprisonment. In their tradition, too, preference for life imprisonment is partly anchored in the belief in the avenging spirit, and it brings an opportunity for rehabilitation to the offender and promotes human dignity as much as possible.

---

67 Schabas WA. 1997. "African Perspectives on Abolition of the Death Penalty", in Schabas WA (ed). *The International Sourcebook on Capital Punishment*. Boston: Northeastern University Press, 30-65, 37. See also Constitution of Zimbabwe Amendment (No. 13) Act 1993, where Article 15(1) provided that "No person shall be subjected to torture or to inhuman or degrading punishment or other such treatment". See also, for example, Chenwi LM. 2007. *Towards the Abolition of the Death Penalty in Africa: A Human Rights Perspective*. Pretoria: Pretoria University Law Press, 108.
68 Schabas, "African Perspectives on Abolition of the Death Penalty", 32.
69 Jamal P. 2015. "Muslims Spread into Zimbabwe", *New Zimbabwe*, 8 February.
70 Interview conducted by the authors with Sadiki, Lemba Elder, Chinyika, Gutu (Masvingo), 21 February 2016.

The option for life imprisonment resonates with the views of inmates on death row in Zimbabwe, who have petitioned for a life imprisonment because they said the death penalty was inhumane and degrading and unconstitutional.[71] In this way, the Lemba Muslim views are consistent with those of other religions such as African Christianity and Shona traditional religion in Zimbabwe pertaining to the abolitionist stance.

IS THE DEATH PENALTY CONSISTENT WITH AFRICAN RELIGIOUS HERITAGE?: CRITICAL REFLECTIONS

From the perceptions of the various religious traditions, legal and secular players on the question of the consistency of capital punishment in light of African religious heritage, a number of reflections can be made. From a purely legal perspective, Section 48 of the Constitution of Zimbabwe can be regarded as a well-drafted provision, because it paves the way for the abolition of the death penalty without saying so expressly. For instance, the court may still opt not to impose the death penalty, even if the murder in question was committed in aggravating circumstances. In fact, a moratorium in Zimbabwe has resulted in the absence death sentences and of hangmen, as no person has been executed since 2004.[72] Even so, it can be asked: How significant has the moratorium and other policies by government not to pursue the death penalty been for the past decade in Zimbabwe? Why has the government adopted a soft policy on the death penalty? Does the government's action in any way reflect the death penalty's inconsistency with African religious heritage in Zimbabwe?

Responses to the foregoing questions constitute some of the critical reflections attempted here. From a legal front, Zimbabwe is one of the countries in Southern Africa categorised as retentionist for retaining the death penalty, which remained the law even after the colonial period.[73] Even so, the moratorium on executions has been a positive policy on the death penalty in Zimbabwe since 2004. As a result of the moratorium, Zimbabwe is a state that is in between abolition and retention when it comes to the death penalty. The

---

71 Muzulu P. 2016. "Death Penalty Challenged", *News Day*, 14 September.
72 In Zimbabwe, the moratorium has gained momentum due to the life histories of government ministers such as Vice President Emmerson Mnangagwa, who escaped the hangman's noose by a whisker because of being under age, as noted above. In addition, Emmerson Mnangagwa, a lawyer by training, is the Minister of Justice, Legal and Parliamentary Affairs in Zimbabwe. Of late, Zimbabwe has also been criticised for lawlessness at the backdrop of the Land Reform Programme and could be reforming its stance to be in sync with contemporary human rights trends. In addition, the Christian churches, through platforms like the Zimbabwe Catholic Bishops Conference, Evangelical Fellowship of Zimbabwe, and the Zimbabwe Council of Churches, have exerted pressure on government to respect human rights. These could be the circumstances surrounding the adoption of the moratorium.
73 ACHPR, *Study on the Question of the Death Penalty in Africa*, 25; Schabas, "African Perspectives on Abolition of the Death Penalty", 33.

disadvantage of a moratorium is that Zimbabwe may resume executions any time. This suggests that Zimbabwe has a hesitant and half-hearted approach to the abolition of the practice. Nevertheless, it is important to consider that the government's soft stance on the death penalty came about because the vice president of Zimbabwe, Emmerson Mnangagwa, spoke about the death sentence from personal experience. In addition, Mnangagwa is currently both Vice President and the Minister of Legal and Parliamentary Affairs and has influence in policy formulations in Zimbabwe. Further important to note is the fact that most legislators in government, besides being advocates for the reclamation of African identity and heritage, are also active Christians from various denominations who attended missionary education. Therefore, this has influenced the Zimbabwean government to take African religious heritage seriously in matters that affect human dignity, such as capital punishment.

Whereas the policy considerations noted above are significant, one of the interesting positive elements on capital punishment is its selective application by age and gender. Instead of it being regarded as a constitutional flaw for exempting women and males between 18 and 21 years, as well as those above 70, it can be argued that the government needs to extend this "olive branch" to all citizens.[74] This wider application of exemption from the death penalty would be consistent with values within African religious heritage.

On the religious heritage front, important points for reflection exist. As a way of promoting life and shunning bloodshed at all costs, all the three African religious traditions covered in the study teach the idea of reformation and forgiveness. In the Shona traditional religion, for instance, the concept of *ubuntu/unhu*, anchored on the idea of humanness and communal love, is of pivotal importance in determining the discrepancy between the death penalty and values in the Shona tradition. This Shona perspective forms part of the indigenous African human rights culture, which says a person is a person because of others. The continued mushrooming of death row numbers[75] and absence of a hangman have been interpreted from an Afrocentric perspective

---

74 "A child under 10 years old is considered too young to understand that what they are doing is a crime and so cannot be convicted of a criminal offence (unless it can be proven that they fully realised what they were doing was wrong)." In the British law, this is called *doli incapax*, which means "incapable of wrong doing". So, it becomes very positive for the Zimbabwean Constitution to exempt the 18-21 age group as incapable of doing wrong. See Okon, "Hudud Punishments in Islamic Criminal Law".

75 Agere, "Death Penalty Raises Stink". The source says 117 people are waiting to be hanged. Some of the inmates have been on the death row for over 20 years. This has resulted in emotional stress that violates human rights as the condemned prisoners are "the living dead". The expression "the living dead" can be seen in ambivalence. On the one hand, it reveals the demeaning environment of near hopelessness that the inmates endure as they await execution. On the other hand, the phrase reminds one of John S Mbiti's reference to ancestors as the dead who are living in the spiritual realm (*Nyikadzimu*). The prison conditions place the inmates in "limbo". See Mbiti, *African Religions and Philosophy*.

premised on fear of *ngozi* and respect for human rights that upholds human life at all costs. Similar to the African communitarian system and solidarity, the African Christian faith espoused by JMAC is one based on mutual sharing – "If one member suffers, all suffer with it" (1 Corinthians 12:26). Therefore, theologically speaking, the death penalty "represents the sinful mutilation of the image of God in which human beings are created."[76] The same concern was shared by the Lemba Muslims. Hence, as much as possible, life must be preserved, since no one has the right to kill in God's stead.

CONCLUSION

This chapter concludes that African religious heritage and law can complement each other in resolving the legality of the death penalty in Zimbabwe. By using the religious heritage lens, it can also be concluded that no one has the right to kill except God. The biblical story of Cain and Abel (Genesis 4:1-15) is instructive, as it teaches that revenge is only for God not for humanity. This is a moral foundation for what legal systems should do to overturn the ideology of "an eye for an eye" with a command for reform and forgiveness. As this chapter has demonstrated, the death penalty is inconsistent with African religious heritage and must be abolished both *de facto* and *de jure* in Zimbabwe. After all, Section 48(1) of the Constitution of Zimbabwe also recommends against the mandatory death sentence on the rationale that every person has the right to life. This is a legal flaw in the Constitution of Zimbabwe, which needs urgent amendment.

---

[76] Parratt J. 2008. "Christianity, Ethnicity, and Structural Violence: The Northeast India Case", in Kalu OU (ed). *Interpreting Contemporary Christianity: Global Processes and Local Identities*. Grand Rapids, MI: William B. Eerdmans Publishing Company, 340.

Index

INDEX

A

Addis Ababa, 17, 18, 42, 43
Adetona, Abdul Lateef, 360, 364
African Charter on Human and Peoples' Rights (ACHPR), 76-77
African Indigenous/Independent/Initiated Churches (AIC), 360, 379-380
African Traditional Religions (ATR) (also African Indigenous Religion (AIR) (see also Irreecha; Shona Mwari religion of), 21, 24 n8, 31, 157, 161, 162, 166, 158, 167, 205-219, 358, 361-362, 371 n5, 373, 374, 377-379, 381, 384, 385
    ancestors in, 158, 161, 162, 165, 168, 341-342, 345, 349
    burial practices of, 159, 336, 338, 341-342, 343-344, 350-351
    water resources management practices of in Zimbabwe, 205, 206, 207-209, 213-216, 217-219
African traditional heritage (see also customary law), 157-179, 333
    individual in, 158, 160, 161, 162-167, 168
    individual rights in, 157-163, 167-169
    collective rights in, 157, 158, 159, 162, 163, 167-168
    family/clan in, 158, 159, 161, 162, 163-167
African Union, 76, 292
Afrocentricity, 191-192, 371-372, 382, 387
Agré, Cardinal Bernard, 140, 145-148, 154
Al-Zakzaky, Yaqoub, 101, 102 n11
Anglican, 67, 130, 146, 306, 342, 362
apartheid, 55, 67, 77, 87, 88, 171, 173, 185, 236, 264, 271-275, 276, 277, 281, 283, 284, 285, 287, 289, 323
Asmal, Kader, 171, 173, 174, 175
Axum, 6, 14-17, 39
avenging spirits (see *ngozi*)

B

Baha'i, 158, 242
Benin, 91-97
    African traditional religions in (see also Vodoun), 91-97
    Catholic Church in, 91, 95
    constitutional law of, 94, 95
    diaspora Africans and, 91-93, 95
    Ouida 92 festival in, 91-94
    secularism in, 91, 94-95
Benson, Iain, 184
Berger, Peter, 357, 359

Bible (see also Zimbabwe, biblical political rhetoric in), 4, 60, 63, 71, 87, 125, 148, 181, 194, 224, 231, 234, 248, 254, 306, 379, 384, 388
    Genesis, 388
    1 and 2 Kings, 81
    Psalms, 256
    Isaiah, 83, 380
    Acts, 380
    Romans, 86, 379
    1 Corintians, 388
Boko Haram, 116, 118
Botswana, 294, 295
Buddhism, 97, 158, 242
burials (see graves)

C

Cameroon, 293, 294, 305
Catholicism (see Roman Catholic Church)
Christianity (see also Ethiopian Orthodox Tewahedo Church; Ghana, Baptist churches in; Kenya, Pentecostal charismatic churches in; Nigeria; Roman Catholic Church; Protestantism), 3, 4, 5, 6 n20, 7, 8, 9, 10, 11, 12, 13, 14, 15, 16, 17, 18, 19, 21, 22 n4, 24 n8, 33, 34, 35, 36, 38, 39, 40, 41, 42, 43, 44, 46, 47, 51, 52 n18, 56, 59, 63 n62, 65, 68, 69, 70, 73, 78-79, 80, 81, 82, 87, 88, 91, 94, 96, 97, 121, 122, 128, 129, 130, 131, 136, 143, 147, 157, 158, 167, 171, 174, 175, 176, 177, 181, 182, 205, 211, 221, 222, 223, 231, 232, 233, 234, 236, 237, 242, 244 n13, 255, 256, 266, 274, 291, 292, 303-312, 315, 317, 318, 324, 327, 331, 348, 372, 373, 374, 377, 379-380, 382, 384, 385, 386, 387, 388
Christian Association of Nigeria (CAN), 110-111, 112, 117, 353, 361
Coertzen, Pieter, 176
colonialism (see also precolonial and postcolonialism), 53, 73, 80, 82, 83, 89, 92, 108, 125, 126, 127, 128, 135, 191, 192, 196, 197, 198, 205, 211, 212, 218, 221, 222, 224, 225-226, 230-231, 232-236, 268-271, 272, 274, 275, 276, 277, 279, 281, 284, 285, 288, 302, 303, 307, 311, 315, 324, 328, 371, 372, 376, 382, 383, 386
Commission for the Promotion and Protection of the Rights of Cultural, Religious and Linguistic Communities (CRL Commission), 337, 342-343
conversion, religious, 4, 6 n20, 14, 18, 19
Coote, Robert P, 79, 83
Coote, Mary, 79, 83

Coroner Law System (CLS) in, 353, 355, 363-368
  Christians and, 365, 366, 367
  Muslims and, 364-365, 366-369
  religious objections to, 365, 366, 369
  survey of attitudes toward, 365-368
corruption, 252, 254, 256, 257
Côte d'Ivoire, 51, 139-155
  Catholic Church in, 140, 142-144, 148-149, 154-155
  glaè mask in, 139-140, 150-154, 155
  media in, 139-143, 145-149
  politics of, 139-155
  Wê people of, 139, 150-153, 155
customary law, 158, 160, 166-167, 168, 208, 209, 218, 219, 372, 378, 382

D

Deacon, Janette, 325, 326-327, 328, 330
death penalty,
  Afrocentric reading of, 371, 372, 374, 386-388
  history in Zimbabwe of, 375-377
  legal regime of, 371, 373, 374, 382-386
  religion and, 371, 374, 375, 377-382, 386-388
Derg, 5, 16
Deya, Gilbert, 249-250
development (social, cultural, political, legal), 33, 34-38, 39, 43-44, 47, 52, 72-73, 74-81, 132, 197, 198, 203, 205, 207, 210, 212, 215, 219, 243, 292, 297, 309, 310, 311, 315, 322, 324, 331, 336, 338, 343, 344, 345, 350, 360, 383
Durham, W Cole (Jr), 106

E

Ethiopia (see also Ethiopian Orthodox Tewahedo Church; Irreecha), 3-19, 21-32, 33-47, 190 n8, 192, 193, 194, 198
  constitutional law of, 4, 5, 6, 10, 14, 16-17, 22, 27-28, 29, 31, 32, 36, 37-38, 47
  Ethiopian People's Revolutionary Democratic Front (EPRDF), 5, 11-12, 18, 21-22
  ethnic federalism in, 22, 31, 35-36
  forbearance narratives in, 3, 8-10, 12-13, 39
  government/state of, 3, 4-5, 11-12, 14, 16, 19, 21, 23, 24, 25, 26, 27, 28, 29, 31, 32, 35, 36, 37, 40, 41, 42, 47
  history of, 3, 4, 6, 7-8, 10, 11-12, 14-15, 21 n2, 35-36, 37, 38, 39, 41
  Irreecha ritual in (see also Irreecha), 21-32
  as "Christian island", 5, 21, 35
  Muslims in, 3, 5-7, 11-14, 21, 22 n4, 24 n8, 34-35, 39-44, 42, 47
  national identity of, 4-5, 11-12, 22, 23 n6, 25, 31, 32, 38, 42-43

religious coexistence in, 3, 11, 14 n53, 19, 34, 36, 39, 43, 46
religious "cohabitation" in, 33-34, 37, 41, 44-46, 47
religious demography of, 4-5, 17, 34
religious freedom in, 3, 12, 16-17, 21-22, 29, 31, 34, 37, 41-42, 47
religious intolerance in, 3, 11, 12, 14-19, 43-44
religious pluralism in, 33, 34-38, 44, 46
religious tolerance in, 3-19, 8-10, 11-14, 14-18
secularism in, 5, 16, 21, 25, 27-28, 30, 31, 32
Ethiopian Orthodox Tewahedo Church, 3, 4-5, 6 n20, 10, 12, 14, 15, 16, 17, 21, 23, 24, 35, 36, 39
Evangelical Christians, 21, 23, 24, 59, 91, 244 n13, 253, 256, 296, 383 n72

F

"The Freedom of a Christian" (see also Luther, Martin), 291, 303-309, 311
Furseth, Inger, 357, 359

G

Gbagbo, Laurent, 141, 142, 145-149, 153, 154
Ghana, 51-70
  Aliens Compliance Order of 1969 in, 52, 54, 57
  American missionary influence in, 51-52, 53, 54-55, 57, 58, 59, 60, 61, 62, 63, 64, 68, 70
  Baptist churches in, 51-70
  Baptist church schism in, 53-70
  church and state in, 52-53, 65-69
  Ghana Baptist Commission (GBC) in, 51-70
  Ghana Baptist Convention-Southern Baptist Convention (GBC-SBC) in, 64-70
  Ghana Baptist Mission (GBM) in, 51-70
  government/state of, 65-68, 69-70
  Nigerian Baptist Convention (NBC) in, 51, 52
  Nigerian Baptist Mission (NBM) in, 51, 52
  Southern Baptist Convention (SBC) in, 51, 53
Gilbert Deya Ministries International, 249-250
glaè mask (see Côte d'Ivoire)
globalisation, 33, 167, 205, 324, 358, 376
Gnonsoa, Angèle, 140, 150, 151, 152, 154
graves and burial sites
  burial rights, 333, 346, 347, 348, 349
  cultural significance of, 334, 347
  regulation of, 315, 316, 318 n24, 334, 335, 340
  reuse/relocation of, 315, 317, 318-319, 321, 324, 327, 328 n89, 329, 330, 331, 333, 340-346, 349-350
Great Zimbabwe Monuments, 221-237
  and the Abrahmic religions, 231-234
  African discourses on, 225-229
  colonial policies toward, 221, 222, 224, 225, 226, 228, 229, 230, 231, 232, 236

heritage management of, 222, 226, 227, 234-239
indigenous religions and, 231, 232, 233 n94, 234, 236, 237
legal protections and challenges in heritage management of, 222, 229, 230, 234-236
non-African origins controversy surrounding, 222-225
political discourses of dominance and, 230-234
religious significance of, 222, 224, 225, 226-229, 236
Solomonic legacy of, 222, 224, 231, 234
Green, M Christian, 292, 311
Gunda, Masiiwa Rajies, 79, 82, 83

H

hate speech
libertarian principles and, 259, 263
protection of human dignity and, 259, 260, 261, 263, 264, 265, 269
South African perspective on, 259, 262-269
United States perspective on, 259-269
heritage, 21, 23, 25, 27, 28, 33, 34, 35, 36, 38, 44, 47, 54, 91, 167, 189, 191
authorisation/legitimisation of, 25-28, 29, 30, 329, 335, 341, 344, 345
and "authorised heritage discourses", 26, 236
cultural, 23, 28, 29, 30, 54, 191, 208 n16, 213, 216, 232, 234, 235, 236, 272, 284, 322, 325, 329, 334, 335, 335, 339, 341, 345, 350
definition/meaning of, 26, 328, 329, 330
and ethnic identity, 26, 27, 29, 30
experts/professionals and, 24, 26, 27-29, 30, 222, 345
intangible, 23, 25, 29, 30, 33, 222, 235, 236, 315, 324, 325, 326, 327, 331
local communities and, 335, 336, 342, 344, 345, 346, 350
management of, 203, 205, 222, 234-236, 315, 316, 318-319, 322, 323, 326, 330, 335, 336, 344
political, 80, 81-87, 89, 139, 381-387
as process and discourse, 25-26, 28
religion and, 58-60, 70, 81-87, 176, 191, 208, 333, 335, 345, 350-351, 377-382, 386-388
right to, 336, 339, 346
tangible, 235, 236, 324
and tourism (see also Irreecha, "cul-touristic" turn regarding), 23-30, 221, 224, 235, 335, 344
Hinduism, 130, 172, 179, 182, 242, 335
HIV/AIDS, 245, 246, 247, 254, 255, 303, 309
homosexuality (see also *Minister of Home Affairs v. Fourie*; South Africa, same-sex marriage in), 160, 262, 266, 355-356, 359
in African culture, 302-303
African laws against, 293-295
dignity and, 291, 296, 297, 298, 299, 300, 301, 302, 304, 305, 308, 309, 310, 312

equality and, 291, 298, 299, 300, 304, 310
human rights and, 203, 291, 292, 296, 302, 304
human rights (see also homosexuality, human rights and), 33, 34 n6, 37, 71, 75, 76, 77, 106, 115, 117, 167, 374, 376, 386 n72, 387, 388

I

International Covenant on Civil and Political Rights (ICCPR), 75, 269
Irreecha,
"cul-touristic" turn regarding, 24, 25, 26-32
as cultural festival, 23-25, 26-28, 29, 30, 32
at Hora Arsedi, 22, 23 n6, 24, 25, 27, 29
and Oromo ethnic identity, 22, 23, 26, 29, 30
and Oromo national identity, 22 n4, 23-24, 25, 27, 30, 31
as ritual/spiritual, 22-23, 24, 25, 26-27, 28, 29, 30, 31
as worship of Waaqa (creator/sky god), 22, 24, 25, 27, 30
Islam (see also Muslims), 3, 5-7, 9, 10, 12, 13, 15, 19, 21, 22 n4, 33, 34, 35, 36, 38, 39, 40, 42, 43, 78, 97, 101, 102, 103, 105, 107, 108, 109, 110, 111, 117, 121, 125, 126, 127, 128, 130, 131, 132, 158, 221, 228, 229, 232, 233, 242, 335, 353, 356, 357, 358, 359, 360, 361, 364, 365, 367, 369, 371 n5, 371, 373, 374, 377, 380-382, 385
Islamic law/*sharia* (see also Kenya, Kadhi Courts in), 113, 126 n25, 127, 131, 380-381, 382 n51
Islamic Movement of Nigeria, 101, 102, 103, 114-115

J

Jama'atu Nasril Islam (JNI), 110-112, 117
Jebel, Ahmedin, 7-8, 13, 15
Jehovah's Witnesses, 50, 130
Johane Marange Apostolic Church (JMAC), 379-378, 384-385, 388
Jubilee Christian Centre (JCC), 250-251
Judaism, 36, 158, 221, 222, 229, 231, 232, 233, 234, 236, 237

K

Kairos Theology, 87-89
Kanyari, Victor, 246-248, 249, 256
Kenya, 121-136, 241-257
Bomas Draft Constitution of, 128-132
constitution of, 121-136, 244, 253
constitutional reform in, 122, 128-131
Independence Constitution of, 124-128, 132-136
Kadhi Courts in, 121, 122, 125-136
Muslim-Christian relations in, 121, 122, 136
Muslims in, 121, 122, 125, 126, 127, 128, 130, 131, 132, 133, 134, 135, 136

Pentecostal and charismatic churches in, 130, 241-257
secular state ideal in, 122-125, 136
Wanjikyu Draft Constitution of, 129
Kérékou, Mathieu, 91, 95
Kiuna, Allan, 250-251
Kiuna, Kathy, 250-251

L

Lalibela, 14, 16-17
land, 69, 96, 189-203, 209, 216
denial/distribution of, 13-14, 16-17, 18, 19, 35, 196
holy/sacred, 14, 15, 210, 213
management, 190, 191, 192, 193, 194, 200-202, 203, 213
ownership of, 10, 12, 13, 189, 191, 192, 193, 194-197, 203, 209, 236
use of, 189, 190, 191, 192, 193, 194, 195, 197-200, 201, 202, 203, 209, 222, 227, 228, 230, 231, 235, 236
Langa, Pius, 182-185, 269
Lemba Muslims (of Zimbabwe), 372, 373, 374, 380-382, 385-386, 388
Levine, Donald, 35-36
Luther, Martin (see also "The Freedom of a Christian"), 291, 304-309, 311

M

Malherbe, Rassie, 174-175
Mali, 93, 179
Mandela, Nelson, 270, 271 n2
Markakis, John, 4-5
Mauch, Karl, 224, 227, 231-232
Mbiti, John S, 162, 164-165, 207, 354
Mecca, 6, 14
Minister of Home Affairs v. Fourie, 291-292, 295-302, 304, 307, 308, 311
missionaries (see also Ghana, American Missionary influence in), 108, 231
Mnangagwa, Emmerson, 87, 383, 386 n72, 387
morality and ethics, 44-46, 241, 242, 245, 253-257, 292, 298, 301, 305, 307, 309, 310, 311
Mozambique, 223, 377 n31
Mugabe, Grace, 71, 79, 80, 81-87, 89
Mugabe, Robert, 73-77, 81-87, 89
Muigai, Githu, 252, 253
Muslims (see also Ethiopia; Kenya; Nigeria; Lemba Muslims), 91, 94 n9, 142, 143, 228-229, 232-233, 236, 266, 335, 374, 381, 385

N

Nejashi, King (Ethiopia), 6, 14-15, 39
Ndoro, Webber, 224, 327, 329
Nduta, Lucy, 246-248

Neno Evangelism Ministries, 248-249
Ng'ang'a, James Maina, 248-249
ngozi (avenging spirits), 345-359, 372, 375, 378-379, 381, 383, 384, 388
Nigeria (see also Coroner Law System (CLS)), 51, 52, 101-119, 179, 257, 292, 293, 294, 353-369
African traditional religions in, 361-361
Christians in, 108, 110, 111-112, 117, 353, 354, 355, 356, 357, 358, 359, 360-361, 362, 365, 366, 367
constitutional law of, 103, 104, 105, 106, 107, 108, 113, 114, 115-118, 119
Kaduna State government in, 103, 104, 105, 112, 114-115, 116
military of, 102, 109, 110, 113, 114, 115, 116, 119
Muslims in, 101, 102, 107-114, 117, 353-354, 355, 356, 359-360, 361, 364-369
Pentecostal and charismatic churches in, 256, 360
Regulation of Religious Preaching Edicts of 1984 and 1987, 107, 110
Regulation of Religious Preaching Law of 1996, 103, 105, 107, 113, 119
religious freedom in, 103, 104-107, 115, 116, 118
religious pluralism in, 117, 118, 355-363
Religious Preaching Bill, 2016, 103, 105, 110-115, 117, 118, 119
secularism in, 102, 355-359, 362-363
Shi'a Muslims in, 101-103, 104, 110, 111, 112, 113, 114-115, 116, 119
Sufi Muslims in, 108, 109, 110, 111, 112

N

Ntho-Ntho, Albertina, 174, 181

O

Organisation of the African Unity (OAU), 76, 77
O'Regan, Kate, 182-184
Oromia/Oromo people (see Irreecha)
Orthodox Christianity (see Ethiopia, Ethiopian Orthodox Tewahedo Church)
Ouattara, Alassane, 142, 145, 146 149, 153
Owuor, David, 241 n2

P

Pentecostal and charismatic churches and movements (see also Kenya; Nigeria), 23, 24 n8, 58, 59, 60, 63, 303, 360, 384 n65
Pillay, Sunali, 171, 179, 182-185
pluralism (see religious pluralism)
Pope John Paul II, 95, 96, 155
postcolonialism, 82, 135, 157, 190, 192, 198, 205, 211, 290, 293, 302, 307, 318, 372, 376, 383
precolonial, 302, 377, 378
Prophet Mohammed, 6, 15, 102

Protestantism (see also Anglicans; Evangelical Christians; Ghana, Baptist churches in; Kenya, Pentecostal charismatic churches in; Nigeria, Pentecostal charismatic churches in), 3 n2, 4 n5, 24, 37 n17, 91

Q

Quran, 43, 109, 125, 364, 381-382, 383

R

Radebe, Lerato, 172, 178-179, 181-182, 185
Rastafarianism, 189-203
   diet of, 191 n11, 194, 198, 199, 202
   environmental principles of, 193, 200, 201-202
   history in Zimbabwe of, 192-193
   Ital livity principle of, 190, 193, 194, 197, 198, 199 n40, 200, 202
   land ownership, use and management practices of, 194-202
   theology of land of, 193-194
   wearing of dreadlocks in, 171, 172, 177, 178-179, 180, 181-182, 185
religious freedom (see also Ethiopia; Nigeria; South Africa; Zimbabwe), 75-78, 84, 85, 89, 123-124, 183, 293, 303-311, 320
religious pluralism (see also Ethiopia; Nigeria), 136, 244, 355
Remba, people of Zimbabwe, 221, 222, 227-229, 232, 233, 234, 236
Repstad, Pål, 357, 359
revolution (political), 5, 21, 22 n4, 65, 66, 67, 73 n17, 91, 94, 102, 193, 276
Rhodes, Cecil John, 221, 225, 227, 230 n76
"Rhodes Must Fall" campaign, 272, 273, 275, 277, 285, 289
   black consciousness and, 271, 289
   censorship and, 281-284
   deep diversity and, 273, 281, 284-288, 289
   iconoclasm of, 273, 275-284, 286, 289
   politics of memory and, 274, 276, 277, 278, 282, 284, 285, 286, 287, 288, 289
   politics of recognition and, 273, 282, 284-288, 289
Roman Catholicism (see also papal encyclicals), 21, 23, 74, 81, 83
Roman-Dutch law, 157, 217, 315, 316-321, 331, 372

S

Sachs, Albie, 291, 292, 296, 297
Salvation Healing Ministry, 246-248
same-sex marriage (see South Africa, same-sex marriage in)
secularism (see also Benin; Ethiopia; Kenya; Nigeria), 56, 142-143, 155, 175, 181, 182, 186, 311, 312, 386
Selassie, Haile I, Emperor, 5, 16, 18, 190 n8, 193, 194, 197, 198

sharia (see Islamic law)
Shona (people of Zimbabwe), 80, 86, 205, 206-209, 211, 212, 213-217, 218, 219, 221, 222, 227, 228, 232 n93, 234, 236, 374-375, 377-379, 382, 383-384, 386, 387
   Mwari religion of, 205, 207, 214, 216, 219, 227, 374
Smith, Ian, 73, 82, 230, 383
Smith, Laurajane, 25-26, 28, 29
Soglo, Nicéphore, 92, 93, 96
South Africa, 74, 75 n22, 76 n26, 87-88, 157-169, 171-186, 259-270, 271-289, 291-312, 315-331, 333-351
   Bushman Relics Protection Act of 1911, 321-322
   constitutional law of (see also *Minister of Home Affairs v. Fourie*), 84, 157-160, 171, 173, 174, 175, 177, 178, 179, 180, 181, 182-185, 263-266, 269, 273, 275, 277, 278-281, 291, 292, 295-302, 315, 316, 317, 323, 324, 328, 336-340, 341, 346-347, 350
   Council for the Protection and Promotion of Religious Rights and Freedoms in, 339
   Extension and Security of Tenure Act (ESTA), 346-348, 250
   National Heritage Council in, 350-351
   National Heritage Resources Act (NHRA), 273, 278, 279, 308, 310, 311, 312, 315, 323-331, 333, 334-336, 339, 341, 344-345, 350
   National Monuments Act of 1969, 321-323
   National Monuments Council of, 325, 328, 329
   National Policy on Religion and Education (NPRE) in, 171, 172-177, 179-182, 185-186
   religious freedom in, 336, 337, 339, 346, 347, 350
   religious observances in public schools in, 171-186
   same-sex marriage in, 291-312
South African Charter of Religious Rights and Freedoms, 333, 339-340, 350
South Africa Council of Churches (SACC), 87-89
South African Heritage Resources Agency (SAHRA), 328, 329, 330, 334, 335, 341, 344
South African Human Rights Commission (SAHRC), 267
Synagogue, Church of All Nations (SCOAN), 355, 369

T

Taylor, Charles, 33, 273, 284, 286-287, 289, 311
theology (see also Kairos theology; Rastafarianism, theology of land), 5, 64, 60, 61, 71, 72, 79, 81, 82, 123, 162, 173, 177, 182, 197, 214, 252, 256, 291, 295, 304, 306-311, 354, 374, 379, 380, 388
Tutu, Desmond, 146, 296

U

ubuntu (humanity), 158, 169, 264, 310, 379, 387
Uganda, 293, 294, 296
Ukah, Asonzeh, 355

UNESCO, 227, 235, 236, 325
United Nations Charter, 269, 338
United Nations Declaration on the Rights of Indigenous Peoples (UNDRIP), 338-339
United States,
   constitutional law of, 51, 125, 259-262, 263, 265
   freedom of speech in, 259-262
   State Department, 16, 66, 68, 69, 77-78
Universal Declaration of Human Rights (UDHR), 33, 75, 77, 269
Usman dan Fodio, 107-108

V

Verner, WE, 63, 66, 67
Verstraelen, Frans J, 79-80
Vodoun, 91, 92, 93, 95

W

women (see also Kiuna, Kathy; Mugabe, Grace; Nduta, Lucy), 81, 89, 168, 172, 241, 243, 250, 257
   as central to traditional water management, 215-216
World Tourism Association (UNWTO), 335

X

Xhosa, 158, 161, 163, 164, 165

Y

Yoruba, 51, 83, 354, 362

Z

Zambia, 296, 305
Zewde, Bahru, 35, 36
Zimbabwe, 71-89, 189-203, 205-219, 221-237, 371-388
   avenging spirits (see *ngozi*)
   biblical political rhetoric in, 71, 79 81, 82, 83, 86, 87
   Chimurenga liberation war in, 80, 85, 87, 89, 189-190, 194, 196, 382-383
   citizenship in, 71-73, 76, 77, 79, 80, 81, 89
   constitutional law of, 71, 72, 73-75, 76-77, 78, 80, 84, 85, 89, 372, 374, 376-377, 379, 381, 383, 385-386, 387-388
   death penalty in, 371-388
   Land Reform Programme in, 189-190, 191, 196, 197, 386n72
   religious demographics of, 78
   religious freedom in, 71, 72-73, 76-79, 84, 85, 89
   Unilateral Declaration of Independence (UDI) of, 73, 82
   water management policies in, 209-210, 211, 212, 217, 219
Zimbabwe African National Union (ZANU), 73-74
Zimbabwe African National Union Patriotic Front (ZANU-PF), 74, 80, 84-86, 89, 189, 197
Zimbabwe African People's Union (ZAPU), 73-74

www.ingramcontent.com/pod-product-compliance
Lightning Source LLC
Chambersburg PA
CBHW082058230426

43670CB00017B/2883